THE OFFICIAL®
PRICE GUIDE TO

COLLECTOR
PLATES

PRICE GUIDE TO

COLLECTOR
PLATES

Rinker Enterprises

SIXTH EDITION

House of Collectibles • New York

Table of Contents

Acknowledgments vii

What Is a Collector Plate? 1

The History of Collector Plates 7

Manufacturers: A Few Histories 15
    Anna–Perenna Porcelain, Inc. 15
    Bareuther 16
    Bing and Grondahl 16
    Fenton Art Glass Company 17
    Frankoma Pottery 18
    Dave Grossman Creations 19
    Hadley Companies 19
    Edna Hibel Studio 21
    Pemberton & Oakes 21
    Pickard, Inc. 22
    Rockwell Museum 23
    Royal Copenhagen 24

Gallery Of Artists 25
    Dave Barnhouse 25
    Thomas Kinkade 26
    Lena Liu 27
    Terry Redlin 28

Collecting Tips 29

How to Display Your Plates 35

Caring for Your Plates 39

Investing in Collector Plates 43

Buying and Selling Collector Plates 45

Fakes and Imitations 61

State–of–the–Market Report 63

Glossary 69

Publications 74

List Of Manufacturers 75

How to Use This Book 79

Collector Plate Listings 81

Artist Index 555

Series Index 563

Acknowledgments

The collector plate community — manufacturers, dealers, collectors, etc. — willingly and enthusiastically assisted in the gathering and/or providing of information for this project. A general expression of thanks and gratitude to everyone for their strong support.

We want to especially thank Tamra Armstrong (Information Specialist) of Fenton, Karen Meyer of The Hadley Companies, Andy Plotkin (Vice President) of Edna Hibel Studios, Stephani Perlmutter of the Media Connection representing Cavanaugh, Lauri Repp of Dave Grossman Creations, Jenny Rose of Waterford/Wedgwood, Ginny Sexton (Manager of Public Relations) of The Bradford Exchange, and Jay Voss of Pickard Fine China for the information and illustrations that they provided.

Cherie Souhrada, David Souhrada, and Linda Kruger of *Collectors News & The Antique Reporter* (PO Box 156, Grundy Center, IA 50638) deserve special acknowledgment. Over half the illustrations in this book came from *Collectors News'* photographic archives. *Collectors News* is one of only two trade newspapers that stuck with collector plates through thick and thin. *Collectors News* continually runs articles about modern collectibles and devotes one issue per year exclusively to this important collecting category.

Rinker Enterprises, Inc. (5093 Vera Cruz Road, Emmaus, PA 18049) prepared the text, typeset the information, and did the page layout for this book. Terese J. Oswald was project director during its initial stages. Dana N. Morykan directed the project and did the typesetting and page layout. Nancy Butt assisted in the acquisition and identification of the illustrations. Harry L. Rinker provided general supervision.

The revisions and enhancements that led to the current edition of this work were initiated by Stephen H. Sterns, then Senior Editor, at House of Collectibles. Timothy J. Kochuba, General Manager of House of Collectibles, provided overall guidance. Randy Ladenheim–Gil supervised the project throughout its final stages. Alex Klapwald handled the production process. Alessandra Gouldner and Simon Vukelj of the House of Collectibles staff also aided the project.

COLLECTORS' INFORMATION BUREAU

The Collectors' Information Bureau [5065 Shoreline Road, Suite 200, Barrington, IL 60010; (847) 842-2200] is a not–for–profit business league that serves as a clearinghouse for limited edition collectibles and provides answers to questions from collectors about secondary market values for their favorite collectibles.

In addition, the organization produces several publications that help collectors locate, buy, and sell limited edition collectibles. We especially recommend the following two titles:

Directory to Limited Edition Collectibles Stores
Directory to Secondary Market Retailers

The Collectors' Information Bureau also publishes a general price guide that covers the entire limited edition and modern collectibles field — bells, cottages, dolls, figurines, graphics, ornaments, plates, and steins. It is revised annually and available at your favorite bookstore, dealer, or shop specializing in limited edition material, or from booksellers of antiques and collectibles titles.

What Is a Collector Plate?

The limited edition plate traces its beginnings to the 1895 blue and white porcelain Christmas plate produced by Bing & Grondahl. The concept has weathered the storms of flooded markets, slipshod, opportunistic manufacturers, and wildly fluctuating economic conditions. Indeed, millions of people around the globe buy them.

Limited edition plates are made in every shape, size, subject matter, and material imaginable. It is the word *imagination* that suggests the key to the future of collector plates. Technology and artistic creativity continue to produce innovations in both the aesthetic and production phases.

DEFINING LIMITED EDITION COLLECTIBLES

In 1989 the Collectibles and Platemaker's Guild and the National Association of Limited Edition Dealers adopted the following *Statement of Integrity* as a means of defining limited edition collectibles:

STATEMENT OF INTEGRITY
Definitions for Limited Edition Collectibles

Original — one of a kind created by the artist.

Edition Limited by Number — A reproduction of an original, the edition limited by a number pre–announced at the time the collectible is announced. Each piece may, or may not, be sequentially numbered.

Edition Limited by Firing Days — A reproduction of an original limited by number of announced firing days.

Open Edition — A reproduction of an original with no limit on time of production or the number of pieces produced and no announcement of edition size.

Sold Out or Closed — No longer available from the producer (Sold Out applies to both Numbered Limited Editions and Time Limited Editions).

Retired — No longer available from the producer and none of the pieces will ever be produced again.

Suspended — Not available from producer — production suspended.

Collectibles and Platemakers Guild Adopted Feb. 7, 1989	National Association of Limited Edition Dealers Adopted May 5, 1989

Production run information is usually recorded on the back of each plate, along with the backstamp, which is the trademark of the manufacturer. Other information often included is the name of the plate, the series title, the artist, and the date it was made. Sometimes plates are even hand–numbered in the order in which they were produced.

WHY COLLECT LIMITED EDITION PLATES?

Why do millions of people around the world collect limited edition plates? One has only to see the plates to understand their popularity. Every subject imaginable is portrayed. As new themes and styles are created, they immediately find their way to the face of a plate.

Beautiful horses running in the wind, a child gazing adoringly at his mother, Snoopy and Charlie Brown engaged in a battle of wits — all of these and more make up the range of subject matter that appears on collector plates. Plates are produced on such a wide variety of topics in order to appeal to the collector that lurks in each of us.

A particularly popular theme is that of the world's children, in all their infinite, playful varieties. We have all been children. Seeing these touching reminders of our youth evokes pleasant sensations and memories. Even the most diehard noncollector is hard pressed not to respond to a childhood scene that parallels his own.

Animal lovers are also taken care of by the manufacturers of collector plates. Almost every animal and bird has been immortalized on a plate. The depictions can vary from traditional, realistic, Audubon–like renditions to comic relief caricatures.

If you are a student of art but your budget is limited, there are plates based on the works of contemporary artists, many with collectibles in other forms such as figurines, and prints by famous fine artists available to you.

Indeed, most plate collectors display their plates as artwork and derive the same sense of pleasure and satisfaction from them that they would from original paintings.

You can also compare limited edition plates to limited edition prints. Both are produced by fine artists in a limited edition, both have investment potential, and both are aesthetically pleasing. However, the affordability of collector plates gives them quite an edge over prints.

Appreciation of collector plates is further enhanced by the knowledge that the price difference between a limited edition plate and an original work of art is vast. A lovely plate can be bought for $25 to $85, whereas an important painting of the same genre would run to thousands of dollars.

MAKING A CERAMIC LIMITED EDITION PLATE

How are ceramic plates produced? Few people understand how ceramic limited edition plates are made. Obviously, the artist does not paint each plate individually. How is the original painting reproduced onto a ceramic plate?

The answer is via a ceramic decal. Before you turn up your nose, dispel any preconceived notions about decals. Ceramic decals bear no resemblance to bumper stickers or to the old–fashioned fruit and flowers with which your grandmother decorated her kitchen cabinets. The making of a ceramic decal is a very involved, highly artistic and extremely technical process that generally takes a year or two from the planning stage to the finished plate.

First, the artist meets with the producer to discuss the concept for the plate or series. The artist then produces the original painting from which the decal will be produced. To do this, he often uses a matte that precisely outlines the shape of the plate.

At this point the producer meets with the decal manufacturer. There are many key decisions to be made at this crucial stage. One of the most important is the choice of a method for making the decal. There are three basic techniques that can be used: screen printing, offset lithography, or litho/screen combination. Each of these methods has its advantages and disadvantages. It is crucial to select the process best suited to the special requirements presented by the original artwork.

Screen printing produces opaque colors, and varying the amount of color can also produce a textured look. However, extremely fine detail work and subtle shading cannot be adequately achieved using this process.

Offset multicolored lithography, on the other hand, permits extremely fine detail and tonal gradations. This is possible because of the basic premise of lithography, which is the use of tiny dots of color. The dots can vary in size and in distance from each other, thus permitting delicate shading. However, its high cost and lack of certain colors, including white, make this process less than desirable for some projects.

If neither of these two processes will produce the desired results, a combination of the two is used. This is referred to as litho/screen combination printing. Screen printed colors are added to a lithographic decal when brightness is needed. An example of this would be using a silkscreen white for highlighting on a predominantly offset decal. Sometimes waves or clouds are best presented in silkscreen, which gives them a heavier appearance, a sense of depth.

Color chemists now become involved. They are experts in knowing how the various ceramic colors will fire on the different blank plates available. The color chemist is responsible for choosing the various colors that will match the original painting. Unlike the artist, he or she is restricted by the printing process chosen. When the color chemist has completed this task, the process moves to the making of the color transparency. A series of negatives is made by photographing the original artwork using various filters and screens. From these negatives the color separations are made.

Time for another decision. There are two basic approaches to color separations: four–color camera–separation and hand–separation.

The first is a process which is similar to that used in the printing of magazines. In essence, the color separation is a photographic positive of one color. The difference is that in ceramic decals the colors are not totally transparent and a true magenta is not available. As a consequence, the results are not as true to the original as they are in nonceramic printing, from the standpoint of both color and detail.

In the four–color process there are four sheets of clear acetate, each one containing a portion of the total image done in varying shades of one color, which is applied in dots. The colors used are yellow, magenta (red), cyan (blue), and black. When these sheets are layered on top of each other and precisely aligned, the desired image and colors appear. The coloration of each sheet must be perfect if the original artwork is to be faithfully reproduced. The industry has developed computerized scanners that scan the original artwork and print the color separations. The result, although not as accurate as the work of a skilled color separator, continues to show progress.

The hand–separation method is considerably more time consuming, sometimes taking several months to complete. Separate "boards" must be made for each color, from six or seven to as many as thirty or more. A "proofing" process of transferring individual color dot patterns from a metal plate to special composition paper is arduous as well. This hand–separation method produces an unparalleled richness of color but does move away somewhat from the artist's original colors.

Whether to apply only one of these processes, or to utilize a combination of the two, using additional "picked colors" to improve on the standard process, is a tough decision. For instance, skin tones of a child may be done by hand while the rest of the image is done by the camera process. This requires an expertise gained only by experience, knowing what each decision will mean when the final product goes to the oven for firing.

Printing plates are made for each color separation, regardless of the separation method used. The printing of the decal is an arduous procedure. Decals are printed on special paper that has a very shiny, smooth film on one side. This paper dissolves when dipped in water prior to transferring the decal to the blank plate for firing. Decal paper also is unique in that it always lies perfectly flat, permitting the layers of colored ceramic powder to be applied precisely.

Blank sheets of decal paper are placed in an offset printing press and are individually printed with a very thin layer of varnish, the pattern of which is determined by the color separation. The sheet then goes to a dusting machine, where the special ceramic color powder is applied. When fired, this powder "paints" the plate.

Only the varnished areas hold the powder, and only one color per day can be printed. The decals are reinserted each day, and new color is added until each decal is completed. If the plate requires twenty colors, it will take twenty days to print the decals alone. They are constantly checked throughout the printing process for correct alignment of the colored powder. The different colors must be perfectly aligned so that there will be no overlapping of color or gaps in the design on the finished plate.

When all of the colors have been applied to the decal, it is sealed with a thin top layer of clear lacquer. This lacquer is organic and dissolves without a trace during the firing of the plate. Its only job is to hold the colors in place while the decal is transferred to the blank ceramic plate.

David Jacobs of Design Point Decal, Inc., of New Hyde Park, New York, a leading decal manufacturer whose skills have been used by Pemberton & Oakes and The Hamilton Collection, puts it all in perspective:

> Producing the ceramic transfer is perhaps the most difficult, time–consuming and exacting art form in the world. No one has yet invented an automated, mechanical, or photographic method that can satisfactorily reproduce an artist's original hand–painted design, decoration, or image on a ceramic transfer. Unlike painting or printing on paper or canvas, in which the final results of color are immediately evident, the printing of the ceramic transfer gives no valid indication of its final colors until it is actually fired in the kiln. Even after ceramic decals emerge from the press, the final colors are not evident and are haunted by the unknown judge— how the decal will fire in the kiln. The ceramic decal is plagued with so many natural and man–made variations that its creation has been described as involving 10,000 times more headaches than printing with a standard four–color process.

When the decals are finished, they are sent to the plate manufacturer, where they will be transferred to the blank, back–stamped plates for firing. Hand–decorated detail work may also be added at this time, such as the application of a gold border. If everyone along the way has done his job perfectly, the finished plate will be a true reproduction of the original painting. The process is very exacting, as some plates require several firings.

OTHER MATERIALS

Since the vast majority of limited edition plates are made from pottery or porcelain and decorated with ceramic decals, understanding this very complicated procedure gives us an added appreciation for the finished product. However, this is by no means the only method or material used.

Wedgwood makes its plates with unglazed stained jasperware, which features applied white bas–relief figures in a classical motif. Studio di Volteradici executes its sculpted plates in ivory alabaster. Incolay Studios has come up with a new material made from crushed rock with a marble–like appearance. Lalique of France uses lead crystal with etched details. The Franklin Mint, River Shore, Danbury Mint, and Reed and Barton, to name a few, produce sculpted metal plates made from gold, silver, pewter, or damascene. Another new material, toriart, was devised by the House of Anri. It consists of wood resin that is molded and hand–painted in bright colors. One of the most unusual plates is the exquisite stained glass plate "Old Ironsides," produced by the United States Historical Society. The stained glass portion is surrounded by a polished pewter rim. It has been acclaimed by collectors and has already made a permanent place for itself in the plate world.

IN SUMMARY

The diversity of material, theme, size, shape, and price of limited edition plates is no doubt responsible for the tremendous popularity of this collectible field. Welcome to the wonderful world of collector plates!

The History of Collector Plates

Although decorative plates have fascinated people for centuries, the hobby of collecting is a fairly recent occurrence. Elaborate designs on plates date from the third and fourth centuries, e.g., an ornamental plate called "The Paris Plate."

Through the centuries two key discoveries laid the foundation for the production of the first collector plate. The initial discovery occurred in China, where the process for making porcelain was perfected. When the formula was finally brought to Europe, English and Continental manufacturers began making fine ceramic wares.

A desire for decoration led to the second major discovery. In 1888 Arnold Krog, director of Royal Copenhagen, one of the oldest porcelain factories in Denmark, perfected the underglazing process. Underglazed decoration was produced by dipping an object into a transparent glaze after it had been painted in cobalt blue glaze. The two glazes fused to produce a fuzzy blue and white surface.

Many porcelain factories in Europe produced controlled production sets of decorative plates or commemorative issues in honor of celebrated guests visiting their countries. These specimens, although limited in their production size, were the forerunners of the modern collector plates. They didn't qualify as *limited* by today's standards. Although the production run was limited initially, if enough people requested the item, the manufacturer made more. These plates prepared the public for acceptance of the collector plate concept.

THE BIRTH OF THE MODERN COLLECTOR PLATE

There was a custom in Denmark for many years, as the story goes, of the wealthy giving gifts to their servants at Christmastime. To celebrate the holidays, they would fill plates with cakes and cookies to take to their servants. Over the years the plates became more and more decorative. Eventually the recipients valued the plates more highly than the treats found on them. Soon people started hanging the plates on the wall.

In 1895 Harald Bing, of Bing & Grondahl, decided to produce a decorative plate designed especially for this gift–giving custom. He also wanted to test the value of adding novelty giftware items to his current product line.

This plate, which is considered the first true *collector plate*, carried a design of the Copenhagen skyline in winter. It was named "Behind the Frozen Window" and inscribed with the date 1895. The swishes of white against a blue background were a design by Franz August Hallin.

Though the company did not plan this plate as a series, the use of a date encouraged the company to issue another Christmas plate for 1896. Sales of the 1895 plate satisfied expectations, and Bing & Grondahl has been issuing Christmas plates ever since. This is the oldest collector plate series and is also the largest in terms of the number of plates produced. While it is certainly the most challenging and costly for a hobbyist to assemble, it is by no means impossible.

Bing & Grondahl, Christmas Series 1898, Roses and Star

Bing & Grondahl, Christmas Series 1912, Going to Church

Bing & Grondahl's success produced imitators. Most of the earliest series to follow were short–lived. Rorstrand of Sweden began producing a series of plates in 1904. The series ended after twenty–two years. Porsgrund, another Norwegian company, issued a Christmas plate in 1909. It was the only one they made.

Rosenthal, a German manufacturer, marketed Christmas plates between 1905 and 1909. Hutschenreuther and KPM–Berlin also produced early plates, both surviving only a few years.

In 1908 Royal Copenhagen, another Danish company, introduced a Christmas plate series that still continues in production. The success of Royal Copenhagen's Christmas plate series roughly paralleled that of Bing & Grondahl.

Collector plate production slowed during World War I, from 1914 to 1918, due to the scarcity of materials. Buying also slowed because few Europeans could afford to buy luxury items during the economic depressions that followed both World War I and World War II. No one could foresee the complex level of buying, selling, and trading that occurs today.

BEGINNING OF THE POST–WORLD WAR II COLLECTOR PLATE PHENOMENON

Lalique, a French glassworks company, made the first plate issued as something other than giftware. In 1965 Lalique announced its intention of producing an *annual* plate for collectors. Unlike earlier manufacturers, who made no special concessions to collectors, Lalique proclaimed that its first plate would be limited — not only in length of time produced but in *actual number* as well. This new approach broadened the plate horizon. The contemporary collector plate was born. Lalique produced just two thousand specimens of its 1965 plate, a thousand of which were placed in the hands of U.S. distributors. Lalique apparently was well aware that the concept of a *collector plate in limited edition* would be received more favorably in America than anywhere else. The issue price was set at $25.

The venture was a resounding success. For the next several years the porcelain trade and related industries tracked the rising growth of the collector plate market. Lalique kept producing annual plates, as did the old–line firms. Collector interest built. As early as 1968, collectors were combing the market for 1965 Lalique plates. When an example was found it was priced at four times the original retail price.

Secondary market values rose on earlier plates, even though they had not been manufactured with any announced limit on quantities. The late 1960's secondary market was a paradise for any willing buyer or any investor with the slightest foresight. Half–century–old plates, whose numbers in existence had vastly diminished over the years, could be purchased for modest sums. Even when bought at double or triple original retail price, the cost was a mere fraction of present day values. And this was less than thirty years ago!

The 1965 Lalique plate became the subject of tremendous speculation. No other plate issued up to that time had generated so much collecting activity. Some observers cynically commented on inflated prices, noting that they were sure to go down, leaving owners holding overpriced, hard–to–sell examples. The plate eventually reached a high of $1,800. Today it books at $1,250. Yes, some plate speculators lost money. However, the value drop never reached the levels predicted by the critics. A $1,225 return on an initial $25 investment thirty years ago still far exceeds what one would have realized by putting the $25 in a bank savings account.

What did the 1965 Lalique plate prove? First, the American public would respond favorably to high–quality, limited edition plates, not only favorably but in great numbers, and with a passion. Second, they were not scared off by the speculative secondary market. In fact, they seemed encouraged by it. As the price of the 1965 Lalique rose, so did the demand.

Lalique's success was not lost on other ceramic manufacturers. A collector plate market was clearly established. Product was needed to fuel the market. By the early 1970s dozens of manufacturers entered the limited edition plate field.

COLLECTOR PLATES IN THE 1970s

The next important event instrumental in establishing the present–day collector plate market occurred in 1969. In that year Wedgwood, the most prestigious earthenware company in Great Britain, inaugurated a series of Christmas plates. Wedgwood, with roots dating to the eighteenth century, was a legend in the industry. The year 1969 marked Wedgwood's two–hundredth anniversary, the perfect starting date for a line of annual plates. Its first annual plate was in blue with a white sculptured likeness of Windsor Castle. It read: "Christmas 1969."

Wedgwood was collector–conscious. It planned its entry into the annual market with collectors specifically in mind. As such, Wedgwood did more in terms of drawing other companies into the collector plate field than did Lalique or any of its predecessors. Just like the 1965 Lalique plate, the Wedgwood plates's price was set at $25. Wedgwood never published the production numbers for its 1969 plate. Although not promoted as a limited edition, Wedgwood assured its customers that they would indeed be owning an item of some exclusivity. After production ceased, the company destroyed the mold and thereby rendered further production, authorized or unauthorized, impossible. This was a promise to the public that no previous manufacturer had made prior to that time.

Demand soon exceeded supply. Examples appeared quickly on the secondary market. During 1970 the price rose and topped at $240. The pace of buying and selling, especially in the United States, and the rate of price increase exceeded that of the 1965 Lalique plate.

Dozens of companies soon began producing collector plates, an activity that proved very beneficial to the market. With more and more plates being issued, another buyer entered the market: the hobbyist who not only wanted to collect but who wanted (in the early 1970s, anyway) one example of every plate produced.

What was the collector plate market potential? No one in the early 1970s knew. America was unquestionably a nation of collectors. There were doubters who felt that the initial collecting enthusiasm could not be sustained. It was and continued to grow.

The Franklin Mint of Franklin Center, Pennsylvania, took a very innovative step in 1970. This organization, operating since 1964, had dealt mainly in commemorative medals and other numismatic items. The company wanted to make a splash when it entered the collector plate market. The Franklin Mint contracted with Norman Rockwell, America's most recognized illustrator, to design its plate. In addition, Franklin Mint decided to produce the plate in sterling silver, not ceramics, thereby capturing the collector market from several distinct angles. For those who collected Rockwell, the plate was a must. Buyers also came from the ranks of silver investors, a field previously uninterested in collector plates.

With that kind of varied appeal, the 1970 Rockwell–designed plate's success was assured, even at the very high issue price of $100 — the most expensive collector plate offered up to that time. Fearing that the price might place it out of reach for the average buyer and that the concept of a colorless plate would not necessarily be appealing, some gift shops hesitated to order it. Those who put confidence in the 1970 Franklin plate were rewarded. It sold extremely well. When it entered the secondary market, its value jumped wildly. Thereafter, Franklin Mint became one of the leaders of the plate industry, offering collectors' editions in not only silver but also porcelain and crystal. The scope of Franklin Mint's plate production has become so extensive that many collectors now specialize exclusively in the works of this company.

The early 1970s was a period of intense activity for plate collecting, molding the hobby into its present proportions. Collector magazines and the general press began running stories about plate collecting. Specialized publications for the hobby made an appearance. Shows were held. Clubs and associations were founded.

The number of manufacturers issuing plates and the types of plates offered on the market multiplied at an unprecedented rate: collector editions in glass, silver, pewter, wood, and other materials followed. Collectible ornaments and figurines arrived on the scene. In the late 1980s they would challenge plates for leadership in the limited edition marketplace.

On the secondary market, competition between hobbyists and investors drove some values to astronomical heights. Prices changed so rapidly that dealers could scarcely keep track. Published advertisements became obsolete a few weeks after release. Naturally, this state of affairs created enormous confusion. Speculation was rampant.

Manufacturers and dealers of collector plates needed to react quickly before the problems became counterproductive and caused long–term harm. Specific problems were addressed, chief among them the controversy over use of the term "limited edition." It became apparent that some manufacturers, while labeling their plates limited editions, had produced them in very large quantities—the editions were either not truly limited or limited to such high numbers that the edition carried no exclusivity. Restraint and honesty was requested.

Second, a number of lesser quality plates appeared on the market. This was the result of a certain amount of bandwagoning, or quick entry into the field, by manufacturers whose standards of quality were lower than the initial manufacturers.

Third, the speculative fever needed to be brought under control. It was inevitable that speculation should occur. The circumstances invited it. It appeared to anyone watching the market in the years from 1970 to 1972 that investment buyers had lost all sense of reason and were pumping huge sums of money into anything called limited edition — not just plates but medals, prints, statuettes, and other items. Serious collectors attempted to use judgment in their buying, but even they were at a disadvantage because of the newness of the hobby. They could not help but be influenced by the wild movement of prices.

Many certainly felt justified in paying $300 or $400 for a plate whose issue price had been one–tenth that much. Waiting could have meant paying an even higher figure while watching the price soar completely out of reach. If collectors alone or collectors combined with a minor sprinkling of investors constituted the market, things would not have reached the panic level. Prices would have advanced but at a much slower and steadier pace.

The ideal market is one with price stability. Slow growth allows more time for all concerned (including the dealers) to plan their course of action. As things stood, many people bought in a rush and sold in a rush.

By 1973 so many plates appeared on the secondary market that supply began to exceed demand. Prices decreased on a number of editions, including quality plates that did not deserve to get caught up in this tornado of speculation and profiteering.

Plate collecting had been called a "fad," a passing fancy from which the public would soon turn. The first indication of market weakness was seized on as proof that these assertions were correct. Actually, the events of 1973 were the best thing that could have happened to the hobby. They shook plate collecting out of the fantasy world into which it had been led by speculators and profiteers and brought it back to earth. The way was opened for serious collectors, fair–minded dealers, and responsible manufacturers to take over.

Some manufacturers went out of business, primarily those firms whose plates had been bought largely by investors and attracted only a minimal hobbyist following. Some plate prices dipped by 50 percent or more within one calendar year in the mid–1970s. Once again, these were mainly editions that had no special claim on the collector's attention, whose prices had risen out of all proportion to their quality, originality, or edition size.

*Goebel/Hummel, 1973
Annual Plate, Globe Trotter*

The sudden dose of reality drove home a clear message: plate collecting was not going to be a paradise for quick–buck artists and entrepreneurs. It was shaping itself into an activity of genuine prestige, where quality and reputation carried weight and the inferior product or questionable sales approach would be recognized as such.

Several key manufacturers, one of whom was The Franklin Mint, re–evaluated their sales literature. No longer were collector plates hyped as long–term potential investments, but rather as the collectibles they are. It took some manufacturers and distributors longer than others to follow The Franklin Mint's lead. This reorganization of the market caused pain and financial loss to many individuals, especially those from low– and middle–income families who "invested" much of their life savings into collector plates. There was a lesson learned — one that extended even beyond plates into other hobbies: there is no such thing as instant money. Serious collectors uniformly applauded it.

By the end of the 1970s, the youthful exuberance of the collector plate market was ending. The phenomenal annual growth experienced by collector plates in the early and mid–1970s leveled. The speculative secondary market saw prices decline more often than rise. The speculative bubble burst. Several manufacturers discontinue collector plate production.

COLLECTOR PLATES IN THE 1980s AND 1990s

The collector plate market matured in the 1980s. Once again, the market was the provenance of manufacturers, collectors, and dealers willing to make a long–term commitment. The number of new plate issues declined sharply. This actually helped the market by providing collectors with more focused buying opportunities and allowing them to buy without becoming financially overextended.

Two central selling themes — artist and subject matter — dominate the collector plate market of the 1980s and 1990s. Collector plate manufacturers carefully follow several contemporary art mediums, the most important of which is limited edition prints. When an artist achieves national recognition, a collector plate series often follows. The 1980s witnessed the arrival of Ben Black and Rusty Money. Thomas Kinkade arrived in the 1990s.

In the 1980s collector plate manufacturers increased their reliance on crossover buyers. A crossover buyer is an individual who is buying the plate primarily for its subject matter, e.g., a plate containing an image of a favorite movie or music star. Clearly, one of the major image shifts in the collector plate field was the arrival of the personality–driven plate image.

By the mid–1980s, the secondary collector plate market had virtually disappeared. Those who owned plates were unwilling to sell them for prices substantially below that which they paid. Best to store them and wait for the market to improve. The recession of the late 1980s and early 1990s further reinforced this approach.

If collector plates were king of the limited edition market in the 1970s, collectible figurines reign supreme in the late 1990s. While collector plates remain an important part of the contemporary collectibles market, figurines, ornaments, and prints enjoy a much stronger market share. However, what comes around, goes around.

As this book goes to press, signs of a collector plate renaissance are positive. First, several new manufacturers have entered the collector plate field. Many specialize in small runs and focus on a single theme. Fewer and fewer manufacturers are "limiting" their production, preferring to emphasize long–term rather than limited collectibility.

Second, the secondary market for collector plates is beginning to show signs of renewed activity. While interest is selective, several 1970s plate series are beginning to attract new collectors. Secondary prices have bottomed out. The climb upward will be gradual and cautious. Those willing to be patient just a little while longer will be rewarded.

Third, there is a growing negative collector reaction to collectibles made from plastic, i.e., resin. Collectors like the firm, solid feel of ceramics. Plastic will never convey the same sense of timelessness as ceramic. The exact impact this will have on the collector plate market will be determined in the years ahead.

Manufacturers: A Few Histories

ANNA–PERENNA PORCELAIN, INC.

Anna–Perenna Porcelain, Inc., is an international firm specializing in fine art on limited edition collector plates. Offerings of this firm are made of the finest hard–paste Bavarian porcelain, created in a tradition dating back many generations. The firm also makes miniature figurines, limited edition sculptures, and carousel music boxes.

The firm was founded in 1977 by Klaus D. Vogt, former president of Rosenthal, U.S.A. Vogt was fascinated by the possibilities of fine art on fine porcelain and left Rosenthal to pursue this new art medium.

The name Anna–Perenna is derived from the Roman goddess of spring. From her name the English words for "annual" and "perennial" also stem. This international firm required a name that could be pronounced easily in English, German, and French, and Anna–Perenna filled the bill. Even more appropriately, this goddess was also the protectorate of the arts.

Anna–Perenna Porcelain has commissioned some of the world's most celebrated and unique artists to create original artwork for collector plates. Each Anna–Perenna artist submits paintings "in the round," and as near to the actual size of the plate as possible, as Vogt stresses that this is the only way to achieve fidelity in the creation of multicolor art on porcelain plates.

Anna–Perenna artists include Count Lennart Bernadotte, creator of a collection inspired by his Island of Mainau; Ken Danby, Canadian Reflections of Youth Series artist; Thaddeus "Uncle Tad" Krumeich, creator of numerous cat–subject plates; Frank Russell and Gertrude Barrer, who introduced the triptych concept to the plate world; actress–turned–artist Elke Sommer; Margaret Kane, creator of the unique Masquerade Fantasy plates; and Pat Buckley Moss, artist for American Silhouettes, Annual Christmas, Celebration Series, Carousel Triptych, the Four Seasons Quartet, and the Heartland Series. Also on the roster are Canadian–Indian master artist Norval Morrisseau, cartoonist–turned–plate–artist Al Hirschfeld, and Nori Peter, famous for her Eskimo subjects.

BAREUTHER

In 1867 a German sculptor founded a porcelain factory in Waldsassen, Bavaria. Johann Matthaeus Ries, with one small porcelain kiln and one anular brick kiln, began producing dinnerware, vases, and giftware. The factory grew and flourished but was sold in 1884 by Ries's son to Oskar Bareuther. The porcelain factory, called Bareuther, has since grown into one of the world's leading factories.

In 1967, to celebrate Bareuther's 100th anniversary, the company issued the first in a series of Christmas plates. Each plate in the series, which still continues today, is decorated in cobalt blue underglaze with an inscription of the year and "Weihnachten." The artist for the first issue was Hans Mueller, who was himself a son of a Bareuther artist. He joined the factory in 1952 as an artist after studying at the Porcelain Academy in Selb. He was promoted to chief designer in 1968.

Since the Christmas Series was so widely accepted, Bareuther released in 1969 the first issues in a Mother's Day Series and a Father's Day Series. These are also done in underglazed cobalt blue with inscriptions "Mutterag" and "Vaterag." A Thanksgiving Day Series was started in 1971, with the first issue titled "First Thanksgiving." To commemorate the first ten years of the very successful Christmas Series, a "Jubilee Plate" was issued in 1977.

Today the Bareuther factory enjoys much popularity with hobbyists in the collectors' market. They continue to produce a new issue each year in their three collector plate series and fine dinnerware and giftware items that are exported to at least thirty countries. The factory's seven hundred employees include sixty painters and sixty printers, who strive to keep Bareuther items as highly respected and valued as they have been for over one hundred years.

BING & GRONDAHL

When Frederick Grondahl, a porcelain modeler, and Meyer and Jacob Bing, merchant brothers, joined in 1853 to form a porcelain factory, one of today's most widely recognized companies was born. They began their production of bisque plaques the next year from designs by a well–known Danish sculptor named Thorwaldsen. Within ten years their production was such that they decided to add figurines and dinnerware to their line.

With the advent of underglazing by Arnold Krog of Royal Copenhagen, a new aspect of porcelain design began to be experimented with in the Bing & Grondahl factory. The process was much popularized at the World Exhibition in Paris in 1900 by a painter named Willumsen. For years only the

"Copenhagen blue" was used to color porcelain wares, but Bing & Grondahl later discovered that other colors, such as black, brown, green, and flesh tones, could withstand the intense heat of a high–gloss firing.

In 1895 Harald Bing decided to make a decorative plate for Christmas. His idea was, first of all, for a functional plate, but he also wanted to add some decoration to an old Danish custom. Traditionally, the wealthy would bring gifts of plates of cakes and cookies to their servants in celebration of the holiday. The plates became more and more decorative through the years. To carry on the tradition, Bing designed a blue and white snow scene that, although intended for practical use, became the first "collectible" plate.

The 1895 plate showed the Copenhagen skyline from "Behind a Frozen Window." The swishes of white against the blue background, as designed by Franz August Hallin, beautifully depicted a Danish winter. Many subsequent issues picture snowy Danish landscapes incorporated with the Christmas holiday.

In addition to Christmas plates, Bing & Grondahl produced Mother's Day and Olympic plates and commemorative issues. The same quality has applied to each item in its line of production. For instance, the hours of hand labor painstakingly used in producing one figurine would add up to weeks of artists' and craftsmens' skillful work.

Today, the quality of Bing & Grondahl products is assured to any buyer by the traditional three–tower backstamp. It depicts the towers used in the coat of arms of the city of Copenhagen.

The factory, located in the heart of the city, uses several tons of clay daily in producing its artware, dinnerware, and figurines. Some 1,300 workers skillfully monitor and produce about 10 million pieces each year. Its line of production also includes bells, cameos for jewelry, thimbles, and even high–voltage insulators.

FENTON ART GLASS COMPANY

In 1905 two brothers, John and Frank Fenton, opened a glass–decorating business in Martins Ferry, West Virginia, called the Fenton Art Glass Company. In a short time the business, although relatively small, began to appear as a threat of competition to the companies who were supplying Fenton with glass "blanks" for decoration. Consequently, the companies soon refused to deliver any more glass. Within the next two years, the Fenton brothers decided to alleviate the problem by producing their own glass.

The plant, now located in Williamstown, drew skilled glassworkers— one in particular who worked with colors and helped teach other glassworkers to make carnival glass. Many variations have been produced through the years by Fenton because of the many glass treatments that were tried and perfected by craftsmen. Colors were added: caramel slag, or chocolate glass; Burmese, a greenish–yellow shade; milk glass, white and opaque; and Vasa Murrihina, a transparent glass with suspended flakes of mica that appear as silver or gold

With these innovative ideas put to practice, the company, as a natural step of succession, entered the collector plate market. Fenton had already gained a reputation for its glasswares and was being sought by collectors all over. In 1970 the first issue in the American Craftsman Series was released. The series was created to honor the craftsmen who built America, and the first issue was appropriately titled "Glassmaker." Also in 1970, the Christmas in America Series began with the first issue — "Little Brown Church in the Vale" — produced in carnival, blue satin, and brown glass.

The Fenton Art Glass Company is still producing decorative plates and offers designs from its own artists in the decorating department as well as scenes from Currier & Ives. The products made today are different from those first pieces produced in 1907, but all are quality wares from the Fenton Art Glass Company.

FRANKOMA POTTERY

In 1927 a young man of twenty–three moved from Chicago to Norman, Oklahoma, to become an instructor of art and ceramics at the University of Oklahoma. Because of his involvement in studies and geological surveys of the Oklahoma clays, John Frank set a goal to open the first pottery there to produce wares made only from Oklahoma clays. He founded the Frankoma Pottery in 1933, and with one kiln, a butter churn to mix the clay, and fruit jars of glaze, he began making pottery for everyday uses. A clay from Ada was originally used, but on discovering a red–burning clay in Sapula, Frank chose this clay to be the substance from which all Frankoma pottery is made.

Frank and his wife, Grace Lee, struggled through some hard times trying to make their pottery a success. They had grown into a small factory by 1938, when they moved to Sapula to further their studies on clays. The next years were hard, and with their seven employees the Franks developed a once–fired process, where the clay and glaze are fired at the same time as the maturing point of the clay. The rugged, everyday earthenware was durable and beautiful with its bright–colored glazes, but the Frank family decided to try something new.

In 1965 Frank designed a decorative plate that became the first Christmas plate annually produced in America. Inspired by the Christmas story, Frank chose "Good Will Toward Men" as the title of this first in a series that still continues today. A Della Robbia white glaze has a unique effect on each Christmas theme shown in bas–relief. Another series titled Teenagers of the Bible was started in 1973, and a Madonnas Series was designed by

Grace Lee. Each issue for each series is produced for one year, and then the mold is destroyed on Christmas Eve.

After Frank's death in 1973, his daughter Joneice continued to design the two series originated by her father. For more information see Phyllis and Tom Bess' *Frankoma and Other Oklahoma Potteries,* Schiffer Publishing, 1995.

DAVE GROSSMAN CREATIONS

Dave Grossman Creations began producing collectibles in 1973, most notably figurines inspired by the works of Norman Rockwell. The company began and has remained in St. Louis, Missouri since 1968 and is owned and run solely by Dave Grossman. Mr. Grossman originally began his business by creating and marketing metal sculptures and has since expanded into many areas of collectible art.

Mr. Grossman is a native of St. Louis. After graduating from the University of Missouri, he was commissioned to do architectural sculptures for banks, hospitals, hotels, and other public and private buildings. One of his works is in the Lincoln Center in New York. He was also commissioned to create sculptures for Presidents Johnson and Nixon.

In 1973 Dave Grossman Creations became the first company to produce a collectible line inspired by the work of Norman Rockwell, doing so under a license from Curtis Publishing Company. In addition to its Rockwell items and annual ornament, the firm produced a Christmas plate, water globe, and figurine each year.

The Grossman organization also has other licensed lines including the "Original Emmett Kelly Collection," the "Gone With the Wind" collection, and "The Wizard of Oz." Emmett Kelly was the most famous circus clown of all time, and this line is licensed through his estate. "Gone With the Wind" and "The Wizard of Oz" are licensed through Turner Entertainment Company.

Grossman also produces other figurine lines and plans to expand on existing lines while marketing new collectibles. Mr. Grossman takes pride in the quality of his work and his devotion to the collector.

HADLEY COMPANIES

The Hadley Companies history is a chronicle of its founder, Ray E. Johnson, who turned his passion for antiques and wildlife into a multimillion dollar art business. While vacationing in rural Wisconsin in the summer of 1975, Johnson came upon a wood carver whose antique lathe created the best reproduction duck decoy Johnson had ever seen. Fascinated by the discovery, Johnson returned to Minnesota where he and two friends replicated the carver's machine. Within weeks, the trio set about producing wooden decoys for amateur carvers in a tiny roadside shop in St. Bonifacius, a small community west of Minneapolis.

In the fall of 1976, Johnson launched his first Wooden Bird retail gallery. He soon increased its carvings to more than fifty intricately painted decorative birds. In 1978, wildlife artist Terry Redlin added his limited edition prints to the offering, beginning a long and prosperous relationship between the two wildlife art enthusiasts.

By the early 1980s, The Wooden Bird had begun publishing limited edition art by other talented American artists. In 1985, it adopted the corporate identity of The Hadley Companies to reflect its growing diversification and national distribution network. Hadley's publishing department manages the production of master editions of canvas lithographs and repligraphs, as well as premium art books, greeting cards, and collectibles in porcelain and glass. Collector plates alone account for nearly 40 percent of the department's production.

Hadley House artists create works which reflect the core tastes of the American public. Particularly popular are themes depicting wildlife and nature, nostalgia, landscapes, and Americana. Nationally prominent artists Terry Redlin (voted America's most popular artist for three consecutive years), Steve Hanks, Mike Capser, Darrell Bush, Dave Barnhouse, John Banovich, Stephen Hamrick, Lesley Harrison, Les Didier, Nancy Howe, Jon Van Zyle, Bryan Moon, Al Agnew, and Jerry Raedeke are represented.

Today this international art enterprise commands a prominent position in the art and collectibles marketplace. Relying on inspired leadership, the strength of its artist roster and a seasoned management team, The Hadley Companies is poised to continue its phenomenal ascent in the decades ahead.

1995 Annual Christmas Series,
Sharing the Evening,
Terry Redlin.

EDNA HIBEL STUDIO

Since the founding of the Edna Hibel Gallery in 1960, this private company has been dedicated to the publishing and distribution of all the collectibles, gifts, decorative accessories, and original fine arts of one of America's best loved and most versatile artists, Edna Hibel. All the products are created by Edna Hibel, who, by virtue of her recent selection by the U.S. National Archives to commemorate the 75th anniversary of women obtaining the right to vote, has been referred to as the heart and conscience of America.

Edna Hibel's first collector plate in 1973 revived the entire plate market. Hibel, now seventy–nine, is renowned for depicting the love between mothers and children and many of her collector plates show this subject matter. Other Hibel plates show children's heads and flower girls.

Thousands of galleries and stores across the country and overseas handle Hibel's work in all of its forms. Dealers and collectors are invited each year to HibelFest, the world's largest solo–artist exhibition in Florida, Massachusetts, and Illinois. Members of the Edna Hibel Society are invited to exclusive art tours and events at the Hibel Museum of Art in Palm Beach, Florida. This museum is the world's only nonprofit museum dedicated to the art of a living American woman. In addition, Hibel's artwork was commissioned by the Foundation for the U.S. National Archives to commemorate the 75th anniversary of the ratification of the 19th Amendment to the U.S. Constitution.

The work of Edna Hibel has been exhibited in prestigious museums and galleries on four continents, including the National Museum of Women in the Arts (Washington, D.C.), United Nations (New York City), the National Museum of Costa Rica, the National Museum of Fine Arts (Brazil), the Russian Academy of Art, and the China National Art Gallery (Beijing).

PEMBERTON & OAKES

Pemberton & Oakes Galleries entered the limited edition field in 1977 to provide high–quality, affordable art to American art collectors. To begin the company's entry into this field, President John Hugunin selected Chicago–based artist Donald Zolan, who has displayed a remarkable ability to capture real–life children in situations that showed the wonder and joy of early childhood.

Pemberton & Oakes issued its first limited edition plate, the famous "Erik and Dandelion" by Donald Zolan, in 1978. Zolan began winning Favorite Living Plate Artist awards, in addition to Plate of the Year accolades, in both the United States and Canada.

"I wanted to see what would happen," Hugunin recalls, "if we pushed the level of plate quality as high as possible and yet kept a tight ceiling on both price and quantity. The result has been a string of award–winning plates that has sold out rapidly and then appreciated even more rapidly on the secondary market. I get letters all the time from collectors who bought their Zolan plates because they were touched by the art but who are also pleased as punch that their plates are worth a whole lot more than they paid for them."

Pemberton & Oakes has also produced major series of collector plates by artists Robert Anderson and Shell Fisher, and it produces the annual "Nutcracker Ballet" plate, which depicts a scene from Tchaikovsky's immortal Christmas ballet.

PICKARD, INC.

Pickard, Inc. was established in Edgerton, Wisconsin in 1893 by Wilder Austin Pickard, and moved to Chicago in 1897. For some forty years the Pickard China Studio, as the firm was then known, was a decorating company specializing in hand–painted art pieces and dessert and tea sets. Many of the original artists were from the Art Institute of Chicago. The staff was increased by renowned ceramic artists from all the countries of Europe. Since most of the china was manufactured abroad at the time, the Pickard studios imported blank ware to be decorated. These early pieces are now sought after by collectors.

When Wilder's son Austin entered the business, he longed for the day that Pickard would no longer be dependent upon outside sources. He dreamed of manufacturing in Illinois as fine a china as could be found anywhere in the world. In 1930, experiments began. It took seven years before the secret Pickard formula was developed — a delicate blend of many different clays and minerals considered worthy to bear Pickard's proud new "Lion" trademark. Further experiments produced a formula for glaze that is considered by many experts as the finest in the industry.

Production was moved to Antioch, in the lakes region of northern Illinois, in 1937. This peaceful setting proved ideal for the painstaking craftsmanship and skilled handwork necessary to produce top quality ware. Pickard became known for creating a beautiful warm white china as well as lovely decorations.

Austin's son, Henry A. "Pete" Pickard, represented the third generation to enter the business and served as president from 1966 until his retirement in 1994. Pete's brother–in–law, Eben C. Morgan Jr., is the current president and carries on the family management that has directed the company for more than a hundred years.

Pickard, Inc. manufactures a wide spectrum of collector plates, the range of subjects including reproductions of religious works such as "Alba Madonna" by the old masters, the "Lockhart Wildlife Series," "Children of Renoir," "Mother's Love Series" and "Let's Pretend" by Irene Spencer, and "Gems of Nature" by Cyndi Nelson. "The Presidential Bowl," celebrating the bicentennial of the U.S. presidency, was introduced in 1989. The first order was placed personally by President George Bush. Since Pickard, Inc. began producing limited edition collector plates and bowls, the company has been the recipient of several awards including "Best Manufacturer of Limited Editions" by readers of *Plate Collector* magazine for seven consecutive years.

ROCKWELL MUSEUM

In 1975 Donald and Marshall Stoltz opened a museum of the largest and most complete exhibit of the works of one of America's best–known artists. Norman Rockwell was the artist who told a pictorial history, clearly and with great detail, of the life of the typical American.

Rockwell was born in 1894, and as early as age five he began drawing. Although he never finished high school, he studied at Chase School of Art and at the National Academy of Art. He also received a degree, a doctorate in Fine Arts, from the University of Vermont. Rockwell's illustrations and paintings reflect a sense of real life, as if he had frozen a moment of life just so he could reproduce it to every exact detail. He gained the American people's attention, if not their hearts, with his illustrations for the covers of the *Saturday Evening Post* and *Boy's Life*.

The Norman Rockwell Museum in Philadelphia represents the reality of a dream after the Stoltz brothers had collected Rockwell's works for over thirty years. In 1978 a selection of twelve works was chosen to portray moments of American life on collector plates. Production of the American Family Series began, and what was originally meant to be a collection of only twelve expanded into a whole new series called American Family Series II. Then, after Rockwell died that same year, a special plate was issued titled "Rockwell Remembered," to pay tribute to his meaningful career.

Since then Rockwell's works have been the subjects of many plates made by the Museum and by many other companies. However, the Museum marks each piece they produce with a seal of authenticity. This seal is round and carries the Museum's name and a silhouette of Rockwell.

A celebration of his life is carried on by the Museum and the Stoltz brothers. The words of Marshall Stoltz express the respect and love for Rockwell illustrations that much of America feels today: "Norman Rockwell was a master at his craft. No one captured America like Rockwell."

ROYAL COPENHAGEN

In the early 1770s a Dane name Frantz Heinrich Muller founded the oldest porcelain factory in Denmark. Four years later, when the company was granted royal privileges, it was named Royal Copenhagen, as it is known today. In 1867 the firm lost its royal status, but this didn't stop its success. When Arnold Krog became the company's director in 1885, he began developing a technique that proved to be a great asset to the field of ceramics.

Royal Copenhagen wares are perhaps best known for a soft appearance common to many plates and figurines. This process, known as underglaze painting, was perfected by Krog in 1888. The method of dipping an object into a transparent glaze after it has been colorfully painted sparked great interest in factories all over Europe. Carving a mold to develop the artist's design in relief worked very well with the underglazed effect to create a unique design since made famous by Royal Copenhagen.

Many companies have used the underglazing process, but a highly recognizable trademark distinguishes Royal Copenhagen from the rest. It consists of three wavy blue lines. Each stands for one of the principal Danish waterways: The Sound, The Great Belt, and The Little Belt. Although there have been minor variations, the trademark has remained steady, just as the quality of its products has. Royal Copenhagen has traditionally drawn talented sculptors and artists to create the right effect for each of its products: the delicacy of porcelain, the sturdiness of stoneware, and the bright colors of faience.

Since its first Christmas plate was produced in 1908, the factory has designed collector plates for eighty years. The company employs 1,700 workers, craftsmen, and technicians. The factory's painters alone comprise 650 of these. Each person does his job in creating Christmas, Mother's Day, historical, and special issue plates. Each strives to continue the traditions that were set many years ago by the original skilled artisans of the Royal Copenhagen porcelain factory.

Gallery of Artists

DAVE BARNHOUSE

Dave Barnhouse is a self–described "country boy" from Richmond, Ohio, who grew up in small towns and has no intention of leaving their environs either physically or emotionally. In commenting on his art he says, "I want to make people feel as if they were back home on a Friday evening, so they can experience the warmth of a cozy fire and smell the homemade bread and cookies coming from the oven."

As soon as he could hold a pencil, Dave started expressing his artistic talents. One of his first drawings was a threshing machine on his grandfather's farm in Ohio. After an early fascination with old farm equipment, he began to paint sports and aviation subjects, teaching himself to work primarily with oils.

Currently, Mr. Barnhouse has settled into the Americana genre. Whether the scene is a summer evening in the small village of Richmond, a sunny afternoon in the countryside or a night scene in a country town getting ready for the annual dance, the warm feeling of good times shines through.

Mr. Barnhouse has exhibited his originals in art shows throughout the country. *U.S.ART* named Barnhouse an "Artist to Watch" in its December, 1994 issue. He was also included in *InformArt's* "Top 10 Hottest New Artists" in the 1995 Annual Resource issue. In 1994 the artist took Best of Show at the Stuebenville Art Show in Stuebenville, Ohio.

THOMAS KINKADE

A unifying element infuses all of the árt of Thomas Kinkade — the luminous glow of light. This mastery has earned him the title of the "painter of light."

Kinkade's subjects vary but for the most part they are traditional gardens, pastoral and landscape scenes, and English cottages. His first collector's plate, issued in 1991, was the award–winning "Chandler's Cottage," part of the Garden Cottages of England Series. Since then, his art work has been featured on eleven more plate series — including Home for the Holidays, Home Is Where the Heart Is, and Thomas Kinkade's Lamplight Village — winning additional awards along the way. He was one of the first artists to be selected for induction into The Bradford Exchange Plate Artist Hall of Fame in 1995.

Thomas Kinkade was born in 1958 in California. By the age of sixteen he already was an accomplished painter in oil. After studies at the University of California at Berkeley and the Art Center College of Design in Pasadena, he spent two years doing background paintings for the movies — personally creating over 600 paintings for the acclaimed, animated feature film, "Fire and Ice." He credits this early experience for providing the foundation for his success in plate art and the other media in which he works.

As a tribute to his wife and two young daughters, Kinkade hides letters and numbers signifying their birthdates, anniversaries and initials within his work. Collectors are most familiar with "N" (for his wife Nanette), which he integrates into each work. Yet another symbol to be found in every Kinkade work is a fish — a symbol of Christianity — and the inscription "John 3:16," a reference to a Bible verse that is special to him. He also occasionally includes a likeness of himself, his wife or his daughters.

Kinkade maintains a rigorous six–day–a–week painting schedule. In addition to his work, his life revolves around his church and his family, with whom he lives in a village in the coastal foothills of Northern California.

LENA LIU

Lena Liu's delicate, pastel–hued scenes of nature have captivated plate collectors since the debut of her first series, On Gossamer Wings, in 1988. Ten subsequent collections showcasing her work have been introduced in the past eight years, including Floral Greetings from Lena Liu and Lena Liu's Hummingbird Treasury. Along the way she has earned numerous honors, including Artist of the Year in both the United States and Canada and Plate of the Year in the United States. Liu was one of the first artists inducted into the Bradford Exchange Plate Artist Hall of Fame in 1995.

Her distinctive style is the result of her personal experience with both Eastern and Western cultures. An intriguing mix of romance and realism, it brought a new look to nature–themed collector plates, combining highly detailed subjects with softly colored backgrounds.

Raised in Taiwan, she was trained from a young age in traditional Oriental painting by Chinese masters. In 1972, Liu moved to the United States to study architecture. She soon discovered that architecture wasn't for her and began painting full time in 1977.

From the beginning, she was deeply attracted to nature as a subject because of its lack of "cultural barriers." It was also an important theme in Oriental art and one that she had painted extensively while studying in Taiwan. Instead of continuing to follow strictly in the footsteps of her instructors — as is the custom in Taiwan — Liu gradually began to develop a style of her own, using her previous training as a foundation.

Working on a silk canvas, the artist uses natural dyes, extremely wide brushes and a "wet on wet" technique to create a blurred effect for the background. Then when the background is dry, Liu paints details in the foreground, producing the striking contrast that is the hallmark of her work.

An enthusiastic gardener and bird watcher, Liu often gets inspiration for her watercolors by looking out the window into the backyard of the Potomoc, Maryland home she shares with her husband Bill and their two dogs.

TERRY REDLIN

Few artists can rival the standards of excellence achieved by Master Artist Terry Redlin over the past eighteen years. For three consecutive years, 1992–94, Redlin has been named America's most popular artist by *U.S. ART* magazine. His use of earthy colors, blazing sunrises and sunsets and nostalgic themes are often cited as the reasons for his immense popularity.

Redlin traces his interest in the out–of–doors to his childhood in Watertown, South Dakota. He earned a degree from the St. Paul School of Associated Arts and spent twenty–five years working in commercial art. In his leisure time he researched wildlife subjects and settings.

In 1977 Redlin burst onto the wildlife scene when his painting "Winter Snows" appeared on the cover of *The Farmer* magazine. In 1979 he changed careers, deciding to concentrate on painting wildlife full time. From 1981 to 1984, Redlin won several competitions, including the Minnesota Duck Stamp and Trout Stamp contests, and placed second in the Federal Duck Stamp Competition. He was honored as Artist of the Year for Ducks Unlimited, both National and Minnesota.

In 1985, Redlin broadened his scope to an entirely new artistic direction, limited edition collector plates. To date, he has released more than twenty editions, many of which are now available only on the secondary market.

The National Association of Limited Editions Dealers has three times presented him with the "Lithograph of the Year" award for excellence in the medium.

In 1987 Redlin began exploring his interest in Americana subjects and nostalgic scenes of yesteryear, painting several images for his American Memories™ and Country Doctor™ Collections. Since then his annual Christmas prints have attracted thousands of collectors from coast to coast. His induction into *U.S. ART's* Hall of Fame in July, 1992, followed the magazine's poll of 900 galleries nationwide.

Terry Redlin is truly one of the country's most widely collected painters of wildlife and Americana.

Collecting Tips

Many individuals buy their first collector plate to use as a decorative accent in their home or office and not with the intent to start a new hobby. Soon the joy of owning one plate creates a desire to own a second, third, and so forth. Before one realizes it, he has become a collector plate collector. A new hobby has begun.

Collector plates also are frequently given as gifts. Many individuals are nudged along the collecting path in that fashion. No decision is made to collect, much less how to collect. The enjoyment from the gift sparks the desire to obtain more.

Many beginners experience so much satisfaction in buying plates that appeal to their aesthetic senses, that they rarely look deeper. Certainly they know about the plate hobby and that some individuals are buying in a more sophisticated way. They have heard of the various refinements of plate collecting — it would be hard to live in today's world and not have heard of them. However, not all plate owners develop into full–blown collectors. On subsequent visits to the gift shop it may be a gilt candlestick or a framed tapestry that excites their attention. They have an "eye" for decorative quality and for art. They could develop into masterful plate collectors — but they are pulled in other directions.

GETTING SERIOUS

Inevitably, some individuals develop into serious collectors. Their purchases are made with more discrimination and a sense of real direction. They acquire knowledge along with their plates. They move beyond the level of starry–eyed child looking at an ice cream cone or methodical and precise decorator wanting a certain shade of green. They think about artists and artistic quality. Most importantly, they develop the critical judgment skills that allow them to determine if a plate is merely gift shop ware or something special and magical.

DEVELOP A COLLECTION PHILOSOPHY

Many individuals begin their collecting by buying everything they like. Pretty often counts more than manufacturing quality or reputation of the illustrator. They probably made a number of good buys along the way. Some plates probably increased in value.

However, rather than having a meaningful nucleus of a collection, the odds are quite good that their collection is nothing more than miscellaneous plates — a gift shop assortment. Once they realize this, they will undoubtedly begin reproaching themselves for not becoming serious in buying sooner.

To the majority of collectors, developing a collection philosophy is a necessary ingredient. This is more true today when the number of available plates has so enormously increased. No one can own them all, not even a tenth of them. One cannot approach the hobby like Britannia embracing the world. The best approach is to choose some aspect of the hobby that deeply excites, keep the plates that relate to it, sell or trade the balance, and move forward.

SPECIALIZE

This is called *specializing*. Serious collectors specialize by turning their eyes, emotions, and checkbooks toward one class of plates. The chosen group becomes, for that person, the hobby. One disciplines oneself to treat all other plates as nonexistent.

By so doing collectors create many advantages for themselves, e.g., eliminating confusion and becoming experts on one type of plate much more rapidly than they would if they tried to track the entire market. Each acquisition, regardless of price, is significant because it complements what is already owned. It fits like a piece in a puzzle.

Perhaps best of all, when (and if) the time arrives for selling, one is likely to find buyers more enthusiastic about a specialized collection as opposed to one whose examples are mixed and matched.

In choosing a suitable specialty, it is wise to take many considerations into account. Some involve the plates themselves, but most revolve around the hobbyist's personality, tastes, and financial circumstances. It is advisable that a beginner or prospective collector become thoroughly acquainted with plates before stepping into the batter's box. False starts on collections are usually made because the individual is not aware of the variety of plates that exist on the market.

This book will help. It contains a wealth of information on plate collecting and the current plate market. However, there is no substitute for the real thing. Reading about plates is not the same as handling them. An excellent approach for any beginner is to visit the shops where collector plates are sold. Browse rather than buy — do not be afraid to look around. The more shops visited before buying, the better.

SPACE AND MONEY

Two obvious considerations are money and space. One can hardly buy what one cannot afford, nor display a large collection in a confined area. Few hobbyists have unlimited budgets or vast quantities of display and storage space. Neither the lack of space nor money need pose a serious handicap. Outstanding collections of plates have been assembled by hobbyists on tight budgets and those living in cramped apartments. More and careful planning is the key. Hobbyists who must make every dollar and inch of wall space count make the best buyers. They do not spend impulsively. They put together a collection in which real pride can be taken.

It is smart at the outset to develop a budget for collector plates that becomes part of your monthly budget — a certain sum that can be set aside weekly and left to accumulate until it has grown sufficiently to make a purchase. Beginners frequently are so enthusiastic that they spend their moneys as soon as they are available — no rainy day funds and no funds for when that special buy becomes available. This is understandable.

When one starts a collection and has nothing, the natural desire is to see it grow. Each new purchase is a measure of progress. However, beware of buying addiction, a collecting disease that some collectors develop whereby they need to make a purchase every day to feel satisfied. Stop to realize that good collections are worked on for years by their owners. Acquire at a leisurely pace. Make acquisitions here and there. Enjoy and admire each acquired plate. Do not buy in a panic just to watch your collection build.

You will have dry spells in your collecting when money is needed for other purposes or, for one reason or another, time passes without any fresh acquisitions. This opportunity to slow down and reflect on what you already own should be savored.

SETS AND SERIES

Collectors have different philosophies and motivations. Some prefer working toward a specific goal — collecting sets and/or series. This is a common approach among stamp and coin collectors. It applies just as well to plates.

The most obvious, of course, is to build a set. Another is to make a collection of annual plates (which is known as a *series collection*). Collecting sets and series makes it easy to budget funds for collecting. Be flexible. Prices often change before the collection is completed.

Also, a close estimate can be made of the length of time needed to complete the collection. One can choose a short series or set in the low price range and complete it quickly or select one of the long–running annual plates and accept a greater challenge. Of course, the longer it takes to complete a collection, the more uncertainty about the total cost involved. The market could rise substantially along the way. However, this should not be regarded as a deterrent. If you build a collection whose components rise rapidly in value, you automatically own a good investment. No one expects you to regret this situation.

There is yet another factor to be weighed. In set collecting, you continually add to the set until it is complete. Series collecting is slightly different if series plates are still being manufactured. To maintain a completed series collection as truly *complete*, new releases must be added. This should be done as soon as possible. The key is to buy at the issue price.

Unfortunately, some collectors (well in the minority) can assume a negative approach toward building a set or series collection. Their attention is so firmly riveted on *completion* that they turn a hobby into a hard and cold businesslike exercise. They do not enjoy themselves. They miss the fun and satisfaction of collecting because their minds are constantly on the plates they don't own rather than the ones they do. For these individuals we would have to say that set or series collecting is unwise.

COLLECTING BY MANUFACTURER

Most collectors need a goal toward which to work. In the case of collector plates, it need not necessarily be completing a set or group. Another approach is to assemble a collection in which the works of as many important artists as possible are represented.

Another collecting approach is to focus on a manufacturer. This enjoys strong support among collectors. This is certainly the oldest collecting philosophy when looking at the history of collector plates. Individuals living in European towns where plates were made bought those of local manufacture. With so many companies now producing collector plates, the choice is boundless.

If you choose to focus on a large company that has issued numerous plates and continues to do so, owning one of "every" plate is not realistic. Rather, strive for a good representation of the company's works, leaning toward the issues that have special appeal to you. These may comprise the efforts of favorite artists or issues showing subjects of a topical interest.

Collecting by manufacturer is an advanced collecting approach. Yet, there is no reason why it cannot be suitable for a beginner. The *investment* aspect of such a collection is apparent. Values of collector plates tend to change *by company* much more than by individual issues. There are exceptions to this statement, but it has held true during the past decades of plate collecting. One reason is the concentration of hobbyist interest on manufacturers.

A strong sense of unity and similarity of design are the chief reasons why so many people like to collect plates from a single manufacturer. All the plates, while differing in artist, subject, and even size, have common roots. Their relationship is unmistakable. They "go together." This "going together" not only adds to their visual charm but to their cash value. When such a collection is sold, the chances for a higher resale price are increased. A specialist dealer who makes a practice of stocking the products of that company and has waiting buyers is the first place to look.

Some selectivity is required in manufacturer collecting, as in all approaches to the collector plate hobby. Select a manufacturer with a solid reputation — one whose plates are universally recognized for quality, both in respect to subject themes and execution, and whose plates are not produced in numbers that exceed the demand for them. This does not necessarily mean going automatically for companies with the highest-priced plates. Some firms whose plates are in the moderate price range are worthy of collecting.

Whether a European or American manufacturer is chosen makes little difference, as long as its products are readily available in this country. One point that the collector ought to consider is the *possible fluctuation in availability* with European manufactured plates. Occasionally, quantities of an older foreign plate reach the U.S. market and temporarily upset the domestic selling price. This is a rare occurrence, but you need to be aware that it can happen.

Also, be forewarned to avoid firms that are new or about which little is known. Manufacturers need to prove themselves both on the retail and secondary markets. Products of a brand-new firm fall within the questionable category. They represent excellent bargains if broad collecting interest develops in that firm's plates, disasters if they do not.

COLLECTING BY ARTIST

Collecting by artist is almost as popular as collecting by manufacturer. You may have a favorite artist whose works are featured on plates. If not, study the available plates and see which artist or artists catch your eye. Artist collecting is a basic and sound approach, especially as collector plates are really prints in which ceramics substitute for paper.

You need not apologize for being more interested in the artist than in the plate itself. In a sense, the artist is the plate. The artist's reputation and skills give the plate much of its value and all of its physical beauty.

COLLECTING BY THEME

Another approach to collecting appeals to the tastes of the home decorator. Numerous individuals collect according to theme. The possibilities are endless. The walls of the family rec room might be adorned with a collection of plates immortalizing sports legends such as Mickey Mantle and Michael Jordan. For the outdoorsman, a collection based on birds of prey and animals of the wild holds special interest. Classic movies and musicals are another popular choice. Plates commemorating *The Wizard of Oz, Gone With the Wind,* and *Star Wars* are just a few examples.

The nursery presents another collecting opportunity. Disney, Peanuts, and other cartoon characters, fairy tale and nursery rhyme series, or cute and cuddily puppies and kittens are all appropriate themes.

Holiday decorating might include a series of plates celebrating the birth and life of Jesus. A more secular approach could be plates with Santa's image. The styles exhibited by different artists and manufacturers only add to the variety of interest of the subjects. With imagination and creativity, any room in the home can be enriched with the addition of collector plates.

Mary Engelbreit Society,
Believe Series,
1986, Santa's Treasure.
Photo courtesy of Collectors News

The Bradford Exchange,
Musical Moments from The Wizard of Oz,
1993, Over the Rainbow

How to Display Your Plates

One facet of collecting plates that fascinates and delights hobbyists is the seemingly endless ways to display them. A well–displayed collection adds appeal to any room and can be a source of pleasure for the collector.

Plates are one group of collectibles whose beauty is recognized and admired by all. Visitors to your home need not be collectors to be impressed with your display. Using your imagination and creative talents, you can effectively and beautifully arrange your plate collection in whatever space you have available.

ON THE WALL

There are three basic places to display a group of plates: on a wall, in a cabinet, or via individual stands on top of furniture. Displaying plates on the wall is the most popular method of display and adapts easily to either a small or large collection.

Wooden frames, metal hangers, and hanging aids can be purchased in gift shops and plate stores. Wooden frames are available in many colors, sizes, and shapes. Find one that best compliments your plate's design, motif, and color scheme. A very effective way to show a series is in a shadow box frame — a wooden frame with velvet background that holds more than one plate. Some of these frames have glass fronts. The glass may help you keep your plates dust free, but some glass types can mute the plates' colors. Whatever method you choose, keeping the viewing surfaces free of dust and dirt build–up will enhance the beauty and brilliance of your collection.

There are two types of metal wall hangers. The first consists of two individual plastic or rubber–coated wires, each with a U–shape prong, that hooks the plate at the top and bottom. The two ends of each U are bent to clip over the edge and are the only part of the hanger that is visible from the front. The top and bottom wires are held in place by two springs. The hanger is attached to the plate from the back by clipping the bottom wire prongs over the edge and then stretching the springs until you can hook the top wire prongs into place. The top wire then has a slight bend, which allows you to hang the plate over a nail or hook.

The second type of hanger consists of two half–circle wires that also hook over the top and bottom of the plate. The wires, which are joined together at the center of the hanger, are shorter in length than the diameter of the plate. To attach this hanger, situate it in the center of the plate and then stretch all four ends outward until they reach the rim. Then hook the four prongs over the edges. Another wire attached to the hanger allows you to hang the plate over a nail or hook. This is the least desirable hanger because of the numerous contacts with a plate's rim.

Only buy examples that have some type of coating over the wire and/or prongs. Be very concerned about any potential damage to a plate's rim. Also, buy the correct size. A hanger that is too small puts pressure on the plate and may cause it to crack. Replace hangers every four to five years. Springs do wear out.

Many collector plates can be hung on a wall without using store–bought hangers. Some manufacturers place two holes in the foot rim on the back of the plate. Wire or string can be threaded through each hole and then tied. Be sure to allow enough slack in the wire so that it can be draped over a nail or hook. Before you place the wire over a hook, double–check that the knots are securely tied. This method is fraught with risk. Consider using a hanger even if rim holes are available.

IN THE CABINET

If your collection is fairly small and not likely to grow at a rapid pace, cabinet storage is a satisfctory method of display. If possible, use a cabinet with glass–panel doors. These are expensive when purchased new. However, if you are willing to search, you can find quality pieces at very reasonable prices on the secondhand furniture market.

A glass display cabinet with a lighting attachment, usually a fluorescent bulb placed at the top, is another possibility. These normally have glass shelves rather than wooden ones. Light travels throughout the cabinet. It is best that a display cabinet used for plates does not have wheels on its base. Wheeled cabinets move when bumped. Plates and shelves can fall. It's a disaster no one wants to experience.

When arranging items in a cabinet, don't overcrowd the shelves. Leave at least two inches of space between each plate for easier viewing. Don't trust plates to stand by propping them against the back wall. They may stand temporarily, but any slight trembling of the floor will dislodge them. Instead, use plate stands or racks. You can buy them at most gift shops and specialty plate stores.

If you use a glass–front cabinet for displaying your collection, you will have a distinct advantage over a wall display — your plates will take much longer to collect dust. Plates displayed uncovered on a wall may need to be individually wiped every week whereas only the glass front of the cabinet will need to be dusted that frequently.

ON STANDS

One type of plate stand is made of twisted wire about the thickness of coat–hanger wire. When using these, be very careful that you don't scratch the plate. Put a small piece of felt between the plate edge and the stand.

A second type of plate stand is made of molded plastic and has a groove to hold the bottom of the plate. They are inexpensive and serve the purpose perfectly.

If you buy holders in quantity, you may even be able to purchase them at a discount. They can also be bought secondhand at flea markets or garage sales.

In addition to their use in a cabinet, metal or plastic stands also can be used to display plates on tables, mantels, or any flat surface. Plate stands can be very decorative, complimenting and enhancing a plate's design, or clear plastic and plain, allowing every part of the plate to be visible with nothing to distract from its beauty. If you display your plates on stands, consider how susceptible they are to damage resulting from children or pets. Most plate stands are not designed to be pushed and shoved about.

MIX AND MATCH

Once you've decided where you want to display your collection, the fun begins. The possibilities of combinations for displays are endless. Here are a few suggestions to consider. Use your imagination and enjoy!

You may want to accent your collection or just a few plates with other items that correspond in topic, basic design, or artistic style. If Hummel annuals and anniversary issues are in your collection, try accenting them with other items made by Goebel, such as figurines and wall plaques. If you own one of the candleholders, lamp bases, or music boxes, this will also add variety to your display and may be just perfect for a baby's room.

If you collect topically, accent possibilities abound. Ceramic puppies, puppies on hooked rugs, tapestries, and even paintings can make an attractive display to go along with a theme collection of collector plates with puppy images. If flowers are your hobby, try arranging vases of home-grown flowers to match the floral artwork on your plates. Use dried or silk flowers to add variety. Consider placing your favorite teddy bear on a table next to your plates that depict children playing with *their* favorite toys.

B & J Art Designs,
Old–Fashioned Country Series,
1984, Cristina

If you have nonplate items by the same manufacturer as your plates, e.g., Bing & Grondahl figurines have the same color scheme as Bing & Grondahl plates, display them together. Collector plates of jasperware can be attractively shown in a china or curio cabinet with the many other wares made by Wedgwood. Royal Copenhagen has a Mother and Child Series in plates as well as in figurines. The design of the first plate, a mother and baby robin, was taken directly from one of the company's figurines. Both have the same soft look from the underglazed design and create a very impressive combination.

Another way to add variety to your display is to supplement it with works in other media by the same artist. This might prove costly if the artist is nationally or internationally famous. Many who collect an artist's work acquire paintings, lithographs, or serigraphs first. Later they are attracted to plates by finding the same designs on these ceramic masterpieces that they found in the other media.

GET STARTED

Take time to choose the right colors and styles for *you*. Coordinate your favorite pieces to create a display that any collector would be proud of. Then share your decorated rooms with others, but most of all, *enjoy them yourself!*

Caring for Your Plates

Collector plates require minimum care and attention. There are only a few basic rules to learn. It is true that plates, like all ceramic objects, will break if dropped. Aside from this they are quite sturdy in terms of resistance to deterioration and will endure for a very, very long time.

Proof of the long–term endurance of ceramics is found in art museums where pottery three thousand and four thousand years old is displayed. Many of these pieces, uncovered through archeological digs, were buried beneath the ground for ages. Yet they remain intact. Some 17th and 18th century ceramic examples appear almost as though they were made yesterday.

GENERAL CONSIDERATIONS

Your objective is to maintain your plates in exactly the same condition as when you acquired them. Some thought and preventive maintenance is all that is necessary.

The way plates are stored plays a major role in their preservation. With safe storage there is virtually no need to do anything other than an occasional cleaning to remove the inevitable accumulation of dust.

If it becomes necessary to wash a plate do this only for plates with a glazed surface. A simple wiping with a damp cloth should remove surface dust if it has not been allowed to build up too long. Rub gently. Do it a second or third time since dust sometimes takes a while to loosen. Wiping surfaces that are not glazed only rubs the dirt into the porous surface. Over time, the result is a plate whose surface appears dull, dirty or even stained. Use a feather duster to clean the surfaces of bisque plates. Do it often. At least once a month. Built–up dirt is the enemy.

Glazed surface collector plates can be washed in lukewarm water with mild soap. Do not use hot water and ordinary dish detergent. The latter may be too harsh and might remove some of the delicate surface banding or highlights. For wiping, use a soft cloth. Do not wipe hard. Take care that your fingernails don't come into contact with the plate. It is also wise to remove rings and other jewelry before washing a plate.

Do not wash collector plates under running water. Use a basin. Wash them first in soapy water and rinse them in a separate clear water bath. It may be necessary to rinse them several times. Make certain all soap film is removed. Wash the backs as well as the fronts and edges.

Be extremely careful when washing plates with gold highlights and banding. Often gilding is on the surface, not under the glaze. It can rub off. Better to have a regular feather dusting routine than relying on a water washing for this type of plate.

After washing, dry your plate with another soft cloth, one that will not leave lint particles. You may want to use thick paper towels to prevent lint remnants. Discard each towel as soon as it becomes saturated with water.

Some common grease stains can be successfully removed. The procedure is to use soap and water as outlined above but concentrate wiping in the area of the stain. Periodic checks must me made during the cleaning procedure to measure your progress. Do not wipe longer than is necessary.

Grease stains that appear to have vanished in the washing process sometimes reappear after the plate is dry. The water camouflages them. Rather than wiping too much, it is best to dry the plate and check the results of your efforts. Wash again if necessary.

PACKING FOR SHIPMENT

The dread of every plate collector is the need to move his collection. Plates must be taken down and packed. Concern mounts. How will the plates survive the move?

There is little danger in transporting plates or even in shipping them through the mail provided simple precautions are taken. Dealers mail plates regularly and seldom encounter breakage. When sending plates by mail or by any commercial carrier, pack one plate per container. The original box in which the plate came is often the best shipping container. You can pack more than one in a container, but this increases the risk of breakage and damage.

Assuming you are packing one plate per container, you will want to begin with a sturdy box that is at least three inches larger on all sides than the plate. In other words, for a plate ten inches in diameter, the ideal box would measure sixteen inches by sixteen inches. The box should be about two inches deep and preferably closed on the top and bottom, with a flap-type opening on one end. This is better than a box on which the lid is removable. In any event, the box must be good and strong. If it's flexible at all, it may not be safe enough to do the job.

Wrap the plate in several layers of tissue paper or bubble wrap, securing it with tape. Then wrap in layers of newspapers, again sealing with tape.

This provides a cushion to protect against scraping. Next step is to place a sheet of very heavy cardboard (about the same thickness as the walls of the box) on each side of the plate. These sheets of cardboard should be nearly as large as the box so that they will fit inside tightly. Having done this, tape the edges of the cardboard sheets together to form a sandwich, enclosing the plate inside them. Use regular packing tape to do this. Stuff the box with newspaper or add styrofoam peanuts so that there is no movement. Seal the box flap shut with strong tape. The plate should travel safely.

It is smart to insure the parcel. Obtain a receipt. Mark the parcel "Fragile."

INSURANCE

Are my collector plates covered by my household insurance? If you are a collector and have not asked this question, you should. Even a small collection of twenty–five plates can have a replacement value that exceeds $2,500.

Check your household insurance policy. Many policies now include the following statement in their "PROPERTY NOT ELIGIBLE" section: "Property listed below is not eligible for replacement cost settlement. Any loss will be settled at actual cash value at time of loss but not more than the amount required to repair or replace. / a. antiques, fine arts, paintings and similar articles of rarity or antiquity which cannot be replaced / b. memorabilia, souvenirs, collectors items and similar articles whose age or history contributes to their value." Collector plates fall into the "b" group.

If your household policy does cover your collector plates, make certain of two things. First, you want replacement, not cash value for your collection. Collector plates are appreciating, not depreciating personal property. Second, coverage should include breakage as well as the traditional coverage for fire, theft, etc.

Schedule a policy review with your insurance carrier. Before the meeting, make a list of the plates in your collection. Information should include name of manufacturer, title of plate, size, year of issue, name of artist, series identification, purchase cost, date of purchase, and current value. Make two copies. Keep one with your collection and the other at a location away from your collection. The list does you no good if it is destroyed along with your collection.

Photograph your collection. The ideal approach is to photograph each plate individually. If this is not practical, take a group photograph. Some collectors videotape their collection, incorporating a verbal description of each plate as part of the videotaping process. Again, make a duplicate copy and store it at an alternate location. Review your videotape every three to five years. Videotapes do deteriorate.

If your collection is not adequately covered under your homeowner's policy, you need to buy a fine arts rider, a form of Marine Inland insurance. Do not hesitate to ask for quotes from more than one company. Rates fluctuate between companies. Make certain you know exactly what type of coverage is quoted. Most companies provide only one price quote. It may or may not cover breakage. Insist on two quotes, one for breakage and one for other types of loss. You do not have to take both. You may wish to "self insure" for breakage.

A per loss deductible of $250 or $500 greatly reduces the cost of coverage. The insurance company wants to avoid nuisance claims. Also ask for portal to portal coverage, each plate in the collection is covered from the time you buy it until the time you sell it.

Some insurance companies require that your collection be appraised. The appraiser must be a neutral party, never the owner of the collection nor the dealer who sold a large portion of it.

The mid–1990s witnessed the arrival of several insurance companies, agents, and groups specializing in insuring collections. The International Collectors Insurance Agency (PO Box 6991, Warwick, RI 02887) is one such group. The company specializes in covering ceramics and glass.

The National Association of Collectors (PO Box 2782, Huntersville, NC 28070; 1-800-287-7127) offers a program whereby when you join the Society (an annual fee of $45) you become eligible to buy up to $50,000 of unscheduled insurance at extremely favorable rates. Coverage is on a replacement cost base and is "all risk," covering fire, windstorm, vandalism, theft, vehicle overturn, accidental breakage, and other perils. The program was designed specifically by collectors for collectors. Unlike the program of the International Collectors Insurance Agency that limits its coverage only to ceramic and glass items, the NAC policy covers all antiques and collectibles found in the home.

Investing in Collector Plates

Investment in contemporary collectibles, especially collector plates, reached record proportions in the mid– and late 1970s. Plates attracted more attention than most collectibles because of their limited edition status and the rapid advance in the price of some plates, more the result of speculation fever than common sense. This speculation fever caused disruption and uncertainty in the market. Many buyers with little market knowledge tried to ride the wave. The result was disastrous.

In 1973 a number of the speculators sold off their plates. The market quickly flooded. Prices on some issues dropped dramatically. The market was in a state of shock. The market stabilized in the late 1970s and it has been stable ever since. Today, most buyers recognize that investment is a long–term proposition.

Current investors are more selective in their buying and are holding longer before selling. This is healthy for the market because it takes plates out of circulation for an extended period of time. It allows desire and scarcity to develop on their own. A good investment is one that stands the test of time.

Can you *invest* in collector plates and make a profit? You can. It is work. And, it is risky. Knowledge of plates, the plate market, and basic investment principles is essential. It is not as simple as going out and buying a random selection of plates and putting them away for a certain length of time. Some plates have better investment potential than others.

First, when buying for profit, one must understand what constitutes *profit*. Selling for more than you paid does not necessarily result in a profit. The length of holding time must be taken into account. For example, assume you buy a plate for $70 today and sell it for $100 five years later. It appears that you made a profit, but you did not. Inflation reduces the dollar's buying power each year. The $100 you receive may not buy as much as the $70 you originally spent. You might have actually lost money.

This is why merchants and dealers favor a quick turn around of their capital. The longer something takes to sell, the more it must be sold for in order to realize a good return. If your plate is not rising in value faster than the rate of inflation, it is not a profitable investment.

Also, you bought at retail and will most likely sell at wholesale when you cash in your investment. In selling to a dealer, you do not expect to obtain full retail price. Therefore, your plates need to register a very dramatic price increase, in the neighborhood of twenty–five percent per year or more, to be sold profitably. Some plates do this well; many do not.

As an investor, you have the option of purchasing newly issued editions as they come out and paying the issue price. You also can buy older plates that are now selling for more than their issue price. There is less speculation involved in buying older plates, especially those with an established secondary market. The key is to buy right, i.e., keep a good working margin.

If a plate has moved up twenty percent to thirty percent in price within six months of being sold out, it has a fair chance of doing as well or better over the next several years. Public reaction is difficult to forecast. Even the most knowledgeable experts misjudge the popularity of plates on some occasions. There have been many instances of editions that drew little attention when they first came on the market but rose rapidly in value thereafter. Likewise, there are those that showed all of the favorable signs for investment but just did not catch on as expected.

There are some basic guidelines that apply when attempting to forecast future price movement. Remember, these are guidelines, not absolutes:

1. Since many collectors buy their plates by artist, a new series of plates by an artist with an established collector following is usually considered favorable for investment. If the artist's work has saturated the market, avoid the plate.

2. Edition size plays a role in investment potential, if other qualities are favorable. A low–edition plate by an unknown artist would not generally be considered attractive for investment.

3. Topical themes of popular interest can affect a plates's investment potential.

THE REAL INVESTMENT

The real investment in collector plates is the joy and satisfaction of ownership and the pleasures you receive each time you look at and/or handle them. It is the wise collector who values his plates for their decorative and nostalgic value and not for their potential as an investment.

Fall in love with the plates you buy. Plan on keeping and enjoying them for a lifetime. There is no finer investment than this.

Buying and Selling Collector Plates

What are your collector plate objectives? Do you want to collect, invest, or deal in collector plates? The advice that follows applies to one or more groups, but not universally. Pick and choose the advice that best serves your needs. Ignore what does not apply; think about what does.

You *can* make a profit buying and selling collector plates. If profit is your chief motivation, your approach is different from that of the hobbyist or "fan" of collector plates. As a seller, you may have to pass on plates that appeal to you personally but do not have mass sales appeal. The reverse is also true. If you are buying for profit, you may acquire some editions that are not among your personal favorites.

This is not to say that private collections, built entirely for enjoyment, cannot substantially grow in value. Many collections assembled without the slightest intention on the part of the collector to resell have been sold profitably.

Circumstances in the market at the time you buy and sell are a key factor in determining value, as is the care and selectivity with which plates are acquired. Certain types of collections are more apt to return a profit than others. This has little to do with their size or the sum total of capital invested. If the potential buyer, dealer or private collector, likes the collection, it will sell well.

Collections focusing on popular editions of the major plate manufacturers always fall within the favorable category in respect to resale. They can be sold for a higher percentage of their current retail value than plates produced by less popular manufacturers.

Miscellaneous collections can also arouse dealer interest. Topical collections fall into that category. If you collect plates in which cats are a major image focus you have a very appealing collection. A dealer will pay a higher price when he knows he can resell something quickly.

An artist collection is another example of a miscellaneous collection. Often a company will feature the designs of one artist for a complete series. Chances are great that the artist has done plate and/or series designs for another company. If your collection is a mix and match group focusing on the work of one individual, it is called a "miscellaneous" collection. Most dealers welcome the opportunity to buy a collection based on the works of a popular artist. They already may have standing orders from their customers for some of the plates. You will find ads in hobby and collectible trade publications from dealers seeking to buy plates by specific artists, regardless of manufacturer. Popularity changes. An artist who is in today may be out tomorrow.

SOURCES OF SUPPLY

The major sources of supply for collector plates are specialist dealers, general gift shops, and manufacturers, many of whom sell directly to the public. Begin by acquiring the following two titles from the Collectors' Information Bureau (5065 Shoreline Rd., Ste. 200, Barrington, IL 60010): **Directory To Limited Edition Collectible Stores** and **Directory To Secondary Market Retailers**. Collector plates also are found in a variety of other sale environments: antiques shops, secondhand shops, antiques shows and conventions, auction sales of all kinds, "country" and "estate" sales, flea markets, garage sales, and advertisements in the collector publications and local newspapers.

Begin your quest to acquire collector plates in your own locale. You will be surprised how many plates you will find for sale within an hour's drive from your home. Supplement the local selection through telephone and mail–order purchases. The collector living in a remote rural area has just as many good buying opportunities as an urban dweller. Aggressive buying no matter where you live is the key.

Obviously, you will encounter differences buying from one type of source rather than from another. Prices will vary and so will the selection. Dealers offering the best selections tend to charge full market prices or very close to them. Bargains frequently turn up in locations where just a few plates are found.

Collector plate collectors have a distinct advantage over many other hobbyists. Bargains *are* bargains. If a coin collector or an antiques enthusiast finds an item selling for half or less of book there is a strong possibility the item is a reproduction or fake. Unless the individual is experienced and can confidently make his own appraisal, he has trouble deciding whether the object is indeed a "find" or a worthless reproduction.

Fakes have not invaded the world of collector plates. This is not to say that buying should be done haphazardly without proper examination. While authenticity is not in question, there are other points to consider: the plate's physical condition and whether the it has been correctly identified and/or repaired.

Some plates are very similar to each other, yet from different series. The same artist may be featured in different series with art bearing nearly identical titles. Obviously, these differences can and do influence value. This is why the often–repeated saying, "The back of a plate tells more about it than the front," is worth remembering. Check the back of every plate for the manufacturers' marks, series, title, and edition size. You do not want to be surprised after you get the plate home.

Bargains are most often found at off–the–beaten–path sources. In some cases, the sellers are not aware of current market values and have acquired collector plates from individuals who likewise were unaware of their values. This happens with collector plates more frequently than most collectible items. If a noncollector received a plate as a gift in the early 1970s when the hobby was just becoming established he may think of it more as a decorative gift than an object with potential long–term value. When selling the plate, the individual may be perfectly satisfied to accept $5 or $10 for an item actually worth $100 or more. The dealer who buys it may be familiar with the collector plate hobby, but may not have the necessary reference material on hand to check values, especially if he runs a small secondhand shop or other neighborhood business. Having made the purchase for $10, the dealer does not hesitate to sell for $20 to $30, content to double or triple his money. Had he done his homework, he would have sold it for more.

Finding bargains is exciting. However, if you have specific collecting goals, such as completing an artist collection or assembling a full set of one manufacturer's series, bargains need to be supplemented with purchases from within the regular plate marketplace. It can be exasperating to continually look for a plate and not find it. Yes, bargains save money. However, when you find a plate you need at full retail, you should consider buying it, especially if you have been hunting it for several years. If you want it now, and some collectors do, pay the full retail value and order the plate from a well–stocked supplier.

In the final analysis, take whatever buying approach that suits you the best. Some collectors have a more adventurous spirit than others and more free time and mobility. They enjoy the hunt as much as the capture. Others make buying as painless as possible. Their enjoyment comes from continually admiring the plates that they own.

Buying Direct from the Manufacturer

Some manufacturers sell their plates directly to the public. They advertise in magazines and mail to customer lists they assembled or acquired. If you respond to a manufacturer's magazine ad, you will be placed on its mailing list and receive announcements of future editions. You also are likely to receive announcements from manufacturers with whom you have never done business. You may be puzzled at how they know you are interested in collector plates. Manufacturers do not randomly solicit names from the phone book. The percentage of potential plate buyers in the general population is too small to make this worthwhile. Some manufacturers swap customer names and addresses with other manufacturers. For example, one manufacturer trades names of 500 of its customers for 500 of another company's customers.

Manufacturers frequently sell their mailing lists. The result is that a name from one maker's list gradually gets on almost every maker's list. Few collectors object to this. They want to receive these announcements because it keeps them fully informed on every new issue. Obviously, you cannot buy every plate offered to you. But, *save all literature* received from the manufacturers even if you have no intention of buying their plates. Maintain a filing system for manufacturers' announcements and brochures. This material will prove useful in the future for dating and tracking the value of a particular plate. There is no better way to keep informed about the plate market than to compare these manufacturers' announcements with the offerings of dealers.

The most important step in buying from a manufacturer is to know exactly what you are ordering. Read the description carefully. Pay close attention to the size, material, type of decoration, and other pertinent information. Plates pictured in brochures are not always shown in actual size. If marked *reduced*, this could mean that the actual plate is twice as large as the photograph or even larger. Many times you will find a precise statement of the diameter in the promotional text.

Keep in mind that sales brochures and announcements are sometimes printed before the plate is actually manufactured. The photograph or photographs in the brochure are not the final plate design but a master or "dummy" model that has been prepared strictly for use in advertising. While the actual plate should be very nearly identical to the photograph, sometimes there are minor variations. Rarely, but it happens, the change is major.

As far as the colors are concerned, these will not reproduce 100 percent accurately in the photograph. Even if the photograph is excellent in quality, which most of those in plate brochures are, it will not catch every nuance or subtle tonal quality of the colors appearing on the plate. Do not expect the plate to look precisely like the photograph. Many times the colors are sharper and richer. Be alert for imperfections in a plate. If there is a problem, contact the company, return the plate immediately, and request a replacement.

When you order a plate from a manufacturer, there may be a slight delay, particularly if you order within a "time deadline" announcement. Veteran collectors have learned to be patient and not start watching the mail a week after posting their orders. If you have not received the plate you ordered after six to eight weeks and you have received no announcement from the company about a change in the mailing date, write and ask to know the current status of your order.

When your plate is received, save the box. This adds to a plate's value. Also save all literature that accompanies the plate.

Buying from Plate Dealers

The focus here is on dealers who either specialize only in the sale of collector plates or for whom plates make up a large portion of their stock and trade. They include plate dealers and gift shops, some of whom deal exclusively in newly issued plates and some of whom sell new plates in addition to those no longer available from the manufacturer.

Selling plates that are no longer being produced is the lifeblood of the specialized plate dealer. This is the famed secondary market. Dealers try to triple and quadruple their initial investment. When the value is high, doubling is acceptable. The secondary market has far more risk than the current production market, but also offers a greater profit potential if all goes well.

A merchant selling a plate currently in production tries to sell as close to the manufacturer's announced price as possible. Often he sells for somewhat less than the suggested retail price in order to compete with other dealers. Having bought the plate at the established wholesale level, this leaves only a modest profit margin.

Secondary market items present more flexibility. The dealer buys them not from a wholesaler charging a set price but from the public. The price is negotiated sale by sale. Thus, dealers have more leeway in buying and selling. If the plate is in demand, they sell it at a price well above its initial issue retail price. Because there is no fixed price, dealers try for the best price possible. They succeed more often than they fail.

Dealers try to maintain as comprehensive a stock as possible, especially for plates from the most popular editions and series. The flow of material makes it impossible to have one of every plate in stock. A dealer may be slightly overstocked on a plate at one time and out of stock at another. As more and more are produced, the task of keeping "something for everybody" grows increasingly more challenging. Some dealers have already begun to specialize. Look for this trend to continue in the future. If you are looking for a plate issued by one of the smaller or more obscure manufacturers, you may need to contact several dealers before finding one who has the plate you are seeking.

Browsing in a plate shop, especially one that is well-stocked, is a treat for any collector. You will see many plates you did not know existed. Plates will look quite different "in person" from pictures in books or brochures.

In most cases, the selling price will be marked on a card alongside each plate. This refers to only to that plate. It does not necessarily mean that another plate from the same series is being sold for the same price. After reaching the secondary market, many plates from the same series sell for different prices. One or two plates, usually the first edition from the series, become more popular than the rest.

Just as prices vary in a given shop on plates of the same series, they also vary throughout the trade. Learn to compare prices between shops. Trade periodicals and price guides help you keep up with the market. Do not expect the seller to do this homework for you.

If you want a certain plate and do not find it displayed in the shop, ask for it. In many shops, only a portion of the stock is on display. The dealer may have many other plates in a back room or cellar. Possibly a consignment has just arrived and is in the process of being cataloged and priced. The plate you want may go on display the very next day.

When dealers do not have the plate you want, they may be willing to take your name and address and hunt for it for you. With the connections most dealers have, they locate almost any plate in a very short time. Of course, it might not be at the price you are willing to pay. Therefore, it is essential when asking a dealer to locate a plate for you that you honestly tell him what you are prepared to pay. Once committed, honor your pledge.

If you quote a price that is too low, you could hurt your chances of getting the plate. Chances are the dealer will buy the plate from another dealer and then add on a margin of profit or "commission." The price often is higher than you would pay if you located the plate on your own. When you ask for special service, you pay a premium. If you are unwilling to do this, then continue hunting on your own.

If the dealer issues a list, pick one up before you leave and study it at home. It may be obsolete by the time it's in your hands. Chances are some of the plates already have been sold. Any such list is useful for comparing the dealer's prices to those found in advertisements of other dealers to see just how the prices compare.

If you order a plate from a dealer, when it arrives, examine it for scratches or other damage before paying. If a plate is in a sealed box, open the box and make your inspection *in the shop*, not at home. It may not be easy or even possible to return a plate once you remove it from the shop.

Buying by Mail Order

Collector plates are sold by mail by large specialist dealers (often the very same ones who operate shops), general dealers in collector's items, and private collectors. Plate and antiques trade publications contain page after page of advertisements by individuals willing to sell through the mail. Many advertisements list available plates and the asking prices. Others ask you to send your want list and an SASE (self–addressed, stamped envelope). There are those who list their available plates, but do not price them. Instead, they ask for offers. This form of selling is actually an auction in disguise. Avoid buying from these individuals. If you want to buy at auction, go through traditional auction channels.

Buying via mail is a very satisfactory way of adding to your collection. It gives you a far greater choice of what you buy and from whom. The entire world of collector plates from the earliest to the latest is directly within your grasp. Any slight disadvantages that may be involved, e.g., delays in the mail, are offset by positive factors.

One big plus of mail–order buying is that the selling vehicle often contains advertisements from dozens of dealers, many of whom are offering the same plate. You can compare prices. Find the best deal. Comparing prices in retail shops is not nearly this easy.

Unless the plate you are seeking is scarce, two or more dealers will offer it at the same time. The prices will differ from one seller to the next, sometimes by as much as fifty percent. One seller may be a private collector, another an investor, and another a regular dealer. Their cost of merchandise is different, thus making their selling prices different.

Check out the terms of sale. They also can differ: one seller may pay postage, another may not. The seller offering the lowest price is not automatically the one offering the best buy.

Admittedly, mail order is more suitable for the buyer who knows what he wants and not the beginner unfamiliar with collector plates. If you are a beginner, shop browsing is probably the best initial buying approach. This enables you to view many different plates and get a feel for the breadth and scope of the market's offering. If you are unfamiliar with a plate and order it by mail it may be very different than what you expect. Only order collector plates through the mail that you have seen in person or pictured in a book.

Always read the advertisement and review its listings carefully before placing an order. A well–prepared ad or list gives the name of the manufacturer as well as the series and plate name. It also may provide information on the artist, the year of issue and the size. To save space, some dealers provide only the very basic information. In extreme cases, everything is omitted except the title. The assumption is that the buyer knows what he is buying.

The less information an advertisement provides, the more careful you need to be when buying. This is particularly true if the stated price is far different from the book or trade price at which the plate normally sells. It might be the same scene by the same artist but in a smaller size. There may be unspecified damage. There is absolutely no way of knowing for certain unless you contact the seller and ask for specifics.

Many lists are prepared haphazardly. The seller puts the burden on the buyer to plow through them. Therefore, you need to read any list from top to bottom to find out exactly what it contains.

Do not pay attention to the promotional verbage in advertisements. Dealers may honestly believe that their price is the lowest for a particular plate or series when several other ads on the same page confirm that it is not. There is no way they can know what prices were going to be quoted *at the same time* by other dealers. The more ads you read and the more lists you receive, the better will be your capability of judging the really good buys.

Buying at Flea Markets and Secondhand Shops

Collector plates *do* turn up at flea markets and secondhand (thrift) locations — perhaps not in quite the same quantity as they did a few years ago, but they are certainly available. Sometimes collector plates and ordinary table plates are offered for the same price! You may not get *that* lucky, but if you comb flea markets and thrift shops you will definitely encounter many, many bargains.

Noncollectors and uninformed owners simply do not care. They have something they do not desire and just want to get rid of it. A few dollars is more than satisfactory. The level of "plate awareness" on the part of the general public is not high, but it's growing. Annual plates are more apt to be recognized as having potential value because they carry a date. A plate that does not bear a date often is considered nothing more than a pretty household decoration. You know better. This is why you can find bargains.

The basic problem with plates sold at thrift shops and flea markets is that they are rarely found in the original box. They may be scratched or damaged in some other way. If the seller is unaware of the plate's collector status, he may not handle them carefully. This is why it is absolutely critical that you take extra time to examine plates at thrift shops and flea markets. There is no bargain in buying a collector plate with problems. Avoid purchasing any plate that is not in fine condition or better.

Don't ask for plates at a flea market or thrift shop. Find them yourself. An expression of interest on a buyer's part has a tendency to raise the price. Sellers often do not price items. They want to check out the seller before quoting a price. If you look like you can pay more, you will. They will ask for whatever they feel they can get.

Buying at Auction

Collector plates appear at all types of auctions ranging from on–site and mail auctions containing only collector plates to general auctions held at small auction barns or someone's front yard. Auction buying appeals to many plate collectors. The competition and the showlike atmosphere of auctions are exhilarating. If you fail to get a desired plate, you leave the auction feeling entertained. Auctions are more fun than browsing in a shop. At the very least, if you paid attention, you learned valuable information about how an auction works and strategies used by bidders. Currently there are several mail–order collector plate auctions. Bidding is done by mail, telephone, or fax. Competition is strong. Again, this is a case where you have to know what you are bidding on.

The great attraction of auction sales is that they have the allure of buying below normal retail prices. Anyone bidding at an auction, whether mail–bid or floor–sale, might get lucky and buy a $100 plate for $50 or $60. This does happen. In a typical auction where there are hundreds of plates offered, several dozen will sell below market price. However, most will sell at or near book value. Some, though the beginner finds this hard to understand, will exceed the price asked for the same plate in the dealer's shop down the street.

Auction results are not predictable. Best guesstimates are wrong more often than they are right. Even auctioneers have difficulty forecasting prices. There are dozens of variables that affect price, e.g., who is present, level of competition, weather conditions, economy, etc.

The level of competition changes with each lot. One lot may attract dozens of bidders, another only two or three. One bidder restricts his bids to the plates of a specific manufacturer. Another is a topical collector who bids only on the half dozen railroad theme plates included in the sale. Yet another is a Rockwell collector. One needs a certain Hummel Christmas plate to complete a collection. Some bidders are dealers executing orders for customers or buying for their own stock. The list never ends.

It is inevitable, in any large sale, that some lots draw little or no bidder interest while others become the target of heated competition. There may be two bidders at the sale who have made up their minds to get Lot No. 16. This may be a plate that both have tried to buy at previous auctions, only to come up short. This time, they will bid whatever it takes. When two determined bidders clash on such a lot, the price balloons far above the plate's normal retail value. The successful bidder may or may not have second thoughts afterward. He may well chastise himself for overspending if he finds the same plate in a shop priced much lower within a few months following the auction. But there are many auction buyers who willingly pay more than the book value without feeling guilty. Most dealers and collectors discount this event. However, if the same plate begins to top its book value regularly when sold at auction, market price adjusts upward to reflect the auction prices realized.

Dealers keep a careful watch on auction sale results. Prices realized at auctions always are taken into account when dealers decide how much they can pay to buy a plate or charge to sell it. Most of the plate collecting trends first become apparent at auction. To say that the auctions make the market is much more accurate than to say the market makes the auctions. Hence, it is very important for collectors to track the auction scene, just as dealers do.

Tracking auction results takes time, but the process is relatively simple. Subscribe to those specialized and trade periodicals that carry advertisements for mail and on–site auctions. Obtain copies of auction house catalogs that feature collector plates. Usually a subscription fee is charged. It generally includes the catalogs and prices realized, a list that you receive two or three weeks after the sale. The prices realized list includes the sum at which each item in the sale sold. The list also shows which items were passed (not sold). This also is valuable information.

Every collector plate appears at an auction sooner or later. The more recent and common ones are auctioned repeatedly, sometimes with several examples in the same auction. Dealers often sell slower moving stock at auction. This allows new collectors to enter the collector plate field at a modest cost. Dealers who run mail auctions will not sell their plates for less than cost. If the only bids received for a certain lot fall below the cost or are only marginally above it, the dealer rejects them and returns the plates to inventory. Occasionally, they will sell plates at auction for less than the full retail prices as long as the prices are not ridiculously low. Dealers know that auction bidders like to get bargains and that without bargains there would be very little appeal for auction sales.

At a public auction you have the opportunity to examine the lots before bidding on them. Every auction has a presale exhibit during which the lots are placed on view and can be handled. Always examine any collector plate upon which you plan to bid. Mark the items upon which you wish to bid in the catalog. Note the maximum price you are willing to pay. Deciding on your bid limits *before* the sale is a wise move. You have the chance to deliberate coolly and calmly before the auction begins. Avoid auction fever at all costs.

How much should you bid? The usual advice is: "Bid what the lot is worth to you." This should probably be amended to read, "Bid what the lot is worth to you, in light of the alternatives." First, would you really be happy owning a $50 plate for which you paid $100? Second, what are the chances of finding it on the regular retail market? When found, how much is the price likely to be? If you have established a good rapport with several dealers, you know you can buy virtually any plate you want if you are willing to pay the dealer's price. Use auctions as a method to acquire plates below dealer retail.

Never bid above retail unless the plate is extremely scarce. Even then, exercise control. Collector plates are mass–produced items. Most serious collectors, those who have experience in auction buying and are confident of the actions, limit their bidding to 60% to 70% of book value, approximately two–thirds of the normal retail value. Rarely do they exceed 80% of book. This is a perfectly logical bidding practice. If they lose a plate, what have they really lost? They can always buy the plate from a dealter at retail.

Look over the catalog carefully to see how the sale is organized. Pay close attention to the terms and conditions. Is there a buyer's penalty? If so, how much? Some lots may have a reserve or minimum bid. This is more apt to be the case in a mail–bid sale than at a public auction. If a minimum bid is stated, you are at liberty to bid that amount if you wish. There is no obligation to bid higher. However, the chances are good that someone else also will be bid the minimum bid. If you really want the item, it would be wise to bid slightly more.

Instead of a minimum bid, some auction catalogs provide a low and high estimate for the lot. These estimates aid bidders who are unsure about values. The lots could sell for more or less. It is not unusual for prices to fall outside estimates — high and low. Experienced collectors do not allow estimates to influence them. They know what the plate is worth to them. This is the only value that really counts. If they are smart, this is what they bid and not a penny more.

The disadvantage in bidding by mail is that you cannot watch the results. You do not find out what the plate brought until after the sale. When bidding in person, you can adjust your bids based on your success or failure in bidding on other lots. For example, say there are ten lots in a sale that interest you. If you bid on the first five that come up and get them all, your finances may require you to cease bidding at that point. Some mail auctions allow you to place a limit on how much you spend. To do this, you list your bids in the normal fashion. At the bottom of the bid sheet, write "Please limit total purchases to $100." When your success reaches the $100 level, the auctioneer stops executing your bids.

Read the catalog descriptions carefully to be sure you know exactly what you're bidding on. Description quality varies from auction to auction. Add your own notes made during the preview.

When you bid in a mail auction, it may be as long as two weeks after the sale before you receive the auctioneer's invoice. Do not assume that your bids were unsuccessful if you are not contacted immediately. Of course, you can call the auction house and find out sooner if you prefer. Wait until two days after the sale to call. Employees will be too busy on sale day to help you.

Buying from Other Collectors

You can often buy below market values by dealing directly with other collectors or private individuals who own plates. There are expenses involved. Unless you know of individuals with plates to sell, they may not be easily found without running advertisements. Ads can be placed in your local newspaper and/or in regional trade publications.

Hometown ads are often very effective, especially in localities where there are no plate shops. Anyone in these areas who has plates to sell is glad to find a willing buyer nearby.

Swapping with other collectors is another way to get the collector plates you desire. Plate hobbyists do not swap as much as stamp and coin collectors do. Duplicates are uncommon. Most collectors only buy one example of a plate. Swapping often occurs when a collector's interest shifts. He swaps plates in which he has lost interest for examples that meet his current passion. Swapping is generally done on a wholesale cost basis.

SELLING YOUR PLATES

There are a number of methods available through which one can sell collector plates. Some result in a minimal price received, others offer the potential for a higher return. Each requires hard work, persistence, and flexibility.

Selling to a Dealer

Dealers have to buy plates to replenish their stock. They prefer to buy from private sellers more than from any other source of supply. In fact, it is largely the general public selling to dealers that keeps the secondary market going.

Condition is critical. If your plates have any damage, i.e., chips, cracks, fading, surface defects, etc., they will not find a buyer. The plate needs to be in fine to excellent condition. In addition, the plate should have its original box and all supporting literature. If not, deduct 25% from what you expect to get. Finally, the more recent the plate, the less you are likely to receive for it. Plates made before 1980 do best on the secondary market.

Since plates have established market values, the buyer and seller usually have a fair idea of what they are worth. Actually, this makes it much easier to arrive at a mutually satisfactory price. Haggling is kept to a minimum.

The thought of selling your plates is probably the last thing on your mind if you are collecting actively. However, continual buying and selling keeps the market strong.

Investors carefully plan the sale of their plates. They usually will not sell unless they see a substantial profit. Many investors were badly burned in the late 1970s and early 1980s. As a result many are still holding and hoping. A fast or forced sale made in a hurry because cash is needed for some emergency usually results in a loss. Still it is handy to have plates around! No plate is totally worthless. Forced sales may result in ten to twenty cents on the dollar, but this is better than nothing. If you do take a loss on collector plates in a rush sale, it may be a much smaller loss than on a car, jewelry, or other things you could sell.

Whether or not you make a profit on your plates when selling them to a dealer depends on the current market value. If you bought a plate at $90 when it was issued and the average retail price has now reached $300, you will have no trouble profiting. A dealer will pay around $125 to $150 for the plate, possibly even more it it's a really hot item for which he gets many requests. On the other hand, if your plate has not advanced much in value, a dealer's buying price probably will result in a loss for you. Dealers do not base their buying prices on the original issued prices but on current secondary market values. Everything depends on how much the dealer feels he can get when he sells the plates and how long it will take him to sell.

A dealer who is overstocked on a particular plate will either decline to purchase it or offer a slightly lower sum than usual. Dealers do not accumulate large stocks of any single plate unless they believe the value will rise in the near future. If the dealer is totally out of stock on the plate or plates you want to sell, he might be tempted to pay a bit more. This is why it pays to talk with several dealers before accepting an offer. The offers you receive will vary from one dealer to the next.

Dealers' advertisements in specialized plate and trade publications often state buying prices. In fact, some advertisements show the buying and selling price. You may be surprised at the comparatively small spread, sometimes as little as twenty percent, between a dealer's buying and selling price. Do not assume this applies to the dealer's entire inventory. The advertised plates are usually those in which the dealer specializes. They sometimes will pay sixty percent of the normal retail price for plates that are on their "most wanted" list. Otherwise, buy offers are at one–third or less of book value. When a dealer makes low offer, it is usually because he feels a plate is overpriced on the current market and is anticipating a decrease in value. Another dealer may feel differently and be willing to pay more.

A plate that has just recently gone out of production has less interest to a dealer. The market value at that point will probably be 25% to 35% of the issue price — no more. Some dealers may refuse to buy even at these prices because they have ample inventory. It may take fifteen to twenty years before the situation changes.

The longer you hold you plates before selling, the more likely you are to receive a satisfactory price. Many plates bought in the late 1960s and early 1970s are finally reaching book values that equal and exceed their initial purchase price.

You can sell to a dealer by mail or take your plates to his shop. When selling by mail, send the dealer a list of the plates you want to sell and wait for a reply. Do not ship to him on approval. On your list, state the manufacturer, artist, series name, individual plate titles, and sizes. Include your asking price — for each individual plate and the entire lot.

A critical phase in selling by mail is to pack your plates securely for shipment, and insure them for their full value. If the value exceeds the limit for postal insurance, use a commercial deliver service such as United Parcel Service.

Selling at Auction

Most auctioneers will accept your plates for inclusion in their sales. Some may not if they feel they cannot secure a good price. Be appreciative of such an auctioneer.

You can often do better selling by auction than selling outright. Of course, there is no guarantee of this. Auction selling involves some uncertainty. There is the chance of doing very well, obtaining the full retail value, or experiencing a disappointing sale.

Some auctioneers will let you place minimum selling prices on your plates to prevent them from going for ridiculously low prices. A reserve should not exceed forty percent of initial retail value. Expect to pay a fee to the auctioneer if your plates do not sell. The auctioneer cannot afford to work for free.

Whether to sell by auction or to a dealer is a choice the individual must make based on his circumstances. When cash is needed in a hurry, selling to a dealer is the best route. The auction process can take weeks or months from the time your plates are consigned for sale until the date payment is received. Some auctioneers may make a small cash advance on a large, valuable collection, but this is atypical.

Material sold on consignment is auctioned on a commission basis. The auction house receives a certain percentage of the price on each lot. Most houses work with a percentage of around twenty–five percent, though some charge as much as thirty–five percent. Usually the company's overhead costs determine the size of percentage. An auctioneer who publishes illustrated catalogs charges a higher commission rate. This is not unfair. Large auction houses with attractive catalogs often realize better prices for the items they sell. Even though you are paying a commission that is five percent or ten percent higher, your end return may still be higher.

When items are accepted for sale by an auctioneer, you and the auctioneer sign a contract. The contract carries all of the terms involved in the sale. It specifies the date on which your plates will be sold, the rate of commission, the date on which you can expect to receive payment (usually thirty days after the auction), and other details. Read the contract thoroughly before signing. Ask questions about anything that is not clear. Keep your copy of the contract until you receive payment for you merchandise.

Private Sales

There is a great deal of work and some risk involved in selling your collector plates privately. The reward is a higher rate of return. Only you can decide if you have the time, money, and patience required for selling privately.

Here is a general rule to help you decide if a private sale approach makes sense. If you have extremely common collector plates, i.e., plates that are readily available in the marketplace, a private sale makes no sense. Hard–to–find and scarce plates are the best candidates for private sale.

When selling privately, think sixty to seventy cents on the retail dollar. If a person wanted to pay full price for a plate, he would buy it from a dealer or at a shop. Individuals who buy privately expect to save money.

Begin by placing a classified advertisement in Collector's *Mart Magazine, Collector's News*, or *The Antique Trader Weekly*. You will find their addresses in the "Publications, Museums, and Factory Tours" chapter.

Keep your advertisement short and concise. Cost is per word. In today's computer age, consider listing a telephone number and e–mail address instead of a street address. If you have a large number of plates, ask potential buyers to send an SASE (self–addressed, stamped envelope) for a full listing of your plates.

While advertising in your local newspaper is likely to be expensive, the cost to advertise in your local shopper (penny press) is not. Word of mouth also is important. Tell those friends who have admired your plate collection for years that you are planning on selling some or all of it. There are far more friend to friend private sales than most people realize.

When selling privately, insist on payment in advance. Never send plates on approval. Wait four to five days between the time you deposit a check and the time you send the package just in case the check you received is bad.

When shipping plates you have sold, consider photographing them prior to shipping. This establishes the condition of the plates when they left your hands. Plates are damaged in shipment. Buyers have been known to substitute a bad plate for a good one and then return it claiming the plate was misrepresented.

Who pays for shipping? If the sale totals in the hundreds of dollars, the seller pays. If it is only one or two plates, the buyer. Make certain that you insure any package you ship. A return receipt also is a good idea.

BUYING AND SELLING THROUGH THE BRADFORD EXCHANGE

For more than twenty years, The Bradford Exchange has played a unique dual role in the limited edition plate market, serving collectors interested in acquiring both new releases and back–issue plates

Founded in 1973 by the late J. Roderick MacArthur, The Bradford Exchange is one of the world's most successful marketers of collector's plates. Over the years, it has introduced many innovative series, continually expanding the boundaries of plate collecting in the process.

For example, in the 1970s, the exchange first offered movie plates depicting cinematic classics and unique medium plates featuring three–dimensional sculpting. The 1980s saw the arrival of the first collector plates from the People's Republic of China and Russia, as well as a growing number of series in the nature and wildlife categories.

The company also continues to break ground with limited edition plates boasting various enhancements, including unusual shapes (oval, scalloped edges, square with rounded corners), specially designed decorative borders, music, illumination and motion. In addition, through relationships with key licensors, the exchange is able to offer collector plates portraying popular entertainers (Elvis Presley, Marilyn Monroe), sports legends (Babe Ruth, Joe Montana, Michael Jordan) and Disney movie characters.

However, the marketing of newly issued, or primary market, plates, is only one aspect of the services provided by the exchange. It also operates an organized, orderly secondary market where collectors can buy and sell back–issue plates.

J. Roderick MacArthur remained chairman of The Bradford Exchange until his death in 1984. Under his direction, the exchange continued to innovate and grow. By the end of 1973, Bradford had begun to publish the Current Quotations, which reports on the market activity and trading prices of hundreds of issues. Three years later, the Bradford Museum of Collector's Plates opened to the public.

Bradford took its first step toward international expansion in 1979 when the London, Ontario, office opened its doors. In 1972, computerization came to the U.S. Trading Floor, allowing collectors to place buy and sell orders over the phone for the first time. It also meant that the exchange could provide traders with up–to–the–minute pricing information.

To eliminate the risk of buying and selling plates long–distance, The Bradford Exchange guarantees both ends of the trades it brokers. Only Bradford–recommended plates are eligible for trading on the exchange.

The Bradford Museum of Collector's Plates is located in The Bradford Exchange's international headquarters in Niles, Illinois. It is open from 10 a.m. to 5 p.m., Monday through Friday; and 9 a.m. to 4 p.m. on Saturday and Sunday. The museum is closed on major holidays.

The museum's collection contains almost 800 porcelain, china, crystal, pewter and resin plates, produced by makers from around the world. It traces the development of limited edition throughout the past century, show-casing significant issues such as "Behind the Frozen Window," the very first collector plate issued in 1895 by Bing & Grondahl.

Fakes and Imitations

The hobby of collecting, no matter what you choose to collect, is plagued by fakes and counterfeits. The limited edition plate collector, however, is luckier than most. While the markets for stamps, coins, and antiques are rife with fakes and reproductions, the collector plate field remains relatively pure. Actual fakes are very rare on the U. S. market despite rising prices and the corresponding increase in temptation for counterfeiters.

This does not mean, however, that the inexperienced buyer should not be cautious. Certain pitfalls exist. With a little insight and know–how, you will become informed enough to avoid them.

Any manufactured object of quality that proves successful on the market will draw inexpensive imitations. This is true of cars, clothing, anything. Plates are no exception. The public's rush to buy a plate issued for $50 creates a great incentive for a manufacturer to produce a lesser quality plate with a selling price of $5 or $10. The assumption is that many purchasers of collector plates are not connoisseurs or even *collectors*. They are simply charmed by the physical qualities of the plate. Could they not be just as charmed by a less expensive imitation produced in vast quantities? Unfortunately, the answer is often yes.

Gift shops are being inundated with plates that, while appearing to be collector plates, are nothing more than facsimiles. They seldom carry the designs of noted artists. Those that do are poorly reproduced. Overall workmanship is well below the standard of collector plates. The edition is not limited. In fact, quite the opposite is true. Production is overwhelmingly high and quality is very low.

If you are a novice in this field of collecting be aware that not every plate in a gift shop is a collector plate. When attractively displayed among collector plates, imitations may be deceiving. They may be the same size. They may be just as colorful. When you handle them, they may feel about the same. If you want a true collector plate, don't be fooled. Be prepared.

Become familiar with the names of companies that make collector plates and with their identifying backstamps. Learn to recognize the styles and signatures of your favorite artists. Backstamps and signatures are two important assurances that what you buy is authentic and not an imitation.

Many imitations originate in Hong Kong or Japan. Their designs are similar to themes on collector plates. However, they are produced and imported in quantities large enough to saturate the market. These plates, while not limited in production, obviously sell. Otherwise, the producers and distributors would not profit.

The issue is not whether a plate is a forgery. As mentioned earlier, fakes are virtually nonexistent. The question is whether you want to collect limited edition plates or just hang a pretty plate on your wall for decoration. If you are interested only in collector plates, then your best protection is to restrict your buying to shops which specialize in limited edition collectibles. By dealing with reputable professionals you will save yourself a lot of problems.

Do not expect to find a valuable collector plate in a dime store or large discount store. These plates may be decorative, but they will not be limited in edition with the potential to appreciate in value. The key is to view collecting plates as you would view collecting fine art. You would never expect to purchase quality artwork at bargain basement prices. You get what you pay for.

It is of the utmost importance to educate yourself in this field. Subscribe to the various collector plate periodicals. They are a treasure trove of invaluable information to both the novice and the advanced collector.

Once you have learned to spot designers' styles and manufacturers' hallmarks, you can easily avoid imitation.

*Artists of the World,
DeGrazia's Children of the Sun,
1987, My Little Pink Bird,
Photo courtesy of Collector News*

*Armstrong/Crown Parian
Signature Collection,
1987, Ironing the Waves,
Photo courtesy of Collector News*

State-of-the-Market Report

The collector plate market is alive and well. It survived the speculative craze of the early 1970s, over–production by manufacturers in the middle and late 1970s, the flooding of the secondary market in the late 1970s and early 1980s, and the recession of the late 1980s and early 1990s. Although relatively quiet for the past fifteen years, there are signs that the collector plate market is about to enjoy a collecting renaissance. The signs are early, and they may be misleading. The answer will be obvious in another two to three years.

Harry L. Rinker, national antiques and collectibles expert, postulated his Thirty Years Rule in the mid–1980s. The rule states: "For the first thirty years of anything's life, all its value is speculative."

Rinker assumes it takes approximately thirty years for any modern product to achieve a trustworthy secondary market. Thirty years provides enough time for examples to be bought, sold, bought, and sold again. A pricing structure develops upon which everyone can rely.

When production numbers are high, it takes thirty years for enough examples to be removed from the market so that demand exceeds supply. This especially applies to collector plates where hoarding of new issues was a major factor in the retail sales market of the middle to late 1970s. Large quantities simply have to be discarded. Scarcity is a critical value component.

Finally, it is the marketplace that establishes what is and is not collectible. Not everything becomes collectible. Not every object passes the test of time. Desirability is another key value component. An object can be fifty years old. However, if no one desires it, its value is minimal at best.

Forty years have passed since the first wave of post-World War II collector plates was issued. Plates manufactured in the 1970s will soon be celebrating their thirtieth birthday. There is a viable secondary market for collector plates.

The secondary collector plate market of the mid-1990s is highly selective. Less than twenty–five percent of the plates issued in the 1960s and 1970s have reached a value point equal to their initial retail values. Those that have are doing well. Each year a few more collector plates achieve this plateau.

The decline in secondary market value experienced by collector plates in the late 1970s and 1980s has ended. Do not expect prices to go lower. Values for plates with very limited desirability have leveled at $2 to $5. Common plates, those with some, but limited, collectibility fall within the $5 to $15 range. Those beginning the climb back up the financial ladder sell around $20 to $25. Those collector plates that are viewed as most desirable realize $50 plus with prices in the hundreds common.

Collect plate collectors no longer dominate their market. They face stiff competition from crossover collectors, those individuals interested in the subject matter on the surface of the plate. A plate featuring a Norman Rockwell image has far more value to a Rockwell collector, even in today's weak Rockwell market, than it does to a plate collector. The same holds true for plates featuring images of film, television, or sport personalities.

When the collector plate market faltered in the late 1970s, many manufacturers, dealers, and collectors turned their attention to other collectible fields, e.g., figurines, bells, ornaments, etc. The 1980s was the age of Precious Moments and David Winter cottages. Figurines and cottages still reign supreme in the 1990s.

The controlled manufacture of collector plates actually strengthened the market. Manufacturers paid closer attention to design and quality. Collectors bought more selectively. Extensive hoarding ceased. Some collectors still bought a second or third example of a particular favorite.

Perhaps the greatest news for the collector plate market, both primary and secondary, was the switch from ceramics to plastic resin for most figurines and many cottages. The long–term perceived value of a ceramic item is vastly different from an item made from plastic. The secondary resin figurine and cottage market is experiencing the same initial speculative surge the collector market went through in the early and middle 1970s. The resin bubble will burst and, most likely, soon. As long as collector plate manufacturers stick to ceramic and glass as their principal manufacturing mediums, they will maintain a long–term competitive edge against items made from resin.

During the past few years, home shopping cable television channels have revived a number of contemporary collectibles markets. Dolls and Fenton are two examples. Eventually, companies such as QVC will discover collector plates. Initially, buyers focus on the new products offered. However, within less than five years, many of these buyers shift their attention to vintage examples. When this happens, expect boom times within the secondary collector plate market.

Krause Publications (700 East State Street, Iola, WI 54990) recently acquired Collector's Mart Magazine. Krause is an extremely aggressive company. Each month the number of sale and seeker classified advertising increases. At long last, the collector plate market has a reliable, slick sheet trading vehicle.

Perhaps the most optimistic news of all is that Replacements, Ltd. (PO Box 26029, Greensboro, NC 27420) is entering the secondary resale market for contemporary collectibles. The Bradford Exchange, which deserves kudos for sticking with the modern and secondary plate market through the good and bad times of the past decade, finally has formidable competition. Replacements, Ltd., makes markets, both through its aggressive buying and "for sale" advertising.

Finally, the collector plate price guide you are holding is the first price guide to collector plates that has honestly reported actual market values. Plates that are selling substantially below or near, but still below, their initial retail value have been clearly identified. Prices are realistic and truthful.

In the past and even today, some collector plate price guides refuse to list the secondary market value of a plate below its initial retail price. Such an approach is highly deceiving. Its purpose is to serve as an industry prop.

Yes, the truth sometimes hurts. However, if collector plates are going to enjoy a trustworthy secondary market, the information available must be honestly presented. Once done, accepted, and used, the market can make a major move forward. This edition of The Official Price Guide to Collector Plates represents that all important first step.

Publications, Museums, and Factory Tours

PUBLICATIONS

The number of trade magazines and periodicals has shrunk since the last edition of this book. Further, the amount of coverage given collector plates in the trade literature also has lessened. The good news is that coverage of collector plates in these periodicals over the last year has increased. This is one of the many positive signs that a collecting renaissance is in the wind.

Trade Magazines

Collector's Mart Magazine, Krause Publiscations, 700 E. State St., Iola, WI 54990. Published seven times per year — February, April, June, August, September, October, and December. Covers a wide range of limited edition collectibles including plates, dolls, prints, figurines, and teddy bears.

Trade Newspapers

The Antique Trader, P.O. Box 1050, Dubuque, IA 52001. Weekly tabloid newspaper since 1957. Covers a wide range in the antiques and collectibles field. There are brief, incomplete listings on new plate issues and some occasional editorial on the subject. Contains classifieds for all types of collector items.

Collectors News, P.O. Box 156, Grundy Center, IA 50638. Weekly tabloid newspaper with a section each week on collector plates. Most editorial content appears to be press releases from plate manufacturers.

MUSEUMS AND FACTORY TOURS

As your travels take you across America and abroad, consider stopping at museums and factories that display or show how collector plates are made. Understanding the manufacturing process will greatly enhance your appreciation of the plates in your collection.

Several types of museums are listed. First are museums associated with manufacturers. These often are located at the plant site and included in a plant tour. Second are museums featuring the art work of a specific artist. While you may see only a limited number of collector plates, you will see the original art works that inspired the images that appear on the plates.

Make certain to allow enough time for your visit, usually a minimum of two hours. Given your special interest, you will want to spend time admiring the many treasures you will see.

Finally, all museums have gift shops. Plant tours often end in a shop selling firsts and seconds. Take along enough money so that you can add a special remembrance of your visit to your collection.

The Bradford Museum of Collector's Plates, 9333 North Milwaukee
Ave., Niles, IL 607814; (847) 966-2770
Hours: Monday through Friday, 10:00AM – 5:00PM
Saturday and Sunday, 9:00AM – 4:00PM; Closed major holidays
Admission: $2.00 adults, $1.00 senior citizens, children under 12 free

Department 56 Tour of One Village Place, 6436 City West Parkway
Eden Prairie, MN 55344
Hours: June through August, Fridays, 9:00AM to 3:00 PM
Admission: Free, reservations should be made one week in advance

Fenton Art Glass Company, 420 Caroline Ave., Williamstown, WV
26187; (304) 375-7772
Factory Tour Hours: Monday through Friday, 8:30AM – 2:30PM
Closed Saturday, Sunday, and major holidays
Museum & Gift Shop Hours: January through March, Monday through
Saturday, 8:00AM – 5:00PM; Sunday 12:15PM – 5:00PM
April through December, Monday through Friday, 8:00AM – 8:00PM
Saturday 8:00AM – 5:00PM, Sunday 12:15PM – 5:00PM
Admission: Free

Franklin Mint Museum, U.S. Rte. 1, Franklin Center, PA 19091;
(610) 459-6168
Hours: Monday through Saturday, 9:30AM – 4:30PM
Sunday 1:00PM – 4:30PM
Admission: Free

Frankoma Pottery Tour, 2400 Frankoma Rd., Sapulpa, OK 74067;
(800) 331-3650
Factory Tour Hours: Monday through Friday, 9:30AM – 2:00PM
Gift Shop Hours: Monday through Saturday, 9:00AM – 5:00PM
Sunday 1:00PM – 5:00PM
Admission: Free

Hibel Museum of Art, 150 Royal Poinciana Plaza, Palm Beach, FL
33480; (407) 833-6870
Hours: Tuesday through Saturday, 10:00AM – 5:00PM
Sunday 1:00PM – 5:00PM
Admission: Free

The M.I. Hummel Museum, Inc., 199 Main Plaza, New Braunfels, TX
78131; (800) 456-4866
Hours: Monday through Saturday, 10:00AM – 5:00PM
Sunday 12Noon – 5:00PM
Admission: $5.00 adults, $4.50 senior citizens and groups, $3.00 students
ages 6 to 18, children under 5 free

Incolay Studios Museum, 445 North Fox St., San Fernando, CA 91340;
(816) 365-2521
Hours: By invitation only

Lladro Museum and Galleries, 43 West 57th St., New York, NY 10019;
(212) 838-9341
Hours: Tuesday through Saturday, 10:00AM – 5:30PM
Admisison: Free

The Norman Rockwell Museum, Rte. 183, Stockbridge, MA 01262;
(413) 298-4100
Hours: May through October, 10:00AM – 5:00PM daily
November through April, weekdays 11:00AM – 4:00PM,
weekends 10:00AM – 5:00PM
Admission: $9.00 adults, $2.00 under 18

List of Manufacturers

Anheuser–Busch, Inc.
2700 South Broadway
St. Louis, MO 63118
(314) 577-2000

Anna–Perenna Porcelain, Inc.
71 Weyman Avenue
New Rochelle, NY 10805
(914) 633-3777

ANRI Woodsculptures
1126 South Cedar Ridge
Suite 111
Duncanville, TX 75137
(800) 730-2674

Artists of the World
2915 North 67th Place
Scottsdale, AZ 85251
(602) 946-6361

The B & J Company
P.O. Box 67
Georgetown, TX 78626
(512) 863-8318

Belleek
distributed by Reed & Barton
144 West Britannia Street
Taunton, MA 02780
(800) 822-1824

The Boehm Studio
25 Fairfacts
Trenton, NJ 08638
(800) 257-9400

The Bradford Exchange
9333 North Milwaukee Avenue
Niles, IL 60714
(800) 682-7590

C.U.I., Inc. / Classic Carolina
Collections / Dram Tree
1502 North 23rd Street
Wilmington, NC 28405

Cavanaugh Group International
1000 Holcomb Woods Parkway
Suite 400B
Roswell, GA 30076
(770) 643-1175

Cross Gallery, Inc.
P.O. Box 4181
Jackson, WY 83001
(307) 733-2200

The Danbury Mint
47 Richards Avenue
Norwalk, CT 06857
(203) 853-2000

Department 56, Inc.
P.O. Box 44456
Eden Prairie, MN 55344
(800) 548-8696

Duncan Royale
1141 South Acacia Avenue
Fullerton, CA 92631
(714) 879-1360

Enesco Corporation
225 Windsor Drive
Itasca, IL 60143
(708) 875-5385

Fenton Art Glass Company
700 Elizabeth Street
Williamstown, WV 26187
(304) 375-6122

Fitz and Floyd
13111 North Central Expressway
Dallas, TX 75254
(214) 918-0098

Flambro Imports, Inc.
1530 Ellsworth Industrial Drive
Atlanta, GA 30318
(404) 352-1381

The Franklin Mint
Franklin Center, PA 19091
(610) 459-7494

Gartlan USA, Inc.
575 Route 73 North
Suite A–6
West Berlin, NJ 08091
(609) 753-9229

Georgetown Collection, Inc.
866 Spring Street
P.O. Box 9730
Portland, ME 04104
(800) 626-3330
last plate issued 1993

Goebel United States (Hummel)
Goebel Plaza
P.O. Box 10, Route 31
Pennington, NJ 08534
(609) 737-8700

Dave Grossman Creations, Inc.
1608 North Warson Road
St. Louis, MO 63132
(314) 423-5600

The Hadley Companies
11001 Hampshire Avenue South
Bloomington, MN 55438
(612) 943-8474

The Hamilton Collection
4810 Executive Park Court
P.O. Box 2567
Jacksonville, FL 32232
(904) 279-1300

Edna Hibel Studio
P.O. Box 9967
Riviera Beach, FL 33419
(407) 848-9633

John Hine Studios, Inc.
4456 Campbell Road
P.O. Box 801207
Houston, TX 77280
(713) 690-4477

Incolay Studios, Inc.
445 North Fox Street
San Fernando, CA 91340
(818) 365-2521

Lalique
499 Veterans Boulevard
Carlstadt, NJ 07072
(201) 939-4199

The Lance Corporation
321 Central Street
Hudson, MA 01749
(508) 568-1401

Lenox Collections / Gorham
100 Lenox Drive
Lawrenceville, NJ 08648
(609) 844-1475

Lightpost Publishing
Ten Almaden Boulevard
Ninth Floor
San Jose, CA 95113
(408) 279-4777

Lladro
1 Lladro Drive
Moonachie, NJ 07074
(201) 807-1177

Seymour Mann, Inc.
225 Fifth Avenue
New York, NY 10010
(212) 683-7262

Marty Bell Fine Art, Inc.
9314 Eton Avenue
Chatsworth, CA 91311
(800) 637-4537

Maruri USA Corporation
7541 Woodman Place
Van Nuys, CA 91405
(800) 562-7874
issued one plate only

Miss Martha Originals
P.O. Box 5038
Glencoe, AL 35905
(205) 492-0221

Opa's Haus, Inc.
1600 River Road
New Braunfels, TX 78132
(210) 629-1191

Orrefors of Sweden
140 Bradford Drive
Berlin, NJ 08009]
(609) 768-5400

Pemberton & Oakes
P.O. Box 21907
Santa Barbara, CA 93121

Pickard, Inc.
782 Pickard Avenue
Antioch, IL 60002
(708) 395-3800

Porsgrund USA, Inc.
2920–3000 Wolff Street
Racine, WI 53404
(414) 632-3433

The Raymon Troup Studio
1590 Lewisburg Pike
Franklin, TN 37064
(800) 514-9231

RECO International Corporation
150 Haven Avenue
Port Washington, NJ 11050
(516) 767-2400

River Shore
4810 Executive Park Court
P.O. Box 2567
Jacksonville, FL 32232
(904) 279-1300

The Norman Rockwell Gallery
9200 Center for the Arts Drive
Niles, IL 60714
(708) 581-8326

Roman, Inc.
555 Lawrence Avenue
Roselle, IL 60172
(708) 529-3000

Rosenthal USA
355 Michelle Place
Carlstadt, NJ 07072
(201) 804-8000

Royal Copenhagen, Inc. / Bing &
Grondahl
683 Madison Avenue
New York, NY 10021
(212) 759-6457

Royal Doulton USA, Inc.
701 Cottontail Lane
Somerset, NJ 08873
(908) 356-7880

Royal Worcester Limited
Severn Street
Worcester, England WR1 2NE
9095 23221

Sarah's Attic
126¹/₂ West Broad Street
Chesaning, MI 48616
(517) 845-3990
last plate issued 1994

Schmid
55 Pacella Park Drive
Randolph, MA 02368
(617) 961-3000

U.S. Historical Society
First and Main Streets
Richmond, VA 23219
(804) 648-4736

D. H. Ussher Ltd.
1132 West 15th Street
North Vancouver, British Columbia
Canada V7P1M9
(604) 986-0365

Viletta China Company
10130 Mula
Stafford, TX 77477
(800) 231-5762

Waterford Wedgwood
41 Madison Avenue
New York, NY 10010
(212) 532-5950

Glossary

Alabaster — a fine–grained, somewhat translucent kind of gypsum stone or a mottled kind of calcite that is found in marble. (see also Ivory Alabaster.)

Annual — a term used to describe an item issued once a year, or yearly. When used as a series name, *annual* usually means the series is not a commemorative or a holiday issue.

Art Deco — a classical style of art that emphasized symmetrical and rectilinear shapes, such as the cylinder and the rectangle. It was popular from the 1920s to the 1940s in Europe and the United States.

Art Nouveau — a style of art popular in the 1890s and until about 1920. It emphasized decoration rather than form, expressing this often in a whiplash curve and lines of floral and leaflike designs.

Backstamp — a printed or incised symbol or logo, usually found on the underside of an object, that gives some or all of the information on the object's origin, such as the name of the producer, sponsor, or artist, the title, issue date, number of sequence, and artist's signature.

Banding — a term used to describe hand application of metals, such as gold and silver, to the rim of an item.

Baroque — a French word meaning an irregular shape. It was used to describe a style of art popular in the seventeenth and eighteenth centuries. Baroque art was characteristically displayed by dynamic movements, exaggerated ornamentation, bold contrasts, and massive forms.

Basalt — a dense, fine–grained black volcanic stone. Wedgwood introduced black basalts for ornamental and useful wares.

Bas–Relief — a method of decoration on an object in which the design is raised above a background. This is produced either by pouring a liquid mixture into a mold or by applying to a background an already formed design.

Bisque or Biscuit — a name applied to any pottery item that has been fired in a kiln once but has not been glazed.

Body — the clay or mixture of substances combined to make pottery ware.

Bone Ash — the powder produced when animal bones, usually those of oxen, are crushed and ground. It is an ingredient in bone china that makes it appear whiter and more translucent.

Bone China or Bone Porcelain — ceramic wares that are pure white due to added bone ash. It is softer than hard–paste porcelain but more durable than soft–paste porcelain.

Camber — a shape that has a slightly convex surface. The first camber–shaped collector plate was issued in 1982 by Royal Doulton.

Cameo — a carving in relief that has a color contrasting with its background.

Carnival Glass — inexpensively produced glass made primarily from 1900 to 1925. Items made of carnival glass were originally used as fair prizes. This glass is iridescent and is produced in many colors.

Ceramic — any ware or work of a potter or object made from baked clay.

Certificate of Authenticity — a written statement received when an object is bought that assures the origin and sequence number of an edition.

China — a term originally used for all wares produced in China. It is now used in reference to any hard, vitreous, or glassy ceramic consisting of kaolin, ball clay, china stone, feldspar, and flint.

Cinnabar — a bright red mineral found in hydrothermal deposits of volcanic regions. It is the principal ore of mercury and mercuric sulfide.

Cobalt — a steel–gray metallic element used as a pigment in glazes and tin–enamels. The most common use is in cobalt blue glaze.

Crazing — a mesh of cracks in the glaze on a piece of pottery; also called *crackle* if found in Chinese porcelains.

Crystal — a very clear, brilliant glass of fine quality, well suited for prism cuts by refracting light. Full lead crystal contains at least 24 percent lead.

Damascene — a method of decorating by filling inlaid designs with gold or copper, perfected by Reed & Barton.

Delftware — tin–glazed earthenware that was originally developed in Delft, Holland.

Dresden — a term often used as synonymous with Meissen porcelain. Dresden and Meissen were two cities in East Germany that produced porcelain. The first porcelain produced outside China was discovered by Johann Friedrich Bottger in the Dresden factory in 1709.

Earthenware — any pottery that is not vitrified. It is the largest kind of pottery, including delftware, faience, and majolica.

Edition — the total number produced of one design in a series.

Electroplating — method of covering one metal with another by electrolysis.

Embossing — a method of decoration with raised designs, produced either in a mold or with a stamp.

Enamel — a glassy substance with mineral oxides fused to a surface for decoration.

Engraving — a method of decoration produced by cutting into a surface with tools or acids.

Etching — a method of decoration produced by using acid to cut a design. The surface to be decorated is first covered with a wax; then the acid eats into the areas left bare or carved out with a needle.

Faience — a type of earthenware covered in a tin glaze. Faience is increasingly being used to mean the same as delftware and majolica. The difference is that the Delft faience uses a more refined clay. The name comes from an Italian town called Faenza.

Feldspar — a kind of crystalline rock from which kaolin, one of the main components of porcelain and china, is formed when the rock decomposes.

Fire — the process of heating a piece of clay to high temperatures, transforming it into porcelain or pottery.

Flow Blue — the name given to pottery blue underglaze designs because of the slight fuzziness resulting from glazing over the color blue.

Glaze — a liquid compound that, when fired on a ceramic piece, becomes a glasslike surface. It is used to seal the surface so that it is nonabsorbent.

Glost Fire — a process of firing in a kiln to fuse the glaze.

Hallmark — a stamped or incised mark identifying the manufacturer.

Hard–Paste Porcelain — a vitreous ceramic made primarily of kaolin, or china clay, and petuntse, which is china stone. It is somewhat translucent and when tapped should ring. When chipped, it will have a shell–like or conchoidal shape to the chip.

Incising — a method of cutting designs or inscriptions into the surface of an object for decoration.

Incolay Stone — a material from which Incolay Studios produces art objects that look like cameos. The process for making it is kept secret by the Studio, but it is known that it contains some quartzlike minerals.

Inlaid — a kind of decoration produced by etching into a surface and then filling the etched–out areas with another substance, usually silver or gold.

Iridescence — the intermingling of colors as in a rainbow or as seen in mother–of–pearl. This may be produced by alkaline glazes on ceramic wares.

Ivory Alabaster — a type of fine–grained nontranslucent gypsum, which may acquire a patina with age.

Jasperware — a hard, unglazed stoneware produced by Wedgwood originally in 1775. Color is added to a naturally white body by mixing in metallic oxides. Pale blue is the most common.

Kaolin — a fine white clay used to produce china and porcelain.

Kiln — an oven in which ceramic pieces are fired.

KPM — the abbreviation for Koenigliche Porzellan Manufacture.

Lead Crystal — (see Crystal).

Limited Edition — a term used to describe an item that is produced for a specific period of time or in a specified amount previously decided upon by the manufacturer.

Luster — a film covering an item made of silver, copper, gold, or platinum pigment reduced from an oxide for decoration.

Majolica — any tin–glaze earthenware from Italy.

Mold — the form that shapes ceramic pieces of art. The object is formed either by pressing clay into the mold or by pouring a liquid clay formula into the mold, and the excess water is absorbed, leaving a hardened shape.

Overglaze — an enameled design painted on top of a fired glaze and then fired again at a lower temperature for permanence.

Parian — a hard–paste porcelain named after parian marble. It is a vitrified china that can be fired at a lower temperature, allowing for a greater variety of possible colors for designs.

Pentuntse — a fusible component of hard–paste porcelain.

Porcelain — a fine, hard, white, vitrified material that is generally fired at about 1400 degrees Celsius. Its chief components are kaolin and pentuntse, and when fired they produce a translucent material that will ring when tapped.

Pottery — a general name given to all ceramic wares. In the present market, it sometimes refers only to earthenware, not including porcelain or any ceramic with a vitrified surface.

Queen's Ware — an earthenware developed by Wedgwood for Queen Charlotte of England in 1765. It is cream in color and is also called white ware.

Relief Decoration — a design that is raised above a background. This is produced either by pouring a liquid clay mixture into a mold or by applying an already formed design to an object.

Satin Glass — art glass made with a matte finish rather than a polished finish.

Soft–Paste Porcelain — a porcelain made of white firing clay and silicate, a ground–up mass of glass, sand, or broken china. This very translucent material is also called artificial porcelain and is generally fired at about 1100 degrees Celsius.

Stoneware — a name that applies to all vitrified and nonporous pottery, except porcelain.

Terra Cotta — the name used for clay fired without glaze. This type of clay is more often formed by a potter than by a sculptor, who produces earthenware.

Tin Glaze — a dense lead glaze that is colored white and made opaque by adding ashes of tin. It may also be colored by adding metallic oxides.

Toriart — a method of molding wood shavings into a solid form, perfected by the House of Anri. The forms may then be carved to carry a design or may already have a relief design from the mold.

Translucence — a property of some ceramics in which light can be seen through an object that is not transparent.

Triptych — a set of three paintings with a common theme, usually religious, connected together and often used as an altarpiece.

Underglaze — a method in which colors are painted on ceramic bisque, which is then dipped in glaze and fired a second time.

Vitreous or Vitrification — the condition of a ceramic object when fired that results in a glassy and impermeable surface.

How to Use This Book

This book is designed to be a teaching tool, a checklist, and a pricing aid. It represents a major revision from its predecessor. You will find it easier to read and use. It offers a more realistic look at the collector plate market — indicating for the first time those plates that are attracting collector interest and those that are not — than is available from any other source.

TEACHING TOOL

Take the time to read the chapters in the front of the book. "The History of Collector Plates" offers a detailed look at the origin of the collector plate, how it evolved, and its current role within the world of contemporary collectibles. Several manufacturers and artists provide brief histories of their companies or work. Knowing about a collector plate's maker and artist adds to the personal value of the plate.

Collecting requires a commitment to understanding the hows and whys of any collecting category. This understanding is essential if you wish to become a savvy collector. You will find what you need to know and more in the text chapters preceding the checklist/price guide portion of this book.

Finally, you will find information about periodicals, museums, factory tours, terms (glossary), and names and addresses of manufacturers in the front of this book rather than as appendices in the back. This is information to which the collector plate collector continually refers. It is easier to find up front.

CHECKLIST

You would be making a mistake if you think of this book only as a price guide. It has been designed to serve as a collector plate checklist. The listings for each manufacturer are as complete as possible. With rare exceptions, e.g., Danbury Mint, collector plate manufacturers cooperated fully with this project.

The checklist is organized alphabetically by manufacturer. Use the page heads as a guide to locating the manufacturer in which you are interested. Be creative in your search. For example, Edna Hibel Studios will be found under "H" not "E." We have tried our best to select the key word in a company's title for alphabetizing purposes.

When checking or collecting a specific series, be aware that different plates can have identical or near identical titles. While accuracy is our goal, occasionally manufacturers, wholesalers, retailers, dealers, and other listing sources provide a slightly different title for the same plate. We found title differences between catalog advertisements and the information listed on the back of the plate. Which title is correct? We have tried hard to make the right selection. Hopefully, we have.

PRICE GUIDE

It is time for price honesty in respect to collector plates. In today's market, there frequently is a major difference, down as well as up, between the initial issue retail price and the current secondary market price. The purpose of this book is not to prop the collector plate market. If a plate that initially sold for $25 is now worth $10, you need to know this.

Due to the tremendous price fluctuation at the low end of the collector plate market, we have created three codes for use in this book. They are:

RI = **Recent Issue**. This is a plate that has been issued in the last five years. Any value above its initial retail value is highly speculative. Be forewarned against paying two and three times the retail price for a plate so young. These plates are infants in the market. Their only reliable value is what they sold for initially

NR = **Near Retail.** This is a value assigned to a plate that sells within plus or minus $5 of its initial retail price. It is a plate that is on its way up. It has found collector favor, but has not yet joined the ranks of those plates whose secondary market values significantly exceed their initial retail prices.

BR = **Below Retail**. This indicates plates that are selling for prices that are more than $5 below their initial retail value. In many cases, the plate's value is less than $10. As you review the plates with a **BR** designation, keep in mind the following — the longer a plate falls within this **BR** price range, the less likely it is to ever achieve a profitable status. The one thing that can change this is if its surface image suddenly becomes of interest to crossover collectors.

Prices in this book are retail, i.e., what you would have to pay if you wanted to buy a plate. If you are selling your plates to a dealer expect between twenty–five and thirty cents on the dollar. Hopefully sales via auction will bring a higher figure and a private sale even more. The only individual likely to get full retail is a dealer or specialized shop owner.

Finally, prices in this book are for collector plates in fine condition or better condition with their period boxes and all supporting literature. If the box is missing, deduct ten percent. Subtract another five percent for missing literature. If the plate is damaged in any way, its value diminishes by sixty to seventy–five percent or more.

INDEXES

The book contains two indexes, each designed to make it a simple task to locate the collector plates you own or wish to buy. The **Artist Index** allows you to locate the full range of work by your favorite artist. The **Series Index** provides a quick reference point to a complete list of plates in any series.

COMMENTS INVITED

The Official Price Guide to Collector Plates is a major effort to deal with a complex field. You are encouraged to send your comments and suggestions to: Collector Plates, c/o House of Collectibles, 201 East 50th Street, New York, NY 10022.

Collector Plate Listings

ACCENT ON ART UNITED STATES

		Issue Price	Current Value
Mother Goose			
1978	JACK AND JILL, Oscar Graves, 5,000.................	59.50	80.00
Nobility of the Plains			
1978	THE COMANCHE, Oscar Graves, 12,500	80.00	NR
1979	MOVING DAY, Oscar Graves, 3,500....................	80.00	NR

COUNT AGAZZI ITALY

Children's Hour			
1970	OWL, 2,000	12.50	NR
1971	CAT, 2,000	12.50	NR
1972	PONY, 2,000	12.50	NR
1973	PANDA, 2,000	12.50	NR
Easter			
1971	PLAYING THE VIOLIN, 600	12.50	NR
1972	AT PRAYER, 600	12.50	NR
1973	WINGED CHERUB, 600	12.50	NR
Famous Personalities			
1968	FAMOUS PERSONALITIES, 600	8.00	NR
1970	FAMOUS PERSONALITIES, 1,000	12.50	NR
1973	FAMOUS PERSONALITIES, 600	15.00	NR
Father's Day			
1972	FATHER'S DAY, 144	35.00	NR
1973	FATHER'S DAY, 288	19.50	NR
Mother's Day			
1972	MOTHER'S DAY, 144	35.00	NR
1973	MOTHER'S DAY, 720	19.50	NR
Single Issues			
1969	APOLLO II, 1,000	17.00	NR
1973	PEACE, 720	12.50	NR

ALLISON AND COMPANY UNITED

Late to Party	Issue Price	Current Value
1982 PIECE OF CAKE, Betty Allison, 12,500	35.00	NR
1983 CHEESE PLEASE, Betty Allison, 12,500	35.00	NR
1983 TOAST TO A MOUSE, Betty Allison, 12,500..............	35.00	NR

Nature's Beauty

1981 WINTER'S PEACE, Betty Allison, 7,500	70.00	NR
1982 SUMMER'S JOY, Betty Allison, 7,500	70.00	NR

Summer's Joy
Photo courtesy of *Collectors News*

AMERICAN ARTISTS UNITED STATES

Best of Fred Stone – Mare and Foal

1991 PATIENCE, Fred Stone, 19,500, 6¹/₂"	25.00	NR
1992 WATER TROUGH, Fred Stone, 19,500, 6¹/₂"..............	25.00	RI
1992 PASTURE PEST, Fred Stone, 19,500, 6¹/₂"..............	25.00	RI
1992 KIDNAPPED MARE, Fred Stone, 19,500, 6¹/₂"............	25.00	RI
1993 CONTENTMENT, Fred Stone, 19,500, 6¹/₂"	25.00	RI
1993 ARAB MARE AND FOAL, Fred Stone, 19,500, 6¹/₂".......	25.00	RI

Cats for Cat Lovers

1987 ROMEO AND JULIET, Susan Leigh	29.50	NR

Family Treasures

1981 CORA'S RECITAL, Richard Zolan, 18,500...............	39.50	NR
1982 CORA'S TEA PARTY, Richard Zolan, 18,500	39.50	NR
1983 CORA'S GARDEN PARTY, Richard Zolan, 18,500	39.50	NR

	Issue Price	Current Value

Famous Fillies

1987	LADY'S SECRET, Fred Stone, 9,500	65.00	75.00
1988	RUFFIAN, Fred Stone, 9,500	65.00	75.00
1988	GENUINE RISK, Fred Stone, 9,500......................	65.00	75.00
1992	GO FOR THE WAND, Fred Stone, 9,500.................	65.00	RI

Feathered Friends

1982	PARAKEETS, Linda Crouch, 19,500	29.50	NR

Flower Fantasies

1985	SPRING BLOSSOMS, Donald Zolan, 15 days	24.50	35.00

Fred Stone Classic

1986	THE SHOE – 8,000 WINS, Fred Stone, 9,500	75.00	85.00
1986	THE ETERNAL LEGACY, Fred Stone, 9,500	75.00	85.00
1988	FOREVER FRIENDS, Fred Stone, 9,500	75.00	NR
1989	ALYSHEBA, Fred Stone, 9,500	75.00	NR

Gold Signature

1990	SECRETARIAT FINAL TRIBUTE, Fred Stone, sgd, 4,500 ..	150.00	NR
1990	SECRETARIAT FINAL TRIBUTE, Fred Stone, 7,500	75.00	NR
1991	OLD WARRIORS, Fred Stone, sgd, 4,500	150.00	NR
1991	OLD WARRIORS, Fred Stone, 7,500...................	75.00	NR

Gold Signature II

1991	NORTHERN DANCER, Fred Stone, dbl signature, 1,500 ..	175.00	NR
1991	NORTHERN DANCER, Fred Stone, sgd, 3,000	150.00	NR
1991	NORTHERN DANCER, Fred Stone, 7,500	75.00	NR
1991	KELSO, Fred Stone, dbl signature, 1,500...............	175.00	NR
1991	KELSO, Fred Stone, sgd, 3,000	150.00	NR
1991	KELSO, Fred Stone, 7,500	75.00	NR

Gold Signature III

1992	DANCE SMARTLY – PAT DAY, UP, Fred Stone, dbl signature, 1,500	175.00	RI
1992	DANCE SMARTLY – PAT DAY, UP, Fred Stone, sgd, 3,000	150.00	RI
1992	DANCE SMARTLY – PAT DAY, UP, Fred Stone, 7,500.....	75.00	RI
1993	AMERICAN TRIPLE CROWN — 1937–1946, Fred Stone, sgd, 2,500	195.00	RI
1993	AMERICAN TRIPLE CROWN — 1937–1946, Fred Stone, .. 7,500...	75.00	RI
1993	AMERICAN TRIPLE CROWN — 1948–1978, Fred Stone, sgd, 2,500	195.00	RI
1993	AMERICAN TRIPLE CROWN — 1948–1978, Fred Stone, 7,500...	75.00	RI

Horses of Fred Stone

		Issue Price	Current Value
1982	PATIENCE, Fred Stone, 9,500	55.00	100.00
1982	ARABIAN MARE AND FOAL, Fred Stone, 9,500	55.00	90.00
1982	SAFE AND SOUND, Fred Stone, 9,500	55.00	70.00
1983	CONTENTMENT, Fred Stone, 9,500	55.00	70.00

Mare and Foal

1986	WATER TROUGH, Fred Stone, 12,500	49.50	100.00
1986	TRANQUILITY, Fred Stone, 12,500	49.50	60.00
1986	PASTURE PEST, Fred Stone, 12,500	49.50	85.00
1987	THE ARABIANS, Fred Stone, 12,500	49.50	NR

Mare and Foal II

1989	THE FIRST DAY, Fred Stone, open	35.00	NR
1989	DIAMOND IN THE ROUGH, Fred Stone, retrd	35.00	NR

Diamond in the Rough
Photo courtesy of *Collectors News*

May Queen
Photo courtesy of *Collectors News*

Mother and Child Cats

1983	KITTY LOVE, Phyllis Hollands–Robinson, 19,500	29.50	NR

Noble Tribes

1983	ALGONQUIN, Donald Zolan, 19,500	49.50	65.00
1984	SIOUX, Donald Zolan, 19,500	49.50	65.00

Racing Legends

1989	PHAR LAP, Fred Stone, 9,500	75.00	NR
1989	SUNDAY SILENCE, Fred Stone, 9,500	75.00	NR
1990	JOHN HENRY–SHOEMAKER, Fred Stone, 9,500	75.00	NR

		Issue Price	Current Value
Saturday Evening Post **Covers**			
1983	SANTA'S COMPUTER, Scott Gustafson, 15 days	29.50	35.00

Sport of Kings

1984	MAN O' WAR, Fred Stone, 9,500	65.00	160.00
1984	SECRETARIAT, Fred Stone, 9,500	65.00	200.00
1985	JOHN HENRY, Fred Stone, 9,500	65.00	85.00
1986	SEATTLE SLEW, Fred Stone, 9,500	65.00	NR

The Stallion

| 1983 | BLACK STALLION, Fred Stone, 9,500 .... | 49.50 | 95.00 |
| 1983 | ANDALUSIAN, Fred Stone, 9,500 .... | 49.50 | 70.00 |

Zoe's Cats

1985	THE SNIFFER, Zoe Stokes, 12,500	29.50	NR
1985	WAITING, Zoe Stokes, 12,500	29.50	NR
1985	SUNSHINE, Zoe Stokes, 12,500	29.50	NR
1985	TARZAN, Zoe Stokes, 12,500	29.50	NR

Single Issues

1984	GOING TO GRANDMA'S HOUSE, Donald Zolan, 15,000 ..	29.50	35.00
1986	MAY QUEEN, Zoe Stokes, 21 days	29.95	NR
1987	THE SHOE, Fred Stone, 9,500	75.00	NR

AMERICAN COMMEMORATIVE UNITED STATES

Southern Landmarks

1973	MONTICELLO, 9,800	43.00	95.00
1973	WILLIAMSBURG, 9,800	43.00	95.00
1974	BEAUVOIR, 9,800	43.00	90.00
1974	GABILDO, 9,800	43.00	90.00
1975	HERMITAGE, 9,800	43.00	90.00
1975	OAK HILL, 9,800	43.00	90.00
1976	GOVERNOR TYRON'S PLACE, 9,800	43.00	70.00
1976	MONTPELIER, 9,800	43.00	70.00
1977	ELMSCOURT, 9,800	43.00	60.00
1977	ASHLAND, 9,800	43.00	60.00
1978	MT. VERNON, 9,800	43.00	60.00
1978	WHITE HOUSE, 9,800	43.00	50.00
1979	CURTIS LEE, 9,800	43.00	50.00
1979	DRAYTON HALL, 9,800	43.00	NR
1980	FT. HILL, 9,800	43.00	NR
1980	LIBERTY HALL, 9,800	43.00	NR

AMERICAN CRYSTAL UNITED STATES

Christmas	Issue Price	Current Value
1970 CHRISTMAS	17.50	NR
1971 CHRISTMAS	12.00	NR
1972 CHRISTMAS	12.00	NR
1973 CHRISTMAS	17.00	NR

Mother's Day

1971 MOTHER'S DAY	8.00	NR
1972 MOTHER'S DAY, 2,000	12.00	NR
1973 MOTHER'S DAY	23.00	NR

Single Issue

1969 ASTRONAUT	17.50	NR

AMERICAN EXPRESS UNITED STATES

American Trees of Christmas

1976 DOUGLAS FIR, 1 year	60.00	NR
1977 SCOTCH PINE, 1 year	60.00	NR

Birds of North America

1978 SAW–WHET OWLS, 9,800	38.00	NR
1978 BOB–WHITE QUAIL, 9,800	38.00	NR
1978 OCTOBER CARDINALS, 9,800	38.00	NR
1978 LONG–EARED OWL, 9,800	38.00	NR
1978 EASTERN BLUEBIRDS, 9,800	38.00	NR
1978 AMERICAN WOODCOCK, 9,800	38.00	NR
1978 RUFFED GROUSE, 9,800	38.00	NR
1978 HOUSE WREN, 9,800	38.00	NR

Four Freedoms

1976 FREEDOM OF WORSHIP, 1 year	37.50	NR
1976 FREEDOM FROM WANT, 1 year	37.50	NR
1976 FREEDOM FROM FEAR, 1 year	37.50	NR
1976 FREEDOM OF SPEECH, 1 year	37.50	NR

Roger Tory Peterson

1981 BOB–O–LINK, limited	55.00	NR
1982 BLUE BIRD, limited	55.00	NR
1982 MOCKING BIRD, limited	55.00	NR
1982 SCARLET TANAGER, limited	55.00	NR
1982 ROBIN, limited	55.00	NR
1982 BLUE JAY, limited	55.00	NR

		Issue Price	Current Value
1982	CARDINAL, limited	55.00	NR
1982	WOOD THRUSH, limited	55.00	NR
1982	BALTIMORE ORIOLE, limited	55.00	NR
1982	ROSE–BREASTED GROSBEAK, limited	55.00	NR
1982	BARN SWALLOW, limited	55.00	NR
1982	FLICKER, limited	55.00	NR

AMERICAN HERITAGE UNITED STATES

Africa's Beauties

1983	ELEPHANT FAMILY, Douglas Van Howd, 5,000	65.00	NR
1984	ZEBRA FAMILY, Douglas Van Howd, 5,000	65.00	NR

America's Heritage of Flight

1983	KITTY HAWK, Allen Adams, 5,000	39.50	NR

American Sail

1983	DOWN EASTER IN A SQUALL, Edward Ries, 5,000	39.50	NR
1983	YOUNG AMERICA, Edward Ries, 5,000	39.50	NR

Young America
Photo courtesy of *Collector News*

Battle Wagons

1982	GENERAL QUARTERS, Edward Ries, 5,000	39.50	NR
1983	LAST CRUISE, Edward Ries, 5,000	39.50	NR

		Issue Price	Current Value
Celebrity Clowns			
1982	EMMETT, John Helland, 12,500	50.00	NR
1982	JUDY, John Helland, 12,500	50.00	NR
1982	JIMMY, John Helland, 12,500	50.00	NR
1982	THE SHARK, John Helland, 12,500	50.00	NR
Craftsman Heritage			
1983	DECOY MAKER, Ray Orosz, 5,000	39.50	NR
1983	SAILMAKER, Ray Orosz, 5,000	39.50	NR
Equestrian Love			
1983	ARABIAN DESTINY, 5,000	39.50	NR
Lil' Critters			
1982	INQUISITIVE, Allen Adams, 10,000	40.00	NR
Sawdust Antics			
1983	EMMETT'S EIGHT BALL, John Helland, 5,000	50.00	NR
1983	EMMETT WITH A BANG, John Helland, 5,000	50.00	NR
Vanishing West			
1982	HELLBENT, David Miller, 7,500	60.00	NR
1983	COLD TRAIL, David Miller, 5,000	60.00	NR

AMERICAN HOUSE UNITED STATES

Single Issues			
1972	LANDING OF COLUMBUS, 1,500	100.00	NR
1972	LANDING OF COLUMBUS, 1,000	250.00	NR

AMERICAN LEGACY UNITED STATES

Children to Love			
1982	WENDY, Sue Etem, 10,000	60.00	125.00
1982	JAKE, Sue Etem, 10,000	60.00	70.00
Holidays Around the World			
1984	ELYSA'S CHRISTMAS, Ignacio Gomez, 12,500	39.50	NR
Special Heart			
1982	REACHING TOGETHER, Sue Etem, 40,000	35.00	NR
1983	LOVE IN YOUR HEART, Sue Etem, 40,000	35.00	NR

Walter Brennan

		Issue Price	Current Value
1983	GRAMPA, Walter Brennan, Jr., 10,000 . . . , ...	60.00	NR
1984	TO KISS A WINNER, Walter Brennan, Jr., 10,000	45.00	NR

Love in Your Heart
Photo courtesy of *Collectors News*

AMERICAN ROSE SOCIETY UNITED STATES

All–American Roses

1975	OREGOLD, 9,800	39.00	140.00
1975	ARIZONA, 9,800	39.00	140.00
1975	ROSE PARADE, 9,800	39.00	140.00
1976	YANKEE DOODLE, 9,800	39.00	135.00
1976	AMERICA, 9,800	39.00	135.00
1976	CATHEDRAL, 9,800	39.00	135.00
1976	SEASHELL, 9,800	39.00	135.00
1977	DOUBLE DELIGHT, 9,800	39.00	115.00
1977	PROMINENT, 9,800	39.00	115.00
1977	FIRST EDITION, 9,800	39.00	115.00
1978	COLOR MAGIC, 9,800	39.00	105.00
1978	CHARISMA, 9,800	39.00	100.00
1979	PARADISE, 9,800	39.00	70.00
1979	SUNDOWNER, 9,800	39.00	80.00
1979	FRIENDSHIP, 9,800	39.00	80.00
1980	LOVE, 9,800	49.00	80.00
1980	HONOR, 9,800	49.00	70.00
1980	CHERISH, 9,800	49.00	80.00
1981	BING CROSBY, 9,800	49.00	75.00
1981	WHITE LIGHTNIN', 9,800	49.00	65.00
1981	MARINA, 9,800	49.00	70.00
1982	SHREVEPORT, 9,800	49.00	60.00

		Issue Price	Current Value
1982	FRENCH LACE, 9,800	49.00	65.00
1982	BRANDY, 9,800	49.00	70.00
1982	MON CHERI, 9,800	49.00	55.00
1983	SUN FLARE, 9,800	49.00	70.00
1983	SWEET SURRENDER, 9,800	49.00	55.00
1984	IMPATIENT, 9,800	49.00	55.00
1984	OLYMPIAD, 9,800	49.00	55.00
1984	INTRIGUE, 9,800	49.00	60.00
1985	SHOWBIZ, 9,800	49.50	NR
1985	PEACE, 9,800	49.50	NR
1985	QUEEN ELIZABETH, 9,800	49.50	NR

ANHEUSER–BUSCH, INC.

Archives Plates

1992	1893 COLUMBIAN EXPOSITION N3477, D. Langeneckert, 25 days	27.50	RI
1992	GANYMEDE, D. Langeneckert, 25 days	27.50	RI

Civil War

1992	GENERAL GRANT N3478, D. Langeneckert, 25 days	45.00	RI
1993	GENERAL ROBERT E. LEE N3590, D. Langeneckert, 25 days	45.00	RI
1993	PRESIDENT ABRAHAM LINCOLN N3591, D. Langeneckert, 25 days	45.00	RI

Holiday Plates

1989	WINTER'S DAY N2295, B. Kemper, retrd	30.00	75.00
1990	AN AMERICAN TRADITION N2767, S. Sampson, retrd ...	30.00	75.00
1991	THE SEASON'S BEST N3034, S. Sampson, 25 days	30.00	NR
1992	A PERFECT CHRISTMAS N3440, S. Sampson, 25 days ..	27.50	RI
1993	SPECIAL DELIVERY N4002, N. Koerber, 25 days	27.50	RI

Man's Best Friend

1990	BUDDIES N2615, M. Urdahl, retrd	30.00	50.00
1990	SIX PACK N3005, M. Urdahl, retrd....................	30.00	40.00
1992	SOMETHING'S BREWING N3147, M. Urdahl, 25 days	30.00	RI
1993	OUTSTANDING IN THEIR FIELD N4003, M. Urdahl, 25 days	27.50	RI

1992 Olympic Team

1991	1992 OLYMPIC TEAM WINTER PLATE N3180, 25 days....	35.00	NR
1992	1992 OLYMPIC TEAM SUMMER PLATE N3122, 25 days .	35.00	RI

ANNADOR TRADING COMPANY

Single Issue	Issue Price	Current Value
1987 THE APPRENTICE, Nori Peters, 7,500	45.00	NR

ANNA–PERENNA GERMANY

American Silhouettes I — The Children

1981 FIDDLERS TWO, P. Buckley Moss, 5,000	75.00	85.00
1982 MARY WITH THE LAMBS, P. Buckley Moss, 5,000	75.00	80.00
1982 WAITING FOR TOM, P. Buckley Moss, 5,000	75.00	125.00
1982 RING AROUND THE ROSIE, P. Buckley Moss, 5,000	75.00	140.00

American Silhouettes II — The Family

1982 FAMILY OUTING, P. Buckley Moss, 5,000	75.00	85.00
1982 JOHN AND MARY, P. Buckley Moss, 5,000	75.00	85.00
1982 HOMEMAKERS A–QUILTING, P. Buckley Moss, 5,000	75.00	80.00
1984 LEISURE TIME, P. Buckley Moss, 5,000	75.00	80.00

American Silhouettes III — Valley Life

1982 FROSTY FROLIC, P. Buckley Moss, 5,000	75.00	85.00
1982 HAYRIDE, P. Buckley Moss, 5,000	75.00	80.00
1983 SUNDAY RIDE, P. Buckley Moss, 5,000	75.00	85.00
1984 MARKET DAY, P. Buckley Moss, 5,000	75.00	95.00

Annual Christmas

1984 NOEL, NOEL, P. Buckley Moss, 5,000	67.50	195.00
1985 HELPING HANDS, P. Buckley Moss, 5,000	67.50	175.00
1986 NIGHT BEFORE CHRISTMAS, P. Buckley Moss, 5,000	67.50	125.00
1987 CHRISTMAS SLEIGH, P. Buckley Moss, 5,000	75.00	85.00
1988 CHRISTMAS JOY, P. Buckley Moss, 5,000	75.00	NR
1989 CHRISTMAS CAROL, P. Buckley Moss, 5,000	80.00	NR
1990 CHRISTMAS EVE, P. Buckley Moss, 5,000	80.00	NR
1991 THE SNOWMAN, P. Buckley Moss, 5,000	80.00	NR
1992 CHRISTMAS WARMTH, P. Buckley Moss, 5,000	85.00	NR

Arctic Spring

1983 PATIENCE, Nori Peter, 9,500	75.00	NR

Bashful Bunnies

1981 SPRING'S SURPRISE, Mary Ellen Wehrli, 15,000	62.50	NR
1982 SUMMER'S SUNSHINE, Mary Ellen Wehrli, 15,000	62.50	NR
1982 FALL'S FROLIC, Mary Ellen Wehrli, 15,000	62.50	NR
1983 WINTER'S WONDER, Mary Ellen Wehrli, 15,000	62.50	NR

		Issue Price	Current Value

Birds of Fancy

1978	FIREBIRD, Dr. Irving Burgues, 5,000	110.00	BR

Capricious Clowns

1981	CLOWNS AND UNICORNS, Margaret Kane, 9,800	95.00	BR
1981	MASQUERADE PARTY, Margaret Kane, 9,800	95.00	BR

Celebration

1986	WEDDING JOY, P. Buckley Moss, 5,000	100.00	300.00
1987	THE CHRISTENING, P. Buckley Moss, 5,000	100.00	150.00
1988	THE ANNIVERSARY, P. Buckley Moss, 5,000	100.00	140.00
1989	FAMILY REUNION, P. Buckley Moss, 5,000	100.00	125.00

The Anniversary
Photo courtesy of *Collectors News*

Family Reunion
Photo courtesy of *Collectors News*

Children of Mother Earth

1983	SPRING, Norval Morrisseau, 2,500	250.00	NR
1983	SUMMER, Norval Morrisseau, 2,500	250.00	NR
1983	AUTUMN, Norval Morrisseau, 2,500	250.00	NR
1983	WINTER, Norval Morrisseau, 2,500	250.00	NR

Enchanted Gardens

1978	JUNE DREAM, Carol Burgues, 5,000	75.00	BR
1978	SUMMER DAY, Carol Burgues, 5,000	95.00	100.00

Floral Fantasies

1978	EMPRESS GOLD, Carol Burgues, 5,000	110.00	BR

		Issue Price	Current Value
Flowers of Count Bernadotte			
1982	IRIS, Count Lennart Bernadotte, 17,800	75.00	95.00
1983	CARNATION, Count Lennart Bernadotte, 17,800	75.00	95.00
1983	LILY, Count Lennart Bernadotte, 17,800	75.00	NR
1983	FREESIA, Count Lennart Bernadotte, 17,800.	75.00	NR
1984	ORCHID, Count Lennart Bernadotte, 17,800	75.00	NR
1984	ROSE, Count Lennart Bernadotte, 17,800	75.00	NR
1984	TULIP, Count Lennart Bernadotte, 17,800	75.00	95.00
1984	CHRYSANTHEMUM, Count Lennart Bernadotte, 17,800. .	75.00	NR
Happy Village			
1983	SPRING – SPRING PICNIC, Elke Sommer, 5,000	55.00	NR
1983	SUMMER – ON THE POND, Elke Sommer, 5,000	55.00	NR
1983	AUTUMN – HARVEST DANCE, Elke Sommer, 5,000	55.00	NR
1983	WINTER – SNOW KIDS, Elke Sommer, 5,000	55.00	NR
International Mother Love			
1979	GESA UND KINDER, Edna Hibel, 5,000	195.00	NR
1980	ALEXANDRA UND KINDER, Edna Hibel, 5,000	195.00	NR
Joys of Motherhood			
1979	GESA AND CHILDREN, 5,000.	165.00	NR
1980	ALEXANDRA AND CHILDREN, 5,000	175.00	NR
Masquerade Fantasies			
1981	THE MASQUERADE PARTY, Margaret Kane, 9,800	95.00	NR
1981	CLOWNS AND UNICORNS, Margaret Kane, 9,800	95.00	NR
Oriental Tranquility			
1978	CHUN LI AT POND, Dr. Irving Burgues, 5,000.	100.00	BR
1979	MING TAO ON PATH OF FAITH, Dr. Irving Burgues, 5,000	110.00	BR
Reflection of Youth			
1984	THE SWIMMERS, Ken Danby, 9,500.	75.00	NR
Rhythm and Dance			
1983	BALLROOM, Al Hirschfield, 5,000	29.50	NR
1983	PAS DE DEUX, Al Hirschfield, 5,000	29.50	NR
1983	SWING, Al Hirschfield, 5,000	29.50	NR
1983	JAZZ, Al Hirschfield, 5,000	29.50	NR
1983	AEROBICS, Al Hirschfield, 5,000	29.50	NR
1983	CAKE WALK, Al Hirschfield, 5,000	29.50	NR
1983	CHARLESTON, Al Hirschfield, 5,000	29.50	NR
1983	STRUT, Al Hirschfield, 5,000	29.50	NR

Romantic Love

		Issue Price	Current Value
1979	ROMEO AND JULIET, Frank Russell and Gertrude Barrer, 7,500	95.00	NR
1980	LANCELOT AND GUINEVERE, Frank Russell and Gertrude Barrer, 7,500	95.00	NR
1981	HELEN AND PARIS, Frank Russell and Gertrude Barrer, 7,500	95.00	NR
1982	LOVERS OF TAJ MAHAL, Frank Russell and Gertrude Barrer, 7,500	95.00	NR

Triptych Series

| 1978 | BYZANTINE TRIPTYCH, Frank Russell and Gertrude Barrer, 5,000 | 325.00 | BR |
| 1980 | JERUSALEM TRIPTYCH, Frank Russell and Gertrude Barrer, 5,000 | 350.00 | BR |

Uncle Tad's Cat

1979	OLIVER'S BIRTHDAY, Thaddeus Krumeich, 5,000	75.00	200.00
1980	PEACHES AND CREAM, Thaddeus Krumeich, 5,000	75.00	85.00
1981	PRINCESS AURORA, QUEEN OF THE NIGHT, Thaddeus Krumeich, 5,000	80.00	NR
1981	WALTER'S WINDOW, Thaddeus Krumeich, 5,000	85.00	NR

My Merry Oldsmobile
Photo courtesy of *Collectors News*

Tender Hands
Photo courtesy of *Collectors News*

Uncle Tad's Golden Oldies

1985	MY MERRY OLDSMOBILE	39.50	55.00
1985	DOWN BY THE OLD MILL STREAM	39.50	55.00
1986	RAMONA	39.50	50.00
1987	PADDLIN' MADELINE HOME	39.50	65.00

		Issue Price	Current Value

Uncle Tad's Holiday Cats

1982	JINGLE BELLS, Thaddous Krumeich, 9,800	75.00	NR
1983	POLLYANNA, Thaddeus Krumeich, 9,800	75.00	NR
1984	PUMPKIN, Thaddeus Krumeich, 9,800	75.00	NR
1985	PERRY, BUTTERCUP AND BLACKEYED SUSAN, Thaddeus Krumeich, 9,800	75.00	NR

Uncle Tad's Tick Tock

| 1982 | HICKORY, DICKORY, Thaddeus Krumeich, 5,000 | 150.00 | NR |

Single Issue

| XX | TENDER HANDS, P. Buckley Moss, 5,000 | 80.00 | NR |

ANRI ITALY

Christmas

1971	ST. JAKOB IN GRODEN, J. Malfertheiner, 10,000	37.50	95.00
1972	PIPERS AT ALBEROBELLO, J. Malfertheiner, 1 year	45.00	100.00
1973	ALPINE HORN, J. Malfertheiner, 1 year	45.00	400.00
1974	YOUNG MAN AND GIRL, J. Malfertheiner, 1 year	50.00	95.00
1975	CHRISTMAS IN IRELAND, J. Malfertheiner, 1 year	60.00	85.00
1976	ALPINE CHRISTMAS, J. Malfertheiner, 1 year	65.00	160.00
1977	LEGEND OF HELIGENBLUT, J. Malfertheiner, 6,000	65.00	135.00
1978	KLOCKLER SINGERS, J. Malfertheiner, 6,000	80.00	110.00
1979	MOSS GATHERERS, 6,000	135.00	175.00
1980	WINTRY CHURCHGOING, 6,000	170.00	NR
1981	SANTA CLAUS IN TYROL, 6,000	165.00	185.00

St. Jakob in Groden

Flight into Egypt

Photo courtesy of *Collectors News*

		Issue Price	Current Value
1982	THE STAR SINGERS, 6,000	165.00	NR
1983	UNTO US A CHILD IS BORN, 6,000	165.00	235.00
1984	YULETIDE IN THE VALLEY, 6,000	165.00	NR
1985	GOOD MORNING, GOOD CHEER, J. Malfertheiner, 6,000	165.00	NR
1986	A GRODEN CHRISTMAS, J. Malfertheiner, 6,000	165.00	185.00
1987	DOWN FROM THE ALPS, J. Malfertheiner, 6,000	195.00	235.00
1988	CHRISTKINDLE MARKT, J. Malfertheiner, 6,000	220.00	NR
1989	FLIGHT INTO EGYPT, J. Malfertheiner, 6,000	275.00	NR
1990	HOLY NIGHT, J. Malfertheiner, 6,000	300.00	NR

Disney Four Star Collection

1989	MICKEY MINI PLATE, Disney Studios, 5,000	40.00	NR
1990	MINNIE MINI PLATE, Disney Studios, 5,000	40.00	NR
1991	DONALD MINI PLATE, Disney Studios, 5,000	50.00	NR

Father's Day

1974	ALPINE FATHER AND CHILDREN, 5,000	35.00	100.00
1975	ALPINE FATHER AND CHILDREN, 5,000	45.00	95.00
1976	SAILING, 5,000	50.00	100.00
1977	CLIFF GAZING, 5,000	60.00	95.00

Ferrandiz Annual

1984	PASTORAL JOURNEY, Juan Ferrandiz, 2,000	170.00	NR
1985	A TENDER TOUCH, Juan Ferrandiz, 2,000	170.00	NR

Ferrandiz Christmas

1972	CHRIST IN THE MANGER, Juan Ferrandiz, 2,500	35.00	230.00
1973	CHRISTMAS, Juan Ferrandiz	40.00	225.00
1974	HOLY NIGHT, Juan Ferrandiz, 1 year	50.00	100.00
1975	FLIGHT INTO EGYPT, Juan Ferrandiz, 1 year	60.00	95.00
1976	TREE OF LIFE, Juan Ferrandiz, 1 year	60.00	65.00
1976	MARY AND JOSEPH, Juan Ferrandiz, 1 year	60.00	100.00
1978	LEADING THE WAY, Juan Ferrandiz, 4,000	77.50	180.00
1979	THE DRUMMER, Juan Ferrandiz, 4,000	120.00	175.00
1980	REJOICE, Juan Ferrandiz, 4,000	150.00	160.00
1981	SPREADING THE WORD, Juan Ferrandiz, 4,000	150.00	NR
1982	THE SHEPHERD FAMILY, Juan Ferrandiz, 4,000	150.00	NR
1983	PEACE ATTEND THEE, Juan Ferrandiz, 4,000	150.00	NR

Ferrandiz Mother's Day

1972	MOTHER SEWING, Juan Ferrandiz, 1 year	35.00	200.00
1973	MOTHER AND CHILD, Juan Ferrandiz, 1 year	40.00	150.00
1974	MOTHER HOLDING CHILD, Juan Ferrandiz, 1 year	50.00	150.00
1975	MOTHER AND DOVE, Juan Ferrandiz, 1 year	60.00	150.00
1976	MOTHER KNITTING, Juan Ferrandiz, 1 year	60.00	200.00

		Issue Price	Current Value
1976	GIRL WITH FLOWERS, Juan Ferrandiz, 4,000	65.00	185.00
1977	ALPINE STROLL, Juan Ferrandiz, 1 year	65.00	125.00
1978	THE BEGINNING, Juan Ferrandiz, 3,000	77.50	150.00
1979	ALL HEARTS, Juan Ferrandiz, 3,000	120.00	170.00
1980	SPRING ARRIVALS, Juan Ferrandiz, 3,000..............	150.00	165.00
1981	HARMONY, Juan Ferrandiz, 3,000	150.00	NR
1982	WITH LOVE, Juan Ferrandiz, 3,000	150.00	NR

Ferrandiz Wooden Birthday

1972	BOY, Juan Ferrandiz, 1 year	15.00	70.00
1972	GIRL, Juan Ferrandiz, 1 year	15.00	70.00
1973	BOY, Juan Ferrandiz, 1 year	20.00	90.00
1973	GIRL, Juan Ferrandiz, 1 year	20.00	65.00
1974	BOY, Juan Ferrandiz, 1 year	22.00	70.00
1974	GIRL, Juan Ferrandiz, 1 year	22.00	70.00

Ferrandiz Wooden Wedding

1972	BOY AND GIRL EMBRACING, Juan Ferrandiz, 1 year	40.00	145.00
1973	WEDDING SCENE, Juan Ferrandiz, 1 year	40.00	130.00
1974	WEDDING, Juan Ferrandiz, 1 year	48.00	100.00
1975	WEDDING, Juan Ferrandiz, 1 year	60.00	100.00
1976	WEDDING, Juan Ferrandiz, 1 year	60.00	90.00

Mother's Day

1972	ALPINE MOTHER AND CHILDREN, 5,000	35.00	50.00
1973	ALPINE MOTHER AND CHILDREN, 5,000	45.00	55.00
1974	ALPINE MOTHER AND CHILDREN, 5,000	50.00	NR
1975	ALPINE STROLL, 5,000.............................	60.00	NR
1976	KNITTING, 5,000	60.00	NR

Sarah Kay Annual

1984	A TIME FOR SECRETS, Sarah Kay, 2,500..............	120.00	NR
1985	CAROUSEL MAGIC, Sarah Kay, 2,500	120.00	NR

ANTIQUE TRADER UNITED STATES

Bible Series

1973	DAVID AND GOLIATH, 2,000	10.75	NR
1973	MOSES AND GOLDEN IDOL, 2,000...................	10.75	NR
1973	NOAH'S ARK, 2,000................................	10.75	NR
1973	SAMSON, 2,000	10.75	NR

C. M. Russell

1971	BAD ONE, 2,000	11.95	NR

		Issue Price	Current Value
1971	DISCOVERY OF LAST CHANCE GULCH, 2,000	11.95	NR
1971	DOUBTFUL VISITOR, 2,000	11.95	NR
1971	INNOCENT ALLIES, 2,000	11.95	NR
1971	MEDICINE MAN, 2,000	11.95	NR

Christmas

1971	CHRIST CHILD, 1,500	10.95	NR
1972	FLIGHT INTO EGYPT, 1,500	10.95	NR

Currier & Ives

1969	BASEBALL, 2,000	9.00	NR
1969	FRANKLIN EXPERIMENT, 2,000	9.00	NR
1969	HAYING TIME, 2,000	9.00	NR
1969	WINTER IN COUNTRY, 2,000	9.00	NR

Easter

1971	CHILD AND LAMB, 1,500	10.95	NR
1972	SHEPHERD WITH LAMB, 1,500	10.95	NR

Father's Day

1971	PILGRIM FATHER, 1,500	10.95	NR
1972	DEER FAMILY, 1,000	10.95	NR

Mother's Day

1971	MADONNA AND CHILD, 1,500	10.95	NR
1972	MOTHER CAT AND KITTENS, 1,000	10.95	NR

Thanksgiving

1971	PILGRIMS, 1,500	10.95	NR
1972	FIRST THANKSGIVING, 1,000	10.95	NR

ARABIA OF FINLAND FINLAND

Christmas Annual

1978	INLAND VILLAGE SCENE, 1 year	49.00	NR
1979	FOREST VILLAGE SCENE, 1 year	72.00	NR
1980	SEASIDE VILLAGE SCENE, 1 year	79.00	NR
1981	CHRISTMAS PLATE, 1 year	87.00	NR
1982	CHRISTMAS PLATE, 1 year	95.00	NR

Commemoration Series

1973	Production rare	20.00	70.00
1974	Production rare	20.00	70.00

Kalevala Series

Year	Title	Issue Price	Current Value
1976	VAINOMOINEN'S SOWING SONG, Raija Uosikkinen, 1,996	30.00	230.00
1977	AINO'S FATE, Raija Uosikkinen, 1,008	30.00	NR
1978	LEMMINKAINEN'S CHASE, Raija Uosikkinen, 2,500	39.00	NR
1979	KULLERVO'S REVENGE, Raija Uosikkinen, 1 year	39.50	NR
1980	VAINOMOINEN'S RESCUE, Raija Uosikkinen, 1 year	45.00	60.00
1981	VAINOMOINEN'S MAGIC, Raija Uosikkinen, 1 year	49.50	NR
1982	JOUKAHAINEN SHOOTS THE HORSE, Raija Uosikkinen, 1 year	55.50	NR
1983	LEMMINKAINEN'S ESCAPE, Raija Uosikkinen, 1 year	60.00	85.00
1984	LEMMINKAINEN'S MAGIC FEATHERS, Raija Uosikkinen, 1 year	49.50	90.00
1985	LEMMINKAINEN'S GRIEF, Raija Uosikkinen, 1 year	60.00	NR
1986	OSMATAR CREATING ALE, Raija Uosikkinen, 1 year	60.00	85.00
1987	VAINOMOINEN TRICKS ILMARINEN, Raija Uosikkinen, 1 year	65.00	90.00
1988	HEARS VAINOMOINEN WEEP, Raija Uosikkinen, 1 year	69.00	115.00
1989	FOUR MAIDENS, Raija Uosikkinen, 1 year	75.00	85.00
1990	ANNIKKA, Raija Uosikkinen, 1 year	85.00	105.00
1991	LEMMINKAINEN'S MOTHER SAYS DON'T/WAR, Raija Uosikkinen, 1 year	85.00	NR

ARIZONA ARTISAN UNITED STATES

Christmas

Year	Title	Issue Price	Current Value
1974	MEXICAN CHRISTMAS, 1 year	20.00	NR
1975	NAVAJO CHRISTMAS, 1 year	20.00	NR

Thanksgiving

Year	Title	Issue Price	Current Value
1975	NAVAJO THANKSGIVING, 1 year	15.00	NR

ARLINGTON MINT UNITED STATES

Christmas

Year	Title	Issue Price	Current Value
1972	HANDS IN PRAYER, 1 year	125.00	BR

ARMSTRONG'S/CROWN PARIAN UNITED STATES

American Folk Heroes

Year	Title	Issue Price	Current Value
1983	JOHNNY APPLESEED, Gene Boyer, 50 days	35.00	NR
1984	DAVY CROCKETT, Gene Boyer, 50 days	35.00	NR
1985	BETSY ROSS, Gene Boyer, 50 days	35.00	NR

		Issue Price	Current Value

Beautiful Cats of the World

1979	SHEENA, Douglas Van Howd, sgd, 5,000	60.00	80.00
1979	SHEENA'S CUBS, Douglas Van Howd, sgd, 5,000	60.00	NR
1980	ELISHEBA, Douglas Van Howd, sgd, 5,000	65.00	NR
1980	ELISHEBA'S CUBS, Douglas Van Howd, sgd, 5,000	65.00	NR
1981	ATARAH, Douglas Van Howd, sgd, 5,000	60.00	NR
1982	ATARAH'S CUBS, Douglas Van Howd, sgd, 5,000	60.00	NR

Buck Hill Bears

1986	TIDDLYWINK AND PIXIE, Robert Pearcy, 10,000	29.50	NR
1986	REBECCA AND FRIEND, Robert Pearcy, 10,000	29.50	NR

Companions

1986	ALL BARK AND NO BITE, Robert Pearcy, 10,000	29.50	NR

The Constitution

1987	GUERRIERE, Alan D'Estrehan, 10,000	39.50	45.00
1987	TRIPOLI , Alan D'Estrehan, 10,000	39.50	45.00
1987	JAVA, Alan D'Estrehan, 10,000	39.50	45.00
1987	THE GREAT CHASE, Alan D'Estrehan, 10,000	39.50	45.00

Tripoli
Photo courtesy of *Collectors News*

Blue Boy Woody
Photo courtesy of *Collectors News*

Faces of the World

1988	ERIN (IRELAND), Lisette DeWinne, 14 days	24.50	NR
1988	CLARA (BELGIUM), Lisette DeWinne, 14 days	24.50	NR

		Issue Price	Current Value
1988	LUISA (SPAIN), Lisette DeWinne, 14 days	24.50	NR
1988	TAMIKU (JAPAN), Lisette DeWinne, 14 days	24.50	NR
1988	COLETTE (FRANCE), Lisette DeWinne, 14 days	24.50	NR
1988	HEATHER (ENGLAND), Lisette DeWinne, 14 days	24.50	NR
1988	GRETA (AUSTRIA), Lisette DeWinne, 14 days	24.50	NR
1988	MARIA (ITALY), Lisette DeWinne, 14 days	24.50	NR

Freddie the Freeloader

1979	FREDDIE IN THE BATHTUB, Red Skelton, 10,000	55.00	130.00
1980	FREDDIE'S SHACK, Red Skelton, 10,000	55.00	BR
1981	FREDDIE ON THE GREEN, Red Skelton, 10,000	60.00	BR
1982	LOVE THAT FREDDIE, Red Skelton, 10,000	60.00	BR

Freddie's Adventure

1982	CAPTAIN FREDDIE, Red Skelton, 15,000	60.00	BR
1982	BRONCO FREDDIE, Red Skelton, 15,000	60.00	BR
1983	SIR FREDDIE, Red Skelton, 15,000	62.50	BR
1984	GERTRUDE AND HEATHCLIFFE, Red Skelton, 15,000	62.50	70.00

Freedom Collection of Red Skelton

1990	THE ALL AMERICAN, Red Skelton, sgd, 1,000	195.00	NR
1990	THE ALL AMERICAN, Red Skelton, 9,000	62.50	NR
1991	INDEPENDENCE DAY?, Red Skelton, sgd, 1,000	195.00	250.00
1991	INDEPENDENCE DAY?, Red Skelton, 9,000	62.50	NR
1992	LET FREEDOM RING, Red Skelton, sgd, 1,000	195.00	RI
1992	LET FREEDOM RING, Red Skelton, 9,000	62.50	RI
1993	FREDDIE'S GIFT OF LIFE, Red Skelton, sgd, 1,000	195.00	RI
1993	FREDDIE'S GIFT OF LIFE, Red Skelton, 9,000	62.50	RI

Happy Art (Crown Parian)

1981	WOODY'S TRIPLE SELF–PORTRAIT, Walter Lantz, 10,000	39.50	NR
1981	WOODY'S TRIPLE SELF–PORTRAIT, Walter Lantz, sgd, 1,000 NR		100.00
1983	GOTHIC WOODY, Walter Lantz, 10,000	39.50	NR
1983	GOTHIC WOODY, Walter Lantz, sgd, 1,000	100.00	NR
1984	BLUE BOY WOODY, Walter Lantz, 10,000	39.50	NR
1984	BLUE BOY WOODY, Walter Lantz, sgd, 1,000	100.00	NR

Huggable Puppies

1984	TAKE ME HOME, Robert Pearcy, 10,000	29.50	NR
1985	OH HOW CUTE, Robert Pearcy, 10,000	29.50	NR
1985	PUPPY PALS, Robert Pearcy, 10,000	29.50	NR
1986	WHO, ME?, Robert Pearcy, 10,000	29.50	NR

Infinite Love

		Issue Price	Current Value
1987	A PAIR OF DREAMS, Sue Etem, 14 days	24.50	NR
1987	THE EYES SAY "I LOVE YOU," Sue Etem, 14 days	24.50	NR
1987	ONCE UPON A SMILE, Sue Etem, 14 days..............	24.50	NR
1987	KISS A LITTLE GIGGLE, Sue Etem, 14 days	24.50	NR
1988	LOVE GOES FORTH IN LITTLE FEET, Sue Etem, 14 days .	24.50	NR
1988	BUNDLE OF JOY, Sue Etem, 14 days	24.50	NR
1988	GRINS FOR GRANDMA, Sue Etem, 14 days	24.50	NR
1989	A MOMENT TO CHERISH, Sue Etem, 14 days...........	24.50	NR

Lovable Kittens

1983	THE CAT'S MEOW, Robert Pearcy, 10,000..............	29.50	NR
1984	PURR–SWAYED, Robert Pearcy, 10,000	29.50	NR
1985	THE PRINCE OF PURRS, Robert Pearcy, 10,000	29.50	NR
1986	PET, AND I'LL PURR, Robert Pearcy, 10,000	29.50	NR

Mischief Makers

1986	PUDDLES, Sue Etem, 10,000.........................	39.95	NR
1986	BUCKLES, Sue Etem, 10,000	39.95	NR
1987	TRIX, Sue Etem, 10,000	39.95	NR
1988	NAPS, Sue Etem, 10,000	39.95	NR

A Pair of Dreams
Photo courtesy of *Collectors News*

Puddles
Photo courtesy of *Collectors News*

Moment of Nature

1980	CALIFORNIA QUAIL, John Ruthven, 5,000	39.50	NR
1981	CHICKADEE, John Ruthven, 5,000	39.50	NR
1981	SCREECH OWLS, John Ruthven, 5,000	39.50	NR

North American Birds

1984	CALIFORNIA QUAIL, Jon Roberton, 7,500..............	60.00	NR

		Issue Price	Current Value

Portraits of Childhood

		Issue Price	Current Value
1983	MISS MURRAY, Sir Thomas Lawrence, 7,500	65.00	NR
1984	MASTER LAMBTON, Sir Thomas Lawrence, 7,500	65.00	NR

Reflections of Innocence

1984	ME AND MY FRIEND, Miguel Paredes, 10,000	37.50	NR
1985	MY RAIN BEAU, Miguel Paredes, 10,000	37.50	NR
1986	ROWBOAT RENDEZVOUS, Miguel Paredes, 10,000	37.50	NR
1987	HATCHING A SECRET, Miguel Paredes, 10,000	37.50	NR

Me and My Friend
Photo courtesy of *Collectors News*

Hatching a Secret
Photo courtesy of *Collectors News*

Signature Collection

1986	ANYONE FOR TENNIS?, Red Skelton, 9,000	62.50	NR
1986	ANYONE FOR TENNIS?, Red Skelton, sgd, 1,000	125.00	500.00
1987	IRONING THE WAVES, Red Skelton, 9,000	62.50	75.00
1987	IRONING THE WAVES, Red Skelton, sgd, 1,000	125.00	175.00
1988	THE CLIFFHANGER, Red Skelton, 9,000	62.50	NR
1988	THE CLIFFHANGER, Red Skelton, sgd, 1,000	150.00	NR
1988	HOOKED ON FREDDIE, Red Skelton, 9,000	62.50	NR
1988	HOOKED ON FREDDIE, Red Skelton, sgd, 1,000	175.00	NR

Sporting Dogs

1980	DECOYS, LABRADOR RETRIEVER, John Ruthven, 5,000.	55.00	NR
1981	DUSTY, John Ruthven, 5,000	55.00	NR
1981	RUMMY, John Ruthven, 5,000	55.00	NR
1982	SCARLET, John Ruthven, 5,000	55.00	NR

Statue of Liberty

		Issue Price	Current Value
1985	THE DEDICATION, Alan D'Estrehan, 10,000	39.50	45.00
1986	IMMIGRANTS, Alan D'Estrehan, 10,000................	39.50	45.00
1986	INDEPENDENCE, Alan D'Estrehan, 10,000..............	39.50	45.00
1986	RE–DEDICATION, Alan D'Estrehan, 10,000	39.50	45.00

Anyone For Tennis?
Photo courtesy of *Collectors News*

Immigrants
Photo courtesy of *Collectors News*

Three Graces

1985	THALIA, Michael Perham, 7,500	49.50	NR
1986	AGLIA, Michael Perham, 7,500	49.50	NR
1987	EUPHROSYNE, Michael Perham, 7,500	49.50	NR

Wells Fargo

1979	UNDER SURVEILLANCE, McCarty, 10,000	65.00	NR
1979	PROMISED LAND, McCarty, 10,000	65.00	NR
1982	WINTERSONG, McCarty, 10,000	65.00	NR
1983	TURNING THE LAND, McCarty, 10,000	65.00	NR

Commemorative Issues

1983	70 YEARS YOUNG, Red Skelton, 15,000, 10½"	85.00	NR
1984	FREDDIE THE TORCHBEARER, Red Skelton, 15,000, 8½"	62.50	NR

Single Issues

1978	AFFECTION, Rosemary Calder, 7,500	60.00	NR
1978	SWEET DREAMS, James Daly, 7,500	55.00	NR
1979	CROW BABY, Penni Anne Cross, 7,500	55.00	NR
1979	REVE DE BALLET, Julian Ritter, 7,500	55.00	NR

	Issue Price	Current Value
1980 NAVAJO MADONNA, Ulaf Weidhorst, 7,500	65.00	NR
1981 PAIUTE PALS, Penni Anne Cross, 7,500	60.00	NR
1982 BUON NATALE, Valentino Garavani, 7,500	300.00	NR
1983 BIG SISTER'S BUCKSKINS, Penni Anne Cross, 7,500	55.00	NR
1984 NAVAJO NANNY, Penni Anne Cross, 7,500	55.00	NR
1985 PETE ROSE, Rod Schenken, 9,000	45.00	NR

ART WORLD OF BOURGEAULT UNITED STATES

English Countryside

1981 THE COUNTRY SQUIRE, Robert Bourgeault, 1,500	70.00	250.00
1981 THE WILLOWS, Robert Bourgeault, 1,500	85.00	250.00
1982 ROSE COTTAGE, Robert Bourgeault, 1,500	90.00	250.00
1983 THATCHED BEAUTY, Robert Bourgeault, 1,500	95.00	250.00

English Countryside, Single Issues

1984 THE ANNE HATHAWAY COTTAGE, Robert Bourgeault, 500	150.00	500.00
1986 SUFFOLK PINK, Robert Bourgeault, 50	220.00	250.00
1988 STUART HOUSE, Robert Bourgeault, 50	325.00	500.00
1989 LARK RISE, Robert Bourgeault, 50	450.00	500.00

Royal Gainsborough

1990 THE LISA–CAROLINE, Robert Bourgeault	75.00	NR
1991 A GAINSBOROUGH LADY, Robert Bourgeault	–	NR

Royal Literary Series

1986 JOHN BUNYAN COTTAGE, Robert Bourgeault, 4,500	60.00	75.00
1987 THOMAS HARDY COTTAGE, Robert Bourgeault, 4,500 . . .	65.00	80.00
1988 JOHN MILTON COTTAGE, Robert Bourgeault, 4,500	65.00	80.00
1989 ANNE HATHAWAY COTTAGE, Robert Bourgeault, 4,500 . .	65.00	80.00

Where is England?

1990 FORGET–ME–NOT, Robert Bourgeault, 50	525.00	600.00
1991 THE FLEECE INN, Robert Bourgeault, 50	525.00	600.00
1992 MILBROOK HOUSE, Robert Bourgeault, 50	525.00	RI
1993 COTSWOLD BEAUTY, Robert Bourgeault, 50	525.00	RI

Where is Scotland?

1991 EILEAN DONAN CASTLE, Robert Bourgeault, 50	525.00	600.00

Single Issues

1986 ROSE COTTAGE, Robert Bourgeault, 1,500	150.00	NR
1986 ANNE HATHAWAY COTTAGE, Robert Bourgeault, 500 . . .	250.00	NR

ARTA AUSTRIA

Christmas	Issue Price	Current Value
1973 NATIVITY — IN MANGER, 1,500	50.00	70.00

Mother's Day		
1973 FAMILY WITH PUPPY, 1,500	50.00	70.00

ARTAFFECTS

Adventures of Peter Pan

1990 FLYING OVER LONDON, Tom Newsom, 14 days	29.50	40.00
1990 LOOK AT ME, Tom Newsom, 14 days	29.50	40.00
1990 THE ENCOUNTER, Tom Newsom, 14 days	29.50	40.00
1990 NEVER LAND, Tom Newsom, 14 days.	29.50	40.00

America's Indian Heritage

1987 CHEYENNE NATION, Gregory Perillo, 10 days	24.50	55.00
1988 ARAPAHO NATION, Gregory Perillo, 10 days	24.50	35.00
1988 KIOWA NATION, Gregory Perillo, 10 days	24.50	35.00
1988 SIOUX NATION, Gregory Perillo, 10 days.	24.50	60.00
1988 CHIPPEWA NATION, Gregory Perillo, 10 days	24.50	40.00
1988 CROW NATION, Gregory Perillo, 10 days.	24.50	50.00
1988 NEZ PERCE NATION, Gregory Perillo, 10 days	24.50	50.00
1988 BLACKFOOT NATION, Gregory Perillo, 10 days	24.50	75.00

American Blues Special Occasions

1992 HAPPILY EVER AFTER (WEDDING), Rob Sauber	35.00	RI
1992 THE PERFECT TREE (CHRISTMAS), Rob Sauber	35.00	RI
1992 MY SUNSHINE (MOTHERHOOD), Rob Sauber	35.00	RI

Oh! Oh! A Bunny
Photo courtesy of *Collectors News*

	Issue Price	Current Value
American Maritime Heritage		
1987 U.S.S. CONSTITUTION, Kipp Soldwedel, 14 days	35.00	NR
Angler's Dream		
1983 BROOK TROUT, John Eggert, 9,800	55.00	NR
1983 CHINOOK SALMON, John Eggert, 9,800	55.00	NR
1983 LARGEMOUTH BASS, John Eggert, 9,800	55.00	NR
1983 STRIPED BASS, John Eggert, 9,800	55.00	NR
Arabians		
1986 SILVER STREAK, Gregory Perillo, 3,500	95.00	125.00
Arctic Friends (Vague Shadows)		
1982 SIBERIAN LOVE, Gregory Perillo, 7,500	—	—
1982 SNOW PALS, Gregory Perillo, 7,500, set of 2	100.00	175.00
Baby's Firsts		
1989 VISITING THE DOCTOR, Rob Sauber, 14 days, 6½"	21.50	NR
1989 BABY'S FIRST STEP, Rob Sauber, 14 days, 6½"	21.50	NR
1989 FIRST BIRTHDAY, Rob Sauber, 14 days, 6½"	21.50	NR
1989 CHRISTMAS MORN, Rob Sauber, 14 days, 6½"	21.50	NR
1989 PICTURE PERFECT, Rob Sauber, 14 days, 6½"	21.50	NR
Backstage		
1990 THE RUNAWAY, Barry Leighton–Jones, 14 days	29.50	NR
1990 THE LETTER, Barry Leighton–Jones, 14 days	29.50	NR
1990 BUBBLING OVER, Barry Leighton–Jones, 14 days	29.50	NR
Baker Street		
1983 SHERLOCK HOLMES, Mitchell Hooks, 9,800	55.00	NR
1983 WATSON, Mitchell Hooks, 9,800	55.00	NR
Becker Babies		
1983 SNOW PUFF, Charlotte Becker, limited	29.95	45.00
1984 SMILING THROUGH, Charlotte Becker, limited	29.95	45.00
1984 PALS, Charlotte Becker, limited	29.95	45.00
Bessie's Best		
1984 OH! OH! A BUNNY, Bessie Pease Gutmann, open	29.95	65.00
1984 THE NEW LOVE, Bessie Pease Gutmann, open	29.95	65.00
1984 MY BABY, Bessie Pease Gutmann, open	29.95	65.00
1984 LOOKING FOR TROUBLE, Bessie Pease Gutmann, open .	29.95	65.00
1984 TAPS, Bessie Pease Gutmann, open	29.95	65.00

		Issue Price	Current Value

The Carnival

| 1982 | KNOCK EM' DOWN, Tom Newsom, 19,500 | 35.00 | 50.00 |
| 1982 | CAROUSEL, Tom Newsom, 19,500 | 35.00 | 50.00 |

Chieftains I

1979	CHIEF SITTING BULL, Gregory Perillo, 7,500	65.00	325.00
1979	CHIEF JOSEPH, Gregory Perillo, 7,500	65.00	100.00
1980	CHIEF RED CLOUD, Gregory Perillo, 7,500	65.00	120.00
1980	CHIEF GERONIMO, Gregory Perillo, 7,500	65.00	80.00
1981	CHIEF CRAZY HORSE, Gregory Perillo, 7,500	65.00	140.00

Chief Red Cloud
Photo courtesy of *Collectors News*

Chief Victorio
Photo courtesy of *Collectors News*

Chieftains II

1983	CHIEF PONTIAC, Gregory Perillo, 7,500	70.00	NR
1983	CHIEF VICTORIO, Gregory Perillo, 7,500	70.00	NR
1983	CHIEF TECUMSEH, Gregory Perillo, 7,500	70.00	NR
1983	CHIEF COCHISE, Gregory Perillo, 7,500	70.00	NR
1983	CHIEF BLACK KETTLE, Gregory Perillo, 7,500	70.00	NR

Child's Life

| 1983 | SIESTA, Gregory Perillo, 10,000 | 45.00 | NR |
| 1984 | SWEET DREAMS, Gregory Perillo, 10,000 | 45.00 | NR |

Childhood Delights

| 1983 | AMANDA, Rob Sauber, 7,500 | 45.00 | 75.00 |

		Issue Price	Current Value

Children of the Prairie

Year	Title	Price	Value
1993	TENDER LOVING CARE, Gregory Perillo	29.50	RI
1993	DAYDREAMERS, Gregory Perillo	29.50	RI
1993	PLAY TIME, Gregory Perillo	29.50	RI
1993	THE SENTINEL, Gregory Perillo	29.50	RI
1993	BEACH COMBER, Gregory Perillo	29.50	RI
1993	WATCHFUL WAITING, Gregory Perillo	29.50	RI
1993	PATIENCE, Gregory Perillo	29.50	RI
1993	SISTERS, Gregory Perillo	29.50	RI

Christian Collection

Year	Title	Price	Value
1987	BRING TO ME THE CHILDREN, Alton S. Tobey	35.00	NR
1987	WEDDING FEAST AT CANA, Alton S. Tobey	35.00	NR
1987	THE HEALER, Alton S. Tobey	35.00	NR

Christmas Celebrations of Yesterday

Year	Title	Price	Value
1993	CHRISTMAS ON MAIN STREET, M. Leone	27.00	RI
1993	CHRISTMAS ON THE FARM, M. Leone	27.00	RI
1993	CHRISTMAS EVE, M. Leone	27.00	RI
1993	WREATH MAKER, M. Leone	27.00	RI
1993	CHRISTMAS PARTY, M. Leone	27.00	RI
1993	TRIMMING THE TREE, M. Leone	27.00	RI
1993	CHRISTMAS BLESSINGS, M. Leone	27.00	RI
1993	HOME FOR CHRISTMAS, M. Leone	27.00	RI

Classic American Cars

Year	Title	Price	Value
1989	DUESENBERG, Jim Deneen, 14 days	35.00	NR
1989	CADILLAC, Jim Deneen, 14 days	35.00	NR
1989	CORD, Jim Deneen, 14 days	35.00	NR
1989	RUXTON, Jim Deneen, 14 days	35.00	NR
1990	LINCOLN, Jim Deneen, 14 days	35.00	NR
1990	PACKARD, Jim Deneen, 14 days	35.00	NR
1990	HUDSON, Jim Deneen, 14 days	35.00	NR
1990	PIERCE–ARROW, Jim Deneen, 14 days	35.00	NR

Classic American Trains

Year	Title	Price	Value
1988	HOMEWARD BOUND, Jim Deneen, 14 days	35.00	50.00
1988	A RACE AGAINST TIME, Jim Deneen, 14 days	35.00	60.00
1988	MIDDAY STOP, Jim Deneen, 14 days	35.00	50.00
1988	THE SILVER BULLET, Jim Deneen, 14 days	35.00	65.00
1988	TRAVELING IN STYLE, Jim Deneen, 14 days	35.00	50.00
1988	ROUND THE BEND, Jim Deneen, 14 days	35.00	50.00
1988	TAKING THE HIGH ROAD, Jim Deneen, 14 days	35.00	45.00
1988	COMPETITION, Jim Deneen, 14 days	35.00	40.00

Club Member Limited Edition Redemptions	Issue Price	Current Value
1992 THE PENCIL, Gregory Perillo, 1 year	35.00	RI
1992 STUDIES IN BLACK AND WHITE, 1 year, set of 4	75.00	RI
1993 WATCHER OF THE WILDERNESS, Gregory Perillo, 1 year	60.00	RI

Colts

1985 APPALOOSA, Gregory Perillo, 5,000	40.00	100.00
1985 PINTO, Gregory Perillo, 5,000	40.00	110.00
1985 ARABIAN, Gregory Perillo, 5,000	40.00	100.00
1985 THOROUGHBRED, Gregory Perillo, 5,000	40.00	100.00

Council of Nations

1992 STRENGTH OF THE SIOUX, Gregory Perillo, 14 days	29.50	RI
1992 PRIDE OF THE CHEYENNE, Gregory Perillo, 14 days	29.50	RI
1992 DIGNITY OF THE NEZ PERCE, Gregory Perillo, 14 days	29.50	RI
1992 COURAGE OF THE ARAPAHO, Gregory Perillo, 14 days	29.50	RI
1992 POWER OF THE BLACKFOOT, Gregory Perillo, 14 days	29.50	RI
1992 NOBILITY OF THE ALGONQUIN, Gregory Perillo, 14 days	29.50	RI
1992 WISDOM OF THE CHEROKEE, Gregory Perillo, 14 days	29.50	RI
1992 BOLDNESS OF THE SENECA, Gregory Perillo, 14 days	29.50	RI

Good Sports

1989 PURRFECT GAME, S. Miller–Maxwell, 14 days, 6½"	22.50	NR
1989 ALLEY CATS, S. Miller–Maxwell, 14 days, 6½"	22.50	NR
1989 TEE TIME, S. Miller–Maxwell, 14 days, 6½"	22.50	NR
1989 TWO/LOVE, S. Miller–Maxwell, 14 days, 6½"	22.50	NR
1989 WHAT'S THE CATCH?, S. Miller–Maxwell, 14 days, 6½"	22.50	NR
1989 QUATERBACK SNEAK, S. Miller–Maxwell, 14 days, 6½"	22.50	NR

Great American Trains

1992 THE ALTON LIMITED, Jim Deneen, 75 days	27.00	RI
1992 THE CAPITOL LIMITED, Jim Deneen, 75 days	27.00	RI
1992 THE MERCHANTS LIMITED, Jim Deneen, 75 days	27.00	RI
1992 THE BROADWAY LIMITED, Jim Deneen, 75 days	27.00	RI
1992 THE SOUTHWESTERN LIMITED, Jim Deneen, 75 days	27.00	RI
1992 THE BLACKHAWK LIMITED, Jim Deneen, 75 days	27.00	RI
1992 THE SUNSHINE SPECIAL LIMITED, Jim Deneen, 75 days	27.00	RI
1992 THE PANAMA SPECIAL LIMITED, Jim Deneen, 75 days	27.00	RI

Great Trains

1985 SANTA FE, Jim Deneen, 7,500	35.00	80.00
1985 TWENTIETH CENTURY LTD., Jim Deneen, 7,500	35.00	80.00
1986 EMPIRE BUILDER, Jim Deneen, 7,500	35.00	80.00

Heavenly Angels

1992 HUSH–A–BYE, MaGo, 75 days	27.00	RI

		Issue Price	Current Value
1992	HEAVENLY HELPER, MaGo, 75 days	27.00	RI
1992	HEAVENLY LIGHT, MaGo, 75 days	27.00	RI
1992	THE ANGEL'S KISS, MaGo, 75 days	27.00	RI
1992	CAUGHT IN THE ACT, MaGo, 75 days	27.00	RI
1992	MY ANGEL, MaGo, 75 days	27.00	RI
1992	SLEEPY SENTINEL, MaGo, 75 days	27.00	RI

How Do I Love Thee?

1983	ALAINA, Rob Sauber, 19,500	39.95	45.00
1983	TAYLOR, Rob Sauber, 19,500	39.95	45.00
1983	RENDEZVOUS, Rob Sauber, 19,500	39.95	45.00
1983	EMBRACE, Rob Sauber, 19,500	39.95	45.00

Indian Bridal

1990	YELLOW BIRD, Gregory Perillo, 14 days, 6½"	25.00	NR
1990	AUTUMN BLOSSOM, Gregory Perillo, 14 days, 6½"	25.00	NR
1990	MISTY WATERS, Gregory Perillo, 14 days, 6½"	25.00	NR
1990	SUNNY SKIES, Gregory Perillo, 14 days, 6½"	25.00	NR

Indian Nations

1983	BLACKFOOT, Gregory Perillo, 7,500	–	–
1983	CHEYENNE, Gregory Perillo, 7,500	–	–
1983	APACHE, Gregory Perillo, 7,500	–	–
1983	SIOUX, Gregory Perillo, 7,500, set of 4	140.00	300.00

Legends of the West

1982	DANIEL BOONE, Gregory Perillo, 10,000	65.00	NR
1983	DAVY CROCKETT, Gregory Perillo, 10,000	65.00	NR
1983	KIT CARSON, Gregory Perillo, 10,000	65.00	NR
1983	BUFFALO BILL, Gregory Perillo, 10,000	65.00	NR

Life of Jesus

1992	THE LAST SUPPER, L. Marchetti, 25 days	27.00	RI
1992	THE SERMON ON THE MOUNT, L. Marchetti, 25 days	27.00	RI
1992	THE AGONY IN THE GARDEN, L. Marchetti, 25 days	27.00	RI
1992	THE BLESSING OF THE CHILDREN, L. Marchetti, 25 days	27.00	RI
1992	THE RESURRECTION, L. Marchetti, 25 days	27.00	RI
1992	THE HEALING OF THE SICK, L. Marchetti, 25 days	27.00	RI
1992	THE DESCENT FROM THE CROSS, L. Marchetti, 25 days	27.00	RI

Living in Harmony

1991	PEACEABLE KINGDOM, Gregory Perillo, 75 days	29.50	NR

Magical Moments	Issue Price	Current Value
1981 HAPPY DREAMS, Bessie Pease Gutmann, <1 year	29.95	80.00
1981 HARMONY, Bessie Pease Gutmann, <1 year	29.95	75.00
1982 HIS MAJESTY, Bessie Pease Gutmann, <1 year	29.95	45.00
1982 WAITING FOR DADDY, Bessie Pease Gutmann, <1 year .	29.95	45.00
1982 THANK YOU GOD, Bessie Pease Gutmann, <1 year	29.95	45.00
1983 THE LULLABYE, Bessie Pease Gutmann, <1 year	29.95	45.00

MaGo's Motherhood

1990 SERENITY, MaGo, 14 days	60.00	BR

Maidens

1985 SHIMMERING WATERS, Gregory Perillo, 5,000	50.00	100.00
1985 SNOW BLANKET, Gregory Perillo, 5,000	60.00	100.00
1985 SONG BIRD, Gregory Perillo, 5,000	60.00	100.00

March of Dimes: Our Children, Our Future

1989 A TIME TO BE BORN, Gregory Perillo, 150 days	29.00	NR

Masterpieces of Impressionism

1980 WOMAN WITH PARASOL, Claude Monet, 17,500	35.00	60.00
1981 YOUNG MOTHER SEWING, Mary Cassatt, 17,500	35.00	50.00
1982 SARA IN GREEN BONNET, Mary Cassatt, 17,500	35.00	50.00
1983 MARGOT IN BLUE, Mary Cassatt, 17,500	35.00	45.00

Masterpieces of Rockwell

1980 AFTER THE PROM, Norman Rockwell, 17,500	42.50	90.00
1980 THE CHALLENGER, Norman Rockwell, 17,500	50.00	NR
1982 GIRL AT THE MIRROR, Norman Rockwell, 17,500	50.00	75.00
1982 MISSING TOOTH, Norman Rockwell, 17,500	50.00	NR

Masterpieces of the West

1980 TEXAS NIGHT HERDER, Frank T. Johnson, 17,500	35.00	55.00
1980 INDIAN TRAPPER, Frederic Remington, 17,500	35.00	45.00
1982 COWBOY STYLE, William R. Leigh, 17,500	35.00	NR
1982 INDIAN STYLE, Gregory Perillo, 17,500	35.00	75.00

Melodies of Childhood

1983 TWINKLE, TWINKLE LITTLE STAR, Hector Garrido, 19,500 NR		35.00
1983 ROW, ROW, ROW YOUR BOAT, Hector Garrido, 19,500 . .	35.00	NR
1983 MARY HAD A LITTLE LAMB, Hector Garrido, 19,500	35.00	NR

Motherhood

1983 MADRE, Gregory Perillo, 10,000	50.00	75.00

			Issue Price	Current Value
1984	MADONNA OF THE PLAINS, Gregory Perillo, 3,500		50.00	75.00
1985	ABUELA, Gregory Perillo, 3,500		50.00	75.00
1986	NAP TIME, Gregory Perillo, 3,500		50.00	75.00

Mother's Love

1984	DADDY'S HERE, Bessie Pease Gutmann, limited	29.95	50.00

Mother's Love

1988	FEELINGS, Gregory Perillo, 1 year	35.00	75.00
1989	MOONLIGHT, Gregory Perillo, 1 year	35.00	55.00
1990	PRIDE AND JOY, Gregory Perillo, 1 year	39.50	45.00
1991	LITTLE SHADOW, Gregory Perillo, 1 year	39.50	NR

Nature's Harmony

1982	PEACEABLE KINGDOM, Gregory Perillo, 12,500	100.00	150.00
1982	ZEBRA, Gregory Perillo, 12,500	50.00	NR
1982	BENGAL TIGER, Gregory Perillo, 12,500	50.00	NR
1982	BLACK PANTHER, Gregory Perillo, 12,500	50.00	60.00
1983	ELEPHANT, Gregory Perillo, 12,500	50.00	70.00

North American Wildlife

1989	MUSTANG, Gregory Perillo, 14 days	29.50	45.00
1989	WHITE–TAILED DEER, Gregory Perillo, 14 days	29.50	35.00
1989	MOUNTAIN LION, Gregory Perillo, 14 days	29.50	45.00
1990	AMERICAN BALD EAGLE, Gregory Perillo, 14 days	29.50	NR
1990	TIMBER WOLF, Gregroy Perillo, 14 days	29.50	35.00
1990	POLAR BEAR, Gregory Perillo, 14 days	29.50	40.00
1990	BUFFALO, Gregory Perillo, 14 days	29.50	40.00
1990	BIGHORN SHEEP, Gregory Perillo, 14 days	29.50	40.00

Nursery Pair

1983	IN SLUMBERLAND, Charlotte Becker, open	25.00	40.00
1983	THE AWAKENING, Charlotte Becker, open	25.00	40.00

Old Fashioned Christmas

1993	UP ON THE ROOF TOP, Rob Sauber	29.50	RI
1994	THE TOY SHOPPE, Rob Sauber	29.50	RI
1994	CHRISTMAS DELIGHT, Rob Sauber	29.50	RI
1994	CHRISTMAS EVE, Rob Sauber	29.50	RI

On the Road

1984	PRIDE OF STOCKBRIDGE, Norman Rockwell, open	35.00	55.00
1984	CITY PRIDE, Norman Rockwell, open	35.00	55.00
1984	COUNTRY PRIDE, Norman Rockwell, open	35.00	55.00

		Issue Price	Current Value

Perillo Christmas

1987	SHINING STAR, Gregory Perillo, 1 year	29.50	200.00
1988	SILENT LIGHT, Gregory Perillo, 1 year	35.00	125.00
1989	SNOW FLAKE, Gregory Perillo, 1 year	35.00	45.00
1990	BUNDLE UP, Gregory Perillo, 1 year	39.50	60.00
1991	CHRISTMAS JOURNEY, Gregory Perillo, 1 year	39.50	45.00

Perillo Santas

| 1980 | SANTA'S JOY, Gregory Perillo, 1 year | 29.95 | 40.00 |
| 1981 | SANTA'S BUNDLE, Gregory Perillo, 1 year | 29.95 | 40.00 |

Perillo's Four Seasons

1991	SUMMER, Gregory Perillo, 14 days, 6½"	25.00	NR
1991	AUTUMN, Gregory Perillo, 14 days, 6½"	25.00	NR
1991	WINTER, Gregory Perillo, 14 days, 6½"	25.00	NR
1991	SPRING, Gregory Perillo, 14 days, 6½"	25.00	NR

Plainsmen

| 1978 | BUFFALO HUNT, bronze, Gregory Perillo, 2,500 | 350.00 | 375.00 |
| 1979 | THE PROUD ONE, bronze, Gregory Perillo, 2,500 | 350.00 | 550.00 |

Playful Pets

| 1982 | CURIOSITY, John Henry Dolph, 7,500 | 45.00 | 75.00 |
| 1982 | MASTER'S HAT, John Henry Dolph, 7,500 | 45.00 | 75.00 |

Portraits

1986	CHANTILLY, John Eggert, 14 days	24.50	35.00
1986	DYNASTY, John Eggert, 14 days	24.50	35.00
1986	VELVET, John Eggert, 14 days	24.50	35.00
1986	JAMBALAYA, John Eggert, 14 days	24.50	35.00

Portraits by Perillo, Mini Plates

1989	SMILING EYES, Gregory Perillo, 9,500, 4¼"	19.50	NR
1989	BRIGHT SKY, Gregory Perillo, 9,500, 4¼"	19.50	NR
1989	RUNNING BEAR, Gregory Perillo, 9,500, 4¼"	19.50	NR
1989	LITTLE FEATHER, Gregory Perillo, 9,500, 4¼"	19.50	NR
1990	PROUD EAGLE, Gregory Perillo, 9,500, 4¼"	19.50	NR
1990	BLUE BIRD, Gregory Perillo, 9,500, 4¼"	19.50	NR
1990	WILDFLOWER, Gregory Perillo, 9,500, 4¼"	19.50	NR
1990	SPRING BREEZE, Gregory Perillo, 9,500, 4¼"	19.50	NR

Portraits of American Brides

1986	CAROLINE, Rob Sauber, 10 days	29.50	55.00
1986	JACQUELINE, Rob Sauber, 10 days	29.50	35.00
1987	ELIZABETH, Rob Sauber, 10 days	29.50	40.00

	Issue Price	Current Value
1987 EMILY, Rob Sauber, 10 days	29.50	40.00
1987 MEREDITH, Rob Sauber, 10 days	29.50	40.00
1987 LAURA, Rob Sauber, 10 days	29.50	40.00
1987 SARAH, Rob Sauber, 10 days	29.50	40.00
1987 REBECCA, Rob Sauber, 10 days	29.50	45.00

Pride of America's Indians

1986 BRAVE AND FREE, Gregory Perillo, 10 days	24.50	35.00
1986 DARK–EYED FRIENDS, Gregory Perillo, 10 days	24.50	BR
1986 NOBLE COMPANIONS, Gregory Perillo, 10 days	24.50	BR
1987 KINDRED SPIRITS, Gregory Perillo, 10 days	24.50	NR
1987 LOYAL ALLIANCE, Gregory Perillo, 10 days	24.50	45.00
1987 SMALL AND WISE, Gregory Perillo, 10 days	24.50	NR
1987 WINTER SCOUTS, Gregory Perillo, 10 days	24.50	NR
1987 PEACEFUL COMRADES, Gregory Perillo, 10 days	24.50	30.00

Princesses

1982 LILY OF THE MOHAWKS, Gregory Perillo, 12,500	50.00	85.00
1982 POCAHONTAS, Gregory Perillo, 7,500	50.00	65.00
1982 MINNEHAHA, Gregory Perillo, 7,500	50.00	65.00
1982 SACAJAWEA, Gregory Perillo, 7,500	50.00	85.00

Professionals

1979 THE BIG LEAGUER, Gregory Perillo, 15,000	29.95	45.00
1980 BALLERINA'S DILEMMA, Gregory Perillo, 15,000	32.50	45.00
1981 QUARTERBACK, Gregory Perillo, 15,000	32.50	50.00
1981 RODEO JOE, Gregory Perillo, 15,000	35.00	40.00
1982 MAJOR LEAGUER, Gregory Perillo, 15,000	35.00	50.00
1983 THE HOCKEY PLAYER, Gregory Perillo, 15,000	35.00	50.00

Proud Young Spirits

1990 PROTECTOR OF THE PLAINS, Gregory Perillo, 14 days	29.50	55.00
1990 WATCHFUL EYES, Gregory Perillo, 14 days	29.50	45.00
1990 FREEDOM'S WATCH, Gregory Perillo, 14 days	29.50	40.00
1990 WOODLAND SCOUTS, Gregory Perillo, 14 days	29.50	40.00
1990 FAST FRIENDS, Gregory Perillo, 14 days	29.50	40.00
1990 BIRDS OF A FEATHER, Gregory Perillo, 14 days	29.50	40.00
1990 PRAIRIE PALS, Gregory Perillo, 14 days	29.50	40.00
1990 LOYAL GUARDIAN, Gregory Perillo, 14 days	29.50	40.00

Reflections of Youth

1988 JULIA, MaGo, 14 days	29.50	50.00
1988 JESSICA, MaGo, 14 days	29.50	35.00
1988 SEBASTIAN, MaGo, 14 days	29.50	35.00
1988 MICHELLE, MaGo, 14 days	29.50	35.00

		Issue Price	Current Value
1988	ANDREW, MaGo, 14 days	29.50	35.00
1988	BETH, MaGo, 14 days	29.50	35.00
1988	AMY, MaGo, 14 days	29.50	35.00
1988	LAUREN, MaGo, 14 days	29.50	35.00

Rockwell Americana

1981	SHUFFLETON'S BARBERSHOP, Norman Rockwell, 17,500	75.00	125.00
1982	BREAKING HOME TIES, Norman Rockwell, 17,500	75.00	100.00
1983	WALKING TO CHURCH, Norman Rockwell, 17,500	75.00	100.00

Rockwell Trilogy

1981	STOCKBRIDGE IN WINTER 1, Norman Rockwell, open	35.00	45.00
1982	STOCKBRIDGE IN WINTER 2, Norman Rockwell, open	35.00	45.00
1983	STOCKBRIDGE IN WINTER 3, Norman Rockwell, open	35.00	50.00

Romantic Cities of Europe

1989	VENICE, L. Marchetti, 14 days	35.00	60.00
1989	PARIS, L. Marchetti, 14 days	35.00	45.00
1990	LONDON, L. Marchetti, 14 days	35.00	45.00
1990	MOSCOW, L. Marchetti, 14 days	35.00	NR

Rose Wreaths

1993	SUMMER'S BOUNTY, Knox/Robertson	27.00	RI
1993	VICTORIAN FANTASY, Knox/Robertson	27.00	RI
1993	GENTLE PERSUASION, Knox/Robertson	27.00	RI
1993	SUNSET SPLENDOR, Knox/Robertson	27.00	RI
1994	SWEETHEARTS DELIGHT, Knox/Robertson	27.00	RI
1994	SWEET SUNSHINE, Knox/Robertson	27.00	RI
1994	FLORAL FASCINATION, Knox/Robertson	27.00	RI
1994	LOVE'S EMBRACE, Knox/Robertson	27.00	RI

Sailing Through History

1986	FLYING CLOUD, Kipp Soldwedel, 14 days	29.50	45.00
1986	SANTA MARIA, Kipp Soldwedel, 14 days	29.50	45.00
1986	MAYFLOWER, Kipp Soldwedel, 14 days	29.50	45.00

Simpler Times

1984	LAZY DAZE, Norman Rockwell, 7,500	35.00	55.00
1984	ONE FOR THE ROAD, Norman Rockwell, 7,500	35.00	55.00

Songs of Stephen Foster

1984	OH! SUSANNAH, Rob Sauber, 3,500	60.00	70.00
1984	I DREAM OF JEANIE / LIGHT BROWN HAIR, Rob Sauber, 3,500	60.00	70.00
1984	BEAUTIFUL DREAMER, Rob Sauber, 3,500	60.00	70.00

		Issue Price	Current Value

Special Occasions

			Issue Price	Current Value
1982	DUBBLES, Frances Tipton Hunter, limited		29.95	40.00
1982	BUTTERFLIES, Frances Tipton Hunter, limited		29.95	40.00

Top: Oh! Susannah; left: Beautiful Dreamer; right: I Dream of Jeanie
Photo courtesy of *Collectors News*

Spirits of Nature

1993	PROTECTOR OF THE NATIONS, Gregory Perillo, 3,500 ..	60.00	RI
1993	DEFENDER OF THE MOUNTAIN, Gregory Perillo, 3,500 ..	60.00	RI
1993	SPIRIT OF THE PLAINS, Gregory Perillo, 3,500	60.00	RI
1993	GUARDIAN OF SAFE PASSAGE, Gregory Perillo, 3,500 ..	60.00	RI
1993	KEEPER OF THE FOREST, Gregory Perillo, 3,500	60.00	RI

Storybook Collection

1980	LITTLE RED RIDING HOOD, Gregory Perillo, 18 days	29.95	45.00
1981	CINDERELLA, Gregory Perillo, 18 days	29.95	45.00
1981	HANSEL AND GRETEL, Gregory Perillo, 18 days	29.95	45.00
1982	GOLDILOCKS AND THE THREE BEARS, Gregory Perillo, 18 days 29.95 .... 45.00		

Studies in Black and White — Collector's Club Miniatures

1992	DIGNITY, Gregory Perillo, 1 year	–	–
1992	DETERMINATION, Gregory Perillo, 1 year	–	–
1992	DILIGENCE, Gregory Perillo, 1 year	–	–

		Issue Price	Current Value
1992	DEVOTION, Gregory Perillo, 1 year, set of 14	75.00	RI

Studies of Early Childhood

1990	CHRISTOPHER AND KATE, MaGo, 150 days............	34.90	BR
1990	PEEK–A–BOO, MaGo, 150 days......................	34.90	NR
1990	ANYBODY HOME?, MaGo, 150 days	34.90	NR
1990	THREE–PART HARMONY, MaGo, 150 days.............	34.90	55.00

Tender Moments

1985	SUNSET, Gregory Perillo, 2,000.......................	–	–
1985	WINTER ROMANCE, Gregory Perillo, 2,000, set of 2	150.00	250.00

Thoroughbreds

1984	WHIRLAWAY, Gregory Perillo, 9,500	50.00	150.00
1984	SECRETARIAT, Gregory Perillo, 9,500	50.00	200.00
1984	MAN O' WAR, Gregory Perillo, 9,500	50.00	100.00
1984	SEABISCUIT, Gregory Perillo, 9,500	50.00	100.00

Timeless Love

1989	THE PROPOSAL, Rob Sauber, 14 days.................	35.00	NR
1989	SWEET EMBRACE, Rob Sauber, 14 days	35.00	NR
1990	AFTERNOON LIGHT, Rob Sauber, 14 days.............	35.00	NR
1990	QUIET MOMENTS, Rob Sauber, 14 days	35.00	NR

Christopher and Kate
Photo courtesy of *Collectors News*

Happy Birthday
Photo courtesy of *Collectors News*

Times of Our Lives

		Issue Price	Current Value
1982	THE WEDDING, Rob Sauber, limited, 10¼"............., ..	37.50	NR
1984	HAPPY BIRTHDAY, Rob Sauber, limited, 10¼"..........	37.50	NR
1985	ALL ADORE HIM, Rob Sauber, limited, 10¼"...........	37.50	NR
1985	HOME SWEET HOME, Rob Sauber, limited, 10¼".......	37.50	NR
1986	SWEETHEARTS, Rob Sauber, limited, 10¼"............	37.50	NR
1986	THE ANNIVERSARY, Rob Sauber, limited, 10¼".........	37.50	NR
1987	MOTHERHOOD, Rob Sauber, limited,10¼"..............	37.50	NR
1987	FATHERHOOD, Rob Sauber, limited, 10¼"..............	37.50	NR
1987	SWEET SIXTEEN, Rob Sauber, limited, 10¼"...........	37.50	NR
1988	THE WEDDING, Rob Sauber, limited, 6½"..............	19.50	NR
1988	HAPPY BIRTHDAY, Rob Sauber, limited, 6½"..........	19.50	NR
1988	ALL ADORE HIM, Rob Sauber, limited, 6½"............	19.50	NR
1988	HOME SWEET HOME, Rob Sauber, limited, 6½"........	19.50	NR
1988	SWEETHEARTS, Rob Sauber, limited, 6½"..............	19.50	NR
1988	THE ANNIVERSARY, Rob Sauber, limited, 6½"..........	19.50	NR
1988	MOTHERHOOD, Rob Sauber, limited, 6½"...............	19.50	NR
1988	FATHERHOOD, Rob Sauber, limited, 6½"...............	19.50	NR
1988	THE CHRISTENING, Rob Sauber, limited, 6½"..........	19.50	NR
1989	GOD BLESS AMERICA, Rob Sauber, 14 days, 6½"......	21.50	NR
1989	GOD BLESS AMERICA, Rob Sauber, 14 days, 10¼".....	39.50	NR
1989	VISITING THE DOCTOR, Rob Sauber, 14 days, 10¼"....	39.50	NR
1990	MOTHER'S JOY, Rob Sauber, limited, 6½".............	22.50	NR
1990	MOTHER'S JOY, Rob Sauber, limited, 10¼"............	39.50	NR

Tribal Ponies

1984	ARAPAHO, Gregory Perillo, 3,500......................	65.00	100.00
1984	COMANCHE, Gregory Perillo, 3,500...................	65.00	100.00
1984	CROW, Gregory Perillo, 3,500........................	65.00	150.00

The Tribute

1982	I WANT YOU, James Montgomery Flagg, limited........	29.95	40.00
1982	GEE, I WISH, Howard Chandler Christy, limited.........	29.95	40.00
1983	SOLDIER'S FAIRWELL, Norman Rockwell, limited.......	29.95	40.00

Unicorn Magic

1983	MORNING ENCOUNTER, J. Terreson, 7,500............	50.00	55.00
1983	AFTERNOON OFFERING, J. Terreson, 7,500............	50.00	55.00

War Ponies

1983	SIOUX, Gregory Perillo, 7,500.......................	60.00	115.00
1983	NEZ PERCE, Gregory Perillo, 7,500	60.00	150.00
1983	APACHE, Gregory Perillo, 7,500	60.00	100.00

War Ponies of the Plains

1992	NIGHTSHADOW, Gregory Perillo, 75 days..............	27.00	RI

		Issue Price	Current Value
1992	WINDCATCHER, Gregory Perillo, 75 days	27.00	RI
1992	PRAIRIE PRANCER, Gregory Perillo, 75 days	27.00	RI
1992	THUNDERFOOT, Gregory Perillo, 75 days	27.00	RI
1992	PROUD COMPANION, Gregory Perillo, 75 days	27.00	RI
1992	SUN DANCER, Gregory Perillo, 75 days................	27.00	RI
1992	FREE SPIRIT, Gregory Perillo, 75 days.................	27.00	RI
1992	GENTLE WARRIOR, Gregory Perillo, 75 days	27.00	RI

Winter Mindscape

1989	PEACEFUL VILLAGE, Rob Sauber, 14 days	29.50	55.00
1989	SNOWBOUND, Rob Sauber, 14 days	29.50	35.00
1990	PAPA'S SURPRISE, Rob Sauber, 14 days	29.50	35.00
1990	WELL–TRAVELED ROAD, Rob Sauber, 14 days	29.50	35.00
1990	FIRST FREEZE, Rob Sauber, 14 days	29.50	35.00
1990	COUNTRY MORNING, Rob Sauber, 14 days	29.50	35.00
1990	SLEIGH RIDE, Rob Sauber, 14 days	29.50	35.00
1990	JANUARY THAW, Rob Sauber, 14 days	29.50	35.00

Young Chieftains

1985	YOUNG SITTING BULL, Gregory Perillo, 5,000..........	50.00	100.00
1985	YOUNG JOSEPH, Gregory Perillo, 5,000	50.00	75.00
1985	YOUNG RED CLOUD, Gregory Perillo, 5,000............	50.00	75.00
1985	YOUNG GERONIMO, Gregory Perillo, 5,000	50.00	75.00
1985	YOUNG CRAZY HORSE, Gregory Perillo, 5,000	50.00	75.00

Young Emotions

1986	TEARS, Gregory Perillo, 5,000.........................	–	–
1986	SMILES, Gregory Perillo, 5,000, set of 2	75.00	250.00

Special Issues

1981	APACHE BOY, Gregory Perillo, 5,000	95.00	175.00
1983	PAPOOSE, Gregory Perillo, 3,000	100.00	125.00
1983	INDIAN STYLE, Gregory Perillo, 17,500................	50.00	NR
1984	THE LOVERS, Gregory Perillo, limited	50.00	100.00
1984	NAVAJO GIRL, Gregory Perillo, 3,500	95.00	350.00
1986	NAVAJO BOY, Gregory Perillo, 3,500	95.00	125.00
1987	WE THE PEOPLE, Howard Chandler Christy, limited	35.00	NR

ARTISTS OF THE WORLD UNITED STATES
(See also Fairmont)

Anthony Sidoni Series

1982	THE LITTLE YANKEE, Anthony Sidoni, 15,000	35.00	NR

		Issue Price	Current Value
1983	LITTLE SATCHMO, Anthony Sidoni, 15,000	40.00	NR

Celebration

1993	THE LORD'S CANDLE, Ted DeGrazia, 5,000	39.50	RI
1993	PIÑATA PARTY, Ted DeGrazia, 5,000...................	39.50	RI
1993	HOLIDAY LULLABY, Ted DeGrazia, 5,000..............	39.50	RI
1993	CAROLING, Ted DeGrazia, 5,000	39.50	RI

Children at Play

1985	MY FIRST HORSE, Ted DeGrazia, 15,000	65.00	BR
1986	GIRL WITH SEWING MACHINE, Ted DeGrazia, 15,000 ...	65.00	NR
1987	LOVE ME, Ted DeGrazia, 15,000	65.00	BR
1988	MERRILY, MERRILY, MERRILY, Ted DeGrazia, 15,000....	65.00	NR
1989	MY FIRST ARROW, Ted DeGrazia, 15,000	65.00	80.00
1990	AWAY WITH MY KITE, Ted DeGrazia, 15,000	65.00	80.00

Children of Aberdeen

1979	GIRL WITH LITTLE BROTHER, Kee Fung Ng, 1 year	50.00	BR
1980	THE SAMPAN GIRL, Kee Fung Ng, 1 year	50.00	NR
1981	GIRL WITH LITTLE SISTER, Kee Fung Ng, 1 year	55.00	BR
1982	GIRL WITH SEASHELLS, Kee Fung Ng, 1 year	60.00	NR
1983	GIRL WITH SEABIRDS, Kee Fung Ng, 1 year	60.00	NR
1984	BROTHER AND SISTER, Kee Fung Ng, 1 year...........	60.00	NR

Brother and Sister
Photo courtesy of *Collectors News*

Children Of Don Ruffin

| 1980 | FLOWERS FOR MOTHER, Don Ruffin, 5,000 .... | 50.00 | NR |
| 1981 | LITTLE EAGLE, Don Ruffin, 5,000 .... | 55.00 | NR |

		Issue Price	Current Value
1982	THE LOST MOCCASINS, Don Ruffin, 7,500.............	60.00	NR
1982	SECURITY, Don Ruffin, 7,500	60.00	NR
1984	AMERICANS ALL, Don Ruffin, 7,500	60.00	NR

Children of the Sun

1987	SPRING BLOSSOMS, Ted DeGrazia, 150 days	34.50	40.00
1987	MY LITTLE PINK BIRD, Ted DeGrazia, 150 days.........	34.50	40.00
1987	BRIGHT FLOWERS OF THE DESERT, Ted DeGrazia, 150 days 40.00		34.50
1988	GIFTS FROM THE SUN, Ted DeGrazia, 150 days	34.50	40.00
1988	GROWING GLORY, Ted DeGrazia, 150 days	34.50	40.00
1988	THE GENTLE WHITE DOVE, Ted DeGrazia, 150 days	34.50	40.00
1988	SUNFLOWER MAIDEN, Ted DeGrazia, 150 days.........	34.50	40.00
1989	SUN SHOWERS, Ted DeGrazia, 150 days	34.50	40.00

Children of the World

1976	LOS NIÑOS, Ted DeGrazia, 5,000	35.00	1,000.00
1976	LOS NIÑOS, Ted DeGrazia, sgd, 500	100.00	1,500.00
1977	WHITE DOVE, Ted DeGrazia, 5,000	40.00	150.00
1977	WHITE DOVE, Ted DeGrazia, sgd, 500	100.00	300.00
1978	FLOWER GIRL, Ted DeGrazia, 9,500...................	45.00	NR
1978	FLOWER GIRL, Ted DeGrazia, sgd, 500	100.00	300.00
1979	FLOWER BOY, Ted DeGrazia, 9,500...................	45.00	60.00
1979	FLOWER BOY, Ted DeGrazia, sgd, 500	100.00	300.00
1980	LITTLE COCOPAH INDIAN GIRL, Ted DeGrazia, 9,500....	50.00	65.00
1980	LITTLE COCOPAH INDIAN GIRL, Ted DeGrazia, sgd, 500 .	100.00	300.00
1981	BEAUTIFUL BURDEN, Ted DeGrazia, 9,500	50.00	NR
1981	BEAUTIFUL BURDEN, Ted DeGrazia, sgd, 500	100.00	350.00
1981	MERRY LITTLE INDIAN, Ted DeGrazia, 9,500...........	55.00	90.00
1981	MERRY LITTLE INDIAN, Ted DeGrazia, sgd, 500	100.00	350.00
1983	WONDERING, Ted DeGrazia, 10,000...................	60.00	NR
1984	PINK PAPOOSE, Ted DeGrazia, 10,000................	65.00	BR
1985	SUNFLOWER BOY, Ted DeGrazia, 10,000	65.00	BR

Children of the World, Mini Plates

1980	LOS NIÑOS, Ted DeGrazia, 5,000	15.00	250.00
1981	WHITE DOVE, Ted DeGrazia, 5,000	15.00	30.00
1982	FLOWER GIRL, Ted DeGrazia, 5,000...................	15.00	30.00
1982	FLOWER BOY, Ted DeGrazia, 5,000...................	15.00	30.00
1983	LITTLE COCOPAH INDIAN GIRL, Ted DeGrazia, 5,000....	15.00	45.00
1983	BEAUTIFUL BURDEN, Ted DeGrazia, 5,000	15.00	NR
1984	MERRY LITTLE INDIAN, Ted DeGrazia, 5,000	15.00	NR
1984	WONDERING, Ted DeGrazia, 5,000	15.00	NR
1985	PINK PAPOOSE, Ted DeGrazia, 5,000	15.00	NR
1985	SUNFLOWER BOY, Ted DeGrazia, 5,000................	15.00	NR

Don Ruffin Series

Year	Title	Issue Price	Current Value
1976	NAVAJO LULLABY, Don Ruffin, 9,500 ...	40.00	90.00
1976	NAVAJO LULLABY, Don Ruffin, 500	100.00	230.00
1977	THROUGH THE YEARS, Don Ruffin, 5,000	45.00	150.00
1978	CHILD OF THE PUEBLO, Don Ruffin, 5,000	45.00	75.00
1979	COLIMA MADONNA, Don Ruffin, 5,000	50.00	NR
1980	SUN KACHIMA, Don Ruffin, 5,000	50.00	NR
1981	INNER PEACE, Don Ruffin, 5,000	55.00	NR
1982	MADONNA OF THE CROSS, Don Ruffin, 5,000	60.00	NR
1983	NAVAJO PRINCESS, Don Ruffin, 5,000	60.00	NR
1983	SECURITY, Don Ruffin, 7,500	60.00	NR
1984	AMERICANS ALL, Don Ruffin, 7,500	60.00	NR

Endangered Birds

Year	Title	Issue Price	Current Value
1976	KIRTLAND'S WARBLER, 5,000	195.00	NR
1976	AMERICAN EAGLE, 5,000	195.00	NR
1977	PEREGRINE FALCON, 5,000	200.00	NR

Fiesta of the Children

Year	Title	Issue Price	Current Value
1990	WELCOME TO THE FIESTA, Ted DeGrazia, 150 days	34.50	NR
1990	CASTANETS IN BLOOM, Ted DeGrazia, 150 days	34.50	40.00
1991	FIESTA FLOWERS, Ted DeGrazia, 150 days	34.50	45.00
1991	FIESTA ANGELS, Ted DeGrazia, 150 days	34.50	NR

Floral Fiesta

Year	Title	Issue Price	Current Value
1994	FIESTA FOR MOTHER, Ted DeGrazia, 5,000	39.50	RI
1994	LITTLE FLOWER VENDOR, Ted DeGrazia, 5,000	39.50	RI

Holiday

Year	Title	Issue Price	Current Value
1976	FESTIVAL OF LIGHTS, Ted DeGrazia, 9,500	45.00	115.00
1976	FESTIVAL OF LIGHTS, Ted DeGrazia, sgd, 500	100.00	350.00
1977	BELL OF HOPE, Ted DeGrazia, 9,500	45.00	NR
1977	BELL OF HOPE, Ted DeGrazia, sgd, 500	100.00	200.00
1978	LITTLE MADONNA, Ted DeGrazia, 9,500	45.00	60.00
1978	LITTLE MADONNA, Ted DeGrazia, sgd, 500	100.00	350.00
1979	THE NATIVITY, Ted DeGrazia, 9,500	50.00	70.00
1979	THE NATIVITY, Ted DeGrazia, sgd, 500	100.00	200.00
1980	LITTLE PIMA DRUMMER, Ted DeGrazia, 9,500	50.00	NR
1980	LITTLE PIMA DRUMMER, Ted DeGrazia, sgd, 500	100.00	200.00
1981	A LITTLE PRAYER – CHRISTMAS ANGEL, Ted DeGrazia, 9,500 100.00		BR
1981	A LITTLE PRAYER – CHRISTMAS ANGEL, Ted DeGrazia, sgd, 500 100.00		200.00
1982	BLUE BOY, Ted DeGrazia, 10,000	60.00	NR
1982	BLUE BOY, Ted DeGrazia, sgd, 96	100.00	200.00
1983	HEAVENLY BLESSINGS, Ted DeGrazia, 10,000	65.00	BR

		Issue Price	Current Value
1984	NAVAJO MADONNA, Ted DeGrazia, 10,000	65.00	BR
1985	SAGUARO DANCE, Ted DeGrazia, 10,000	65.00	BR

Holiday Mini Plates

1980	FESTIVAL OF LIGHTS, Ted DeGrazia, 5,000.............	15.00	250.00
1981	BELL OF HOPE, Ted DeGrazia, 5,000	15.00	95.00
1982	LITTLE MADONNA, Ted DeGrazia, 5,000	15.00	95.00
1982	THE NATIVITY, Ted DeGrazia, 5,000	15.00	95.00
1983	LITTLE PIMA DANCER, Ted DeGrazia, 5,000...........	15.00	25.00
1983	LITTLE PRAYER, Ted DeGrazia, 5,000	20.00	NR
1984	BLUE BOY, Ted DeGrazia, 5,000......................	20.00	NR
1984	HEAVENLY BLESSINGS, Ted DeGrazia, 5,000	20.00	NR
1985	NAVAJO MADONNA, Ted DeGrazia, 5,000	20.00	NR
1985	SAGUARO DANCE, Ted DeGrazia, 5,000	20.00	NR

Prowlers of the Clouds

1981	FIRST LIGHT – GREAT HORNED OWL, Larry Toschik, 5,000 NR		55.00
1981	HIS GOLDEN THRONE – SCREECH OWL, Larry Toschik, 5,000 NR		55.00
1982	FREEDOM'S SYMBOL – BALD EAGLE, Larry Toschik, 5,000 NR		60.00
1982	FREEDOM'S CHAMPION – GOLDEN EAGLE, Larry Toschik, 5,000 60.00 .... NR		

Sweetheart Series

1984	WE BELIEVE, Rusty Money, 10,000	40.00	NR

Vel Miller Series

1982	MAMA'S ROSE, Vel Miller, 15,000.....................	35.00	NR
1983	PAPA'S BOY, Vel Miller, 15,000	40.00	NR

Western Series

1986	MORNING RIDE, Ted DeGrazia, 5,000	65.00	75.00
1987	BRONCO, Ted DeGrazia, 5,000.......................	65.00	75.00
1988	APACHE SCOUT, Ted DeGrazia, 5,000	65.00	75.00
1989	ALONE, Ted DeGrazia, 5,000	65.00	75.00

Woodland Friends

1983	SPRING OUTING – WHITETAIL DEER, Larry Toschik, 5,000 NR		60.00
1984	NO REST FOR THE NIGHT SHIFT, Larry Toschik, 5,000 ..	60.00	NR
1984	SPRING OUTING, Larry Toschik, 5,000	60.00	NR

World of Game Birds

		Issue Price	Current Value
1977	MALLARDS – WHISTLING IN, Larry Toschik, 5,000	45.00	80.00
1978	MAYTIME – GAMBEL QUAIL, Larry Toschik, 5,000	45.00	NR
1979	AMERICAN AUTUMN – RING–NECKED PHEASANT, Larry Toschik, 5,000	50.00	NR
1980	NOVEMBER JOURNEY – CANADA GEESE, Larry Toschik, 5,000 NR		50.00

Single Issues

1977	THE STATESMAN, Don Ruffin, 3,500	65.00	BR
1977	THE CLOWN ALSO CRIES, Don Ruffin, 7,500	65.00	BR

Special Issues

1983	DEGRAZIA AND HIS MOUNTAIN, Larry Toschik, 15,000 .	65.00	NR
1984	LITTLE GIRL PAINTS DEGRAZIA, Ted DeGrazia, 12,500 . .	65.00	NR

AVONDALE UNITED STATES

Cameos of Childhood

1978	MELISSA, Frances Taylor Williams, 23,050	65.00	NR
1979	FIRST BORN, Frances Taylor Williams, 12,000	70.00	NR
1980	MELISSA'S BROTHER, Frances Taylor Williams, 8,400 . . .	70.00	NR
1981	DADDY AND I, Frances Taylor Williams, 10,000	75.00	NR

Christmas Annual

1978	...AND THE HEAVENS REJOICED, Frances Taylor Williams, 6,500 90.00 . . . . NR		
1982	...AND THERE CAME THE WISEMEN, Frances Taylor Williams, 6,500	90.00	NR
1983	THE SHEPHERD, Frances Taylor Williams, 6,500	90.00	NR

Mother's Day

1982	A RIBBON FOR HER HAIR, Frances Taylor Williams, 6,500	75.00	NR
1984	JUST LIKE MOTHER, Frances Taylor Williams, 6,500	75.00	NR

Myths of the Sea

1979	POSEIDON, Gregg Appleby, 15,00	70.00	NR
1981	MAIDEN OF THE SEA, Gregg Appleby, 10,000	75.00	NR

Tributes to the Ageless Arts

1979	COURT JESTERS, Almazetta, 10,000	70.00	NR

World of Dance

1979	PRIMA BALLERINA, Almazetta, 15,000	70.00	NR

Single Issues	Issue Price	Current Value
1969 PRINCE OF WALES, 1,000	50.00	NR
1970 THE MAYFLOWER, 1,000	35.00	NR
1973 1,000 YEARS OF ENGLISH MONARCHY, 1,000	30.00	NR

B & J ART DESIGNS UNITED STATES

Old–Fashioned Christmas

1983 CAROL, Jan Hagara, 15,000	45.00	NR

Old–Fashioned Country

1984 CHRISTINA, Jan Hagara, 20,000	39.00	NR
1985 LAUREL, Jan Hagara, 15,000	42.50	NR

Yesterday's Children

1978 LISA AND THE JUMEAU DOLL, Jan Hagara, 5,000	60.00	95.00
1979 ADRIANNE AND THE BYE–LO DOLL, Jan Hagara, 5,000	60.00	90.00
1980 LYDIA AND THE SHIRLEY TEMPLE DOLL, Jan Hagara, 5,000 75.00		60.00
1981 MELANIE AND THE SCARLETT O'HARA DOLL, Jan Hagara, 5,000 60.00		NR

BAREUTHER GERMANY

Christmas

1967 STIFTSKIRCHE, Hans Mueller, 10,000	12.00	85.00
1968 KAPPLKIRCHE, Hans Mueller, 10,000	12.00	25.00
1969 CHRISTKINDLEMARKT, Hans Mueller, 10,000	12.00	20.00
1970 CHAPEL IN OBERNDORF, Hans Mueller, 10,000	12.50	20.00
1971 TOYS FOR SALE, Hans Mueller, from drawing by L. Ricter, 10,000	12.75	20.00
1972 CHRISTMAS IN MUNICH, Hans Mueller, 10,000	14.50	25.00
1973 SLEIGH RIDE, Hans Mueller, 10,000	15.00	NR
1974 BLACK FOREST CHURCH, Hans Mueller, 10,000	19.00	NR
1975 SNOWMAN, Hans Mueller, 10,000	21.50	NR
1976 CHAPEL IN THE HILLS, Hans Mueller, 10,000	23.50	NR
1977 STORY TIME, Hans Mueller, 10,000	24.50	35.00
1978 MITTENWALD, Hans Mueller, 10,000	27.50	NR
1979 WINTER DAY, Hans Mueller, 10,000	35.00	NR
1980 MITTENBERG, Hans Mueller, 10,000	37.50	NR
1980 WALK IN THE FOREST, Hans Mueller, 10,000	39.50	NR
1982 BAD WIMPFEN, Hans Mueller, 10,000	39.50	NR
1983 NIGHT BEFORE CHRISTMAS, Hans Mueller, 10,000	39.50	NR
1984 ZEIL ON THE RIVER MAIN, Hans Mueller, 10,000	42.50	NR

	Issue Price	Current Value
1985 WINTER WONDERLAND, Hans Mueller, 10,000	42.50	NR
1986 CHRISTMAS IN FORCHHEIM, Hans Mueller, 10,000	42.50	65.00
1987 DECORATING THE TREE, Hans Mueller, 10,000	42.50	75.00
1988 ST. COLOMAN CHURCH, Hans Mueller, 10,000	52.50	60.00
1989 SLEIGH RIDE, Hans Mueller, 10,000	52.50	75.00
1990 THE OLD FORGE IN ROTHENBURG, Hans Mueller, 10,000	52.50	NR
1991 CHRISTMAS JOY, Hans Mueller, 10,000	56.50	NR
1992 MARKET PLACE IN HEPPENHEIM, Hans Mueller, 10,000.	59.50	RI
1993 WINTER FUN, Hans Mueller, 10,000	59.50	RI
1994 COMING HOME FOR CHRISTMAS, Hans Mueller, 10,000	59.50	RI

Danish Church

1968 ROSKILDE CATHEDRAL, 1 year	12.00	25.00
1969 RIBE CATHEDRAL, 1 year	12.00	25.00
1970 MARMOR KIRKEN, 1 year	13.00	NR
1977 BUDOLFI KIRKEN, 1 year	15.95	25.00
1978 HADERSLAV CATHEDRAL, 1 year	19.95	NR
1979 HOLMENS CHURCH, 1 year ....:	15.30	20.00

Esteban Murillo Series

1972 FRUIT VENDORS COUNTING MONEY	12.00	45.00
1972 BOYS EATING PASTRY	12.00	45.00
1972 BEGGAR BOYS PLAYING DICE	42.00	NR
1972 BOYS EATING MELONS AND GRAPES	42.00	NR

Father's Day

1969 CASTLE NEWSCHWANSTEIN, Hans Mueller, 1 year	10.50	55.00
1970 CASTLE PFALZ, Hans Mueller, 1 year	12.50	20.00
1971 EJBY CHURCH, 1 year	13.00	NR
1972 KALUNDBORG KIRKEN, 1 year	13.00	20.00
1973 GRUNDTVIG KIRKEN, 1 year	15.00	20.00
1974 BROAGER KIRKEN, 1 year	15.00	20.00
1975 ST. KNUDS KIRKEN, 1 year	20.00	NR
1976 OSTERLAS KIRKEN, 1 year	20.00	NR
1971 CASTLE HEIDELBERG, Hans Mueller, 1 year	12.75	25.00
1972 CASTLE HOHENSCHWANGAN, Hans Mueller, 1 year.....	14.50	25.00
1973 CASTLE KATZ, Hans Mueller, 1 year	15.00	30.00
1974 WURZBURG CASTLE, Hans Mueller, 1 year	19.00	50.00
1975 CASTLE LICHTENSTEIN, Hans Mueller, 1 year	21.50	35.00
1976 CASTLE HOHENZOLLERN, Hans Mueller, 1 year	23.50	30.00
1977 CASTLE ELTZ, Hans Mueller, 1 year	24.50	30.00
1978 CASTLE FALKENSTEIN, Hans Mueller, 1 year	27.50	NR
1979 CASTLE REINSTEIN, Hans Mueller, 2,500	35.00	NR
1980 CASTLE COCHEM, Hans Mueller, 2,500	37.50	NR
1981 CASTLE GUTENFELS, Hans Mueller, 2,500	39.50	NR

		Issue Price	Current Value
1982	CASTLE ZWINGERBERG, Hans Mueller, 2,500	39.50	NR
1983	CASTLE LAUNSTEIN, Hans Mueller, 2,500	39.50	NR
1984	CASTLE NUENSTEIN, Hans Mueller, 2,500	42.50	NR

Mother's Day

1969	MOTHER AND CHILDREN, Ludwig Richter, 5,000	10.50	75.00
1970	MOTHER AND CHILDREN, Ludwig Richter, 5,000	12.50	30.00
1971	MOTHER AND CHILDREN, Ludwig Richter, 5,000	12.75	20.00
1972	MOTHER AND CHILDREN, Ludwig Richter, 5,000	15.00	20.00
1973	MOTHER AND CHILDREN, Ludwig Richter, 5,000	15.00	20.00
1974	MUSICAL CHILDREN, Ludwig Richter, 5,000	19.00	35.00
1975	SPRING OUTING, Ludwig Richter, 5,000	21.50	NR
1976	ROCKING THE CRADLE, Ludwig Richter, 5,000	23.50	NR
1977	NOON FEEDING, Ludwig Richter, 5,000	24.50	NR
1978	BLIND MAN'S BLUFF, Ludwig Richter, 5,000	27.50	NR
1979	MOTHER'S LOVE, Ludwig Richter, 5,000	37.50	NR
1980	THE FIRST CHERRIES, Ludwig Richter, 5,000	37.50	NR
1981	PLAYTIME, Ludwig Richter, 5,000	39.50	NR
1982	SUPPERTIME, Ludwig Richter, 5,000	39.50	NR
1983	ON THE FARM, Ludwig Richter, 5,000	39.50	NR
1984	VILLAGE CHILDREN, Ludwig Richter, 5,000	42.50	NR

Thanksgiving

1971	FIRST THANKSGIVING, 2,500	13.50	35.00
1972	HARVEST, 2,500	14.50	20.00
1973	COUNTRY ROAD IN AUTUMN, 2,500	15.00	NR
1974	OLD MILL, 2,500	19.00	NR
1975	WILD DEER IN FOREST, 2,500	21.50	NR
1976	THANKSGIVING ON FARM, 2,500	23.50	NR
1977	HORSES, Hans Mueller, 2,500	24.50	NR
1978	APPLE HARVEST, Hans Mueller, 2,500	27.50	NR
1979	NOONTIME, Hans Mueller, 2,500	35.00	NR
1980	LONGHORNS, Hans Mueller, 2,500	37.50	NR
1981	GATHERING WHEAT, Hans Mueller, 2,500	39.50	NR
1982	AUTUMN, Hans Mueller, 2,500	39.50	NR
1983	HARROW, Hans Mueller, 2,500	39.50	NR
1984	FARMLAND, Hans Mueller, 2,500	42.50	NR

BARTHMANN GERMANY

Christmas

1977	MARY WITH CHILD, 300	326.00	NR
1978	ADORATION OF CHILD, 500	326.00	NR
1979	HOLY MOTHER OF KASANSKAJA, 500	361.00	NR
1980	HOLY MOTHER BY KYKOS, 500	385.00	NR

BAYEL OF FRANCE FRANCE

Bicentennial	Issue Price	Current Value
1974 LIBERTY BELL, 500	50.00	NR
1975 INDEPENDENCE HALL, 500	60.00	NR
1976 SPREAD EAGLE, 500	60.00	NR

Eagle

1974 EAGLE HEAD, 300	50.00	NR
1974 EAGLE IN FLIGHT, 300	50.00	NR

Flowers

1972 ROSE, 300	50.00	NR
1973 LILIES, 300	50.00	NR
1973 ORCHID, 300	50.00	NR

BEACON PLATE MANUFACTURING UNITED STATES

Pace Setters

1987 FREDERICK DOUGLASS, 2,500	53.50	NR

BELLEEK POTTERY GREAT BRITAIN

Christmas

1970 CASTLE CALDWELL, 7,500	25.00	80.00
1971 CELTIC CROSS, 7,500	25.00	50.00
1972 FLIGHT OF THE EARLS, 7,500	30.00	NR
1973 TRIBUTE TO YEATS, 7,500	38.50	NR
1974 DEVENISH ISLAND, 7,500	45.00	175.00
1975 THE CELTIC CROSS, 7,500	48.00	75.00
1976 DOVE OF PEACE, 7,500	55.00	NR
1977 WREN, 7,500	55.00	NR

Holiday Scenes in Ireland

1991 TRAVELING HOME, 7,500	75.00	NR
1992 BEARING GIFTS, 7,500	75.00	RI

Irish Wildlife

1978 A LEAPING SALMON	55.00	70.00
1979 HARE AT REST	58.50	65.00
1980 THE HEDGEHOG	66.50	NR
1981 RED SQUIRREL	78.00	NR
1982 IRISH SEAL	78.00	NR
1983 RED FOX	85.00	NR

	Issue Price	Current Value

St. Patrick's Day

1986   ST. PATRICK BANISHING THE SNAKES FROM IRELAND, Fergus
Cleary, 10,000 .... 75.00   NR

BENGOUGH CANADA

Christmas

1972   CHARLES DICKENS CHRISTMAS CAROL, 490 .... 125.00   NR

Northwest Mounted Police

1972   1898 DRESS UNIFORM, 1,000 .... 140.00   NR
1972   FIRST UNIFORM, 1,000 .... 140.00   NR

Royal Canadian Police

1972   ORDER DRESS, 1,000 .... 140.00   NR

BERLIN DESIGN GERMANY

Christmas

1970	CHRISTMAS IN BERNKASTEL, 4,000	14.50	125.00
1971	CHRISTMAS IN ROTHENBURG, 20,000	14.50	40.00
1972	CHRISTMAS IN MICHELSTADT, 20,000	15.00	50.00
1973	CHRISTMAS IN WENDELSTEIN, 20,000	20.00	45.00
1974	CHRISTMAS IN BREMEN, 20,000	25.00	40.00
1975	CHRISTMAS IN DORTLAND, 20,000	30.00	NR
1976	CHRISTMAS IN AUGSBURG, 20,000	32.00	50.00
1977	CHRISTMAS IN HAMBURG, 20,000	32.00	NR
1978	CHRISTMAS IN BERLIN, 20,000	36.00	75.00
1979	CHRISTMAS IN GREETSIEL, 20,000	47.50	60.00
1980	CHRISTMAS IN MITTENBERG, 20,000	50.00	NR
1981	CHRISTMAS EVE IN HAHNENKLEE, 20,000	55.00	NR
1982	CHRISTMAS EVE IN WASSERBERG, 20,000	55.00	NR
1983	CHRISTMAS IN OBERNDORF, 20,000	55.00	NR
1984	CHRISTMAS IN RAMSAU, 20,000	55.00	NR
1985	CHRISTMAS IN BAD WIMPFEN, 20,000	55.00	NR
1986	CHIRSTMAS EVE IN GELNHAUS, 20,000	65.00	NR
1987	CHRISTMAS EVE IN GOSLAR, 20,000	65.00	NR
1988	CHRISTMAS EVE IN RUHPOLDING, 20,000	65.00	NR
1989	CHRISTMAS EVE IN FRIEDECHSDADT, 20,000	80.00	NR
1990	CHRISTMAS EVE IN PARTENKIRCHEN, 20,000	80.00	NR
1991	CHRISTMAS EVE IN ALLENDORF, 20,000	80.00	NR

Father's Day

1971   BROOKLYN BRIDGE ON OPENING DAY, 12,000 .... 14.50   20.00

		Issue Price	Current Value
1972	CONTINENT SPANNED, 3,000	15.00	35.00
1973	LANDING OF COLUMBUS, 2,000	18.00	40.00
1974	ADORN'S BALLOON, 1 year	25.00	35.00

Historical

1975	WASHINGTON CROSSING THE DELAWARE, 1 year	30.00	NR
1976	TOM THUMB, 1 year	32.00	NR
1977	ZEPPELIN, 1 year	32.00	NR
1978	BENZ MOTOR CAR MUNICH, 10,000	36.00	NR
1979	JOHANNES GUTENBERG AT MAINZ, 10,000	47.50	NR

Holiday Week of the Family Kappelmann

1984	MONDAY, limited	33.00	NR
1984	TUESDAY, limited	33.00	NR
1985	WEDNESDAY, Detlev Nitschke, limited	33.00	NR
1985	THURSDAY, limited	35.00	NR
1985	FRIDAY, limited	35.00	NR
1986	SATURDAY, limited	35.00	NR
1986	SUNDAY, limited	35.00	BR

Monday
Photo courtesy of *Collectors News*

Mother's Day

1971	GREY POODLES, 20,000	14.50	25.00
1972	FLEDGLINGS, 10,00	15.00	25.00
1973	DUCK FAMILY, 5,000	16.50	40.00
1974	SQUIRRELS, 6,000	22.50	40.00
1975	CATS, 6,000	30.00	40.00
1976	DEER, 6,000	32.00	NR
1977	STORKS, 6,000	32.00	NR

	Issue Price	Current Value
1978 MARE AND FOAL, 6,000	36.00	NR
1979 SWANS WITH CYGNETS, 6,000	47.50	NR
1980 GOAT FAMILY, 6,000	55.00	NR
1981 DACHSHUND AND PUPPIES, 1 year	50.00	NR

BETOURNE STUDIOS FRANCE

Jean–Paul Loup Christmas

1971 NOEL, 300	125.00	1,000.00
1972 NOEL, 300	150.00	700.00
1973 NOEL, 300	175.00	500.00
1974 NOEL, 400	200.00	500.00
1975 NOEL, 250	250.00	500.00
1976 NOEL, 150	300.00	600.00

Mother's Day

1974 MOTHER AND CHILD, 500	250.00	1,200.00
1975 MOTHER'S DAY, 400	285.00	300.00
1976 MOTHER AND CHILD, 250	300.00	600.00

BIEDERMANN & SONS

Single Issues

1993 FOUR CALLING BIRDS, 250	17.50	RI
1994 DRUMMER BOY, 250	20.00	RI

BING & GRONDAHL DENMARK

Bicentennial

1976 E PLURIBUS UNUM, 1 year	50.00	NR

Carl Larsson Miniature

1986 THE FLOWER WINDOW, 15,000	15.00	NR
1986 LUNCH UNDER THE BIRCH TREE, 15,000	15.00	NR
1986 WINTER AND THE OLD BARN, 15,000	15.00	NR
1986 MAMA'S ROOM, 15,000	15.00	NR
1986 IDUNA'S NEW DRESS, 15,000	15.00	NR
1986 WORKING IN THE WOODS, 15,000	15.00	NR
1986 HARVEST, 15,000	15.00	NR
1986 POTATO HARVEST, 15,000	15.00	NR
1986 FISHING, 15,000	15.00	NR
1986 OPENING DAY OF THE CRAYFISH SEASON, 15,000	15.00	NR

		Issue Price	Current Value
1986	AZALEA, 15,000	15.00	NR
1986	APPLE HARVEST, 15,000	15.00	NR

Carl Larsson Series

1977	FLOWERS ON WINDOWSILL, 7,500, set of 4	150.00	NR
1977	BREAKFAST UNDER BIG BIRCH, 7,500, set of 4	150.00	NR
1977	YARD AND WAREHOUSE, 7,500, set of 4	150.00	NR
1977	KITCHEN, 7,500, set of 4	150.00	NR
1978	FIRST BORN, 7,500, set of 4	150.00	NR
1978	ROOM FOR MOTHER AND CHILDREN, 7,500, set of 4	150.00	NR
1978	PORTRAIT OF INGA–MARIA THIEL, 7,500, set of 4	150.00	NR
1978	IDUNA, 7,500, set of 4	150.00	NR
1979	FORESTRY, 7,500, set of 4	150.00	NR
1979	CUTTING GRASS, 7,500, set of 4	150.00	NR
1979	POTATO HARVEST, 7,500, set of 4	150.00	NR
1979	FISHERY, 7,500, set of 4	150.00	NR

Cat Portraits

1987	MANX AND KITTENS, Angela Sayer, 14,500	39.50	NR
1987	PERSIAN AND KITTENS, Angela Sayer, 14,500	39.50	NR
1987	SOMALI AND KITTENS, Angela Sayer, 14,500	39.50	NR
1987	BURMESE AND KITTENS, Angela Sayer, 14,500	39.50	NR

Centennial Collection

1991	CROWS ENJOYING CHRISTMAS, Peter Dahl Jensen, 1 year NR		59.50
1992	COPENHAGEN CHRISTMAS, H. Vlugenring, 1 year	59.50	RI
1993	CHRISTMAS ELF, Henry Thelander, 1 year	59.50	RI
1994	CHRISTMAS IN CHURCH, Henry Thelander, 1 year	59.50	RI
1995	BEHIND THE FROZEN WINDOW, Franz August Hallin, 1 year RI		59.50

Children's Day

1985	THE MAGICAL TEA PARTY, C. Roller, 1 year	24.50	NR
1986	A JOYFUL FLIGHT, C. Roller, 1 year	26.50	NR
1986	THE LITTLE GARDENERS, C. Roller, 1 year	29.50	NR
1988	WASH DAY, C. Roller, 1 year	34.50	NR
1989	BEDTIME, C. Roller, 1 year	37.00	NR
1990	MY FAVORITE DRESS, Sven Vestergaard, 1 year	37.00	NR
1991	FUN ON THE BEACH, Sven Vestergaard, 1 year	45.00	55.00
1992	A SUMMER DAY IN THE MEADOW, Sven Vestergaard, 1 year	45.00	RI
1993	THE CAROUSEL, Sven Vestergaard, 1 year	45.00	RI
1994	THE LITTLE FISHERMAN	45.00	RI

Christmas

Behind the Frozen Window

Sparrows

Crows

Three Wise Men

Expectant Children

Christmas Night

The Old Organist

Amalienborg Castle

Christmas Boat

Outside Lighted Window

Pigeons

Child's Christmas

		Issue Price	Current Value
1897	SPARROWS, Franz August Hallin, 1 year	.75	1,200.00
1898	ROSES AND STAR, Fanny Garde, 1 year	.75	850.00
1899	CROWS, Peter Dahl Jensen, 1 year	.75	1,200.00
1900	CHURCH BELLS, Peter Dahl Jensen, 1 year	.75	1,200.00
1901	THREE WISE MEN, S. Sabra, 1 year	1.00	450.00
1902	GOTHIC CHURCH INTERIOR, Peter Dahl Jensen, 1 year	1.00	300.00
1903	EXPECTANT CHILDREN, Margrethe Hyldahl, 1 year	1.00	250.00
1904	FREDERIKSBERG HILL, Cathinka Olsen, 1 year	1.00	150.00
1905	CHRISTMAS NIGHT, Peter Dahl Jensen, 1 year	1.00	150.00
1906	SLEIGHING TO CHURCH, Peter Dahl Jensen, 1 year	1.00	115.00
1907	LITTLE MATCH GIRL, Ingeborg Plockross, 1 year	1.00	150.00
1908	ST. PETRI CHURCH, Povl Jorgensen, 1 year	1.00	80.00
1909	YULE TREE, Aarestrup, 1 year	1.50	100.00
1910	THE OLD ORGANIST, C. Ersgaard, 1 year	1.50	95.00
1911	ANGELS AND SHEPHERDS, Harold Moltke, 1 year	1.50	95.00
1912	GOING TO CHURCH, Einar Hansen, 1 year	1.50	80.00
1913	BRINGING HOME THE TREE, T. Larsen, 1 year	1.50	90.00
1914	AMALIENBORG CASTLE, T. Larsen, 1 year	1.50	85.00
1915	DOG OUTSIDE WINDOW, Peter Dahl Jensen, 1 year	1.50	130.00
1916	SPARROWS AT CHRISTMAS, J. Bloch Jorgensen, 1 year	1.50	70.00
1917	CHRISTMAS BOAT, Achton Friis, 1 year	1.50	85.00
1918	FISHING BOAT, Achton Friis, 1 year	1.50	90.00
1919	OUTSIDE LIGHTED WINDOW, Achton Friis, 1 year	2.00	70.00
1920	HARE IN SNOW, Achton Friis, 1 year	2.00	90.00
1921	PIGEONS, Achton Friis, 1 year	2.00	60.00
1922	STAR OF BETHLEHEM, Achton Friis, 1 year	2.00	60.00
1923	THE HERMITAGE, Achton Friis, 1 year	2.00	95.00
1924	LIGHTHOUSE, Achton Friis, 1 year	2.50	85.00
1925	CHILD'S CHRISTMAS, Achton Friis, 1 year	2.50	90.00
1926	CHURCHGOERS, Achton Friis, 1 year	2.50	80.00
1927	SKATING COUPLE, Achton Friis, 1 year	2.50	95.00
1928	ESKIMOS, Achton Friis, 1 year	2.50	55.00
1929	FOX OUTSIDE FARM, Achton Friis, 1 year	2.50	100.00
1930	TOWN HALL SQUARE, H. Flugenring, 1 year	2.50	115.00
1931	CHRISTMAS TRAIN, Achton Friis, 1 year	2.50	110.00
1932	LIFE BOAT, H. Flugenring, 1 year	2.50	85.00
1933	KORSOR–NYBORG FERRY, H. Flugenring, 1 year	3.00	90.00
1934	CHURCH BELL IN TOWER, Immanuel Tjerne, 1 year	3.00	90.00
1935	LILLEBELT BRIDGE, Ove Larsen, 1 year	3.00	100.00
1936	ROYAL GUARD, AMALIENBORG, Ove Larsen, 1 year	3.00	80.00
1937	ARRIVAL OF CHRISTMAS GUESTS, Ove Larsen, 1 year	3.00	110.00
1938	LIGHTING THE CANDLES, Immanuel Tjerne, 1 year	3.00	400.00
1939	OLD LOCK–EYE, THE SANDMAN, Immanuel Tjerne, 1 year	3.00	250.00
1940	CHRISTMAS LETTERS, Ove Larsen, 1 year	4.00	215.00
1941	HORSES ENJOYING MEAL, Ove Larsen, 1 year	4.00	175.00
1942	DANISH FARM, Ove Larsen, 1 year	4.00	115.00
1943	RIBE CATHEDRAL, Ove Larsen, 1 year	5.00	290.00

Skating Couple

Christmas Train

Korsor–Nyborg Ferry

Church Bell in Tower

Arrival of Christmas Guests

Old Lock–Eye, The Sandman

Ribe Cathedral

Landsoldaten

Thorvaldsen

Christmas in Copenhagen

Santa Claus

Winter Night

		Issue Price	Current Value
1944	SORGENFRI CASTLE, Ove Larsen, 1 year	5.00	125.00
1945	OLD WATER MILL, Ove Larsen, 1 year	5.00	170.00
1946	COMMEMORATION CROSS, Margrethe Hyldahl, 1 year	5.00	80.00
1947	DYBBOL MILL, Margrethe Hyldahl, 1 year	5.00	190.00
1948	WATCHMAN, Margrethe Hyldahl, 1 year	5.50	90.00
1949	LANDSOLDATEN, Margrethe Hyldahl, 1 year	5.50	150.00
1950	KRONBORG CASTLE, Margrethe Hyldahl, 1 year	5.50	150.00
1951	JENS BANG, Margrethe Hyldahl, 1 year	6.00	150.00
1952	THORVALDSEN MUSEUM, Borge Pramvig, 1 year	6.00	100.00
1953	SNOWMAN, Borge Pramvig, 1 year	7.50	115.00
1954	ROYAL BOAT, Kjeld Bonfils, 1 year	7.00	150.00
1955	KAULUNDBORG CHURCH, Kjeld Bonfils, 1 year	8.00	150.00
1956	CHRISTMAS IN COPENHAGEN, Kjeld Bonfils, 1 year	8.50	275.00
1957	CHRISTMAS CANDLES, Kjeld Bonfils, 1 year	9.00	150.00
1958	SANTA CLAUS, Kjeld Bonfils, 1 year	9.50	125.00
1959	CHRISTMAS EVE, Kjeld Bonfils, 1 year	10.00	110.00
1960	DANISH VILLAGE CHURCH, Kjeld Bonfils, 1 year	10.00	170.00
1961	WINTER HARMONY, Kjeld Bonfils, 1 year	10.50	75.00
1962	WINTER NIGHT, Kjeld Bonfils, 1 year	11.00	55.00
1963	CHRISTMAS ELF, Henry Thelander, 1 year	11.00	70.00
1964	FIR TREE AND HARE, Henry Thelander, 1 year	11.50	50.00
1965	BRINGING HOME THE TREE, Henry Thelander, 1 year	12.00	65.00
1966	HOME FOR CHRISTMAS, Henry Thelander, 1 year	12.00	55.00
1967	SHARING THE JOY, Henry Thelander, 1 year	13.00	50.00
1968	CHRISTMAS IN CHURCH, Henry Thelander, 1 year	14.00	40.00
1969	ARRIVAL OF GUESTS, Henry Thelander, 1 year	14.00	25.00
1970	PHEASANTS IN SNOW, Henry Thelander, 1 year	14.50	NR
1971	CHRISTMAS AT HOME, Henry Thelander, 1 year	15.00	BR
1972	CHRISTMAS IN GREENLAND, Henry Thelander, 1 year	16.50	BR
1973	COUNTRY CHRISTMAS, Henry Thelander, 1 year	19.50	BR
1974	CHRISTMAS IN THE VILLAGE, Henry Thelander, 1 year	22.00	BR
1975	OLD WATER MILL, Henry Thelander, 1 year	27.50	BR
1976	CHRISTMAS WELCOME, Henry Thelander, 1 year	27.50	NR
1977	COPENHAGEN CHRISTMAS, Henry Thelander, 1 year	29.50	BR
1978	CHRISTMAS TALE, Henry Thelander, 1 year	32.00	BR
1979	WHITE CHRISTMAS, Henry Thelander, 1 year	36.50	BR
1980	CHRISTMAS IN WOODS, Henry Thelander, 1 year	42.50	NR
1981	CHRISTMAS PEACE, Henry Thelander, 1 year	49.50	BR
1982	CHRISTMAS TREE, Henry Thelander, 1 year	54.50	BR
1983	CHRISTMAS IN THE OLD TOWN, Henry Thelander, 1 year	54.50	BR
1984	THE CHRISTMAS LETTER, Edvard Jensen, 1 year	54.50	BR
1985	CHRISTMAS EVE AT THE FARMHOUSE, Edvard Jensen, 1 year	54.50	BR
1986	SILENT NIGHT, HOLY NIGHT, Edvard Jensen, 1 year	54.50	BR
1987	THE SNOWMAN'S CHRISTMAS EVE, Edvard Jensen, 1 year	59.50	BR
1988	IN THE KING'S GARDEN, Edvard Jensen, 1 year	59.50	BR
1989	CHRISTMAS ANCHORAGE, Edvard Jensen, 1 year	59.50	BR
1990	CHANGING OF THE GUARDS, Edvard Jensen, 1 year	64.50	NR

Fir Tree and Hare

Home for Christmas

Arrival of Guests

Christmas at Home

Country Christmas

Christmas in the Village

		Issue Price	Current Value
1895	BEHIND THE FROZEN WINDOW, Franz August Hallin, 1 year ..	.50	5,000.00
1990	NEW MOON, Franz August Hallin, 1 year	.50	2,200.00
1991	COPENHAGEN STOCK EXCHANGE, Edvard Jensen, 1 year	69.50	NR
1992	CHRISTMAS AT THE RECTORY, Edvard Jensen, 1 year ..	69.50	RI
1993	FATHER CHRISTMAS IN COPENHAGEN, Edvard Jensen, 1 year	69.50	RI
1994	A DAY AT THE DEER PARK, Edvard Jensen, 1 year	72.50	RI
1995	THE TOWERS OF COPENHAGEN, Jorgen Nielsen	74.50	RI

Christmas in America

1986	CHRISTMAS EVE IN WILLIAMSBURG, Jack Woodson, 1 year .	29.50	70.00
1987	CHRISTMAS EVE AT THE WHITE HOUSE, Jack Woodson, 1 year ...	34.50	60.00
1988	CHRISTMAS EVE AT ROCKEFELLER CENTER, Jack Woodson, 1 year	34.50	60.00
1989	CHRISTMAS IN NEW ENGLAND, Jack Woodson, 1 year .	37.00	60.00
1990	CHRISTMAS EVE AT THE CAPITOL, Jack Woodson, 1 year	39.50	50.00
1991	CHRISTMAS EVE AT INDEPENDENCE HALL, Jack Woodson, 1 year	45.00	60.00
1992	CHRISTMAS IN SAN FRANCISCO, Jack Woodson, 1 year	47.50	RI
1993	COMING HOME FOR CHRISTMAS, Jack Woodson, 1 year	47.50	RI
1994	CHRISTMAS EVE IN ALASKA, Jack Woodson, 1 year	47.50	RI

Christmas in America Anniversary Plate

1991	CHRISTMAS EVE IN WILLIAMSBURG, Jack Woodson, 1 year .	69.50	NR

Composers of Classical Music

1979	BEETHOVEN, 1 year	37.50	NR
1980	BACH, 1 year	37.50	NR
1981	BRAHMS, 1 year	37.50	NR
1982	CHOPIN, 1 year	37.50	NR
1983	HAYDN, 1 year	37.50	NR
1984	EDVARD GRIEG	37.50	NR

Gentle Love

1985	JOANNA AND JON, A. Heesen Cooper, 9,500	45.00	NR
1985	ALEXANDRA AND AMY, A. Heesen Cooper, 9,500	45.00	NR
1985	INGRID AND LISA, A. Heesen Cooper, 9,500	45.00	NR
1985	ELIZABETH AND DAVID, A. Heesen Cooper, 9,500	45.00	NR

Hans Christian Andersen (Ghent Collection)

1979	THUMBELINA, 7,500	42.50	NR
1979	PRINCESS AND THE PEA, 7,500	42.50	NR
1979	WILD SWANS, 7,500	42.50	NR
1980	EMPEROR'S NEW CLOTHES, 7,500	42.50	NR
1980	LITTLE MERMAID, 7,500	42.50	NR
1980	NIGHTINGALE, 7,500	42.50	NR

		Issue Price	Current Value

Heritage

1976	NORSEMAN, 5,000	30.00	NR
1977	NAVIGATORS, 5,000	30.00	NR
1978	DISCOVERY, 5,000	39.50	NR
1979	EXPLORATION, 5,000	39.50	NR
1980	HELMSMAN, 5,000	45.00	NR

Jubilee Five–Year Christmas

1915	FROZEN WINDOW, Franz August Hallin, 1 year	3.00	155.00
1920	CHURCH BELLS, Fanny Garde, 1 year	4.00	65.00
1925	DOG OUTSIDE WINDOW, Peter Dahl Jensen, 1 year	5.00	130.00
1930	THE OLD ORGANIST, C. Ersgaard, 1 year	5.00	170.00
1935	LITTLE MATCH GIRL, E. Plockross, 1 year	6.00	725.00
1940	THREE WISE MEN, S. Sabra, 1 year	10.00	1,850.00
1945	ROYAL GUARD AMALIENBORG CASTLE, T. Larsen, 1 year	10.00	175.00
1950	ESKIMOS, Achton Friis, 1 year	15.00	190.00
1955	DYBBOL MILL, Margarethe Hyldahl, 1 year	20.00	200.00
1960	KRONBORG CASTLE, Margarethe Hyldahl, 1 year	25.00	110.00
1965	CHURCHGOERS, Achton Friis, 1 year	25.00	55.00
1970	AMALIENBORG CASTLE, T. Larsen, 1 year	30.00	NR
1975	HORSES ENJOYING MEAL, Ove Larsen, 1 year	40.00	50.00
1980	HAPPINESS OVER YULE TREE, Aarestrup, 1 year	60.00	75.00
1985	LIFEBOAT AT WORK, Hans Flugenring, 1 year	65.00	95.00
1990	THE ROYAL YACHT DANNEBROG, Kjeld Bonfils, 1 year	95.00	NR

Moments of Truth

1984	HOME IS BEST, Kurt Ard, limited	29.50	BR
1984	THE ROAD TO VIRTUOSITY, Kurt Ard, limited	29.50	BR
1985	FIRST THINGS FIRST, Kurt Ard, limited	29.50	BR
1985	UNFAIR COMPETITION, Kurt Ard, limited	29.50	BR
1986	BORED SICK, Kurt Ard, limited	29.50	BR
1986	FIRST CRUSH, Kurt Ard, limited	29.50	BR

Mother's Day

1969	DOGS AND PUPPIES, Henry Thelander, 1 year	9.75	390.00
1970	BIRD AND CHICKS, Henry Thelander, 1 year	10.00	45.00
1971	CAT AND KITTEN, Henry Thelander, 1 year	11.00	NR
1972	MARE AND FOAL, Henry Thelander, 1 year	12.00	NR
1973	DUCK AND DUCKLINGS, Henry Thelander, 1 year	13.00	25.00
1974	BEAR AND CUBS, Henry Thelander, 1 year	16.50	NR
1975	DOE AND FAWNS, Henry Thelander, 1 year	19.50	BR
1976	SWAN FAMILY, Henry Thelander, 1 year	22.50	NR
1977	SQUIRREL AND YOUNG, Henry Thelander, 1 year	23.50	NR
1978	HERON, Henry Thelander, 1 year	24.50	NR

		Issue Price	Current Value
1979	FOX AND CUBS, Henry Thelander, 1 year	27.50	NR
1980	WOODPECKER AND YOUNG, Henry Thelander, 1 year	29.50	NR
1981	HARE AND YOUNG, Henry Thelander, 1 year	36.50	NR
1982	LIONESS AND CUBS, Henry Thelander, 1 year	39.50	BR
1983	RACCOON AND YOUNG, Henry Thelander, 1 year	39.50	BR
1984	STORK AND NESTLINGS, Henry Thelander, 1 year	39.50	NR
1985	BEAR AND CUBS, Henry Thelander, 1 year	39.50	BR
1986	ELEPHANT WITH CALF, Henry Thelander, 1 year	39.50	NR
1987	SHEEP WITH LAMBS, Henry Thelander, 1 year	42.50	85.00
1988	CRESTED PLOVER AND YOUNG, Henry Thelander, 1 year	47.50	60.00
1988	LAPWING MOTHER WITH CHICKS, Henry Thelander, 1 year	49.50	55.00
1989	COW WITH CALF, Henry Thelander, 1 year	49.50	65.00
1990	HEN WITH CHICKS, L. Jensen, 1 year	49.50	55.00
1991	NANNY GOAT AND HER TWO FRISKY KIDS, L. Jensen, 1 year	54.50	65.00
1992	PANDA WITH CUBS, L. Jensen, 1 year	59.50	RI
1993	ST. BERNARD DOG AND PUPPIES, A. Therkelsen, 1 year	59.50	RI
1994	CAT AND HER KITTENS	59.50	RI
1995	HEDGEHOG WITH YOUNG	59.50	RI

Joanna and Jon
Photo courtesy of *Collectors News*

Raccoon and Young

Mother's Day Five – Year Jubilee

1979	DOG AND PUPPIES, Henry Thelander, 1 year	55.00	NR
1984	SWAN WITH CYGNETS, Henry Thelander, 1 year	65.00	NR

Olympic Games

1972	OLYMPIAD – MUNICH, 1 year	20.00	NR
1976	OLYMPIC MONTREAL, 1 year	29.50	NR
1980	MOSCOW BY NIGHT, 1 year	43.00	NR

		Issue Price	Current Value

Santa Claus Collection

1989	SANTA'S WORKSHOP, Hans H. Hansen, 1 year	59.50	70.00
1990	SANTA'S SLEIGH, Hans H. Hansen, 1 year	59.50	65.00
1991	SANTA'S JOURNEY, Hans H. Hansen, 1 year............	69.50	75.00
1992	SANTA'S ARRIVAL, Hans H. Hansen, 1 year	74.50	RI
1993	SANTA'S GIFTS, Hans H. Hansen, 1 year	74.50	RI

Seasons Remembered

1983	THE WILDFLOWERS OF SUMMER, Verner Munch, 10,000	35.00	NR
1983	AUTUMN SHOWERS, Verner Munch, 10,000	35.00	NR
1983	THE PROMISE OF SPRING, Verner Munch, 10,000	35.00	NR
1983	THE WINTER OF THE SNOWMAN, Verner Munch, 10,000	35.00	NR
1984	THE WILDFLOWERS OF SUMMER, Verner Munch, 7,500	35.00	NR
1984	AUTUMN SHOWERS, Verner Munch, 7,500	35.00	NR
1984	THE PROMISE OF SPRING, Verner Munch, 7,500	35.00	NR
1984	THE WINTER OF THE SNOWMAN, Verner Munch, 7,500 .	35.00	NR

Statue of Liberty

| 1986 | STATUE OF LIBERTY, 10,000 .... | 60.00 | NR |

Summer at Skagen

| 1986 | SUMMER EVENING, limited .... | 34.50 | NR |
| 1987 | LUNCHEON AT KROYER'S, limited .... | 34.50 | NR |

Windjammers

| 1980 | DANMARK, James Mitchell, 10,000 .... | 95.00 | NR |

Left: Christian Radich; right: Amerigo Vespucci

		Issue Price	Current Value
1980	EAGLE, James Mitcholl, 10,000	95.00	NR
1981	GLADAN, James Mitchell, 10,000	95.00	NR
1981	GORDON/FOCK, James Mitchell, 10,000	95.00	NR
1982	AMERIGO VESPUCCI, James Mitchell, 10,000	95.00	NR
1982	CHRISTIAN RADICH, James Mitchell, 10,000	95.00	NR

Young Adventurer Plate

1990	THE LITTLE VIKING, Sven Vestergaard, 1 year	52.50	60.00

Single Issues

1978	MADONNA, 10,000	45.00	NR
1978	SEAGULL, 7,500	75.00	NR
1980	VIKING, 10,000	65.00	NR

BLUE DELFT NETHERLANDS

Christmas

1970	DRAWBRIDGE NEAR BINNEHOF, 1 year	12.00	25.00
1971	ST. LAUREN'S CHURCH, 1 year	12.00	25.00
1972	CHURCH AT BIERKADE, 1 year	12.00	NR
1973	ST. JAN'S CHURCH, 1 year	12.00	NR
1974	DINGERADEEL, 1 year	13.00	NR
1975	MAASSLUIS, 1 year	13.00	NR
1976	MONTELBAANSTOWFR, 1 year	15.00	NR
1977	HARBOUR TOWER OF HOORN, 1 year	19.50	NR
1978	BINNENPOORT GATE, 1 year	21.00	NR

Christmas Story

1982	THE ANGEL GABRIEL FOREBODING MARIA	35.00	NR

Father's Day

1971	FRANCESCO LANA'S AIRSHIP, 1 year	12.00	30.00
1972	DR. JONATHAN'S BALLOON, 1 year	12.00	30.00

Mother's Day

1971	MOTHER AND DAUGHTER OF THE 1600s, 1 year	12.00	NR
1972	MOTHER AND DAUGHTER OF THE ISLE OF URK, 1 year	12.00	NR
1973	REMBRANDT'S MOTHER, 1 year	12.00	NR

Single Issues

1972	OLYMPIAD	12.00	NR
1972	APOLLO II	6.00	NR

BLUE RIVER MILL UNITED STATES

Once Upon a Barn

		Issue Price	Current Value
1986	MAIL POUCH BARN, Ray Day, 5,000	45.00	NR
1986	ROCK CITY BARN, Ray Day, 5,000	45.00	NR
1987	MERAMEC CAVERNS BARN, Ray Day, 5,000	45.00	NR
1987	COCA–COLA BARN, Ray Day, 5,000	45.00	NR

Coca–Cola Barn
Photo courtesy of *Collectors News*

BOEHM, LINDA

Egyptian Treasures of Tutankhamen

1977	THE HEADDRESS, 5,000	50.00	NR
1978	THE MUMMY COLLAR, 5,000	50.00	NR

BOEHM STUDIOS, EDWARD MARSHALL
GREAT BRITAIN

Award–Winning Roses

1979	PEACE ROSE, Boehm Studio Artists, 15,000	45.00	NR
1979	WHITE MASTERPIECE ROSE, Boehm Studio Artists, 15,000 NR		45.00
1979	TROPICANA ROSE, Boehm Studio Artists, 15,000	45.00	NR
1979	ELEGANCE ROSE, Boehm Studio Artists, 15,000	45.00	NR
1979	QUEEN ELIZABETH ROSE, Boehm Studio Artists, 15,000	45.00	NR
1979	ROYAL HIGHNESS ROSE, Boehm Studio Artists, 15,000 .	45.00	NR
1979	ANGEL FACE ROSE, Boehm Studio Artists, 15,000	45.00	NR
1979	MR. LINCOLN ROSE, Boehm Studio Artists, 15,000	45.00	NR

		Issue Price	Current Value

Banquet of Blossoms and Berries

1982	WINTER HOLIDAY BOUQUET, Boehm Studio Artists, 15,000 NR		62.50
1982	THANKSGIVING BOUQUET, Boehm Studio Artists, 15,000	62.50	NR
1982	SCHOOL DAYS BOUQUET, Boehm Studio Artists, 15,000	62.50	NR
1982	INDIAN SUMMER BOUQUET, Boehm Studio Artists, 15,000 NR		62.50
1982	MID–SUMMER BOUQUET, Boehm Studio Artists, 15,000	62.50	NR
1982	AUTUMN BOUQUET, Boehm Studio Artists, 15,000......	62.50	NR

Boehm Owl Collection

1980	BOREAL OWL, Boehm Studio Artists, 15,000...........	45.00	75.00
1980	SNOWY OWL, Boehm Studio Artists, 15,000	45.00	60.00
1980	BARN OWL, Boehm Studio Artists, 15,000	45.00	60.00
1980	SAW–WHET OWL, Boehm Studio Artists, 15,000	45.00	60.00
1980	GREAT HORNED OWL, Boehm Studio Artists, 15,000....	45.00	60.00
1980	SCREECH OWL, Boehm Studio Artists, 15,000	45.00	60.00
1980	SHORT–EARED OWL, Boehm Studio Artists, 15,000	45.00	60.00
1980	BARRED OWL, Boehm Studio Artists, 15,000	45.00	60.00

Butterflies of the World

| 1978 | MONARCH AND DAISY, 5,000 .... | 62.00 | NR |
| 1978 | RED ADMIRAL AND THISTLE, 5,000 .... | 62.00 | NR |

Butterfly

1975	BLUE MOUNTAIN SWALLOWTAILS, 100...............	450.00	NR
1975	JEZABELS, 100......................................	450.00	NR
1976	COMMA WITH LOOPS, 100	450.00	NR
1976	AFRICAN BUTTERFLIES, 100........................	450.00	NR
1976	SOLANDRAS MAXIMA, 100	450.00	NR

Egyptian Commemorative

| 1978 | TUTANKHAMEN, 5,000 .... | 125.00 | 170.00 |
| 1978 | TUTANKHAMEN, hand painted, 225 .... | 975.00 | NR |

European Birds

1973	SWALLOW, 4,319....................................	50.00	NR
1973	CHAFFINCH, 4,319...................................	50.00	NR
1973	COAL TIT, 4,319	50.00	NR
1973	TREE SPARROW, 4,319	50.00	NR
1973	KINGFISHER, 4,319	50.00	NR
1973	GOLD CREST, 4,319.................................	50.00	NR
1973	BLUE TIT, 4,319	50.00	NR
1973	LINNET, 4,319......................................	50.00	NR

	Issue Price	Current Value

Fancy Fowl

1974	PAIR, 85	2,000.00	NR

Favorite Florals

1978	CLEMATIS, 2,500	58.00	NR
1978	RHODODENDRON, 2,500	58.00	NR
1979	BOEHM ORCHID, 2,500	58.00	NR
1979	YELLOW ROSE, 2,500	58.00	NR
1980	SPIDER ORCHID, 2,500	58.00	NR
1980	DAHLIA, 2,500	58.00	NR

Flower Series

1975	LILIES, 100	450.00	490.00
1975	PASSION FLOWERS, 100	450.00	490.00
1975	DOUBLE CLEMATIS, 100	450.00	490.00

Gamebirds of North America

1984	RING–NECKED PHEASANT, Boehm Studio Artists, 15,000	62.50	NR
1984	BOB–WHITE QUAIL, Boehm Studio Artists, 15,000	62.50	NR
1984	AMERICAN WOODCOCK, Boehm Studio Artists, 15,000	62.50	NR
1984	CALIFORNIA QUAIL, Boehm Studio Artists, 15,000	62.50	NR
1984	RUFFED GROUSE, Boehm Studio Artists, 15,000	62.50	NR
1984	WILD TURKEY, Boehm Studio Artists, 15,000	62.50	NR
1984	WILLOW PARTRIDGE, Boehm Studio Artists, 15,000	62.50	NR
1984	PRAIRIE GROUSE, Boehm Studio Artists, 15,000	62.50	NR

Hard Fruits

1975	PLUMS, 100	450.00	NR
1975	PEARS, 100	450.00	NR
1975	PEACHES, 100	450.00	NR
1975	APPLES, 100	450.00	NR

Honor America

1974	AMERICAN BALD EAGLE, 12,000	85.00	NR

Hummingbird Collection

1980	CALLIOPE, Boehm Studio Artists, 15,000	62.50	75.00
1980	BROADBILLED, Boehm Studio Artists, 15,000	62.50	NR
1980	BROADTAIL, Boehm Studio Artists, 15,000	62.50	70.00
1980	RUFOUS FLAME BEARER, Boehm Studio Artists, 15,000	62.50	70.00
1980	STREAMERTAIL, Boehm Studio Artists, 15,000	62.50	NR
1980	BLUE THROATED, Boehm Studio Artists, 15,000	62.50	70.00
1980	CRIMSON TOPAZ, Boehm Studio Artists, 15,000	62.50	NR
1980	BRAZILIAN RUBY, Boehm Studio Artists, 15,000	62.50	70.00

	Issue Price	Current Value

Judaic Commemorative

1979 BLUE, 1,500	45.00	NR
1978 ROSE/GOLD, 75	555.00	NR

Life's Best Wishes (The Hamilton Collection)

1982 LONGEVITY, Boehm Studio Artists	75.00	NR
1982 HAPPINESS, Boehm Studio Artists	75.00	NR
1982 FERTILITY, Boehm Studio Artists	75.00	NR
1982 PROSPERITY, Boehm Studio Artists	75.00	NR

Miniature Roses (The Hamilton Collection)

1982 TOY CLOWN, Boehm Studio Artists, 28 days	39.50	45.00
1982 RISE N' SHINE, Boehm Studio Artists, 28 days	39.50	45.00
1982 CUDDLES, Boehm Studio Artists, 28 days	39.50	45.00
1982 PUPPY LOVE, Boehm Studio Artists, 28 days	39.50	45.00

Musical Maidens of the Imperial Dynasty

1984 THE FLUTE, 15,000	65.00	NR

Oriental Birds

1975 BLUEBACKED FAIRY BLUEBIRDS, 100	400.00	NR
1975 AZURE–WINGED MAGPIES, 100	400.00	NR
1976 GOLDEN–FRONTED LEAFBIRD, 100	400.00	NR
1976 GOLDEN–THROATED BARBET, 100	400.00	NR

Panda

1982 PANDA, HARMONY, 5,000	65.00	NR
1982 PANDA, PEACE, 5,000	65.00	NR

Roses of Excellence

1981 THE LOVE ROSE, Boehm Studio Artists, 1 year	62.00	85.00
1982 WHITE LIGHTNIN', Boehm Studio Artists, 1 year	62.00	70.00
1983 BRANDY, Boehm Studio Artists, 1 year	62.00	NR
1983 SUN FLARE, Boehm Studio Artists, 1 year	62.00	NR

Seashells

1975 VIOLET SPIDER CONCH, 100	450.00	NR
1975 ROOSTER TAIL CONCH, 100	450.00	NR
1976 ORANGE SPIDER CONCH, 100	450.00	NR
1976 CHERAGRA SPIDER CONCH, 100	450.00	NR

Soft Fruits

1975 LOGANBERRIES, 100	450.00	NR

		Issue Price	Current Value
1976	CHERRIES, 100	450.00	NR
1976	STRAWBERRIES, 100	450.00	NR
1976	GRAPES, 100	450.00	NR

Tribute to Award–Winning Roses

1983	IRISH GOLD, Boehm Studio Artists, 15,000	62.50	NR
1983	HANDEL, Boehm Studio Artists, 15,000	62.50	NR
1983	QUEEN ELIZABETH, Boehm Studio Artists, 15,000	62.50	NR
1983	ELIZABETH OF GLAMIS, Boehm Studio Artists, 15,000	62.50	NR
1983	ICEBERG, Boehm Studio Artists, 15,000	62.50	NR
1983	MOUNTBATTEN, Boehm Studio Artists, 15,000	62.50	NR
1983	SILVER JUBILEE, Boehm Studio Artists, 15,000	62.50	NR
1983	PEACE, Boehm Studio Artists, 15,000	62.50	NR

Tribute to Ballet (The Hamilton Collection)

1982	NUTCRACKER, Boehm Studio Artists, 15,000	62.50	NR
1982	FIREBIRD, Boehm Studio Artists, 15,000	62.50	NR
1982	DON QUIXOTE, Boehm Studio Artists, 15,000	62.50	NR
1982	LA BAYADERE, Boehm Studio Artists, 15,000	62.50	NR

Water Birds

1981	CANADA GEESE, Boehm Studio Artists, 15,000	62.50	NR
1981	WOOD DUCK, Boehm Studio Artists, 15,000	62.50	NR
1981	HOODED MERGANSER, Boehm Studio Artists, 15,000	62.50	NR
1981	ROSS'S GEESE, Boehm Studio Artists, 15,000	62.50	NR
1981	COMMON MALLARD, Boehm Studio Artists, 15,000	62.50	NR
1981	CANVAS BACK, Boehm Studio Artists, 15,000	62.50	NR
1981	GREEN–WINGED TEAL, Boehm Studio Artists, 15,000	62.50	NR
1981	AMERICAN PINTAIL, Boehm Studio Artists, 15,000	62.50	NR

Woodland Birds of America

1984	DOWNY WOODPECKER WITH FLOWERING CHERRY BLOSSOMS 75.00		NR

BOHEMIA CZECHOSLOVAKIA

Mother's Day

1974	MOTHER'S DAY, 500	130.00	155.00
1975	MOTHER'S DAY, 500	140.00	160.00
1976	MOTHER'S DAY, 500	150.00	160.00

BONITA MEXICO

Mother's Day	Issue Price	Current Value
1972 MOTHER WITH BABY, Raul Anguiano, 4,000	76.00	05.00

BORSATO

Masterpiece Series

			Issue Price	Current Value
1978	SERENITY, 5,000		75.00	BR
1978	TITIAN, 5,000		75.00	BR

Plaques

1973	GOLDEN YEARS, 750	1,450.00
	1,750.00	
1974	TENDER MUSINGS, 250	1,650.00
	1,900.00	

BOYS TOWN UNITED STATES

Single Issue

1986	REV. EDWARD J. FLANAGAN, FOUNDER OF BOYS TOWN, Michael Engstrom, 5,000	32.00	NR

BRADFORD EXCHANGE RUSSIA

Nutcracker

1993	MARIE'S MAGICAL GIFT	39.87	RI
1993	DANCE OF SUGAR PLUM FAIRY	39.87	RI
1994	WALTZ OF THE FLOWERS	39.87	RI
1994	BATTLE WITH THE MICE KING	39.87	RI

BRADFORD EXCHANGE UNITED STATES
(See also W. S. George)

A Christmas Carol

1993	GOD BLESS US EVERYONE	29.90	RI
1993	GHOST OF CHRISTMAS PRESENT	29.90	RI
1994	A MERRY CHRISTMAS TO ALL	29.90	RI
1994	A VISIT FROM MARLEY'S GHOST	29.90	RI
1994	REMEMBERING CHRISTMAS PAST	29.90	RI
1994	A SPIRIT'S WARNING	29.90	RI
1994	THE TRUE SPIRIT OF CHRISTMAS	29.90	RI
1994	A MERRY CHRISTMAS, BOB	29.90	RI

		Issue Price	Current Value

Baseball Record Breakers
| 1996 | CAL RIPKEN, Jason Walker, 95 days, 8⅛" | 29.95 | RI |

Charles Wysocki's Peppercricket Grove
| 1993 | PEPPERCRICKET FARMS, Charles Wysocki, 95 days | 24.90 | RI |

Cherished Traditions
| 1995 | THE WEDDING RING, Mary Ann Lasher, 95 days, 7" | 29.90 | RI |

Chosen Messengers
1993	THE PATHFINDERS	29.90	RI
1993	THE OVERSEERS	29.90	RI
1994	THE PROVIDERS	32.90	RI
1994	THE SURVEYORS	32.90	RI

Christmas Memories
1993	WINTER'S TALE	29.90	RI
1993	FINISHING TOUCHES	29.90	RI
1994	WELCOME TO OUR HOME	29.90	RI
1994	A CHRISTMAS CELEBRATION	29.90	RI

Classic Cars
1993	1957 CORVETTE	54.90	RI
1993	1956 T–BIRD	54.90	RI
1994	1957 BEL AIR	54.90	RI
1994	1965 MUSTANG	54.90	RI

Commemorating the King
| 1993 | ROCK AND ROLL LEGEND, M. Stutzman, 95 days | 29.75 | RI |

Disney's Musical Memories
| 1995 | THE FAIREST ONE OF ALL, Walt Disney Studios, 95 days, 7½" | 29.90 | RI |

Dog Days
1993	SWEET DREAMS	29.90	RI
1993	PIER GROUP	29.90	RI
1993	WAGON TRAIN	32.90	RI
1994	FIRST FLUSH	32.90	RI
1994	LITTLE RASCALS	32.90	RI
1994	WHERE'D HE GO?	32.90	RI

Family Circles
| 1993 | GREAT GRAY OWL FAMILY | 29.90 | RI |
| 1993 | GREAT HORNED OWL FAMILY | 29.90 | RI |

		Issue Price	Current Value
1993	WINTER LULLABY	29.90	RI
1994	BARRED OWL FAMILY..........................	29.90	RI
1994	SPOTTED OWL FAMILY..........................	29.90	RI
1994	HEAVENLY SLUMBER	29.90	RI
1994	SWEET EMBRACE	32.90	RI
1994	WOODLAND DREAMS..........................	32.90	RI
1994	SNOWY SILENCE	32.90	RI
1994	DREAMY WHISPERS..........................	32.90	RI

Footsteps of the Brave

1993	AT JOURNEY'S END..........................	29.90	RI
1993	AT STORM'S PASSAGE, 95 days	24.90	RI

Forever Glamorous Barbie

1995	ENCHANTED EVENING, 1 year, 8"	49.90	RI

Great Moments in Baseball

1993	JOE DIMAGGIO: THE STREAK, S. Gardner, 95 days	29.90	RI

Heart to Heart

1995	THINKING OF YOU, Raphael, 95 days, heart shaped, 6" h	29.90	RI

Thinking of You

Heirloom Memories

1993	PORCELAIN TREASURES	29.90	RI
1994	RHYTHMS IN LACE	29.90	RI
1994	PINK LEMONADE ROSES	29.90	RI
1994	VICTORIAN ROMANCE	29.90	RI
1994	TEA TIME TULIPS	29.90	RI
1994	TOUCH OF THE IRISH	29.90	RI

Hideaway Lake

1993	RUSTY'S RETREAT	34.90	RI
1993	FISHING FOR DREAMS	34.90	RI

Cal Ripken

The Wedding Ring

The Fairest One of All

Enchanted Evening

Garden Delights

Sultry Yet Regal

Catch a Falling Star

The Buck

Hope's Cottage

		Issue Price	Current Value
1994	SUNSET CABIN	34.90	RI
1994	ECHOES OF MORNING	34.90	RI

Keepsakes of the Heart

1993	FOREVER FRIENDS	29.90	RI
1993	AFTERNOON TEA	29.90	RI
1993	RIDING COMPANIONS	29.90	RI
1994	SENTIMENTAL SWEETHEARTS	29.90	RI

Kingdom of the Unicorn

1993	THE MAGIC BEGINS	29.90	RI
1993	IN CRYSTAL WATERS	29.90	RI
1993	CHASING A DREAM	29.90	RI
1994	THE FOUNTAIN OF YOUTH	29.90	RI

Lena Liu's Country Accents

1995	GARDEN DELIGHTS, Lena Liu, 95 days, oval, 8½"	29.95	RI

Little Bandits

1993	HANDLE WITH CARE	29.90	RI
1993	ALL TIED UP	29.90	RI
1993	EVERYTHING'S COMING UP DAISIES	32.90	RI
1993	OUT OF HAND	32.90	RI
1994	PUPSICLES	32.90	RI
1994	UNEXPECTED GUESTS	32.90	RI

Marilyn: The Golden Collection

1995	SULTRY YET REGAL, Michael Deas, 95 days, 8⅛"	29.95	RI

Me and My Shadow

1994	EASTER PARADE	29.90	RI
1994	A GOLDEN MOMENT	29.90	RI
1994	PERFECT TIMING	29.90	RI
1994	GIDDIYAP	29.90	RI

Musical Moments from the Wizard of Oz

1993	OVER THE RAINBOW, K. Milnazik, 95 days	29.90	RI

Mysterious Case of Fowl Play

1993	INSPECTOR CLAWSEAU	29.90	RI
1994	KOOL CAT	29.90	RI
1994	SNEAKERS AND HIGH–TOP	29.90	RI
1994	TUXEDO	29.90	RI

		Issue Price	Current Value

Nature's Nobility

| 1996 | THE BUCK, < 1 year, 8¼" .... | 39.95 | RI |

New Horizons

1993	BUILDING FOR A NEW GENERATION	29.90	RI
1994	THE POWER OF GOLD	29.90	RI
1994	WINGS OF SNOWY GRANDEUR	32.90	RI
1994	MASTER OF THE CHASE	32.90	RI
1995	COASTAL DOMAIN	32.90	RI
1995	MAJESTIC WINGS	32.90	RI

Nosy Neighbors

| 1995 | CAT NAP, Persis Clayton Weirs, 95 days, 8⅛" .... | 29.90 | RI |

Notorious Disney Villains

1993	THE EVIL QUEEN	29.90	RI
1994	MALEFICENT	29.90	RI
1994	URSELLA	29.90	RI
1994	CRUELLA DE VIL	29.90	RI

Remembering Elvis

| 1995 | THE KING, Nate Giorgio, 95 days, 8⅛" .... | 29.90 | RI |

CatNap

The King

Sacred Circle

| 1993 | BEFORE THE HUNT .... | 29.90 | RI |
| 1993 | SPIRITUAL GUARDIAN .... | 29.90 | RI |

		Issue Price	Current Value
1993	GHOST DANCE	32.90	RI
1994	DEER DANCE	32.90	RI
1994	WOLF DANCE	32.90	RI
1994	PAINTED HORSE	34.90	RI
1994	TRANSFORMATION DANCE	34.90	RI
1994	ELK DANCE	34.90	RI

Sovereigns of the Wild

1993	THE SNOW QUEEN	29.90	RI
1994	LET US SURVIVE	29.90	RI
1994	COOL CATS	29.90	RI
1994	SIBERIAN SNOW TIGERS	29.90	RI
1994	AFRICAN EVENING	29.90	RI
1994	SOVEREIGNS OF THE WILD	29.90	RI

Superstars of Country Music

1993	DOLLY PARTON: ALWAYS LOVE YOU	29.90	RI
1993	KENNY ROGERS: SWEET MUSIC MAN	29.90	RI
1994	BARBARA MANDRELL	32.90	RI
1994	GLEN CAMPBELL: RHINESTONE COWBOY	32.90	RI

Teddy Bear Dreams

1995	CATCH A FALLING STAR, Donna Parker, < 1 year, oval, 7³/₈" RI		49.95

Thomas Kinkade's Scenes of Serenity

1996	HOPE'S COTTAGE, Thomas Kinkade, 95 days, 8¹/₂"	29.95	RI

Thundering Waters

1994	NIAGARA FALLS	34.90	RI
1994	LOWER FALLS, YELLOWSTONE	34.90	RI
1994	BRIDAL VEIL FALLS	34.90	RI
1995	HAVISU FALLS	34.90	RI

Trains of the Great West

1993	MOONLIT JOURNEY	29.90	RI
1993	MOUNTAIN HIDEAWAY	29.90	RI
1993	EARLY MORNING ARRIVAL	29.90	RI
1994	THE SNOWY PASS	29.90	RI

Untamed Spirits

1993	WILD HEARTS	29.90	RI
1994	BREAKAWAY	29.90	RI
1994	FOREVER FREE	29.90	RI

				Issue Price	Current Value
1994	DISTANT THUNDER			29.90	RI

Vanishing Paradises

		Issue Price	Current Value
1993	THE RAINFOREST	29.90	RI
1994	THE PANDA'S WORLD	29.90	RI
1994	SPLENDORS OF INDIA	29.90	RI
1994	AN AFRICAN SAFARI	29.90	RI

World of the Eagle

		Issue Price	Current Value
1993	SENTINEL OF THE NIGHT	29.90	RI
1994	SILENT GUARD	29.90	RI
1994	NIGHT FLYER	32.90	RI
1994	MIDNIGHT DUTY	32.90	RI

BRANTWOOD COLLECTION UNITED STATES

Howe Christmas

		Issue Price	Current Value
1978	VISIT FROM SANTA, 1 year	45.00	NR

John Falter Christmas

		Issue Price	Current Value
1979	CHRISTMAS MORNING, John Falter, 5,000	25.50	NR

Little Clowns

		Issue Price	Current Value
1979	GOING TO CIRCUS, 5,000	29.50	NR

Marien Carlsen Mother's Day

		Issue Price	Current Value
1978	JENNIFER AND JENNY FUR, 1 year	45.00	NR
1979	FOOTBALL BROTHERS, 5,000	45.00	NR

Rockwell Mother's Day

		Issue Price	Current Value
1979	HOMECOMING, 20,000	39.50	NR

Single Issue

		Issue Price	Current Value
1978	TRIBUTE TO ROCKWELL, 1 year	35.00	NR

BRAYMER HALL UNITED STATES

American Folk Art

		Issue Price	Current Value
1982	SPRING CELEBRATION, Fred Wallin, 10,000	24.50	NR
1982	SUMMER BOUNTY, Fred Wallin, 10,000	24.50	NR

Childhood Sonatas

		Issue Price	Current Value
1981	SERENADE, Frank Palmieri, 15,000	28.50	NR
1982	PRELUDE, Frank Palmieri, 15,000	28.50	NR
1983	CAPRICE, Frank Palmieri, 15,000	28.50	NR

Yesterday Dreams

1983	SWING QUARTET, Jack Appleton, 5,000	50.00	NR
1984	SLEIGH BELLES, Jack Appleton, 5,000	50.00	NR

Single Issue

1982	HOW DO I LOVE THEE?, Rob Sauber, 19,500	39.95	NR

Swing Quartet
Photo courtesy of *Collectors News*

BRENTWOOD FINE ARTS UNITED STATES

Nostalgic Memories

1984	FIRST GAME, Marilyn Zapp, 12,500	39.50	NR

BRIANT, PAUL AND SONS UNITED STATES

Christmas

1971	FRUITS OF SPIRIT, 350	125.00	BR
1972	LABOUR OF LOVE, 700	100.00	NR
1973	ANNUNCIATION	100.00	NR

Easter

1972	THE LAST SACRIFICE, 500	85.00	NR

Seven Sacraments

1982	THE GIFT OF THE SPIRIT, Terry Clark, 2,000	110.00	NR

BRIARCREST UNITED STATES

Toys from the Attic

		Issue Price	Current Value
1302	THIS OLE BEAR CHAUNCEY JAMES, James Tuck, 10 days	45.00	NR

BRIMARK LTD. UNITED STATES

Yetta's Holidays

1986	CHRISTMAS BLOCKS, Carol–Lynn Rossel Waugh	29.50	NR

BRINDLE FINE ARTS UNITED STATES

Expressions

1979	QUIET EYES, Claude Hulce, 3,000	60.00	NR

Fantasy in Motion

1978	LITTLE BLUE HORSE, Lenore Béran, 3,000	75.00	NR
1979	HORSE OF A DIFFERENT COLOR, Lenore Béran, 3,000 ..	75.00	NR

Lenore Béran Special

1980	HOMAGE, Lenore Béran, 2,500	125.00	NR

Moods of the Orient

1978	SOFTLY, THE SUN SETS, Lenore Béran, 4,000	75.00	NR
1980	TRANQUIL MORN, Lenore Béran, 3,000	75.00	NR

Those Precious Years

1980	LITTLE CURT AND FRIEND, 3,000	60.00	NR

BYDGO

Christmas

1969	SHEPHERDESS AND SHEEP, 5,000	10.00	NR
1970	CLUMSY HANS, 5,000	10.00	NR
1971	THE FLYING TRUNK, 5,000	10.00	NR
1972	CHINESE NIGHTINGALE, 5,000	10.00	NR

BYLINY PORCELAIN RUSSIA

Flights of Fancy: Ornamental Art of Old Russia

1991	ENCHANTMENT	29.87	NR

		Issue Price	Current Value
1991	RHAPSODY	29.87	NR
1991	SPLENDOR	32.87	NR
1991	RAPTURE	32.87	NR
1991	FANTASIE	32.87	40.00
1991	REVERIE	32.87	60.00

Jewels of the Golden Ring

		Issue Price	Current Value
1990	ST. BASIL'S, MOSCOW	29.87	NR
1991	TRINITY MONASTERY, ZAGORSK	29.87	NR
1991	ROSTOV THE GREAT	32.87	NR
1991	NIKITSKY MONASTERY	32.87	40.00
1991	BORIS AND GLEB MONASTERY	32.87	45.00
1991	YAROSLAVI KREMLIN	34.87	45.00
1991	SUZDAL, PEARL OF THE GOLDEN RING	34.87	75.00
1991	THE GOLDEN GATES OF VLADIMIR	34.87	40.00

Enchantment
Photo courtesy of *Collectors News*

St. Basil's, Moscow
Photo courtesy of *Collectors News*

Legend of the Scarlet Flower

		Issue Price	Current Value
1991	THE ENCHANTED GARDEN	29.87	NR
1991	THE VOICE OF KINDNESS	29.87	55.00
1992	THE SPIRIT OF LOVE	29.87	RI
1992	THE SCARLET FLOWER	32.87	RI
1992	THE MAGIC RING	32.87	RI
1992	MERCHANT'S FAREWELL	32.87	RI

Legend of Tsar Saltan

		Issue Price	Current Value
1991	THE ARRIVAL OF TSAR SALTAN	39.87	NR
1991	THE MAGIC LAND OF PRINCE GUIDON	39.87	60.00

		Issue Price	Current Value
1991	THE SWAN PRINCESS	39.87	60.00
1991	THE MAGIC SQUIRREL	39.87	80.00

Russian Fairy Tale Princesses

1992	LUDMILLA	35.87	RI
1992	THE SNOWMAIDEN	35.87	RI
1992	SLEEPING BEAUTY	35.87	RI
1992	VASILISA THE BEAUTIFUL	35.87	RI

Russian Seasons

1992	WINTER MAJESTY	29.87	RI
1992	SPRINGTIME SPLENDOR	29.87	RI
1992	SUMMERTIME SERENADE	32.87	RI
1992	AUTUMN FANTASIE	32.87	RI
1992	WINTER IDYLL	32.87	RI
1993	SPRINGTIME REJOICE	34.87	RI
1993	SUMMERTIME BOUNTY	34.87	RI
1993	AN AUTUMN MEDLEY	34.87	RI

Tale of Father Frost

1992	FOR ALL BOYS AND GIRLS	29.87	RI
1992	THROUGH FORESTS OF SNOW	29.87	RI
1992	TREE TRIMMING TIME	32.87	RI
1992	THE CIRCLE DANCE	32.87	RI
1993	A SNOWY PLAYLAND	32.87	RI
1993	ON THIS COLD AND WINTRY NIGHT	32.87	RI

Village Life of Russia

1990	A WINTER SLEIGH RIDE	35.87	NR
1990	BRINGING HOME THE HARVEST	35.87	NR

Bringing Home the Harvest
Photo courtesy of *Collectors News*

		Issue Price	Current Value
1991	A CELEBRATION OF FRIENDSHIP	38.87	NR
1991	A VILLAGE WEDDING	38.87	NR
1991	COUNTRY PEDDLER	38.87	NR
1991	TO THE SPRING FESTIVAL	40.87	NR
1991	THE MERRY MUSICIANS	40.87	50.00

CABOCHON — CONTEMPORARY ORIGINALS, INC.   UNITED STATES

Nancy Doyle's Candy Girls

1983	REBECCA, Nancy Doyle, 15,000	50.00	NR

CALIFORNIA PORCELAIN, INC. UNITED STATES

Best of Sascha

1979	FLOWER BOUQUET, Sascha Brastoff, 7,500	65.00	NR

Now Is the Moment

1984	BE STILL, Carolyn Blish, 12,500	35.00	NR

Seed of the People

1984	KEENAH, THE STRONG ONE, Carolyn Blish, 10,000	29.95	NR

Vanishing Animals

1979	ASIAN MONARCH, Gene Dieckhoner, 7,500	40.00	NR
1979	SNOW LEOPARDS, Gene Dieckhoner, 7,500	45.00	NR
1980	PANDAS, Gene Dieckhoner, 7,500	45.00	NR
1981	POLAR BEARS, Gene Dieckhoner, 7,500	50.00	NR

Single Issue

1983	KOALA, Gene Dieckhoner, 5,000	29.95	NR

CANADIAN COLLECTOR PLATES CANADA

Children of the Classics

1982	ANNE OF GREEN GABLES, Will Davies, 15,000	78.00	NR
1983	TOM SAWYER, Will Davies, 15,000	78.00	NR

Days of Innocence

1982	BUTTERFLIES, Will Davies, 15,000	78.00	NR
1983	HE LOVES ME, Will Davies, 15,000	78.00	NR

Discover Canada		Issue Price	Current Value
1979	SAWMILL–KINGS LANDING, James Koirotcad, 10,000 ..	98.00	350.00
1980	QUEBEC WINTER, Krieghoff, 10,000	125.00	150.00
1981	BEFORE THE BATH, Paul Peel, 10,000..................	125.00	NR
1982	THE GRIST MILL, DELTA, James Keirstead, 10,000	125.00	NR
1982	ANGLICAN CHURCH AT MAGNETAWAN, A. J. Casson, 10,000	125.00	NR
1983	MAJESTIC ROCKIES, 10,000...........................	125.00	NR
1983	HABITANTS DRIVING THE SLEIGH, 10,000	125.00	NR
1984	AUTUMN MEMORIES, 10,000	125.00	NR
1984	AFTER THE BATH, 10,000	125.00	NR

CAPO DI MONTE ITALY

Christmas

1972	CHERUBS, 500	55.00	92.00
1973	BELLS AND HOLLY, 500	55.00	NR
1974	CHRISTMAS, 1,000...................................	60.00	NR
1975	CHRISTMAS, 1,000...................................	60.00	NR
1976	CHRISTMAS, 250	65.00	NR

Mother's Day

1973	MOTHER'S DAY, 500..................................	55.00	68.00
1974	MOTHER'S DAY, 500..................................	60.00	68.00
1975	MOTHER'S DAY, 500..................................	60.00	68.00
1976	MOTHER'S DAY, 500..................................	65.00	NR

CARMEL COLLECTION UNITED STATES

Country Friends

1983	MEETING AT THE FENCE, Helen Rampel, 15,000	45.00	NR

Famous Parades

1983	MACY'S THANKSGIVING PARADE, Melanie Taylor Kent, 1 year	39.50	NR

First Performers

1983	DARLING DIANA, Elizabeth Maxwell, 19,500	39.50	NR

Joy of Christmas

1983	CHRISTMAS DELIGHT, Jerome Walczak, 19,500	39.50	NR

Memories of the Heart

1984	PETALS, Elizabeth Maxwell, 15,000....................	28.50	NR

CARSON MINT UNITED STATES

		Issue Price	Current Value
America Has Heart (B & J Art Designs)			
1980	MY HEART'S DESIRE, Jan Hagara, 1 year	24.50	135.00
1981	HEARTS AND FLOWERS, Jan Hagara, 1 year	24.50	40.00
1982	THE HEARTY SAILOR, Jan Hagara, 1 year	28.50	NR
1983	SHANNON'S SWEETHEART, Jan Hagara, 1 year	28.50	NR
Bear Feats			
1983	TEDDY BEAR PICNIC, Susan Anderson, 15,000	37.50	NR
1984	ON THE BEACH, Susan Anderson, 15,000	37.50	NR
Big Top			
1981	THE WHITE FACE, Edward J. Rohn, 60 days	28.50	NR
1982	THE TRAMP, Edward J. Rohn, 60 days	28.50	NR
Hollywood Squares			
1979	PETER MARSHALL, 100 days	28.50	NR
1980	GEORGE GOBEL, 100 days	28.50	NR
The Littlest			
1982	THE LITTLEST STOCKING, June Colbert, 12,500	29.50	NR
1983	LITTLEST SANTA, June Colbert, 12,500	29.50	NR
Magic Afternoons			
1980	ENCHANTED GARDEN, Jo Anne Mix, 5,000	39.50	NR
1981	THE DELIGHTFUL TEA PARTY, 5,000	39.50	NR
Moments in Time			
1979	FREEDOM FLIGHT, 5,000	55.00	NR
Nature's Children			
1982	CANDICE, Don Price, 12,500	29.50	NR
1983	CORY, Don Price, 12,500	29.50	NR
Old–Fashioned Mother's Day (B & J Art Designs)			
1979	DAISIES FROM MARY BETH, Jan Hagara, 1 year	38.00	80.00
1980	DAISIES FROM JIMMY, Jan Hagara, 1 year	37.50	80.00
1981	DAISIES FROM MEG, Jan Hagara, 1 year	37.50	NR
1982	DAISIES FOR MOMMIE, Jan Hagara, 1 year	37.50	NR
To Mom with Love			
1983	A BASKET OF LOVE, Cynthia Knapton, 15,000	37.50	NR

CARTIER FRANCE

Cathedral		Issue Price	Current Value
1972	CHARTRES CATHEDRAL, 12,500	50.00	68.00
1974	CHARTRES MILLOUS, 500	130.00	160.00

CASTLETON CHINA UNITED STATES

Aviation (American Historical)

1972	AMELIA EARHART, 3,500	40.00	62.00
1972	CHARLES LINDBERGH, 3,500	40.00	NR

Bicentennial (Shenango)

1972	A NEW DAWN, 7,600	60.00	NR
1972	TURNING POINT, 7,600	60.00	NR
1973	SILENT FOE, 7,600	60.00	NR
1973	THE STAR–SPANGLED BANNER, 7,600	60.00	NR
1973	U.S.S. CONSTITUTION, 7,600	60.00	NR
1974	ONE NATION, 7,600	60.00	NR
1974	WESTWARD HO, 7,600	60.00	NR

Natural History (American Historical)

1973	PAINTED LADY, 1,500	40.00	NR
1973	ROSEATE SPOONBILL, 1,500	40.00	NR

Single Issue

1976	GENERAL DOUGLAS MACARTHUR, 1,000	30.00	NR

CATALINA PORCELAIN UNITED STATES

Escalera's Christmas

1982	SPECIAL DELIVERY, Rudy Escalera, 19,500	32.50	NR

CERTIFIED RARITIES UNITED STATES

Indian Dancers

1979	EAGLE DANCER, Don Ruffin, 2,500	300.00	320.00
1980	HOOP DANCER, Don Ruffin, 2,500	300.00	320.00

Postal Artists

1978	COLIAS EURYDICE, Stanley Galli, 15,000	60.00	NR
1979	EUYPHYDRYAS PHAETON, Stanley Galli, 7,500	60.00	NR

Renaissance Masters

		Issue Price	Current Value
1978	ALBA MADONNA, 15,000	55.00	BR
1979	PIETA, 5,000	55.00	NR

CHILMARK UNITED STATES

Family Christmas

| 1978 | TRIMMING THE TREE, 10,000 | 65.00 | NR |

Holy Night

| 1979 | WISEMEN, 10,000 | 65.00 | NR |

In Appreciation

| 1978 | FLOWERS OF FIELD, 10,000 | 65.00 | NR |

Twelve Days of Christmas

| 1979 | A PARTRIDGE IN A PEAR TREE, R. Lamb, J. Nussbaum, 10,000 | 89.50 | NR |

CHINESE FINE ARTS CO., INC. UNITED STATES

Eight Immortals

| 1979 | LI T'IEH–KUAI — POVERTY, sgd and dated by sculptor, 300 | 175.00 | NR |

CHING–T'AI–LAN THE PEOPLES REPUBLIC OF CHINA

Winged Jewels: Chinese Cloisonné Birds

1991	AZURE WINGED MAGPIES	95.00	BR
1991	LONG–TAILED TITMOUSE	95.00	NR
1991	ROSY MINIVET	100.00	NR
1991	KINGFISHER	100.00	125.00
1992	ORIOLE	100.00	RI
1992	FLOWERPECKER	105.00	RI
1992	PEKING ROBIN	105.00	RI
1992	SHRIKE	105.00	RI

CHRISTIAN BELL PORCELAIN CANADA

Age of Steam

| 1981 | SYMPHONY IN STEAM, Ted Xaras, 15,000 | 65.00 | 200.00 |

		Issue Price	Current Value
1982	BRIEF ENCOUNTER, Ted Xaras, 15,000	65.00	80.00
1983	NO CONTEST, Ted Xaras, 15,000	65.00	115.00
1984	TIMBER COUNTY, Ted Xaras, 15,000	65.00	BR
1985	WHITE PASS IN YUKON, Ted Xaras, 15,000	65.00	NR

American Steam

1982	HIAWATHA, Ted Xaras, 15,000	65.00	NR
1983	HITTIN' THE DIAMOND, Ted Xaras, 15,000	65.00	NR
1984	MORNING AT THE DEPOT, Ted Xaras, 15,000	65.00	NR
1984	WINTER ON THE BOSTON & MAINE, Ted Xaras, 15,000 .	65.00	NR
1985	ON THE HORSESHOE CURVE, Ted Xaras, 15,000	65.00	NR

Copeland Remembers

1986	POSSESSION IS..., Eric Copeland	65.00	NR

Great Atlantic Liners

1987	R.M.S. QUEEN MARY, Ted Xaras	—	—

Last Spike Centennial (Two–Plate Series)

1986	SPIRAL TUNNEL, Ted Xaras, 7,500	135.00	145.00
1986	BIG HILL, Ted Xaras, 7,500	135.00	145.00

Men of the Rails

1982	ENGINEER, Ted Xaras, <1 year	39.50	NR
1983	PULLMAN PORTER, Ted Xaras, <1 year	39.50	NR
1983	CONDUCTOR, Ted Xaras, <1 year	39.50	NR
1983	NIGHT OPERATOR, Ted Xaras, <1 year	39.50	NR

Preserving a Way of Life

1980	MAKING WAY FOR CARS, 5,000	60.00	NR
1980	ATOP HAY WAGON, 5,000	60.00	NR
1982	SUGARBUSH, Peter Etril Snyder, hand numbered, 10,000	65.00	NR
1982	FISHING FOR REDFIN, Peter Etril Snyder, 10,000	65.00	NR
1982	WHEAT HARVEST, Peter Etril Snyder, 10,000	65.00	NR
1982	RETURNING FROM THE VILLAGE, Peter Etril Snyder, 10,000 ..	65.00	NR
1986	THE NEW HORSE, Peter Etril Snyder, 10,000	65.00	NR

Vanishing Africa

1983	THE SENTINEL, Douglas Manning, 15,000	75.00	NR

Wild North

1983	EMPEROR OF THE NORTH, Douglas Manning, 15,000	75.00	NR

CHRISTIAN FANTASY COLLECTIBLES UNITED STATES

Christian Fantasy

		Issue Price	Current Value
1985	THE LEGEND OF THE PRAYER BEAR I, Tim Hildebrandt, 5,100 .	50.00	NR
1986	THE LEGEND OF THE PRAYER BEAR II, Tim Hildebrandt, 5,100 .	50.00	NR
1987	THE LEGEND OF THE PRAYER BEAR III, Tim Hildebrandt, 5,100	50.00	NR

Fantasy Cookbook

1986	PICNIC IN THE WOODS, Tim Hildebrandt, 7,100	50.00	NR
1987	THE MAGICAL LAGOON, Tim Hildebrandt, 7,100	50.00	NR
1987	A DWARF CELEBRATION, Tim Hildebrandt, 7,100	50.00	NR
1987	THE WIZARD'S MAGICAL FEAST, Tim Hildebrandt, 7,100 .	50.00	NR
1987	A STEW POT, Tim Hildebrandt, 7,100	50.00	NR
1987	THE MERMAID'S HIDDEN WATERFALL, Tim Hildebrandt, 7,100	50.00	NR
1987	TINY CELEBRATION, Tim Hildebrandt, 7,100	50.00	NR
1987	THE ENCHANTED REALM OF ZIR, Tim Hildebrandt, 7,100	50.00	NR

Realms of Wonder I

1986	WIZARD'S GLADE, Tim Hildebrandt, 9,100	50.00	NR
1987	MERMAID'S GROTTO, Tim Hildebrandt, 9,100	50.00	NR
1987	ICE PALACE OF THE FAIRIES, Tim Hildebrandt, 9,100	50.00	NR
1987	MUSHROOM VILLAGE OF THE ELVES, Tim Hildebrandt, 9,100 .	50.00	NR
1987	FOREST OF THE UNICORN, Tim Hildebrandt, 9,100	50.00	NR
1987	THE ELVEN FORTRESS (PEGASUS), Tim Hildebrandt, 9,100	50.00	NR
1987	THE WATER NIXIE, Tim Hildebrandt, 9,100	50.00	NR
1987	DWARVES, Tim Hildebrandt, 9,100	50.00	NR

Realms of Wonder II

1987	WIZARD'S STEED, Tim Hildebrandt, 9,100	50.00	NR
1987	SEA LORD OF LAMURIA, Tim Hildebrandt, 9,100	50.00	NR
1987	COUNCIL OF THE ELVES, Tim Hildebrandt, 9,100	50.00	NR
1987	FAIRIES II, Tim Hildebrandt, 9,100	50.00	NR

Santa's Night Out

1986	SANTA DAYDREAMS, Tim Hildebrandt, 9,100	50.00	NR

CHRISTIAN SELTMANN GERMANY

Luekel's Idyllic Village Life

1986	BLACKSMITH	24.50	NR
1986	THE ARRIVAL OF THE STAGECOACH	24.50	BR
1986	STOP AT THE VILLAGE INN	27.50	BR
1986	IN THE FIELDS AT HARVEST TIME	27.50	NR
1987	ON THE WAY TO THE MARKET	27.50	NR
1987	AT THE VILLAGE FOUNTAIN	27.50	NR

		Issue Price	Current Value
1987	THE FISHERMAN	29.50	NR
1987	DAYTRIP IN THE SUMMERTIME	29.50	NR
1987	THE FARMER'S WEDDING	29.50	NR
1988	ANGLER'S PLEASURE	29.50	NR

Velvet Paws

1991	PLAYMATES	29.00	NR
1991	GYMNASTICS	29.00	40.00
1991	THE MISHAP	32.00	45.00
1992	FRIEND OR FOE?	32.00	RI
1992	UNEXPECTED VISIT	32.00	RI
1992	HIDE AND SEEK	34.00	RI
1992	WATER SPORTS	34.00	RI
1992	IN THE GARDEN	34.00	RI
1992	SWINGING EXERCISE	34.00	RI
1992	DOLL'S PRAM EXPRESS	36.00	RI
1992	PLAYING WITH SOAP BUBBLES	36.00	RI
1993	BIKE CHAMPIONS	36.00	RI
1993	CARNIVAL OF CATS	36.00	RI

CLARISSA'S CREATIONS

Single Issues

1990	LITTLE BALLERINA, C. Johnson, 14 days	48.00	NR
1994	MEMORIES, C. Johnson, 25,000	48.00	RI

CLEVELAND MINT UNITED STATES

Da Vinci Series

1972	LAST SUPPER, 5,000	150.00	BR

COLLECTOR'S TREASURY GREAT BRITAIN

Beauty of Polar Wildlife

1990	BABY SEALS	27.50	NR
1990	POLAR BEAR CUBS	27.50	NR
1991	THE EMPEROR PENGUINS	30.50	45.00
1991	ARCTIC FOX CUBS	30.50	NR
1991	ARCTIC HARE FAMILY	30.50	NR
1991	ARCTIC WOLF FAMILY	32.50	45.00
1991	DALL DHEEP	32.50	BR
1992	REINDEER YOUNG	32.50	RI

COLLECTOR'S WEEKLY UNITED STATES

American Series		Issue Price	Current Value
1971	MISS LIBERTY, 500	12.50	NR
1972	MISS LIBERTY, 900	12.50	NR
1973	EAGLE, 900	9.75	NR

CONTINENTAL MINT UNITED STATES

Tom Sawyer

1976	TAKING HIS MEDICINE, 5,000	60.00	NR
1977	PAINTING FENCE, 5,000	60.00	NR
1978	LOST IN CAVE, 5,000	60.00	NR
1979	SMOKING PIPE, 5,000	60.00	NR

Single Issue

1979	BUTTER GIRL, 5,000	60.00	NR

CREATIVE WORLD UNITED STATES

Aesop's Fables

1979	THE FOX AND THE GRAPES, 9,750	85.00	NR

Four Seasons

1972	FALL, silver plate, 2,000	75.00	NR
1972	FALL, sterling silver, 2,000	125.00	NR
1973	SPRING, silver plate, 2,300	75.00	NR
1973	SPRING, sterling silver, 750	125.00	NR
1973	WINTER, silver plate, 2,000	75.00	NR
1973	WINTER, sterling silver, 2,250	125.00	NR
1974	SUMMER, silver plate, 300	75.00	NR
1974	SUMMER, sterling silver, 750	125.00	NR

Immortals of Early American Literature

1978	VILLAGE SMITHY, Roger Brown, 15,000	50.00	BR
1979	RIP VAN WINKLE, Roger Brown, 15,000	55.00	NR

Living Dolls

1982	ERIKO AND NORIKO, David Smiton, 9,500	49.50	NR
1983	INGRID AND INGEMAR, David Smiton, 9,500	49.50	NR

Prize Collection

1982	FAMILY CARES, 12,500	45.00	NR
1983	WIND IN THE FROLIC, 12,500	45.00	NR

		Issue Price	Current Value
Rockwell Series			
1978	LOOKING OUT TO SEA, Roger Brown, 15,000	50.00	65.00
1978	YANKEE DOODLE, Roger Brown, 15,000	50.00	BR
1979	GIRL AT THE MIRROR, Roger Brown, 15,000	55.00	NR
Wags to Riches			
1982	BENJI THE MOVIE STAR, Murray Karn, 19,500	29.50	NR
1982	BENJI AND TIFFANY, Murray Karn, 19,500	29.50	NR
1983	MERRY CHRISTMAS BENJI, Murray Karn, 19,500	29.50	NR
1984	BENJI'S BARBER SHOP BLUES, Murray Karn, 19,500 . . .	35.00	NR

Merry Christmas Benji
Photo courtesy of *Collectors News*

CRISTAL D'ALBRET FRANCE

Four Seasons			
1972	SUMMER, 1,000	65.00	110.00
1973	AUTUMN, 1,000	75.00	95.00
1974	SPRING, 1,000	75.00	170.00
1975	WINTER, 1,000	88.00	155.00
Single Issue			
1972	BIRD OF PEACE, 3,700	88.00	155.00

CROWN DELFT NETHERLANDS

Christmas			
1969	MAN BY FIRE, 1 year	10.00	30.00
1970	TWO SLEIGH RIDERS, 1 year	10.00	20.00
1971	CHRISTMAS TREE, 1 year	10.00	NR

		Issue Price	Current Value
1972	BAKING FOR CHRISTMAS, 1 year	10.00	NR

Father's Day

1970	FATHER'S DAY, 1 year	10.00	NR
1971	FATHER'S DAY, 1 year	10.00	NR
1972	FATHER'S DAY, 1 year	10.00	NR
1973	FATHER'S DAY, 1 year	10.00	NR

Mother's Day

1970	SHEEP, 1 year	10.00	NR
1971	STORK, 1 year...	10.00	NR
1972	DUCKS, 1 year	10.00	NR
1973	MOTHER'S DAY, 1 year	10.00	NR

CUI — CAROLINA COLLECTION — DRAM TREE

Christmas

1991	CHECKIN' IT TWICE EDITION I, CUI, 4,950..............	39.50	NR

Classic Cars

1992	1957 CHEVY, G. Geivette, 28 days	40.00	RI

Corvette

1992	1953 CORVETTE, G. Geivette, 28 days..................	40.00	RI

DU Great American Sporting Dogs

1992	BLACK LAB EDITION I, J. Killen, 20,000	40.00	RI
1993	GOLDEN RETRIEVER EDITION II, J. Killen, 28 days	40.00	RI
1993	SPRINGER SPANIEL EDITION III, J. Killen, 28 days	40.00	RI
1993	YELLOW LABRADOR EDITION IV, J. Killen, 28 days......	40.00	RI
1993	ENGLISH SETTER EDITION V, J. Killen, 28 days	40.00	RI
1993	BRITTANY SPANIEL EDITION VI, J. Killen, 28 days	40.00	RI

Environmental

1991	RAINFOREST MAGIC EDITION I, C. L. Bragg, 4,950	39.50	NR
1992	FIRST BREATH, M. Hoffman, 4,950	40.00	RI

Girl in the Moon

1991	MILLER GIRL IN THE MOON EDITION I, CUI, 9,950	39.50	NR

Native American

1991	HUNT FOR THE BUFFALO EDITION I, P. Kethley, 4,950 ...	39.50	NR

		Issue Price	Current Value
1992	STORY TELLER, P. Kethley, 1,050	40.00	RI

Winterfest

1992	SKATING PARTY, T. Stortz, 45 days	29.50	RI

CURATOR COLLECTION UNITED STATES
(See also Artaffects)

Becker Babies

1983	SNOWPUFF, Charlotte Becker, limited	29.95	45.00
1984	SMILING THROUGH, Charlotte Becker, limited	29.95	45.00
1984	PALS, Charlotte Becker, limited	29.95	45.00

Classic Circus

1983	THE FAVORITE CLOWN, 17,500	39.95	NR

Gift Edition

1982	THE WEDDING, Rob Sauber	37.50	NR
1984	HAPPY BIRTHDAY, Rob Sauber	37.50	NR
1985	ALL ADORE HIM, Rob Sauber	37.50	NR
1985	HOME SWEET HOME, Rob Sauber	37.50	NR
1986	THE ANNIVERSARY, Rob Sauber	37.50	NR
1986	SWEETHEARTS, Rob Sauber	37.50	NR
1986	THE CHRISTENING, Rob Sauber	37.50	NR
1987	MOTHERHOOD, Rob Sauber	37.50	NR
1987	FATHERHOOD, Rob Sauber	37.50	NR
1987	SWEET SIXTEEN, Rob Sauber	37.50	NR

Great Trains

1985	SANTA FE, Jim Deneen, 7,500	35.00	80.00
1985	TWENTIETH CENTURY LTD., Jim Deneen, 7,500	35.00	80.00
1986	EMPIRE BUILDER, Jim Deneen, 7,500	35.00	80.00

Magical Moments

1981	HAPPY DREAMS, Bessie Pease Gutmann, <1 year	29.95	85.00
1981	HARMONY, Bessie Pease Gutmann, <1 year	29.95	75.00
1982	HIS MAJESTY, Bessie Pease Gutmann, <1 year	29.95	45.00
1982	WAITING FOR DADDY, Bessie Pease Gutmann, <1 year	29.95	45.00
1982	THANK YOU GOD, Bessie Pease Gutmann, <1 year	29.95	45.00
1983	LULLABY, Bessie Pease Gutmann, <1 year	29.95	45.00

Masterpieces of Impressionism

1980	WOMAN WITH PARASOL, Claude Monet, 17,500	35.00	60.00

		Issue Price	Current Value
1981	YOUNG MOTHER SEWING, Mary Cassatt, 17,500	35.00	50.00
1982	SARA IN GREEN BONNET, Mary Cassatt, 17,500	35.00	50.00
1983	MARGOT IN BLUE, Mary Cassatt, 17,500	35.00	45.00

Masterpieces of Rockwell

1980	AFTER THE PROM, Norman Rockwell, 17,500	42.50	120.00
1980	THE CHALLENGER, Norman Rockwell, 17,500	50.00	65.00
1982	GIRL AT THE MIRROR, Norman Rockwell, 17,500	50.00	85.00
1982	MISSING TOOTH, Norman Rockwell, 17,500	50.00	65.00

Masterpieces of the West

1980	TEXAS NIGHT HERDER, Frank T. Johnson, 17,500	35.00	55.00
1980	INDIAN TRAPPER, Frederic Remington, 17,500	35.00	45.00
1982	COWBOY STYLE, William R. Leigh, 17,500	35.00	NR
1982	INDIAN STYLE, Gregory Perillo, 17,500	35.00	75.00

Mother's Love

1984	CONTENTMENT, Norman Rockwell, 7,500	35.00	NR

Nursery Pair

1983	IN SLUMBERLAND, Charlotte Becker, limited	25.00	40.00
1983	THE AWAKENING, Charlotte Becker, limited	25.00	40.00

On the Road

1984	PRIDE OF STOCKBRIDGE, Norman Rockwell, limited	35.00	55.00
1984	CITY PRIDE, Norman Rockwell, limited	35.00	55.00
1984	COUNTRY PRIDE, Norman Rockwell, limited	35.00	55.00

Playful Pets

1982	CURIOSITY, John Henry Dolph, 7,500	45.00	60.00
1982	MASTER'S HAT, John Henry Dolph, 7,500	45.00	60.00

Portraits

1986	CHANTILLY, John Eggert, 14 days	24.50	35.00
1986	DYNASTY, John Eggert, 14 days	24.50	35.00
1986	VELVET, John Eggert, 14 days	24.50	35.00
1986	JAMBALAYA, John Eggert, 14 days	24.50	35.00

Portraits of American Brides

1987	CAROLINE, Rob Sauber, 10 days	29.50	55.00
1987	JACQUELINE, Rob Sauber, 10 days	29.50	35.00
1987	ELIZABETH, Rob Sauber, 10 days	29.50	40.00
1987	EMILY, Rob Sauber, 10 days	29.50	40.00

		Issue Price	Current Value
1987	MEREDITH, Rob Sauber, 10 days	29.50	40.00
1987	LAURA, Rob Sauber, 10 days	29.50	40.00
1987	SARAH, Rob Sauber, 10 days	29.50	40.00
1987	REBECCA, Rob Sauber, 10 days	29.50	45.00

Rockwell Americana

1981	SHUFFLETON'S BARBERSHOP, Norman Rockwell, 17,500	75.00	125.00
1982	BREAKING HOME TIES, Norman Rockwell, 17,500	75.00	100.00
1983	WALKING TO CHURCH, Norman Rockwell, 17,500.......	75.00	100.00

Rockwell Trilogy

1981	STOCKBRIDGE IN WINTER I, Norman Rockwell, <1 year .	35.00	45.00
1982	STOCKBRIDGE IN WINTER II, Norman Rockwell, <1 year	35.00	45.00
1983	STOCKBRIDGE IN WINTER III, Norman Rockwell, <1 year	35.00	50.00

Sailing through History

1986	FLYING CLOUD, Kipp Soldwedel, 14 days	29.50	45.00
1986	SANTA MARIA, Kipp Soldwedel, 14 days	29.50	45.00
1986	MAYFLOWER, Kipp Soldwedel, 14 days	29.50	45.00

Simpler Times

1984	LAZY DAZE, Norman Rockwell, 7,500	35.00	55.00
1984	ONE FOR THE ROAD, Norman Rockwell, 7,500	35.00	55.00

Special Occasions

1981	BUBBLES, Frances Tipton Hunter, <1 year	29.95	40.00
1982	BUTTERFLIES, Frances Tipton Hunter, <1 year	29.95	40.00

Tribute Series

1982	I WANT YOU, James Montgomery Flagg, limited	29.95	40.00
1982	GEE, I WISH I WERE A MAN, Howard Chandler Christy, limited	29.95	40.00
1983	SOLDIER'S FAREWELL, Norman Rockwell, limited	29.95	40.00

DANBURY MINT UNITED STATES

Bicentennial Silver

1973	BOSTON TEA PARTY, 7,500...........................	125.00	NR
1974	FIRST CONTINENTAL CONGRESS, 7,500	125.00	NR
1975	PAUL REVERE'S RIDE, 7,500	125.00	NR
1976	DECLARATION OF INDEPENDENCE, 7,500	125.00	NR
1977	WASHINGTON AT VALLEY FORGE, 7,500	125.00	NR
1978	MOLLY PITCHER, 7,500	125.00	NR
1979	BON HOMME RICHARD, 7,500........................	125.00	NR

		Issue Price	Current Value

Christmas

1975	SILENT NIGHT, <1 year	24.50	NR
1976	JOY TO THE WORLD, <1 year	27.50	NR
1977	AWAY IN THE MANGER, <1 year	28.50	NR
1978	THE FIRST NOEL, <1 year	29.50	NR

Currier & Ives Silver

1972	THE ROAD WINTER, 7,500	125.00	NR
1973	CENTRAL PARK WINTER, 7,500	125.00	NR
1974	WINTER IN THE COUNTRY, 7,500	125.00	NR
1975	AMERICAN HOMESTEAD, 7,500	125.00	NR
1976	AMERICAN WINTER EVENING, 7,500	125.00	135.00
1977	WINTER MORNING, 7,500	125.00	135.00

Great American Masterpieces Silver

1975	MONA LISA, 7,500	125.00	NR
1975	THE LAST SUPPER, 7,500	135.00	NR
1976	SUNFLOWER, 7,500	135.00	NR
1976	BLUE BOY, 7,500	135.00	NR

Michelangelo Crystal

1977	PIETA, <1 year	75.00	NR
1978	HOLY FAMILY, <1 year	75.00	NR
1978	MOSES, <1 year	75.00	NR
1979	CREATION OF ADAM, <1 year	75.00	NR

Michelangelo Silver

1973	PIETA, 7,500	125.00	140.00
1973	HOLY FAMILY, 7,500	125.00	140.00
1973	MOSES, 7,500	125.00	140.00
1973	CREATION OF ADAM, 7,500	125.00	140.00

Pewter

1977	CHRISTMAS CAROL	27.50	NR

Single Issue

1977	OFFICIAL AMERICA'S CUP, <1 year	20.00	NR
1977	TALL SHIPS, <1 year	21.00	NR
1977	QUEEN'S SILVER JUBILEE, <1 year	85.00	NR

D'ARCEAU LIMOGES FRANCE

Cambier Four Seasons

1978	LA JEUNE FILLE D'ETE, Guy Cambier, 15,000	105.00	120.00

	Issue Price	Current Value
1979 LA JEUNE FILLE D'HIVER, Guy Cambier, 15,000	105.00	NR
1980 LA JEUNE FILLE DU PRINTEMPS, Guy Cambier, 15,000 ..	105.00	NR
1980 LA JEUNE FILLE D'AUTOMNE, Guy Cambier, 15,000	105.00	125.00

Christmas

	Issue Price	Current Value
1975 LA FRUITE EN EGYPTE, Andre Restieau	24.32	35.00
1976 DANS LA CRECHE, Andre Restieau	24.32	30.00
1977 LE REFUS D'HÈBERGEMENT, Andre Restieau	24.32	30.00
1978 LA PURIFICATION, Andre Restieau, 1 year	26.81	NR
1979 L'ADORATION DES ROIS, Andre Restieau, 1 year	26.81	40.00
1980 JOYEUSE NOUVELLE, Andre Restieau, 1 year	28.74	NR
1981 GUIDES PAR L'ETOILE, Andre Restieau, 1 year..........	28.74	NR
1982 THE ANNUNCIATION, Andre Restieau, 1 year	30.74	45.00

Josephine and Napoleon

	Issue Price	Current Value
1984 L'EMPERATRICE JOSEPHINE, limited	29.32	NR
1984 BONAPARTE TRAVERSANT LES ALPES, limited	29.32	NR
1984 THE MEETING, limited	29.32	NR

Lafayette Legacy

	Issue Price	Current Value
1973 THE SECRET CONTRACT, Andre Restieau	14.82	NR
1973 NORTH ISLAND LANDING, Andre Restieau	19.82	NR
1974 CITY TAVERN MEETING, Andre Restieau	19.82	NR
1974 BATTLE OF BRANDYWINE, Andre Restieau	19.82	NR
1975 MESSAGE TO FRANKLIN, Andre Restieau	19.82	NR
1975 SIEGE AT YORKTOWN, Andre Restieau	14.82	NR

Les Femmes du Siècle

	Issue Price	Current Value
1976 SCARLET EN CRINOLINE, Francois Ganeau	14.80	40.00
1976 SARAH EN TOURNURE, Francois Ganeau...............	19.87	30.00
1976 COLETTE, Francois Ganeau	19.87	30.00
1977 LEA, Francois Ganeau	19.87	30.00
1977 ALBERTINE, Francois Ganeau, 1 year	22.74	NR
1977 DAISY, Francois Ganeau, 1 year	22.74	NR
1977 MARLENE, Francois Ganeau, 1 year	22.74	NR
1978 HELENE, Francois Ganeau, 1 year	22.74	NR
1978 SOPHIE, Francois Ganeau, 1 year....................	22.74	50.00
1979 FRANCOISE, Francois Ganeau, 1 year	22.74	50.00
1979 BRIGITTE, Francois Ganeau, 1 year	22.74	50.00

Les Noels de France

	Issue Price	Current Value
1986 THE MAGICAL WINDOW, Jean–Claude Guidou, 150 days	28.47	50.00

Les Sites Parisiens de Louis Dali

	Issue Price	Current Value
1979 L'ARC DE TRIOMPHE, Louis Dali	22.94	NR

		Issue Price	Current Value
1980	LA CATHEDRALE NOTRE DAME, Louis Dali.............	22.94	30.00
1981	LA PLACE DE LA CONCORDE, Louis Dali	22.94	30.00
1981	L'ÉGLISE SAINT – PIERRE ET LE SACRÉ – COEUR DE MONT- MARTRE, Louis Dali	22.94	30.00
1982	LE MARCHÉ AUX FLEURS ET LA CONCIERGERIE, Louis Dali, 1 year...	26.83	NR
1982	LA POINTE DU VERT GALANT, Louis Dali, 1 year	26.83	NR
1983	LE JARDIN DES TUILERIES, Louis Dali, 1 year	26.83	NR
1983	LE MOULIN ROUGE, Louis Dali, 1 year	26.83	NR
1983	LE PONT ALEXANDRE, Louis Dali, 1 year	26.83	NR
1983	L'OPERA, Louis Dali, 1 year..........................	26.83	NR
1983	LA TOUR EIFFEL, Louis Dali, 1 year	26.83	NR
1983	L'HOTEL DE VILLE DE PARIS, Louis Dali, 1 year	26.83	NR

Les Tres Riches Heures

1979	JANVIER, Jean Dutheil, 1 year	75.48	NR
1980	AVRIL, Jean Dutheil, 1 year	75.48	NR
1981	AOUT, Jean Dutheil, 1 year...........................	75.48	NR
1982	JUIN, Jean Dutheil, 1 year	75.48	NR
1984	MAI, Jean Dutheil, 1 year............................	75.48	NR

Juin
Photo courtesy of *Collectors News*

DAUM FRANCE

Art Nouveau

1979	WATER LILIES, 4,000	125.00	NR
1980	LILY POND, 4,000	150.00	NR
1981	SWAN, 4,000	170.00	NR

Famous Musicians

		Issue Price	Current Value
1971	BACH, 2,000	75.00	NR
1971	BEETHOVEN, 2,000	75.00	NR
1971	MOZART, 2,000	75.00	NR
1971	WAGNER, 2,000	75.00	NR
1972	DEBUSSY, 2,000	75.00	NR
1972	GERSHWIN, 2,000	75.00	NR

Four Seasons

1970	AUTUMN, Raymond Corbin, 2,000	150.00	NR
1970	WINTER, Raymond Corbin, 2,000	150.00	NR
1970	SPRING, Raymond Corbin, 2,000	150.00	NR
1970	SUMMER, Raymond Corbin, 2,000	150.00	NR

Nymphea

| 1979 | WATERLILIES, 4,000 | 125.00 | 140.00 |
| 1980 | LILY POND, 4,000 | 150.00 | 170.00 |

Salvador Dali

| 1970 | CECI N'EST PAS UNE ASSIETTE, 2,000 | 475.00 | NR |
| 1970 | TRIOMPHALE, 2,000 | 475.00 | NR |

DAVENPORT POTTERY GREAT BRITAIN

Attwell's Silver Linings

| 1988 | THANK GOD FOR FIDO | 24.50 | NR |
| 1988 | RAINBOWS | 24.50 | 30.00 |

Thank God for Fido
Photo courtesy of *Collectors News*

Rainbows
Photo courtesy of *Collectors News*

		Issue Price	Current Value
1988	HOW GOOD OF GOD	24.50	30.00
1988	A BIT OF LOVE	24.50	55.00

Cottages of Olde England

1991	HOLLYHOCK COTTAGE	75.00	80.00
1991	LILAC COTTAGE	75.00	85.00
1991	WILD ROSF COTTAGE	75.00	135.00
1991	CATTAIL COTTAGE	75.00	130.00

Gardens of Victoria

1989	THE QUEEN VICTORIA ROSE	60.00	NR
1989	THE CROWN ORCHID	60.00	75.00
1990	THE EMPRESS OF INDIA	65.00	NR
1990	THE ROYAL CARNELIA	65.00	75.00
1990	THE REGAL CLEMATIS	65.00	100.00
1991	THE SOVEREIGN POPPY	65.00	100.00

Toby Plate Collection

1984	TOBY FILLPOT, Wilfred Blandford	35.00	NR
1984	FALSTAFF, Douglas Tootle	35.00	BR
1985	JACK TAR, Douglas Tootle	40.00	NR
1986	MR. PICKWICK, Douglas Tootle	40.00	BR
1986	FRIAR TUCK, Douglas Tootle	40.00	NR
1986	LONG JOHN SILVER	40.00	BR

Toby Fillpot
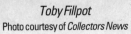
Photo courtesy of *Collectors News*

Tale of Peter Rabbit

Treasury of Classic Children's Verse	Issue Price	Current Value
1986 ALL THINGS BRIGHT AND BEAUTIFUL	29.00	NR
1986 PIRATE STORY	29.00	NR
1987 THE STAR	29.00	35.00
1987 ANIMAL CRACKERS	32.00	NR
1987 TARTARY	32.00	50.00
1987 LOOKING–GLASS RIVER	32.00	40.00
1988 THE KITE	34.00	50.00
1988 AT THE ZOO	34.00	55.00

World of Beatrix Potter

	Issue Price	Current Value
1991 TALE OF PETER RABBIT	59.00	110.00
1992 TALE OF TOM KITTEN	59.00	RI
1992 TALE OF JEMIMA PUDDLEDUCK	64.00	RI
1992 TALE OF TWO BED MICE	64.00	RI
1992 TALE OF JEREMY FISHER	64.00	RI
1993 TALE OF BENJAMIN BUNNY	69.00	RI
1993 TALE OF MRS. TIGGY–WINKLE	69.00	RI
1993 TALE OF THE TAILOR OF GLOUCHESTER	69.00	RI

DAVID KAPLAN STUDIOS UNITED STATES

Fiddler's People

	Issue Price	Current Value
1978 FIDDLER ON THE ROOF, Rik Vig, 7,500	60.00	NR
1979 TEVYA, Rik Vig, 7,500	60.00	NR
1980 MIRACLE OF LOVE, Rik Vig, 7,500	60.00	NR
1981 THE WEDDING, Rik Vig, 7,500	60.00	NR

DAYBRAKE MARKETING CANADA

Single Issue

	Issue Price	Current Value
1984 ERNIE'S FARM FRIENDS, Tammy Laye, 7,500	50.00	NR

DELOS APOLLO GREECE

Great Love Stories of Greek Mythology

	Issue Price	Current Value
1988 APHRODITE AND ADONIS	65.00	BR
1989 EROS AND PSYCHE	65.00	NR
1989 DAPHNE AND APOLLO	65.00	NR
1989 PYGMALION AND GALATEA	65.00	NR

DELPHI   UNITED STATES

Beatles Collection

		Issue Price	Current Value
1991	THE BEATLES, LIVE IN CONCERT, Nate Giorgio, 150 days	24.75	40.00
1991	HELLO AMERICA, Nate Giorgio, 150 days	24.75	45.00
1991	A HARD DAY'S NIGHT, Nate Giorgio, 150 days	27.75	50.00
1992	BEATLES '65, Nate Giorgio, 150 days	27.75	RI
1992	HELP, Nate Giorgio, 150 days	27.75	RI
1992	THE BEATLES AT SHEA STADIUM, Nate Giorgio, 150 days	29.75	RI
1992	RUBBER SOUL, Nate Giorgio, 150 days	29.75	RI
1992	YESTERDAY AND TODAY, Nate Giorgio, 150 days	29.75	RI

Beatles '67–'70

1992	SGT. PEPPER THE 25TH ANNIVERSARY, D. Sivavec, 150 days	27.75	RI
1992	ALL YOU NEED IS LOVE, D. Sivavec, 150 days	27.75	RI

The Beatles, Live in Concert
Photo courtesy of *Collectors News*

'68 Comeback Special
Photo courtesy of *Collectors News*

Commemorating the King

1993	THE ROCK AND ROLL LEGEND, M. Stutzman, 95 days	29.75	RI
1993	LAS VEGAS, LIVE	29.75	RI
1993	BLUES AND BLACK LEATHER	29.75	RI
1994	PRIVATE PRESLEY	29.75	RI
1994	GOLDEN BOY	29.75	RI
1994	SCREEN IDOL	29.75	RI
1994	OUTSTANDING YOUNG MAN	29.75	RI
1994	THE TIGER: FAITH, SPIRIT AND DISCIPLINE	29.75	RI

		Issue Price	Current Value

Dream Machines

1988	'56 T–BIRD, P. Palma, 150 days ...., ...	24.75	NR
1988	'57 'VETTE, P Palma, 150 days	24.75	NR
1989	'58 BIARRITZ, P. Palma, 150 days	27.75	NR
1989	'56 CONTINENTAL, P. Palma, 150 days	27.75	NR
1989	'57 BEL AIR, P. Palma, 150 days	27.75	50.00
1989	'57 CHRYSLER 300C, P. Palma, 150 days	27.75	NR

Elvis on the Big Screen

1992	ELVIS IN LOVING YOU, B. Emmett, 150 days	29.75	RI
1992	ELVIS IN G.I. BLUES, B. Emmett, 150 days	29.75	RI
1992	VIVA LAS VEGAS, B. Emmett, 150 days	32.75	RI
1993	ELVIS IN BLUE HAWAII, B. Emmett, 150 days	32.75	RI
1993	ELVIS IN JAILHOUSE ROCK, B. Emmett, 150 days	32.75	RI
1993	ELVIS IN SPINOUT....................................	34.75	RI
1993	ELVIS IN SPEEDWAY	34.75	RI
1993	ELVIS IN HARUM SCARUM	34.75	RI

Elvis Presley Hit Parade

1992	HEARTBREAK HOTEL, Nate Giorgio, 150 days	29.75	RI
1992	BLUE SUEDE SHOES, Nate Giorgio, 150 days	29.75	RI
1992	HOUND DOG, Nate Giorgio, 150 days	32.75	RI
1992	BLUE CHRISTMAS, Nate Giorgio, 150 days.............	32.75	RI
1992	RETURN TO SENDER, Nate Giorgio, 150 days...........	32.75	RI
1993	TEDDY BEAR, Nate Giorgio, 150 days..................	34.75	RI

Elvis Presley: In Performance

1990	'68 COMEBACK SPECIAL, B. Emmett, 150 days	24.75	50.00
1991	KING OF LAS VEGAS, B. Emmett, 150 days	24.75	50.00
1991	ALOHA FROM HAWAII, B. Emmett, 150 days	27.75	50.00
1991	BACK IN TUPELO, 1956, B. Emmett, 150 days	27.75	65.00
1991	IF I CAN DREAM, B. Emmett, 150 days	27.75	50.00
1991	BENEFIT FOR THE U.S.S. ARIZONA, B. Emmett, 150 days	29.75	50.00
1991	MADISON SQUARE GARDEN 1972, B. Emmett, 150 days .	29.75	60.00
1991	TAMPA 1955, B. Emmett, 150 days	29.75	50.00
1991	CONCERT IN BATON ROUGE 1974, B. Emmett, 150 days .	29.75	45.00
1992	ON STAGE IN WICHITA 1974, B. Emmett, 150 days	31.75	RI
1992	IN THE SPOTLIGHT: HAWAII '72, B. Emmett, 150 days ...	31.75	RI
1992	TOUR FINALE: INDIANAPOLIS 1977, B. Emmett, 150 days	31.75	RI

Elvis Presley: Looking at a Legend

1988	ELVIS AT GATES OF GRACELAND, B. Emmett, 150 days ..	24.75	85.00
1989	JAILHOUSE ROCK, B. Emmett, 150 days	24.75	80.00
1989	THE MEMPHIS FLASH, B. Emmett, 150 days.............	27.75	55.00
1989	HOMECOMING, B. Emmett, 150 days	27.75	50.00
1990	ELVIS AND GLADYS, B. Emmett, 150 days..............	27.75	60.00

		Issue Price	Current Value
1990	A STUDIO SESSION, B. Emmett, 150 days	27.75	40.00
1990	ELVIS IN HOLLYWOOD, B. Emmett, 150 days	29.75	55.00
1990	ELVIS ON HIS HARLEY, B. Emmett, 150 days	29.75	70.00
1990	STAGE DOOR AUTOGRAPHS, B. Emmett, 150 days	29.75	55.00
1991	CHRISTMAS AT GRACELAND, B. Emmett, 150 days	32.75	70.00
1991	ENTERING SUN STUDIO, B. Emmett, 150 days	32.75	50.00
1991	GOING FOR THE BLACK BELT, B. Emmett, 150 days	32.75	45.00
1991	HIS HAND IN MINE, B. Emmett, 150 days	32.75	75.00
1991	LETTERS FROM FANS, B. Emmett, 150 days	32.75	60.00
1991	CLOSING THE DEAL, B. Emmett, 150 days	34.75	60.00
1992	ELVIS RETURNS TO THE STAGE, B. Emmett, 150 days ...	34.75	RI

Fabulous Cars of the Fifties

		Issue Price	Current Value
1993	'57 RED CORVETTE, open	24.75	RI
1993	'57 WHITE T–BIRD, open	24.75	RI
1993	'57 BLUE BELAIR, open	27.75	RI
1993	'59 PINK CADILLAC, open..........................	27.75	RI
1994	'56 LINCOLN PREMIER, open........................	27.75	RI
1994	'59 RED FORD FAIRLANE, open	27.75	RI

Indiana Jones

		Issue Price	Current Value
1989	INDIANA JONES, V. Gadino, 150 days	24.75	NR
1989	INDIANA JONES AND HIS DAD, V. Gadino, 150 days	24.75	40.00
1990	INDIANA JONES/DR. SCHNEIDER, V. Gadino, 150 days ..	27.75	NR
1990	A FAMILY DISCUSSION, V. Gadino, 150 days	27.75	50.00
1990	YOUNG INDIANA JONES, V. Gadino, 150 days	27.75	50.00
1991	INDIANA JONES/THE HOLY GRAIL, V. Gadino, 150 days .	27.75	50.00

In the Footsteps of the King

		Issue Price	Current Value
1993	GRACELAND: MEMPHIS, TENNESSEE	29.75	RI
1994	ELVIS' BIRTHPLACE: TUPELO, MISSISSIPPI	29.75	RI
1994	ELVIS' DAY JOB: MEMPHIS, TENNESSEE..............	32.75	RI
1994	FLYING G RANCH: WALLS, MISSISSIPPI	32.75	RI
1994	THE LAUDERDALE COURTS	32.75	RI
1994	PATRIOTIC SOLDIER: BAD NAUHEIM, WEST GERMANY .	34.75	RI

Legends of Baseball

		Issue Price	Current Value
1992	BABE RUTH: THE CALLED SHOT, B. Benger, 150 days ...	24.75	RI
1992	LOU GEHRIG: THE LUCKIEST MAN, J. Barson, 150 days .	24.75	RI

Magic of Marilyn

		Issue Price	Current Value
1992	FOR OUR BOYS IN KOREA 1954, C. Notarile, 150 days ...	24.75	RI
1992	OPENING NIGHT 1954, C. Notarile, 150 days	24.75	RI
1993	RISING STAR 1954, C. Notarile, 150 days	27.75	RI
1993	STOPPING TRAFFIC..................................	27.75	RI

			Issue Price	Current Value
1993	STRASBERG'S CLASS		27.75	RI
1993	PHOTO OPPORTUNITY		27.75	RI
1993	SHINING STAR		27.75	RI
1993	CURTAIN CALL		27.75	RI

Marilyn Monroe Collection

1989	MARILYN MONROE/SEVEN-YEAR ITCH, C. Notarile, 150 days	24.75	80.00
1990	DIAMONDS/GIRLS BEST FRIEND, C. Notarile, 150 days	24.75	80.00
1991	MARILYN MONROE/RIVER OF NO RETURN, C. Notarile, 150 days	27.75	80.00
1992	HOW TO MARRY A MILLIONAIRE, C. Notarile, 150 days	27.75	RI
1992	THERE'S NO BUSINESS/SHOW BUSINESS, C. Notarile, 150 days	27.75	RI
1992	MARILYN MONROE IN NIAGARA, C. Notarile, 150 days	29.75	RI
1992	MY HEART BELONGS TO DADDY, C. Notarile, 150 days	29.75	RI
1992	MARILYN MONROE/CHERIE IN BUS STOP, C. Notarile, 150 days	29.75	RI
1992	MARILYN MONROE IN ALL ABOUT EVE, C. Notarile, 150 days	29.75	RI
1992	MARILYN MONROE IN MONKEY BUSINESS, C. Notarile, 150 days	31.75	RI
1992	MARILYN MONROE IN DON'T BOTHER TO KNOCK, C. Notarile, 150 days	31.75	RI
1992	MARILYN MONROE/WE'RE NOT MARRIED, C. Notarile, 150 days	31.75	RI

Elvis at Gates of Graceland

Marilyn Monroe in The Seven-Year Itch

Portraits of the King

1991	LOVE ME TENDER, D. Zwierz, 150 days	27.75	45.00
1991	ARE YOU LONESOME TONIGHT?, D. Zwierz, 150 days	27.75	55.00
1991	I'M YOURS, D. Zwierz, 150 days	30.75	50.00
1991	TREAT ME NICE, D. Zwierz, 150 days	30.75	50.00
1992	THE WONDER OF YOU, D. Zwierz, 150 days	30.75	RI
1992	YOU'RE A HEARTBREAKER, D. Zwierz, 150 days	32.75	RI
1992	JUST BECAUSE, D. Zwierz, 150 days	32.75	RI

		Issue Price	Current Value
1992	FOLLOW THAT DREAM, D. Zwierz, 150 days	32.75	RI

Take Me Out to the Ballgame

| 1993 | WRIGLEY FIELD, D. Henderson, 95 days . . . . | 29.75 | RI |

DEPARTMENT 56

A Christmas Carol

1991	THE CRATCHIT'S CHRISTMAS PUDDING, 5706-1, R. Innocenti, 18,000	60.00	RI
1992	MARLEY'S GHOST APPEARS TO SCROOGE, 5721-5, R. Innocenti, 18,000	60.00	RI
1993	THE SPIRIT OF CHRISTMAS PRESENT, 5722-3, R. Innocenti, 18,000	60.00	RI

Dickens' Village

| 1987 | DICKENS' VILLAGE PORCELAIN PLATES, 5917-0, Department 56, closed, set of 4 . . . . | 140.00 | NR |

DE PAUW STUDIOS UNITED STATES

Single Issue

| 1976 | BICENTENNIAL LINCOLN, 2,400 . . . . | 30.00 | 70.00 |

DEVONSHIRE USA UNITED STATES

Single Issue

| 1987 | A TIMELESS TRADITION, Carlo Beninati, 30 days . . . . | 29.50 | NR |

DOMINION CHINA COMPANY CANADA

Birds of the North

1990	GOLDEN FLIGHT: CANADA GEESE	34.80	NR
1990	WINTER WINGS: SNOW GEESE	34.80	NR
1990	TRANQUIL BEAUTY: TRUMPETER SWANS	37.80	NR
1991	MORNING LIGHT: COMMON LOONS	37.80	NR
1991	ROCKY PERCH: HOMED PUFFINS	37.80	NR
1991	BARROW'S GOLDEN EYE	37.80	NR
1991	FLYING IN: KING ELDER DUCKS	39.80	45.00
1991	ON THE WING: BLUE BILLS	39.80	75.00

Heartfelt Traditions

		Issue Price	Current Value
1992	JOY TO THE WORLD	34.80	RI
1992	COME ALL YE FAITHFUL	34.80	RI
1993	A MIDNIGHT CLEAR	34.80	RI
1993	WE GATHER TOGETHER	34.80	RI

Joys of Childhood

1992	YOU'LL PLAY GOALIE!	29.80	RI
1992	TOASTY WARM	29.80	RI
1992	MAKING A FRIEND	32.80	RI
1992	LUNCHTIME	32.80	RI
1992	SNOW ANGELS	32.80	RI
1993	BEDTIME STORY	34.80	RI
1993	LET'S GO!	34.80	RI
1993	TIME TO GO HOME	34.80	RI

Lords of the Wilderness

1992	HIS DOMAIN: MOOSE	34.80	RI
1992	MOUNTAIN KINGDOM: GRIZZLY	34.80	RI
1992	PRINCELY REALM: WHITE–TAILED DEER	37.80	RI
1992	ROYAL PRESENCE: ELK	37.80	RI

Portraits of the Wild

1991	READY: WHITE–TAILED DEER	29.80	NR
1991	NOT THIS YEAR: MULE DEER	29.80	NR
1992	CHANGING DIRECTION: ELK	32.80	RI
1992	FROSTY MORNING: BUFFALO	32.80	RI
1992	GRAND VIEW: JASPER RAMS	32.80	RI
1992	BELOW THE PEAK: ANTELOPE	34.80	RI
1992	ABOVE AND BEYOND: MOUNTAIN GOATS	34.80	RI
1992	PROUD DOMAIN: MOOSE	34.80	RI

Proud Passage

1992	THE RETURN HOME	29.80	RI
1993	SPRING LANDING	29.80	RI
1993	AT THE NEST	32.80	RI
1993	FAMILY PORTRAIT	32.80	RI
1993	LEARNING TO FLY	32.80	RI
1993	TAKING OFF	32.80	RI

Reflections of Canadian Childhood

1986	DREAMS OF GLORY	24.80	NR
1987	QUIET MOMENT	24.80	NR
1987	PICK OF THE CROP	27.80	NR
1988	WISHFUL THINKING	27.80	NR
1988	SUNDAY BEST	27.80	NR

		Issue Price	Current Value
1988	PEACEMAKER	27.80	NR
1988	AUTUMN YEARNING	29.80	NR
1989	WINNING WAYS	29.80	NR

"The Loon" Voice of the North

		Issue Price	Current Value
1991	KEEPING THEM SAFE	34.80	45.00
1991	EARLY START	34.80	50.00
1992	REGAL WINGS	37.80	RI
1992	TIME TO FLY	37.80	RI
1992	QUIET REPAST	37.80	RI
1992	SILENT SNOW	39.80	RI
1992	TAKE TO THE AIR	39.80	RI
1992	KEPT WITH CARE	39.80	RI

Treasures of the Arctic

		Issue Price	Current Value
1990	KINGS OF THE HILL	29.80	NR
1991	SPIRITS OF THE WILD	29.80	NR
1991	SPRING ON THE MOUNTAIN	32.80	NR
1991	MOTHER'S WATCHFUL EYE	32.80	NR
1991	A RESTING PLACE	32.80	NR
1991	ON THE TRAIL	32.80	48.00

Dreams of Glory
Photo courtesy of *Collectors News*

Kings of the Hill
Photo courtesy of *Collectors News*

Victorian Christmas

		Issue Price	Current Value
1989	COMING HOME	39.80	NR
1990	SKATING ON THE POND	39.80	NR
1991	TRIMMING THE TREE	44.80	NR

		Issue Price	Current Value
1992	JOYFUL CAROLERS ....,,,, ...	44.80	RI
1993	WINDOW SHOPPING	44.80	RI
1994	A WINTER PASTIME	46.80	RI

Coming Home
Photo courtesy of *Collectors News*

Wild and Free: Canada's Big Game

1988	THE GRIZZLY BEAR	29.80	NR
1989	THE MOOSE	29.80	NR
1989	THE BIGHORN SHEEP	32.80	NR
1989	THE WHITE–TAILED DEER	32.80	NR
1990	THE ELK	32.80	NR
1990	THE POLAR BEAR	32.80	NR
1990	THE PRONGHORN	34.80	NR
1990	THE CINNAMON BEAR	34.80	NR

Wings Upon the Wind

1986	THE LANDING, Donald Pentz	21.80	75.00
1986	THE NESTING	21.80	30.00
1986	THE COURTSHIP	24.80	30.00
1987	THE FAMILY.......................................	24.80	NR
1987	SOUTHWARD BOUND.............................	24.80	30.00
1987	WINTER HOME....................................	24.80	NR

DRESDEN GERMANY

Christmas

1971	SHEPHERD SCENE, 3,500	15.00	50.00
1972	NIKLAS CHURCH, 6,000...........................	15.00	25.00
1973	SCHWANSTEIN, 6,000.............................	18.00	35.00
1974	VILLAGE SCENE, 5,000	20.00	30.00

		Issue Price	Current Value
1975	ROTHENBURG SCENE, 5,000	24.00	30.00
1976	VILLAGE CHURCH, 5,000	26.00	35.00
1977	OLD MILL, 5,000	28.00	NR

Mother's Day

1972	DOE AND FAWN, Hans Waldheimer, 8,000	15.00	20.00
1973	MARE AND COLT, Hans Waldheimer, 6,000	16.00	25.00
1974	TIGER AND CUB, Hans Waldheimer, 5,000	20.00	25.00
1975	DACHSHUND FAMILY, Hans Waldheimer, 5,000	24.00	NR
1976	MOTHER OWL AND YOUNG, Hans Waldheimer, 5,000 ...	26.00	NR
1977	CHAMOIS, Hans Waldheimer, 5,000	28.00	NR

DUNCAN ROYALE UNITED STATES

History of Santa Claus I

1985	MEDIEVAL, Susie Morton, 10,000	40.00	65.00
1985	KRIS KRINGLE, Susie Morton, 10,000	40.00	60.00
1985	PIONEER, Susie Morton, 10,000	40.00	NR
1986	SODA POP, Susie Morton, 10,000	40.00	60.00
1986	CIVIL WAR, Susie Morton, 10,000	40.00	NR
1986	THOMAS NAST SANTA, Thomas Nast, 10,000	40.00	70.00
1986	RUSSIAN, Susie Morton, 10,000	40.00	NR
1986	WASSAIL, Susie Morton, 10,000	40.00	NR
1986	ST. NICK, Susie Morton, 10,000	40.00	70.00
1986	BLACK PETER, Susie Morton, 10,000	40.00	NR
1986	VICTORIAN, Susie Morton, 10,000	40.00	NR
1986	DEDT MOROZ, Susie Morton, 10,000	40.00	NR
	Set of 12	480.00	NR

History of Santa Claus II

1986	LORD OF MISRULE, T. Holter Bruckner, 10,000	80.00	NR

EBELING AND REUSS UNITED STATES

Christmas

1982	A TIME OF SONG AND CAROLING, Joan Walsh Anglund, 7,500	15.00	NR

ELEGANCE OF BRONZE

Knapp Series

1978	NAVAJO MADONNA, 2,500	285.00	NR

ENESCO UNITED STATES

Christmas Love

Year	Description	Issue Price	Current Value
1986	I'M SENDING YOU A WHITE CHRISTMAS, 101834, Samuel Butcher, 1 year	45.00	60.00
1987	MY PEACE I GIVE UNTO THEE, 102954, Samuel Butcher, 1 year	45.00	75.00
1988	MERRY CHRISTMAS DEER, 520284, Samuel Butcher, 1 year	50.00	80.00
1989	MAY YOUR CHRISTMAS BE A HAPPY HOME, 523003, Samuel Butcher, 1 year	50.00	60.00

My Peace I Give unto Thee
Photo courtesy of *Collectors News*

Tell Me the Story of Jesus
Photo courtesy of *Collectors News*

Little Bible Friends

Year	Description	Issue Price	Current Value
1981	THE NATIVITY, Lucas, 25,000	40.00	NR
1982	FLIGHT INTO EGYPT, Lucas, 25,000	40.00	NR
1982	THE LAST SUPPER, Lucas, 25,000	40.00	NR

Memories of Yesterday

Year	Description	Issue Price	Current Value
1993	LOOK OUT — SOMETHING GOOD IS COMING YOUR WAY!, 530298, Samuel Butcher, 1 year	50.00	RI

Precious Moments Christmas Blessings

Year	Description	Issue Price	Current Value
1990	WISHING YOU A MERRY CHRISTMAS, 523801, Samuel Butcher, 1 year	50.00	60.00
1991	BLESSINGS FROM ME TO THEE, 523680, Samuel Butcher, 1 year	50.00	NR
1992	BUT THE GREATEST OF THESE IS LOVE, 527742, Samuel Butcher, 1 year	50.00	RI
1993	WISHING YOU THE SWEETEST CHRISTMAS, 530204, Samuel Butcher, 1 year	50.00	RI

		Issue Price	Current Value

Precious Moments Christmas Collection

1981	COME LET US ADORE HIM, E5646, Biel and Butcher, 15,000...	40.00	50.00
1982	LET HEAVEN AND NATURE SING, E2347, Biel and Butcher, 15,000...	40.00	NR
1983	WE THREE KINGS, E9256, Biel and Butcher, 15,000......	40.00	NR
1984	UNTO US A CHILD IS BORN, E5395, Samuel Butcher, 15,000 ..	40.00	NR

Precious Moments Four Seasons

1985	VOICE OF SPRING, 12106, Samuel Butcher, 1 year	40.00	90.00
1985	SUMMER'S JOY, 12114, Samuel Butcher, 1 year	40.00	80.00
1986	AUTUMN'S PRAISE, 12122, Samuel Butcher, 1 year	40.00	70.00
1986	WINTER'S SONG, 12130, Samuel Butcher, 1 year	40.00	70.00

Precious Moments Inspired Thoughts

1980	LOVE ONE ANOTHER, E5215, Samuel Butcher, 15,000....	40.00	50.00
1981	MAKE A JOYFUL NOISE, E7174, Samuel Butcher, 15,000 .	40.00	NR
1982	I BELIEVE IN MIRACLES, E9257, Samuel Butcher, 15,000 .	40.00	NR
1984	LOVE IS KIND, E2847, Samuel Butcher, 15,000	40.00	NR

Precious Moments Joy of Christmas

1982	I'LL PLAY MY DRUM FOR HIM, E2357, Samuel Butcher, 1 year .	40.00	90.00
1983	CHRISTMASTIME IS FOR SHARING, E0505, Samuel Butcher, 1 year..	40.00	65.00
1984	THE WONDER OF CHRISTMAS, E5396, Samuel Butcher, 1 year	40.00	60.00
1985	TELL ME THE STORY OF JESUS, 15237, Samuel Butcher, 1 year	40.00	50.00

Precious Moments Mother's Love

1980	MOTHER SEW DEAR, E5217, Samuel Butcher, 15,000	40.00	NR
1981	THE PURR–FECT GRANDMA, E7173, Samuel Butcher, 15,000 .	40.00	NR
1982	THE HAND THAT ROCKS THE FUTURE, E9256, Samuel Butcher, 15,000..	40.00	NR
1983	LOVING THY NEIGHBOR, E2848, Samuel Butcher, 15,000 .	40.00	NR

Precious Moments — Open Editions

1980	THE LORD BLESS YOU AND KEEP YOU, E5216, Samuel Butcher	30.00	40.00
1981	REJOICING WITH YOU, E7172, Samuel Butcher.........	30.00	NR
1982	OUR FIRST CHRISTMAS TOGETHER, E2378, Samuel Butcher .	30.00	45.00
1982	JESUS LOVES ME – BOY HOLDING TEDDY BEAR, E9275, Samuel Butcher	30.00	45.00
1982	JESUS LOVES ME – GIRL WITH TEDDY BEAR, E9276, Samuel Butcher	30.00	45.00
1994	BRING THE LITTLE ONES TO JESUS, 531359, Samuel Butcher, 1 year..	50.00	RI

R. J. ERNST ENTERPRISES UNITED STATES
(See also Viletta China)

		Issue Price	Current Value

Bare Innocence

| 1986 | FREE AT LAST, Glen Banse, 10 days | 24.50 | NR |

Beautiful World

1981	TAHITIAN DREAMER, Susie Morton, 27,500	27.50	NR
1982	FLIRTATION, Susie Morton, 27,500	27.50	NR
1983	ELKE OF OSLO, Susie Morton, 27,500	27.50	NR

Busy Bears

1986	HEADING SOUTH, Simon Devoche, 100 days	19.50	NR
1986	BREAKFAST BREAK, Simon Devoche, 100 days	19.50	NR
1986	FALL FUN, Simon Devoche, 100 days	19.50	NR
1986	FLYING LOW, Simon Devoche, 100 days	19.50	NR

Children of the Past

| 1986 | BOY WITH HOOP, Peter Quidley, 90 days | 29.50 | NR |

Classy Cars

1982	THE 26T, Scott Kuhnly, 20 days	24.50	30.00
1982	THE 31A, Scott Kuhnly, 20 days	24.50	NR
1983	THE PICKUP, Scott Kuhnly, 20 days	24.50	NR
1983	THE PANEL VAN, Scott Kuhnly, 20 days	24.50	30.00

Country Cousins

| 1986 | YEP THAT'S IT, William Powell, 30 days | 24.50 | NR |
| 1986 | SHE'S ALL YOURS, William Powell, 30 days | 24.50 | NR |

Daddy's Little Girl

| 1986 | LOOK AT ME, DADDY, John Letostak, 90 days | 29.95 | NR |

Elvira

| 1986 | NIGHT ROSE, Susie Morton, 90 days | 29.50 | NR |

Fishing Boats

| 1983 | SUNSET AT MONTEREY, Scott Kuhnly, <1 year | 24.50 | NR |

Fogg and Steam

| 1986 | PRIDE OF THE NORTHWEST, Howard Fogg, 7,500 | 39.50 | NR |
| 1986 | AUTUMN IN NEW ENGLAND, Howard Fogg, 7,500 | 39.50 | NR |

		Issue Price	Current Value

Fondest Memories

| 1986 | MOTHER'S PEARLS, Ann Marry–Kenyon, limited .... | 60.00 | NR |
| 1986 | A TOUCHING MOMENT, Ann Marry–Kenyon, limited .... | 60.00 | NR |

Go for the Gold

| 1985 | VALERIE, Susie Morton, 5,000 .... | 29.50 | NR |

Hollywood Greats

1981	JOHN WAYNE, Susie Morton, 27,500	29.95	85.00
1981	GARY COOPER, Susie Morton, 27,500..................	29.95	40.00
1982	CLARK GABLE, Susie Morton, 27,500	29.95	75.00
1984	ALAN LADD, Susie Morton, 27,500	29.95	75.00

Liebchen

1983	AUTUMN LIEBCHEN, Von Ault, <1 year	19.50	NR
1983	SPRING LIEBCHEN, Von Ault, <1 year	19.50	NR
1983	SUMMER LIEBCHEN, Von Ault, <1 year................	19.50	NR
1983	WINTER LIEBCHEN, Von Ault, <1 year	19.50	NR

Little Misses Young and Fair

1983	HEART OF A CHILD, Alan Murray, 29,000...............	60.00	NR
1984	WHERE WILDFLOWERS GROW, Alan Murray, 29,000	60.00	NR
1986	FINAL TOUCH, Alan Murray, 29,000	60.00	NR

Final Touch
Photo courtesy of *Collectors News*

Love Story

| 1982 | CHAPTER I, Adam Shields, <1 year.................... | 24.50 | NR |
| 1983 | CHAPTER II, Adam Shields, <1 year .... | 24.50 | NR |

Me and Mom

		Issue Price	Current Value
1986	BEACH BABY, Susie Morton, 5,000	29.50	NR
1986	WHAT'S THIS?, Susie Morton, 5,000	29.50	NR

Mommy and Me

1982	FIRST TEA, Rusty Money, <1 year	35.00	NR
1983	BABY'S SLEEPING, Rusty Money, <1 year	35.00	NR

Baby's Sleeping
Photo courtesy of *Collectors News*

Breakfast Time
Photo courtesy of *Collectors News*

My Fair Ladies

1982	LADY SABRINA, Rusty Money, 29,000	50.00	NR
1983	LADY VICTORIA, Rusty Money, 29,000	50.00	NR

Narrow Gauge

1983	HALFWAY TO ALAMOSA, Jack Hamilton, <1 year	29.50	NR
1984	DOWN FROM RICO, Jack Hamilton, limited	29.50	NR

The Performance

1980	ACT I, Bonnie Porter, 5,000	65.00	BR

Rufus and Roxanne

1980	LOVE IS..., C. Kelly, 19,900	14.95	NR

Seems Like Yesterday

1981	STOP AND SMELL THE ROSES, Rusty Money, 10 days ...	24.50	NR
1982	HOME BY LUNCH, Rusty Money, 10 days	24.50	NR
1982	LISA'S CREEK, Rusty Money, 10 days	24.50	NR

			Issue Price	Current Value
1983	IT'S GOT MY NAME ON IT, Rusty Money, 10 days	....	24.50	NR
1983	MY MAGIC HAT, Rusty Money, 10 days	....	24.50	NR
1984	LITTLE PRINCE, Rusty Money, 10 days	....	24.50	NR

Shades of Time

1986	SCENT AND SATIN, Alan Murray, 5,000	....	45.00	NR

So Young, So Sweet

1982	GIRL WITH STRAW HAT, Susie Morton, 10 days	....	39.50	NR
1983	MY FAVORITE NECKLACE, Susie Morton, 10 days	....	39.50	NR
1983	BREAKFAST TIME, Susie Morton, 10 days	....	39.50	NR

Star Trek

1984	MR. SPOCK, Susie Morton, 90 days	....	29.50	95.00
1984	DR. MCCOY – MEDICAL OFFICER, Susie Morton, 90 days		29.50	65.00
1985	SULU, Susie Morton, 90 days	....	29.50	45.00
1985	SCOTTY, Susie Morton, 90 days	....	29.50	50.00
1985	UHURA, Susie Morton, 90 days	....	29.50	55.00
1985	CHEKOV, Susie Morton, 90 days	....	29.50	55.00
1985	CAPTAIN KIRK, Susie Morton, 90 days	....	29.50	95.00
1985	BEAM US DOWN, SCOTTY, Susie Morton, 90 days	......	29.50	75.00
1985	THE ENTERPRISE, Susie Morton, 90 days	....	29.50	85.00

Star Trek Commemorative

1986	THE TROUBLE WITH TRIBBLES, Susie Morton, limited	..	29.50	NR
1987	MIRROR, MIRROR, Susie Morton, limited	....	29.50	NR
1987	A PIECE OF THE ACTION, Susie Morton, limited	....	29.50	NR
1987	THE DEVIL IN THE DARK, Susie Morton, limited	....	29.50	NR
1987	AMOK TIME, Susie Morton, limited	....	29.50	NR
1987	THE CITY ON THE EDGE OF FOREVER, Susie Morton, limited		29.50	NR
1987	JOURNEY TO BABEL, Susie Morton, limited	....	29.50	NR
1988	THE MENAGERIE, Susie Morton, limited	....	29.50	NR

This Land Is Our Land

1986	SAND DUNES, Gage Taylor, 5,000	....	29.50	NR

Turn of the Century

1981	RIVERBOAT HONEYMOON, Rusty Money,10 days	....	35.00	NR
1982	CHILDREN'S CAROUSEL, Rusty Money, 10 days	....	35.00	NR
1984	FLOWER MARKET, Rusty Money, 10 days	....	35.00	NR
1985	BALLOON RACE, Rusty Money, 10 days	....	35.00	NR

Women of the West (Viletta)

1979	EXPECTATIONS, Donald Putnam, 10,000	....	39.50	NR

		Issue Price	Current Value
1981	SILVER DOLLAR SAL, Donald Putnam, 10,000	39.50	NR
1982	SCHOOL MARM, Donald Putnam, 10,000	39.50	NR
1983	DOLLY, Donald Putnam, 10,000	39.50	NR

Yesterday

1982	AMBER, Glenice,10 days	24.50	NR
1983	ELMER, Glenice,10 days	24.50	NR
1976	KATIE, Glenice, 10 days.............................	24.50	NR

Single Issues

1978	DEGRAZIA BY MARCO, J. Marco, 5,000	65.00	NR
1983	TRIBUTE TO HENRY FONDA, Susie Morton, 10 days.....	45.00	NR
1984	MARILYN MONROE, Susie Morton, 61 days	29.50	NR

Single Issues, Commemoratives

1981	JOHN LENNON, Susie Morton, 30 days	39.50	60.00
1982	ELVIS PRESLEY, Susie Morton, 30 days	39.50	85.00
1982	MARILYN MONROE, Susie Morton, 30 days	39.50	55.00
1983	JUDY GARLAND, Susie Morton, 30 days	39.50	60.00
1983	JOHN WAYNE, Susie Morton, 2,500	39.50	60.00

ESCALERA PRODUCTION ART UNITED STATES

Olympiad Triumphs Collection

1984	TRACK, Rudy Escalera, 19,500	60.00	NR
1984	FIELD EVENTS, Rudy Escalera, 19,500	60.00	NR
1984	BASKETBALL, Rudy Escalera, 19,500	60.00	NR
1984	SWIMMING, Rudy Escalera, 19,500	60.00	NR
1984	SOCCER, Rudy Escalera, 19,500	60.00	NR
1984	BASEBALL AND TENNIS, Rudy Escalera, 19,500	60.00	NR
1984	BOXING, Rudy Escalera, 19,500	60.00	NR
1984	GYMNASTICS, Rudy Escalera, 19,500	60.00	NR

EVERGREEN PRESS UNITED STATES

Catalina Island

1986	AVALON BAY, Roger Upton, 5,000	39.95	NR
1986	PLEASURE PIER, Roger Upton, 5,000	39.95	NR
1987	CATALINA CALLS, Frank Loudin, 5,000	39.95	NR
1987	REFLECTIONS, Frank Loudin, 5,000	39.95	NR
1987	CASINO WAY, Frank Loudin, 5,000	39.95	NR

FAIRMONT CHINA UNITED STATES

		Issue Price	Current Value
America's Most Beloved			
1980	JOHN WAYNE, Clarence Thorpe, 5,000	13.95	NR
1981	PORTRAIT OF ROCKWELL, Clarence Thorpe, 15,000	40.00	NR
1980	MUSIC MAKER, Norman Rockwell, 15,000	19.95	NR
1981	THE TINKERER, Norman Rockwell, 15,000..............	19.95	NR
Annual			
1984	LITTLE BALLERINA, Anthony Sidoni, 5,000	29.95	NR
1984	ORGAN GRINDER, Anthony Sidoni, 5,000	29.95	NR
Child of America			
1979	ESKIMO GIRL, Laura Johnson, 3,000	48.00	NR
Children of the World			
1976	LOS NIÑOS, Ted DeGrazia, 5,000......................	35.00	1,000.00
1976	LOS NIÑOS, Ted DeGrazia, sgd, 500	100.00	1,500.00
1977	WHITE DOVE, Ted DeGrazia, 5,000	40.00	150.00
1977	WHITE DOVE, Ted DeGrazia, sgd, 500	100.00	300.00
1978	FLOWER GIRL, Ted DeGrazia, 9,500...................	45.00	NR
1978	FLOWER GIRL, Ted DeGrazia, sgd, 500	100.00	300.00
1979	FLOWER BOY, Ted DeGrazia, 9,500	45.00	60.00
1979	FLOWER BOY, Ted DeGrazia, sgd, 500	100.00	300.00
1980	LITTLE COCOPAH INDIAN GIRL, Ted DeGrazia, 9,500	50.00	65.00
1980	LITTLE COCOPAH INDIAN GIRL, Ted DeGrazia, sgd, 500 .	100.00	300.00
1981	BEAUTIFUL BURDEN, Ted DeGrazia, 9,500	50.00	NR
1981	BEAUTIFUL BURDEN, Ted DeGrazia, sgd, 500	100.00	350.00
1981	MERRY LITTLE INDIAN, Ted DeGrazia, 9,500	55.00	90.00
1981	MERRY LITTLE INDIAN, Ted DeGrazia, sgd, 500.........	100.00	350.00
1983	WONDERING, Ted DeGrazia, 10,000	60.00	NR

Wondering
Photo courtesy of *Collectors News*

		Issue Price	Current Value
1984	PINK PAPOOSE, Ted DeGrazia, 10,000	65.00	BR
1985	SUNFLOWER BOY, Ted DeGrazia, 10,000	65.00	BR

Early Works

1979	OLD MAN WINTER, Norman Rockwell, 15,000	19.95	50.00
1980	THE INVENTOR, Norman Rockwell, 15,000	19.95	NR
1980	READY FOR SCHOOL, Norman Rockwell, 15,000	19.95	NR

Famous Clowns

1976	FREDDIE THE FREELOADER, Red Skelton, 10,000	55.00	375.00
1977	W. C. FIELDS, Red Skelton, 10,000	55.00	BR
1978	HAPPY, Red Skelton, 10,000	55.00	75.00
1979	THE PLEDGE, Red Skelton, 10,000	55.00	NR

Gnome Four Seasons

1980	LITTLE SWINGER, Rien Poortvliet, 15,000	29.50	NR
1980	GNOME DE BLOOM, Rien Poortvliet, 15,000	29.50	NR
1980	THE LOOKOUTS, Rien Poortvliet, 15,000	29.50	NR
1980	FIRST SKATER, Rien Poortvliet, 15,000	29.50	NR
1981	SPRING SHARING, Rien Poortvliet, 15,000	29.95	NR
1981	FUN AND GAMES, Rien Poortvliet, 15,000	29.95	NR
1981	UP, UP AND AWAY, Rien Poortvliet, 15,000	29.95	NR
1981	FIRST SKIER, Rien Poortvliet, 15,000	29.95	NR
1982	GNOME KNOWLEDGE, Rien Poortvliet, 15,000	29.95	NR
1982	THE BERRY PICKERS, Rien Poortvliet, 15,000	29.95	NR
1982	GNOME MADE, Rien Poortvliet, 15,000	29.95	NR
1982	KEEP THE GNOME FIRES BURNING, Rien Poortvliet, 15,000 . .	29.95	NR

Gnome Holiday

1980	GNOME BLUES, Rien Poortvliet, 5,000	24.50	NR
1981	GIFT OF LOVE, Rien Poortvliet, 5,000	29.95	NR

Hobo Joe

1982	DO NOT DISTURB, Ron Lee, 7,500	50.00	NR

Israeli Commemorative (Ghent Collection)

1978	THE PROMISED LAND, Alton S. Tobey, 5,738	79.00	85.00

Legend of the Gnomes

1984	BIRTHDAY PLANTING, Rien Poortvliet, 15,000	29.95	NR
1984	FOREST FIRST AID, Rien Poortvliet, 15,000	29.95	NR
1984	GNOME HOME, Rien Poortvliet, 15,000	29.95	NR
1984	GNOME KNOW HOW, Rien Poortvliet, 15,000	29.95	NR

		Issue Price	Current Value
1984	HAPPY PASTIME, Rien Poortvliet, 15,000	29.95	NR
1984	LABOR OF LOVE, Rien Poortvliet, 15,000	29.95	NR
1984	LITTLE COUNSELOR, Rien Poortvliet, 15,000	29.95	NR
1984	WINTER SHARING, Rien Poortvliet, 15,000	29.95	NR

Long Road West

1981	THE TRAILBLAZERS, Jim Henson, 20,000	40.00	NR
1981	PRAIRIE SCHOONER PIONEER, Jim Henson, 20,000	40.00	NR
1981	PONY EXPRESS, Jim Henson, 20,000	40.00	NR
1981	THE PEACE MAKERS, Jim Henson, 20,000	40.00	NR
1981	COWBOYS OF THE WEST, Jim Henson, 20,000	40.00	NR
1981	LAWMEN OF THE WEST, Jim Henson, 20,000	40.00	NR

Lords of the Plains

1979	SITTING BULL, Richard Nickerson, 5,000	60.00	NR

Memory Annual (Ghent Collection)

1977	MEMORY PLATE, 1,977	77.00	85.00
1978	MEMORY PLATE, 1,978	78.00	85.00
1979	MEMORY PLATE, 1,979	80.00	NR
1980	MEMORY PLATE, 1,980	80.00	NR

Passing of Plains Indians (Collector's Heirlooms)

1979	CHEYENNE CHIEFTAIN, Andre Bouche, 7,500	65.00	NR

Playful Memories

1981	RENEE, Sue Etem, 10,000	39.50	BR
1982	JEREMY, Sue Etem, 10,000	42.50	BR
1983	JAMIE, Sue Etem, 10,000	42.50	BR
1983	RANDY, Sue Etem, 10,000	45.00	BR

Ruthven Birds Feathered Friends

1978	CHICKADEES, John Ruthven, 5,000	39.50	NR
1981	SCREECH OWLS, John Ruthven, 5,000	39.50	NR

Spencer Annual

1977	PATIENT ONES, Irene Spencer, 10,000	42.50	100.00
1978	YESTERDAY, TODAY AND TOMORROW, Irene Spencer, 10,000 85.00		47.50

Spencer Special

1978	HUG ME, Irene Spencer, 10,000	55.00	95.00
1978	SLEEP LITTLE BABY, Irene Spencer, 10,000	65.00	NR

		Issue Price	Current Value

Timeless Moments

1978	TENDERNESS, Clarence Thorpe, 5,000	45.00	NR
1979	RENAISSANCE, Clarence Thorpe, 5,000	45.00	NR
1980	COMING IN GLORY, Clarence Thorpe, 5,000	39.95	NR

Vanishing Americana

| 1984 | AMERICAN EAGLE, Clarence Thorpe, 15,000 .... | 13.50 | NR |
| 1984 | THE COUNTRY DOCTOR, Clarence Thorpe, 15,000 .... | 13.50 | NR |

When I Grow Up

1981	I'LL BE LOVED, Ann Hershenburgh, 7,500	29.95	NR
1981	I'LL BE LIKE MOMMY, Ann Hershenburgh, 7,500	29.95	NR
1981	I'LL BE FIRST LADY, Ann Hershenburgh, 7,500	29.95	NR
1981	I'LL BE A STAR, Ann Hershenburgh, 7,500	29.95	NR

Single Issues

1978	THE FENCE, St. Clair, 5,000	45.00	NR
1978	SIOUX WARRIOR, Olaf Wieghorst, 5,000	65.00	95.00
1978	THE SCOUT, Olaf Wieghorst, 5,000	65.00	NR
1983	MY LITTLE SHELTIE, Clarence Thorpe, 5,000	39.95	NR
1984	THE ORGAN GRINDER, Anthony Sidoni, 5,000	29.95	NR

FENTON ART GLASS UNITED STATES

Alliance

1975	LAFAYETTE AND WASHINGTON, blue satin glass, 1 year	15.00	30.00
1975	LAFAYETTE AND WASHINGTON, red satin glass, 1 year .	17.50	30.00
1975	LAFAYETTE AND WASHINGTON, white satin glass, 1 year	15.00	30.00
1976	LAFAYETTE AND WASHINGTON, blue satin glass, 1 year	15.00	30.00
1976	LAFAYETTE AND WASHINGTON, chocolate glass, 1 year	17.50	30.00
1976	LAFAYETTE AND WASHINGTON, white satin glass, 1 year	15.00	30.00

American Craftsman Carnival

1970	GLASSMAKER, 1 year	10.00	50.00
1970	GLASSMAKER, black, 600	10.00	125.00
1970	GLASSMAKER, 200	10.00	200.00
1971	PRINTER, 1 year	10.00	60.00
1972	BLACKSMITH, 1 year	10.00	125.00
1973	SHOEMAKER, 1 year	12.50	50.00
1974	PIONEER COOPER, 1 year..........................	12.50	45.00
1975	SILVERSMITH REVERE, 1 year......................	12.50	50.00
1976	GUNSMITH, 1 year	13.50	35.00
1977	POTTER, 1 year..................................	15.00	25.00
1978	WHEELWRIGHT, 1 year	15.00	NR
1979	CABINETMAKER, 1 year...........................	15.00	NR

		Issue Price	Current Value
1980	TANNER, 1 year	16.50	NR
1981	HOUSEWRIGHT, 1 year	17.50	NR

The Glassmaker

The Printer

The Blacksmith

Pioneer Cooper

Childhood Treasure

1983	TEDDY BEAR, Diane Johnson, 15,000	45.00	NR

Christmas In America

1970	LITTLE BROWN CHURCH IN VALE, carnival glass, 1 year	12.50	NR
1970	LITTLE BROWN CHURCH IN VALE, blue satin glass, 1 year	12.50	50.00

		Issue Price	Current Value
1971	LITTLE BROWN CHURCH IN VALE, white satin glass, 1 year ..	12.50	35.00
1971	OLD BRICK CHURCH, carnival glass, 1 year	12.50	NR
1971	OLD BRICK CHURCH, blue satin glass, 1 year...........	12.50	40.00
1971	OLD BRICK CHURCH, white satin glass, 1 year	12.50	30.00
1972	TWO– HORNED CHURCH, carnival glass, 1 year	12.50	NR
1972	TWO–HORNED CHURCH, blue satin glass, 1 year	12.50	40.00
1972	TWO–HORNED CHURCH, white satin glass, 1 year	12.50	25.00
1973	SAINT MARY'S/MOUNTAINS, carnival glass, 1 year	12.50	NR
1973	SAINT MARY'S/MOUNTAINS, blue satin glass, 1 year ...	12.50	35.00
1973	SAINT MARY'S/MOUNTAINS, white satin glass, 1 year ..	12.50	25.00
1974	NATION'S CHURCH, carnival glass, 1 year	13.50	NR
1974	NATION'S CHURCH, blue satin glass, 1 year	13.50	30.00
1974	NATION'S CHURCH, white satin glass, 1 year	13.50	25.00
1975	BIRTHPLACE OF LIBERTY, carnival glass, 1 year	13.50	NR
1975	BIRTHPLACE OF LIBERTY, blue satin glass, 1 year	13.50	30.00
1975	BIRTHPLACE OF LIBERTY, white satin glass, 1 year	13.50	25.00
1976	OLD NORTH CHURCH, carnival glass, 1 year	15.00	NR
1976	OLD NORTH CHURCH, blue satin glass, 1 year..........	15.00	25.00
1976	OLD NORTH CHURCH, white satin glass, 1 year.........	15.00	25.00
1977	SAN CARLOS BOROMEO DE CARMELO, carnival glass, 1 year	15.00	NR
1977	SAN CARLOS BOROMEO DE CARMELO, blue satin glass, 1 year	15.00	NR
1977	SAN CARLOS BOROMEO DE CARMELO, white satin glass, 1 year	15.00	NR
1978	CHURCH OF THE HOLY TRINITY, carnival glass, 1 year ...	15.00	NR
1978	CHURCH OF THE HOLY TRINITY, blue satin glass, 1 year .	15.00	NR
1978	CHURCH OF THE HOLY TRINITY, white satin glass, 1 year	15.00	NR
1979	SAN JOSE Y MIGUEL DE AQUAYO, carnival glass, 1 year	15.00	NR
1979	SAN JOSE Y MIGUEL DE AQUAYO, blue satin glass, 1 year NR		15.00
1979	SAN JOSE Y MIGUEL DE AQUAYO, white satin glass, 1 year ..	15.00	NR
1980	CHRIST CHURCH, ALEXANDRIA, VA, carnival glass, 1 year ...	16.50	NR
1980	CHRIST CHURCH, ALEXANDRIA, VA, blue satin glass, 1 year..	16.50	NR
1980	CHRIST CHURCH, ALEXANDRIA, VA, white satin glass, 1 year	16.50	NR
1981	MISSION OF SAN XAVIER DEL BAC, carnival glass, 1 year ...	18.50	NR
1981	MISSION OF SAN XAVIER DEL BAC, blue satin glass, 1 year ..	18.50	NR
1981	MISSION OF SAN XAVIER DEL BAC, white satin glass, 1 year .	18.50	NR
1981	MISSION OF SAN XAVIER DEL BAC, florentine glass, 1 year ..	25.00	NR

Currier & Ives Limited Edition

1980	WINTER IN THE COUNTRY – THE OLD GRIST MILL, Anthony Rosena, 1 year	25.00	NR
1981	HARVEST, Anthony Rosena, 1 year.....................	25.00	NR
1982	THE OLD HOMESTEAD IN WINTER, Anthony Rosena, 1 year .	25.00	NR
1983	WINTER PASTIME, Anthony Rosena, 1 year............	25.00	NR

Designer Series

1983	DOWN HOME, Gloria Fina, 1,000	65.00	NR
1983	LIGHTHOUSE POINT, Gloria Fina, 1,000	65.00	NR

Hand Painted Christmas Classic

		Issue Price	Current Value
1979	NATURE'S CHRISTMAS, 1 year	35.00	NR
1980	GOING HOME, 1 year	38.50	NR
1981	ALL IS CALM, 1 year	42.50	NR
1982	COUNTRY CHRISTMAS, 1 year	42.50	NR

Mother's Day I

1971	MADONNA WITH SLEEPING CHILD, carnival glass, 1 year	10.75	30.00
1971	MADONNA WITH SLEEPING CHILD, blue satin glass, 1 year	10.75	35.00
1972	MADONNA OF THE GOLDFINCH, carnival glass, 1 year	12.50	35.00
1972	MADONNA OF THE GOLDFINCH, blue satin glass, 1 year	12.50	30.00
1972	MADONNA OF THE GOLDFINCH, white satin glass, 1 year	12.50	25.00
1973	SMALL COWPER MADONNA, carnival glass, 1 year	12.50	30.00
1973	SMALL COWPER MADONNA, blue satin glass, 1 year	12.50	30.00
1973	SMALL COWPER MADONNA, white satin glass, 1 year	12.50	20.00
1974	MADONNA OF THE GROTTO, carnival glass, 1 year	13.50	25.00
1974	MADONNA OF THE GROTTO, blue satin glass, 1 year	13.50	25.00
1974	MADONNA OF THE GROTTO, white satin glass, 1 year	13.50	20.00
1975	TADDEI MADONNA, carnival glass, 1 year	13.50	30.00
1975	TADDEI MADONNA, blue satin glass, 1 year	13.50	30.00
1975	TADDEI MADONNA, white satin glass, 1 year	13.50	25.00
1976	HOLY NIGHT, carnival glass, 1 year	13.50	25.00
1976	HOLY NIGHT, blue satin glass, 1 year	13.50	NR
1976	HOLY NIGHT, white satin glass, 1 year	13.50	NR

Mother's Day 1976

1977	MADONNA AND CHILD WITH POMEGRANATE, carnival glass, 1 year	15.00	NR
1977	MADONNA AND CHILD WITH POMEGRANATE, blue satin glass, 1 year	15.00	NR
1977	MADONNA AND CHILD WITH POMEGRANATE, white satin glass, 1 year	15.00	NR

		Issue Price	Current Value
1978	MADONNINA, carnival glass, 1 year	15.00	NR
1978	MADONNINA, blue satin glass, 1 year	15.00	NR
1978	MADONNINA, white satin glass, 1 year	15.00	NR
1979	MADONNA OF THE ROSE HEDGE, carnival glass, 1 year	15.00	NR
1979	MADONNA OF THE ROSE HEDGE, blue satin glass, 1 year	15.00	NR
1979	MADONNA OF THE ROSE HEDGE, white satin glass, 1 year	15.00	NR
1979	MADONNA OF THE ROSE HEDGE, ruby iridescent, 5,000	35.00	BR

Mother's Day II

1990	MOTHER SWAN, Linda Everson, opal satin glass	45.00	NR
1991	MOTHER'S WATCHFUL EYE, Martha Reynolds, opal satin glass	45.00	NR
1992	LET'S PLAY WITH MOM, Martha Reynolds, opal satin glass	49.50	RI
1993	MOTHER DEER, Martha Reynolds, opal satin glass	49.50	RI
1994	LOVING PUPPY, Martha Reynolds, opal satin glass	49.50	RI

Mother's Day, Hand Painted

1980	NEW BORN, Linda Everson, custard satin glass	28.50	NR
1981	GENTLE FAWN, Linda Everson, custard satin glass	32.50	NR
1982	NATURE'S AWAKENING, Linda Everson, custard satin glass	35.00	NR
1983	WHERE'S MOM, Linda Everson, custard satin glass	35.00	NR
1984	PRECIOUS PANDA, Linda Everson, custard satin glass	35.00	NR
1985	MOTHER'S LITTLE LAMB, Linda Everson, custard satin glass	45.00	NR

Valentine's Day

1972	ROMEO AND JULIET, carnival glass, 1 year	15.00	25.00
1972	ROMEO AND JULIET, blue satin glass, 1 year	15.00	25.00

FINE ARTS MARKETING CANADA

Autumn Flights

1986	CANADIAN GEESE, Jerold Bishop, 5,000	55.00	NR
1986	MALLARD DUCKS, Jerold Bishop, 5,000	55.00	NR

Turn, Turn, Turn

1986	AUTUMN BACK HOME, Jerold Bishop, 5,000	50.00	NR
1986	WINTER MEMORIES, Jerold Bishop, 5,000	50.00	NR

FIREHOUSE COLLECTIBLES UNITED STATES

This Ole Bear

1984	BUSTER AND SAM, Janet Tuck, 5,000	39.50	NR
1984	MATILDA JANE, Janet Tuck, 5,000	39.50	NR

FITZ AND FLOYD, INC.

Fitz and Floyd Annual Christmas Plate

Year	Description	Issue Price	Current Value
1992	NUTCRACKER SUITE'S "THE MAGIC OF THE NUTCRACKER," R. Havins, closed	65.00	RI
1993	CHARLES DICKENS' "A CHRISTMAS CAROL," T. Kerr, 5,000	70.00	RI

Myth of Santa Claus

1993	RUSSIAN SANTA, R. Havins, 5,000	70.00	RI

Twelve Days of Christmas

1993	A PARTRIDGE IN A PEAR TREE, T. Kerr, 5,000	70.00	RI

Wonderland

1993	A MAD TEA PARTY, R. Havins, 5,000	70.00	RI

FLAMBRO IMPORTS

Emmett Kelly, Jr.

1983	WHY ME?, Plate I, C. Kelly, 10,000	40.00	225.00
1984	BALLOONS FOR SALE, Plate II, C. Kelly, 10,000	40.00	200.00
1985	BIG BUSINESS, Plate III, C. Kelly, 10,000	40.00	160.00
1986	AND GOD BLESS AMERICA, Plate IV, C. Kelly, 10,000	40.00	170.00
1988	'TIS THE SEASON, D. Rust, 10,000	40.00	60.00
1989	LOOKING BACK — 65TH BIRTHDAY, D. Rust, 6,500	50.00	115.00
1991	WINTER, D. Rust, 10,000	60.00	NR
1992	SPRING, D. Rust, 10,000	60.00	RI
1992	SUMMER, D. Rust, 10,000	60.00	RI
1992	AUTUMN, D. Rust, 10,000	60.00	RI

Raggedy Ann & Andy

1988	70 YEARS YOUNG, C. Beylon, 10,000	35.00	45.00

THE FLEETWOOD COLLECTION UNITED STATES

Birds and Flowers of the Meadow and Garden

1980	BALTIMORE ORIOLE AND MORNING GLORY, Don Balke, limited	39.00	NR
1980	GOLDFINCH AND BULLTHISTLE, Don Balke, limited	39.00	NR
1980	CARDINAL AND LUPINE, Don Balke, limited	39.00	NR
1980	EASTERN BLUE BIRD AND BLACKEYED SUSAN, Don Balke, limited	39.00	NR
1980	CAPPED CHICKADEE AND NEW ENGLAND ASTER, Don Balke, limited	39.00	NR
1980	ROBIN AND CRABAPPLE, Don Balke, limited	39.00	NR

		Issue Price	Current Value
1980	PAINTED BUNTING AND BLACKBERRY, Don Balke, limited	39.00	NR
1980	GOLDEN CROWNED KINGLET AND DOWNY PHLOX, Don Balke, limited	39.00	NR
1980	REDBREASTED NUTHATCH AND JAPANESE HONEYSUCKLE, Don Balke, limited	39.00	NR
1980	MAGNOLIA WARBLER AND COMMON DAY LILY, Don Balke, limited	39.00	NR
1980	HUMMINGBIRD AND FIRE PINK, Don Balke, limited	39.00	NR
1980	SCARLET TANAGER AND BLUE COLUMBINE, Don Balke, limited	39.00	NR

Blossoms of China

1982	PEONY, Ren Yu, 7,500	49.50	NR
1982	HERBACEOUS PEONY, Ren Yu, 7,500	49.50	NR
1982	CHRYSANTHEMUM, Ren Yu, 7,500	49.50	NR
1982	MAGNOLIA, Ren Yu, 7,500	49.50	NR
1982	PLUM BLOSSOM, Ren Yu, 7,500	49.50	NR
1982	NARCISSUS, Ren Yu, 7,500	49.50	NR

Christmas

1980	MAGI, Fritz Wegner, 5,000	45.00	55.00
1981	HOLY CHILD, Fritz Wegner, 7,500	49.50	NR
1982	THE SHEPHERDS, Fritz Wegner, 5,000	50.00	NR
1985	COMING HOME FOR CHRISTMAS, F. Jacques, 5,000	50.00	NR

Golden Age of Sail

1981	FLYING CLOUD, Charles Lundgren, 5,000	39.00	NR
1982	NEW WORLD, Charles Lundgren, 5,000	39.00	NR
1982	YOUNG AMERICA, Charles Lundgren, 5,000	39.00	NR
1982	COURIER, Charles Lundgren, 5,000	39.00	NR
1982	SEA WITCH, Charles Lundgren, 5,000	39.00	NR
1983	GREAT REPUBLIC, Charles Lundgren, 5,000	39.00	NR

Mother's Day

1980	COTTONTAILS, Don Balke, 5,000	45.00	60.00
1981	RACCOONS, Don Balke, 5,000	45.00	NR
1982	WHITETAIL DEER, Don Balke, 5,000	50.00	NR
1983	CANADA GEESE, Don Balke, 5,000	50.00	NR

Pandas of Wu Zuoren

1981	MOTHER AND BABY, Wu Zuoren, 5,000	39.00	NR
1981	SLEEPING PANDA, Wu Zuoren, 5,000	39.00	NR
1981	TWO PANDAS, Wu Zuoren, 5,000	39.00	NR
1981	MOTHER AND BABY PLAYING, Wu Zuoren, 5,000	39.00	NR
1981	MOTHER HOLDING BABY, Wu Zuoren, 5,000	39.00	NR
1981	PANDA ON A ROCK, Wu Zuoren, 5,000	39.00	NR

		Issue Price	Current Value
Royal Wedding			
1981	PRINCE CHARLES/LADY DIANA, Jeffrey Mathews, 9,500	49.50	65.00
1986	PRINCE ANDREW/SARAH FERGUSON, Jeffrey Mathews, 10,000	50.00	NR
Statue of Liberty			
1986	STATUE OF LIBERTY, Jeffrey Mathews, 10,000	50.00	NR
Tsarevich's Bride			
1981	AN ARROW IN THE AIR, A. M. Kurkin, 7,500	50.00	60.00
1982	BOYER'S COURTYARD, A. M. Kurkin, 7,500	50.00	60.00
1982	RICH MERCHANT'S YARD, A. M. Kurkin, 7,500	50.00	60.00
1983	MOUTH OF A FROG, A. M. Kurkin, 7,500	50.00	60.00
Single Issue			
1982	MOM'S APPLE PIE, Gene Boyer, <1 year	29.00	NR

FONTANA

Christmas			
1972	18TH CENTURY COUPLE WITH DOG, 2,000	35.00	BR
1973	SLEIGHING, 1,000	35.00	BR
Mother's Day			
1973	MOTHER AND CHILD, 2,000	35.00	BR

FOSTORIA GLASS UNITED STATES

American Milestones			
1971	BETSY ROSS FLAG, 5,000	12.50	25.00
1972	NATIONAL ANTHEM, 8,000	12.50	NR
1973	WASHINGTON CROSSING DELAWARE, 1 year	12.50	NR
1974	SPIRIT OF '76, 1 year	13.00	NR
1975	MOUNT RUSHMORE, 1 year	16.00	NR
State Plates			
1971	CALIFORNIA, 6,000	12.50	NR
1971	NEW YORK, 12,000	12.50	NR
1971	OHIO, 3,000	12.50	NR
1972	FLORIDA, 1 year	12.50	NR
1972	HAWAII, 1 year	12.50	NR
1972	PENNSYLVANIA, 1 year	12.50	NR
1972	MASSACHUSETTS, 1 year	13.00	NR
1972	TEXAS, 1 year	13.00	NR

		Issue Price	Current Value
1973	MICHIGAN, 1 year ....,,.	13.50	NR

FOUNTAINHEAD

As Free as the Wind

1989	AS FREE AS THE WIND, Mario Fernandez	295.00	375.00

Wings of Freedom

1985	COURTSHIP FLIGHT, Mario Fernandez, 2,500...........	250.00	2,000.00
1986	WINGS OF FREEDOM, Mario Fernandez, 2,500	250.00	1,000.00

Courtship Flight
Photo courtesy of *Collectors News*

FRANKLIN MINT UNITED STATES

American Revolution

1976–77	BOSTON TEA PARTY, Steven Dohanos, 3,596.........	75.00	NR
1976–77	PATRICK HENRY URGES ARMED RESISTANCE, Paul Calle, 3,596	75.00	NR
1976–77	PAUL REVERE'S RIDE, John Falter, 3,596.............	75.00	NR
1976–77	THE BATTLE OF CONCORD BRIDGE, Paul Rickert, 3,596	75.00	NR
1976–77	THE CAPTURE OF FORT TICONDEROGA, Dean Fausett, 3,596 .	75.00	NR
1976–77	THE BATTLE OF BUNKER HILL, Alton S. Tobey, 3,596 ..	75.00	NR
1976–77	THE SIGNING OF THE DECLARATION, Gordon Phillips, 3,596 ..	75.00	NR
1976–77	WASHINGTON CROSSES THE DELAWARE, Alexander Farnham, 3,596	75.00	NR
1976–77	BURGOYNE DEFEATED AT SARATOGA, Don Stone, 3,596	75.00	NR
1976–77	WINTER AT VALLEY FORGE, Isa Barratt, 3,596........	75.00	NR

		Issue Price	Current Value
1976–77	BONHOMME RICHARD DEFEATS SERAPIS, John Pike, 3,596	75.00	NR
1976–77	VICTORY AT YORKTOWN, John Chumley, 3,596	75.00	NR

Annual

1977	TRIBUTE TO THE ARTS, 1,901	280.00	300.00
1978	TRIBUTE TO NATURE, 435	280.00	300.00

Arabian Nights

1981–82	ALADDIN AND HIS WONDERFUL LAMP, Christopher McEwan, 690	27.50	NR
1981–82	ALI BABA AND FORTY THIEVES, Christopher McEwan, 690 . .	27.50	NR
1981–82	THE CITY OF BRASS, Christopher McEwan, 690	27.50	NR
1981–82	THE FAIR PERSIAN, Christopher McEwan, 690	27.50	NR
1981–82	THE FISHERMAN, Christopher McEwan, 690	27.50	NR
1981–82	THE MAGIC HORSE, Christopher McEwan, 690	27.50	NR
1981–82	THE MERCHANT AND THE GENIE, Christopher McEwan, 690	27.50	NR
1981–82	PRINCE AGIB, Christopher McEwan, 690	27.50	NR
1981–82	PRINCE CAMARAIZAMAN AND THE PRINCESS BADOURA, Christopher McEwan, 690	27.50	NR
1981–82	SINBAD THE SAILOR, Christopher McEwan, 690	27.50	NR
1981–82	THE VIZIER WHO WAS PUNISHED, Christopher McEwan, 690	27.50	NR
1981–82	THE YOUNG KING OF THE EBONY ISLES, Christopher McEwan, 690	27.50	NR

Audubon Society

1972	THE GOLDFINCH, James Fenwick Lansdowne, 10,193 . . .	125.00	BR
1972	THE WOOD DUCK, James Fenwick Lansdowne, 10,193 . .	125.00	BR
1973	THE CARDINAL, James Fenwick Lansdowne, 10,193	125.00	BR
1973	THE RUFFED GROUSE, James Fenwick Lansdowne, 10,193 . . .	125.00	BR

Bernard Buffet

1973	GAZELLE, Bernard Buffet, 570	150.00	275.00
1974	PANDA, Bernard Buffet, 408	150.00	250.00
1975	GIRAFFE, Bernard Buffet, 333	150.00	250.00
1976	LION, Bernard Buffet, 263	150.00	250.00
1977	RHINOCEROS, Bernard Buffet, 200	150.00	250.00

Bicentennial

1973	JEFFERSON DRAFTING DECLARATION OF INDEPENDENCE, 8556	175.00	210.00
1974	JOHN ADAMS CHAMPIONS CAUSE OF INDEPENDENCE, 8,442	175.00	210.00
1975	CAESAR RODNEY DECIDES VOTE ON INDEPENDENCE, 8,319	175.00	210.00
1976	JOHN HANCOCK SIGNS DECLARATION OF INDEPENDENCE, 10,166	175.00	210.00

		Issue Price	Current Value

Birds

1972	CARDINAL, Richard Evans Younger, 13,939	125.00	135.00
1972	BOB WHITE, Richard Evans Younger, 13,939	125.00	135.00
1972	MALLARDS, Richard Evans Younger, 13,939	125.00	135.00
1973	AMERICAN BALD EAGLE, Richard Evans Younger, 13,939	125.00	145.00

Birds and Flowers of Beautiful Cathay

1981–82	BEGINNING OF WINTER, Wei Tseng Yang	35.00	NR
1981–83	BIG SNOW, Wei Tseng Yang	35.00	NR
1981–83	CHING CHE (AWAKENING OF INSECTS), Wei Tseng Yang	35.00	NR
1981–83	CH'ING MING (PURE BRIGHTNESS), Wei Tseng Yang	35.00	NR
1981–83	CH'UN FEN (DIVISION OF SPRING), Wei Tseng Yang	35.00	NR
1981–83	COLD DEW, Wei Tseng Yang	35.00	NR
1981–83	HSIA CHIH (ARRIVAL OF SUMMER), Wei Tseng Yang	35.00	NR
1981–83	HSIAO HAN (SMALL COLD), Wei Tseng Yang	35.00	NR
1981–83	HSIAO MAN (RIPENING GRAIN), Wei Tseng Yang	35.00	NR
1981–83	HSIAO SHU, Wei Tseng Yang	35.00	NR
1981–83	KU YU (CORN RAIN), Wei Tseng Yang	35.00	NR
1981–83	LI CH'IU (BEGINNING OF AUTUMN), Wei Tseng Yang	35.00	NR
1981–83	LI CH'UN (BEGINNING OF SPRING), Wei Tseng Yang	35.00	NR
1981–83	LI HSIA (BEGINNING OF SUMMER), Wei Tseng Yang	35.00	NR
1981–83	LIMIT OF HEAT, Wei Tseng Yang	35.00	NR
1981–83	MANG CHUNG (GRAIN IN THE EAR), Wei Tseng Yang	35.00	NR
1981–83	SCARLET FINCHES AND CHRYSANTHEMUMS, Wei Tseng Yang	35.00	NR
1981–83	SMALL SNOW, Wei Tseng Yang	35.00	NR
1981–83	TA HAN (GREAT COLD), Wei Tseng Yang	35.00	NR
1981–83	TA SHUS (GREAT HEAT), Wei Tseng Yang	35.00	NR
1981–83	WHITE DEW, Wei Tseng Yang	35.00	NR
1981–83	WINTER SOLSTICE, Wei Tseng Yang	35.00	NR
1981–83	YU SHUI (RAIN WATER), Wei Tseng Yang	35.00	NR

Birds and Flowers of the Orient

1979–80	ROOSTER AND MORNING GLORY, Naoka Nobata, 32,373	55.00	NR
1979–80	LOTUS AND WATER FOWL, Naoka Nobata, 32,373	55.00	NR
1979–80	MAPLE TREE AND SHRIKE, Naoka Nobata, 32,373	55.00	NR
1979–80	WHITE CRANE AND THE PINE, Naoka Nobata, 32,373	55.00	NR
1979–80	WHITE EYE AND PEACH, Naoka Nobata, 32,373	55.00	NR
1979–80	MANDARIN DUCK AND IRIS, Naoka Nobata, 32,373	55.00	NR
1979–80	EGRET AND WATER LILY, Naoka Nobata, 32,373	55.00	NR
1979–80	TREE SPARROW AND CHRYSANTHEMUM, Naoka Nobata, 32,373	55.00	NR
1979–80	WREN AND NARCISSUS, Naoka Nobata, 32,373	55.00	NR
1979–80	BUSH WARBLER AND APRICOT, Naoka Nobata, 32,373	55.00	NR
1979–80	CHINESE BLUE PIE AND CHERRY, Naoka Nobata, 32,373	55.00	NR
1979–80	PEONY AND PEACOCK, Naoka Nobata, 32,373	55.00	NR

		Issue Price	Current Value

Butterflies of the World

		Issue Price	Current Value
1977–79	SOUTH AMERICA, 481	240.00	275.00
1977–79	AUSTRALIA, 481	240.00	275.00
1977–79	NORTH AMERICA, 481	240.00	275.00
1977–79	EUROPE, 481	240.00	275.00
1977–79	AFRICA, 481	240.00	275.00
1977–79	ASIA, 481	240.00	275.00

Calendar

1981	TURN–OF–THE–CENTURY SCENE, Deborah Bell Jarratt, 5,634	55.00	NR
1982	TURN–OF–THE–CENTURY CHILDREN, Margaret Murphy, 5,634	58.00	NR
1983	CHILDREN CELEBRATING VICTORIAN MONTHS, Kate Lloyd Jones	55.00	NR
1984	CHILDREN WITH TEDDY BEARS, Margaret Murphy	55.00	NR

Carol Lawson Annual

1981	STORYTIME, Carol Lawson, 1 year	35.00	NR
1982	TEACHER'S PET, Carol Lawson, 1 year	35.00	NR
1983	TEATIME SURPRISE, Carol Lawson, 1 year	35.00	NR

Christmas

1976	SILENT NIGHT, 19,286	65.00	NR
1977	DECK THE HALLS, 9,185	75.00	NR
1978	WE THREE KINGS, 6,737	75.00	NR
1979	HARK THE HERALD ANGELS SING, 4,784	75.00	NR
1980	JOY TO THE WORLD	125.00	NR
1981	O HOLY NIGHT	125.00	NR

Christmas — International

1981	CHRISTMAS IN FRANCE, Yves Beaujard	35.00	NR
1982	CHRISTMAS IN ENGLAND, Peter D. Jackson	35.00	NR
1983	CHRISTMAS IN AMERICA, William Plummer	35.00	NR

Clipper Ships

1982–83	ARIEL, L. J. Pearce	55.00	NR
1982–83	CHALLENGE, L. J. Pearce	55.00	NR
1982–83	CUTTY SARK, L. J. Pearce	55.00	NR
1982–83	FLYING CLOUD, L. J. Pearce	55.00	NR
1982–83	GREAT REPUBLIC, L. J. Pearce	55.00	NR
1982–83	MARCO POLO, L. J. Pearce	55.00	NR
1982–83	NIGHTINGALE, L. J. Pearce	55.00	NR
1982–83	ORIENTAL, L. J. Pearce	55.00	NR
1982–83	PATRIARCH, L. J. Pearce	55.00	NR
1982–83	RED JACKET, L. J. Pearce	55.00	NR
1982–83	SEA WITCH, L. J. Pearce	55.00	NR
1982–83	THERMOPYLAE, L. J. Pearce	55.00	NR

Cobblestone Kids

		Issue Price	Current Value
1982	MAKING FRIENDS, Debbie Bell Jarratt	65.00	NR
1983	A STITCH IN TIME, Debbie Bell Jarratt	65.00	NR
1983	EXTRA! EXTRA!, Debbie Bell Jarratt	65.00	NR
1983	FEEDING THE RACCOON, Debbie Bell Jarratt	65.00	NR
1983	JUST DUCKY, Debbie Bell Jarratt	65.00	NR

Country Diary

1984	JANUARY – DECEMBER, Geoff Mowery, limited, set of 12	660.00	NR

Country Year

1980–82	COUNTRY PATH IN MAY, Peter Barratt, 89,173	55.00	NR
1980–82	JANUARY–LAMBING SEASON, Peter Barratt, 89,173 .	55.00	NR
1980–82	OCTOBER–COLOURS OF AUTUMN, Peter Barratt, 89,173	55.00	NR
1980–82	WHEAT FIELDS IN AUGUST, Peter Barratt, 89,173	55.00	NR
1980–82	SEPTEMBER ON THE MOORS, Peter Barratt, 89,173 . .	55.00	NR
1980–82	JUNE IN A COTTAGE GARDEN, Peter Barratt, 89,173 . .	55.00	NR
1980–82	COUNTRY CHURCH IN MARCH, Peter Barratt, 89,173 .	55.00	NR
1980–82	SECLUDED STREAM IN NOVEMBER, Peter Barratt, 89,173 . . .	55.00	NR
1980–82	WOODLANDS IN APRIL, Peter Barratt, 89,173	55.00	NR
1980–82	COUNTRY LANE IN DECEMBER, Peter Barratt, 89,173 .	55.00	NR
1980–82	JULY BESIDE THE RIVER, Peter Barratt, 89,173	55.00	NR
1980–82	FEBRUARY ON THE COAST, Peter Barratt, 89,173	55.00	NR

Currier & Ives

1977–79	WINTER PASTIME, Currier & Ives, 1,836	39.50	45.00
1977–79	PREPARING FOR MARKET, Currier & Ives, 1,836	39.50	45.00
1977–79	WINTER IN THE COUNTRY, Currier & Ives, 1,836	39.50	45.00
1977–79	AMERICAN HOMESTEAD–WINTER, Currier & Ives, 1,836	39.50	45.00
1977–79	AMERICAN FOREST SCENE, Currier & Ives, 1,836	39.50	45.00
1977–79	AMERICAN HOMESTEAD–SUMMER, Currier & Ives, 1,836 . . .	39.50	45.00
1977–79	AMERICAN HOMESTEAD–AUTUMN, Currier & Ives, 1,836 . . .	39.50	45.00
1977–79	HAYING TIME–THE LAST LOAD, Currier & Ives, 1,836 .	39.50	45.00
1977–79	CATCHING A TROUT, Currier & Ives, 1,836	39.50	45.00
1977–79	YOSEMITE VALLEY, Currier & Ives, 1,836	39.50	45.00

Days of the Week

1979–80	MONDAY'S CHILD IS FAIR OF FACE, Caroline Ebborn, 1,890 . . .	39.00	NR
1979–80	TUESDAY'S CHILD IS FULL OF GRACE, Caroline Ebborn, 1,890 .	39.00	NR
1979–80	WEDNESDAY'S CHILD IS FULL OF WOE, Caroline Ebborn, 1,890	39.00	NR
1979–80	THURSDAY'S CHILD HAS FAR TO GO, Caroline Ebborn, 1,890 .	39.00	NR
1979–80	FRIDAY'S CHILD IS LOVING AND GIVING, Caroline Ebborn, 1,890	39.00	NR
1979–80	SATURDAY'S CHILD WORKS HARD FOR A LIVING, Caroline Ebborn, 1,890	39.00	NR

		Issue Price	Current Value
1979–80	SUNDAY'S CHILD IS BORN ON THE SABBATH DAY, Caroline Ebborn, 1,890	39.00	NR

Easter

1973	RESURRECTION, Evangelos Frudakis, 7,116	175.00	185.00
1974	HE IS RISEN, Abram Belski, 3,719	185.00	195.00
1975	THE LAST SUPPER, Oriol Sunyer, 2,004	200.00	225.00
1976	THE CRUCIFIXION, Marguerite Gaudin, 3,904	250.00	300.00
1977	RESURRECTION, 1,206	250.00	300.00

Fairy Tales Miniatures

1979–84	THE THREE BEARS, Carol Lawson, 15,207	14.50	NR
1979–84	LITTLE RED RIDING HOOD, Carol Lawson, 15,207	14.50	NR
1979–84	THE LITTLE MERMAID, Carol Lawson, 15,207	14.50	NR
1979–84	SNOW WHITE AND THE SEVEN DWARFS, Carol Lawson, 15,207	14.50	NR
1979–84	ALADDIN AND THE WONDERFUL LAMP, Carol Lawson, 15,207	14.50	NR
1979–84	THE SNOW QUEEN, Carol Lawson, 15,207	14.50	NR
1979–84	TOM THUMB, Carol Lawson, 15,207	14.50	NR
1979–84	ALI BABA, Carol Lawson, 15,207	14.50	NR
1979–84	JACK AND THE BEANSTALK, Carol Lawson, 15,207	14.50	NR
1979–84	PUSS IN BOOTS, Carol Lawson, 15,207	14.50	NR
1979–84	THE FROG PRINCE, Carol Lawson, 15,207	14.50	NR
1979–84	CINDERELLA, Carol Lawson, 15,207	14.50	NR
1979–84	PRINCESS AND THE PEA, Carol Lawson, 15,207	14.50	NR
1979–84	THE PIED PIPER, Carol Lawson, 15,207	14.50	NR
1979–84	VALIANT LITTLE TAILOR, Carol Lawson, 15,207	14.50	NR
1979–84	THE UGLY DUCKLING, Carol Lawson, 15,207	14.50	NR
1979–84	THE THREE LITTLE PIGS, Carol Lawson, 15,207	14.50	NR
1979–84	RAPUNZEL, Carol Lawson, 15,207	14.50	NR
1979–84	THE LITTLE MATCH GIRL, Carol Lawson, 15,207	14.50	NR
1979–84	THUMBELINA, Carol Lawson, 15,207	14.50	NR
1979–84	THE NIGHTINGALE, Carol Lawson, 15,207	14.50	NR
1979–84	THE STEADFAST TIN SOLDIER, Carol Lawson, 15,207	14.50	NR
1979–84	THE GOOSE THAT LAID THE GOLDEN EGGS, Carol Lawson, 15,207	14.50	NR
1979–84	HENNY–PENNY, Carol Lawson, 15,207	14.50	NR
1979–84	EAST OF THE SUN AND WEST OF THE MOON, Carol Lawson, 15,207	14.50	NR
1979–84	BILLY GOAT'S GRUFF, Carol Lawson, 15,207	14.50	NR
1979–84	SINBAD THE SAILOR, Carol Lawson, 15,207	14.50	NR
1979–84	BEAUTY AND THE BEAST, Carol Lawson, 15,207	14.50	NR
1979–84	THE RED SHOES, Carol Lawson, 15,207	14.50	NR
1979–84	RUMPELSTILTSKIN, Carol Lawson, 15,207	14.50	NR
1979–84	SLEEPING BEAUTY, Carol Lawson, 15,207	14.50	NR
1979–84	THE TWELVE DANCING PRINCESSES, Carol Lawson, 15,207	14.50	NR

	Issue Price	Current Value
1979–84 HANSEL AND GRETEL, Carol Lawson, 15,207	14.50	NR
1979 04 SNOW WHITE AND ROSE RED, Carol Lawson, 15,207 .	14.50	NR
1979–84 THE BRONZE RING, Carol Lawson, 15,207	14.50	NR
1979–84 JORINDA AND JORINDEL, Carol Lawson, 15,207	14.50	NR
1979–84 PINOCCHIO, Carol Lawson, 15,207	14.50	NR
1979–84 THE GOLDEN GOOSE, Carol Lawson, 15,207..........	14.50	NR
1979–84 THE SORCERER'S APPRENTICE, Carol Lawson, 15,207	14.50	NR
1979–84 TOWN MOUSE AND COUNTRY MOUSE, Carol Lawson, 15,207	14.50	NR
1979–84 SIX SWANS, Carol Lawson, 15,207..................	14.50	NR
1979–84 MAID MALEEN, Carol Lawson, 15,207	14.50	NR
1979–84 THE GINGERBREAD BOY, Carol Lawson, 15,207	14.50	NR

Flowers of the American Wilderness

	Issue Price	Current Value
1978–80 NEW ENGLAND, Jeanne Holgate, 8,759	39.00	NR
1978–80 ALASKA, Jeanne Holgate, 8,759	39.00	NR
1978–80 EVERGLADES OF FLORIDA, Jeanne Holgate, 8,759	39.00	NR
1978–80 MISSISSIPPI DELTA, Jeanne Holgate, 8,759	39.00	NR
1978–80 CALIFORNIA, Jeanne Holgate, 8,759	39.00	NR
1978–80 ROCKY MOUNTAINS, Jeanne Holgate, 8,759	39.00	NR
1978–80 CAPE COD, Jeanne Holgate, 8,759	39.00	NR
1978–80 NORTHWEST, Jeanne Holgate, 8,759................	39.00	NR
1978–80 SOUTHWEST, Jeanne Holgate, 8,759	39.00	NR
1978–80 APPALACHIAN MOUNTAINS, Jeanne Holgate, 8,759 .	39.00	NR
1978–80 PRAIRIES, Jeanne Holgate, 8,759	39.00	NR
1978–80 GREAT LAKES, Jeanne Holgate, 8,759	39.00	NR

Flowers of the Year

	Issue Price	Current Value
1976 JANUARY, Leslie Greenwood, 27,394	50.00	NR
1976 FEBRUARY, Leslie Greenwood, 27,394	50.00	NR
1977 MARCH, Leslie Greenwood, 27,394.....................	50.00	NR
1977 APRIL, Leslie Greenwood, 27,394	50.00	NR
1977 MAY, Leslie Greenwood, 27,394.......................	50.00	NR
1978 JUNE, Leslie Greenwood, 27,394......................	50.00	NR
1978 JULY, Leslie Greenwood, 27,394	50.00	NR
1978 AUGUST, Leslie Greenwood, 27,394	50.00	NR
1978 SEPTEMBER, Leslie Greenwood, 27,394	50.00	NR
1978 OCTOBER, Leslie Greenwood, 27,394	50.00	NR
1978 NOVEMBER, Leslie Greenwood, 27,394	50.00	NR
1978 DECEMBER, Leslie Greenwood, 27,394	50.00	NR

Four Seasons Champleve

	Issue Price	Current Value
1975 SPRING BLOSSOMS, Rene Restoueux, 2,648	240.00	BR
1975 SUMMER BOUQUET, Rene Restoueux, 2,648	240.00	BR
1976 AUTUMN GARLAND, Rene Restoueux, 2,648	240.00	BR
1976 WINTER SPRAY, Rene Restoueux, 2,648	240.00	BR

		Issue Price	Current Value
Game Birds of the World			
1978–80	CHINESE RING–NECKED PHEASANT, Basil Ede, 76,294	55.00	NR
1978–80	RED–LEGGED PARTRIDGE, Basil Ede, 76,294	55.00	NR
1978–80	COMMON SNIPE, Basil Ede, 76,294	55.00	NR
1978–80	COMMON PARTRIDGE, Basil Ede, 76,294	55.00	NR
1978–80	ROCK PTARMIGAN, Basil Ede, 76,294	55.00	NR
1978–80	WOODCOCK, Basil Ede, 76,294	55.00	NR
1978–80	COMMON PHEASANT, Basil Ede, 76,294	55.00	NR
1978–80	HAZEL GROUSE, Basil Ede, 76,294	55.00	NR
1978–80	RED GROUSE, Basil Ede, 76,294	55.00	NR
1978–80	BLACK GROUSE, Basil Ede, 76,294	55.00	NR
1978–80	CAPERCAILLIE, Basil Ede, 76,294	55.00	NR
1978–80	COMMON QUAIL, Basil Ede, 76,294	55.00	NR
Garden Birds of the World			
1984	AMERICAN ROBIN, Basil Ede, sgd, limited	55.00	NR
1984	BLACKBIRD, Basil Ede, sgd, limited	55.00	NR
1984	BLACK–CAPPED CHICKADEE, Basil Ede, sgd, limited	55.00	NR
1984	CARDINAL, Basil Ede, sgd, limited	55.00	NR
1984	EASTERN BLUEBIRD, Basil Ede, sgd, limited	55.00	NR
1984	GOLDFINCH, Basil Ede, sgd, limited	55.00	NR
1984	GREAT TITMOUSE, Basil Ede, sgd, limited	55.00	NR
1984	KINGFISHER, Basil Ede, sgd, limited	55.00	NR
1984	MOCKINGBIRD, Basil Ede, sgd, limited	55.00	NR
1984	SONG THRUSH, Basil Ede, sgd, limited	55.00	NR
1984	SWALLOW, Basil Ede, sgd, limited	55.00	NR
1984	WHITE–BREASTED NUTHATCH, Basil Ede, sgd, limited	55.00	NR
Garden Year			
1984	JANUARY – DECEMBER, David Hurrell, sgd, limited, set of 12	330.00	NR
Grimm's Fairy Tales			
1978	SLEEPING BEAUTY, Carol Lawson, 27,006	42.00	NR
1978	TWELVE DANCING PRINCESSES, Carol Lawson, 27,006	42.00	NR
1979	BREMEN TOWN MUSICIANS, Carol Lawson, 27,006	42.00	NR
1979	GOLDEN GOOSE, Carol Lawson, 27,006	42.00	NR
1979	HANSEL AND GRETEL, Carol Lawson, 27,006	42.00	NR
1979	RAPUNZEL, Carol Lawson, 27,006	42.00	NR
1979	SNOW WHITE AND THE SEVEN DWARFS, Carol Lawson, 27,006	42.00	NR
1979	FROG PRINCE, Carol Lawson, 27,006	42.00	NR
1979	RED RIDING HOOD, Carol Lawson, 27,006	42.00	NR
1979	RUMPELSTILTSKIN, Carol Lawson, 27,006	42.00	NR
1979	CINDERELLA, Carol Lawson, 27,006	42.00	NR
1979	SHOEMAKER AND THE ELVES, Carol Lawson, 27,006	42.00	NR
Hans Christian Andersen			
1976	PRINCESS AND THE PEA, Pauline Ellison, 16,875	38.00	70.00

		Issue Price	Current Value
1976	UGLY DUCKLING, Pauline Ellison, 16,875	38.00	70.00
1976	LITTLE MERMAID, Pauline Ellison, 16,875	38.00	70.00
1976	EMPEROR'S NEW CLOTHES, Pauline Ellison, 16,875	38.00	70.00
1976	STEADFAST TIN SOLDIER, Pauline Ellison, 16,875	38.00	70.00
1976	LITTLE MATCH GIRL, Pauline Ellison, 16,875	38.00	70.00
1977	SNOW QUEEN, Pauline Ellison, 16,875	38.00	70.00
1977	RED SHOES, Pauline Ellison, 16,875	38.00	70.00
1977	TINDER BOX, Pauline Ellison, 16,875	38.00	70.00
1977	NIGHTINGALE, Pauline Ellison, 16,875	38.00	70.00
1977	THUMBELINA, Pauline Ellison, 16,875	38.00	70.00
1977	SHEPHERDESS AND CHIMNEY SWEEP, Pauline Ellison, 16,875	38.00	70.00

Hometown Memories

1979	COUNTRY FAIR, Jo Sickbert, 4,715	29.00	NR
1980	RED SCHOOLHOUSE, Jo Sickbert, 4,715	29.00	NR
1981	SUNDAY PICNIC, Jo Sickbert, 4,715	29.00	NR
1982	SKATING PARTY, Jo Sickbert, 4,715	29.00	NR

International Gallery of Flowers

1980–81	WHEAT, BLACK–EYED SUSAN, COLUMBINE, MAYFLOWER, CALIFORNIA POPPY, Jeanne Holgate, 4,294	55.00	NR
1980–81	ORCHID, Marion Ruff Sheehan, 4,294	55.00	NR
1980–81	IRISES, Claus Caspari, 4,294	55.00	NR
1980–81	CAMELIAS, Anne Marie Trechslin, 4,294	55.00	NR
1980–81	CHERRY BLOSSOMS, Yoai Ohta, 4,294	55.00	NR
1980–81	ENGLISH SPRING WILD FLOWERS, Mary Grierson, 4,294	55.00	NR
1980–81	FUCHSIAS, Raphael Henri/Charles Ghislain, 4,294	55.00	NR
1980–81	FLAME AZALEAS, Martha Prince, 4,294	55.00	NR
1980–81	ROSES, Gabriele Gossner, 4,294	55.00	NR
1980–81	ENGLISH GARDEN FLOWERS, Barbara Everard, 4,294	55.00	NR
1980–81	TULIPS, Elizabeth Riemer–Gerbardt, 4,294	55.00	NR
1980–81	DESERT PEA, Paul Jones, 4,294	55.00	NR

James Wyeth

1972	ALONG THE BRANDYWINE, James Wyeth, 19,760	125.00	140.00
1973	WINTER FOX, James Wyeth, 10,394	125.00	NR
1974	RIDING TO THE HUNT, James Wyeth, 10,751	150.00	NR
1975	SKATING ON THE BRANDYWINE, James Wyeth, 8,058	175.00	BR
1976	BRANDYWINE BATTLEFIELD, James Wyeth, 6,968	180.00	NR

John James Audubon

1973	THE WOOD THRUSH, John James Audubon, 5,273	150.00	BR
1973	THE BALD EAGLE, John James Audubon, 3,040	150.00	BR
1974	THE NIGHT HERON, John James Audubon, 3,005	150.00	BR
1974	AUDUBON'S WARBLER, John James Audubon, 3,034	150.00	BR

		Issue Price	Current Value
Joys of the Victorian Year			
1983	JANUARY – DECEMBER, Kate Lloyd–Jones, limited, set of 12 .	660.00	NR

Mark Twain

1977	WHITEWASHING THE FENCE, Yves Beaujard, 2,645	38.00	55.00
1977	STEALING A KISS, Yves Beaujard, 2,645	38.00	45.00
1977	TRAVELING THE RIVER, Yves Beaujard, 2,645	38.00	45.00
1977	RAFTING DOWN THE RIVER, Yves Beaujard, 2,645	38.00	NR
1978	RIDING A BRONC, Yves Beaujard, 2,645	38.00	NR
1978	JUMPING FROG FENCE, Yves Beaujard, 2,645	38.00	NR
1978	FACING A CHARGING KNIGHT, Yves Beaujard, 2,645	38.00	NR
1978	DISGUISING HUCK, Yves Beaujard, 2,645	38.00	NR
1978	LIVING ALONG THE RIVER, Yves Beaujard, 2,645	38.00	NR
1978	LEARNING TO SMOKE, Yves Beaujard, 2,645	38.00	NR
1978	FINGER PRINTING PAYS OFF, Yves Beaujard, 2,645	38.00	NR

Mother's Day

1977	A MOTHER'S LOVE, Adelaid Sundin, 12,392	65.00	NR
1978	A MOTHER'S JOY, Deborah Bell	65.00	NR
1979	A MOTHER'S GIFT, Deborah Bell, 1 year	75.00	NR

Mother's Day by Spencer

1972	MOTHER AND CHILD, Irene Spencer, 21,987	125.00	175.00
1973	MOTHER AND CHILD, Irene Spencer, 6,154	125.00	140.00
1974	MOTHER AND CHILD, Irene Spencer, 5,116	150.00	160.00
1975	MOTHER AND CHILD, Irene Spencer, 2,704	175.00	180.00
1976	MOTHER AND CHILD, Irene Spencer, 1,858	180.00	190.00

Poor Richard

1979–81	HASTE MAKES WASTE, 13,133	12.50	NR
1979–81	WHEN THE WELL'S DRY, WE KNOW THE WORTH OF WATER, 13,133	12.50	NR
1979–81	LOVE THY NEIGHBOR, YET DON'T PULL DOWN YOUR HEDGE, 13,133	12.50	NR
1979–81	DILIGENCE IS THE MOTHER OF GOOD LUCK, 13,133	12.50	NR
1979–81	WHO PLEASURE GIVES, SHALL JOY RECEIVE, 13,133	12.50	NR
1979–81	THE ROTTEN APPLE SPOILS HIS COMPANION, 13,133	12.50	NR
1979–81	A SPOONFUL OF HONEY WILL CATCH MORE FLIES THAN A GALLON OF VINEGAR, 13,133	12.50	NR
1979–81	THERE'S A TIME TO WINK AS WELL AS A TIME TO SEE, 13,133	12.50	NR
1979–81	A TRUE FRIEND SAVED IS A PENNY EARNED, 13,133	12.50	NR
1979–81	GREAT TALKERS, LITTLE DOERS, 13,133	12.50	NR
1979–81	EARLY TO BED, AND EARLY TO RISE, MAKES A MAN HEALTHY, WEALTHY AND WISE, 13,133	12.50	NR
1979–81	LOST TIME IS NEVER FOUND AGAIN, 13,133	12.50	NR

		Issue Price	Current Value
1979–81	THE WORST WHEEL OF THE CART MAKES THE MOST NOISE, 13,133	12.50	NR
1979–81	KEEP THY SHOP AND THY SHOP WILL KEEP THEE, 13,133	12.50	NR
1979–81	AN EMPTY BAG CANNOT STAND UPRIGHT, 13,133	12.50	NR
1979–81	'TIS EASIER TO PREVENT BAD HABITS THAN TO BREAK THEM, 13,133	12.50	NR
1979–81	THE GOLDEN AGE NEVER WAS THE PRESENT AGE, 13,133	12.50	NR
1979–81	NO GAINS WITHOUT PAINS, 13,133	12.50	NR
1979–81	YOU CANNOT PLUCK ROSES WITHOUT FEAR OF THORNS, 13,133	12.50	NR
1979–81	BEWARE OF LITTLE EXPENSES, A SMALL LEAK WILL SINK A GREAT SHIP, 13,133	12.50	NR
1979–81	NOW I'VE A SHEEP AND A COW, EVERY BODY BIDS ME GOOD MORNING, 13,133	12.50	NR
1979–81	A QUARRELSOME MAN HAS NO GOOD NEIGHBOURS, 13,133	12.50	NR
1979–81	LOVE AND BE LOVED, 13,133	12.50	NR
1979–81	LOOK BEFORE, OR YOU'LL FIND YOURSELF BEHIND, 13,133	12.50	NR

Presidential Inaugural

1973	NIXON/AGNEW, Gilroy Roberts, 10,483	150.00	160.00
1974	FORD, Mico Kaufman, 11	3,500.00	3,600.00
1974	FORD, Mico Kaufman, 1,141	200.00	225.00
1977	CARTER, Julian Harris, 928	225.00	230.00

Robert's Zodiac

1973–80	ARIES, Gilroy Roberts	150.00	165.00
1973–80	TAURUS, Gilroy Roberts	150.00	165.00
1973–80	GEMINI, Gilroy Roberts	150.00	165.00
1973–80	CANCER, Gilroy Roberts	150.00	165.00
1973–80	LEO, Gilroy Roberts	150.00	165.00
1973–80	VIRGO, Gilroy Roberts	150.00	165.00
1973–80	LIBRA, Gilroy Roberts	150.00	165.00
1973–80	SCORPIO, Gilroy Roberts	150.00	165.00
1973–80	SAGITTARIUS, Gilroy Roberts	150.00	165.00
1973–80	CAPRICORN, Gilroy Roberts	150.00	165.00
1973–80	AQUARIUS, Gilroy Roberts	150.00	165.00
1973–80	PISCES, Gilroy Roberts	150.00	165.00

Rockwell American Sweethearts

1977	YOUNGSTERS AT PLAY, Norman Rockwell, 1,004	120.00	160.00
1977	TEENAGERS TOGETHER, Norman Rockwell, 1,004	120.00	160.00
1978	BRIDE AND GROOM, Norman Rockwell, 1,004	120.00	160.00
1978	PROUD PARENTS, Norman Rockwell, 1,004	120.00	160.00
1978	GRADUATION DAY, Norman Rockwell, 1,004	120.00	160.00
1979	RETIREMENT KISS, Norman Rockwell, 1,004	120.00	160.00

Rockwell Christmas

		Issue Price	Current Value
1970	BRINGING HOME THE TREE, Norman Rockwell, 18,321 ..	100.00	310.00
1971	UNDER THE MISTLETOE, Norman Rockwell, 24,792	100.00	175.00
1972	THE CAROLERS, Norman Rockwell, 29,074	125.00	165.00
1973	TRIMMING THE TREE, Norman Rockwell, 18,010	125.00	170.00
1974	HANGING THE WREATH, Norman Rockwell, 12,822	175.00	BR
1975	HOME FOR CHRISTMAS, Norman Rockwell, 11,059	180.00	190.00

Seven Seas

1976	ATLANTIC OCEAN, James Wyeth, 2,799	120.00	NR
1977	CARIBBEAN SEA, James Wyeth, 2,799	120.00	NR
1978	INDIAN OCEAN, James Wyeth, 2,799...................	120.00	NR
1979	PACIFIC OCEAN, James Wyeth, 2,799	120.00	NR
1980	ARCTIC OCEAN, James Wyeth, 2,799...................	120.00	NR
1981	MEDITERRANEAN SEA, James Wyeth, 2,799	120.00	NR
1982	SOUTH CHINA SEA, James Wyeth, 2,799	120.00	NR

Songbirds of the World

1977–81	BALTIMORE ORIOLE, Arthur Singer, 20,225	55.00	NR
1977–81	BOHEMIAN WAXWING, Arthur Singer, 20,225........	55.00	NR
1977–81	MAGNOLIA WARBLER, Arthur Singer, 20,225	55.00	NR
1977–81	BOBOLINK, Arthur Singer, 20,225	55.00	NR
1977–81	WESTERN BLUEBIRD, Arthur Singer, 20,225	55.00	NR
1977–81	CARDINAL, Arthur Singer, 20,225	55.00	NR
1977–81	EUROPEAN GOLDFINCH, Arthur Singer, 20,225	55.00	NR
1977–81	WOOD THRUSH, Arthur Singer, 20,225	55.00	NR
1977–81	SCARLET TANAGER, Arthur Singer, 20,225	55.00	NR
1977–81	BARN SWALLOW, Arthur Singer, 20,225	55.00	NR
1977–81	BLUETHROAT, Arthur Singer, 20,225.................	55.00	NR
1977–81	TURQUOISE WREN, Arthur Singer, 20,225	55.00	NR

Songbirds of the World Miniatures

1980–83	GOLDFINCH, Colin Newman	14.50	NR
1980–83	PAINTED BUNTING, Colin Newman	14.50	NR
1980–83	BLUE TIT, Colin Newman	14.50	NR
1980–83	CHAFFINCH, Colin Newman	14.50	NR
1980–83	YELLOWHAMMER, Colin Newman...................	14.50	NR
1980–83	EUROPEAN ROBIN, Colin Newman	14.50	NR
1980–83	CARDINAL, Colin Newman	14.50	NR
1980–83	GOLDEN–FRONTED LEAFBIRD, Colin Newman	14.50	NR
1980–83	REDSTART, Colin Newman.........................	14.50	NR
1980–83	RUFOUS OVENBIRD, Colin Newman	14.50	NR
1980–83	GOLDEN ORIOLE, Colin Newman	14.50	NR
1980–83	DIAMOND FIRETAIL FINCH, Colin Newman	14.50	NR
1980–83	RUFOUS BELLIED NITAVA, Colin Newman	14.50	NR
1980–83	ASIAN FAIRY BLUEBIRD, Colin Newman	14.50	NR
1980–83	BARN SWALLOW, Colin Newman	14.50	NR

		Issue Price	Current Value
1980 83	WESTERN TANAGER, Colin Newman	14.50	NR
1980–83	BLUE JAY, Colin Newman	14.50	NR

Tales of Enchantment

1982	ALICE IN WONDERLAND, Carol Lawson, limited	55.00	NR
1982	PETER PAN, Carol Lawson, limited	55.00	NR
1982	THE WIND IN THE WILLOWS, Carol Lawson, limited	55.00	NR

Thanksgiving by Dohanos

1972	THE FIRST THANKSGIVING, Steven Dohanos, 10,142	125.00	150.00
1973	AMERICAN WILD TURKEY, Steven Dohanos, 3,547	125.00	150.00
1974	THANKSGIVING PRAYER, Steven Dohanos, 5,150	150.00	NR
1975	FAMILY THANKSGIVING, Steven Dohanos, 3,025	175.00	200.00
1976	HOME FROM THE HUNT, Steven Dohanos, 3,474	175.00	200.00

Western Series

1972	HORIZONS WEST, Richard Baldwin, sterling silver, 5,860	150.00	160.00
1972	HORIZONS WEST, Richard Baldwin, 22KT gold, 67	2,200.00	2,350.00
1973	MOUNTAIN MAN, Gordon Phillips, sterling silver, 5,860	150.00	185.00
1973	MOUNTAIN MAN, Gordon Phillips, 22KT gold, 67	2,200.00	2,350.00
1973	PROSPECTOR, Gus Shaefer, sterling silver, 5,860	150.00	185.00
1973	PROSPECTOR, Gus Shaefer, 22KT gold, 69	2,200.00	2,350.00
1973	PLAINS HUNTER, John Weaver, sterling silver, 5,860	150.00	185.00
1973	PLAINS HUNTER, John Weaver, 22KT gold, 67	2,200.00	2,350.00

Woodland Birds of the World

1980–82	BLUE JAY, Arthur Singer, 5,507	65.00	NR
1980–82	WHITE–WINGED CROSSBILL, Arthur Singer, 5,507	65.00	NR
1980–82	PAINTED REDSTART, Arthur Singer, 5,507	65.00	NR
1980–82	RIVOLI'S HUMMINGBIRD, Arthur Singer, 5,507	65.00	NR
1980–82	CHAFFINCH, Arthur Singer, 5,507	65.00	NR
1980–82	COLLARED TROGON, Arthur Singer, 5,507	65.00	NR
1980–82	EVENING GROSBEAK, Arthur Singer, 5,507	65.00	NR
1980–82	GREAT SPOTTED WOODPECKER, Arthur Singer, 5,507	65.00	NR
1980–82	RAINBOW LORIKEET, Arthur Singer, 5,507	65.00	NR
1980–82	TAWNY OWL, Arthur Singer, 5,507	65.00	NR
1980–82	WOODLAND KINGFISHER, Arthur Singer, 5,507	65.00	NR
1980–82	GOLDEN PHEASANT, Arthur Singer, 5,507	65.00	NR

Woodland Year

1980 83	FAWNS IN THE JUNE MEADOW, Peter Barratt	55.00	NR
1980–83	BUTTERFLY CHASE IN MAY, Peter Barratt	55.00	NR
1980–83	RABBITS IN A JULY FIELD, Peter Barratt	55.00	NR
1980–83	STRIPED SKUNKS AT A MARCH STREAM, Peter Barratt	55.00	NR
1980–83	SQUIRRELING FOR NUTS IN JANUARY, Peter Barratt	55.00	NR

		Issue Price	Current Value
1980–83	CURIOUS RACCOONS AT AN APRIL POND, Peter Barratt	55.00	NR
1980–83	AMERICAN MARTEN IN THE NOVEMBER PINES, Peter Barratt	55.00	NR
1980–83	THE PLAYFUL BADGERS IN OCTOBER, Peter Barratt..	55.00	NR
1980–83	COZY DORMOUSE IN THE DECEMBER WOODS, Peter Barratt	55.00	NR
1980–83	WOODCHUCKS IN FEBRUARY THAW, Peter Barratt ..	55.00	NR
1980–83	OTTER AT SEPTEMBER WATERFALL, Peter Barratt ...	55.00	NR

World's Great Porcelain Houses

1981–83	CROWN STAFFORDSHIRE	19.50	NR
1981–83	MOSA	19.50	NR
1981–83	HUTSCHENREUTHER	19.50	NR
1981–83	HAVILAND	19.50	NR
1981–83	WEDGWOOD	19.50	NR
1981–83	LANGENTHAL	19.50	NR
1981–83	PORSGRUND	19.50	NR
1981–83	NORITAKE	19.50	NR
1981–83	ROSTRAND	19.50	NR
1981–83	FRANKLIN	19.50	NR
1981–83	AK KAISER	19.50	NR
1981–83	THE ROYAL COPENHAGEN	19.50	NR
1981–83	ROYAL DOULTON	19.50	NR
1981–83	ZSOLNAY	19.50	NR
1981–83	OKURA	19.50	NR
1981–83	VERBANO	19.50	NR
1981–83	LILIEN PORZELAN	19.50	NR
1981–83	ROYAL WORCESTER	19.50	NR
1981–83	GINORY	19.50	NR
1981–83	LLADRO	19.50	NR
1981–83	FRANCISCAN	19.50	NR
1981–83	RAYNAUD	19.50	NR

Single Issues

1976	LIBERTY TREE CRYSTAL, 10,927	120.00	130.00
1976	PARTRIDGE IN A PEAR TREE, 1,453	150.00	185.00
1977	INFANT, Abram Belski, 290	210.00	275.00
1977	LAFAYETTE AND WASHINGTON, 546	275.00	325.00
1977	OLD–FASHIONED THANKSGIVING, Norman Rockwell, 1,361	185.00	225.00
1977	THE SKATING PARTY, Vincent Miller, 908	55.00	BR
1978	AIR FORCE ASSOCIATION	95.00	105.00
1978	BEN FRANKLIN, PRINTER, 281	65.00	NR
1978	CINDERELLA, Pauline Ellison, 29,439	55.00	NR
1978	ORIENTAL	32.50	NR
1979	BUTTERFLY, set of 4	38.00	NR
1979	PETER PAN, Carol Lawson, 5,391	39.00	NR
1979	PRINCE AND PRINCESS, T. Okamoto	85.00	NR
1979	UNIVERSITY OF PENNSYLVANIA, T. T. McKenzie, 226 ...	125.00	140.00

		Issue Price	Current Value
1980	ANGEL WITH TRUMPET, Maureen Jensen, 8,696	17.50	NR
1980	GREAT EGRETS, J. Fenwick Lansdowne, 2,384..........	65.00	NR
1980	LE JOUR DES AMOUREUS, Raymond Peynet, 5,332	50.00	NR
1981	ROYAL WEDDING BOUQUET, Mary Grierson	75.00	NR
1983	THE BARN OWL, Basil Ede, limited	95.00	NR

FRANKOMA POTTERY UNITED STATES

Bicentennial

1972	PROVOCATIONS, John Frank, 1 year	5.00	40.00
1973	PATRIOTS–LEADERS, John Frank, 1 year	5.00	40.00
1974	BATTLES FOR INDEPENDENCE, Joniece Frank, 1 year ..	5.00	40.00
1975	VICTORIES FOR INDEPENDENCE, Joniece Frank, 1 year .	5.00	40.00
1976	SYMBOLS OF FREEDOM, Joniece Frank, 1 year	6.00	40.00

Christmas

1965	GOODWILL TOWARD MEN, John Frank, 1 year	3.50	300.00
1966	JOY TO THE WORLD, John Frank, 1 year	3.50	90.00
1967	GIFTS FOR THE CHRIST CHILD, John Frank, 1 year	3.50	75.00
1968	FLIGHT INTO EGYPT, John Frank, 1 year	3.50	55.00
1969	LAID IN A MANGER, John Frank, 1 year	4.50	40.00
1970	KING OF KINGS, John Frank, 1 year	4.50	40.00
1971	NO ROOM IN THE INN, John Frank, 1 year	4.50	35.00
1972	SEEKING THE CHRIST CHILD, John Frank, 1 year	5.00	35.00
1973	THE ANNUNCIATION, John Frank, 1 year	5.00	35.00
1974	SHE LOVED AND CARED, Joniece Frank, 1 year	5.00	35.00
1975	PEACE ON EARTH, Joniece Frank, 1 year	5.00	35.00
1976	THE GIFT OF LOVE, Joniece Frank, 1 year	6.00	30.00
1977	BIRTH OF ETERNAL LIFE, Joniece Frank, 1 year	6.00	30.00
1978	ALL NATURE REJOICED, Joniece Frank, 1 year	7.50	30.00
1979	THE STAR OF HOPE, Joniece Frank, 1 year	7.50	30.00
1980	UNTO US A CHILD IS BORN, Joniece Frank, 1 year	10.00	30.00
1981	O COME LET US ADORE HIM, Joniece Frank, 1 year	12.00	25.00
1982	THE WISE MEN REJOICE, Joniece Frank, 1 year	12.00	25.00
1983	THE WISE MEN BRING GIFTS, Joniece Frank, 1 year....	12.00	25.00
1984	FAITH, HOPE AND LOVE, Joniece Frank, 1 year	12.00	25.00
1985	THE ANGELS WATCHED, Joniece Frank, 1 year.........	12.00	25.00
1986	FOR THEE I PLAY MY DRUM, Joniece Frank, 1 year	12.00	25.00
1987	GOD'S CHOSEN FAMILY, Joniece Frank, 1 year	12.00	25.00
1988	THE GUIDING LIGHT	—	25.00
1989	THE BLESSING OF CHRISTMAS	—	25.00
1990	THE ANGELS REJOICE	—	25.00
1991	LET THERE BE PEACE	—	20.00
1992	AND HE CALLED HIS NAME JESUS	—	RI
1993	PROCLAIMING THE MIRACLE	—	RI

		Issue Price	Current Value
1994	THE FIRST CHRISTMAS CAROL	—	RI

Madonna Plates

1977	THE GRACE MADONNA, Grace Lee Frank, 1 year	12.50	25.00
1978	MADONNA OF LOVE, Grace Lee Frank, 1 year	12.50	25.00
1981	THE ROSE MADONNA, Grace Lee Frank, 1 year	15.00	NR
1986	THE YOUTHFUL MADONNA, Grace Lee Frank, 1 year ...	15.00	NR

Teenagers of the Bible

1972	JESUS THE CARPENTER, John Frank, 1 year	5.00	40.00
1974	DAVID THE MUSICIAN, John Frank, 1 year	5.00	40.00
1975	JONATHAN THE ARCHER, John Frank, 1 year	5.00	40.00
1976	DORCAS THE SEAMSTRESS, Joniece Frank, 1 year	6.00	45.00
1977	PETER THE FISHERMAN, Joniece Frank, 1 year	6.00	30.00
1978	MARTHA THE HOMEMAKER, Joniece Frank, 1 year.....	7.50	30.00
1979	DANIEL THE COURAGEOUS, Joniece Frank, 1 year	7.50	30.00
1980	RUTH THE DEVOTED, Joniece Frank, 1 year	10.00	30.00
1981	JOSEPH THE DREAMER, Joniece Frank, 1 year	12.00	30.00
1982	MARY THE MOTHER, Joniece Frank, 1 year	12.00	30.00

Wildlife

1972	BOBWHITE QUAIL, 1,000	—	80.00
1973	WHITE–TAILED DEER, 1,000	—	80.00
1974	PRAIRIE CHICKEN, 1,000	—	80.00
1975	LARGEMOUTH BASS, 1,000	—	80.00
1977	GRAY SQUIRREL, 1,000	—	70.00
1978	WILD TURKEY, 1,000	—	70.00
1979	BUFFALO, 1,000	—	70.00

Single Issues

1971	CONESTOGA WAGON, John Frank, 2,000, 8½"	–	85.00
1977	THE BRAILLE SYSTEM, Joniece Frank, 500, 9"	–	65.00
1989	OKLAHOMA LAND RUN	–	15.00
1993	FRANKOMA 60TH ANNIVERSARY, Joniece Frank	–	RI
XX	THE SOONER STATE, OKLAHOMA	–	RI
XX	TEXAS STATE PLATE	–	RI

FUKAGAWA JAPAN

Warabe No Haiku

1977	BENEATH PLUM BRANCH, Shunsute Suetomi, 1 year ...	38.00	45.00
1978	CHILD OF STRAW, Shunsute Suetomi, 1 year	42.00	NR
1979	DRAGON DANCE, Shunsute Suetomi, 1 year	42.50	NR
1980	MASK DANCING, Shunsute Suetomi, 1 year	42.00	90.00

FURSTENBERG GERMANY

		Issue Price	Current Value
Christmas			
1971	RABBITS, 7,000	15.00	30.00
1972	SNOWY VILLAGE, 6,000	15.00	20.00
1973	CHRISTMAS EVE, 4,000	18.00	35.00
1974	SPARROWS, 4,000	20.00	30.00
1975	DEER FAMILY, 4,000	22.00	30.00
1976	WINTER BIRDS, 4,000	25.00	NR

Deluxe Christmas

1971	WISE MEN, E. Grossberg, 1,500	45.00	NR
1972	HOLY FAMILY, E. Grossberg, 2,000	45.00	NR
1973	CHRISTMAS EVE, E. Grossberg, 2,000	60.00	NR

Easter

1971	SHEEP, 3,500	15.00	100.00
1972	CHICKS, 6,000	15.00	40.00
1973	BUNNIES, 4,000	16.00	60.00
1974	PUSSYWILLOW, 4,000	20.00	30.00
1975	EASTER WINDOW, 4,000	22.00	NR
1976	FLOWER COLLECTING, 4,000	25.00	NR

Mother's Day

1972	HUMMINGBIRDS, 6,000	15.00	40.00
1973	HEDGEHOGS, 5,000	16.00	30.00
1974	DOE AND FAWN, 4,000	20.00	NR
1975	SWANS, 4,000	22.00	NR
1976	KOALA BEARS, 4,000	25.00	NR

Muninger's Romantic Winter Impressions

1987	ICE SKATERS/EVENING SUN	34.50	NR
1987	ICE FISHERS/VILLAGE POND	34.50	NR
1987	REFRESHMENTS/WINTER FEST	37.50	NR
1987	VISIT OF THE PEDDLER	37.50	NR
1988	ON THE WAY TO CHURCH	37.50	NR
1988	A REST AFTER WORK	37.50	NR
1988	RETURN OF THE WOODCUTTERS	39.50	NR
1988	FIRST SIGNS OF SPRING	39.50	NR

Olympic

1972	MUNICH, J. Poluszynski, 5,000	20.00	45.00
1976	MONTREAL, J. Poluszynski, 5,000	37.50	NR

Wild Beauties

1989	BY THE WAYSIDE	34.50	NR

		Issue Price	Current Value
1989	AT THE POND	34.50	NR
1989	ON THE WALL	37.50	NR
1990	BETWEEN THE ROCKS	37.50	NR
1991	IN THE GLADE	37.50	NR
1991	IN THE BOG	37.50	NR
1991	AT THE WATERFALL	39.50	NR
1991	IN THE UNDERGROWTH	39.50	60.00
1991	BY THE CORNFIELD	42.50	70.00
1992	BY THE CASTLE RUIN	42.50	RI
1992	AT THE FOUNTAIN	42.50	RI

By the Wayside
Photo courtesy of *Collectors News*

GARTLAN USA, INC. UNITED STATES

Al Barlick

1991	PLATE, M. Taylor, open, 3¹/₄"	16.00	NR

Bob Cousy

1993	SIGNED PLATE, M. Taylor, 950, 10¹/₄"	175.00	RI
1993	PLATE, M. Taylor, 5,000, 8¹/₂"	49.00	RI
1993	PLATE, M. Taylor, open, 3¹/₄"	19.00	RI

Brett and Bobby Hull

1991	HOCKEY'S GOLDEN BOYS, sgd, M. Taylor, 950, 10¹/₄"	250.00	325.00
1991	HOCKEY'S GOLDEN BOYS, M. Taylor, 10,000, 8¹/₂"	45.00	NR
1991	HOCKEY'S GOLDEN BOYS, M. Taylor, open, 3¹/₄"	16.00	NR
1992	PLATE, sgd, M. Taylor, artist proof, 300	350.00	RI

		Issue Price	Current Value
1993	SIGNED PLATE, M. Taylor, 950, 10¹/₄"	175.00	RI
1993	PLATE, M. Taylor, 10,000, 8¹/₂"	49.00	RI
1993	PLATE, M. Taylor, open, 3¹/₄"	19.00	R

Carlton Fisk

		Issue Price	Current Value
1992	SIGNED PLATE, M. Taylor, 950, 10¹/₄"	150.00	RI
1992	SIGNED PLATE, M. Taylor, artist proof, 300, 10¹/₄'	175.00	225.00
1992	PLATE, M. Taylor, 10,000, 8¹/₂"	45.00	RI
1992	PLATE, M. Taylor, open, 3¹/₄"	19.00	RI

Carlton Fisk Collection
Photo courtesy of *Collectors News*

Coaching Classics — John Wooden

		Issue Price	Current Value
1989	COLLECTOR PLATE, sgd, M. Taylor, 1,975, 10¹/₄"	100.00	NR
1989	COLLECTOR PLATE, M. Taylor, 10,000, 8¹/₂"	45.00	NR
1989	COLLECTOR PLATE, M. Taylor, open, 3¹/₄"	16.00	NR

Darryl Strawberry

		Issue Price	Current Value
1990	SIGNED PLATE, M. Taylor, 2,500, 10¹/₄"	125.00	NR
1990	PLATE, M. Taylor, 10,000, 8¹/₂"	45.00	NR
1990	PLATE, M. Taylor, open, 3¹/₄"	16.00	NR

George Brett Gold Crown Collection

		Issue Price	Current Value
1986	GEORGE BRETT "BASEBALL'S ALL STAR," John Martin, sgd, 2,000, 10¹/₄"	100.00	200.00
1986	GEORGE BRETT "BASEBALL'S ALL STAR," John Martin, open, 3¹/₄"	12.95	20.00

Gordy Howe

		Issue Price	Current Value
1992	SIGNED PLATE, M. Taylor, 2,358, 10¹/₄"	150.00	RI

		Issue Price	Current Value
1992	SIGNED PLATE, M. Taylor, artist proof, 250, 10¼"	195.00	RI
1992	SIGNED PLATE, M. Taylor, 10,000, 8½"................	45.00	RI
1992	SIGNED PLATE, M. Taylor, open, 3¼".................	19.00	RI

Joe Montana

1991	SIGNED PLATE, M. Taylor, 2,250, 10¼"................	125.00	NR
1991	SIGNED PLATE, M. Taylor, artist proof, 250, 10¼"	195.00	NR
1991	PLATE, M. Taylor, 10,000, 8½"	45.00	NR
1991	PLATE, M. Taylor, open, 3¼"	16.00	NR

Johnny Bench

| 1989 | COLLECTOR PLATE, M. Taylor, sgd, 1,989, 10¼" .... | 100.00 | 150.00 |
| 1989 | COLLECTOR PLATE, M. Taylor, open, 3¼".............. | 16.00 | NR |

Kareem Abdul–Jabbar Sky–Hook Collection

| 1989 | KAREEM ABDUL–JABBAR "PATH OF GLORY," M. Taylor, sgd, 1,989, 10¼" .... | 100.00 | 150.00 |
| 1989 | COLLECTOR PLATE, M. Taylor, closed, 3¼" .... | 16.00 | NR |

Ken Griffey Jr.

1992	SIGNED PLATE, M. Taylor, 1,989, 10¼"................	125.00	RI
1992	SIGNED PLATE, M. Taylor, artist proof, 300, 10½"	195.00	RI
1992	PLATE, M. Taylor, 10,000, 8½"	45.00	RI
1992	PLATE, M. Taylor, open, 3¼"	19.00	RI

Kristi Yamaguchi

1993	SIGNED PLATE, M. Taylor, 950, 10¼"	150.00	RI
1993	PLATE, M. Taylor, 5,000, 8½"........................	49.00	RI
1993	PLATE, M. Taylor, open, 3¼"	19.00	RI

Kristi Yamaguchi
Photo courtesy of *Collectors News*

	Issue Price	Current Value

Luis Aparicio

1990	SIGNED PLATE, M. Taylor, 1,984, 10¼"	125.00	NR
1990	SIGNED PLATE, M. Taylor, artist proof, 250, 10¼"	150.00	NR
1990	PLATE, M. Taylor, 10,000, 8½"	45.00	NR
1990	PLATE, M. Taylor, open, 3¼"	16.00	NR

Magic Johnson Gold Rim Collection

1987	MAGIC JOHNSON "THE MAGIC SHOW," R. Winslow, sgd, 1,987, 10¼"	100.00	350.00
1987	MAGIC JOHNSON "THE MAGIC SHOW," R. Winslow, closed, 3¼" 14.50	30.00	

Mike Schmidt "500th" Home Run Edition

1987	MIKE SCHMIDT "POWER AT THE PLATE," Christopher Paluso, sgd, 1,987, 10¼"	100.00	300.00
1987	MIKE SCHMIDT "POWER AT THE PLATE," Christopher Paluso, open, 3¼"	14.50	NR
1987	MIKE SCHMIDT, Christopher Paluso, artist proof, 56	150.00	NR

Pete Rose Diamond Collection

1988	PETE ROSE "THE REIGNING LEGEND," Forbes, sgd, 950, 10¼" 225.00		195.00
1988	PETE ROSE "THE REIGNING LEGEND," Forbes, sgd, artist proof, 50, 10¼"	300.00	400.00
1988	PETE ROSE "THE REIGNING LEGEND," Forbes, open, 3¼" 14.50		NR

Pete Rose Platinum Edition

1985	PETE ROSE "THE BEST OF BASEBALL," Ted Sizemore, sgd, 4,192, 10¼"	100.00	175.00
1985	PETE ROSE, "THE BEST OF BASEBALL," Ted Sizemore, open, 3¼" 12.95	20.00	

Phil Esposito

1992	SIGNED PLATE, M. Taylor, 1,984, 10¼"	150.00	RI
1992	SIGNED PLATE, M. Taylor, artist proof, 250, 10¼"	195.00	RI
1992	PLATE, M. Taylor, 10,000, 8½"	49.00	RI
1992	PLATE, M. Taylor, open, 3¼"	19.00	RI

Rod Carew

1991	HITTING FOR THE HALL, M. Taylor, sgd, 950, 10¼"	150.00	NR
1991	HITTING FOR THE HALL, M. Taylor, 10,000, 8½"	45.00	NR
1991	HITTING FOR THE HALL, M. Taylor, open, 3¼"	16.00	NR

Roger Staubach Sterling Collection

1987	ROGER STAUBACH, Charles Soileau, sgd, 1,979, 10¼"	100.00	NR
1987	ROGER STAUBACH, Charles Soileau, open, 3¼"	12.95	20.00

Round Tripper

		Issue Price	Current Value
1986	REGGIE JACKSON, John Martin, open, 3¹/₄"	12.50	NR

Sam Snead

1993	SIGNED PLATE, M. Taylor, 950, 10¹/₄"	175.00	RI
1993	PLATE, M. Taylor, 5,000, 8¹/₂"	49.00	RI
1993	PLATE, M. Taylor, open, 3¹/₄"	19.00	RI

Tom Seaver

1992	SIGNED PLATE, M. Taylor, 1,992, 10¹/₄"	150.00	RI
1992	SIGNED PLATE, M. Taylor, artist proof, 250, 10¹/₄"	195.00	RI
1992	SIGNED PLATE, M. Taylor, 10,000, 8¹/₂"	45.00	RI
1992	SIGNED PLATE, M. Taylor, open, 3¹/₄"	19.00	RI

Tom Seaver
Photo courtesy of *Collectors News*

Wayne Gretzky
Photo courtesy of *Collectors News*

Wayne Gretzky

1989	COLLECTOR PLATE, M. Taylor, sgd by Gretzky and Howe, 1,851, 10¹/₄"	225.00	300.00
1989	COLLECTOR PLATE, M. Taylor, sgd by Gretzky and Howe, artist proof, 300, 10¹/₄"	300.00	425.00
1989	COLLECTOR PLATE, M. Taylor, 10,000, 8¹/₂"	45.00	60.00
1989	COLLECTOR PLATE, M. Taylor, open, 3¹/₄"	16.00	NR

Whitey Ford

1990	SIGNED PLATE, M. Taylor, 2,360, 10¹/₄"	125.00	135.00
1990	SIGNED PLATE, M. Taylor, artist proof, 250, 10¹/₄"	175.00	NR
1990	PLATE, M. Taylor, 10,000, 8¹/₂"	45.00	NR
1990	PLATE, M. Taylor, open, 3¹/₄"	16.00	NR

	Issue Price	Current Value

Yogi Berra

1989	COLLECTOR PLATE, M. Taylor, sgd, 2,150, 10¹/₄'	125.00	135.00
1989	COLLECTOR PLATE, M. Taylor, sgd, artist proof, 250, 10¹/₄" NR		175.00
1989	COLLECTOR PLATE, M. Taylor, 10,000, 8¹/₂"	45.00	NR
1989	COLLECTOR PLATE, M. Taylor, open, 3¹/₄"	16.00	NR

W. S. GEORGE UNITED STATES

Alaska: The Last Frontier

1991	ICY MAJESTY, H. Lambson, 150 days	34.50	NR
1991	AUTUMN GRANDEUR, H. Lambson, 150 days	34.50	NR
1992	MOUNTAIN MONARCH, H. Lambson, 150 days	37.50	RI
1992	DOWN THE TRAIL, H. Lambson, 150 days	37.50	RI
1992	MOONLIGHT LOOKOUT, H. Lambson, 150 days........	37.50	RI
1992	GRACEFUL PASSAGE, H. Lambson, 150 days	39.50	RI
1992	ARCTIC JOURNEY, H. Lambson, 150 days	39.50	RI
1992	SUMMIT DOMAIN, H. Lambson, 150 days	39.50	RI

Along an English Lane

1993	SUMMER'S BRIGHT WELCOME, M. Harvey, 95 days	29.50	RI
1993	GREETING THE DAY, M. Harvey, 95 days..............	29.50	RI
1993	FRIENDS AND FLOWERS	29.50	RI
1993	COTTAGE AROUND THE BEND	29.50	RI

America's Pride

1992	MISTY FJORDS, R. Richert, 150 days	29.50	RI
1992	RUGGED SHORES, R. Richert, 150 days	29.50	RI
1992	MIGHTY SUMMIT, R. Richert, 150 days...............	32.50	RI
1993	LOFTY REFLECTIONS, R. Richert, 150 days	32.50	RI
1993	TRANQUIL WATERS, R. Richert, 150 days	32.50	RI
1993	MOUNTAIN MAJESTY	34.50	RI
1993	CANYON CLIMB	34.50	RI
1993	GOLDEN VISTA	34.50	RI

America the Beautiful

1988	YOSEMITE FALLS, H. Johnson, 150 days	34.50	NR
1989	THE GRAND CANYON, H. Johnson, 150 days..........	34.50	NR
1989	YELLOWSTONE RIVER, H. Johnson, 150 days.........	37.50	NR
1989	THE GREAT SMOKEY MOUNTAINS, H. Johnson, 150 days	37.50	NR
1990	THE EVERGLADES, H. Johnson, 150 days	37.50	NR
1990	ACADIA, H. Johnson, 150 days	37.50	NR
1990	THE GRAND TETONS, H. Johnson, 150 days	39.50	NR
1990	CRATER LAKE, H. Johnson, 150 days	39.50	NR

Art Deco

		Issue Price	Current Value
1989	A FLAPPER WITH GREYHOUNDS, M. McDonald, 150 days	39.50	45.00
1990	TANGO DANCERS, M. McDonald, 150 days	39.50	60.00
1990	ARRIVING IN STYLE, M. McDonald, 150 days	39.50	60.00
1990	ON THE TOWN, M. McDonald, 150 days	39.50	70.00

Baby Cats of the Wild

		Issue Price	Current Value
1992	MORNING MISCHIEF, Charles Frace, 95 days	29.50	RI
1993	TOGETHERNESS, Charles Frace, 95 days	29.50	RI
1993	THE BUDDY SYSTEM, Charles Frace, 95 days	32.50	RI
1993	NAP TIME, Charles Frace, 95 days	32.50	RI

Bear Tracks

		Issue Price	Current Value
1992	DENALI FAMILY, J. Seerey–Lester, 150 days	29.50	RI
1993	THEIR FIRST SEASON, J. Seerey–Lester, 150 days	29.50	RI
1993	HIGH COUNTRY CHAMPION	29.50	RI
1993	HEAVY GOING	29.50	RI
1993	BREAKING COVER	29.50	RI
1993	ALONG THE ICE FLOW	29.50	RI

Beloved Hymns of Childhood

		Issue Price	Current Value
1988	THE LORD'S MY SHEPHERD, Cicely Mary Barker, 150 days	29.50	40.00
1988	AWAY IN A MANGER, Cicely Mary Barker, 150 days	29.50	35.00
1989	NOW THANK WE ALL OUR GOD, Cicely Mary Barker, 150 days	32.50	NR
1989	LOVE DIVINE, Cicely Mary Barker, 150 days	32.50	NR
1989	I LOVE TO HEAR THE STORY, Cicely Mary Barker, 150 days	32.50	NR
1989	ALL GLORY, LAUD AND HONOUR, Cicely Mary Barker, 150 days	32.50	NR
1990	ALL PEOPLE ON EARTH DO DWELL, Cicely Mary Barker, 150 days	34.50	NR
1990	LOVING SHEPHERD OF THY SHEEP, Cicely Mary Barker, 150 days	34.50	NR

The Lord's My Shepherd
Photo courtesy of *Collectors News*

Let the Children Come to Me
Photo courtesy of *Collectors News*

Black Tie Affair: The Penguin

		Issue Price	Current Value
1992	LITTLE EXPLORER, C. Jagodits, 150 days	29.50	RI
1992	PENGUIN PARADE, C. Jagodits, 150 days	29.50	RI
1992	BABY–SITTERS, C. Jagodits, 150 days	29.50	RI
1992	BELLY FLOPPING, C. Jagodits, 150 days	29.50	RI

Blessed are the Children

1990	LET THE CHILDREN COME TO ME, W. Rane, 150 days ..	29.50	45.00
1990	I AM THE GOOD SHEPHERD, W. Rane, 150 days	29.50	45.00
1991	WHOEVER WELCOMES/CHILD, W. Rane, 150 days	32.50	40.00
1991	HOSANNA IN THE HIGHEST, W. Rane, 150 days	32.50	NR
1991	JESUS HAD COMPASSION ON THEM, W. Rane, 150 days	32.50	50.00
1991	BLESSED ARE THE PEACEMAKERS, W. Rane, 150 days .	34.50	55.00
1991	I AM THE VINE, YOU ARE THE BRANCHES, W. Rane, 150 days	34.50	50.00
1991	SEEK AND YOU WILL FIND, W. Rane, 150 days	34.50	NR

Bonds of Love

1989	PRECIOUS EMBRACE, B. Burke, 150 days	29.50	NR
1990	CHERISHED MOMENT, B. Burke, 150 days	29.50	NR
1991	TENDER CARESS, B. Burke, 150 days	32.50	NR
1992	LOVING TOUCH, B. Burke, 150 days	32.50	RI
1992	TREASURED KISSES, B. Burke, 150 days	32.50	RI
1994	ENDEARING WHISPER	32.50	RI

Charles Vickery's Romantic Harbors

1993	ADVENT OF THE GOLDEN BOUGH, Charles Vickery, 95 days ..	34.50	RI
1993	CHRISTMAS TREE SCHOONER, Charles Vickery	34.50	RI
1993	PRELUDE TO THE JOURNEY, Charles Vickery	34.50	RI
1993	SHIMMERING LIGHT OF DUSK, Charles Vickery	34.50	RI

Cherished Moment
Photo courtesy of *Collectors News*

Great Blue Heron
Photo courtesy of *Collectors News*

		Issue Price	Current Value

Christmas Story

1992	GIFTS OF THE MAGI, Hector Garrido, 150 days	29.50	RI
1993	REST ON THE FLIGHT INTO EGYPT, Hector Garrido, 150 days .	29.50	RI
1993	JOURNEY OF THE MAGI, Hector Garrido, 150 days......	29.50	RI
1993	THE NATIVITY, Hector Garrido, 150 days...............	29.50	RI
1993	THE ANNUNCIATION, Hector Garrido, 150 days.........	29.50	RI
1993	ADORATION OF THE SHEPHERDS, Hector Garrido, 150 days .	29.50	RI

Classic Waterfowl

1988	MALLARDS AT SUNRISE, L. Kaatz, 150 days	36.50	BR
1988	GEESE IN THE AUTUMN FIELDS, L. Kaatz, 150 days.....	36.50	NR
1989	GREEN WINGS/MORNING MARSH, L. Kaatz, 150 days ..	39.50	BR
1989	CANVASBACKS, BREAKING AWAY, L. Kaatz, 150 days ...	39.50	BR
1989	PINTAILS IN INDIAN SUMMER, L. Kaatz, 150 days......	39.50	BR
1990	WOOD DUCKS TAKING FLIGHT, L. Kaatz, 150 days......	39.50	BR
1990	SNOW GEESE AGAINST NOVEMBER SKIES, L. Kaatz, 150 days	41.50	NR
1990	BLUEBILLS COMING IN, L. Kaatz, 150 days	41.50	NR

Columbus Discovers America: The 500th Anniversary

1992	UNDER FULL SAIL, J. Penalva, 150 days...............	29.50	RI
1992	ASHORE AT DAWN, J. Penalva, 150 days	29.50	RI
1992	COLUMBUS RAISES THE FLAG, J. Penalva, 150 days ...	32.50	RI
1992	BRINGING TOGETHER TWO CULTURES, J. Penalva, 150 days	32.50	RI
1992	THE QUEEN'S APPROVAL, J. Penalva, 150 days	32.50	RI
1992	TREASURES FROM THE NEW WORLD, J. Penalva, 150 days .	32.50	RI

Country Bouquets

1991	MORNING SUNSHINE, G. Kurz, 150 days	29.50	45.00
1991	SUMMER PERFUME, G. Kurz, 150 days	29.50	50.00
1991	WARM WELCOME, G. Kurz, 150 days	32.50	50.00
1991	GARDEN'S BOUNTY, G. Kurz, 150 days	32.50	65.00

Country Nostalgia

1989	THE SPRING BUGGY, M. Harvey, 150 days	29.50	NR
1989	THE APPLE CIDER PRESS, M. Harvey, 150 days	29.50	NR
1989	THE VINTAGE SEED PLANTER, M. Harvey, 150 days	29.50	40.00
1989	THE OLD HAND PUMP, M. Harvey, 150 days	32.50	50.00
1990	THE WOODEN BUTTER CHURN, M. Harvey, 150 days ...	32.50	40.00
1990	THE DAIRY CANS, M. Harvey, 150 days................	32.50	NR
1990	THE FORGOTTEN PLOW, M. Harvey, 150 days	34.50	NR
1990	THE ANTIQUE SPINNING WHEEL, M. Harvey, 150 days ..	34.50	NR

Critic's Choice: Gone with the Wind

1991	MARRY ME, SCARLETT, P. Jennis, 150 days	27.50	40.00
1991	WAITING FOR RHETT, P. Jennis, 150 days	27.50	50.00

		Issue Price	Current Value
1001	A DECLARATION OF LOVE, P. Jennis, 150 days	30.50	50.00
1991	THE PARIS HAT, P. Jennis, 150 days	30.50	45.00
1991	SCARLETT ASKS FOR A FAVOR, P. Jennis, 150 days	30.50	55.00
1992	SCARLETT GETS HER WAY, P. Jennis, 150 days	32.50	RI
1992	THE SMITTEN SUITOR, P. Jennis, 150 days	32.50	RI
1992	SCARLETT'S SHOPPING SPREE, P. Jennis, 150 days	32.50	RI
1992	THE BUGGY RIDE, P. Jennis, 150 days	32.50	RI
1992	SCARLETT GETS DOWN TO BUSINESS, P. Jennis, 150 days ..	34.50	RI
1993	SCARLETT'S HEART IS WITH TARA	34.50	RI
1993	AT CROSS PURPOSES	34.50	RI

Delicate Balance: Vanishing Wildlife

1992	TOMORROW'S HOPE, G. Beecham, 95 days............	29.50	RI
1993	TODAY'S FUTURE, G. Beecham, 95 days	29.50	RI
1993	PRESENT DREAMS	32.50	RI
1993	EYES ON THE NEW DAY	32.50	RI

Dr. Zhivago

1990	ZHIVAGO AND LARA, G. Bush, 150 days	39.50	NR
1991	LOVE POEMS FOR LARA, G. Bush, 150 days	39.50	NR
1991	ZHIVAGO SAYS FAREWELL, G. Bush, 150 days	39.50	NR
1991	LARA'S LOVE, G. Bush, 150 days	39.50	55.00

Elegant Birds

1988	THE SWAN, J. Faulkner, 150 days	32.50	NR
1988	GREAT BLUE HERON, J. Faulkner, 150 days	32.50	NR
1989	SNOWY EGRET, J. Faulkner, 150 days	32.50	NR
1989	THE ANHINGA, J. Faulkner, 150 days	35.50	NR
1989	THE FLAMINGO, J. Faulkner, 150 days	35.50	NR
1990	SANDHILL AND WHOOPING CRANE, J. Faulkner, 150 days ...	35.50	NR

Enchanted Garden

1993	A PEACEFUL RETREAT, E. Antonaccio, 95 days	24.50	RI

Eyes of the Wild

1993	EYES IN THE MIST, D. Pierce, 95 days	29.50	RI
1993	EYES IN THE PINES	29.50	RI
1993	EYES ON THE SKY	29.50	RI
1993	EYES OF GOLD	29.50	RI
1993	EYES OF SILENCE	29.50	RI
1993	EYES IN THE SNOW...............................	29.50	RI
1994	EYES OF WONDER................................	29.50	RI
1994	EYES OF STRENGTH	29.50	RI

Faces of Nature

		Issue Price	Current Value
1992	CANYON OF THE CAT, J. Kramer Cole, 150 days	29.50	RI
1992	WOLF RIDGE, J. Kramer Cole, 150 days	29.50	RI
1993	TRAIL OF THE TALISMAN, J. Kramer Cole, 150 days	29.50	RI
1993	WOLFPACK OF THE ANCIENTS, J. Kramer Cole, 150 days	29.50	RI
1993	TWO BEARS CAMP, J. Kramer Cole, 150 days	29.50	RI
1993	WINTERING WITH THE WAPITI, J. Kramer Cole, 150 days	29.50	RI
1993	WITHIN SUNRISE....................................	29.50	RI
1993	WAMBLI, OKIYE	29.50	RI

Eyes in the Mist

Canyon of the Cat
Photo courtesy of *Collectors News*

Federal Duck Stamps

1990	THE LESSER SCAUP, N. Anderson, 150 days	27.50	35.00
1990	MALLARD, N. Anderson, 150 days	27.50	40.00
1990	THE RUDDY DUCKS, N. Anderson, 150 days	30.50	NR
1990	CANVASBACKS, N. Anderson, 150 days	30.50	NR
1991	PINTAILS, N. Anderson, 150 days....................	30.50	NR
1991	WIGEONS, N. Anderson, 150 days	30.50	NR
1991	CINNAMON TEAL, N. Anderson, 150 days.............	32.50	NR
1991	FULVOUS WISTLING DUCK, N. Anderson, 150 days	32.50	50.00
1991	SNOW GOOSE, N. Anderson, 150 days	32.50	NR
1991	THE REDHEADS	32.50	45.00

Feline Fancy

1993	GLOBETROTTERS	34.50	RI
1993	LITTLE ATHLETES	34.50	RI
1993	YOUNG ADVENTURERS	34.50	RI
1993	THE GEOGRAPHERS	34.50	RI

Field Birds of North America

		Issue Price	Current Value
1991	WINTER COLORS: RING–NECKED PHEASANT, D. Bush, 150 days	39.50	45.00
1991	IN DISPLAY: RUFFED GOOSE, D. Bush, 150 days	39.50	NR
1991	MORNING LIGHT: BOBWHITE QUAIL, D. Bush, 150 days	42.50	NR
1991	MISTY CLEARING: WILD TURKEY, D. Bush, 150 days	42.50	80.00
1992	AUTUMN MOMENT: AMERICAN WOODCOCK, D. Bush, 150 days	42.50	RI
1992	SEASON'S END: WILLOW PTARMIGAN, D. Bush, 150 days	42.50	RI

Flash of Cats

1993	MOONLIGHT CHASE: COUGAR, J. Seerey–Lester, 150 days	29.50	RI

Floral Fancies

1993	SITTING SOFTLY	34.50	RI
1993	SITTING PRETTY	34.50	RI
1993	SITTING SUNNY	34.50	RI
1993	SITTING PINK	34.50	RI

Flowers from Grandma's Garden

1990	COUNTRY CUTTINGS, G. Kurz, 150 days	24.50	45.00
1990	THE MORNING BOUQUET, G. Kurz, 150 days	24.50	40.00
1991	HOMESPUN BEAUTY, G. Kurz, 150 days	27.50	40.00
1991	HARVEST IN THE MEADOW, G. Kurz, 150 days	27.50	40.00
1991	GARDENER'S DELIGHT, G. Kurz, 150 days	27.50	45.00
1991	NATURE'S BOUNTY, G. Kurz, 150 days	27.50	60.00
1991	A COUNTRY WELCOME, G. Kurz, 150 days	29.50	55.00
1991	THE SPRINGTIME ARRANGEMENT, G. Kurz, 150 days	29.50	50.00

Flowers of your Garden

1988	ROSES, V. Morley, 150 days	24.50	30.00
1988	LILACS, V. Morley, 150 days	24.50	70.00
1988	DAISIES, V. Morley, 150 days	27.50	NR
1988	PEONIES, V. Morley, 150 days	27.50	NR
1988	CHRYSANTHEMUMS, V. Morley, 150 days	27.50	NR
1989	DAFFODILS, V. Morley, 150 days	27.50	NR
1989	TULIPS, V. Morley, 150 days	29.50	NR
1989	IRISES, V. Morley, 150 days	29.50	NR

Garden of the Lord

1992	LOVE ONE ANOTHER, C. Gillies, 150 days	29.50	RI
1992	PERFECT PEACE, C. Gillies, 150 days	29.50	RI
1992	TRUST IN THE LORD, C. Gillies, 150 days	32.50	RI
1992	THE LORD'S LOVE, C. Gillies, 150 days	32.50	RI
1992	THE LORD BLESS YOU, C. Gillies, 150 days	32.50	RI
1992	ASK IN PRAYER, C. Gillies, 150 days	34.50	RI
1993	PEACE BE WITH YOU, C. Gillies, 150 days	34.50	RI

Gardens of Paradise

		Issue Price	Current Value
1992	TRANQUILITY, L. Chang, 150 days	29.50	RI
1992	SERENITY, L. Chang, 150 days	29.50	RI
1993	SPLENDOR, L. Chang, 150 days	32.50	RI
1993	HARMONY, L. Chang, 150 days	32.50	RI
1993	BEAUTY	32.50	RI
1993	ELEGANCE	32.50	RI
1993	GRANDEUR	32.50	RI
1993	MAJESTY	32.50	RI

Gentle Beginnings

1991	TENDER LOVING CARE, W. Nelson, 150 days	34.50	NR
1991	A TOUCH OF LOVE, W. Nelson, 150 days	34.50	50.00
1991	UNDER WATCHFUL EYES, W. Nelson, 150 days	37.50	50.00
1991	LAP OF LOVE, W. Nelson, 150 days	37.50	85.00
1991	HAPPY TOGETHER, W. Nelson, 150 days	37.50	60.00
1991	FIRST STEPS, W. Nelson, 150 days	37.50	75.00

Glorious Songbirds

1991	CARDINALS ON A SNOWY BRANCH, R. Cobane, 150 days	29.50	NR
1991	INDIGO BUNTINGS AND/BLOSSOMS, R. Cobane, 150 days	29.50	NR
1991	CHICKADEES AMONG THE LILACS, R. Cobane, 150 days	32.50	NR
1991	GOLDFINCHES IN/THISTLE, R. Cobane, 150 days	32.50	NR
1991	CEDAR WAXWING/WINTER BERRIES, R. Cobane, 150 days	32.50	NR
1991	BLUEBIRDS IN A BLUEBERRY BUSH, R. Cobane, 150 days	34.50	NR
1991	BALTIMORE ORIOLES/AUTUMN LEAVES, R. Cobane, 150 days	34.50	50.00
1991	ROBINS WITH DOGWOOD IN BLOOM, R. Cobane, 150 days	34.50	50.00

Golden Age of the Clipper Ships

1989	THE TWILIGHT UNDER FULL SAIL, Charles Vickery, 150 days	29.50	NR
1989	THE BLUE JACKET AT SUNSET, Charles Vickery, 150 days	29.50	NR
1989	YOUNG AMERICA, HOMEWARD, Charles Vickery, 150 days	32.50	NR
1990	FLYING CLOUD, Charles Vickery, 150 days	32.50	NR
1990	DAVY CROCKETT AT DAYBREAK, Charles Vickery, 150 days	32.50	NR
1990	GOLDEN EAGLE CONQUERS WIND, Charles Vickery, 150 days	32.50	NR
1990	THE LIGHTNING IN LIFTING FOG, Charles Vickery, 150 days	34.50	NR
1990	SEA WITCH, MISTRESS/OCEANS, Charles Vickery, 150 days	34.50	NR

Gone with the Wind: Golden Anniversary

1988	SCARLETT AND HER SUITORS, H. Rogers, 150 days	24.50	50.00
1988	THE BURNING OF ATLANTA, H. Rogers, 150 days	24.50	45.00
1988	SCARLETT AND ASHLEY AFTER THE WAR, H. Rogers, 150 days	27.50	55.00
1988	THE PROPOSAL, H. Rogers, 150 days	27.50	70.00
1989	HOME TO TARA, H. Rogers, 150 days	27.50	45.00
1989	STROLLING IN ATLANTA, H. Rogers, 150 days,	27.50	40.00
1989	A QUESTION OF HONOR, H. Rogers, 150 days,	29.50	40.00

	Issue Price	Current Value
1989 SCARLETT'S RESOLVE, H. Rogers, 150 days, ...	29.50	45.00
1989 FRANKLY MY DEAR, H. Rogers, 150 days, ...	29.50	50.00
1989 MELANIE AND ASHLEY, H. Rogers, 150 days, ...	32.50	NR
1990 A TOAST TO BONNIE BLUE, H. Rogers, 150 days,.......	32.50	50.00
1990 SCARLETT AND RHETT'S HONEYMOON, H. Rogers, 150 days,	32.50	45.00

The Burning of Atlanta
Photo courtesy of *Collectors News*

Grand Safari: Images of Africa

1992 A MOMENT'S REST, Charles Frace, 150 days	34.50	RI
1992 ELEPHANTS OF KILIMANJARO, Charles Frace, 150 days .	34.50	RI
1992 UNDIVIDED ATTENTION, Charles Frace, 150 days	37.50	RI
1993 QUIET TIME IN SAMBURU, Charles Frace, 150 days	37.50	RI
1993 LONE HUNTER, Charles Frace, 150 days	37.50	RI
1993 THE GREATER KUDO, Charles Frace, 150 days	37.50	RI

Heart of the Wild

1991 A GENTLE TOUCH, G. Beecham, 150 days	29.50	NR
1992 MOTHER'S PRIDE, G. Beecham, 150 days	29.50	RI
1992 AN AFTERNOON TOGETHER, G. Beecham, 150 days	32.50	RI
1992 QUIET TIME?, G. Beecham, 150 days..................	32.50	RI

Hollywood's Glamour Girls

1989 JEAN HARLOW — DINNER AT EIGHT, E. Dzenis, 150 days	29.50	NR
1990 LANA TURNER — POSTMAN RINGS TWICE, E. Dzenis, 150 days	29.50	NR
1990 CAROLE LOMBARD — THE GAY BRIDE, E. Dzenis, 150 days .	29.50	NR
1990 GRETA GARBO — IN GRAND HOTEL, E. Dzenis, 150 days	29.50	NR

Hometown Memories

1993 MOONLIGHT SKATERS, H. T. Becker, 150 days	29.50	RI

		Issue Price	Current Value
1993	MOUNTAIN SLEIGH RIDE, H. T. Becker, 150 days	29.50	RI
1993	HEADING HOME	29.50	RI
1993	A WINTER RIDE	29.50	RI

Last of Their Kind: The Endangered Species

1988	PANDA, W. Nelson, 150 days	27.50	NR
1988	SNOW LEOPARD, W. Nelson, 150 days	27.50	NR
1989	RED WOLF, W. Nelson, 150 days.....................	30.50	NR
1989	ASIAN ELEPHANT, W. Nelson, 150 days	30.50	NR
1990	SLENDER–HORNED GAZELLE, W. Nelson, 150 days	30.50	NR
1990	BRIDLED WALLABY, W. Nelson, 150 days.............	30.50	NR
1990	BLACK–FOOTED FERRET, W. Nelson, 150 days	33.50	NR
1990	SIBERIAN TIGER, W. Nelson, 150 days	33.50	45.00
1991	VICUNA, W. Nelson, 150 days	33.50	NR
1991	PRZEWALSKI'S HORSE, W. Nelson, 150 days	33.50	NR

Lena Liu's Basket Bouquets

1992	ROSES, Lena Liu, 150 days	29.50	RI
1992	PANSIES, Lena Liu, 150 days.........................	29.50	RI
1992	TULIPS AND LILACS, Lena Liu, 150 days	32.50	RI
1992	IRISES, Lena Liu, 150 days	32.50	RI
1992	LILIES, Lena Liu, 150 days...........................	32.50	RI
1992	PARROT TULIPS, Lena Liu, 150 days..................	32.50	RI
1992	PEONIES, Lena Liu, 150 days	32.50	RI
1993	BEGONIAS, Lena Liu, 150 days	32.50	RI
1993	MAGNOLIAS, Lena Liu, 150 days	32.50	RI
1993	CALLA LILIES	32.50	RI
1993	ORCHIDS	32.50	RI
1993	HYDRANGEAS	32.50	RI

Lena Liu's Flower Fairies

| 1993 | MAGIC MAKERS, Lena Liu, 95 days .... | 29.50 | RI |

Lena Liu's Hummingbird Treasury

1992	RUBY–THROATED HUMMINGBIRD, Lena Liu, 150 days .	29.50	RI
1992	ANNA'S HUMMINGBIRD, Lena Liu, 150 days	29.50	RI
1992	VIOLET–CROWNED HUMMINGBIRD, Lena Liu, 150 days	32.50	RI
1992	RUFOUS HUMMINGBIRD, Lena Liu, 150 days	32.50	RI
1993	WHITE–EARED HUMMINGBIRD, Lena Liu, 150 days	32.50	RI
1993	BROAD–BILLED HUMMINGBIRD	34.50	RI
1993	CALLIOPE HUMMINGBIRD............................	34.50	RI
1993	ALLEN'S HUMMINGBIRD	34.50	RI

Little Angels

| 1992 | ANGELS WE HAVE HEARD ON HIGH, B. Burke, 150 days | 29.50 | RI |

		Issue Price	Current Value
1992	O TANNENBAUM, B. Burke, 150 days	29.50	RI
1993	JOY TO THE WORLD, B. Burke, 150 days	32.50	RI
1993	HARK THE HERALD ANGELS SING, B. Burke, 150 days	32.50	RI
1993	IT CAME UPON A MIDNIGHT CLEAR	32.50	RI
1993	FIRST NOEL	32.50	RI

Ruby–Throated Hummingbird

Angels We Have Heard on High
Photo courtesy of *Collectors News*

Loving Look: Duck Families

1990	FAMILY OUTING, B. Langton, 150 days	34.50	NR
1991	SLEEPY START, B. Langton, 150 days	34.50	NR
1991	QUIET MOMENT, B. Langton, 150 days	37.50	NR
1991	SAFE AND SOUND, B. Langton, 150 days	37.50	NR
1991	SPRING ARRIVALS, B. Langton, 150 days	37.50	NR
1991	FAMILY TREE, B. Langton, 150 days	37.50	50.00

Majestic Horse

1992	CLASSIC BEAUTY: THOROUGHBRED, P. Wildermuth, 150 days	34.50	RI
1992	AMERICAN GOLD: QUARTERHORSE, P. Wildermuth, 150 days	34.50	RI
1992	REGAL SPIRIT: THE ARABIAN, P. Wildermuth, 150 days	34.50	RI
1992	WESTERN FAVORITE: AMERICAN PAINT HORSE, P. Wildermuth, 150 days	34.50	RI

Memories of a Victorian Childhood

1992	YOU'D BETTER NOT POUT, 150 days	29.50	RI
1992	SWEET SLUMBER, 150 days	29.50	RI
1992	THROUGH THICK AND THIN, 150 days	32.50	RI
1992	AN ARMFUL OF TREASURES, 150 days	32.50	RI

		Issue Price	Current Value
1993	A TRIO OF BOOKWORMS, 150 days	32.50	RI
1993	PUGNACIOUS PLAYMATE, 150 days	32.50	RI

Nature's Legacy

1990	BLUE SNOW AT HALF DOME, J. Sias, 150 days	24.50	NR
1991	MISTY MORNING/MT. MCKINLEY, J. Sias, 150 days	24.50	NR
1991	MOUNT RANIER, J. Sias, 150 days	27.50	NR
1991	HAVASU CANYON, J. Sias, 150 days	27.50	NR
1991	AUTUMN SPLENDOR IN THE SMOKEY MOUNTAINS, J. Sias, 150 days	27.50	NR
1991	WINTER PEACE IN YELLOWSTONE PARK, J. Sias, 150 days	29.50	NR
1991	GOLDEN MAJESTY/ROCKY MOUNTAINS, J. Sias, 150 days	29.50	NR
1991	RADIANT SUNSET OVER THE EVERGLADES, J. Sias, 150 days	29.50	NR

Blue Snow at Half Dome
Photo courtesy of *Collectors News*

Nature's Lovables

1990	THE KOALA, Charles Frace, 150 days	27.50	NR
1991	NEW ARRIVAL, Charles Frace, 150 days	27.50	35.00
1991	CHINESE TREASURE, Charles Frace, 150 days	27.50	NR
1991	BABY HARP SEAL, Charles Frace, 150 days	30.50	40.00
1991	BOBCAT: NATURE'S DAWN, Charles Frace, 150 days	30.50	NR
1991	CLOUDED LEOPARD, Charles Frace, 150 days	32.50	NR
1991	ZEBRA FOAL, Charles Frace, 150 days	32.50	45.00
1991	BANDIT, Charles Frace, 150 days	32.50	45.00

Nature's Playmates

1991	PARTNERS, Charles Frace, 150 days	29.50	NR
1991	SECRET HEIGHTS, Charles Frace, 150 days	29.50	NR
1991	RECESS, Charles Frace, 150 days	32.50	50.00

			Issue Price	Current Value
1991	DOUBLE TROUBLE, Charles Frace, 150 days		32.50	NR
1991	PALS, Charles Frace, 150 days		32.50	NR
1992	CURIOUS TRIO, Charles Frace, 150 days		34.50	RI
1992	PLAYMATES, Charles Frace, 150 days		34.50	RI
1992	SURPRISE, Charles Frace, 150 days		34.50	RI
1992	PEACE ON ICE, Charles Frace, 150 days		36.50	RI
1992	AMBASSADORS, Charles Frace, 150 days		36.50	RI

Nature's Poetry

1989	MORNING SERENADE, Lena Liu, 150 days	24.50	40.00
1989	SONG OF PROMISE, Lena Liu, 150 days	24.50	35.00
1990	TENDER LULLABYE, Lena Liu, 150 days	27.50	35.00
1990	NATURE'S HARMONY, Lena Liu, 150 days	27.50	35.00
1990	GENTLE REFRAIN, Lena Liu, 150 days	27.50	NR
1990	MORNING CHORUS, Lena Liu, 150 days	27.50	NR
1990	MELODY AT DAYBREAK, Lena Liu, 150 days	29.50	NR
1991	DELICATE ACCORD, Lena Liu, 150 days	29.50	NR
1991	LYRICAL BEGINNINGS, Lena Liu, 150 days	29.50	NR
1991	SONG OF SPRING, Lena Liu, 150 days	32.50	NR
1991	MOTHER'S MELODY, Lena Liu, 150 days	32.50	NR
1991	CHERUB CHORALE, Lena Liu, 150 days	32.50	NR

On Golden Wings

1993	MORNING LIGHT	29.50	RI
1993	EARLY RISERS	29.50	RI
1993	AS DAY BREAKS	32.50	RI
1993	DAYLIGHT FLIGHT	32.50	RI
1994	WINTER DAWN	32.50	RI
1994	FIRST LIGHT	32.50	RI

On Gossamer Wings

1988	MONARCH BUTTERFLIES, Lena Liu, 150 days	24.50	NR
1988	WESTERN TIGER SWALLOWTAILS, Lena Liu, 150 days	24.50	35.00
1988	RED–SPOTTED PURPLE, Lena Liu, 150 days	27.50	45.00
1988	MALACHITES, Lena Liu, 150 days	27.50	NR
1988	WHITE PEACOCKS, Lena Liu, 150 days	27.50	35.00
1988	EASTERN TAILED BLUES, Lena Liu, 150 days	27.50	NR
1988	ZEBRA SWALLOWTAILS, Lena Liu, 150 days	29.50	NR
1988	RED ADMIRALS, Lena Liu, 150 days	29.50	NR

On the Wing

1992	WINGED SPLENDOR, T. Humphrey, 150 days	29.50	RI
1992	RISING MALLARD, T. Humphrey, 150 days	29.50	RI
1992	GLORIOUS ASCENT, T. Humphrey, 150 days	32.50	RI
1992	TAKING WING, T. Humphrey, 150 days	32.50	RI

		Issue Price	Current Value
1992	UPWARD BOUND, T. Humphrey, 150 days	32.50	RI
1993	WONDROUS MOTION, T. Humphrey, 150 days	34.50	RI
1993	SPRINGING FORTH, T. Humphrey, 150 days...........	34.50	RI
1993	ON THE WING.....................................	34.50	RI

On Wings of Snow

		Issue Price	Current Value
1991	THE SWANS, Lena Liu, 150 days	34.50	40.00
1991	THE DOVES, Lena Liu, 150 days	34.50	50.00
1991	THE PEACOCKS, Lena Liu, 150 days	37.50	50.00
1991	THE EGRETS, Lena Liu, 150 days	37.50	55.00
1991	THE COCKATOOS, Lena Liu, 150 days	37.50	65.00
1991	THE HERONS, Lena Liu, 150 days....................	37.50	NR

Our Woodland Friends

		Issue Price	Current Value
1989	FASCINATION, C. Brenders, 150 days	29.50	NR
1990	BENEATH THE PINES, C. Brenders, 150 days	29.50	NR
1990	HIGH ADVENTURE, C. Brenders, 150 days	32.50	NR
1990	SHY EXPLORERS, C. Brenders, 150 days	32.50	NR
1991	GOLDEN SEASON: GRAY SQUIRREL, C. Brenders, 150 days .	32.50	NR
1991	FULL HOUSE: FOX FAMILY, C. Brenders, 150 days	32.50	45.00
1991	A JUMP INTO LIFE: SPRING FAWN, C. Brenders, 150 days ...	34.50	NR
1991	FOREST SENTINEL: BOBCAT, C. Brenders, 150 days	34.50	NR

Passions of Scarlett O'Hara

		Issue Price	Current Value
1992	FIERY EMBRACE, P. Jennis, 150 days	29.50	RI
1992	PRIDE AND PASSION, P. Jennis, 150 days	29.50	RI
1992	DREAMS OF ASHLEY, P. Jennis, 150 days..............	32.50	RI
1992	AS GOD IS MY WITNESS, P. Jennis, 150 days	34.50	RI

Fiery Embrace

Backyard Treasure: Chickadee
Photo courtesy of *Collectors News*

		Issue Price	Current Value
1993	BRAVE SCARLETT	34.50	RI
1992	THE FOND FAREWELL, P. Jennis, 150 days.............	32.50	RI
1992	THE WALTZ, P. Jennis, 150 days	32.50	RI
1993	NIGHTMARE	34.50	RI
1993	EVENING PRAYERS	34.50	RI
1993	NAP TIME	36.50	RI
1993	DANGEROUS ATTRACTION	36.50	RI
1993	THE END OF AN ERA	36.50	RI

Petal Pals

1992	GARDEN DISCOVERY, L. Chang, 150 days	24.50	RI
1992	FLOWERING FASCINATION, L. Chang, 150 days	24.50	RI
1993	ALLURING LILIES, L. Chang, 150 days	24.50	RI
1993	SPRINGTIME OASIS, L. Chang, 150 days	24.50	RI
1993	BLOSSOMING ADVENTURE, L. Chang, 150 days........	24.50	RI
1993	DANCING DAFFODILS, L. Chang, 150 days.............	24.50	RI
1993	SUMMER SURPRISE, L. Chang, 150 days	24.50	RI
1993	MORNING MELODY..................................	24.50	RI

Poetic Cottages

1992	GARDEN PATHS OF OXFORDSHIRE, C. Valente, 150 days	29.50	RI
1992	TWILIGHT AT WOODGREEN POND, C. Valente, 150 days	29.50	RI
1992	STONEWALL BROOK BLOSSOMS, C. Valente, 150 days .	32.50	RI
1992	BEDFORDSHIRE EVENING SKY, C. Valente, 150 days	32.50	RI
1993	WISTERIA SUMMER, C. Valente, 150 days	32.50	RI
1993	WILTSHIRE ROSE ARBOR, C. Valente, 150 days	32.50	RI
1993	ALDERBURY GARDENS, C. Valente, 150 days	32.50	RI
1993	HAMPSHIRE SPRING SPLENDOR, C. Valente, 150 days .	32.50	RI

Portraits of Christ

1991	FATHER, FORGIVE THEM, J. Salamanca, 150 days	29.50	65.00
1991	THY WILL BE DONE, J. Salamanca, 150 days...........	29.50	50.00
1991	THIS IS MY BELOVED SON, J. Salamanca, 150 days	32.50	40.00
1991	LO, I AM WITH YOU, J. Salamanca, 150 days	32.50	50.00
1991	BECOME AS LITTLE CHILDREN, J. Salamanca, 150 days	32.50	60.00
1991	PEACE I LEAVE WITH YOU, J. Salamanca, 150 days.....	34.50	50.00
1992	FOR GOD SO LOVED THE WORLD, J. Salamanca, 150 days ..	34.50	RI
1992	I AM THE WAY, THE TRUTH AND THE LIFE, J. Salamanca, 150 days	34.50	RI
1992	WEEP NOT FOR ME, J. Salamanca, 150 days	34.50	RI
1992	FOLLOW ME, J. Salamanca, 150 days	34.50	RI

Portraits of Exquisite Birds

1990	BACKYARD TREASURE: CHICKADEE, C. Brenders, 150 days..	29.50	NR
1990	THE BEAUTIFUL BLUEBIRD, C. Brenders, 150 days	29.50	NR

		Issue Price	Current Value
1991	SUMMER GOLD: THE ROBIN, C. Brenders, 150 days ...	32.50	NR
1991	THE MEADOWLARK'S SONG, C. Brenders, 150 days	32.50	NR
1991	IVORY–BILLED WOODPECKER, C. Brenders, 150 days ..	32.50	NR
1991	RED–WINGED BLACKBIRD, C. Brenders, 150 days......	32.50	NR

Purebred Horses of the Americas

1989	THE APPALOOSA, D. Schwartz, 150 days	34.50	NR
1989	THE TENNESSEE WALKER, D. Schwartz, 150 days	34.50	NR
1990	THE QUARTERHORSE, D. Schwartz, 150 days	37.50	NR
1990	THE SADDLEBRED, D. Schwartz, 150 days.............	37.50	NR
1990	THE MUSTANG, D. Schwartz, 150 days	37.50	NR
1990	THE MORGAN, D. Schwartz, 150 days	37.50	65.00

Rare Encounters

1993	SOFTLY, SOFTLY, J. Seerey–Lester, 95 days	29.50	RI
1993	BLACK MAGIC, J. Seerey–Lester, 95 days	29.50	RI
1993	FUTURE SONG	32.50	RI
1993	HIGH AND MIGHTY	32.50	RI
1993	LAST SANCTUARY....................................	32.50	RI
1993	SOMETHING STIRRED	34.50	RI

Romantic Gardens

1989	THE WOODLAND GARDEN, C. Smith, 150 days.........	29.50	NR
1989	THE PLANTATION GARDEN, C. Smith, 150 days	29.50	NR
1990	THE COTTAGE GARDEN, C. Smith, 150 days	32.50	NR
1990	THE COLONIAL GARDEN, C. Smith, 150 days	32.50	NR

Scenes of Christmas Past

1987	HOLIDAY SKATERS, L. Garrison, 150 days	27.50	40.00
1988	CHRISTMAS EVE, L. Garrison, 150 days	27.50	35.00
1989	THE HOMECOMING, L. Garrison, 150 days.............	30.50	NR
1990	THE TOY STORE, L. Garrison, 150 days...............	30.50	NR
1991	THE CAROLLERS, L. Garrison, 150 days	30.50	NR
1992	FAMILY TRADITIONS, L. Garrison, 150 days	30.50	RI
1993	HOLIDAY PAST	30.50	RI
1994	A GATHERING OF FAITH	32.50	RI

Secret World of the Panda

1990	A MOTHER'S CARE, J. Bridgett, 150 days	27.50	NR
1991	A FROLIC IN THE SNOW, J. Bridgett, 150 days	27.50	NR
1991	LAZY AFTERNOON, J. Bridgett, 150 days	30.50	NR
1991	A DAY OF EXPLORING, J. Bridgett, 150 days	30.50	NR
1991	A GENTLE HUG, J. Bridgett, 150 days	32.50	NR
1991	A BAMBOO FEAST, J. Bridgett, 150 days	32.50	70.00

		Issue Price	Current Value

Soaring Majesty

1991	FREEDOM, Charles Frace, 150 days	29.50	NR
1991	THE NORTHERN GOSHHAWK, Charles Frace, 150 days	29.50	40.00
1991	PEREGRINE FALCON, Charles Frace, 150 days	32.50	NR
1991	RED–TAILED HAWK, Charles Frace, 150 days	32.50	NR
1991	THE OSPREY, Charles Frace, 150 days	32.50	BR
1991	THE GYRFALCON, Charles Frace, 150 days	34.50	40.00
1991	THE GOLDEN EAGLE, Charles Frace, 150 days	34.50	40.00
1992	RED–SHOULDERED HAWK, Charles Frace, 150 days	34.50	RI

Sonnets in Flowers

1992	SONNET OF BEAUTY, G. Kurz, 150 days	29.50	RI
1992	SONNET OF HAPPINESS, G. Kurz, 150 days	34.50	RI
1992	SONNET OF LOVE, G. Kurz, 150 days	34.50	RI
1992	SONNET OF PEACE, G. Kurz, 150 days	34.50	RI

Sound of Music: Silver Anniversary

1991	THE HILLS ARE ALIVE, V. Gadino, 150 days	29.50	NR
1992	LET'S START AT THE VERY BEGINNING, V. Gadino, 150 days	29.50	RI
1992	SOMETHING GOOD, V. Gadino, 150 days	32.50	RI
1992	MARIA'S WEDDING DAY, V. Gadino, 150 days	32.50	RI

Spirit of Christmas

1990	SILENT NIGHT, J. Sias, 150 days	29.50	NR
1991	JINGLE BELLS, J. Sias, 150 days	29.50	NR
1991	DECK THE HALLS, J. Sias, 150 days	32.50	40.00
1991	I'LL BE HOME FOR CHRISTMAS, J. Sias, 150 days	32.50	45.00
1991	WINTER WONDERLAND, J. Sias, 150 days	32.50	NR
1991	O CHRISTMAS TREE, J. Sias, 150 days	32.50	NR

The Toy Store
Photo courtesy of *Collectors News*

Running with the Wind

		Issue Price	Current Value

Spirits of the Sky

1992	TWILIGHT GLOW, C. Fisher, 150 days	29.50	RI
1992	FIRST LIGHT, C. Fisher, 150 days	29.50	RI
1992	EVENING GLIMMER, C. Fisher, 150 days	32.50	RI
1992	GOLDEN DUSK, C. Fisher, 150 days	32.50	RI
1993	SUNSET SPLENDOR, C. Fisher, 150 days	32.50	RI
1993	AMBER FLIGHT, C. Fisher, 150 days	34.50	RI
1993	WINGED RADIANCE	34.50	RI
1993	DAYS END	34.50	RI

Symphony of Shimmering Beauty

1991	IRIS QUARTET, Lena Liu, 150 days	29.50	50.00
1991	TULIP ENSEMBLE, Lena Liu, 150 days	29.50	35.00
1991	POPPY PASTORALE, Lena Liu, 150 days	32.50	40.00
1991	LILY CONCERTO, Lena Liu, 150 days	32.50	55.00
1991	PEONY PRELUDE, Lena Liu, 150 days	32.50	40.00
1991	ROSE FANTASY, Lena Liu, 150 days	34.50	50.00
1991	HIBISCUS MEDLEY, Lena Liu, 150 days	34.50	40.00
1992	DAHLIA MELODY, Lena Liu, 150 days	34.50	RI
1992	HOLLYHOCK MARCH, Lena Liu, 150 days	34.50	RI
1992	CARNATION SERENADE, Lena Liu, 150 days	36.50	RI
1992	GLADIOLUS ROMANCE, Lena Liu, 150 days	36.50	RI
1992	ZINNIA FINALE, Lena Liu, 150 days	36.50	RI

'Tis the Season

1993	A WORLD DRESSED IN SNOW	29.50	RI
1993	A TIME FOR TRADITION	29.50	RI
1993	WE SHALL COME REJOICING	29.50	RI
1993	OUR FAMILY TREE	29.50	RI

Tomorrow's Promise

1992	CURIOSITY: ASIAN ELEPHANTS, W. Nelson, 150 days	29.50	RI
1992	PLAYTIME PANDAS, W. Nelson, 150 days	29.50	RI
1992	INNOCENCE: RHINOS, W. Nelson, 150 days	32.50	RI
1992	FRISKINESS: KIT FOXES, W. Nelson, 150 days	32.50	RI

Touching the Spirit

1993	RUNNING WITH THE WIND, J. Kramer Cole, 95 days	29.50	RI
1993	KINDRED SPIRITS	29.50	RI
1983	THE MARKING TREE	29.50	RI
1993	WAKAN TNAKA	29.50	RI
1993	HE WHO WATCHES	29.50	RI
1994	TWICE TRAVELLED TRAIL	29.50	RI
1994	KEEPER OF THE SECRET	29.50	RI
1994	CAMP OF THE SACRED DOGS	29.50	RI

Treasury of Songbirds

		Issue Price	Current Value
1992	SPRINGTIME SPLENDOR, R. Stine, 150 days	29.50	RI
1992	MORNING'S GLORY, R. Stine, 150 days	29.50	RI
1992	GOLDEN DAYBREAK, R. Stine, 150 days	32.50	RI
1992	AFTERNOON CALM, R. Stine, 150 days	32.50	RI
1992	DAWN'S RADIANCE, R. Stine, 150 days	32.50	RI
1993	SCARLET SUNRISE, R. Stine, 150 days	34.50	RI
1993	SAPPHIRE DAWN, R. Stine, 150 days	34.50	RI
1993	ALLURING DAYLIGHT	34.50	RI

Vanishing Gentle Giants

1991	JUMPING FOR JOY, A. Casay, 150 days	32.50	NR
1991	SONG OF THE HUMPBACK, A. Casay, 150 days	32.50	NR
1991	MONARCH OF THE DEEP, A. Casay, 150 days	35.50	NR
1991	TRAVELERS OF THE SEA, A. Casay, 150 days	35.50	65.00
1991	WHITE WHALE OF THE NORTH, A. Casay, 150 days	35.50	65.00
1991	UNICORN OF THE SEA, A. Casay, 150 days	35.50	NR

Victorian Cat

1990	MISCHIEF WITH THE HATBOX, H. Bonner, 150 days	24.50	40.00
1991	STRING QUARTET, H. Bonner, 150 days	24.50	50.00
1991	DAYDREAMS, H. Bonner, 150 days	27.50	35.00
1991	FRISKY FELINES, H. Bonner, 150 days	27.50	40.00
1991	KITTENS AT PLAY, H. Bonner, 150 days	27.50	40.00
1991	PLAYING IN THE PARLOR, H. Bonner, 150 days	29.50	50.00
1991	PERFECTLY POISED, H. Bonner, 150 days	29.50	50.00
1992	MIDDAY REPOSE, H. Bonner, 150 days	29.50	RI

Victorian Cat Caper

1992	WHO'S THE FAIREST OF THEM ALL?, F. Paton, 150 days	24.50	RI

Who's the Fairest of Them All?

		Issue Price	Current Value
1992	PUSS IN BOOTS, 150 days	24.50	RI
1992	MY BOWL IS EMPTY, W. Hepple, 150 days	27.50	RI
1992	A CURIOUS KITTY, W. Hepple, 150 days	27.50	RI
1992	VANITY FAIR, W. Hepple, 150 days	27.50	RI
1992	FORBIDDEN FRUIT, W. Hepple, 150 days	29.50	RI
1993	THE PURR–FECT PEN PAL, W. Hepple, 150 days	29.50	RI
1993	THE KITTEN EXPRESS, W. Hepple, 150 days	29.50	RI

Wild Innocents

1992	MOONLIGHT CHASE: COUGAR	29.50	RI
1993	REFLECTIONS, Charles Frace, 95 days	29.50	RI
1993	SPIRITUAL HEIR	29.50	RI
1993	LION CUB	29.50	RI
1993	SUNNY SPOT	29.50	RI

Wild Spirits

1992	SOLITARY WATCH, T. Hirata, 150 days	29.50	RI
1992	TIMBER GHOST, T. Hirata, 150 days	29.50	RI
1992	MOUNTAIN MAGIC, T. Hirata, 150 days	32.50	RI
1993	SILENT GUARD, T. Hirata, 150 days	32.50	RI
1993	SLY EYES, T. Hirata, 150 days	32.50	RI
1993	MIGHTY PRESENCE	34.50	RI
1993	QUIET VIGIL	34.50	RI
1993	LONE VANGUARD	34.50	RI

Windows of Glory

1993	KING OF KINGS, J. Welty, 95 days	29.90	RI

Wings of Winter

1992	MOONLIGHT RETREAT, D. Rust, 150 days	29.50	RI
1992	TWILIGHT SERENADE, D. Rust, 150 days	29.50	RI
1992	SILENT SUNSET, D. Rust, 150 days	29.50	RI

Winter's Majesty

1992	THE QUEST, Charles Frace, 150 days	34.50	RI
1992	THE CHASE, Charles Frace, 150 days	34.50	RI
1993	ALASKAN FRIEND, Charles Frace, 150 days	34.50	RI
1993	AMERICAN COUGAR, Charles Frace, 150 days	34.50	RI
1993	ON WATCH, Charles Frace, 150 days	34.50	RI
1993	SOLITUDE, Charles Frace, 150 days	34.50	RI

Wonders of the Sea

1991	STAND BY ME, Ray Harm, 150 days	34.50	NR
1991	HEART TO HEART, Ray Harm, 150 days	34.50	NR
1991	WARM EMBRACE, Ray Harm, 150 days	34.50	NR

	Issue Price	Current Value
1991 A FAMILY AFFAIR, Ray Harm, 150 days	34.50	NR

World's Most Magnificent Cats

	Issue Price	Current Value
1991 FLEETING ENCOUNTER, Charles Frace, 150 days	24.50	35.00
1991 COUGAR, Charles Frace, 150 days	24.50	50.00
1991 ROYAL BENGAL, Charles Frace, 150 days	27.50	NR
1991 POWERFUL PRESENCE, Charles Frace, 150 days	27.50	45.00
1991 JAGUAR, Charles Frace, 150 days.	27.50	40.00
1991 THE CLOUDED LEOPARD, Charles Frace, 150 days	29.50	45.00
1991 THE AFRICAN LEOPARD, Charles Frace, 150 days.	29.50	40.00
1991 MIGHTY WARRIOR, Charles Frace, 150 days	29.50	50.00
1992 THE CHEETAH, Charles Frace, 150 days.	31.50	RI
1992 SIBERIAN TIGER, Charles Frace, 150 days	31.50	RI

GEORGE WASHINGTON MINT UNITED STATES

Indians

	Issue Price	Current Value
1972 CURLEY, Sawyer, gold, 100	2,000.00	2,250.00
1972 CURLEY, Sawyer, sterling silver, 7,300	150.00	BR
1973 TWO MOONS, Sawyer, gold, 100	2,000.00	2,250.00
1973 TWO MOONS, Sawyer, sterling silver, 7,300	150.00	BR

Mother's Day

	Issue Price	Current Value
1972 WHISTLER'S MOTHER, gold, 100	2,000.00	2,250.00
1972 WHISTLER'S MOTHER, sterling silver, 9,800	150.00	BR
1973 MOTHERHOOD, gold, 100	2,000.00	2,250.00
1973 MOTHERHOOD, sterling silver, 9,800	175.00	BR

N. C. Wyeth

	Issue Price	Current Value
1972 UNCLE SAM'S AMERICA, N. C. Wyeth, gold, 100	2,000.00	2,250.00
1972 UNCLE SAM'S AMERICA, N. C. Wyeth, sterling silver, 9,800 . .	150.00	BR
1973 MASSED FLAGS, N. C. Wyeth, gold, 100	2,000.00	2,250.00
1973 MASSED FLAGS, N. C. Wyeth, sterling silver, 2,300	150.00	BR

Picasso

	Issue Price	Current Value
1972 DON QUIXOTE, gold, 100	2,000.00	2,300.00
1972 DON QUIXOTE, sterling silver, 9,800	125.00	155.00
1974 RITES OF SPRING, sterling silver, 9,800	150.00	185.00

Remington Series

	Issue Price	Current Value
1972 RATTLESNAKE, Frederic Remington, 100	2,000.00	2,200.00
1972 RATTLESNAKE, Frederic Remington, 800	250.00	390.00
1974 COMING THROUGH THE RYE, Frederic Remington, 2,500	300.00	365.00

Single Issues	Issue Price	Current Value
1972 LAST SUPPER, L. Da Vinci	125.00	140.00
1973 ISRAEL ANNIVERSARY, 10,000	300.00	335.00

GEORGETOWN

Hearts in Song

1993 BUFFALO CHILD, C. Theroux, 35 days	29.95	RI

GHENT COLLECTION UNITED STATES
(See also Bing & Grondahl, Fairmont, Gorham and Villetta)

American Bicentennial Wildlife

1976 AMERICAN BALD EAGLE, Harry J. Moeller, 2,500	95.00	NR
1976 AMERICAN WHITE–TAILED DEER, Edward J. Bierly, 2,500	95.00	NR
1976 AMERICAN BISON, Charles Frace, 2,500	95.00	NR
1976 AMERICAN WILD TURKEY, Albert Earl Gilbert, 2,500	95.00	NR

April Fool Annual

1978 APRIL FOOL'S DAY, Norman Rockwell, 10,000	35.00	50.00
1979 APRIL FOOL'S DAY, Norman Rockwell, 10,000	35.00	NR
1980 APRIL FOOL'S DAY, Norman Rockwell, 10,000	37.50	NR

Caverswall Christmas Carol

1979 GOOD KING WENCESLAS, Holmes Gray, 2,500	300.00	NR
1980 THE FIRST NOEL, Holmes Gray, 2,500	300.00	NR

Christmas Wildlife

1974 CARDINALS IN SNOW, Albert Earl Gilbert, 10,030	20.00	55.00
1975 WE THREE KINGS, Harry J. Moeller, 12,750	29.00	40.00
1976 PARTRIDGES AND PEAR TREE, Guy Tudor, 12,750	32.00	50.00
1977 FOXES AND EVERGREEN, Edward J. Bierly, 12,750	32.00	50.00
1978 SNOWY OWLS, Jay H. Matterness, 12,750	32.00	NR

Country Diary of an Edwardian Lady

1979 APRIL, Edith Holden, 10,000	80.00	NR
1979 JUNE, Edith Holden, 10,000	80.00	NR
1980 JANUARY, Edith Holden, 10,000	80.00	NR
1980 MAY, Edith Holden, 10,000	80.00	NR
1980 SEPTEMBER, Edith Holden, 10,000	80.00	NR
1980 DECEMBER, Edith Holden, 10,000	80.00	NR
1981 JULY, Edith Holden, 10,000	80.00	NR
1981 OCTOBER, Edith Holden, 10,000	80.00	NR

	Issue Price	Current Value
Fausett Mural Plates		
1976 FROM SEA TO SHINING SEA, 1,970	76.00	230.00
Lands of Fable		
1981 XANADU, F. F. Long, 17,500	55.00	NR
1982 ATLANTIS, F. F. Long, 17,500	55.00	NR
Mother's Day		
1975 COTTONTAIL, Harry J. Moeller, 12,750	22.00	40.00
1976 MALLARD FAMILY, Guy Tudor, 12,750	29.00	40.00
1977 CHIPMUNKS AND TRILLIUM, Albert Earl Gilbert, 12,750 .	32.00	40.00
1978 RACCOON FAMILY, Edward J. Bierly, 12,750	32.00	NR
1979 MAYTIME ROBINS, Jay H. Matterness, 12,750	32.00	NR
Single Issues		
1979 PILGRIM OF PEACE, Alton S. Tobey, 15 days	29.50	NR
1980 1970s DECADE PLATE, Alton S. Tobey, 5,000	80.00	NR

GNOMES UNITED UNITED STATES

	Issue Price	Current Value
Gnome Patrol		
1979 NUMBER ONE, Edith McLennan Choma, 5,000	45.00	60.00
1980 GREAT GOO ROO YU–HOO, Edith McLennan Choma, 5,000 . .	48.00	NR
1981 FLEAFUT, Edith McLennan Choma, 5,000	50.00	NR
Single Issue		
1982 GNOME ON THE RANGE, Rex T. Reed, 10,000	23.00	NR

GOEBEL/SCHMID COLLECTION GERMANY

	Issue Price	Current Value
American Heritage		
1979 FREEDOM AND JUSTICE SOARING, Gunther Granget, 15,000	100.00	NR
1980 WILD AND FREE, Gunther Granget, 10,000	120.00	NR
1981 WHERE BUFFALO ROAM, Gunther Granget, 5,000	125.00	NR
Annual Crystal		
1978 PRAYING GIRL, 1 year	45.00	NR
1979 PRAYING BOY, 1 year	50.00	NR
1980 PRAYING ANGEL, 15,000	50.00	NR
1981 GIRL WITH TEDDY BEARS, 10,000	50.00	NR
Bavarian Forest		
1980 OWLS, 7,500	150.00	NR

		Issue Price	Current Value
1981	DEER, 7,500	150.00	NR

Brastoff Series

1979	STAR STEED, 15,000................................	125.00	140.00

Charlot Byi Series

1973	SANTA AT TREE, 1 year.............................	16.50	NR
1974	SANTA AND GIRL, 1 year	22.00	NR
1975	UP AND AWAY, 1 year	25.00	NR
1976	BOY WITH TEDDY BEAR, 1 year	25.00	NR
1977	JOY TO THE WORLD, 1 year	25.00	NR

Christmas in Kinderland

1982	A GIFT OF JOY, 10,000	49.50	60.00
1983	A MIDNIGHT CLEAR, 10,000	49.50	NR

MI Hummel Club Exclusive — Celebration
(Goebel Collectors Club)

1986	VALENTINE GIFT, Hum738, M. I. Hummel, limited.......	90.00	NR
1987	VALENTINE JOY, Hum737, M. I. Hummel, limited	98.00	BR
1988	DAISIES DON'T TELL, Hum736, M. I. Hummel, limited ..	115.00	BR
1989	IT'S COLD, Hum735, M. I. Hummel, limited	120.00	BR

MI Hummel Collectibles Anniversary Plates

1975	STORMY WEATHER, 280, M. I. Hummel, 1 year	100.00	BR
1980	SPRING DANCE, 281, M. I. Hummel, 1 year	225.00	BR
1985	AUF WIEDERSEHEN, 282, M. I. Hummel, 1 year........	225.00	250.00

MI Hummel Collectibles — Annual Plates

1971	HEAVENLY ANGEL, 264, M. I. Hummel, 1 year..........	25.00	600.00
1972	HEAR YE, HEAR YE, 265, M. I. Hummel, 1 year	30.00	50.00
1973	GLOBE TROTTER, 266, M. I. Hummel, 1 year	32.50	75.00
1974	GOOSE GIRL, 267, M. I. Hummel, 1 year..............	40.00	50.00
1975	RIDE INTO CHRISTMAS, 268, M. I. Hummel, 1 year	50.00	BR
1976	APPLE TREE GIRL, 269, M. I. Hummel, 1 year..........	50.00	BR
1977	APPLE TREE BOY, 270, M. I. Hummel, 1 year..........	52.50	80.00
1978	HAPPY PASTIME, 271, M. I. Hummel, 1 year	65.00	BR
1979	SINGING LESSON, 272, M. I. Hummel, 1 year	90.00	BR
1980	SCHOOL GIRL, 273, M. I. Hummel, 1 year	100.00	BR
1981	UMBRELLA BOY, 274, M. I. Hummel, 1 year............	100.00	BR
1982	UMBRELLA GIRL, 275, M. I. Hummel, 1 year...........	100.00	125.00
1983	THE POSTMAN, 276, M. I. Hummel, 1 year.............	108.00	195.00
1984	LITTLE HELPER, 277, M. I. Hummel, 1 year	108.00	BR
1985	CHICK GIRL, 278, M. I. Hummel, 1 year	110.00	BR

		Issue Price	Current Value
1986	PLAYMATES, 279, M. I. Hummel, 1 year	125.00	165.00
1987	FEEDING TIME, 280, M. I. Hummel, 1 year	125.00	400.00
1988	LITTLE GOAT HERDER, 284, M. I. Hummel, 1 year	145.00	BR
1989	FARM BOY, 285, M. I. Hummel, 1 year	160.00	BR
1990	SHEPHERD'S BOY, 286, M. I. Hummel, 1 year	170.00	250.00
1991	JUST RESTING, 287, M. I. Hummel, 1 year	196.00	BR
1992	WAYSIDE HARMONY, 288, M. I. Hummel, 1 year	210.00	RI
1993	DOLL BATH, 289, M. I. Hummel, 1 year	210.00	RI

The Postman
Photo courtesy of *Collectors News*

Chick Girl
Photo courtesy of *Collectors News*

MI Hummel — Friends Forever

1992	MEDITATION, 292, M. I. Hummel, open	180.00	RI
1993	FOR FATHER, 293, M. I. Hummel, open	195.00	RI

MI Hummel — The Little Homemakers

1988	LITTLE SWEEPER, Hum745, M. I. Hummel, closed......	45.00	60.00
1989	WASH DAY, Hum746, M. I. Hummel, closed	50.00	NR
1990	A STITCH IN TIME, Hum747, M. I. Hummel, closed	50.00	NR
1991	CHICKEN LICKEN, Hum748, M. I. Hummel, closed	70.00	NR

MI Hummel — Little Music Maker

1984	LITTLE FIDDLER, 744, M. I. Hummel, 1 year	30.00	50.00
1985	SERENADE, 741, M. I. Hummel, 1 year	30.00	NR
1986	SOLOIST, 743, M. I. Hummel, 1 year	35.00	NR
1987	BAND LEADER, 742, M. I. Hummel, 1 year	40.00	NR

		Issue Price	Current Value

Mothers

1975	RABBITS, 1 year	45.00	NR
1976	CATS, 1 year	45.00	NR
1977	PANDAS, 1 year	45.00	NR
1978	DEER, 1 year	50.00	NR
1979	OWL, 1 year, 10,000	65.00	NR
1980	RACCOONS, 10,000	75.00	NR

Native Companions

1982	RACHEL, Eddie LePage, 10,000	49.50	NR
1983	HUMMINGBIRD, Eddie LePage, 10,000	49.50	NR
1983	RABBIT DANCER, Eddie LePage, 10,000	49.50	NR

North American Wildlife

1980	BEAVER, Lissa Calvert, 10,000	126.00	NR
1982	HARP SEALS, Lissa Calvert, 10,000	126.00	NR
1983	POLAR BEAR, Lissa Calvert, 10,000	126.00	NR

Old Testament

1978	TWELVE TRIBES OF ISRAEL, 10,000	125.00	NR
1979	TEN COMMANDMENTS, 10,000	175.00	NR
1980	TRADITION, 10,000	225.00	NR

Robson Christmas

1975	FLIGHT TO EGYPT, pewter, 1 year	45.00	NR
1975	FLIGHT TO EGYPT, porcelain, 1 year	50.00	NR

Wildlife

1974	ROBIN, 1 year	45.00	65.00
1975	BLUE TITMOUSE, 1 year	50.00	NR

Cerises
Photo courtesy of *Collectors News*

		Issue Price	Current Value
1976	BARN OWL, 1 year . . . . , , , ...	50.00	NR
1977	BULLFINCH, 1 year	50.00	NR
1978	SEA GULL, 1 year	55.00	NR

Winged Fantasies

1982	STRAWBERRIES, Toller Cranston, 10,000	49.50	NR
1983	BACCHANALIA, Toller Cranston, 10,000	49.50	NR
1984	CERISES, Toller Cranston, 10,000	49.50	NR
1984	BRAMBLEBERRIES, Toller Cranston, 10,000	49.50	NR

Single Issues

1979	CHRISTMAS, 200	5,000.00	5,200.00
1982	THIS IS WHAT IT'S ALL ABOUT, Irene Spencer	49.50	NR

GORHAM COLLECTION UNITED STATES

American Artists

1976	APACHE MOTHER AND CHILD, R. Donnelly, 9,800	25.00	55.00

America's Cup

1975	COURAGEOUS, 5,000	50.00	NR

America's Cup Set

1975	AMERICA 1861, 1,000	200.00	NR
1975	PURITAN, 1,000	200.00	NR
1975	RELIANCE, 1,000	200.00	NR
1975	RANGER, 1,000	200.00	NR
1975	COURAGEOUS, 1,000	200.00	NR

April Fool Annual (Ghent Collection)

1978	APRIL FOOL'S DAY, Norman Rockwell, 10,000	35.00	50.00
1979	APRIL FOOL'S DAY, Norman Rockwell, 10,000	35.00	NR
1980	APRIL FOOL'S DAY, Norman Rockwell, 10,000	37.50	NR

Audubon American Wildlife Heritage (Volair)

1977	HOUSE MOUSE, 2,500	90.00	NR
1977	ROYAL LOUISIANA HERON, 2,500	90.00	NR
1977	VIRGINIA DEER, 2,500	90.00	NR
1977	SNOWY OWL, 2,500	90.00	NR

Barrymore

1971	QUIET WATERS, 15,000	25.00	NR

		Issue Price	Current Value
1972	SAN PEDRO HARBOR, 15,000	25.00	NR
1972	NANTUCKET, sterling, 1,000	100.00	NR
1972	LITTLE BOATYARD, sterling, 1,000	100.00	145.00

Bas Relief

1981	SWEET SONG SO YOUNG, Norman Rockwell, 17,500	100.00	NR
1981	BEGUILING BUTTERCUP, Norman Rockwell, 17,500	62.50	NR
1982	FLOWERS IN TENDER BLOOM, Norman Rockwell, 17,500	100.00	NR
1982	FLYING HIGH, Norman Rockwell, 17,500	62.50	NR

Bicentennial

1971	BURNING OF THE GASPEE, pewter, R. Pailthorpe, 5,000	35.00	NR
1972	BURNING OF THE GASPEE, silver, R. Pailthorpe, 750	500.00	NR
1972	THE 1776 PLATE, china, 18,500	17.50	35.00
1972	THE 1776 PLATE, silver, Gorham, 500	500.00	NR
1972	THE 1776 PLATE, vermeil, Gorham, 250	750.00	800.00
1972	BOSTON TEA PARTY, pewter, R. Pailthorpe, 5,000	35.00	NR
1973	BOSTON TEA PARTY, silver, R. Pailthorpe, 750	550.00	575.00
1976	1776 BICENTENNIAL, china, Gorham, 8,000	17.50	35.00

Boy Scout

1975	OUR HERITAGE, Norman Rockwell, 18,500	19.50	40.00
1976	A SCOUT IS LOYAL, Norman Rockwell, 18,500	19.50	30.00
1977	THE SCOUTMASTER, Norman Rockwell, 18,500	19.50	30.00
1977	A GOOD SIGN ALL OVER THE WORLD, Norman Rockwell, 18,500	19.50	25.00
1978	POINTING THE WAY, Norman Rockwell, 18,500	19.50	25.00
1978	CAMPFIRE STORY, Norman Rockwell, 18,500	19.50	25.00
1980	BEYOND THE EASEL, Norman Rockwell, 18,500	45.00	NR

Charles Russell

1980	IN WITHOUT KNOCKING, Charles Russell, 9,800	38.00	65.00
1981	BRONC TO BREAKFAST, Charles Russell, 9,800	38.00	65.00
1982	WHEN IGNORANCE IS BLISS, Charles Russell, 9,800	45.00	65.00
1983	COWBOY LIFE, Charles Russell, 9,800	45.00	75.00

Children's Television Workshop Christmas

1981	SESAME STREET CHRISTMAS, 1 year	17.50	NR
1982	SESAME STREET CHRISTMAS, 1 year	17.50	NR
1983	SESAME STREET CHRISTMAS, 1 year	19.50	NR

Christmas

1974	TINY TIM, Norman Rockwell, 1 year	12.50	35.00
1975	GOOD DEEDS, Norman Rockwell, 1 year	17.50	35.00
1976	CHRISTMAS TRIO, Norman Rockwell, 1 year	19.50	NR

		Issue Price	Current Value
1977	YULETIDE RECKONING, Norman Rockwell, 18,500	19.50	30.00
1978	PLANNING CHRISTMAS VISIT, Norman Rockwell, 1 year	24.50	NR
1979	SANTA'S HELPERS, Norman Rockwell, 1 year	24.50	NR
1980	LETTER TO SANTA, Norman Rockwell, 1 year	27.50	NR
1981	SANTA PLANS HIS VISIT, Norman Rockwell, 1 year	29.50	50.00
1982	THE JOLLY COACHMAN, Norman Rockwell, 1 year	29.50	NR
1983	CHRISTMAS DANCERS, Norman Rockwell, 1 year	29.50	NR
1984	CHRISTMAS MEDLEY, Norman Rockwell, 17,500	29.95	NR
1985	HOME FOR THE HOLIDAYS, Norman Rockwell, 17,500 . .	29.95	NR
1986	MERRY CHRISTMAS GRANDMA, Norman Rockwell, 17,500 .	29.50	65.00
1987	THE HOMECOMING, Norman Rockwell, 17,500	35.00	50.00
1988	DISCOVERY, Norman Rockwell, 17,500	37.50	NR

Clowns (Brown and Bigelow)

		Issue Price	Current Value
1977	THE RUNAWAY, Norman Rockwell, 7,500	45.00	65.00
1978	IT'S YOUR MOVE, Norman Rockwell, 7,500	45.00	55.00
1979	UNDERSTUDY, Norman Rockwell, 7,500	45.00	NR
1980	THE IDOL, Norman Rockwell, 7,500	45.00	NR

Cowboys (Brown and Bigelow)

		Issue Price	Current Value
1980	SHARING AN APPLE, 5,000	35.00	40.00
1980	SPLIT DECISION, 5,000	35.00	40.00
1980	HIDING OUT, 5,000	35.00	40.00

Encounters, Survival and Celebration

		Issue Price	Current Value
1982	A FINE WELCOME, John Clymer, 7,500	50.00	70.00
1983	WINTER TRAIL, John Clymer, 7,500	50.00	95.00
1983	ALOUETTE, John Clymer, 7,500	62.50	NR
1983	THE TRADER, John Clymer, 7,500	62.50	NR
1983	WINTER CAMP, John Clymer, 7,500	62.50	70.00
1983	THE TRAPPER TAKES A WIFE, John Clymer, 7,500	62.50	NR

Four Seasons — A Boy and His Dog

		Issue Price	Current Value
1971	BOY MEETS HIS DOG, Norman Rockwell, 1 year	—	—
1971	ADVENTURES BETWEEN ADVENTURES, Norman Rockwell, 1 year — . . . . —		
1971	THE MYSTERIOUS MALADY, Norman Rockwell, 1 year . .	—	—
1971	PRIDE OF PARENTHOOD, Norman Rockwell, 1 year	—	—
	Set of 4	50.00	200.00

Four Seasons — Ages of Love

		Issue Price	Current Value
1973	GAILY SHARING VINTAGE TIME, Norman Rockwell, 1 year	—	—
1973	FLOWERS IN TENDER BLOOM, Norman Rockwell, 1 year	—	—
1973	SWEET SONG SO YOUNG, Norman Rockwell, 1 year	—	—
1973	FONDLY WE DO REMEMBER, Norman Rockwell, 1 year .	—	—
	Set of 4	60.00	150.00

		Issue Price	Current Value

Four Seasons — Dad's Boy

1980	SKI SKILLS, Norman Rockwell, 1 year	—	—
1980	IN HIS SPIRITS, Norman Rockwell, 1 year	—	—
1980	TROUT DINNER, Norman Rockwell, 1 year	—	—
1980	CAREFUL AIM, Norman Rockwell, 1 year	—	—
	Set of 4	135.00	BR

Four Seasons — Going on Sixteen

1977	CHILLING CHORE, Norman Rockwell, 1 year	—	—
1977	SWEET SERENADE, Norman Rockwell, 1 year	—	—
1977	SHEAR AGONY, Norman Rockwell, 1 year	—	—
1977	PILGRIMAGE, Norman Rockwell, 1 year	—	—
	Set of 4	75.00	90.00

Four Seasons — Grand Pals

1976	SNOW SCULPTURING, Norman Rockwell, 1 year	—	—
1976	SOARING SPIRITS, Norman Rockwell, 1 year	—	—
1976	FISH FINDERS, Norman Rockwell, 1 year	—	—
1976	GHOSTLY GOURDS, Norman Rockwell, 1 year	—	—
	Set of 4	70.00	125.00

Four Seasons — Grandpa and Me

1974	GAY BLADES, Norman Rockwell, 1 year	—	—
1974	DAY DREAMERS, Norman Rockwell, 1 year	—	—
1974	GOIN' FISHING, Norman Rockwell, 1 year	—	—
1974	PENSIVE PALS, Norman Rockwell, 1 year	—	—
	Set of 4	60.00	90.00

Four Seasons — A Helping Hand

1979	YEAR END COURT, Norman Rockwell, 1 year	—	—
1979	CLOSED FOR BUSINESS, Norman Rockwell, 1 year	—	—
1979	SWATTER'S RIGHTS, Norman Rockwell, 1 year	—	—
1979	COAL SEASON'S COMING, Norman Rockwell, 1 year	—	—
	Set of 4	100.00	NR

Four Seasons — Landscape

1980	SUMMER RESPITE, Norman Rockwell, 1 year	45.00	55.00
1981	AUTUMN REFLECTIONS, Norman Rockwell, 1 year	45.00	55.00
1982	WINTER DELIGHT, Norman Rockwell, 1 year	50.00	NR
1983	SPRING RECESS, Norman Rockwell, 1 year	60.00	NR

Four Seasons — Life with Father

1982	BIG DECISION, Norman Rockwell, 1 year	—	—
1982	BLASTING OUT, Norman Rockwell, 1 year	—	—
1982	CHEERING THE CHAMPS, Norman Rockwell, 1 year	—	—

		Issue Price	Current Value
1982	A TOUGH ONE, Norman Rockwell, 1 year	—	—
	Set of 4 .. ., ...	100.00	150.00

Four Seasons — Me and My Pals

1975	A LICKIN' GOOD BATH, Norman Rockwell, 1 year	—	—
1975	YOUNG MAN'S FANCY, Norman Rockwell, 1 year	—	—
1975	FISHERMAN'S PARADISE, Norman Rockwell, 1 year	—	—
1975	DISASTROUS DARING, Norman Rockwell, 1 year	—	—
	Set of 4...	70.00	100.00

Four Seasons — Old Buddies

1983	SHARED SUCCESS, Norman Rockwell, 1 year	—	—
1983	ENDLESS DEBATE, Norman Rockwell, 1 year	—	—
1983	HASTY RETREAT, Norman Rockwell, 1 year	—	—
1983	FINAL SPEECH, Norman Rockwell, 1 year	—	—
	Set of 4...	115.00	NR

Four Seasons — Old Timers

1981	CANINE SOLO, Norman Rockwell, 1 year	—	—
1981	SWEET SURPRISE, Norman Rockwell, 1 year	—	—
1981	LAZY DAYS, Norman Rockwell, 1 year	—	—
1981	FANCY FOOTWORK, Norman Rockwell, 1 year	—	—
	Series of 4	100.00	NR

Four Seasons – Tender Years

1978	NEW YEAR LOOK, Norman Rockwell, 1 year	—	—
1978	SPRING TONIC, Norman Rockwell, 1 year..............	—	—
1978	COOL AID, Norman Rockwell, 1 year	—	—
1978	CHILLY RECEPTION, Norman Rockwell, 1 year	—	—
	Set of 4...	100.00	NR

Four Seasons – Traveling Salesman

1984	TRAVELING SALESMAN, Norman Rockwell, 1 year......	—	—
1984	COUNTRY PEDDLER, Norman Rockwell, 1 year..........	—	—
1984	EXPERT SALESMAN, Norman Rockwell, 1 year	—	—
1984	HORSE TRADER, Norman Rockwell, 1 year	—	—
	Set of 4...	115.00	NR

Four Seasons – Young Love

1972	DOWNHILL DARING, Norman Rockwell, 1 year	—	—
1972	BEGUILING BUTTERCUP, Norman Rockwell, 1 year	—	—
1972	FLYING HIGH, Norman Rockwell, 1 year	—	—
1972	A SCHOLARLY PACE, Norman Rockwell, 1 year.........	—	—
	Set of 4...	60.00	125.00

	Issue Price	Current Value

Gallery of Masters

1971	MAN WITH A GILT HELMET, Rembrandt, 10,000	50.00	NR
1972	SELF–PORTRAIT WITH SASKIA, Rembrandt, 10,000	50.00	NR
1973	THE HONORABLE MRS. GRAHAM, Gainsborough, 7,500	50.00	NR

Grandpa and Me (Brown and Bigelow)

1977	GAY BLADES, 1 year	55.00	NR

Irene Spencer

1975	DEAR CHILD, Irene Spencer, 10,000	37.50	110.00
1976	PROMISES TO KEEP, Irene Spencer, 10,000	40.00	55.00

Julian Ritter

1977	CHRISTMAS VISIT, Julian Ritter, 9,800	24.50	30.00
1978	VALENTINE FLUTTERING HEART, Julian Ritter 7,500	45.00	NR

Julian Ritter – Fall in Love

1977	ENCHANTMENT, Julian Ritter, 5,000	—	—
1977	FROLIC, Julian Ritter, 5,000	—	—
1977	GUTSY GAL, Julian Ritter, 5,000	—	—
1977	LONELY CHILL, Julian Ritter, 5,000	—	—
	Set of 4	100.00	NR

Julian Ritter – To Love a Clown

1978	AWAITED REUNION, Julian Ritter, 5,000	120.00	NR
1978	TWOSOME TIME, Julian Ritter, 5,000	120.00	NR
1978	SHOWTIME BECKONS, Julian Ritter, 5,000	120.00	NR
1978	TOGETHER IN MEMORIES, Julian Ritter, 5,000	120.00	NR

Leaders of Tomorrow (Kern Collectibles)

1980	FUTURE PHYSICIAN, Leo Jansen, 9,800	50.00	65.00
1981	FUTURE FARMER, Leo Jansen, 9,800	50.00	NR
1982	FUTURE FLORIST, Leo Jansen, 9,800	50.00	NR
1983	FUTURE TEACHER, Leo Jansen, 9,800	50.00	NR

Lewis and Clark Expedition (The Hamilton Collection)

1981	IN THE BITTERROOTS, John Clymer, 10 days	55.00	75.00
1981	SACAJAWEA AT THE BIG WATER, John Clymer, 10 days	55.00	65.00
1981	THE LEWIS CROSSING, John Clymer, 10 days	55.00	NR
1981	CAPTAIN CLARK AND THE BUFFALO GANG, John Clymer, 10 days	55.00	NR
1982	THE SALT MAKER, John Clymer, 10 days	55.00	NR
1982	UP THE JEFFERSON, John Clymer, 10 days	55.00	NR
1982	ARRIVAL OF SERGEANT PRYOR, John Clymer, 10 days	55.00	NR
1982	VISITORS AT FORT CLATSOP, John Clymer, 10 days	55.00	NR

	Issue Price	Current Value

Leyendecker Annual Christmas

1988	CHRISTMAS HUG, J. C. Leyendecker, 10,000	37.50	NR

Little Men

1977	COME RIDE WITH ME, Lorraine Trester, 1 year	50.00	NR

Moppets Anniversary

1976	MOPPET COUPLE, 20,000	13.00	NR

Moppets Christmas

1973	CHRISTMAS MARCH, 20,000	10.00	35.00
1974	DECORATING THE TREE, 20,00.....................	12.00	NR
1975	BRINGING HOME THE TREE, 20,000	13.00	NR
1976	CHRISTMAS TREE, 10,000..........................	13.00	NR
1977	PLACING THE STAR, 18,500	13.00	NR
1978	THE PRESENTS, 18,500	10.00	NR
1979	MOPPETS, 18,500	12.00	NR
1980	MOPPETS CHRISTMAS, 1 year	12.00	NR
1981	MOPPETS CHRISTMAS, 1 year	12.00	NR
1982	MOPPETS CHRISTMAS, 1 year	12.00	NR
1983	MOPPETS CHRISTMAS, 1 year	12.00	NR

Moppets Mother's Day

1973	MOTHER'S DAY, 20,000	10.00	30.00
1974	MOTHER'S DAY, 20,000	12.00	20.00
1975	MOTHER'S DAY, 20,000	13.00	NR
1976	MOTHER'S DAY, 20,000	13.00	NR
1977	MOTHER'S DAY, 18,500	13.00	NR
1978	MOTHER'S DAY, 18,500	10.00	NR

Mother's Day (Brown and Bigelow)

1980	FAMILY CIRCUS, 5,000............................	25.00	NR

Museum Doll

1983	LYDIA, Gorham, 5,000.............................	29.00	125.00
1984	BELTON BEBE, Gorham, 5,000	29.00	55.00
1984	CHRISTMAS LADY, Gorham, 7,500	32.50	NR
1985	LUCILLE, Gorham, 5,000	29.00	NR
1985	JUMEAU, Gorham, 5,000	29.00	NR

Omnibus Muralis

1976	200 YEARS WITH OLD GLORY, 15,000	60.00	NR
1977	LIFE OF CHRIST, 15,000	60.00	NR

		Issue Price	Current Value

Pastoral Symphony

1982	WHEN I WAS A CHILD, Bettie Felder, 7,500	42.50	50.00
1983	GATHER THE CHILDREN, Bettie Felder, 7,500	42.50	50.00
1984	SUGAR AND SPICE, Bettie Felder, 7,500	42.50	50.00
1985	HE LOVES ME, Bettie Felder, 7,500	42.50	50.00

Presidential Series

| 1976 | KENNEDY, Norman Rockwell, 9,800 | 30.00 | 55.00 |
| 1976 | EISENHOWER, Norman Rockwell, 9,800 | 30.00 | 35.00 |

Remington Western

1973	NEW YEAR ON THE CIMARRON, Frederic Remington, 1 year	25.00	45.00
1973	AIDING A COMRADE, Frederic Remington, 1 year	25.00	75.00
1973	THE FLIGHT, Frederic Remington, 1 year	25.00	60.00
1973	FIGHT FOR THE WATER HOLE, Frederic Remington, 1 year	25.00	75.00
1975	OLD RAMOND, Frederic Remington, 1 year	30.00	50.00
1975	A BREED, Frederic Remington, 1 year	30.00	50.00
1976	CAVALRY OFFICER, Frederic Remington, 5,000	37.50	55.00
1976	A TRAPPER, Frederic Remington, 5,000	37.00	55.00

Time Machine Teddies

1986	MISS EMILY, BEARING UP, Beverly Port, 5,000	32.50	NR
1987	BIG BEAR, THE TOY COLLECTOR, Beverly Port, 5,000	32.50	NR
1988	HUNNY MUNNY, Beverly Port, 5,000	37.50	NR

Traveling Salesman (Brown and Bigelow)

1977	TRAVELING SALESMAN, 7,500	35.00	NR
1978	COUNTRY PEDDLAR, 7,500	40.00	NR
1979	HORSE TRADER, 7,500	40.00	NR

Wilderness Wings (Brown and Bigelow)

1978	GLIDING IN, 5,000	35.00	NR
1979	TAKING OFF, 5,000	40.00	NR
1980	JOINING UP, 5,000	45.00	NR
1981	CANVASBACKS, 5,000	47.50	NR
1982	MOMENT OF REST, David Maass, 5,000	30.00	NR
1983	MOURNING DOVES, David Maass, 5,000	30.00	NR

Single Issues

1970	AMERICAN FAMILY TREE, Norman Rockwell, 5,000	17.00	100.00
1974	BIG THREE, Norman Rockwell, 10,000	17.50	NR
1974	THE GOLDEN RULE, Norman Rockwell, 1 year	12.50	30.00
1974	WEIGHING IN, Norman Rockwell, 10,000	12.50	70.00
1975	BENJAMIN FRANKLIN, Norman Rockwell, 18,500	19.50	35.00
1976	THE MARRIAGE LICENSE, Norman Rockwell, 1 year	37.50	55.00
1976	BLACK REGIMENT 1778, F. Quagon, 7,500	25.00	60.00

		Issue Price	Current Value
1976	WAGON TRAIN, <1 year ....,,..	19.50	NR
1976	MEMORIAL PLATE, Norman Rockwell, 1 year	37.50	NR
1978	TRIPLE SELF–PORTRAIT, Norman Rockwell, 1 year	37.50	70.00
1980	THE ANNUAL VISIT, Norman Rockwell, 1 year	32.50	NR
1981	A DAY IN THE LIFE OF A BOY, Norman Rockwell, 1 year .	50.00	80.00
1981	A DAY IN THE LIFE OF A GIRL, Norman Rockwell, 1 year	50.00	90.00

GRANDE COPENHAGEN DENMARK

Christmas

1975	ALONE TOGETHER, 1 year	24.50	NR
1976	CHRISTMAS WREATH, 1 year	24.50	NR
1977	FISHWIVES AT GAMMELSTRAND, 1 year	26.50	NR
1978	HANS CHRISTIAN ANDERSEN, 1 year	32.50	NR
1979	PHEASANTS, 1 year................................	34.50	NR
1980	SNOW QUEEN IN THE TIVOLI, Frode Bahnsen, <1 year ..	39.50	NR
1981	LITTLE MATCH GIRL IN NYHAVN, Frode Bahnsen, 1 year	42.50	NR
1982	SHEPHERDESS/CHIMNEY SWEEP, Frode Bahnsen, 1 year	45.00	NR
1983	LITTLE MERMAID NEAR KRONBORG, Frode Bahnsen, 1 year 120.00		45.00
1984	SANDMAN AT AMALIENBORG, Frode Bahnsen, 1 year ...	45.00	60.0

Ugly Duckling

1985	NOT LIKE THE OTHERS.............................	29.00	BR
1985	HE WILL GROW UP STRONG	29.00	NR
1986	COME WITH US	32.00	NR
1986	YOU DON'T UNDERSTAND ME	32.00	NR
1986	WHAT BEAUTIFUL BIRDS...........................	32.00	NR
1986	MOST BEAUTIFUL OF ALL	32.00	45.00

Not Like the Others
Photo courtesy of *Collectors News*

		Issue Price	Current Value

Single Issue

| 1976 | BICENTENNIAL – GREAT SEAL, 1 year | 35.00 | NR |

GRANDE DANICA DENMARK

Mother's Day

1977	DOG WITH PUPPIES, 10,000	25.00	NR
1978	STORKS, 10,000	25.00	NR
1979	BADGERS, 10,000	25.00	NR

Mother's Day — Kate Greenaway

1971	KATE GREENAWAY	14.95	NR
1972	KATE GREENAWAY	14.95	NR
1973	KATE GREENAWAY	16.95	NR
1974	KATE GREENAWAY	16.95	NR

GREENTREE POTTERIES UNITED STATES

American Landmarks

| 1970 | MT. RUSHMORE, 2,000 | 10.00 | NR |
| 1971 | NIAGARA FALLS, 2,000 | 10.00 | NR |

Grant Wood

1971	STUDIO, 2,000	10.00	NR
1972	ANTIOCH SCHOOL, 2,000	10.00	NR
1973	AT STONE CITY, 2,000	10.00	NR
1974	ADOLESCENCE, 2,000	10.00	NR
1975	BIRTHPLACE, 2,000	10.00	NR
1976	AMERICAN GOTHIC, 2,000	10.00	NR

Kennedy

| 1972 | CENTER FOR PERFORMING ARTS, 2,000 | 20.00 | NR |
| 1973 | BIRTHPLACE, BROOKLINE, MASS., 2,000 | 12.00 | NR |

Mississippi River

| 1973 | DELTA QUEEN, 2,000 | 20.00 | NR |
| 1973 | TRI–CENTENNIAL, 2,000 | 20.00 | NR |

Motorcar

| 1972 | 1929 PACKARD DIETRICH CONVERTIBLE, 2,000 | 20.00 | NR |
| 1973 | MODEL "A" FORD, 2,000 | 20.00 | NR |

GROLIER UNITED STATES

		Issue Price	Current Value

Snow White and the Seven Dwarfs

1984	AT THE WISHING WELL, Disney Studios, 15,000	24.95	NR

Three Little Pigs 50th Anniversary

1984	FIFER PIG, Disney Studios, 15,000	14.95	NR

DAVE GROSSMAN CREATIONS UNITED STATES

Boy Scout Annual

1981	CAN'T WAIT, BSP–01, Rockwell–inspired, 10,000	30.00	40.00
1982	A GUIDING HAND, BSP–02, Rockwell–inspired, 10,000 ..	30.00	35.00
1983	TOMORROW'S LEADER, BSP–03, Rockwell–inspired, 10,000..	30.00	40.00

Children of the Week

1978	MONDAY'S CHILD, Barbard, 5,000	30.00	NR
1979	TUESDAY'S CHILD, Barbard, 5,000	30.00	NR
1979	WEDNESDAY'S CHILD, Barbard, 5,000	30.00	NR
1980	THURSDAY'S CHILD, Barbard, 5,000	30.00	NR
1980	FRIDAY'S CHILD, Barbard, 5,000	30.00	40.00
1981	SATURDAY'S CHILD, Barbard, 5,000	30.00	45.00
1981	SUNDAY'S CHILD, Barbard, 5,000	30.00	50.00

Christmas

1978	PEACE, Barbard, 5,000	55.00	BR
1979	SANTA, Barbard, 5,000	55.00	BR

Emmett Kelly Christmas

1986	CHRISTMAS CAROL, Barry Leighton–Jones, 1 year	20.00	NR
1987	CHRISTMAS WREATH, Barry Leighton–Jones, 1 year ...	20.00	NR
1988	CHRISTMAS DINNER, Barry Leighton–Jones, 1 year	20.00	NR
1989	CHRISTMAS FEAST, Barry Leighton–Jones, 1 year	22.00	NR
1990	JUST WHAT I NEEDED, Barry Leighton–Jones, 1 year ...	24.00	NR
1991	EMMETT THE SNOWMAN, Barry Leighton–Jones, 1 year	25.00	NR
1992	CHRISTMAS TUNES, Barry Leighton–Jones, 1 year	25.00	RI
1993	DOWNHILL–CHRISTMAS PLATE, Barry Leighton–Jones, 2 years	30.00	RI
1994	HOLIDAY SKATER, 2 years	30.00	RI
1995	MERRY CHRISTMAS MR. SCROOGE, 2 years	30.00	RI

Magic People

1982	MUSIC FOR A QUEEN, Lynn Lupetti, 10,000	65.00	NR
1983	FANTASY FESTIVAL, Lynn Lupetti, 10,000..............	65.00	NR
1983	BUBBLE CHARIOT, Lynn Lupetti, 10,000	65.00	NR

Fantasy Festival
Photo courtesy of *Collectors News*

	Issue Price	Current Value

Margaret Keane

			Issue Price	Current Value
1976	BALLOON GIRL, Margaret Keane, 1 year		25.00	40.00
1977	MY KITTY, Margaret Keane, 1 year		25.00	NR
1978	BEDTIME, Margaret Keane, 1 year		25.00	NR

Miniature Bas–Relief

1981	NO SWIMMING, RMP–81, Rockwell–inspired		25.00	40.00

Native American

1991	LONE WOLF, E. Roberts, 10,000		45.00	NR
1992	TORTOISE LADY, E. Roberts, 10,000		45.00	RI

Norman Rockwell Collection

1978	YOUNG DOCTOR, RDP–26, Rockwell–inspired, 5,000		50.00	60.00
1979	BUTTERBOY, RP–01, Rockwell–inspired, 1 year		40.00	NR
1979	LEAP FROG, NRP–79, Rockwell–inspired, 1 year		50.00	75.00
1980	BACK TO SCHOOL, RMP–80, Rockwell–inspired, 1 year		24.00	30.00
1980	LOVERS, NRP–80, Rockwell–inspired, 1 year		60.00	70.00
1980	CHRISTMAS TRIO, RXP–80, Rockwell–inspired, 1 year		75.00	90.00
1981	DREAMS OF LONG AGO, NRP–81, Rockwell–inspired, 1 year		60.00	75.00
1981	SANTA'S GOOD BOYS, RXP–81, Rockwell–inspired, 1 year		75.00	90.00
1982	LOVE LETTER, RMP–82, Rockwell–inspired, 1 year		27.00	40.00
1982	THE AMERICAN MOTHER, RGP–42, Rockwell–inspired, 17,500		45.00	NR
1982	DOCTOR AND THE DOLL, NRP–82, Rockwell–inspired, 1 year		65.00	75.00
1982	FACES OF CHRISTMAS, RXP–82, Rockwell–inspired, 1 year		75.00	90.00
1983	DREAMBOAT, RGP–83, Rockwell–inspired, 1 year		24.00	30.00
1983	DOCTOR AND THE DOLL, RMP–83, Rockwell–inspired, 1 year		27.00	NR
1983	CIRCUS, NRP–83, Rockwell–inspired, 9,500		65.00	NR
1983	CHRISTMAS CHORES, RXP–83, Rockwell–inspired, 9,500		75.00	85.00

		Issue Price	Current Value
1984	BIG MOMENT, RMP 04, Rockwell–inspired, 1 year......	27.00	NR
1984	VISIT WITH NORMAN ROCKWELL, NRP–84, Rockwell–inspired, 9,500	65.00	75.00
1984	TINY TIM, RXP–84, Rockwell–inspired, 9,500	75.00	85.00

Big Moment
Photo courtesy of *Collectors News*

Visit with Norman Rockwell
Photo courtesy of *Collectors News*

Norman Rockwell — Huckleberry Finn

1979	THE SECRET, HFP–01, Rockwell–inspired, 10,000	40.00	NR
1980	LISTENING, HFP–02, Rockwell–inspired, 10,000........	40.00	NR
1980	NO KINGS NOR DUKES, HFP–03, Rockwell–inspired, 10,000 .	40.00	NR
1980	THE SNAKE ESCAPES, HFP–04, Rockwell–inspired, 10,000 ..	40.00	NR

Norman Rockwell — Tom Sawyer

1975	WHITEWASHING FENCE, TSP–01, Rockwell–inspired, 1 year	60.00	BR
1976	FIRST SMOKE, TSP–02, Rockwell–inspired, 1 year......	60.00	BR
1977	TAKE YOUR MEDICINE, TSP–03, Rockwell–inspired, 1 year	63.00	BR
1978	LOST IN CAVE, TSP–04, Rockwell–inspired, 1 year......	70.00	BR

Saturday Evening Post

1991	DOWNHILL DARING, BRP–91, Rockwell–inspired, 1 year	25.00	NR
1991	MISSED, BRP–101, Rockwell–inspired, 1 year...........	25.00	NR
1992	CHOOSIN' UP, BUP–102, Rockwell–inspired, 1 year	25.00	RI

Single Issue

1990	EMMETT KELLY COMMEMORATIVE...................	25.00	NR

HACKETT AMERICAN UNITED STATES

(See also Fairmont)

		Issue Price	Current Value

Classical American Beauties

		Issue Price	Current Value
1978	COLLEEN, Michael Vincent, 7,500	60.00	NR
1979	HEATHER, Michael Vincent, 7,500	60.00	NR
1980	DAWN, Michael Vincent, 7,500	60.00	NR
1982	EVE, Michael Vincent, 7,500	60.00	NR

Corita Kent Annual

1983	BELINDA, Chuck Oberstein, 7,500	39.50	NR

Crazy Cats

1982	DAISY KITTEN, Sadako Mano, 7,500	42.50	NR
1982	DAISY CAT, Sadako Mano, 7,500	42.50	NR

Days Remembered

1982	FIRST BIRTHDAY, David Smith, 19,500	29.50	NR
1983	FIRST HAIRCUT, David Smith, 19,500	35.00	NR

Early Discoveries

1982	LET'S PLAY, Rudy Escalera, 7,500	42.50	NR

Endangered Species

1980	CALIFORNIA SEA OTTERS, Sadako Mano, 7,500	35.00	75.00
1981	ASIAN PANDAS, Sadako Mano, 7,500	37.50	65.00
1982	AUSTRALIAN KOALAS, Sadako Mano, 7,500	37.50	NR
1982	RIVER OTTERS, Sadako Mano, 7,500	39.50	NR

Escalera's Father's Day

1982	DADDY'S ROSE, Rudy Escalera, 7,500	42.50	NR
1983	DADDY'S WISH, Rudy Escalera, 7,500	42.50	NR

Everyone's Friends

1982	SPRINGTIME, Sadako Mano, 7,500	42.50	NR
1982	AUTUMN BANDIT, Sadako Mano, 7,500	42.50	NR
1983	SNOW BUNNIES, Sadako Mano, 10,000	42.50	NR
1984	SUMMER'S BANDIT, Sadako Mano, 10,000	42.50	NR

Famous Planes of Yesterday

1983	SPIRIT OF ST. LOUIS, Robert Banks, 5,000	39.50	NR
1984	BYRD ANTARCTIC, Robert Banks, 5,000	39.50	NR
1984	WINNIE MAE, Robert Banks, 5,000	39.50	NR

Fashions by Irene

		Issue Price	Current Value
1900	ELEGANT LADY, Virginia Fisher, 15,000	45.00	NR

Favorite Dreams

| 1983 | DADDY'S SAILOR, Christopher Paluso, 7,500 .... | 39.50 | NR |
| 1984 | DADDY'S ENGINEER, Christopher Paluso, 7,500 .... | 39.50 | NR |

Friends of the Forest

1981	FOREST ALERT, David Smith, 7,500	50.00	NR
1982	BROOKSIDE PROTECTION, David Smith, 7,500	50.00	NR
1982	MOUNTAIN GUARDIAN, David Smith, 7,500	50.00	NR
1983	FRIENDS OF THE FOREST, David Smith, 7,500	50.00	NR

Summer's Bandit
Photo courtesy of *Collectors News*

Spirit of St. Louis
Photo courtesy of *Collectors News*

Byrd Antarctic
Photo courtesy of *Collectors News*

		Issue Price	Current Value

Golfing Great

1984	GARY PLAYER GRAND SLAM EDITION, Cassidy J. Alexander, 3,000	125.00	NR
1984	GARY PLAYER CHAMPION EDITION, Cassidy J. Alexander, <1 year	45.00	NR

Grandparents

1984	GRANDPA'S DELIGHT, Greensmith, 10,000	27.50	NR

Horses in Action

1981	THE CHALLENGE, Violet Parkhurst, 7,500	50.00	NR
1982	COUNTRY DAYS, Violet Parkhurst, 7,500	50.00	NR
1982	FAMILY PORTRAIT, Violet Parkhurst, 7,500	50.00	NR
1983	ALL GROWN UP, Violet Parkhurst, 7,500	50.00	NR

Huggable Moments

1983	NAPTIME, Irish McCalla, 10,000	39.50	NR
1983	PLAYTIME, Irish McCalla, 10,000	39.50	NR

Impressions

1982	WINDY DAY, Jo Anne Mix, 7,500	42.50	NR
1982	SUNNY DAY, Jo Anne Mix, 7,500	42.50	NR
1983	SUMMER'S DAY, Jo Anne Mix, 7,500	42.50	NR

Kelly's Stable

1982	MY CHAMPION, C. Kelly, 15,000	42.50	NR
1983	GLORY BOUND, C. Kelly, 15,000	42.50	NR
1983	ARABIAN SPRING, C. Kelly, 15,000	42.50	NR

Landfalls

1982	SAN FRANCISCO BAY, Bob Russell, 7,500	39.50	NR
1983	NEWPORT HARBOR, Bob Russell, 7,500	39.50	NR

Little Friends

1984	TINY CREATURES, David Smith, 5,000	35.00	NR
1984	FOREST FRIENDS, David Smith, 5,000	35.00	NR

Little Orphans

1982	SURPRISE PACKAGE, Ozz Franca, 19,500	29.50	NR
1983	CASTAWAY, Ozz Franca, 19,500	32.50	NR
1984	FURRY SURPRISE, Ozz Franca, 19,500	35.00	NR

Memorable Impressions

1983	BEACHCOMBER, Ivan Anderson, 7,500	39.50	NR

		Issue Price	Current Value
1983	BEACH GIRL, Ivan Anderson, 7,500	39.50	NR

Beachcomber
Photo courtesy of *Collectors News*

Milestone Automobiles

1983	'57 CHEVY, Carl Pape, 5,000	39.50	NR
1984	'57 THUNDERBIRD, Carl Pape, 5,000	39.50	NR
1984	'53 CORVETTE, Carl Pape, 5,000	39.50	NR

Mix Annual Christmas

1982	CHRISTMAS LOVE, Jo Anne Mix, 7,500	39.50	NR

Mother and Child

1981	MOTHER'S LOVE, Ozz Franca, 7,500	42.50	NR
1982	TENDERNESS, Ozz Franca, 7,500	42.50	NR
1983	SERENITY, Ozz Franca, 7,500	42.50	NR
1984	NAVAJO MADONNA, Ozz Franca, 7,500	42.50	NR

Ocean Moods

1981	SUNSET TIDES, Violet Parkhurst, 5,000	50.00	NR
1981	MOONLIGHT FLIGHT, Violet Parkhurst, 5,000	50.00	NR
1982	MORNING SURF, Violet Parkhurst, 5,000	50.00	NR
1982	AFTERNOON SURF, Violet Parkhurst, 5,000	50.00	NR

Ocean Stars

1982	SEA HORSE, Carl Pope, 7,500	42.50	NR
1982	DOLPHINS, Carl Pope, 7,500	42.50	NR
1983	WHALES, Carl Pope, 10,000	42.50	NR

		Issue Price	Current Value

Parkhurst Annual Christmas

1981	CHRISTMAS TEAR, Violet Parkhurst, 7,500	39.50	NR
1982	CHRISTMAS MORNING, Violet Parkhurst, 7,500	39.50	NR
1983	NIGHT BEFORE CHRISTMAS, Violet Parkhurst, 7,500 ...	39.50	NR

Parkhurst Annual Mother's Day

| 1981 | DAISIES FOR MOTHER, Violet Parkhurst, 7,500 .... | 39.50 | NR |

Parkhurst Diamond Collection

| 1982 | CHANCE ENCOUNTER, Violet Parkhurst, 1,500 .... | 300.00 | NR |

Peaceful Retreat

1982	REFUGE, Joan Horton, 19,500	29.50	NR
1983	SOLITUDE, Joan Horton, 19,500	29.50	NR
1983	TRANQUILITY, Joan Horton, 19,500	35.00	NR
1984	SECLUSION, Joan Horton, 19,500	35.00	NR

Tranquility
Photo courtesy of *Collectors News*

Seclusion
Photo courtesy of *Collectors News*

Playful Memories

1981	RENEE, Sue Etem, 10,000	39.50	BR
1982	JEREMY, Sue Etem, 10,000	42.50	BR
1983	JAMIE, Sue Etem, 10,000	42.50	BR
1983	RANDY, Sue Etem, 10,000	45.00	BR

Prairie Children

| 1982 | YOUNG PIONEER, Louise Sigle, 19,500 .... | 32.50 | NR |
| 1983 | ADAM, Louise Sigle, 19,500 .... | 35.00 | NR |

		Issue Price	Current Value
Puzzling Moments			
1983	THE PROBLEM SOLVER, William Selden, 7,500.........	39.50	NR
1983	PRACTICE MAKES PERFECT, Louise Sigle, 19,500	39.50	NR
Reflections of the Sea			
1983	GOLDEN SHORES, Violet Parkhurst, 5,000	42.50	NR
1984	SUMMER SANDS, Violet Parkhurst, 5,000	39.50	NR
1984	BIG SUR, Violet Parkhurst, 5,000	39.50	NR
Sadako's Helpers			
1983	ARTIST'S PAL, Sadako Mano, 7,500...................	39.50	NR
1983	ARTIST'S HELPER, Sadako Mano, 7,500...............	39.50	NR
Sadako Mano's Christmas			
1983	SANTA'S SPECIAL GIFT, Sadako Mano, 5,000	39.50	NR
1984	A GIFT FROM SANTA, Sadako Mano, 5,000	39.50	NR
Save the Whales			
1980	TRUST AND LOVE, 10,000	30.00	NR
Sensitive Moments			
1983	SHARING THE BEAUTY, Rudy Escalera, 5,000	39.50	NR
Side by Side			
1982	MY HERO, Jo Anne Mix, 19,500	32.50	45.00
1983	SIPPIN' SODA, Jo Anne Mix, 19,500	35.00	NR
Snow Babies			
1981	CANADIAN HARP SEALS, Violet Parkhurst, 5,000	39.50	65.00
1981	POLAR BEAR CUBS, Violet Parkhurst, 5,000	39.50	NR
1982	SNOW LEOPARDS, Violet Parkhurst, 5,000	42.50	NR
1982	ARCTIC FOXES, Violet Parkhurst, 5,000...............	42.50	NR
Special Moments			
1982	APRIL, Rudy Escalera, 7,500	42.50	NR
1983	RACHAEL, Rudy Escalera, 7,500	42.50	NR
Summer Fun			
1983	FISHING TOGETHER, Gina Conche, 7,500	39.50	NR
1984	SWINGING TOGETHER, Gina Conche, 7,500............	39.50	NR
Sunbonnet Babies			
1984	SUNDAY – SATURDAY, Charlotte Gutshall, limited, set of 7 .	136.50	NR

		Issue Price	Current Value

Sunday Best

| 1981 | STACEY, Jo Anne Mix, 7,500 | 42.50 | NR |
| 1982 | LAURIE, Jo Anne Mix, 7,500 | 42.50 | NR |

Owl and the Pussycat

| 1983 | THE OWL, Lenore Béran, 5,000 | 40.00 | NR |
| 1983 | THE PUSSYCAT, Lenore Béran, 5,000 | 40.00 | NR |

True Love

1982	HOG HEAVEN, Sadako Mano, 15,000	42.50	NR
1983	FROG HEAVEN, Sadako Mano, 15,000	39.50	NR
1983	OTTER HEAVEN, Sadako Mano, 15,000	39.50	NR
1984	OWL HEAVEN, Sadako Mano, 15,000	39.50	NR

Waterbird Families

1981	MARSH VENTURE, Dave Chapple, 7,500	42.50	NR
1982	AFTERNOON SWIM, Dave Chapple, 7,500	42.50	NR
1983	NESTING WOOD DUCKS, Dave Chapple, 10,000	42.50	NR
1983	RETURNING HOME, Dave Chapple, 10,000	42.50	NR

Wonderful World of Clowns

1981	KISS FOR A CLOWN, Chuck Oberstein, 5,000	39.50	NR
1981	RAINBOW'S END, Chuck Oberstein, 5,000	39.50	NR
1982	HAPPY DAYS, Chuck Oberstein, 5,000	39.50	NR
1982	FILLING POP'S SHOES, Chuck Oberstein, 5,000	42.50	NR

Wondrous Years

| 1981 | AFTER THE RAINS, Rudy Escalera, 5,000 | 39.50 | NR |
| 1982 | I GOT ONE, Rudy Escalera, 5,000 | 42.50 | NR |

World of Ozz Franca

1982	IMAGES, Ozz Franca, 7,500	42.50	NR
1982	LOST AND FOUND, Ozz Franca, 7,500	42.50	NR
1983	BEST FRIENDS, Ozz Franca, 7,500	42.50	NR

Yesterday's Impressions

| 1983 | GLORIA, Kalan, 5,000 | 39.50 | NR |

Single Issues

1982	JOHN LENNON TRIBUTE, Cassidy J. Alexander, 10,000	45.00	NR
1982	JOHN WAYNE, Cassidy J. Alexander, 10,000	39.50	BR
1983	BILL ROGERS, 7,991	42.50	NR
1983	BILL ROGERS/KING OF THE ROAD, 2,009	95.00	NR
1983	HENRY FONDA, Cassidy J. Alexander, 10,000	39.50	NR
1983	JOHN WAYNE – MILITARY, 10,000	42.50	NR

		Issue Price	Current Value
1983	LAUREL AND HARDY, Cassidy J. Alexander, 15,000	42.50	NR
1983	NOLAN RYAN/INNINGS PITCHED, 1,598	100.00	NR
1983	NOLAN RYAN, 8,402	42.50	NR
1983	STEVE GARVEY, Christopher Paluso, 10,000	60.00	NR
1983	STEVE GARVEY, 1,269	100.00	NR
1983	REGGIE JACKSON, Christopher Paluso, 10,000	60.00	NR
1983	REGGIE JACKSON, 464.............................	100.00	200.00
1983	TOM SEAVER, 6,728	42.50	NR
1983	TOM SEAVER/STRIKE OUT, 3,272....................	100.00	NR
1984	FOREVER YOURS, Cassidy J. Alexander, 15,000	42.50	NR
1984	KING REMEMBERED (ELVIS PRESLEY), Cassidy J. Alexander, 10,000	50.00	NR
1984	AMERICAN FRONTIER, Cassidy J. Alexander, 5,000	39.50	NR
1984	SALVATION ARMY, William Selden, 5,000	32.50	NR

Sunday
Photo courtesy of *Collectors News*

John Lennon Tribute
Photo courtesy of *Collectors News*

HADLEY COMPANIES

American Memories

1987	COMING HOME, Terry Redlin, 9,500..................	85.00	NR
1988	LIGHTS OF HOME, Terry Redlin, 9,500	85.00	NR
1989	HOMEWARD BOUND, Terry Redlin, 9,500..............	85.00	NR
1991	FAMILY TRADITIONS, Terry Redlin, 9,500.............	85.00	NR

Annual Christmas

| 1991 | HEADING HOME, Terry Redlin, 9,500, 9¼" .... | 65.00 | NR |

Winter Wonderland

Almost Home

Things Worth Keeping

The New Arrival

House Call

Morning Rounds

		Issue Price	Current Value
1992	PLEASURES OF WINTER, Terry Redlin, 19,500, 9¼"	65.00	RI
1993	WINTER WONDERLAND, Terry Redlin, 19,500, 9¼"	65.00	RI
1994	ALMOST HOME, Terry Redlin, 19,500, 9¼"	65.00	RI
1995	SHARING THE EVENING, Terry Redlin, 45 days, 8¼"	29.95	RI

Birds of Prey

1990	FALCON, M. Dumas, 5,000............................	75.00	NR
1990	EAGLE, M. Dumas, 5,000	75.00	NR
1990	OWL, M. Dumas, 5,000..............................	75.00	NR
1990	HAWK, M. Dumas, 5,000	75.00	NR

Cherished Moments

1993	THINGS WORTH KEEPING, Steve Hanks, 5,000.........	40.00	RI
XX	THE NEW ARRIVAL, Steve Hanks, 15,000	42.95	RI

Country Doctors

1995	HOUSE CALL, Terry Redlin, 45 days	29.95	RI
1995	MORNING ROUNDS, Terry Redlin, 45 days	29.95	RI
1995	OFFICE HOURS, Terry Redlin, 45 days	29.95	RI
1995	WEDNESDAY AFTERNOON, Terry Redlin, 45 days	29.95	RI

Glow Series

1985	EVENING GLOW, Terry Redlin, 5,000	55.00	475.00
1985	MORNING GLOW, Terry Redlin, 5,000	55.00	225.00
1985	TWILIGHT GLOW, Terry Redlin, 5,000	55.00	110.00
1988	AFTERNOON GLOW, Terry Redlin, 5,000	55.00	NR

Legacy Series

1990	LOON, J. Meger, 7,500	60.00	NR
1991	TIMBERWOLVES, J. Meger, 7,500	60.00	NR
1992	EAGLE, J. Meger, 7,500.............................	60.00	RI
1992	MOOSE, J. Meger, 7,500.............................	60.00	RI

Loons

1989	QUIET WATER, L. Didier, 9,500	45.00	NR

Lovers Collection

1992	LOVERS, Ozz Franca, 9,500	50.00	RI

Mountain Majesty

1990	AMERICAN BALD EAGLE, T. Blaylock, 5,000............	50.00	NR
1991	TRUMPETER PASS, T. Blaylock, 5,000.................	50.00	NR
1992	DAYBREAK ON CINNAMON CREEK, T. Blaylock, 5,000 ...	50.00	RI
1993	BRING UP A GRANDCHILD, T. Blaylock, 5,000..........	50.00	RI

Office Hours

Wednesday Afternoon

Young Warrior

Pink Navajo

Autumn Evening

Summertime

	Issue Price	Current Value

Nature Collection

1989	ALGONQUIN SUMMER, M. Dumas, 5,000..............	50.00	NR

Navajo Visions Suite

1993	NAVAJO FANTASY, Ozz Franca, 5,000..................	50.00	RI
1993	YOUNG WARRIOR, Ozz Franca, 5,000	50.00	RI

Navajo Woman

1990	FEATHERED HAIR TIES, Ozz Franca, 5,000	50.00	NR
1991	NAVAJO SUMMER, Ozz Franca, 5,000	50.00	NR
1992	TURQUOISE NECKLACE, Ozz Franca, 5,000	50.00	RI
1993	PINK NAVAJO, Ozz Franca, 5,000	50.00	RI

Retreat Series

1987	MORNING RETREAT, Terry Redlin, 9,500	65.00	110.00
1987	EVENING RETREAT, Terry Redlin, 9,500	65.00	NR
1988	GOLDEN RETREAT, Terry Redlin, 9,500	65.00	95.00
1989	MOONLIGHT RETREAT, Terry Redlin, 9,500	65.00	NR

Seasons

1994	AUTUMN EVENING, Terry Redlin, 45 days, $8^1/4$"	29.95	RI
1995	SUMMERTIME, Terry Redlin, 45 days, $8^1/4$".............	29.95	RI
1995	WINTERTIME, Terry Redlin, 45 days, $8^1/4$"..............	29.95	RI

That Special Time

1991	EVENING SOLITUDE, Terry Redlin, 9,500	65.00	NR
1992	AROMA OF FALL, Terry Redlin, 9,500..................	65.00	RI
1993	WELCOME TO PARADISE, Terry F lin, 9,500	65.00	RI

Wildlife Memories

1994	SHARING THE SOLITUDE, Terry F llin, 19,500, $9^1/4$"....	65.00	RI
1994	COMFORTS OF HOME, Terry Red 19,500, $9^1/4$".......	65.00	RI
1994	BEST FRIENDS, Terry Redlin, 19,! $9^1/4$"	65.00	RI
1994	PURE CONTENTMENT, Terry Red 19,500, $9^1/4$".......	65.00	RI

Windows to the Wild

1990	MASTER'S DOMAIN, Terry Redlin 500...............	65.00	NR
1991	WINTER WINDBREAK, Terry Redl 9,500	65.00	NR
1992	EVENING COMPANY, Terry Redlin 500	65.00	RI
1993	NIGHT MAPLING, Terry Redlin, 9, l	65.00	RI

Winner's Circle

1991	FRIENDS, J. K. Pyrah, 5,000	50.00	NR

Wintertime

Welcome to Paradise

Comforts of Home

Winter Windbreak

Winter Grotto—Cardinal

The Quest—Loons

		Issue Price	Current Value
1993	ROSIE, J. K. Pyrah, 5,000	50.00	RI

Winter Grotto Collection

1990	WINTER GROTTO – CARDINAL, L. Didier, 5,000	55.00	NR
1992	THE QUEST – LOONS, L. Didier, 5,000	55.00	RI

Single Issues

1995	PEEKING OUT, Steve Hanks, 15,000, 9¼"	42.95	RI
1995	PICKETS AND VINES, Mike Capser, 45 days, 8¼"	29.95	RI
1995	REPAIRS, Dave Barnhouse, 45 days, 8¼"	29.95	RI

Peeking Out

Pickets and Vines

Repairs

HALLMARK GALLERIES

Days to Remember — Norman Rockwell

		Issue Price	Current Value
1992	SWEET SONG SO YOUNG, pewter medallion, D. Unruh, 9,500 .	45.00	RI
1992	SLEEPING CHILDREN, pewter medallion, D. Unruh, 9,500	45.00	RI
1992	A BOY MEETS HIS DOG, pewter medallion, D. Unruh, 9,500 ...	45.00	RI
1992	FISHERMAN'S PARADISE, pewter medallion, D. Unruh, 9,500 .	45.00	RI
1993	BREAKING HOME TIES, D. Unruh, 9,500	35.00	RI

Enchanted Garden

1992	SWAN LAKE (tile), E. Richardson, 9,500	35.00	RI
1992	FAIRY BUNNY TALE: BEGINNING (tile), E. Richardson, 14,500 .	25.00	RI
1992	FAIRY BUNNY TALE: BEGINNING II (tile), E. Richardson, 14,500 35.00 .... RI		
1992	NEIGHBORHOOD DREAMER, E. Richardson, 9,500	45.00	RI

Innocent Wonders

1992	DINKY TOOT, Thomas Blackshear, 9,500	35.00	RI
1992	PINKY POO, Thomas Blackshear, 9,500	35.00	RI
1993	POCKETS, Thomas Blackshear, 9,500	35.00	RI

Majestic Wilderness

1992	VIXEN AND KITS, M. Newman, 9,500..................	35.00	RI
1992	TIMBER WOLVES, porcelain, M. Newman, 9,500	35.00	RI

Tobin Fraley Carousels

1992	PHILADELPHIA TOBOGGAN CO. 1920, pewter medallion, Tobin Fraley, 9,500	45.00	RI
1993	MAGICAL RIDE, Tobin Fraley, 9,500	35.00	RI

HAMILTON/BOEHM

Award–Winning Roses

1979	PEACE ROSE, Boehm Studio Artists, 15,000	45.00	60.00
1979	WHITE MASTERPIECE ROSE, Boehm Studio Artists, 15,000 ...	45.00	60.00
1979	TROPICANA ROSE, Boehm Studio Artists, 15,000	45.00	60.00
1979	ELEGANCE ROSE, Boehm Studio Artists, 15,000	45.00	55.00
1979	QUEEN ELIZABETH ROSE, Boehm Studio Artists, 15,000 .	45.00	55.00
1979	ROYAL HIGHNESS ROSE, Boehm Studio Artists, 15,000 ..	45.00	55.00
1979	ANGEL FACE ROSE, Boehm Studio Artists, 15,000	45.00	55.00
1979	MR. LINCOLN ROSE, Boehm Studio Artists, 15,000	45.00	55.00

Gamebirds of North America

1984	RING–NECKED PHEASANT, Boehm Studio Artists, 15,000	62.50	NR
1984	BOB–WHITE QUAIL, Boehm Studio Artists, 15,000	62.50	NR

		Issue Price	Current Value
1984	AMERICAN WOODCOCK, Boehm Studio Artists, 15,000 ..	62.50	NR
1984	CALIFORNIA QUAIL, Boehm Studio Artists, 15,000	62.50	NR
1984	RUFFED GROUSE, Boehm Studio Artists, 15,000	62.50	NR
1984	WILD TURKEY, Boehm Studio Artists, 15,000	62.50	NR
1984	WILLOW PARTRIDGE, Boehm Studio Artists, 15,000	62.50	NR
1984	PRAIRIE GROUSE, Boehm Studio Artists, 15,000	62.50	NR

Hummingbird Collection

1980	CALLIOPE HUMMINGBIRD, Boehm Studio Artists, 15,000	62.50	75.00
1980	BROADBILLED HUMMINGBIRD, Boehm Studio Artists, 15,000	62.50	NR
1980	BROADTAIL HUMMINGBIRD, Boehm Studio Artists, 15,000 ..	62.50	NR
1980	RUFOUS FLAME BEARER HUMMINGBIRD, Boehm Studio Artists, 15,000	62.50	NR
1980	STREAMERTAIL HUMMINGBIRD, Boehm Studio Artists, 15,000	62.50	NR
1980	BLUE–THROATED HUMMINGBIRD, Boehm Studio Artists, 15,000	62.50	NR
1980	CRIMSON TOPAZ HUMMINGBIRD, Boehm Studio Artists, 15,000	62.50	NR
1980	BRAZILIAN RUBY HUMMINGBIRD, Boehm Studio Artists, 15,000	62.50	NR

Owl Collection

1980	BOREAL OWL, Boehm Studio Artists, 15,000	45.00	75.00
1980	SNOWY OWL, Boehm Studio Artists, 15,000	45.00	65.00
1980	BARN OWL, Boehm Studio Artists, 15,000	45.00	65.00
1980	SAW–WHET OWL, Boehm Studio Artists, 15,000	45.00	65.00
1980	GREAT HORNED OWL, Boehm Studio Artists, 15,000	45.00	65.00
1980	SCREECH OWL, Boehm Studio Artists, 15,000	45.00	65.00
1980	SHORT–EARED OWL, Boehm Studio Artists, 15,000	45.00	65.00
1980	BARRED OWL, Boehm Studio Artists, 15,000	45.00	65.00

Water Birds

1981	CANADA GEESE, Boehm Studio Artists, 15,000	62.50	NR
1981	WOOD DUCKS, Boehm Studio Artists, 15,000	62.50	NR
1981	HOODED MERGANSER, Boehm Studio Artists, 15,000...	62.50	NR
1981	ROSS'S GEESE, Boehm Studio Artists, 15,000..........	62.50	NR
1981	COMMON MALLARD, Boehm Studio Artists, 15,000	62.50	NR
1981	CANVASBACK, Boehm Studio Artists, 15,000	62.50	NR
1981	GREEN–WINGED TEAL, Boehm Studio Artists, 15,000...	62.50	NR
1981	AMERICAN PINTAIL, Boehm Studio Artists, 15,000	62.50	NR

THE HAMILTON COLLECTION UNITED STATES

(See also Boehm Studios, Gorham, Heinrich Porzellan, Metal Arts Co.,
Pickard China, Porcelaine Ariel, Royal Devon, and Viletta China)

America at Work

1984	THE SCHOOL TEACHER, Norman Rockwell, 10 days	29.50	NR

		Issue Price	Current Value
1984	THE PIANO TUNER, Norman Rockwell, 10 days.........	29.50	NR
1984	THE ZOO KEEPER, Norman Rockwell, 10 days..........	29.50	NR
1984	THE CLEANING LADIES, Norman Rockwell, 10 days.....	29.50	NR
1984	THE HATCHECK GIRL, Norman Rockwell, 10 days	29.50	NR
1984	THE ARTIST, Norman Rockwell, 10 days	29.50	NR
1984	THE CENSUS TAKER, Norman Rockwell, 10 days	29.50	NR

America's Greatest Sailing Ships

1988	U.S.S. CONSTITUTION, T. Freeman, 14 days	29.50	40.00
1988	GREAT REPUBLIC, T. Freeman, 14 days................	29.50	35.00
1988	AMERICA, T. Freeman, 14 days	29.50	55.00
1988	CHARLES W. MORGAN, T. Freeman, 14 days	29.50	35.00
1988	EAGLE, T. Freeman, 14 days.........................	29.50	50.00
1988	BONHOMME RICHARD, T. Freeman, 14 days	29.50	45.00
1988	GERTRUDE L. THEBAUD, T. Freeman, 14 days..........	29.50	45.00
1988	ENTERPRISE, T. Freeman, 14 days	29.50	45.00

American Civil War

1990	GENERAL ROBERT E. LEE, D. Prechtel, 14 days	37.50	50.00
1990	GENERALS GRANT AND LEE AT APPOMATTOX, D. Prechtel, 14 days	37.50	50.00
1990	GENERAL THOMAS "STONEWALL" JACKSON, D. Prechtel, 14 days	37.50	55.00
1990	ABRAHAM LINCOLN, D. Prechtel, 14 days	37.50	60.00
1991	GENERAL J.E.B. STUART, D. Prechtel, 14 days	37.50	45.00
1991	GENERAL PHILIP SHERIDAN, D. Prechtel, 14 days......	37.50	45.00
1991	A LETTER FROM HOME, D. Prechtel, 14 days	37.50	60.00
1991	GOING HOME, D. Prechtel, 14 days	37.50	45.00
1992	ASSEMBLING THE TROOPS, D. Prechtel, 14 days.......	37.50	RI
1992	STANDING WATCH, D. Prechtel, 14 days..............	37.50	RI

American Rose Garden

1988	AMERICAN SPIRIT, P. J. Sweany, 14 days..............	29.50	NR
1988	PEACE ROSE, P. J. Sweany, 14 days.................	29.50	NR
1989	WHITE KNIGHT, P. J. Sweany, 14 days...............	29.50	NR
1989	AMERICAN HERITAGE, P. J. Sweany, 14 days	29.50	NR
1989	ECLIPSE, P. J. Sweany, 14 days.....................	29.50	NR
1989	BLUE MOON, P. J. Sweany, 14 days	29.50	NR
1989	CORAL CLUSTER, P. J. Sweany, 14 days..............	29.50	NR
1989	PRESIDENT HERBERT HOOVER, P. J. Sweany, 14 days ..	29.50	NR

Andy Griffith

1992	SHERIFF ANDY TAYLOR, R. Tanenbaum, 28 days	29.50	RI
1992	A STARTLING CONCLUSION, R. Tanenbaum, 28 days ...	29.50	RI
1993	MAYBERRY SING–A–LONG, R. Tanenbaum, 28 days	29.50	RI

		Issue Price	Current Value
1993	AUNT BEE'S KITCHEN, R. Tanenbaum, 28 days	29.50	RI

Angler's Prize

1991	TROPHY BASS, M. Susinno, 15 days	29.50	40.00
1991	BLUE RIBBON TROUT, M. Susinno, 15 days	29.50	NR
1991	SUN DANCERS, M. Susinno, 15 days...................	29.50	NR
1991	FRESHWATER BARRACUDA, M. Susinno, 15 days	29.50	NR
1991	BRONZEBACK FIGHTER, M. Susinno, 15 days	29.50	NR
1991	AUTUMN BEAUTY, M. Susinno, 15 days	29.50	NR
1992	OLD MOONEYES, M. Susinno, 15 days	29.50	RI
1992	SILVER KING, M. Susinno, 15 days	29.50	RI

Beauty of Winter

1992	SILENT NIGHT, 28 days..............................	19.50	RI
1992	MOONLIGHT SLEIGH RIDE, 28 days	19.50	RI

Best of Baseball

1993	THE LEGENDARY MICKEY MANTLE, R. Tanenbaum, 28 days ..	29.50	RI
1993	THE IMMORTAL BABE RUTH, R. Tanenbaum, 28 days ...	29.50	RI
1993	THE GREAT WILLIE MAYS, R. Tanenbaum, 28 days	29.50	RI
1993	THE UNBEATABLE DUKE SNIDER, R. Tanenbaum, 28 days	29.50	RI
1993	THE EXTRAORDINARY LOU GEHRIG, R. Tanenbaum, 28 days .	29.50	RI

Bialosky® & Friends

1992	FAMILY ADDITION, P. & A. Bialosky, 28 days	29.50	RI
1993	SWEETHEART, P. & A. Bialosky, 28 days	29.50	RI
1993	LET'S GO FISHING, P. & A. Bialosky, 28 days	29.50	RI
1993	U.S. MAIL, P & A. Bialosky, 28 days	29.50	RI
1993	SLEIGH RIDE, P. & A. Bialosky, 28 days	29.50	RI
1993	HONEY FOR SALE, P. & A. Bialosky, 28 days	29.50	RI
1993	BREAKFAST IN BED, P. & A. Bialosky, 28 days	29.50	RI

Big Cats of the World

1989	AFRICAN SHADE, Douglas Manning, 14 days	29.50	NR
1989	VIEW FROM ABOVE, Douglas Manning, 14 days	29.50	NR
1990	ON THE PROWL, Douglas Manning, 14 days	29.50	NR
1990	DEEP IN THE JUNGLE, Douglas Manning, 14 days	29.50	NR
1990	SPIRIT OF THE MOUNTAIN, Douglas Manning, 14 days..	29.50	NR
1990	SPOTTED SENTINEL, Douglas Manning, 14 days	29.50	NR
1990	ABOVE THE TREETOPS, Douglas Manning, 14 days	29.50	NR
1990	MOUNTAIN SWELLER, Douglas Manning, 14 days	29.50	NR
1992	JUNGLE HABITAT, Douglas Manning, 14 days	29.50	RI
1992	SOLITARY SENTRY, Douglas Manning, 14 days.........	29.50	RI

Birds of the Temple Gardens

1989	DOVES OF FIDELITY, J. Cheng, 14 days	29.50	NR
1989	CRANES OF ETERNAL LIFE, J. Cheng, 14 days	29.50	NR

		Issue Price	Current Value
1989	HONORABLE SWALLOWS, J. Cheng, 14 days	29.50	NR
1989	ORIENTAL WHITE EYES OF BEAUTY, J. Cheng, 14 days ..	29.50	NR
1989	PHEASANTS OF GOOD FORTUNE, J. Cheng, 14 days	29.50	NR
1989	IMPERIAL GOLDCREST, J. Cheng, 14 days.............	29.50	NR
1989	GOLDFINCHES OF VIRTUE, J. Cheng, 14 days	29.50	NR
1989	MAGPIES: BIRDS OF GOOD OMEN, J. Cheng, 14 days ...	29.50	NR

Bundles of Joy

1988	AWAKENING, Bessie Pease Gutmann, 14 days	24.50	100.00
1988	HAPPY DREAMS, Bessie Pease Gutmann, 14 days	24.50	75.00
1988	TASTING, Bessie Pease Gutmann, 14 days.............	24.50	45.00
1988	SWEET INNOCENCE, Bessie Pease Gutmann, 14 days ..	24.50	30.00
1988	TOMMY, Bessie Pease Gutmann, 14 days.............	24.50	45.00
1988	A LITTLE BIT OF HEAVEN, Bessie Pease Gutmann, 14 days ...	24.50	75.00
1988	BILLY, Bessie Pease Gutmann, 14 days	24.50	40.00
1988	SUN KISSED, Bessie Pease Gutmann, 14 days	24.50	40.00

Butterfly Garden

1987	SPICEBUSH SWALLOWTAIL, P. J. Sweany, 14 days	29.50	NR
1987	COMMON BLUE, P. J. Sweany, 14 days	29.50	NR
1987	ORANGE SULPHUR, P. J. Sweany, 14 days.............	29.50	NR
1987	MONARCH, P. J. Sweany, 14 days....................	29.50	NR
1987	TIGER SWALLOWTAIL, P. J. Sweany, 14 days	29.50	NR
1987	CRIMSON–PATCHED LONGWING, P. J. Sweany, 14 days.	29.50	NR
1988	MORNING CLOAK, P. J. Sweany, 14 days	29.50	NR
1988	RED ADMIRAL, P. J. Sweany, 14 days	29.50	40.00

Cameo Kittens

1993	GINGER SNAP, Q. Lemond, 28 days	29.50	RI
1993	CAT TAILS, Q. Lemond, 28 days	29.50	RI
1993	LADY BLUE, Q. Lemond, 28 days	29.50	RI

Carefree Days

1982	AUTUMN WANDERER, Thornton Utz, 10 days	24.50	NR
1982	BEST FRIENDS, Thornton Utz, 10 days	24.50	NR
1982	FEEDING TIME, Thornton Utz, 10 days................	24.50	NR
1982	BATHTIME VISITOR, Thornton Utz, 10 days	24.50	NR
1982	FIRST CATCH, Thornton Utz, 10 days.................	24.50	NR
1982	MONKEY BUSINESS, Thornton Utz, 10 days...........	24.50	NR
1982	TOUCHDOWN, Thornton Utz, 10 days	24.50	NR
1982	NATURE HUNT, Thornton Utz, 10 days................	24.50	NR

Child's Best Friend

1985	IN DISGRACE, Bessie Pease Gutmann, 14 days	24.50	90.00
1985	THE REWARD, Bessie Pease Gutmann, 14 days	24.50	60.00

		Issue Price	Current Value
1985	WHO'S SLEEPY, Bessie Pease Gutmann, 14 days	24.50	55.00
1985	GOOD MORNING, Bessie Pease Gutmann, 14 days	24.50	45.00
1985	SYMPATHY, Bessie Pease Gutmann, 14 days	24.50	55.00
1985	ON THE UP AND UP, Bessie Pease Gutmann, 14 days ...	24.50	55.00
1985	MINE, Bessie Pease Gutmann, 14 days	24.50	60.00
1985	GOING TO TOWN, Bessie Pease Gutmann, 14 days	24.50	50.00

In Disgrace
Photo courtesy of *Collectors News*

Childhood Reflections

1991	HARMONY, Bessie Pease Gutmann, 14 days	29.50	60.00
1991	KITTY'S BREAKFAST, Bessie Pease Gutmann, 14 days...	29.50	NR
1991	FRIENDLY ENEMIES, Bessie Pease Gutmann, 14 days ...	29.50	NR
1991	SMILE, SMILE, SMILE, Bessie Pease Gutmann, 14 days .	29.50	NR
1991	LULLABY, Bessie Pease Gutmann, 14 days	29.50	NR
1991	OH! OH! A BUNNY, Bessie Pease Gutmann, 14 days	29.50	NR
1991	LITTLE MOTHER, Bessie Pease Gutmann, 14 days	29.50	NR
1991	THANK YOU, GOD, Bessie Pease Gutmann, 14 days	29.50	NR

Children of the American Frontier

1986	IN TROUBLE AGAIN, Don Crook, 10 days	24.50	NR
1986	TUBS AND SUDS, Don Crook, 10 days	24.50	NR
1986	A LADY NEEDS A LITTLE PRIVACY, Don Crook, 10 days .	24.50	NR
1986	THE DESPERADOES, Don Crook, 10 days	24.50	NR
1986	RIDERS WANTED, Don Crook, 10 days	24.50	NR
1987	A COWBOY'S DOWNFALL, Don Crook	24.50	NR
1987	RUNAWAY BLUES, Don Crook, 10 days...............	24.50	NR
1987	A SPECIAL PATIENT, Don Crook, 10 days	24.50	NR

Chinese Blossoms of the Four Seasons

1985	SPRING PEONY BLOSSOM, 9,800	95.00	NR

		Issue Price	Current Value
1985	SUMMER LOTUS BLOSSOM, 9,800	95.00	NR
1985	AUTUMN CHRYSANTHEMUM, 9,800	95.00	NR
1985	WINTER PLUM BLOSSOM, 9,800	95.00	NR

Chinese Symbols of the Universe

		Issue Price	Current Value
1984	THE DRAGON, Mou–Sien Tseng, 7,500	90.00	NR
1984	THE PHOENIX, Mou–Sien Tseng, 7,500	90.00	NR
1984	THE TIGER, Mou–Sien Tseng, 7,500	90.00	NR
1984	THE TORTOISE, Mou–Sien Tseng, 7,500	90.00	NR
1984	MAN, Mou–Sien Tseng, 7,500	90.00	NR

Classic Sporting Dogs

		Issue Price	Current Value
1989	GOLDEN RETRIEVERS, B. Christie, 14 days	24.50	55.00
1989	LABRADOR RETRIEVERS, B. Christie, 14 days	24.50	60.00
1989	BEAGLES, B. Christie, 14 days	24.50	35.00
1989	POINTERS, B. Christie, 14 days	24.50	30.00
1989	SPRINGER SPANIELS, B. Christie, 14 days	24.50	40.00
1990	GERMAN SHORT–HAIRED POINTERS, B. Christie, 14 days 35.00		24.50
1990	IRISH SETTERS, B. Christie, 14 days	24.50	35.00
1990	BRITTANY SPANIELS, B. Christie, 14 days	24.50	50.00

Classic TV Westerns

		Issue Price	Current Value
1990	THE LONE RANGER AND TONTO, K. Milnazik, 14 days...	29.50	50.00
1990	BONANZA™, K. Milnazik, 14 days	29.50	60.00
1990	ROY ROGERS AND DALE EVANS, K. Milnazik, 14 days ..	29.50	55.00
1991	RAWHIDE, K. Milnazik, 14 days	29.50	45.00
1991	WILD WILD WEST, K. Milnazik, 14 days	29.50	60.00
1991	HAVE GUN, WILL TRAVEL, K. Milnazik, 14 days	29.50	45.00
1991	THE VIRGINIAN, K. Milnazik, 14 days	29.50	35.00
1991	HOPALONG CASSIDY, K. Milnazik, 14 days	29.50	60.00

Coral Paradise

		Issue Price	Current Value
1989	THE LIVING OASIS, Higgins Bond, 14 days	29.50	NR
1990	RICHES OF THE CORAL SEA, Higgins Bond, 14 days	29.50	NR
1990	TROPICAL PAGEANTRY, Higgins Bond, 14 days	29.50	NR
1990	CARIBBEAN SPECTACLE, Higgins Bond, 14 days	29.50	NR
1990	UNDERSEA VILLAGE, Higgins Bond, 14 days	29.50	NR
1990	SHIMMERING REEF DWELLERS, Higgins Bond, 14 days.	29.50	NR
1990	MYSTERIES OF THE GALAPAGOS, Higgins Bond, 14 days	29.50	NR
1990	FOREST BENEATH THE SEA, Higgins Bond, 14 days.....	29.50	NR

Council of Nations

		Issue Price	Current Value
1992	STRENGTH OF THE SIOUX, Gregory Perillo, 14 days	29.50	RI
1992	PRIDE OF THE CHEYENNE, Gregory Perillo, 14 days	29.50	RI

		Issue Price	Current Value
1992	DIGNITY OF THE NEZ PERCE, Grogory Perillo, 14 days . . .	29.50	RI
1992	COURAGE OF THE ARAPAHO, Gregory Perillo, 14 days . .	29.50	RI
1992	POWER OF THE BLACKFOOT, Gregory Perillo, 14 days . . .	29.50	RI
1992	NOBILITY OF THE ALGONQUIN, Gregory Perillo, 14 days	29.50	RI
1992	WISDOM OF THE CHEROKEE, Gregory Perillo, 14 days . .	29.50	RI
1992	BOLDNESS OF THE SENECA, Gregory Perillo, 14 days . . .	29.50	RI

Country Garden Calendar Collection (Bing & Grondahl)

1984	SEPTEMBER, Linda Thompson, 12,500	55.00	NR
1984	OCTOBER, Linda Thompson, 12,500	55.00	NR
1984	NOVEMBER, Linda Thompson, 12,500	55.00	NR
1984	DECEMBER, Linda Thompson, 12,500	55.00	NR
1984	JANUARY, Linda Thompson, 12,500	55.00	NR
1984	FEBRUARY, Linda Thompson, 12,500	55.00	NR
1984	MARCH, Linda Thompson, 12,500	55.00	NR
1984	APRIL, Linda Thompson, 12,500	55.00	NR
1984	MAY, Linda Thompson, 12,500	55.00	NR
1984	JUNE, Linda Thompson, 12,500	55.00	NR
1984	JULY, Linda Thompson, 12,500	55.00	NR
1984	AUGUST, Linda Thompson, 12,500	55.00	NR

Country Garden Cottage

1992	RIVERBANK COTTAGE, E. Dertner, 28 days	29.50	RI
1992	SUNDAY OUTING, E. Dertner, 28 days	29.50	RI
1992	SHEPHERD'S COTTAGE, E. Dertner, 28 days	29.50	RI
1993	DAYDREAM COTTAGE, E. Dertner, 28 days	29.50	RI
1993	GARDEN GLORIOUS, E. Dertner, 28 days	29.50	RI
1993	THIS SIDE OF HEAVEN, E. Dertner, 28 days	29.50	RI
1993	SUMMER SYMPHONY, E. Dertner, 28 days	29.50	RI
1993	APRIL COTTAGE, E. Dertner, 28 days	29.50	RI

Country Kitties

1989	MISCHIEF MAKERS, G. Gerardi, 14 days	24.50	45.00
1989	TABLE MANNERS, G. Gerardi, 14 days	24.50	35.00
1989	ATTIC ATTACK, G. Gerardi, 14 days	24.50	45.00
1989	ROCK AND ROLLERS, G. Gerardi, 14 days	24.50	30.00
1989	JUST FOR THE FERN OF IT, G. Gerardi, 14 days	24.50	30.00
1989	ALL WASHED UP, G. Gerardi, 14 days	24.50	40.00
1989	STROLLER DERBY, G. Gerardi, 14 days	24.50	40.00
1989	CAPTIVE AUDIENCE, G. Gerardi, 14 days	24.50	40.00

Country Season of Horses

1990	FIRST DAY OF SPRING, J. M. Vass, 14 days	29.50	NR
1990	SUMMER SPLENDOR, J. M. Vass, 14 days	29.50	NR

		Issue Price	Current Value
1990	A WINTER'S WALK, J. M. Vass, 14 days	29.50	NR
1990	AUTUMN GRANDEUR, J. M. Vass, 14 days	29.50	NR
1990	CLIFFSIDE BEAUTY, J. M. Vass, 14 days	29.50	NR
1990	FROSTY MORNING, J. M. Vass, 14 days	29.50	NR
1990	CRISP COUNTRY MORNING, J. M. Vass, 14 days	29.50	NR
1990	RIVER RETREAT, J. M. Vass, 14 days..................	29.50	NR

Country Summer

1985	BUTTERFLY BEAUTY, N. Noel, 10 days..................	29.50	NR
1985	THE GOLDEN PUPPY, N. Noel, 10 days	29.50	NR
1985	THE ROCKING CHAIR, N. Noel, 10 days................	29.50	NR
1985	MY BUNNY, N. Noel, 10 days	29.50	NR
1985	THE BRAHMA CALF, N. Noel, 10 days	29.50	NR
1985	THE TRICYCLE, N. Noel, 10 days	29.50	NR
1988	THE PIGLET, N. Noel, 10 days	29.50	NR
1988	TEAMMATES, N. Noel, 10 days	29.50	NR

Curious Kittens

1990	RAINY DAY FRIENDS, B. Harrison, 14 days	29.50	NR
1990	KEEPING IN STEP, B. Harrison, 14 days................	29.50	NR
1990	DELIGHTFUL DISCOVERY, B. Harrison, 14 days	29.50	NR
1990	CHANCE MEETING, B. Harrison, 14 days...............	29.50	NR
1990	ALL WOUND UP, B. Harrison, 14 days	29.50	NR
1990	MAKING TRACKS, B. Harrison, 14 days..............	29.50	NR
1990	PLAYING CAT AND MOUSE, B. Harrison, 14 days	29.50	NR
1990	A PAW'S IN THE ACTION, B. Harrison, 14 days	29.50	NR
1990	LITTLE SCHOLAR, B. Harrison, 14 days	29.50	NR
1990	CAT BURGLAR, B. Harrison, 14 days	29.50	NR

Daughter's of the Sun

1993	SUN DANCER, K. Thayer, 28 days	29.50	RI
1993	SHINING FEATHER, K. Thayer, 28 days	29.50	RI
1993	DELIGHTED DANCER, K. Thayer, 28 days	29.50	RI
1993	EVENING DANCER, K. Thayer, 28 days	29.50	RI
1993	A SECRET GLANCE, K. Thayer, 28 days	29.50	RI

Dear to My Heart

1990	CATHY, Jan Hagara, 14 days	29.50	NR
1990	ADDIE, Jan Hagara, 14 days.........................	29.50	NR
1990	JIMMY, Jan Hagara, 14 days	29.50	NR
1990	DACY, Jan Hagara, 14 days	29.50	NR
1990	PAUL, Jan Hagara, 14 days	29.50	NR
1991	SHELLY, Jan Hagara, 14 days........................	29.50	NR
1991	JENNY, Jan Hagara, 14 days	29.50	NR

		Issue Price	Current Value
1991	JOY, Jan Hagara, 14 days	29.50	NR

Delights of Childhood

1989	CRAYON CREATIONS, J. Lamb, 14 days	29.50	NR
1989	LITTLE MOTHER, J. Lamb, 14 days	29.50	NR
1990	BATHING BEAUTY, J. Lamb, 14 days	29.50	NR
1990	IS THAT YOU, GRANNY?, J. Lamb, 14 days	29.50	NR
1990	NATURE'S LITTLE HELPER, J. Lamb, 14 days	29.50	NR
1990	SO SORRY, J. Lamb, 14 days	29.50	NR
1990	SHOWER TIME, J. Lamb, 14 days	29.50	NR
1990	STORYTIME FRIENDS, J. Lamb, 14 days	29.50	NR

Elvis Remembered

1989	LOVING YOU, Susan Morton, 90 days	37.50	85.00
1989	EARLY YEARS, Susan Morton, 90 days	37.50	80.00
1989	TENDERLY, Susan Morton, 90 days	37.50	85.00
1989	THE KING, Susan Morton, 90 days	37.50	100.00
1989	FOREVER YOURS, Susan Morton, 90 days	37.50	85.00
1989	ROCKIN' IN THE MOONLIGHT, Susan Morton, 90 days	37.50	80.00
1989	MOODY BLUES, Susan Morton, 90 days	37.50	85.00
1989	ELVIS PRESLEY, Susan Morton, 90 days	37.50	100.00

English Country Cottages

1990	PERIWINKLE TEA ROOM, M. Bell, 14 days	29.50	45.00
1991	GAMEKEEPER'S COTTAGE, M. Bell, 14 days	29.50	75.00
1991	GINGER COTTAGE, M. Bell, 14 days	29.50	60.00
1991	LARKSPUR COTTAGE, M. Bell, 14 days	29.50	NR
1991	THE CHAPLAIN'S COTTAGE, M. Bell, 14 days	29.50	NR
1991	LORNA DOONE COTTAGE, M. Bell, 14 days	29.50	NR
1991	MURRIE COTTAGE, M. Bell, 14 days	29.50	NR
1991	LULLABYE COTTAGE, M. Bell, 14 days	29.50	NR

Eternal Wishes of Good Fortune

1983	FRIENDSHIP, Shuho and Senkin Kage, limited	34.95	NR
1983	LOVE, Shuho and Senkin Kage, limited	34.95	NR
1983	FERTILITY, Shuho and Senkin Kage, limited	34.95	NR
1983	PURITY AND PERFECTION, Shuho and Senkin Kage, limited	34.95	NR
1983	ILLUSTRIOUS OFFSPRING, Shuho and Senkin Kage, limited	34.95	NR
1983	PEACE, Shuho and Senkin Kage, limited	34.95	NR
1983	LONGEVITY, Shuho and Senkin Kage, limited	34.95	NR
1983	IMMORTALITY, Shuho and Senkin Kage, limited	34.95	NR
1983	MARITAL BLISS, Shuho and Senkin Kage, limited	34.95	NR
1983	BEAUTY, Shuho and Senkin Kage, limited	34.95	NR
1983	FORTITUDE, Shuho and Senkin Kage, limited	34.95	NR
1983	YOUTH, Shuho and Senkin Kage, limited	34.95	NR

Fairy Tales of Old Japan

		Issue Price	Current Value
1984	THE OLD MAN WHO MADE CHERRY TREES BLOSSOM, Shigekasu Hotta, 10 days	39.50	NR
1984	LITTLE ONE INCH, Shigekasu Hotta, 10 days	39.50	NR
1984	MY LORD BAG OF RICE, Shigekasu Hotta, 10 days	39.50	NR
1984	THE TONGUE–CUT SPARROW, Shigekasu Hotta, 10 days	39.50	NR
1984	THE BAMBOO CUTTER AND THE MOON CHILD, Shigekasu Hotta, 10 days	39.50	NR
1984	THE FISHER LAD, Shigekasu Hotta, 10 days	39.50	NR
1984	THE MAGIC TEA KETTLE, Shigekasu Hotta, 10 days	39.50	NR

The Old Man Who Made Cherry Trees Blossom
Photo courtesy of *Collectors News*

Farmyard Friends

1992	MISTAKEN IDENTITY, J. Lamb, 28 days	29.50	RI
1992	LITTLE COWHANDS, J. Lamb, 28 days	29.50	RI
1993	SHREDDING THE EVIDENCE, J. Lamb, 28 days	29.50	RI
1993	PARTNERS IN CRIME, J. Lamb, 28 days	29.50	RI
1993	FOWL PLAY, J. Lamb, 28 days	29.50	RI
1993	FOLLOW THE LEADER, J. Lamb, 28 days	29.50	RI
1993	PONY TALES, J. Lamb, 28 days	29.50	RI
1993	AN APPLE A DAY, J. Lamb, 28 days	29.50	RI

Favorite American Songbirds

1989	BLUE JAYS OF SPRING, D. O'Driscoll, 14 days	29.50	NR
1989	RED CARDINALS OF WINTER, D. O'Driscoll, 14 days	29.50	NR
1989	ROBINS AND APPLE BLOSSOMS, D. O'Driscoll, 14 days	29.50	NR
1989	GOLDFINCHES OF SUMMER, D. O'Driscoll, 14 days	29.50	NR
1990	AUTUMN CHICKADEES, D. O'Driscoll, 14 days	29.50	NR
1990	BLUEBIRDS AND MORNING GLORIES, D. O'Driscoll, 14 days	29.50	NR
1990	TUFTED TITMOUSE AND HOLLY, D. O'Driscoll, 14 days	29.50	NR
1991	CAROLINA WRENS OF SPRING, D. O'Driscoll, 14 days	29.50	NR

		Issue Price	Current Value
The Fierce and the Free			
1992	BIG MEDICINE, F. McCarthy, 28 days	29.50	RI
1993	LAND OF THE WINTER HAWK, F. McCarthy, 28 days	29.50	RI
1993	WARRIOR OF SAVAGE SPLENDOR, F. McCarthy, 28 days	29.50	RI

Fifty Years of Oz

1989	FIFTY YEARS OF OZ, Thomas Blackshear, 14 days	37.50	150.00

Flower Festivals of Japan

1985	CHRYSANTHEMUM, N. Hara, 10 days	45.00	55.00
1985	HOLLYHOCK, N. Hara, 10 days	45.00	55.00
1985	PLUM BLOSSOM, N. Hara, 10 days	45.00	55.00
1985	MORNING GLORY, N. Hara, 10 days	45.00	55.00
1985	CHERRY BLOSSOM, N. Hara, 10 days	45.00	55.00
1985	IRIS, N. Hara, 10 days	45.00	55.00
1985	LILY, N. Hara, 10 days	45.00	55.00
1985	PEACH BLOSSOM, N. Hara, 10 days	45.00	55.00

Garden of Verses

1983	PICTURE BOOKS IN WINTER, Jessie Wilcox Smith, 10 days . .	24.50	NR
1983	LITTLE DROPS OF WATER, Jessie Wilcox Smith, 10 days	24.50	NR
1983	A CHILD'S QUESTION, Jessie Wilcox Smith, 10 days	24.50	NR
1983	LOOKING GLASS RIVER, Jessie Wilcox Smith, 10 days . .	24.50	NR
1983	THE LITTLE BUSY BEE, Jessie Wilcox Smith, 10 days . . .	24.50	NR
1983	AT THE SEASIDE, Jessie Wilcox Smith, 10 days	24.50	NR
1983	THE TEA PARTY, Jessie Wilcox Smith, 10 days	24.50	NR
1983	FOREIGN LANDS, Jessie Wilcox Smith, 10 days	24.50	NR
1983	THE HAYLOFT, Jessie Wilcox Smith, 10 days	24.50	NR
1983	AMONG THE POPPIES, Jessie Wilcox Smith, 10 days . . .	24.50	NR
1983	FIVE O'CLOCK TEA, Jessie Wilcox Smith, 10 days	24.50	NR
1983	I LOVE LITTLE KITTY, Jessie Wilcox Smith, 10 days	24.50	NR

Gardens of the Orient

1983	FLOWERING OF SPRING, Shunsute Suetomi, <1 year . . .	19.50	NR
1983	FESTIVAL OF MAY, Shunsute Suetomi, <1 year	19.50	NR
1983	CHERRY BLOSSOM BROCADE, Shunsute Suetomi, <1 year	19.50	NR
1983	A WINTER'S REPOSE, Shunsute Suetomi, <1 year	19.50	NR
1983	THE GARDEN SANCTUARY, Shunsute Suetomi, <1 year .	19.50	NR
1983	SUMMER'S GLORY, Shunsute Suetomi, <1 year	19.50	NR
1983	JUNE'S CREATION, Shunsute Suetomi, <1 year	19.50	NR

Gentle Arts of the Geisha

1983	IKEBANA, Yasuhiko Adachi, limited	21.50	NR

Glory of Christ

1992	THE ASCENSION, C. Micarelli, 48 days	29.50	RI

		Issue Price	Current Value
1992	JESUS TEACHING, C. Micarelli, 48 days	29.50	RI
1993	THE LAST SUPPER, C. Micarelli, 48 days	29.50	RI
1993	THE NATIVITY, C. Micarelli, 48 days	29.50	RI
1993	THE BAPTISM OF CHRIST, C. Micarelli, 48 days	29.50	RI
1993	JESUS HEALS THE SICK, C. Micarelli, 48 days	29.50	RI
1993	JESUS WALKS ON WATER, C. Micarelli, 48 days	29.50	RI
1993	DESCENT FROM THE CROSS, C. Micarelli, 48 days	29.50	RI

Golden Age of American Railroads

		Issue Price	Current Value
1991	THE BLUE COMET, Theodore Xaras, 15 days	29.50	NR
1991	THE MORNING LOCAL, Theodore Xaras, 15 days	29.50	NR
1991	THE PENNSYLVANIA K–4, Theodore Xaras, 15 days	29.50	NR
1991	ABOVE THE CANYON, Theodore Xaras, 15 days	29.50	NR
1991	PORTRAIT IN STEAM, Theodore Xaras, 15 days	29.50	NR
1991	THE SANTA FE SUPER CHIEF, Theodore Xaras, 15 days	29.50	NR
1991	BIG BOY, Theodore Xaras, 15 days	29.50	NR
1991	THE EMPIRE BUILDER, Theodore Xaras, 15 days	29.50	NR
1992	AN AMERICAN CLASSIC, Theodore Xaras, 15 days	29.50	RI
1992	FINAL DESTINATION, Theodore Xaras, 15 days	29.50	RI

Golden Classics

		Issue Price	Current Value
1987	SLEEPING BEAUTY, Carol Lawson, 14 days	37.50	NR
1987	RUMPELSTILTSKIN, Carol Lawson, 14 days	37.50	NR
1987	JACK AND THE BEANSTALK, Carol Lawson, 14 days	37.50	NR
1987	SNOW WHITE AND ROSE RED, Carol Lawson, 14 days	37.50	NR
1987	HANSEL AND GRETEL, Carol Lawson, 14 days	37.50	NR
1987	CINDERELLA, Carol Lawson, 14 days	37.50	NR
1987	THE GOLDEN GOOSE, Carol Lawson, 14 days	37.50	NR
1987	THE SNOW QUEEN, Carol Lawson, 14 days	37.50	NR

Good Sports

		Issue Price	Current Value
1990	WIDE RETRIEVER, J. Lamb, 14 days	29.50	55.00
1990	DOUBLE PLAY, J. Lamb, 14 days	29.50	65.00
1990	HOLE IN ONE, J. Lamb, 14 days	29.50	45.00
1990	THE BASS MASTERS, J. Lamb, 14 days	29.50	40.00
1990	SPOTTED ON THE SIDELINE, J. Lamb, 14 days	29.50	40.00
1990	SLAP SHOT, J. Lamb, 14 days	29.50	45.00
1991	NET PLAY, J. Lamb, 14 days	29.50	50.00
1991	BASSETBALL, J. Lamb, 14 days	29.50	35.00
1992	BOXER REBELLION, J. Lamb, 14 days	29.50	RI
1992	GREAT TRY, J. Lamb, 14 days	29.50	RI

Great Fighter Planes of World War II

		Issue Price	Current Value
1992	OLD CROW, R. Waddey, 14 days	29.50	RI
1992	BIG HOG, R. Waddey, 14 days	29.50	RI

			Issue Price	Current Value
1992	P–47 THUNDERBOLT, R. Waddey, 14 days..............		29.50	RI
1992	P–40 FLYING TIGER, R. Waddey, 14 days		29.50	RI
1992	F4F WILDCAT, R. Waddey, 14 days		29.50	RI
1992	P–38F LIGHTNING, R. Waddey, 14 days		29.50	RI
1993	F6F HELLCAT, R. Waddey, 14 days		29.50	RI
1993	P–39M AIRACOBRA, R. Waddey, 14 days		29.50	RI

Great Mammals of the Sea

		Issue Price	Current Value
1991	ORCA TRIO, Wyland, 14 days.........................	35.00	45.00
1991	HAWAII DOLPHINS, Wyland, 14 days	35.00	40.00
1991	ORCA JOURNEY, Wyland, 14 days	35.00	40.00
1991	DOLPHIN PARADISE, Wyland, 14 days	35.00	45.00
1991	CHILDREN OF THE SEA, Wyland, 14 days	35.00	45.00
1991	KISSING DOLPHINS, Wyland, 14 days	35.00	40.00
1991	ISLANDS, Wyland, 14 days...........................	35.00	45.00
1991	ORCAS, Wyland, 14 days	35.00	45.00

Greatest Show on Earth

		Issue Price	Current Value
1981	CLOWNS, Franklin Moody, 10 days....................	30.00	70.00
1981	ELEPHANTS, Franklin Moody, 10 days	30.00	NR
1981	AERIALISTS, Franklin Moody, 10 days	30.00	NR
1981	GREAT PARADE, Franklin Moody, 10 days	30.00	NR
1981	MIDWAY, Franklin Moody, 10 days	30.00	NR
1981	EQUESTRIANS, Franklin Moody, 10 days	30.00	NR
1981	LION TAMER, Franklin Moody, 10 days	30.00	NR
1981	GRANDE FINALE, Franklin Moody, 10 days	30.00	NR

Growing Up Together

		Issue Price	Current Value
1990	MY VERY BEST FRIENDS, P. Brooks, 14 days	29.50	NR
1990	TEA FOR TWO, P. Brooks, 14 days	29.50	NR
1990	TENDER LOVING CARE, P. Brooks, 14 days	29.50	NR
1990	PICNIC PALS, P. Brooks, 14 days	29.50	NR
1991	NEWFOUND FRIENDS, P. Brooks, 14 days	29.50	NR
1991	KITTEN CABOODLE, P. Brooks, 14 days...............	29.50	NR
1991	FISHING BUDDIES, P. Brooks, 14 days	29.50	NR
1991	BEDTIME BLESSINGS, P. Brooks, 14 days	29.50	NR

I Love Lucy Plate Collection

		Issue Price	Current Value
1989	CALIFORNIA, HERE WE COME, J. Kritz, 14 days.........	29.50	55.00
1989	IT'S JUST LIKE CANDY, J. Kritz, 14 days	29.50	65.00
1990	THE BIG SQUEEZE, J. Kritz, 14 days	29.50	70.00
1990	EATING THE EVIDENCE, J. Kritz, 14 days..............	29.50	75.00
1990	TWO OF A KIND, J. Kritz, 14 days	29.50	70.00
1991	QUEEN OF THE GYPSIES, J. Kritz, 14 days.............	29.50	50.00
1992	NIGHT AT THE COPA, J. Kritz, 14 days	29.50	RI

		Issue Price	Current Value
1992	A RISING PROBLEM, J. Kritz, 14 days	29.50	RI

Japanese Blossoms of Autumn

1985	BELLFLOWER, Koseki and Ebihara, 10 days	45.00	NR
1985	ARROWROOT, Koseki and Ebihara, 10 days	45.00	NR
1985	WILD CARNATION, Koseki and Ebihara, 10 days	45.00	NR
1985	MAIDEN FLOWER, Koseki and Ebihara, 10 days	45.00	NR
1985	PAMPAS GRASS, Koseki and Ebihara, 10 days	45.00	NR
1985	BUSH CLOVER, Koseki and Ebihara, 10 days	45.00	NR
1985	PURPLE TROUSERS, Koseki and Ebihara, 10 days	45.00	NR

Japanese Floral Calendar

1981	NEW YEAR'S DAY, Shuho and Senkin Kage, 10 days	32.50	NR
1982	EARLY SPRING, Shuho and Senkin Kage, 10 days	32.50	NR
1982	SPRING, Shuho and Senkin Kage, 10 days	32.50	NR
1982	GIRL'S DOLL DAY FESTIVAL, Shuho and Senkin Kage, 10 days .	32.50	NR
1982	BUDDHA'S BIRTHDAY, Shuho and Senkin Kage, 10 days .	32.50	NR
1982	EARLY SUMMER, Shuho and Senkin Kage, 10 days	32.50	NR
1982	BOY'S DOLL DAY FESTIVAL, Shuho and Senkin Kage, 10 days .	32.50	NR
1982	SUMMER, Shuho and Senkin Kage, 10 days............	32.50	NR
1982	AUTUMN, Shuho and Senkin Kage, 10 days	32.50	NR
1983	FESTIVAL OF THE FULL MOON, Shuho and Senkin Kage, 10 days	32.50	NR
1983	LATE AUTUMN, Shuho and Senkin Kage, 10 days	32.50	NR
1983	WINTER, Shuho and Senkin Kage, 10 days.............	32.50	NR

Jeweled Hummingbirds Plate Collection

1989	RUBY–THROATED HUMMINGBIRDS, James Landenberger, 14 days	37.50	NR
1989	GREAT SAPPHIRE WING HUMMINGBIRDS, James Landenberger, 14 days	37.50	NR
1989	RUBY–TOPAZ HUMMINGBIRDS, James Landenberger, 14 days	37.50	NR
1989	ANDEAN EMERALD HUMMINGBIRDS, James Landenberger, 14 days	37.50	NR
1989	GARNET–THROATED HUMMINGBIRDS, James Landenberger, 14 days	37.50	NR
1989	BLUE–HEADED SAPPHIRE HUMMINGBIRDS, James Landenberger, 14 days	37.50	NR
1989	PEARL CORONET HUMMINGBIRDS, James Landenberger, 14 days	37.50	NR
1989	AMETHYST–THROATED SUNANGETS, James Landenberger, 14 days	37.50	NR

Last Warriors

1993	WINTER OF '41, C. Ren, 28 days	29.50	RI

		Issue Price	Current Value

Lisi Martin Christmas

1992	SANTA'S LITTLEST REINDEER, Lisi Martin, 28 days	29.50	RI
1993	NOT A CREATURE WAS STIRRING, Lisi Martin, 28 days ..	29.50	RI
1993	CHRISTMAS DREAMS, Lisi Martin, 28 days	29.50	RI
1993	THE CHRISTMAS STORY, Lisi Martin, 28 days	29.50	RI
1993	TRIMMING THE TREE, Lisi Martin, 28 days	29.50	RI
1993	A TASTE OF THE HOLIDAYS, Lisi Martin, 28 days	29.50	RI
1993	THE NIGHT BEFORE CHRISTMAS, Lisi Martin, 28 days ..	29.50	RI

Little House on the Prairie

1985	FOUNDER'S DAY PICNIC, Eugene Christopherson, 10 days	29.50	40.00
1985	THE WOMEN'S HARVEST, Eugene Christopherson, 10 days ..	29.50	NR
1985	MEDICINE SHOW, Eugene Christopherson, 10 days	29.50	NR
1985	CAROLINE'S EGGS, Eugene Christopherson, 10 days	29.50	NR
1985	MARY'S GIFT, Eugene Christopherson, 10 days	29.50	NR
1985	A BELL FOR WALNUT GROVE, Eugene Christopherson, 10 days	29.50	NR
1985	INGALLS' FAMILY CHRISTMAS, Eugene Christopherson, 10 days	29.50	NR
1985	THE SWEETHEART TREE, Eugene Christopherson, 10 days ...	29.50	NR

Little Ladies

1989	PLAYING BRIDESMAID, M. H. Bogart, 14 days	29.50	75.00
1990	THE SEAMSTRESS, M. H. Bogart, 14 days	29.50	50.00
1990	LITTLE CAPTIVE, M. H. Bogart, 14 days	29.50	45.00
1990	PLAYING MAMA, M. H. Bogart, 14 days	29.50	55.00
1990	SUSANNA, M. H. Bogart, 14 days	29.50	50.00
1990	KITTY'S BATH, M. H. Bogart, 14 days	29.50	55.00
1990	A DAY IN THE COUNTRY, M. H. Bogart, 14 days	29.50	50.00
1991	SARAH, M. H. Bogart, 14 days	29.50	45.00
1991	FIRST PARTY, M. H. Bogart, 14 days	29.50	NR
1991	THE MAGIC KITTEN, M. H. Bogart, 14 days	29.50	NR

Little Rascals

1985	THREE FOR THE SHOW, 10 days	24.50	35.00
1985	MY GAL, 10 days	24.50	NR
1985	SKELETON CREW, 10 days	24.50	NR
1985	ROUGHIN' IT, 10 days	24.50	NR
1985	SPANKY'S PRANKS, 10 days	24.50	NR
1985	BUTCH'S CHALLENGE, 10 days	24.50	NR
1985	DARLA'S DEBUT, 10 days	24.50	NR
1985	PETE'S PAL, 10 days	24.50	NR

Little Shopkeepers

1990	SEW TIRED, G. Gerardi, 15 days	29.50	NR
1991	BREAK TIME, G. Gerardi, 15 days	29.50	NR
1991	PURRFECT FIT, G. Gerardi, 15 days	29.50	NR
1991	TOYING AROUND, G. Gerardi, 15 days	29.50	35.00

		Issue Price	Current Value
1991	CHAIN REACTION, G. Gerardi, 15 days	29.50	45.00
1991	INFERIOR DECORATORS, G. Gerardi, 15 days	29.50	35.00
1991	TULIP TAG, G. Gerardi, 15 days	29.50	35.00
1991	CANDY CAPERS, G. Gerardi, 15 days	29.50	35.00

Lore of the West

1993	A MILE IN HIS MOCASSINS, L. Danielle, 28 days	29.50	RI

Lucy Collage

1993	LUCY, M. Weistling, 28 days	37.50	RI

Madonna and Child

1992	MADONNA DELLA SEIDA, R. Sanzio, 28 days	37.50	RI
1992	VIRGIN OF THE ROCKS, L. DaVinci, 28 days	37.50	RI
1992	MADONNA OF ROSARY, B. E. Murillo, 28 days..........	37.50	RI
1992	SISTINE MADONNA, R. Sanzio, 28 days	37.50	RI
1992	VIRGIN ADORING CHRIST CHILD, A. Correggio, 28 days .	37.50	RI
1992	VIRGIN OF THE GRAPE, P. Mignard, 28 days............	37.50	RI

Majestic Birds of Prey

1983	GOLDEN EAGLE, C. Ford Riley, 12,500	55.00	65.00
1983	COOPER'S HAWK, C. Ford Riley, 12,500	55.00	65.00
1983	GREAT HORNED OWL, C. Ford Riley, 12,500	55.00	65.00
1983	BALD EAGLE, C. Ford Riley, 12,500	55.00	65.00
1983	BARRED OWL, C. Ford Riley, 12,500	55.00	65.00
1983	SPARROW HAWK, C. Ford Riley, 12,500	55.00	65.00
1983	PEREGRINE FALCON, C. Ford Riley, 12,500	55.00	65.00
1983	OSPREY, C. Ford Riley, 12,500	55.00	65.00

Majesty of Flight

1989	THE EAGLE SOARS, T. Hirata, 14 days	37.50	50.00
1989	REALM OF THE RED–TAIL, T. Hirata, 14 days	37.50	NR
1989	COASTAL JOURNEY, T. Hirata, 14 days	37.50	45.00
1989	SENTRY OF THE NORTH, T. Hirata, 14 days	37.50	50.00
1989	COMMANDING THE MARSH, T. Hirata, 14 days	37.50	NR
1990	THE VANTAGE POINT, T. Hirata, 14 days	29.50	45.00
1990	SILENT WATCH, T. Hirata, 14 days	29.50	50.00
1990	FIERCE AND FREE, T. Hirata, 14 days	29.50	45.00

Man's Best Friend

1992	SPECIAL DELIVERY, L. Picken, 28 days................	29.50	RI
1992	MAKING WAVES, L. Picken, 28 days	29.50	RI
1992	GOOD CATCH, L. Picken, 28 days	29.50	RI
1993	TIME FOR A WALK, L. Picken, 28 days	29.50	RI

		Issue Price	Current Value
1993	FAITHFUL FRIEND, L. Picken, 28 days	29.50	RI
1993	LET'S PLAY BALL, L. Picken, 28 days	29.50	RI
1993	SITTING PRETTY, L. Picken, 28 days....................	29.50	RI
1993	BEDTIME STORY, L. Picken, 28 days...................	29.50	RI

Mixed Company

1990	TWO AGAINST ONE, P. Cooper, 14 days	29.50	NR
1990	A STICKY SITUATION, P. Cooper, 14 days	29.50	NR
1990	WHAT'S UP?, P. Cooper, 14 days	29.50	NR
1990	ALL WRAPPED UP, P. Cooper, 14 days................	29.50	NR
1990	PICTURE PERFECT, P. Cooper, 14 days	29.50	NR
1991	A MOMENT TO UNWIND, P. Cooper, 14 days	29.50	NR
1991	OLÉ, P. Cooper, 14 days	29.50	NR
1991	PICNIC PROWLERS, P. Cooper, 14 days	29.50	NR

Mystic Warriors

1992	DELIVERANCE, C. Ren, 28 days	29.50	RI
1992	MYSTIC WARRIOR, C. Ren, 28 days	29.50	RI
1992	SUN SEEKER, C. Ren, 28 days	29.50	RI
1992	TOP GUN, C. Ren, 28 days	29.50	RI
1992	MAN WHO WALKS ALONE, C. Ren, 28 days	29.50	RI
1992	WINDRIDER, C. Ren, 28 days	29.50	RI
1992	SPIRIT OF THE PLAINS, C. Ren, 28 days	29.50	RI
1993	BLUE THUNDER, C. Ren, 28 days	29.50	RI
1993	SUN GLOW, C. Ren, 28 days........................	29.50	RI
1993	PEACE MAKER, C. Ren, 28 days	29.50	RI

Nature's Nightime Realm

1992	BOBCAT, G. Murray, 28 days	29.50	RI
1992	COUGAR, G. Murray, 28 days.......................	29.50	RI
1993	JAGUAR, G. Murray, 28 days	29.50	RI
1993	WHITE TIGER, G. Murray, 28 days...................	29.50	RI
1993	LYNX, G. Murray, 28 days	29.50	RI
1993	LION, G. Murray, 28 days	29.50	RI
1993	SNOW LEOPARDS, G. Murray, 28 days	29.50	RI

Nature's Quiet Moments

1988	A CURIOUS PAIR, R. Parker, 14 days	37.50	NR
1988	NORTHERN MORNING, R. Parker, 14 days	37.50	NR
1988	JUST RESTING, R. Parker, 14 days....................	37.50	NR
1989	WAITING OUT THE STORM, R. Parker, 14 days	37.50	NR
1989	CREEKSIDE, R. Parker, 14 days......................	37.50	NR
1989	AUTUMN FORAGING, R. Parker, 14 days..............	37.50	NR
1989	OLD MAN OF THE MOUNTAIN, R. Parker, 14 days.......	37.50	NR
1989	MOUNTAIN BLOOMS, R. Parker, 14 days	37.50	NR

Noble American Indian Women

		Issue Price	Current Value
1989	SACAJAWEA, D. Wright, 14 days	29.50	45.00
1990	POCAHONTAS, D. Wright, 14 days	29.50	45.00
1990	MINNEHAHA, D. Wright, 14 days	29.50	35.00
1990	PINE LEAF, D. Wright, 14 days	29.50	45.00
1990	LILY OF THE MOHAWK, D. Wright, 14 days	29.50	35.00
1990	WHITE ROSE, D. Wright, 14 days	29.50	45.00
1991	LOZEN, D. Wright, 14 days	29.50	35.00
1991	FALLING STAR, D. Wright, 14 days	29.50	45.00

Noble Owls of America

1986	MORNING MIST, J. Seerey–Lester, 15,000	55.00	75.00
1987	PRAIRIE SUNDOWN, J. Seerey–Lester, 15,000	55.00	75.00
1987	WINTER VIGIL, J. Seerey–Lester, 15,000	55.00	75.00
1987	AUTUMN MIST, J. Seerey–Lester, 15,000	55.00	75.00
1987	DAWN IN THE WILLOWS, J. Seerey–Lester, 15,000	55.00	75.00
1987	SNOWY WATCH, J. Seerey–Lester, 15,000	55.00	90.00
1988	HIDING PLACE, J. Seerey–Lester, 15,000	55.00	75.00
1988	WAITING FOR DUSK, J. Seerey–Lester, 15,000	55.00	75.00

North American Ducks

1991	AUTUMN FLIGHT, R. Lawrence, 15 days	29.50	NR
1991	THE RESTING PLACE, R. Lawrence, 15 days	29.50	NR
1991	TWIN FLIGHT, R. Lawrence, 15 days	29.50	NR
1991	MISTY MORNING, R. Lawrence, 15 days	29.50	NR
1992	SPRINGTIME THAW, R. Lawrence, 15 days	29.50	RI
1992	SUMMER RETREAT, R. Lawrence, 15 days	29.50	RI
1992	OVERCAST, R. Lawrence, 15 days	29.50	RI
1992	PERFECT PINTAILS, R. Lawrence, 15 days	29.50	RI

North American Gamebirds

1990	RING–NECKED PHEASANT, J. Killen, 14 days	37.50	NR
1990	BOBWHITE QUAIL, J. Killen, 14 days	37.50	45.00
1990	RUFFED GROUSE, J. Killen, 14 days	37.50	NR
1990	GAMBEL QUAIL, J. Killen, 14 days	37.50	NR
1990	MOURNING DOVE, J. Killen, 14 days	37.50	45.00
1990	WOODCOCK, J. Killen, 14 days	37.50	45.00
1991	CHUKAR PARTRIDGE, J. Killen, 14 days	37.50	45.00
1991	WILD TURKEY, J. Killen, 14 days	37.50	45.00

North American Waterbirds

1988	WOOD DUCKS, R. Lawrence, 14 days	37.50	55.00
1988	HOODED MERGANSERS, R. Lawrence, 14 days	37.50	55.00
1988	PINTAILS, R. Lawrence, 14 days	37.50	45.00
1988	CANADA GEESE, R. Lawrence, 14 days	37.50	45.00
1989	AMERICAN WIDGEONS, R. Lawrence, 14 days	37.50	55.00

		Issue Price	Current Value
1989	CANVASBACKS, R. Lawrence, 14 days	37.50	55.00
1989	MALLARD PAIR, R. Lawrence, 14 days	37.50	60.00
1989	SNOW GEESE, R. Lawrence, 14 days	37.50	45.00

Nutcracker Ballet

1978	CLARA, Shell Fisher, 28 days	29.50	40.00
1979	GODFATHER, Shell Fisher, 28 days	29.50	NR
1979	SUGAR PLUM FAIRY, Shell Fisher, 28 days	29.50	NR
1979	SNOW QUEEN AND KING, Shell Fisher, 28 days	29.50	NR
1980	WALTZ OF THE FLOWERS, Shell Fisher, 28 days	29.50	NR
1980	CLARA AND THE PRINCE, Shell Fisher, 28 days	29.50	NR

Official Honeymooners Plate Collection

1987	THE HONEYMOONERS, D. Kilmer, 14 days	24.50	110.00
1987	THE HUCKLEBUCK, D. Kilmer, 14 days	24.50	55.00
1987	BABY, YOU'RE THE GREATEST, D. Kilmer, 14 days	24.50	55.00
1988	THE GOLFER, D. Kilmer, 14 days	24.50	75.00
1988	THE TV CHEFS, D. Kilmer, 14 days	24.50	50.00
1988	BANG! ZOOM!, D. Kilmer, 14 days	24.50	55.00
1988	THE ONLY WAY TO TRAVEL, D. Kilmer, 14 days	24.50	75.00
1988	THE HONEYMOON EXPRESS, D. Kilmer, 14 days	24.50	60.00

Our Cherished Seas

1992	WHALE SONG, Sy Barlowe, 48 days	37.50	RI
1992	LIONS OF THE SEA, Sy Barlowe, 48 days	37.50	RI
1992	FLIGHT OF THE DOLPHINS, Sy Barlowe, 48 days	37.50	RI
1992	PALACE OF THE SEALS, Sy Barlowe, 48 days	37.50	RI
1992	ORCA BALLET, Sy Barlowe, 48 days	37.50	RI
1992	EMPERORS OF THE ICE, Sy Barlowe, 48 days	37.50	RI
1992	SEA TURTLES, Sy Barlowe, 48 days	37.50	RI
1992	SPLENDOR OF THE SEA, Sy Barlowe, 48 days	37.50	RI

Passage to China

1983	EMPRESS OF CHINA, R. Massey, 15,000	55.00	NR
1983	ALLIANCE, R. Massey, 15,000	55.00	NR
1985	GRAND TURK, R. Massey, 15,000	55.00	NR
1985	SEA WITCH, R. Massey, 15,000	55.00	NR
1985	FLYING CLOUD, R. Massey, 15,000	55.00	NR
1985	ROMANCE OF THE SEAS, R. Massey, 15,000	55.00	NR
1985	SEA SERPENT, R. Massey, 15,000	55.00	NR
1985	CHALLENGE, R. Massey, 15,000	55.00	NR

Petals and Purrs

1988	BLUSHING BEAUTIES, B. Harrison, 14 days	24.50	45.00
1988	SPRING FEVER, B. Harrison, 14 days	24.50	40.00

		Issue Price	Current Value
1988	MORNING GLORIES, B. Harrison, 14 days.............	24.50	35.00
1988	FORGET–ME–NOT, B. Harrison, 14 days	24.50	35.00
1989	GOLDEN FANCY, B. Harrison, 14 days	24.50	30.00
1989	PINK LILIES, B. Harrison, 14 days	24.50	30.00
1989	SUMMER SUNSHINE, B. Harrison, 14 days	24.50	30.00
1989	SIAMESE SUMMER, B. Harrison, 14 days..............	24.50	30.00

Portraits from Oz

		Issue Price	Current Value
1989	DOROTHY, Thomas Blackshear, 14 days	29.50	100.00
1989	SCARECROW, Thomas Blackshear, 14 days	29.50	85.00
1989	TIN MAN, Thomas Blackshear, 14 days	29.50	85.00
1990	COWARDLY LION, Thomas Blackshear, 14 days	29.50	75.00
1990	GLINDA, Thomas Blackshear, 14 days.................	29.50	75.00
1990	WIZARD, Thomas Blackshear, 14 days	29.50	80.00
1990	WICKED WITCH, Thomas Blackshear, 14 days	29.50	80.00
1990	TOTO, Thomas Blackshear, 14 days	29.50	155.00

Portraits of the Bald Eagle

		Issue Price	Current Value
1993	RULER OF THE SKY, J. Pitcher, 28 days	37.50	RI
1993	IN BOLD DEFIANCE, J. Pitcher, 28 days................	37.50	RI
1993	MASTER OF THE SUMMER SKIES, J. Pitcher, 28 days ...	37.50	RI
1993	SPRING'S SENTINEL, J. Pitcher, 28 days	37.50	RI

Portraits of Childhood

		Issue Price	Current Value
1981	BUTTERFLY MAGIC, Thornton Utz, 28 days.............	24.95	35.00
1982	SWEET DREAMS, Thornton Utz, 28 days	24.95	NR
1983	TURTLE TALK, Thornton Utz, 28 days	24.95	NR
1984	FRIENDS FOREVER, Thornton Utz, 28 days	24.95	NR

Precious Moments

		Issue Price	Current Value
1979	FRIEND IN THE SKY, Thornton Utz, 28 days.............	21.50	50.00
1980	SAND IN HER SHOE, Thornton Utz, 28 days	21.50	35.00
1980	SNOW BUNNY, Thornton Utz, 28 days	21.50	30.00
1980	SEASHELLS, Thornton Utz, 28 days	21.50	30.00
1981	DAWN, Thornton Utz, 28 days	21.50	30.00
1982	MY KITTY, Thornton Utz, 28 days.....................	21.50	30.00

Precious Moments Bible Story

		Issue Price	Current Value
1991	COME LET US ADORE HIM, Samuel Butcher, 28 days ...	29.50	NR
1992	THEY FOLLOWED THE STAR, Samuel Butcher, 28 days ..	29.50	RI
1992	THE FLIGHT INTO EGYPT, Samuel Butcher, 28 days	29.50	RI
1992	THE CARPENTER SHOP, Samuel Butcher, 28 days	29.50	RI
1992	JESUS IN THE TEMPLE, Samuel Butcher, 28 days.......	29.50	RI
1992	THE CRUCIFIXION, Samuel Butcher, 28 days	29.50	RI
1993	HE IS NOT HERE, Samuel Butcher, 28 days	29.50	RI

		Issue Price	Current Value
Precious Moments Classics			
1993	GOD LOVETH A CHEERFUL GIVER, Samuel Butcher, 28 days . .	35.00	RI
1993	A JOYFUL NOISE, Samuel Butcher, 28 days	35.00	RI
Precious Portraits			
1987	SUNBEAM, Bessie Pease Gutmann, 14 days	24.50	NR
1987	MISCHIEF, Bessie Pease Gutmann, 14 days	24.50	35.00
1987	PEACH BLOSSOM, Bessie Pease Gutmann, 14 days	24.50	35.00
1987	GOLDILOCKS, Bessie Pease Gutmann, 14 days	24.50	40.00
1987	FAIRY GOLD, Bessie Pease Gutmann, 14 days	24.50	40.00
1987	BUNNY, Bessie Pease Gutmann, 14 days	24.50	40.00
Princesses of the Plains			
1993	PRAIRIE FLOWER, D. Wright, 28 days	29.50	RI
1993	SNOW PRINCESS, D. Wright, 28 days	29.50	RI
1993	WILD FLOWER, D. Wright, 28 days	29.50	RI
1993	NOBLE BEAUTY, D. Wright, 28 days	29.50	RI
Proud Indian Families			
1991	THE STORYTELLER, K. Freeman, 15 days	29.50	35.00
1991	THE POWER OF THE BASKET, K. Freeman, 15 days	29.50	35.00
1991	THE NAMING CEREMONY, K. Freeman, 15 days	29.50	35.00
1992	PLAYING WITH TRADITION, K. Freeman, 15 days	29.50	RI
1992	PREPARING THE BERRY HARVEST, K. Freeman, 15 days .	29.50	RI
1992	CEREMONIAL DRESS, K. Freeman, 15 days	29.50	RI
1992	SOUNDS OF THE FOREST, K. Freeman, 15 days	29.50	RI
1992	THE MARRIAGE CEREMONY, K. Freeman, 15 days	29.50	RI
1993	THE JEWELRY MAKER, K. Freeman, 15 days	29.50	RI
1993	BEAUTIFUL CREATIONS, K. Freeman, 15 days	29.50	RI
Proud Nation			
1989	NAVAJO LITTLE ONE, R. Swanson, 14 days	24.50	45.00
1989	IN A BIG LAND, R. Swanson, 14 days	24.50	35.00
1989	OUT WITH MAMA'S FLOCK, R. Swanson, 14 days	24.50	35.00
1989	NEWEST LITTLE SHEEPHERDER, R. Swanson, 14 days . .	24.50	35.00
1989	DRESSED UP FOR THE POWWOW, R. Swanson, 14 days .	24.50	35.00
1989	JUST A FEW DAYS OLD, R. Swanson, 14 days	24.50	40.00
1989	AUTUMN TREAT, R. Swanson, 14 days	24.50	45.00
1989	UP IN THE RED ROCKS, R. Swanson, 14 days	24.50	30.00
Quiet Moments of Childhood			
1991	ELIZABETH'S AFTERNOON TEA, D. Green, 14 days	29.50	NR
1991	CHRISTINA'S SECRET GARDEN, D. Green, 15 days	29.50	NR
1991	ERIC AND ERIN'S STORYTIME, D. Green, 15 days	29.50	NR
1992	JESSICA'S TEA PARTY, D. Green, 15 days	29.50	RI
1992	MEGAN AND MONIQUE'S BAKERY, D. Green, 15 days . . .	29.50	RI

		Issue Price	Current Value
1992	CHILDREN'S DAY BY THE SEA, D. Green, 15 days	29.50	RI
1992	JORDAN'S PLAYFUL PUPS, D. Green, 15 days	29.50	RI
1992	DANIEL'S MORNING PLAYTIME, D. Green, 15 days	29.50	RI

Quilted Countryside: Mel Steele Signature Collection

1991	THE OLD COUNTRY STORE, M. Steele, 15 days	29.50	NR
1991	WINTER'S END, M. Steele, 15 days	29.50	NR
1991	THE QUILTER'S CABIN, M. Steele, 15 days	29.50	NR
1991	SPRING CLEANING, M. Steele, 15 days	29.50	NR
1991	SUMMER HARVEST, M. Steele, 15 days	29.50	NR
1991	THE COUNTRY MERCHANT, M. Steele, 15 days	29.50	NR
1992	WASH DAY, M. Steele, 15 days	29.50	RI
1992	THE ANTIQUES STORE, M. Steele, 15 days	29.50	RI

Republic Pictures Film Library Collection

1992	SHOW WITH LAREDO, Susan Morton, 28 days	37.50	RI
1992	THE RIDE HOME, Susan Morton, 28 days	37.50	RI
1992	ATTACK AT TARAWA, Susan Morton, 28 days	37.50	RI
1992	THOUGHTS OF ANGELIQUE, Susan Morton, 28 days	37.50	RI
1992	WAR OF THE WILDCATS, Susan Morton, 28 days	37.50	RI
1992	THE FIGHTING SEABEES, Susan Morton, 28 days	37.50	RI
1992	THE QUIET MAN, Susan Morton, 28 days	37.50	RI
1992	ANGEL AND THE BADMAN, Susan Morton, 28 days	37.50	RI
1992	SANDS OF IWO JIMA, Susan Morton, 28 days	37.50	RI
1992	FLYING TIGERS, Susan Morton, 28 days	37.50	RI

Rockwell Home of the Brave

1981	REMINISCING, Norman Rockwell, 18,000	35.00	75.00
1981	HERO'S WELCOME, Norman Rockwell, 18,000	35.00	50.00
1981	BACK TO HIS OLD JOB, Norman Rockwell, 18,000	35.00	NR
1981	WAR HERO, Norman Rockwell, 18,000	35.00	NR
1982	WILLIE GILLIS IN CHURCH, Norman Rockwell, 18,000	35.00	NR
1982	WAR BOND, Norman Rockwell, 18,000	35.00	NR
1982	UNCLE SAM TAKES WINGS, Norman Rockwell, 18,000	35.00	NR
1982	TAKING MOTHER OVER THE TOP, Norman Rockwell, 18,000	35.00	NR

Rockwell's Saturday Evening Post Baseball Plates

1992	100TH YEAR OF BASEBALL, Norman Rockwell, open	19.50	RI
1993	THE ROOKIE, Norman Rockwell, open	19.50	RI
1993	THE DUGOUT, Norman Rockwell, open	19.50	RI
1993	BOTTOM OF THE SIXTH, Norman Rockwell, open	19.50	RI

Romantic Castles of Europe

1990	LUDWIG'S CASTLE, D. Sweet, 19,500	55.00	NR

		Issue Price	Current Value
1991	PALACE OF THE MOORS, D. Sweet, 19,500	55.00	NR
1991	SWISS ISLE FORTRESS, D. Sweet, 19,500	55.00	NR
1991	THE LEGENDARY CASTLE OF LEEDS, D. Sweet, 19,500	55.00	NR
1991	DAVINCI'S CHAMBORD, D. Sweet, 19,500	55.00	NR
1991	EILEAN DONAN, D. Sweet, 19,500	55.00	NR
1992	ELTZ CASTLE, D. Sweet, 19,500	55.00	RI
1992	KYLEMORE ABBEY, D. Sweet, 19,500	55.00	RI

Romantic Victorian Keepsake

1992	DEAREST KISS, J. Grossman, 28 days	35.00	RI
1993	FIRST LOVE, J. Grossman, 28 days	35.00	RI
1993	AS FAIR AS A ROSE, J. Grossman, 28 days	35.00	RI
1993	SPRINGTIME BEAUTY, J. Grossman, 28 days	35.00	RI
1993	SUMMERTIME FANCY, J. Grossman, 28 days	35.00	RI
1993	BONNIE BLUE EYES, J. Grossman, 28 days	35.00	RI

Saturday Evening Post Plate Collection

1989	THE WONDERS OF RADIO, Norman Rockwell, 14 days	35.00	60.00
1989	EASTER MORNING, Norman Rockwell, 14 days	35.00	55.00
1989	THE FACTS OF LIFE, Norman Rockwell, 14 days	35.00	45.00
1990	THE WINDOW WASHER, Norman Rockwell, 14 days	35.00	45.00
1990	FIRST FLIGHT, Norman Rockwell, 14 days	35.00	55.00
1990	TRAVELING COMPANION, Norman Rockwell, 14 days	35.00	50.00
1990	JURY ROOM, Norman Rockwell, 14 days	35.00	50.00
1990	FURLOUGH, Norman Rockwell, 14 days	35.00	45.00

Seasons of the Bald Eagle

1991	AUTUMN IN THE MOUNTAINS, J. Pitcher, 14 days	37.50	NR
1991	WINTER IN THE VALLEY, J. Pitcher, 14 days	37.50	NR
1991	SPRING ON THE RIVER, J. Pitcher, 14 days	37.50	NR
1991	SUMMER ON THE SEACOAST, J. Pitcher, 14 days	37.50	NR

Small Wonders of the Wild

1989	HIDEAWAY, Charles Frace, 14 days	29.50	NR
1990	YOUNG EXPLORERS, Charles Frace, 14 days	29.50	NR
1990	THREE OF A KIND, Charles Frace, 14 days	29.50	75.00
1990	QUIET MORNING, Charles Frace, 14 days	29.50	NR
1990	EYES OF WONDER, Charles Frace, 14 days	29.50	NR
1990	READY FOR ADVENTURE, Charles Frace, 14 days	29.50	NR
1990	UNO, Charles Frace, 14 days	29.50	NR
1990	EXPLORING A NEW WORLD, Charles Frace, 14 days	29.50	NR

Spock® Commemorative Wall Plaque

1993	SPOCK® COMMEMORATIVE WALL PLAQUE, 2,500	195.00	RI

Sporting Generation

		Issue Price	Current Value
1991	LIKE FATHER, LIKE SON, J. Lamb, 14 days	29.50	NR
1991	GOLDEN MOMENTS, J. Lamb, 14 days	29.50	NR
1991	THE LOOKOUT, J. Lamb, 14 days	29.50	NR
1992	PICKING UP THE SCENT, J. Lamb, 14 days	29.50	RI
1992	FIRST TIME OUT, J. Lamb, 14 days	29.50	RI
1992	WHO'S TRACKING WHO?, J. Lamb, 14 days	29.50	RI
1992	SPRINGING INTO ACTION, J. Lamb, 14 days	29.50	RI
1992	POINT OF INTEREST, J. Lamb, 14 days	29.50	RI

Springtime of Life

1985	TEDDY'S BATHTIME, Thornton Utz, 14 days	29.50	NR
1985	JUST LIKE MOMMY, Thornton Utz, 14 days	29.50	NR
1985	AMONG THE DAFFODILS, Thornton Utz, 14 days	29.50	NR
1985	MY FAVORITE DOLLS, Thornton Utz, 14 days	29.50	NR
1985	AUNT TILLIE'S HATS, Thornton Utz, 14 days	29.50	NR
1985	LITTLE EMILY, Thornton Utz, 14 days	29.50	NR
1985	GRANNY'S BOOTS, Thornton Utz, 14 days	29.50	NR
1985	MY MASTERPIECE, Thornton Utz, 14 days	29.50	NR

Stained Glass Gardens

1989	PEACOCK AND WISTERIA, 15,000	55.00	NR
1989	GARDEN SUNSET, 15,000	55.00	NR
1989	THE COCKATOO'S GARDEN, 15,000	55.00	NR
1989	WATERFALL AND IRIS, 15,000	55.00	NR
1990	ROSES AND MAGNOLIAS, 15,000	55.00	NR
1990	A HOLLYHOCK SUNRISE, 15,000	55.00	NR
1990	PEACEFUL WATERS, 15,000	55.00	NR
1990	SPRINGTIME IN THE VALLEY, 15,000	55.00	NR

Star Trek: The Next Generation

1993	CAPTAIN JEAN–LUC PICARD, Thomas Blackshear, 28 days	35.00	RI
1993	COMMANDER WILLIAM RIKER, Thomas Blackshear, 28 days	35.00	RI

Star Trek 25th Anniversary Commemorative Collection

1991	SPOCK, Thomas Blackshear, 14 days	35.00	85.00
1991	KIRK, Thomas Blackshear, 14 days	35.00	55.00
1992	MCCOY, Thomas Blackshear, 14 days	35.00	RI
1992	UHURA, Thomas Blackshear, 14 days	35.00	RI
1992	SCOTTY, Thomas Blackshear, 14 days	35.00	RI
1993	SULU, Thomas Blackshear, 14 days	35.00	RI
1993	CHEKOV, Thomas Blackshear, 14 days	35.00	RI

Star Trek 25th Anniversary Commemorative Plate

1991	STAR TREK 25TH ANNIVERSARY COMMEMORATIVE PLATE, Thomas Blackshear, 14 days	37.50	75.00

Star Wars	Issue Price	Current Value
1987 HAN SOLO, Thomas Blackshear, 14 days	29.50	NR
1007 R2–D2 AND WICKET, Thomas Blackshear, 14 days	29.50	50.00
1987 LUKE SKYWALKER AND DARTH VADER, Thomas Blackshear, 14 days	29.50	65.00
1987 PRINCESS LEIA, Thomas Blackshear, 14 days	29.50	65.00
1987 THE IMPERIAL WALKERS, Thomas Blackshear, 14 days	29.50	65.00
1987 LUKE AND YODA, Thomas Blackshear, 14 days	29.50	65.00
1987 SPACE BATTLE, Thomas Blackshear, 14 days	29.50	300.00
1987 CREW IN COCKPIT, Thomas Blackshear, 14 days	29.50	70.00

Star Wars 10th Anniversary Commemorative

1990 STAR WARS 10TH ANNIVERSARY COMMEMORATIVE PLATE, Thomas Blackshear, 15 days	39.50	95.00

Star Wars Trilogy

1993 STAR WARS, M. Weistling, 28 days	37.50	RI
1993 THE EMPIRE STRIKES BACK, M. Weisting, 28 days	37.50	RI
1993 RETURN OF THE JEDI, M. Weisting, 28 days	37.50	RI

Stars of the Circus

1983 GUNTHER GEBEL–WILLIAMS, Franklin Moody, limited	29.50	NR

Story of Heidi

1981 HEIDI, 14,750	45.00	NR
1981 GRANDFATHER, 14,750	45.00	NR
1981 GRANDMOTHER, 14,750	45.00	NR
1981 HEIDI AND PETER, 14,750	45.00	NR
1982 KITTENS, 14,750	45.00	NR
1982 MOUNTAIN CURE, 14,750	45.00	NR

Story of Noah's Ark

1981 TWO BY TWO...EVERY LIVING CREATURE, Laetitia, 12,500	45.00	NR
1982 IN DIVINE HARMONY, Laetitia, 12,500	45.00	NR
1982 FINALLY A RAINBOW, Laetitia, 12,500	45.00	NR
1982 THE ARK BECKONS, Laetitia, 12,500	45.00	NR

Summer Days of Childhood

1983 MOUNTAIN FRIENDS, Thornton Utz, 10 days	29.50	NR
1983 GARDEN MAGIC, Thornton Utz, 10 days	29.50	NR
1983 LITTLE BEACHCOMBER, Thornton Utz, 10 days	29.50	NR
1983 BLOWING BUBBLES, Thornton Utz, 10 days	29.50	NR
1983 THE BIRTHDAY PARTY, Thornton Utz, 10 days	29.50	NR
1983 PLAYING DOCTOR, Thornton Utz, 10 days	29.50	NR
1983 A STOLEN KISS, Thornton Utz, 10 days	29.50	NR
1983 KITTY'S BATHTIME, Thornton Utz, 10 days	29.50	NR

		Issue Price	Current Value
1983	COOLING OFF, Thornton Utz, 10 days.................	29.50	NR
1983	FIRST CUSTOMER, Thornton Utz, 10 days.............	29.50	NR
1983	A JUMPING CONTEST, Thornton Utz, 10 days..........	29.50	NR
1983	BALLOON CARNIVAL, Thornton Utz, 10 days	29.50	NR

Mountain Friends
Photo courtesy of *Collectors News*

Tale of Genji

1985	SERENE AUTUMN MOON, Shigekasu Hotta, 10 days	45.00	NR
1985	DRAGON AND PHOENIX BOATS, Shigekasu Hotta, 10 days ..	45.00	NR
1985	ROMANTIC DUET, Shigekasu Hotta, 10 days	45.00	NR
1985	WAVES OF THE BLUE OCEAN DANCE, Shigekasu Hotta, 10 days	45.00	NR
1985	EVENING FACES, Shigekasu Hotta, 10 days	45.00	NR
1985	THE ARCHERY MEET, Shigekasu Hotta, 10 days	45.00	NR
1985	MOON VIEWING, Shigekasu Hotta, 10 days	45.00	NR
1985	THE TABLE GAME, Shigekasu Hotta, 10 days	45.00	NR

Thornton Utz 10th Anniversary Commemorative

1989	DAWN, Thornton Utz, 14 days	29.50	NR
1989	JUST LIKE MOMMY, Thornton Utz, 14 days	29.50	NR
1989	PLAYING DOCTOR, Thornton Utz, 14 days	29.50	NR
1989	MY KITTY, Thornton Utz, 14 days	29.50	NR
1989	TURTLE TALK, Thornton Utz, 14 days	29.50	NR
1989	BEST FRIENDS, Thornton Utz, 14 days	29.50	NR
1989	AMONG THE DAFFODILS, Thornton Utz, 14 days	29.50	NR
1989	FRIENDS IN THE SKY, Thornton Utz, 14 days...........	29.50	NR
1989	TEDDY'S BATHTIME, Thornton Utz, 14 days	29.50	NR
1989	LITTLE EMILY, Thornton Utz, 14 days	29.50	NR

		Issue Price	Current Value

Timeless Expressions of the Orient

		Issue Price	Current Value
1990	FIDELITY, M. Tsang, 15,000	75.00	95.00
1991	FEMININITY, M. Tsang, 15,000	75.00	NR
1991	LONGEVITY, M. Tsang, 15,000	75.00	NR
1991	BEAUTY, M. Tsang, 15,000	55.00	NR
1992	COURAGE, M. Tsang, 15,000	55.00	RI

Treasured Days

1987	ASHLEY, Higgins Bond, 14 days	24.50	45.00
1987	CHRISTOPHER, Higgins Bond, 14 days	24.50	45.00
1987	SARA, Higgins Bond, 14 days	24.50	30.00
1987	JEREMY, Higgins Bond, 14 days	24.50	45.00
1987	AMANDA, Higgins Bond, 14 days	24.50	45.00
1988	NICHOLAS, Higgins Bond, 14 days	24.50	45.00
1988	LINDSAY, Higgins Bond, 14 days	24.50	45.00
1988	JUSTIN, Higgins Bond, 14 days	24.50	45.00

Treasures of the Chinese Mandarins

Note: The designs for this series are adaptations of art objects found in the National Palace Museum in Taipei, Taiwan.

1981	THE BIRD OF PARADISE, 2,500	75.00	135.00
1982	THE GUARDIANS OF HEAVEN, 2,500	75.00	105.00
1982	THE TREE OF IMMORTALITY, 2,500	75.00	95.00
1982	THE DRAGON OF ETERNITY, 2,500	75.00	85.00

Unbridled Spirit

1992	SURF DANCER, C. DeHaan, 28 days	29.50	RI
1992	WINTER RENEGADE, C. DeHaan, 28 days	29.50	RI
1992	DESERT SHADOWS, C. DeHaan, 28 days	29.50	RI
1993	PAINTED SUNRISE, C. DeHaan, 28 days	29.50	RI
1993	DESERT DUEL, C. DeHaan, 28 days	29.50	RI
1993	MIDNIGHT RUN, C. DeHaan, 28 days	29.50	RI
1993	MOONLIGHT MAJESTY, C. DeHaan, 28 days	29.50	RI
1993	AUTUMN REVERIE, C. DeHaan, 28 days	29.50	RI
1993	BLIZZARD'S PERIL, C. DeHaan, 28 days	29.50	RI

Utz Mother's Day

1983	A GIFT OF LOVE, Thorton Utz, 1 year	27.50	40.00
1983	MOTHER'S HELPING HAND, Thorton Utz, 1 year	27.50	NR
1983	MOTHER'S ANGEL, Thorton Utz, 1 year	27.50	NR

Vanishing Rural America

1991	QUIET REFLECTIONS, J. Harrison, 14 days	29.50	45.00
1991	AUTUMN'S PASSAGE, J. Harrison, 14 days	29.50	45.00
1991	STOREFRONT MEMORIES, J. Harrison, 14 days	29.50	45.00
1991	COUNTRY PATH, J. Harrison, 14 days	29.50	35.00

		Issue Price	Current Value
1991	WHEN THE CIRCUS CAME TO TOWN, J. Harrison, 14 days	29.50	35.00
1991	COVERED IN FALL, J. Harrison, 14 days	29.50	45.00
1991	AMERICA'S HEARTLAND, J. Harrison, 14 days	29.50	35.00
1991	RURAL DELIVERY, J. Harrison, 14 days	29.50	35.00

Victorian Christmas Memories

1992	A VISIT FROM ST. NICHOLAS, J. Grossman, 28 days	29.50	RI
1993	CHRISTMAS DELIVERY, J. Grossman, 28 days	29.50	RI
1993	CHRISTMAS ANGELS, J. Grossman, 28 days	29.50	RI

Victorian Playtime

1991	A BUSY DAY, M. H. Bogart, 15 days	29.50	NR
1991	LITTLE MASTERPIECE, M. H. Bogart, 15 days	29.50	NR
1991	PLAYING BRIDE, M. H. Bogart, 15 days	29.50	NR
1991	WAITING FOR A NIBBLE, M. H. Bogart, 15 days	29.50	NR
1991	TEA AND GOSSIP, M. H. Bogart, 15 days	29.50	NR
1991	CLEANING HOUSE, M. H. Bogart, 15 days	29.50	NR
1991	A LITTLE PERSUASION, M. H. Bogart, 15 days	29.50	NR
1991	PEEK–A–BOO, M. H. Bogart, 15 days	29.50	NR

West of Frank McCarthy

1991	ATTACKING THE IRON HORSE, Frank McCarthy, 14 days	37.50	55.00
1991	ATTEMPT ON THE STAGE, Frank McCarthy, 14 days	37.50	50.00
1991	THE PRAYER, Frank McCarthy, 14 days	37.50	50.00
1991	ON THE OLD NORTH TRAIL, Frank McCarthy, 14 days	37.50	50.00
1991	THE HOSTILE THREAT, Frank McCarthy, 14 days	37.50	45.00
1991	BRINGING OUT THE FURS, Frank McCarthy, 14 days	37.50	45.00
1991	KIOWA RAIDER, Frank McCarthy, 14 days	37.50	45.00
1991	HEADED NORTH, Frank McCarthy, 14 days	37.50	NR

Winged Reflections

1989	FOLLOWING MAMA, R. Parker, 14 days	37.50	NR
1989	ABOVE THE BREAKERS, R. Parker, 14 days	37.50	NR
1989	AMONG THE REEDS, R. Parker, 14 days	37.50	NR
1989	FREEZE UP, R. Parker, 14 days	37.50	NR
1989	WINGS ABOVE THE WATER, R. Parker, 14 days	29.50	NR
1990	SUMMER LOON, R. Parker, 14 days	29.50	NR
1990	EARLY SPRING, R. Parker, 14 days	29.50	NR
1990	AT THE WATER'S EDGE, R. Parker, 14 days	29.50	NR

Winter Rails

1992	WINTER CROSSING, Theodore Xaras, 28 days	29.50	RI
1993	COAL COUNTRY, Theodore Xaras, 28 days	29.50	RI
1993	DAYLIGHT RUN, Theodore Xaras, 28 days	29.50	RI

		Issue Price	Current Value
1993	BY SEA OR RAIL, Theodore Xaras, 28 days	29.50	RI
1993	COUNTRY CROSSROADS, Theodore Xaras, 28 days	29.50	RI
1993	TIMBER LINE, Theodore Xaras, 28 days	29.50	RI
1993	THE LONG HAUL, Theodore Xaras, 28 days	29.50	RI

Winter Wildlife

1989	CLOSE ENCOUNTERS, J. Seerey–Lester, 15,000	55.00	NR
1989	AMONG THE CATTAILS, J. Seerey–Lester, 15,000	55.00	NR
1989	THE REFUGE, J. Seerey–Lester, 15,000	55.00	NR
1989	OUT OF THE BLIZZARD, J. Seerey–Lester, 15,000	55.00	NR
1989	FIRST SNOW, J. Seerey–Lester, 15,000	55.00	NR
1989	LYING IN WAIT, J. Seerey–Lester, 15,000	55.00	NR
1989	WINTER HIDING, J. Seerey–Lester, 15,000.............	55.00	NR
1989	EARLY SNOW, J. Seerey–Lester, 15,000	55.00	NR

Wizard of Oz Commemorative

1988	WE'RE OFF TO SEE THE WIZARD, Thomas Blackshear, 14 days	24.50	175.00
1988	DOROTHY MEETS THE SCARECROW, Thomas Blackshear, 14 days	24.50	110.00
1989	THE TIN MAN SPEAKS, Thomas Blackshear, 14 days	24.50	130.00
1989	A GLIMPSE OF THE MUNCHKINS, Thomas Blackshear, 14 days	24.50	110.00
1989	THE WITCH CASTS A SPELL, Thomas Blackshear, 14 days	24.50	115.00
1989	IF I WERE KING OF THE FOREST, Thomas Blackshear, 14 days	24.50	100.00
1989	THE GREAT AND POWERFUL OZ, Thomas Blackshear, 14 days	24.50	100.00
1989	THERE'S NO PLACE LIKE HOME, Thomas Blackshear, 14 days	24.50	100.00

Wonder of Christmas

1991	SANTA'S SECRET, John McClelland, 28 days	29.50	NR
1992	MY FAVORITE ORNAMENT, John McClelland, 28 days ...	29.50	RI
1992	WAITING FOR SANTA, John McClelland, 28 days	29.50	RI
1993	THE CAROLER, John McClelland, 28 days	29.50	RI

Woodland Encounters

1991	WANT TO PLAY?, G. Giordano, 14 days	29.50	NR
1991	PEEK–A–BOO!, G. Giordano, 14 days...................	29.50	NR
1991	LUNCHTIME VISITOR, G. Giordano, 14 days	29.50	NR
1991	ANYONE FOR A SWIM?, G. Giordano, 14 days	29.50	NR
1991	NATURE SCOUTS, G. Giordano, 14 days	29.50	NR
1991	MEADOW MEETING, G. Giordano, 14 days	29.50	NR
1991	HI NEIGHBOR, G. Giordano, 14 days..................	29.50	NR
1992	FIELD DAY, G. Giordano, 14 days	29.50	RI

World of Zolan

1992	FIRST KISS, Donald Zolan, 28 days	29.50	RI

			Issue Price	Current Value
1992	MORNING DISCOVERY, Donald Zolan, 28 days		29.50	RI
1993	LITTLE FISHERMAN, Donald Zolan, 28 days		29.50	RI
1993	LETTER TO GRANDMA, Donald Zolan, 28 days		29.50	RI
1993	TWILIGHT PRAYER, Donald Zolan, 28 days		29.50	RI
1993	FLOWERS FOR MOTHER, Donald Zolan, 28 days		29.50	RI

Year of the Wolf

1993	BROKEN SILENCE, A. Agnew, 28 days	29.50	RI
1993	LEADER OF THE PACK, A. Agnew, 28 days	29.50	RI

Single Issues

1983	PRINCESS GRACE, Thornton Utz, 21 days	39.50	55.00
1993	THE OFFICIAL HONEYMOONER'S COMMEMORATIVE PLATE, D. Bobnick, 28 days...............................	37.50	RI

HAMILTON MINT UNITED STATES

Kennedy

1974	Gold on pewter, 1 year...............................	40.00	NR
1974	Pewter, 1 year	25.00	40.00

Picasso (Sculpted by Alfred Brunettin)

Note: This series was also produced in 18K gold in editions of only 51.

1972	LE GOURMET, sterling silver, 5,000	125.00	NR
1972	THE TRAGEDY, sterling silver, 5,000..................	125.00	NR
1973	THE LOVERS, sterling silver, 5,000	125.00	NR

Single Issue

1971	ST. PATRICK, H. Alvin Sharpe........................	75.00	NR

HAMPTON HOUSE STUDIOS

Single Issue

1977	NANCY WARD/CHEROKEE NATION, B. Hampton, 3,000 ..	48.00	300.00

HANTAN PORCELAIN WORKS CHINA

Chinese and American Historical (China Trade Corporation)

1982	THE EAGLE AND THE PANDA, Zhu Bohua, 10,000.......	195.00	215.00

HAVILAND FRANCE

Bicentennial	Issue Price	Current Value
1972 BURNING OF THE GASPEE, Remy Hetreau, 10,000	39.95	45.00
1973 BOSTON TEA PARTY, Remy Hetreau, 10,000	39.95	NR
1974 CONTINENTAL CONGRESS, Remy Hetreau, 10,000	39.95	NR
1975 PAUL REVERE, Remy Hetreau, 10,000	39.95	50.00
1976 THE DECLARATION, Remy Hetreau, 10,000	39.95	45.00

Christmas

	Issue Price	Current Value
1970 PARTRIDGE, Remy Hetreau, 30,000	25.00	110.00
1971 TWO TURTLE DOVES, Remy Hetreau, 30,000	25.00	45.00
1972 THREE FRENCH HENS, Remy Hetreau, 30,000	27.50	40.00
1973 FOUR CALLING BIRDS, Remy Hetreau, 30,000	27.50	40.00
1974 FIVE GOLDEN RINGS, Remy Hetreau, 30,000	30.00	NR
1975 SIX GEESE A–LAYING, Remy Hetreau, 30,000	32.50	BR
1976 SEVEN SWANS, Remy Hetreau, 30,000	38.00	BR
1977 EIGHT MAIDS, Remy Hetreau, 30,000	40.00	45.00
1978 NINE LADIES DANCING, Remy Hetreau, 30,000	45.00	NR
1979 TEN LORDS A–LEAPING, Remy Hetreau, 30,000	50.00	NR
1980 ELEVEN PIPERS PIPING, Remy Hetreau, 30,000	55.00	NR
1981 TWELVE DRUMMERS, Remy Hetreau, 30,000	60.00	NR

Fleurs et Rubans

	Issue Price	Current Value
1981 ORCHIDEE, 5,000	120.00	NR
1981 LYS, 7,500	120.00	NR
1981 PIVOINE, 7,500	120.00	NR
1981 PAVOT (POPPY), 7,500	120.00	NR
1981 AIL SAUVAGE (WILD GARLIC), 7,500	120.00	NR
1982 HIBISCUS, 7,500	120.00	NR

French Collection Mother's Day

	Issue Price	Current Value
1973 BREAKFAST, Remy Hetreau, 10,000	29.95	BR
1974 THE WASH, Remy Hetreau, 10,000	29.95	BR
1975 IN THE PARK, Remy Hetreau, 10,000	30.00	NR
1976 TO MARKET, Remy Hetreau, 10,000	38.00	NR
1977 WASH BEFORE DINNER, Remy Hetreau, 10,000	38.00	NR
1978 AN EVENING AT HOME, Remy Hetreau, 10,000	40.00	NR
1979 HAPPY MOTHER'S DAY, Remy Hetreau, 10,000	30.00	45.00
1980 A CHILD AND HIS ANIMALS, Remy Hetreau, 10,000	55.00	NR

Historical

	Issue Price	Current Value
1968 MARTHA WASHINGTON, 2,500	35.00	80.00
1969 LINCOLN, 2,500	100.00	BR
1970 GRANT, 3,000	100.00	BR
1971 HAYES, 2,500	100.00	BR

		Issue Price	Current Value

1001 Arabian Nights

1979	MAGIC HORSE, Liliane Tellier, 5,000	54.50	NR
1980	ALADDIN AND HIS LAMP, Liliane Tellier, 5,000	54.50	NR
1981	SCHEHERAZADE, Liliane Tellier, 5,000	54.50	NR
1982	SINBAD THE SAILOR, Liliane Tellier, 5,000	54.50	NR

Theatre des Saisons

1978	SPRING, 5,000	120.00	140.00
1978	SUMMER, 5,000	120.00	140.00
1978	AUTUMN, 5,000	120.00	140.00
1978	WINTER, 5,000	120.00	140.00

Traditional Christmas Cards

| 1986 | DECK THE HALLS, Elisa Stone, 2,000 | 75.00 | NR |

Visit from Saint Nicholas

1980	NIGHT BEFORE CHRISTMAS, 1 year	55.00	NR
1981	CHILDREN WERE NESTLED, 5,000	60.00	NR
1982	FOR YOU, SANTA, 5,000	60.00	NR
1982	WHEN WHAT TO MY WONDERING EYES..., 1,500	60.00	NR
1985	HAPPY CHRISTMAS TO ALL, Loretta Jones	60.00	NR

HAVILAND AND PARLON FRANCE

Christmas Madonnas

1972	MADONNA AND CHILD, Raphael, 5,000	35.00	80.00
1973	MADONNINA, Feruzzi, 5,000	40.00	100.00
1974	COWPER MADONNA AND CHILD, Raphael, 5,000	42.50	60.00
1975	MADONNA AND CHILD, Murillo, 5,000	42.50	NR
1976	MADONNA AND CHILD, Botticelli, 5,000	45.00	NR
1977	MADONNA AND CHILD, Bellini, 5,000	48.00	55.00
1978	MADONNA AND CHILD, Fra Filippo Lippi, 7,500	48.00	70.00
1979	MADONNA OF THE EUCHARIST, Botticelli, 7,500	49.50	100.00

Lady and the Unicorn

1977	TO MY ONLY DESIRE, 20,000	45.00	NR
1978	SIGHT, 20,000	45.00	NR
1979	SOUND, 20,000	47.50	NR
1980	TOUCH, 15,000	52.50	100.00
1981	SCENT, 10,000	59.00	NR
1982	TASTE, 10,000	59.00	NR

Mother's Day

| 1975 | MOTHER AND CHILD, 15,000 | 37.50 | 80.00 |

Touch

Scent

Taste

Orioles

Photo courtesy of *Collectors News*

		Issue Price	Current Value
1976	PINKY AND BABY, 15,000	42.50	BR
1977	AMY AND SNOOPY, 15,000	45.00	BR

Songbirds

		Issue Price	Current Value
1980	CARDINALS, Patti Canaris, 5,000	65.00	90.00
1981	BLUE BIRDS, Patti Canaris, 5,000.....................	70.00	NR
1982	ORIOLES, Patti Canaris, 5,000........................	70.00	NR
1982	GOLDFINCHES, Patti Canaris, 5,000	70.00	NR

Tapestry I

			Issue Price	Current Value

Note: These plates are reproductions of medieval tapestries from the collection at The Cloisters in New York City.

1971	UNICORN IN CAPTIVITY, 10,000	35.00	130.00
1972	START OF THE HUNT, 10,000	35.00	60.00
1973	CHASE OF THE UNICORN, 10,000	35.00	100.00
1974	END OF THE HUNT, 10,000	37.50	90.00
1975	UNICORN SURROUNDED, 10,000	40.00	50.00
1976	BROUGHT TO THE CASTLE, 10,000	42.50	NR

Unicorn in Captivity

Start of the Hunt

End of the Hunt

Unicorn Surrounded

Single Issues	Issue Price	Current Value
1971 CHINA TRADE PLATE	30.00	BR
1971 EMPRESS	60.00	NR
1972 MEISSEN PLATE.....................................	30.00	BR
1973 PEACEABLE KINGDOM, Nan Lee, 5,000................	30.00	65.00
1977 ASTROLOGICAL MAN, 5,000.........................	50.00	NR
1978 SCARAB, 2,500....................................	100.00	NR

HEINRICH PORZELLAN GERMANY

Fairies of the Fields and Flowers

1982 RAGGED ROBIN, Cicely Mary Barker, 10 days	49.50	NR
1982 THE WILLOW FAIRY, Cicely Mary Barker, 10 days	49.50	NR
1983 ELDERBERRY FAIRY, Cicely Mary Barker, <1 year	49.50	NR
1983 VETCH FAIRY, Cicely Mary Barker, <1 year	49.50	NR
1984 NARCISSUS, Cicely Mary Barker, <1 year	49.50	NR
1984 NASTURTIUM, Cicely Mary Barker, <1 year.............	49.50	NR

Flower Fairy

1979 THE LAVENDER FAIRY, Cicely Mary Barker, 21 days	35.00	50.00
1980 THE SWEET PEA FAIRY, Cicely Mary Barker, 21 days	35.00	NR
1980 THE CANDY TUFT FAIRY, Cicely Mary Barker, 21 days ...	35.00	NR
1981 THE HELIOTROPE FAIRY, Cicely Mary Barker, 21 days ...	35.00	NR
1981 THE BLACKTHORN FAIRY, Cicely Mary Barker, 21 days ..	35.00	NR
1981 THE APPLE BLOSSOM FAIRY, Cicely Mary Barker, 21 days	35.00	NR

Flower Fairy II

1985 COLUMBINE, Cicely Mary Barker, 21 days	35.00	NR
1985 CORNFLOWER, Cicely Mary Barker, 21 days............	35.00	NR
1985 MALLOW, Cicely Mary Barker, 21 days	35.00	NR
1985 BLACK MEDICK, Cicely Mary Barker, 21 days	35.00	NR
1985 CANTERBURY BELL, Cicely Mary Barker, 21 days	35.00	NR
1985 FUCHSIA, Cicely Mary Barker, 21 days.................	35.00	NR

Russian Fairy Tales — The Firebird

1981 IN SEARCH OF THE FIREBIRD, Boris Zvorykin, 27,500...	70.00	NR
1981 IVAN AND TSAREVNA ON THE GREY WOLF, Boris Zvorykin, 27,500	70.00	NR
1981 THE WEDDING OF IVAN AND TSAREVNA ELENA THE FAIR, Boris Zvorykin, 27,500	70.00	100.00

Russian Fairy Tales — Maria Morevna

1982 MARIA MOREVNA AND TSAREVICH IVAN, Boris Zvorykin, 27,500	70.00	85.00

		Issue Price	Current Value
1983	KOSHCHEY CARRIES OFF MARIA MOREVNA, Boris Zvorykin, 27,500	70.00	NR
1983	TSAREVICH IVAN AND THE BEAUTIFUL CASTLE, Boris Zvorykin, 27,500	70.00	90.00

Russian Fairy Tales — The Red Knight

1981	THE RED KNIGHT, Boris Zvorykin, 27,500	70.00	BR
1981	VASSILISSA AND HER STEPSISTERS, Boris Zvorykin, 27,500	70.00	BR
1981	VASSILISSA IS PRESENTED TO THE TSAR, Boris Zvorykin, 27,500	70.00	BR

Russian Fairy Tales — Snow Maiden

1980	THE SNOW MAIDEN, Boris Zvorykin, 27,500	70.00	100.00
1981	SNEGUROCHKA AT THE COURT OF THE TSAR BERENDEI, Boris Zvorykin, 27,500	70.00	BR
1981	SNEGUROCHKA AND LEL THE SHEPHERD BOY, Boris Zvorykin, 27,500	70.00	BR

HEIRLOOM TRADITIONS UNITED STATES

Cinema Classics

1985	HIGH NOON, Susan Edison, 10,000	35.00	NR
1986	YOUNG AT HEART, Susan Edison, 10,000	35.00	NR
1986	RIO GRANDE, Susan Edison, 10,000	35.00	NR

Hollywood's View of Christmas

1986	CHARLES DICKENS' CHRISTMAS CAROL, Susan Edison, 10,000	35.00	NR

Single Issues

1985	IT'S A WONDERFUL LIFE	35.00	NR
1986	VARGA, Alberto Vargas, 10,000	45.00	NR
1986	BARRY MANILOW, 20,000	35.00	NR
1986	MISS AMERICA, 1927, Louis Icart, 7,500	50.00	65.00

EDNA HIBEL STUDIOS GERMANY

Allegro (Hutschenreuther)

1978	PLATE AND BOOK, Edna Hibel, 7,500	120.00	135.00

Arte Ovale (Rosenthal Porcelain)

1980	TAKARA, Edna Hibel, cobalt blue, 1,000	595.00	1,750.00
1980	TAKARA, Edna Hibel, gold, 300	1,000.00	3,300.00

		Issue Price	Current Value
1980	TAKARA, Edna Hibel, blanco, 700	450.00	950.00
1984	TARO–KUN, Edna Hibel, cobalt blue, 1,000	595.00	650.00
1984	TARO–KUN, Edna Hibel, gold, 300	1,000.00	1,700.00
1984	TARO–KUN, Edna Hibel, blanco, 700	450.00	495.00

Christmas Annual

1985	ANGELS' MESSAGE, Edna Hibel, 1 year	45.00	NR
1986	GIFT OF THE MAGI, Edna Hibel, 1 year.................	45.00	NR
1987	FLIGHT INTO EGYPT, Edna Hibel, 1 year	49.00	NR
1988	ADORATION OF THE SHEPHERDS, Edna Hibel, 1 year ...	49.00	NR
1989	PEACEFUL KINGDOM, Edna Hibel, 1 year	49.00	NR
1990	THE NATIVITY, Edna Hibel, 1 year	49.00	NR

Gift of the Magi
Photo courtesy of *Collectors News*

The Nativity

David Series

1979	THE WEDDING OF DAVID AND BATHSHEBA, Edna Hibel, 5,000	250.00	300.00
1980	DAVID, BATHSHEBA AND SOLOMON, Edna Hibel, 5,000 .	275.00	300.00
1982	DAVID THE KING, Edna Hibel, 5,000	275.00	300.00
1982	DAVID THE KING, Edna Hibel, cobalt A/P, 25	275.00	1,200.00
1984	BATHSHEBA, Edna Hibel, 10,000	275.00	300.00
1984	BATHSHEBA, Edna Hibel, cobalt A/P, 100	275.00	1,200.00

Edna Hibel Holiday

1991	THE FIRST HOLIDAY, Edna Hibel, 1 year................	49.00	75.00
1991	THE FIRST HOLIDAY, Edna Hibel, gold, 1,000.............	99.00	150.00
1992	THE CHRISTMAS ROSE, Edna Hibel, 1 year	49.00	RI

The Christmas Rose
Photo courtesy of *Collectors News*

A Time to Embrace

Molly and Annie

Jaclyn and Rene

Tammy and Kali Jo

Abby and Lisa

		Issue Price	Current Value
1992	THE CHRISTMAS ROSE, Edna Hibel, gold, 1,000	99.00	RI
1993	HOLIDAY JOY, Edna Hibel, 1 year	49.00	RI
1993	HOLIDAY JOY, Edna Hibel, gold, 1,000	99.00	RI

Eroica

1990	COMPASSION, Edna Hibel, 10,000	49.50	65.00
1992	DARYA, Edna Hibel, 10,000	49.50	RI

Famous Women and Children

1980	PHARAOH'S DAUGHTER AND MOSES, Edna Hibel, gold, 2,500	350.00	625.00
1980	PHARAOH'S DAUGHTER AND MOSES, Edna Hibel, cobalt blue, 500	350.00	1,350.00
1982	CORNELIA AND HER JEWELS, Edna Hibel, gold, 2,500 ...	350.00	495.00
1982	CORNELIA AND HER JEWELS, Edna Hibel, cobalt blue, 500 ...	350.00	1,350.00
1982	ANNA AND THE CHILDREN OF THE KING OF SIAM, Edna Hibel, gold, 2,500	350.00	495.00
1982	ANNA AND THE CHILDREN OF THE KING OF SIAM, Edna Hibel, cobalt blue, 500	350.00	1,350.00
1984	MOZART AND THE EMPRESS MARIA THERESA, Edna Hibel, gold, 2,500	350.00	395.00
1984	MOZART AND THE EMPRESS MARIA THERESA, Edna Hibel, cobalt blue, 500	350.00	975.00

Flower Girl Annual

1985	LILY, Edna Hibel, 15,000	79.00	NR
1986	IRIS, Edna Hibel, 15,000	79.00	NR
1987	ROSE, Edna Hibel, 15,00 0	79.00	NR
1988	CAMELLIA, Edna Hibel, 15,000	79.00	165.00
1989	PEONY, Edna Hibel, 15,000	79.00	125.00
1992	WISTERIA, Edna Hibel, 15,000	79.00	RI

International Mother Love French

1985	YVETTE AVEC SES INFANTS, Edna Hibel, 5,000	125.00	NR
1991	LIBERTÉ, EGALITÉ, FRATERNITÉ, Edna Hibel, 5,000	95.00	NR

International Mother Love German

1979	GESA UND KINDER, Edna Hibel, 5,000	195.00	NR
1980	ALEXANDRA UND KINDER, Edna Hibel, 5,000	195.00	NR

March of Dimes: Our Children, Our Future

1990	A TIME TO EMBRACE, Edna Hibel, 150 days............	29.00	NR

Mother and Child

1973	COLETTE AND CHILD, Edna Hibel, 15,000	40.00	460.00

Sarah and Tess

Jessica and Kate

Elizabeth, Jordan and Janie

Holly and Talia

A Tender Moment
Photo courtesy of *Collectors News*

		Issue Price	Current Value
1974	SAYURI AND CHILD, Edna Hibel, 15,000	40.00	165.00
1975	KRISTINA AND CHILD, Edna Hibel, 15,000	50.00	125.00
1976	MARILYN AND CHILD, Edna Hibel, 15,000	55.00	115.00
1977	LUCIA AND CHILD, Edna Hibel, 15,000	60.00	90.00
1982	KATHLEEN AND CHILD, Edna Hibel, 15,000	85.00	NR

Mother's Day

1992	MOLLY AND ANNIE, Edna Hibel, <1 year	39.00	RI
1992	MOLLY AND ANNIE, Edna Hibel, gold, 2,500	95.00	RI
1992	MOLLY AND ANNIE, Edna Hibel, platinum, 500	275.00	RI
1993	OLIVIA AND HILDY, Edna Hibel, <1 year	39.00	RI
1993	OLIVIA AND HILDY, Edna Hibel, gold, 2,500	95.00	RI
1993	OLIVIA AND HILDY, Edna Hibel, platinum, 500	275.00	RI
1994	JACLYN AND RENE, Edna Hibel, <1 year	39.00	RI
1994	JACLYN AND RENE, Edna Hibel, gold, 2,500	95.00	RI
1994	JACLYN AND RENE, Edna Hibel, platinum, 500	275.00	RI
1995	TAMMY AND KALI JO, Edna Hibel, <1 year	39.00	RI
1995	TAMMY AND KALI JO, Edna Hibel, gold, 2,500	95.00	RI
1995	TAMMY AND KALI JO, Edna Hibel, platinum, 500	275.00	RI

Mother's Day Annual

1984	ABBY & LISA, Edna Hibel, <1 year	29.50	NR
1985	ERICA & JAMIE, Edna Hibel, <1 year	29.50	NR
1986	EMILY & JENNIFER, Edna Hibel, <1 year	29.50	NR
1987	CATHERINE & HEATHER, Edna Hibel, <1 year	34.50	NR
1988	SARAH & TESS, Edna Hibel, <1 year	34.90	NR
1989	JESSICA & KATE, Edna Hibel, <1 year	34.90	NR
1990	ELIZABETH, JORDAN & JANIE, Edna Hibel, <1 year	36.90	NR
1991	MICHELE & ANNA, Edna Hibel, <1 year	36.90	NR

Museum Commemorative I

1977	THE FLOWER GIRL OF PROVENCE, Edna Hibel, 12,750	175.00	400.00

Museum Commemorative II

1980	DIANA, Edna Hibel, 3,000	350.00	375.00

Nobility of Children

1976	LA CONTESSA ISABELLA, Edna Hibel, 12,750	120.00	NR
1977	LE MARQUIS MAURICE PIERRE, Edna Hibel, 12,750	120.00	NR
1978	BARONESSE JOHANNA – MARYKE VAN VOLLENDAM TOT MARKEN, Edna Hibel, 12,750	130.00	140.00
1979	CHIEF RED FEATHER, Edna Hibel, 12,750	140.00	160.00

Nordic Families

1987	A TENDER MOMENT, Edna Hibel, 7,500	79.00	95.00

Oriental Gold

		Issue Price	Current Value
1975	YASUKO, Edna Hibel, 2,000	275.00	650.00
1976	MR. OBATA, Edna Hibel, 2,000	275.00	500.00
1978	SAKURA, Edna Hibel, 2,000	295.00	400.00
1979	MICHIO, Edna Hibel, 2,000	325.00	375.00

Scandinavian Mother and Child

1987	PEARL AND FLOWERS, Edna Hibel, 7,500	55.00	225.00
1989	ANEMONE AND VIOLET, Edna Hibel, 7,500	75.00	90.00
1990	HOLLY AND TALIA, Edna Hibel, 7,500	75.00	85.00

To Life Annual

1986	GOLDEN'S CHILD, Edna Hibel, 5,000	99.00	275.00
1987	TRIUMPH! EVERONE A WINNER!, Edna Hibel, 19,500	55.00	75.00
1988	THE WHOLE EARTH BLOOMED AS A SACRED PLACE, Edna Hibel, 15,000	85.00	90.00
1989	LOVERS OF THE SUMMER PALACE, Edna Hibel, 5,000	65.00	75.00
1992	PEOPLE OF THE FIELDS, Edna Hibel, 5,000	49.00	RI

Tribute to All Children

1984	GISELLE, Edna Hibel, 19,500	55.00	NR
1984	GERARD, Edna Hibel, 19,500	55.00	NR
1985	WENDY, Edna Hibel, 19,500	55.00	NR
1986	TODD, Edna Hibel, 19,500	55.00	NR

World I Love

1981	LEAH'S FAMILY, Edna Hibel, 17,500	85.00	175.00
1982	KAYLIN, Edna Hibel, 17,500	85.00	175.00
1983	EDNA'S MUSIC, Edna Hibel, 17,500	85.00	175.00
1984	O'HANA, Edna Hibel, 17,500	85.00	175.00

JOHN HINE N.A. LTD.

David Winter Plate Collection

1991	A CHRISTMAS CAROL, M. Fisher, 10,000	30.00	30.00
1991	COTSWOLD VILLAGE PLATE, M. Fisher, 10,000	30.00	30.00
1992	CHICHESTER CROSS PLATE, M. Fisher, 10,000	30.00	RI
1992	LITTLE MILL PLATE, M. Fisher, 10,000	30.00	RI
1992	OLD CURIOSITY SHOP, M. Fisher, 10,000	30.00	RI
1992	SCROOGE'S COUNTING HOUSE, M. Fisher, 10,000	30.00	RI
1993	DOVE COTTAGE, M. Fisher, 10,000	30.00	RI
1993	LITTLE FORGE, M. Fisher, 10,000	30.00	RI

HISTORIC PROVIDENCE MINT UNITED STATES

Alice in Wonderland

		Issue Price	Current Value
1986	THE TEA PARTY, George Terp, 45 days	29.50	NR
1986	THE CATERPILLAR, George Terp, 45 days	29.50	NR
1986	THE WHITE KNIGHT, George Terp, 45 days	29.50	NR
1986	THE DUCHESS AND COOK, George Terp, 45 days	29.50	NR
1986	OFF WITH THEIR HEADS!, George Terp, 45 days	29.50	NR
1986	RED AND WHITE QUEENS, George Terp, 45 days	29.50	NR
1986	THE WHITE RABBIT, George Terp, 45 days	29.50	NR
1986	TALKING FLOWERS, George Terp, 45 days	29.50	NR
1986	TWEEDLEDEE–TWEEDLEDUM, George Terp, 45 days	29.50	NR
1986	WALRUS AND CARPENTER, George Terp, 45 days	29.50	NR
1986	LION AND UNICORN, George Terp, 45 days	29.50	NR
1986	HUMPTY DUMPTY, George Terp, 45 days	29.50	NR

America the Beautiful

1981	SPACIOUS SKIES, Ben Essenburg, 17,500	37.50	NR
1981	AMBER WAVES OF GRAIN, Ben Essenburg, 17,500	37.50	NR
1981	PURPLE MOUNTAINS MAJESTY, Ben Essenburg, 17,500	37.50	NR
1981	GOD SHED HIS GRACE, Ben Essenburg, 17,500	37.50	NR
1981	CROWN THY GOOD WITH BROTHERHOOD, Ben Essenburg, 17,500	37.50	NR
1981	FROM SEA TO SHINING SEA, Ben Essenburg, 17,500	37.50	NR

Children of the Seasons

1980	CHILDREN OF SPRING, 3,000	107.50	NR

Lil' Peddlers

1986	FORGET ME NOTS, Lee Dubin	29.50	NR
1986	POPPIN' CORN, Lee Dubin	29.50	NR
1986	BALLOONS 'N THINGS, Lee Dubin	29.50	NR
1986	PENNY CANDY, Lee Dubin	29.50	NR
1986	TODAY'S CATCH, Lee Dubin	29.50	NR
1986	JUST PICKED, Lee Dubin	29.50	NR
1986	COBBLESTONE DELI, Lee Dubin	29.50	NR
1986	CHIMNEY SWEEP, Lee Dubin	29.50	NR
1986	APPLE A DAY, Lee Dubin	29.50	NR
1986	EXTRA, EXTRA, Lee Dubin	29.50	NR
1986	OPEN FRESH, Lee Dubin	29.50	NR
1986	COOLIN' OFF, Lee Dubin	29.50	NR

Vanishing American Barn

1983	LOG BARN, Harris Hien, 14,500	39.50	NR
1983	APPALACHIAN BARN, Harris Hien, 14,500	39.50	NR
1983	BUCKS COUNTY BARN, Harris Hien, 14,500	39.50	NR
1983	ROUND BARN, Harris Hien, 14,500	39.50	NR
1983	LANCASTER BARN, Harris Hien, 14,500	39.50	NR

		Issue Price	Current Value
1983	VICTORIAN BARN, Harris Hien, 14,500	39.50	NR
1983	NEW ENGLAND BARN, Harris Hien, 14,500	39.50	NR
1983	THATCHED BARN, Harris Hien, 14,500	39.50	NR
1983	HUDSON RIVER BARN, Harris Hien, 14,500	39.50	NR
1983	SOUTHERN TOBACCO FARM, Harris Hien, 14,500	39.50	NR
1983	FOREBAY BARN, Harris Hien, 14,500	39.50	NR
1983	CONNECTED BARN, Harris Hien, 14,500	39.50	NR

Single Issue

1979	THE CHILDREN'S YEAR, 3,000	95.00	NR

HORNSEA GREAT BRITAIN

Christmas

1979	C–NATIVITY, 10,000	24.00	50.00
1980	H–MARY AND CHILD, 10,000	28.00	50.00
1981	R–THREE WISEMEN, 10,000	28.00	50.00

HOUSE OF GLOBAL ART UNITED STATES

American Heritage

1979	FREEDOM AND JUSTICE SOARING, Gunther Granget, 15,000	100.00	NR
1980	WILD AND FREE, Gunther Granget, 10,000	120.00	NR
1981	WHERE BUFFALO ROAM, Gunther Granget, 5,000	125.00	NR

Annual Crystal

1978	PRAYING GIRL, 1 year	45.00	BR
1979	PRAYING BOY, 1 year	50.00	BR
1980	PRAYING ANGEL, 15,000	50.00	NR
1981	GIRL WITH TEDDY BEARS, 10,000	50.00	NR

Bavarian Forest

1980	OWLS, 7,500	150.00	NR
1981	DEER, 7,500	150.00	NR

Blue–Button Trains Christmas

1983	BY THE FIREPLACE, Helen Nyce, 10,000	30.00	NR
1983	DOWN THE STAIRS, Helen Nyce, 10,000	30.00	NR

Christmas Morning in Dingle Dell

1983	BILLIE BUMP'S CHRISTMAS, Grace Drayton, 19,000	30.00	NR

	Issue Price	Current Value
1983 DOLLY CELEBRATES CHRISTMAS, Grace Drayton, 10,000	30.00	NR

Dolly Dingle World Traveler

	Issue Price	Current Value
1982 DOLLY DINGLE VISITS GERMANY, Grace Drayton, 10,000	30.00	NR
1982 DOLLY DINGLE VISITS ITALY, Grace Drayton, 10,000	30.00	NR
1982 DOLLY DINGLE VISITS HOLLAND, Grace Drayton, 10,000	30.00	NR
1982 DOLLY DINGLE VISITS SPAIN, Grace Drayton, 10,000 ...	30.00	NR
1982 DOLLY DINGLE VISITS SCOTLAND, Grace Drayton, 10,000 ...	30.00	NR
1982 DOLLY DINGLE VISITS FRANCE, Grace Drayton, 10,000 ..	30.00	NR

English Countryside Cats Collection

	Issue Price	Current Value
1983 JAMES, Sharon Jervis, 10,000	35.00	NR
1983 HENRY, Sharon Jervis, 10,000	35.00	NR
1983 LILY, Sharon Jervis, 10,000	35.00	NR
1983 LUCY, Sharon Jervis, 10,000	35.00	NR

HOYLE PRODUCTS UNITED STATES

Bygone Days

	Issue Price	Current Value
1983 BREAKFAST WITH TEDDY, Jessie Wilcox Smith, 12,500 .	35.00	NR
1983 A FLOWER BASKET, Jessie Wilcox Smith, 12,500	35.00	NR

Breakfast with Teddy
Photo courtesy of *Collectors News*

Family Circus Christmas

	Issue Price	Current Value
1980 CHRISTMAS, Bil Keane, 5,000	25.00	NR
1981 CHRISTMAS, Bil Keane, 5,000	30.00	NR

		Issue Price	Current Value

Gothic Romance

| 1982 | MOONLIGHT ROMANCE, Jondar, 5,000 .... | 30.00 | NR |

Hilda

| 1982 | TOASTING MARSHMALLOWS, 5,000 .... | 25.00 | NR |

Mother's Day

| 1980 | MOTHER'S DAY, Bil Keane, 5,000 .... | 25.00 | NR |

Norman Rockwell Clowns

1977	THE RUNAWAY, Norman Rockwell, 7,500	45.00	75.00
1978	IT'S YOUR MOVE, Norman Rockwell, 7,500	45.00	65.00
1979	THE UNDERSTUDY, Norman Rockwell, 7,500	45.00	NR
1980	THE IDOL, Norman Rockwell, 7,500	45.00	NR

Norman Rockwell Salesman

1977	THE TRAVELING SALESMAN, Norman Rockwell, 7,500 ..	35.00	NR
1978	THE COUNTRY PEDDLER, Norman Rockwell, 7,500	40.00	NR
1979	THE HORSE TRADER, Norman Rockwell, 7,500	40.00	NR
1980	THE EXPERT SALESMAN, Norman Rockwell, 7,500	45.00	NR

Nostalgia

1981	PEPSI COLA GIRL, 5,000	25.00	65.00
1982	OLYMPIA GIRL, 5,000	30.00	NR
1982	SAVANNAH BEER GIRL, 5,000	30.00	NR
1982	DR. PEPPER GIRL, 5,000	30.00	NR

Nostalgia – Children

| 1983 | PEAR'S SOAP AD, 12,500 .... | 35.00 | NR |

Nostalgia Magazine Covers

| 1983 | LADIES' HOME JOURNAL, Hayden Hayden, 12,500 ...... | 35.00 | NR |

Rare Rockwell

| 1980 | MRS. O'LEARY'S COW, Norman Rockwell, 7,500 .... | 30.00 | NR |
| 1981 | COME AND GET IT, Norman Rockwell, 7,500 .... | 30.00 | NR |

Remember When

1982	A SURPRISE FOR KITTY, M. Humphrey, 10,000	30.00	NR
1982	WASHDAY, M. Humphrey, 10,000	30.00	NR
1983	PLAYING GRANDMOTHER, M. Humphrey, 10,000	30.00	NR
1983	THE PHYSICIAN, M. Humphrey, 10,000	30.00	NR

		Issue Price	Current Value
Western Series			
1977	SHARING AN APPLE, 5,000	35.00	NR
1978	SPLIT DECISION, 5,000	35.00	NR
1979	HIDING OUT, 5,000	35.00	NR
1980	IN TROUBLE, 5,000	35.00	NR
Wilderness Wings			
1978	GLIDING IN, David Maass, 5,000	35.00	NR
1979	TAKEOFF, 5,000.......................................	40.00	NR
1980	JOINING UP, 5,000	45.00	NR
1981	CANVASBACKS, 5,000	47.50	NR
Wings of the Wild			
1982	CINNAMON TEAL, David Maass, 5,000	30.00	NR
1982	MOMENT OF REST, David Maass, 5,000	30.00	NR
1983	MOURNING DOVES, David Maass, 5,000	30.00	NR

HUDSON PEWTER UNITED STATES

		Issue Price	Current Value
America's Sailing Ships			
1979	U.S.S. CONSTITUTION, 5,000	35.00	NR
Child's Christmas			
1978	BEDTIME STORY, Albert Petitto, 10,000	35.00	NR
1979	LITTLEST ANGELS, Albert Petitto, 10,000..............	35.00	NR
1980	HEAVEN'S CHRISTMAS TREE, Albert Petitto, 10,000.....	42.50	NR
1981	FILLING THE SKY, Albert Petitto, 10,000	47.50	NR
Mother's Day			
1979	CHERISHED, 10,000	15.00	35.00
Songbirds of the Four Seasons			
1979	HUMMINGBIRD, 7,500	35.00	NR
'Twas the Night before Christmas			
1982	NOT A CREATURE WAS STIRRING, Andrea Hollis, 10,000	47.50	NR
1983	VISIONS OF SUGAR PLUMS, Andrea Hollis, 10,000	47.50	NR
1984	HIS EYES HOW THEY TWINKLED, Andrea Hollis, 10,000.	47.50	NR
1985	HAPPY CHRISTMAS TO ALL, Andrea Hollis, 10,000......	47.50	NR
1986	BRINGING HOME THE TREE, Andrea Hollis, 10,000	47.50	NR
Single Issue			
1976	BICENTENNIAL	42.00	NR

HUTSCHENREUTHER GERMANY

		Issue Price	Current Value
Allegro Ensemble			
1978	ALLEGRO, Edna Hibel, 7,500	—	—
1978	FLUTIST, Edna Hibel, 7,500	—	—
	Set of 2..	120.00	140.00

Arzberg

1986	BODO AND THE BOAT, Kathia Berger, limited	47.50	NR

Birds of Paradise

1981	BLUE BIRD OF PARADISE, Ole Winther, 10,000	175.00	NR
1981	RAGGIS GREAT BIRD OF PARADISE, Ole Winther, 10,000	175.00	NR

Birth Plates

1978	BIRTH PLATE, Ole Winther, 10,000	165.00	NR

Bouquets of the Seasons

1987	SPRING MORNING	24.50	NR
1987	EASTER BOUQUET.................................	24.50	NR
1987	SUMMER PROMISE...............................	27.50	NR
1987	SUMMER GLORY	27.50	NR
1988	AUTUMN TINTS	27.50	NR
1988	AUTUMN MEMORIES	27.50	NR
1988	WINTER TWILIGHT	29.50	NR
1988	FROSTY BEAUTY	29.50	NR

Christmas

1978	CHRISTMAS, Ole Winther, 2,000	260.00	NR
1979	CHRISTMAS, Ole Winther, 2,500.....................	295.00	NR
1980	CHRISTMAS, Ole Winther, 1 year	360.00	NR
1981	CHRISTMAS, Ole Winther, 1 year	400.00	NR
1982	CHRISTMAS CONCERTO, Ole Winther, 1 year	400.00	NR
1983	THE ANNUNCIATION, Ole Winther, 1 year	135.00	NR
1984	HOLY NIGHT, Ole Winther, 1 year	135.00	NR

Country Birds of the Year

1983	LESSER SPOTTED WOODPECKER, Martin Camm, 15 days	29.95	NR
1983	LONG TAILED TIT, Martin Camm, 15 days..............	29.95	NR
1986	JANUARY, Martin Camm, open	29.50	NR
1986	FEBRUARY, Martin Camm, open	29.50	NR
1986	MARCH, Martin Camm, open.........................	29.50	NR
1986	APRIL, Martin Camm, open	29.50	NR
1986	MAY, Martin Camm, open	29.50	NR
1986	JUNE, Martin Camm, open	29.50	NR
1986	JULY, Martin Camm, open	29.50	NR

		Issue Price	Current Value
1986	AUGUST, Martin Camm, open	29.50	NR
1986	SEPTEMBER, Martin Camm, open	29.50	NR
1986	OCTOBER, Martin Camm, open	29.50	NR
1986	NOVEMBER, Martin Camm, open	29.50	NR
1986	DECEMBER, Martin Camm, open	29.50	NR

Der Ring des Nibelungen

1986	MOTIF I – DAS RHEINGOLD, Charlotte and William Hallett, 5,000	125.00	NR
1986	MOTIF II – DIE WALKUERE, Charlotte and William Hallett, 5,000	125.00	NR
1986	MOTIF III – SIEGFRIED, Charlotte and William Hallett, 5,000	125.00	NR
1986	MOTIF IV – GOETTERDAEMMERUNG, Charlotte and William Hallett, 5,000	125.00	NR

Early Memories

1983	DO THEY BITE?, James Keirstead, 7,500	72.50	NR
1983	TUG OF WAR, James Keirstead, 7,500	72.50	NR
1983	THE EXPLORERS, James Keirstead, 7,500	72.50	NR
1983	MY TURN, James Keirstead, 7,500	72.50	NR

Enchanted Seasons of a Unicorn

1985	JOYOUS SPRING, Charlotte and William Hallett, 12,500	39.50	NR
1985	PEACEFUL SUMMER, Charlotte and William Hallett, 12,500	39.50	NR
1985	GLORIOUS AUTUMN, Charlotte and William Hallett, 12,500	39.50	NR
1985	WINTER'S TRANQUILITY, Charlotte and William Hallett, 12,500	39.50	NR

Enchantment

1979	PRINCESS SNOWFLAKE, Dolores Valenza, 5,000	50.00	60.00
1979	BLOSSOM QUEEN, Dolores Valenza, 5,000	62.50	NR
1980	PRINCESS MARINA, Dolores Valenza, 5,000	87.50	NR
1981	PRINCESS STARBRIGHT, Dolores Valenza, 2,500	87.50	NR
1981	HARVEST QUEEN, Dolores Valenza, 5,000	87.50	NR
1982	PRINCESS AURA, Dolores Valenza, 5,000	87.50	NR

Flowers that Never Fade

1982	ANNUAL, Ole Winther, 1 year	27.50	NR
1983	ANNUAL, Ole Winther, 1 year	27.50	NR
1984	ANNUAL, Ole Winther, 1 year	27.50	NR

Friendship Annual

1978	FRIENDSHIP, Ole Winther, 1 year	80.00	NR

Glory of Christmas

1982	THE NATIVITY, Charlotte and William Hallett, 25,000	80.00	100.00
1983	THE ANGELS, Charlotte and William Hallett, 25,000	80.00	90.00

	Issue Price	Current Value
1984 THE SHEPHERDS, Charlotte and William Hallett, 25,000 ..	80.00	NR
1985 THE WISEMEN, Charlotte and William Hallett, 25,000....	80.00	NR

The Angels   *Toward the Sun*

Gunther Granget

1972 SPARROWS, AMERICAN, Gunther Granget, 5,000	50.00	175.00
1972 SPARROWS, EUROPEAN, Gunther Granget, 5,000	30.00	70.00
1973 KILDEER, AMERICAN, Gunther Granget, 2,500	75.00	100.00
1973 SQUIRREL, AMERICAN, Gunther Granget, 2,500	75.00	85.00
1973 SQUIRREL, EUROPEAN, Gunther Granget, 2,500	35.00	55.00
1974 PARTRIDGE, AMERICAN, Gunther Granget, 2,500	75.00	90.00
1976 RABBITS, AMERICAN, Gunther Granget, 2,500	90.00	NR
1976 FREEDOM IN FLIGHT, Gunther Granget, 5,000	100.00	BR
1976 FREEDOM IN FLIGHT, gold, Gunther Granget, 200	200.00	NR
1976 WRENS, Gunther Granget, 2,500	100.00	110.00
1977 BEARS, Gunther Granget, 2,500	100.00	NR
1978 FOXES' SPRING JOURNEY, Gunther Granget, 1,000	125.00	200.00

Hans Achtziger

1979 HEADING SOUTH, Hans Achtziger, 5,000	150.00	NR
1980 PLAYFUL FLIGHT, Hans Achtziger, 5,000	187.50	NR
1981 TROPICAL SKIES, Hans Achtziger, 5,000	245.00	NR
1982 CARRIED BY THE WIND, Hans Achtziger, 5,000	250.00	NR
1983 TOWARD THE SUN, Hans Achtziger, 5,000	250.00	NR
1985 OVER LAND AND SEA, Hans Achtziger, 5,000	250.00	NR

Hummingbirds

1982 SWORD–BILLED HUMMINGBIRD, Ole Winther	—	—
1982 TRAIN–BEARER, Ole Winther........................	—	—

		Issue Price	Current Value
1982	RUFOUC HUMMINGBIRD, Ole Winther	—	—
1982	HELIOTHRIX, Ole Winther.............................	—	—
1982	HORNED SUNGEM, Ole Winther	—	—
1982	VERVIAN HUMMINGBIRD, Ole Winther	—	—
	Set of 6...	200.00	NR

Kathia's Cats

1983	IN A FLOWER BASKET, Kathia Berger	18.50	NR
1983	IN THE PASTURE, Kathia Berger	18.50	NR
1983	CONVERSATION WITH A SEAGULL, Kathia Berger	18.50	NR
1983	MY FAVORITE PLACE, Kathia Berger	18.50	NR
1983	PLAY IN THE SNOW, Kathia Berger....................	18.50	NR
1983	BODO AND THE BOAT, Kathia Berger	47.50	NR

Legend of St. George

1985	THE KNIGHT, Charlotte and William Hallett, 5,000	100.00	NR
1985	THE LADY KNIGHT, Charlotte and William Hallett, 5,000 ..	100.00	NR
1985	THE CONTEST, Charlotte and William Hallett, 5,000......	100.00	NR
1985	THE WEDDING, Charlotte and William Hallett, 5,000.....	100.00	NR

Legendary Animals

1982	GRIFFIN, Charlotte and William Hallett, 12,500	—	—
1982	UNICORN, Charlotte and William Hallett, 12,500	—	—
1982	PEGASUS, Charlotte and William Hallett, 12,500	—	—
1982	DRAGON, Charlotte and William Hallett, 12,500.........	—	—
	Set of 4...	175.00	NR

Love for All Seasons

1981	THE RIDE OUT, Charlotte and William Hallett, 10,000	125.00	NR
1982	THE MINSTREL SONG, Charlotte and William Hallett, 10,000 ..	125.00	NR
1982	AFFECTION, Charlotte and William Hallett, 10,000	125.00	NR
1982	THE TOURNAMENT, Charlotte and William Hallett, 10,000	125.00	NR
1983	THE FALCON HUNT, Charlotte and William Hallett, 10,000	125.00	NR
1983	WINTER ROMANCE, Charlotte and William Hallett, 10,000	125.00	NR

Mother and Child Annual

1978	MOTHER AND CHILD, Ole Winther, 2,500	65.00	NR
1979	MOTHER AND CHILD, Ole Winther, 2,500	65.00	NR
1980	MOTHER AND CHILD, Ole Winther, 2,500.............	87.50	NR
1981	MOTHER AND CHILD, Ole Winther, 2,500	87.50	NR
1982	MOTHER AND CHILD, Ole Winther, 2,500..............	87.50	NR
1983	MOTHER AND CHILD, Ole Winther, 2,500..............	87.50	NR

Mother and Child II

1983	MOTHER AND CHILD, Ole Winther, 1 year	47.50	NR

		Issue Price	Current Value
1984	MOTHER AND CHILD, Ole Winther, 1 year	47.50	NR

Museum Commemorative

1978	FLOWER GIRL OF PROVENCE, Edna Hibel, 12,750	175.00	215.00

Plate of the Month

1978	JANUARY – WREN, Ole Winther......................	—	—
1978	FEBRUARY – GREAT TITMOUSE, Ole Winther	—	—
1978	MARCH – PEEWEE, Ole Winther	—	—
1978	APRIL – STARLING, Ole Winther......................	—	—
1978	MAY – CUCKOO, Ole Winther	—	—
1978	JUNE – NIGHTINGALE, Ole Winther	—	—
1978	JULY – LARK, Ole Winther	—	—
1978	AUGUST – SWALLOW, Ole Winther	—	—
1978	SEPTEMBER – BLACKBIRD, Ole Winther	—	—
1978	OCTOBER – PIGEON, Ole Winther.....................	—	—
1978	NOVEMBER – WOODCOCK, Ole Winther	—	—
1978	DECEMBER – BULLFINCH, Ole Winther	—	—
	Set of 12	324.00	NR

Richard Wagner

1986	TANNHAEUSER, Charlotte and William Hallett, 5,000	125.00	NR
1986	PARSIFAL, Charlotte and William Hallett, 5,000	125.00	NR

Ruthven Songbirds

1972	BLUEBIRD AND GOLDFINCH, John Ruthven, 5,000	100.00	BR
1973	MOCKINGBIRD AND ROBIN, John Ruthven, 5,000	100.00	BR

Songbirds of North America

1981	ROSE–BREASTED GROSBEAK, Ole Winther, 12,500	60.00	NR
1981	EASTERN BLUEBIRD, Ole Winther, 12,500	60.00	NR
1981	AMERICAN GOLDFINCH, Ole Winther, 12,500	60.00	NR
1981	MOCKINGBIRD, Ole Winther, 12,500	60.00	NR

Spring in the World of Birds

1985	THE PHEASANTS, Hans Achtziger, 2,500	325.00	NR
1986	HERON, Hans Achtziger, 2,500	350.00	NR

Unicorns in Dreamer's Garden

1986	THE SIGHT OF WONDERS, Charlotte and William Hallett, 12,500	—	—
1986	THE SMELL OF ROSES, Charlotte and William Hallett, 12,500 ..	—	—
1986	THE SOUND OF MELODIES, Charlotte and William Hallett, 12,500	—	—
1986	THE TASTE OF SWEETNESS, Charlotte and William Hallett, 12,500	—	—

		Issue Price	Current Value
1986	THE TOUCH OF A DREAM, Charlotte and William Hallett, 12,500 Set of 5	— 197.50	— NR

Waterbabies

1983	TOM AND THE DRAGON FLY (#1), Sandy Nightingale, limited	45.00	NR
1983	THE FAIRIES TAKE CARE OF TOM (#2), Sandy Nightingale, limited	45.00	NR
1983	TOM AND MRS. DO AS YOU WOULD BE DONE BY (#3), Sandy Nightingale, limited.................................	45.00	NR
1984	TOM AND THE SWEET–CHEST, Sandy Nightingale, 15 days ..	45.00	NR
1984	ELLIE TEACHES TOM, Sandy Nightingale, 15 days	45.00	NR
1984	TOM TAKES CARE OF THE BABY, Sandy Nightingale, 15 days .	45.00	NR
1984	TOM MEETS ELLIE AGAIN, Sandy Nightingale, 15 days ..	45.00	NR

Tom and the Dragon Fly   *The Fairies Take Care of Tom*

Wedding

1979	WEDDING PLATE, Ole Winther, 10,000	210.00	235.00

Zodiac

1978	AQUARIUS, Ole Winther, 2,000	125.00	135.00
1978	ARIES, Ole Winther, 2,000	125.00	135.00
1978	CANCER, Ole Winther, 2,000.........................	125.00	135.00
1978	CAPRICORN, Ole Winther, 2,000	125.00	135.00
1978	GEMINI, Ole Winther, 2,000	125.00	135.00
1978	LEO, Ole Winther, 2,000	125.00	135.00
1978	LIBRA, Ole Winther, 2,000	125.00	135.00
1978	PISCES, Ole Winther, 2,000.........................	125.00	135.00
1978	SAGITTARIUS, Ole Winther, 2,000	125.00	135.00
1978	SCORPIO, Ole Winther, 2,000	125.00	135.00

			Issue Price	Current Value
1978	TAURUS, Ole Winther, 2,000	....	125.00	135.00
1978	VIRGO, Ole Winther, 2,000	....	125.00	135.00

Single Issues

1970	UN COMMEMORATIVE	....	8.00	15.00
1973	CHRISTMAS	....	37.00	45.00

IMPERIAL UNITED STATES

America the Beautiful

1969	U. S. CAPITOL, 500	....	17.50	NR
1970	MOUNT RUSHMORE, 500	....	17.50	NR
1971	STATUE OF LIBERTY, 500	....	17.50	NR
1972	MONUMENT VALLEY, ARIZONA, 500	....	17.50	NR
1973	LIBERTY BELL, 500	....	17.50	NR
1974	GOLDEN GATE, 500	....	19.95	NR
1975	MT. VERNON, 500	....	19.95	NR

Christmas

1970	PARTRIDGE, carnival glass, 1 year	....	12.00	30.00
1970	PARTRIDGE, crystal, 1 year	....	15.00	25.00
1971	TURTLEDOVES, carnival glass, 1 year	....	12.00	35.00
1971	TURTLEDOVES, crystal, 1 year	....	16.50	30.00
1972	HENS, carnival glass, 1 year	....	12.00	30.00
1972	HENS, crystal, 1 year	....	16.50	25.00
1973	COLLY BIRDS, carnival glass, 1 year	....	12.00	35.00
1973	COLLY BIRDS, crystal, 1 year	....	16.50	25.00
1974	GOLDEN RINGS, carnival glass, 1 year	....	12.00	20.00
1974	GOLDEN RINGS, crystal, 1 year	....	16.50	25.00
1975	GEESE, carnival glass, 1 year	....	14.00	35.00
1975	GEESE, crystal, 1 year	....	19.00	25.00
1976	SWANS, carnival glass, 1 year	....	16.00	NR
1976	SWANS, crystal, 1 year	....	21.00	NR
1977	MAIDS, carnival glass, 1 year	....	18.00	NR
1977	MAIDS, crystal, 1 year	....	23.00	NR
1978	DRUMMERS, carnival glass, 1 year	....	20.00	30.00
1978	DRUMMERS, crystal, 1 year	....	25.00	NR
1979	PIPERS, carnival glass, 1 year	....	22.00	NR
1979	PIPERS, crystal, 1 year	....	27.00	NR
1980	LADIES, carnival glass, 1 year	....	24.00	NR
1980	LADIES, crystal, 1 year	....	29.00	NR
1981	LORDS, carnival glass, 1 year	....	28.00	NR
1981	LORDS, crystal, 1 year	....	34.00	NR

	Issue Price	Current Value

Coin Plates

1971	KENNEDY COIN	15.00	NR
1972	IKE COIN	15.00	NR
1976	BICENTENNIAL COIN	20.00	NR

IMPERIAL CHING–TE CHEN
PEOPLES REPUBLIC OF CHINA

THE

Beauties of the Red Mansion

1986	PAO–CHAI, Z. HuiMin, 115 days	27.92	BR
1986	YUAN–CHUN, Z. HuiMin, 115 days	27.92	BR
1987	HSI–FENG, Z. HuiMin, 115 days	30.92	BR
1987	HSI–CHUN, Z. HuiMin, 115 days	30.92	BR
1987	MIAO–YU, Z. HuiMin, 115 days	30.92	BR
1987	YING–CHUN, Z. HuiMin, 115 days	30.92	BR
1988	TAI–YU, Z. HuiMin, 115 days	32.92	BR
1988	LI–WAN, Z. HuiMin, 115 days	32.92	BR
1988	KO–CHING, Z. HuiMin, 115 days	32.92	BR
1988	HSIANG–YUN, Z. HuiMin, 115 days	34.92	BR
1988	TAN–CHUN, Z. HuiMin, 115 days	34.92	BR
1989	CHIAO–CHIEH, Z. HuiMin, 115 days	34.92	BR

Blessings from a Chinese Garden

1988	THE GIFT OF PURITY, A. Song Mao, 175 days	39.92	BR
1988	THE GIFT OF GRACE, A. Song Mao, 175 days	39.92	BR
1989	THE GIFT OF BEAUTY, A. Song Mao, 175 days	42.92	BR
1989	THE GIFT OF HAPPINESS, A. Song Mao, 175 days	42.92	BR
1990	THE GIFT OF TRUTH, A. Song Mao, 175 days	42.92	NR
1990	THE GIFT OF JOY, A. Song Mao, 175 days	42.92	NR

China's Imperial Palace: The Forbidden City

1990	PAVILION OF 10,000 SPRINGS, S. Fu, 150 days	39.92	BR
1990	FLYING KITES ON A SPRING DAY, S. Fu, 150 days	39.92	BR
1990	PAVILION/FLOATING JADE GREEN, S. Fu, 150 days	42.92	NR
1991	THE LANTERN FESTIVAL, S. Fu, 150 days	42.92	NR
1991	NINE DRAGON SCREEN, S. Fu, 150 days	42.92	NR
1991	THE HALL OF THE CULTIVATING MIND, S. Fu, 150 days	42.92	BR
1991	DRESSING THE EMPRESS, S. Fu, 150 days	45.92	NR
1991	PAVILION OF FLOATING CUPS, S. Fu, 150 days	45.92	NR

Flower Goddesses of China

1991	THE LOTUS GODDESS, Z. HuiMin, 175 days	34.92	BR
1991	THE CHRYSANTHEMUM GODDESS, Z. HuiMin, 175 days	34.92	BR
1991	THE PLUM BLOSSOM GODDESS, Z. HuiMin, 175 days	37.92	BR

		Issue Price	Current Value
1991	THE PEONY BLOSSOM GODDESS, Z. HuiMin, 175 days ..	37.92	55.00
1991	THE NARCISSUS BLOSSOM GODDESS, Z. HuiMin, 175 days .	37.92	60.00
1991	THE CAMELIA BLOSSOM GODDESS, Z. HuiMin, 175 days	37.92	50.00

Flying Kites on a Spring Day
Photo courtesy of *Collectors News*

The Lotus Goddess
Photo courtesy of *Collectors News*

Garden of Satin Wings

1992	A MORNING DREAM, J. Xue–Bing, 115 days	29.92	RI
1993	AN EVENING MIST, J. Xue–Bing, 115 days	29.92	RI
1993	A GARDEN WHISPER, J. Xue–Bing, 115 days...........	29.92	RI
1993	AN ENCHANTING INTERLUDE	29.92	RI

Legends of West Lake

1989	LADY WHITE, J. Xue–Bing, 175 days	29.92	NR
1990	LADY SILKWORM, J. Xue–Bing, 175 days	29.92	40.00
1990	LAUREL PEAK, J. Xue–Bing, 175 days	39.92	NR
1990	RISING SUN TERRACE, J. Xue–Bing, 175 days..........	32.92	40.00
1990	THE APRICOT FAIRY, J. Xue–Bing, 175 days	32.92	BR
1990	BRIGHT PEARL, J. Xue–Bing, 175 days	32.92	BR
1990	THREAD OF SKY, J. Xue–Bing, 175 days	34.92	NR
1991	PHOENIX MOUNTAIN, J. Xue–Bing, 175 days	34.92	BR
1991	ANCESTORS OF TEA, J. Xue–Bing, 175 days	34.92	BR
1991	THREE POOLS MIRRORING/MOON, J. Xue–Bing, 175 days	36.92	NR
1991	FLY–IN PEAK, J. Xue–Bing, 175 days	36.92	NR
1991	THE CASE OF THE FOLDING FANS, J. Xue–Bing, 175 days	36.92	NR

Maidens of the Folding Sky

1992	LADY LU, J. Xue–Bing, 175 days	29.92	RI

	Issue Price	Current Value
1992 MISTRESS YANG, J. Xue–Bing, 175 days	29.92	RI
1992 BRIDE YEN CHUN, J. Xue–Bing, 175 days	32.92	RI
1993 PARROT MAIDEN, J. Xue–Bing, 175 days	32.92	RI

Scenes from the Summer Palace

1988 THE MARBLE BOAT, A. Song Mao, 175 days	29.92	BR
1988 JADE BELT BRIDGE, A. Song Mao, 175 days	29.92	NR
1989 HALL THAT DISPELS THE CLOUDS, A. Song Mao, 175 days	32.92	NR
1989 THE LONG PROMENADE, A. Song Mao, 175 days	32.92	BR
1989 GARDEN/HARMONIOUS PLEASURE, A. Song Mao, 175 days	32.92	BR
1989 THE GREAT STAGE, A. Song Mao, 175 days	32.92	BR
1989 SEVENTEEN ARCH BRIDGE, A. Song Mao, 175 days	34.92	BR
1990 BOATERS ON KUMMING LAKE, A. Song Mao, 175 days	34.92	BR

INCOLAY STUDIOS UNITED STATES

Enchanted Moments

1984 TIFFANY'S WORLD, Rosemary Calder, 7,500	95.00	NR
1985 JENNIFER'S WORLD, Rosemary Calder, 7,500	95.00	NR

Four Elements, Micro Plate

1983 AIR, Artisans of Incolay Studios	25.00	NR
1983 FIRE, Artisans of Incolay Studios	25.00	NR
1983 WATER, Artisans of Incolay Studios	25.00	NR
1983 EARTH, Artisans of Incolay Studios	25.00	NR
Set of 4	95.00	NR

Great Romances of History

1979 ANTONY AND CLEOPATRA, Carl Romanelli	65.00	NR
1980 TAJ MAHAL LOVERS, Carl Romanelli	65.00	NR
1981 LANCELOT AND GUINEVERE, Carl Romanelli	65.00	NR
1982 LORD NELSON AND LADY HAMILTON, Carl Romanelli	70.00	NR

Life's Interludes

1979 UNCERTAIN BEGINNING, James Roberts	95.00	NR
1980 FINALLY FRIENDS, James Roberts, 1 year	95.00	NR

Love Sonnets of Shakespeare

1986 SHALL I COMPARE THEE, limited	55.00	NR

Romantic Poets

1977 SHE WALKS IN BEAUTY, Gayle Bright Appleby	60.00	80.00
1978 A THING OF BEAUTY IS A JOY FOREVER, Gayle Bright Appleby	60.00	NR

		Issue Price	Current Value
1979	ODE TO A SKYLARK, Gayle Bright Appleby	65.00	NR
1980	SHE WAS A PHANTOM OF DELIGHT, Gayle Bright Appleby	65.00	NR
1981	THE KISS, Roger Akers	65.00	NR
1982	MY HEART LEAPS UP, Roger Akers	70.00	NR
1983	I STOOD TIPTOE, Roger Akers	70.00	NR
1984	THE DREAM, Roger Akers	70.00	NR
1985	THE RECOLLECTION, Roger Akers	70.00	NR

Voyage of Ulysses

1984	THE ISLE OF CIRCE, Alan Brunettin, 1 year	50.00	60.00
1985	THE SIRENS, Alan Brunettin, 1 year	50.00	NR
1986	OYGIA, ISLE OF CALYPSO, Alan Brunettin, 1 year	55.00	NR
1986	THE RETURN OF ULYSSES, Alan Brunettin, 1 year	55.00	NR
1986	THE REUNION, Alan Brunettin, 1 year	55.00	NR

The Return of Ulysses
Photo courtesy of *Collectors News*

INTERNATIONAL ART SOCIETY LTD. UNITED STATES

Erte Collection

1982	APPLAUSE, Erte	75.00	90.00

INTERNATIONAL SILVER UNITED STATES

Bicentennial

1972	SIGNING DECLARATION, Manuel de Oliveira, 7,500	40.00	310.00
1973	PAUL REVERE, Manuel de Oliveira, 7,500	40.00	160.00

		Issue Price	Current Value
1974	CONCORD BRIDGE, Manuel de Oliveira, 7,500	40.00	115.00
1075	CROSSING DELAWARE, Manuel de Oliveira, 7,500	50.00	80.00
1976	VALLEY FORGE, Manuel de Oliveira, 7,500..............	50.00	65.00
1977	SURRENDER AT YORKTOWN, Manuel de Oliveira, 7,500 .	50.00	60.00

Christmas

1974	TINY TIM, Carl Sundberg, 7,500......................	75.00	NR
1975	CAUGHT, Beverly Chase, 7,500	75.00	NR
1976	BRINGING HOME THE TREE, Albert Petitto, 7,500	75.00	NR
1977	CHRISTMAS BALL, Albert Petitto, 7,500	75.00	NR
1978	ALLELUIA, Albert Petitto, 7,500	75.00	NR
1979	REJOICE, Albert Petitto, 7,500	100.00	NR

INTERNATIONAL MUSEUM UNITED STATES

Letter Writer's

1982	PORTRAIT OF MICHELANGELO, 15,000	37.50	NR
1982	MRS. JOHN DOUGLAS, 15,000......................	37.50	NR
1983	DON ANTONIO, 15,000	37.50	NR
1983	LOVELY READER, 15,000	37.50	NR
1984	LADY WRITING LETTER, 15,000	37.50	NR

Stamp Art

1979	GINGERBREAD SANTA, 9,900	29.00	90.00
1980	MADONNA AND CHILD, 9,900......................	37.50	75.00
1981	BOTICELLI'S MADONNA AND CHILD, 9,900	45.00	60.00
1982	MADONNA OF THE GOLDFINCH, 9,900	45.00	NR
1983	RAPHAEL'S MADONNA, 9,900	39.50	NR

Superheroes

1983	SUPERMAN, limited	29.50	NR

INTERPACE UNITED STATES

Architects of Democracy

1974	GEORGE WASHINGTON, 1,776	—	—
1974	JOHN ADAMS, 1,776...............................	—	—
1974	THOMAS JEFFERSON, 1,776	—	—
1974	ALEXANDER HAMILTON, 1,776	—	—
	Set of 4...	225.00	280.00

Modigliani Series

1972	CARYATID, 10,000.................................	60.00	70.00

ISRAEL CREATIONS (NAAMAN LTD.)

Commemorative		Issue Price	Current Value
1967	WAILING WALL, 5,000	7.50	30.00
1967	TOWER OF DAVID, 5,000	7.50	30.00
1968	MASADA, 5,000	17.50	25.00
1969	RACHEL'S TOMB, 5,000	17.50	25.00
1970	TIBERIAS, 5,000	8.00	25.00
1971	NAZARETH, 5,000	9.00	25.00
1972	BETHSHEBA, 5,000	9.00	25.00
1973	ACRE, 5,000	9.00	25.00

ANTHONY JACKSON UNITED STATES

Single Issue

1982	PRESIDENTIAL PLATE, Anthony C. Jackson, 5,000	195.00	NR

GEORG JENSEN DENMARK

Chagall Series

1972	THE LOVERS, 12,500	50.00	120.00

Christmas

1972	DOVES, 1 year	15.00	55.00
1973	CHRISTMAS EVE, 1 year	15.00	40.00
1974	CHRISTMAS STORY, 1 year	17.50	25.00
1975	WINTER SCENE, 1 year	22.50	50.00
1976	CHRISTMAS IN THE COUNTRY, 1 year	27.00	35.00

Mother's Day

1973	MOTHER AND CHILD, 1 year	15.00	40.00
1974	SWEET DREAMS, 1 year	17.50	30.00
1975	A MOTHER'S WORLD, 1 year	22.50	30.00

SVEND JENSEN DENMARK

Anniversary

1980	HANS CHRISTIAN ANDERSEN'S HOME	60.00	75.00

Christmas/Andersen Fairy Tales

1970	HANS CRISTIAN ANDERSEN HOUSE, Gerhard Sausmark, 20,136	14.50	85.00

	Issue Price	Current Value
1971 LITTLE MATCH GIRL, Mado Stage, 20,000	15.00	40.00
1972 MAID OF COPENHAGEN, Edvard Eriksen, 22,122	16.50	45.00
1973 THE FIR TREE, Svend Otto, 11,000	22.00	40.00
1974 CHIMNEY SWEEP, Svend Otto, 11,000	25.00	NR
1975 THE UGLY DUCKLING, Svend Otto, 1 year	27.50	NR
1976 THE SNOW QUEEN, Mads Stage, 1 year	27.50	40.00
1977 THE SNOWMAN, Svend Otto, 1 year	29.50	40.00
1978 LAST DREAM OF THE OLD OAK TREE, Svend Otto, 1 year	32.00	45.00
1979 OLD STREET LAMP, Svend Otto, 1 year	36.50	NR
1980 WILLIE WINKIE, Svend Otto, 1 year	42.50	NR
1981 UTTERMOST PART OF THE SEA, Svend Otto, 1 year	49.50	NR
1982 TWELVE BY THE MAILCOACH, Svend Otto, 1 year	54.50	NR
1983 THE STORY OF THE YEAR, Svend Otto, 1 year	54.50	NR
1984 THE NIGHTINGALE, Svend Otto, 1 year	54.50	NR

Mother's Day

	Issue Price	Current Value
1970 BOUQUET FOR MOTHER, Maggi Baaring, 13,740	14.50	75.00
1971 MOTHER'S LOVE, Nulle Oigaard, 14,310	15.00	40.00
1972 GOOD NIGHT, Mads Stage, 11,018	16.50	35.00
1973 FLOWERS FOR MOTHER, Mads Stage, 11,000	20.00	35.00
1974 DAISIES FOR MOTHER, Mads Stage, 11,000	25.00	35.00
1975 SURPRISE FOR MOTHER, Mads Stage, 15,000	27.50	NR
1976 COMPLETE GARDENER, Mads Stage, 1 year	27.50	NR
1977 LITTLE FRIENDS, Mads Stage, 1 year	29.50	NR
1978 DREAMS, Mads Stage, 1 year	32.00	NR
1979 PROMENADE, Mads Stage, 1 year	36.50	NR
1980 NURSERY SCENE, Mads Stage, 1 year	42.50	NR
1981 DAILY DUTIES, Mads Stage, 1 year	49.50	NR
1982 MY BEST FRIEND, Mads Stage, 1 year	54.50	NR
1983 AN UNEXPECTED MEETING, Mads Stage, 1 year	54.50	NR
1984 WHO ARE YOU?, Mads Stage, 1 year..................	54.50	NR

JM COMPANY UNITED STATES

Competitive Sports

1979 DOWNHILL RACING SLALOM, Hal Reed, 5,000	30.00	NR

Love

1980 LOVE'S SERENADE, Hal Reed, 5,000	50.00	NR

Oriental Birds

1976 WINDOW AT TIGER SPRING TEMPLE, Hal Reed, 10,000 .	39.00	NR

JOSAIR FRANCE

Bicentennial		Issue Price	Current Value
1972	AMERICAN EAGLE, 400	250.00	NR
1973	AMERICAN FLAG, 400	250.00	NR
1974	ABRAHAM LINCOLN, 400	250.00	NR
1975	GEORGE WASHINGTON, 400	250.00	NR
1976	DECLARATION OF INDEPENDENCE, 400	250.00	NR

JUDAIC HERITAGE SOCIETY UNITED STATES
(See also Avondale and Villeta China)

Great Jewish Women

1976	GOLDA MEIR, 4,000	35.00	NR
1976	HENRIETTA SZOLD, 4,000	35.00	NR
1976	EMMA LAZARUS, 4,000	35.00	NR

Heritage

1976	RABBI, 4,000	35.00	NR
1976	HASIDIM, 4,000	35.00	NR
1976	SHTETL, 4,000	35.00	NR

Israel's 30th Anniversary Commemorative

1979	L'CHAYIM TO ISRAEL, 10,000	59.50	NR
1979	PROPHECY OF ISAIAH, 10,000	59.50	NR

Jerusalem Wedding

1979	BRIDE OF JERUSALEM, 6,000	65.00	BR
1979	HASIDIC DANCERS, 6,000	65.00	BR

Jewish Holidays

1972	PESACH, gold, 25	1,900.00	NR
1972	PESACH, silver, 2,000	150.00	NR
1972	PURIM, silver, 2,000	150.00	NR
1973	CHANUKAH, gold, 100	1,900.00	NR
1973	CHANUKAH, silver, 2,000	150.00	NR
1974	PURIM, silver, 1,000	150.00	NR
1979	CHANUKAH, 2,500	50.00	NR
1979	PURIM, 2,500	50.00	NR
1979	SHAVOUTH, 2,500	50.00	NR
1979	ROSH HASHANA, 2,500	50.00	NR
1979	SIMCHAT TORAH, 2,500	50.00	NR
1979	PESACH, 2,500	50.00	NR

Single Issues

		Issue Price	Current Value
1977	JACOB AND ANGEL, 5,000 . . . . ,,, ...	45.00	NR
1977	HATIKVAH, copper, 5,000	55.00	NR
1977	HATIKVAH, gold plate, 1,000	75.00	NR
1977	HATIKVAH, sterling silver, 500	180.00	NR
1980	SHALOM—PEACE, 6,000	95.00	NR

KAISER GERMANY

Anniversary

1972	LOVE BIRDS, Toni Schoener, 12,000	16.50	30.00
1973	IN THE PARK, Toni Schoener, 7,000	16.50	25.00
1974	CANOEING, Toni Schoener, 7,000	20.00	30.00
1975	TENDER MOMENT, Kurt Bauer, 7,000	25.00	NR
1976	SERENADE, Toni Schoener, 7,000	25.00	NR
1977	SIMPLE GIFT, Toni Schoener, 1 year	25.00	NR
1978	VIKING TOAST, Toni Schoener, 1 year	30.00	NR
1979	ROMANTIC INTERLUDE, Hannelore Blum, 1 year	32.00	NR
1980	LOVE AT PLAY, Hannelore Blum, 1 year	40.00	NR
1981	RENDEZVOUS, Hannelore Blum, 1 year	40.00	NR
1982	BETROTHAL, Kurt Bauer, 1 year	40.00	NR
1983	SUNDAY AFTERNOON, Toni Schoener, 1 year	40.00	NR

Bicentennial

1976	SIGNING DECLARATION, J. Trumball, 1,000	75.00	150.00

Bird Dogs

XX	COCKER SPANIEL, J. Francis, 19,500	39.50	NR
XX	BEAGLE, J. Francis, 19,500	39.50	NR
XX	ENGLISH SETTER, J. Francis, 19,500	39.50	NR
XX	BLACK LABRADOR, J. Francis, 19,500	39.50	NR
XX	GERMAN SHORT–HAIR POINTER, J. Francis, 19,500	39.50	NR
XX	GOLDEN LABRADOR, J. Francis, 19,500	39.50	NR
XX	ENGLISH POINTER, J. Francis, 19,500	39.50	NR
XX	IRISH SETTER, J. Francis, 19,500	39.50	NR

Childhood Memories

1985	WAIT A LITTLE, A. Schlesinger, 9,800	29.00	NR

Children's Prayer

1982	NOW I LAY ME DOWN TO SLEEP, Willy Freuner, 5,000 . . .	29.50	NR
1982	SAYING GRACE, Willy Freuner, 5,000	29.50	NR

Christmas

1970	WAITING FOR SANTA CLAUS, Toni Schoener, 1 year	12.50	25.00

		Issue Price	Current Value
1971	SILENT NIGHT, Kurt Bauer, 10,000	13.50	20.00
1972	COMING HOME FOR CHRISTMAS, Kurt Bauer, 10,000 ...	16.50	25.00
1973	HOLY NIGHT, Toni Schoener, 8,000	18.00	40.00
1974	CHRISTMAS CAROLERS, Kurt Bauer, 8,000.............	25.00	NR
1975	BRINGING HOME THE TREE, Joann Northcott, 1 year ...	25.00	NR
1976	CHRIST THE SAVIOUR IS BORN, Carlo Maratti, 1 year ...	25.00	35.00
1977	THE THREE KINGS, Toni Schoener, 1 year.............	25.00	NR
1978	SHEPHERDS IN THE FIELD, Toni Schoener, 1 year	30.00	NR
1979	CHRISTMAS EVE, Hannelore Blum, 1 year	32.00	40.00
1980	JOYS OF WINTER, Hannelore Blum, 1 year.............	40.00	NR
1981	ADORATION OF THREE KINGS, Kurt Bauer, 1 year	40.00	NR
1982	BRINGING HOME THE TREE, Kurt Bauer, 1 year	40.00	NR

Dance, Ballerina, Dance

1982	FIRST SLIPPERS, Robert Clarke, 14,500	47.50	NR
1983	AT THE BARRE, Robert Clarke, 14,500	47.50	NR
XX	THE RECITAL, Robert Clarke, 14,500	47.50	NR
XX	PIROUETTE, Robert Clarke, 14,500	47.50	NR
XX	SWAN LAKE, Robert Clarke, 14,500	47.50	NR
XX	OPENING NIGHT, Robert Clarke, 14,500................	47.50	NR

Egyptian

1978	KING TUT, 15,000	65.00	80.00
1980	NEFERTITI, 10,000	275.00	350.00
1980	TUTANKHAMEN, 10,000	275.00	350.00

Fairy Tales

1982	THE FROG KING, Gerda Neubacher, 50 days	39.50	50.00
1983	PUSS IN BOOTS, Gerda Neubacher, 50 days	39.50	NR

Little Red Riding Hood
Photo courtesy of *Collectors News*

Hansel and Gretel
Photo courtesy of *Collectors News*

Cinderella
Photo courtesy of *Collectors News*

		Issue Price	Current Value
1983	LITTLE RED RIDING HOOD, Gerda Neubacher	39.50	NR
1984	HANSEL AND GRETEL, Gerda Neubacher, limited	39.50	NR
1984	CINDERELLA, Gerda Neubacher, limited	39.50	NR
1984	SLEEPING BEAUTY, Gerda Neubacher, limited	39.50	NR

Famous Horses

1983	SNOW KNIGHT, Adolf Lohmann, 3,000	95.00	NR
1984	NORTHERN DANCER, Adolf Lohmann, 3,000	95.00	NR

Famous Lullabies

1985	SLEEP BABY SLEEP, Gerda Neubacher	39.50	NR
1986	ROCKABYE BABY, Gerda Neubacher	39.50	NR
1986	A MOCKINGBIRD, Gerda Neubacher	39.50	NR
1986	AU CLAIR DE LUNE, Gerda Neubacher	39.50	NR
1987	WELSH LULLABYE, Gerda Neubacher	39.50	NR
1988	BRAHMS' LULLABYE, Gerda Neubacher	39.50	NR

Four Seasons

1981	SPRING, Ivo Cenkovcan, 1 year	50.00	NR
1981	SUMMER, Ivo Cenkovcan, 1 year	50.00	NR
1981	AUTUMN, Ivo Cenkovcan, 1 year	50.00	NR
1981	WINTER, Ivo Cenkovcan, 1 year	50.00	NR

Garden and Songbirds

1973	CARDINAL, Wolfgang Gawantka, 2,000	200.00	250.00
1973	BLUE TITMOUSE, Wolfgang Gawantka, 2,000	200.00	250.00

Glen Loates' Feathered Friends

		Issue Price	Current Value
1978	BLUE JAYS, Glen Loates, 10,000	70.00	100.00
1979	CARDINALS, Glen Loates, 10,000	80.00	90.00
1980	CEDAR WAXWINGS, Glen Loates, 10,000	80.00	NR
1981	GOLDFINCH, Glen Loates, 10,000	80.00	NR

Graduate

1986	BOY, K. McKernan, 7,500............................	39.50	NR
1986	GIRL, K. McKernan, 7,500	39.50	NR

Happy Days

1981	THE AEROPLANE, Gerda Neubacher, 5,000	75.00	NR
1982	JULIE, Gerda Neubacher, 5,000	75.00	NR
1982	WINTER FUN, Gerda Neubacher, 5,000	75.00	NR
1983	THE LOOKOUT, Gerda Neubacher, 5,000	75.00	NR

Harmony and Nature

1985	SPRING ENCORE, John Littlejohn, 9,800	39.50	NR

Little Clowns

1981	THE RED MASK, Lorraine Trester, 9,500	35.00	NR
1982	PIGTAILS AND PUPPIES, Lorraine Trester, 9,500	35.00	NR
1983	CONCERTINA, Lorraine Trester, 9,500	35.00	NR

Little Men

1977	COME RIDE WITH ME, Lorraine Trester, 9,500	60.00	NR
1980	A MAGICAL MOMENT, Lorraine Trester, 9,500	60.00	NR
1983	DAY TO REMEMBER, Lorraine Trester, 9,500............	60.00	NR

Memories of Christmas

1983	THE WONDER OF CHRISTMAS, Gerda Neubacher, closed	42.50	NR
1984	A CHRISTMAS DREAM, Gerda Neubacher, closed	39.50	NR
1985	CHRISTMAS EVE, Gerda Neubacher, closed	39.50	NR
1986	A VISIT WITH SANTA, Gerda Neubacher, closed	39.50	NR

Mother's Day

1971	MARE AND FOAL, Toni Schoener, 1 year...............	13.00	25.00
1972	FLOWERS FOR MOTHER, Toni Schoener, 8,000	16.50	NR
1973	CAT AND KITTENS, Toni Schoener, 7,000	17.00	40.00
1974	FOX AND YOUNG, Toni Schoener, 7,000................	20.00	40.00
1975	GERMAN SHEPHERD WITH PUPS, Toni Schoener, 7,000 .	25.00	85.00
1976	SWAN AND CYGNETS, Toni Schoener, 7,000	25.00	NR
1977	MOTHER RABBIT WITH YOUNG, Joann Northcott, 1 year	25.00	NR
1978	HEN AND CHICKS, Toni Schoener, 1 year	30.00	50.00

	Issue Price	Current Value
1979 MOTHER'S DEVOTION, Nori Peter, 1 year	32.00	40.00
1980 RACCOON FAMILY, Joann Northcott, 1 year	40.00	NR
1981 SAFE NEAR MOTHER, Hannelore Blum	40.00	NR
1982 PHEASANT FAMILY, Kurt Bauer	40.00	NR
1983 TENDER CARD, Kurt Bauer	40.00	65.00

Oberammergau Passion Play

1970 OBERAMMERGAU, Toni Schoener, 1 year	25.00	NR
1970 OBERAMMERGAU, Kurt Bauer, 1 year	40.00	NR
1991 OBERAMMERGAU, sepia, 700	38.00	NR
1991 OBERAMMERGAU, cobalt, 400	64.00	NR

On the Farm

1981 THE DUCK, Adolf Lohmann, 1 year	50.00	75.00
1982 THE ROOSTER, Adolf Lohmann, 1 year	50.00	75.00
1983 THE POND, Adolf Lohmann, 1 year	50.00	75.00
1983 THE HORSES, Adolf Lohmann, 1 year	50.00	75.00
XX WHITE HORSE, Adolf Lohmann, 1 year	50.00	75.00
XX DUCKS ON THE POND, Adolf Lohmann, 1 year	50.00	75.00
XX GIRL WITH GOATS, Adolf Lohmann, 1 year	50.00	75.00
XX GIRL FEEDING ANIMALS, Adolf Lohmann, 1 year	50.00	75.00

Passion Play

1970 THE LAST SUPPER, Toni Schoener, 1 year	25.00	NR
1980 THE CRUCIFIXION, Kurt Bauer, 1 year	40.00	NR

People of the Midnight Sun

1978 NORTHERN LULLABY, Nori Peter, 15,000	65.00	NR
1979 ILAGA, MY FRIEND, Nori Peter, 15,000	75.00	NR
1980 MOTHERHOOD, Nori Peter, 15,000	85.00	NR
1981 ODARK AND SON SAMIK, Nori Peter, 15,000	90.00	NR
1982 ANANA WITH LITTLE MUTAK, Nori Peter, 15,000	90.00	NR
1983 THE HUNTER'S REWARD, Nori Peter, 15,000	90.00	NR

Racing for Pride and Profit

1984 THE AGING VICTOR, Roger Horton, 9,500	50.00	NR
1985 SECOND GOES HUNGRY, Roger Horton, 9,500	50.00	NR
1986 NO TIME TO BOAST, Roger Horton, 9,500	50.00	NR
1987 FIRST FISH TO MARKET, Roger Horton, 9,500	50.00	NR
1988 GYPSY TRADERS, Roger Horton, 9,500	50.00	NR

Romantic Portraits

1981 LILIE, Gerda Neubacher, 5,000	200.00	225.00
1982 CAMELIA, Gerda Neubacher, 5,000	175.00	200.00

		Issue Price	Current Value
1983	ROSE, Gerda Neubacher, 5,000	175.00	185.00
1984	DAISY, Gerda Neubacher, 5,000	175.00	NR

Traditional Fairy Tales

1983	CINDERELLA, Dorothea King, limited	39.50	NR
1983	JACK AND THE BEANSTALK, Dorothea King, limited	39.50	NR
1984	THREE LITTLE PIGS, Dorothea King, limited	39.50	NR
1985	GOLDILOCKS, Dorothea King, limited	39.50	NR
1985	DICK WITTINGTON, Dorothea King, limited	39.50	NR

Treasures of Tutankhamen

1978	THE GOLDEN MASK, 3,247	90.00	120.00
1978	THE GOLDEN THRONE, 3,247	90.00	120.00
1978	THE HORUS FALCON, 3,247	90.00	120.00
1978	THE IVORY CHEST, 3,247	90.00	120.00

Water Fowl

1985	MALLARD DUCKS, Edward J. Bierly, 19,500	55.00	75.00
1985	CANVASBACK DUCKS, Edward J. Bierly, 19,500	55.00	75.00
1985	WOOD DUCKS, Edward J. Bierly, 19,500	55.00	75.00
1985	PINTAIL DUCKS, Edward J. Bierly, 19,500	55.00	75.00

Wildflowers

1986	TRILLIUM, Gerda Neubacher, 9,500	39.50	55.00
1987	SPRING BEAUTY, Gerda Neubacher, 9,500	45.00	55.00
1987	WILD ASTERS, Gerda Neubacher, 9,500	45.00	55.00
1987	WILD ROSES, Gerda Neubacher, 9,500	49.50	55.00

Wildlife

1973	LITTLE CRITTERS, 5,000, set of 6	100.00	125.00

Woodland Creatures

1985	SPRINGTIME FROLIC, R. Orr, 10 days	37.50	NR
1985	FISHING TRIP, R. Orr, 10 days	37.50	NR
1985	RESTING IN THE GLEN, R. Orr, 10 days	37.50	NR
1985	MEADOWLAND VIGIL, R. Orr, 10 days	37.50	NR
1985	MORNING LESSON, R. Orr, 10 days	37.50	NR
1985	FIRST ADVENTURE, R. Orr, 10 days	37.50	NR
1985	THE HIDING PLACE, R. Orr, 10 days	37.50	NR
1985	STARTLED SENTRY, R. Orr, 10 days	37.50	NR

Yachts

1972	CETONIA, Kurt Bauer, 1,000	50.00	NR

		Issue Price	Current Value
1972	WESTWARD, Kurt Bauer, 1,000	50.00	NR

Yesterday's World

1978	A TIME FOR DREAMING, Lorraine Trester, 5,000	70.00	NR
1979	SUMMER IS FOREVER, Lorraine Trester, 5,000	75.00	NR
1980	SUNDAY AFTERNOON, Lorraine Trester, 5,000	80.00	NR
1984	BREATH OF SPRING, Lorraine Trester, 5,000	80.00	NR

Single Issue

1973	TORONTO HORSE SHOW, 1,000	29.00	40.00

DAVID KAPLAN STUDIOS UNITED STATES

Loveables

1982	LITTLE ANGEL, Sol Dember, 10,000	40.00	NR

KEIRSTEAD GALLERY CANADA

Sisters

1987	BRENDA'S MILL, James Keirstead, 4,000	55.00	NR

Single Issue

1985	DAWN, PEGGY'S COVE, James Keirstead, 7,500	98.00	NR

KERA DENMARK

Christmas

1967	KOBENHAVN, 1 year	6.00	25.00
1968	FORSTE, 1 year	6.00	20.00
1969	ANDERSEN'S HOUSE, 1 year	6.00	20.00
1970	LANGELINIE, 1 year	6.00	15.00
1971	LITTLE PETER, 1 year	6.00	15.00

Moon

1969	APOLLO II, 1 year	6.00	NR
1970	APOLLO 13, 1 year	6.00	NR

Mother's Day

1970	MOTHER'S DAY, 1 year	6.00	NR
1971	MOTHER'S DAY, 1 year	6.00	NR

KERN COLLECTIBLES UNITED STATES
(See also Gorham, Haviland & Parlon and Pickard)

		Issue Price	Current Value

Adventures of the Old West

1981	GRIZZLY AMBUSH, Harland Young, 7,500	65.00	NR
1982	THE TRIAN ROBBERS, Harland Young, 7,500	65.00	NR
1983	BANK HOLDUP, Harland Young, 7,500	65.00	NR
1985	NATURE STRIKES, Harland Young, 7,500	75.00	NR

Butterflies

| 1983 | MONARCHS, Patti Canaris, 7,500 | 75.00 | NR |

Nature Strikes
Photo courtesy of *Collectors News*

Elizabeth
Photo courtesy of *Collectors News*

Navajo Pixie
Photo courtesy of *Collectors News*

Morning Sun
Photo courtesy of *Collectors News*

Children of the Southwest

Year	Title	Issue Price	Current Value
1984	NAVAJO PIXIE, Jay Schmidt, 7,500	36.00	NR
1984	MORNING SUN, Jay Schmidt, 7,500	36.00	NR

Child's World

Year	Title	Issue Price	Current Value
1983	KATHIE, Leo Jansen, 9,800	45.00	NR
1983	MEREDITH, Leo Jansen, 9,800	45.00	NR
1984	FREDDIE, Leo Jansen, 9,800	45.00	NR
1984	JAMIE, Leo Jansen, 9,800	45.00	NR

Christmas of Yesterday

Year	Title	Issue Price	Current Value
1978	CHRISTMAS CALL, Marvin Nye, 5,000	45.00	NR
1979	WOODCUTTER'S CHRISTMAS, Marvin Nye, 5,000	50.00	NR
1980	BAKING CHRISTMAS GOODIES, Marvin Nye, 5,000	65.00	NR
1981	SINGING CHRISTMAS CAROLS, Marvin Nye, 5,000	55.00	NR

Companions

Year	Title	Issue Price	Current Value
1978	CUBS, Gregory Perillo, 5,000	40.00	90.00
1978	MIGHTY SIOUX, Gregory Perillo, 5,000	40.00	70.00
1979	NATURE GIRL, Gregory Perillo, 5,000	50.00	NR
1980	BUFFALO BOY, Gregory Perillo, 5,000	50.00	65.00
1981	SHEPHERDS, Gregory Perillo, 5,000	55.00	NR

Country Friends

Year	Title	Issue Price	Current Value
1984	ELIZABETH, Leesa Hoffman, 7,500	35.00	NR

Favorite Pets

Year	Title	Issue Price	Current Value
1981	SCHNAUZERS, Leo Jansen, 7,500	39.95	85.00
1982	COCKER SPANIELS, Leo Jansen, 7,500	39.95	NR
1983	POINTERS, Leo Jansen, 7,500	39.95	NR

Great Achievements in Art

Year	Title	Issue Price	Current Value
1980	THE ARABIAN, Harland Young, 3,000	65.00	170.00
1981	THE LONGHORNS, Harland Young, 3,000	60.00	NR

Horses of Harland Young

Year	Title	Issue Price	Current Value
1982	QUARTERHORSES, Harland Young, 10,000	55.00	NR
1983	ARABIANS, Harland Young, 10,000	55.00	NR
1984	MUSTANGS, Harland Young, 10,000	55.00	NR

Kitty Cats

Year	Title	Issue Price	Current Value
1983	MORRIE, Leo Jansen, 7,500	39.00	NR
1984	TATTOO, Leo Jansen, 7,500	39.00	NR

		Issue Price	Current Value

Leaders of Tomorrow

1980	FUTURE PHYSICIAN, Leo Jansen, 9,800	50.00	65.00
1981	FUTURE FARMER, Leo Jansen, 9,800	50.00	NR
1982	FUTURE FLORIST, Leo Jansen, 9,800	50.00	NR
1983	FUTURE TEACHER, Leo Jansen, 9,800	50.00	NR

Linda's Little Loveables

1978	THE BLESSING, Linda Avey, 7,500	30.00	40.00
1978	APPRECIATION, Linda Avey, 7,500	37.50	NR
1979	ADOPTED BURRO, Linda Avey, 7,500	42.50	NR

Mother's Day

1976	MOTHER AND CHILDREN, Leslie De Mille, 7,500	40.00	NR
1977	DARCY, Edward Runci, 7,500	50.00	NR
1978	MOMENT TO REFLECT, Edward Runci, 5,000	55.00	NR
1979	FULFILLMENT, Edward Runci, 5,000	45.00	NR
1980	A RENEWAL OF FAITH, Edward Runci, 5,000	45.00	NR

North American Game Birds

1983	CANADIAN GEESE, Derk Hansen, 7,500	60.00	NR
1984	MALLARDS, Derk Hansen, 7,500	60.00	NR
1984	PHEASANTS, Derk Hansen, 7,500	60.00	NR

Portrait of Innocence

1977	JOHNNIE AND DUKE, Leo Jansen, 7,500	40.00	55.00
1978	RANDY AND REX, Leo Jansen, 7,500	42.50	65.00
1979	FURRY FRIENDS, Leo Jansen, 7,500	47.50	NR
1980	BENJI'S BURRO, Leo Jansen, 7,500	50.00	115.00

School Days

| 1982 | APPLE FOR MY TEACHER, Marvin Nye, 7,500 | 65.00 | BR |
| 1983 | THE ARITHMETIC LESSON, Marvin Nye, 7,500 | 65.00 | BR |

Sugar and Spice

1976	DANA AND DEBBIE, Leo Jansen, 7,500	40.00	130.00
1977	BECKY AND BABY, Leo Jansen, 7,500	42.50	75.00
1978	JEANNETTE AND JULIE, Leo Jansen, 7,500	47.50	60.00
1980	RAMONA AND RACHEL, Leo Jansen, 7,500	50.00	100.00

This Little Pig Went to Market

1982	THIS LITTLE PIG WENT TO MARKET, Linda Nye, 9,800	39.95	NR
1983	THIS LITTLE PIG STAYED HOME, Linda Nye, 9,800	42.50	NR
1984	THIS LITTLE PIG HAD ROAST BEEF, Linda Nye, 9,800	45.00	NR
1985	THIS LITTLE PIG HAD NONE, Linda Nye, 9,800	45.00	NR

		Issue Price	Current Value

Tribal Companions

| 1984 | MY BEST FRIEND, Derk Hansen, 6,000 . . . . | 35.00 | NR |

Zoological Garden

| 1983 | ELEPHANTS, Mike Carroll, 5,000 . . . . | 55.00 | NR |
| 1984 | TIGERS, Mike Carroll, 5,000 . . . . | 55.00 | NR |

Single Issue

| 1984 | CHAMP, Leo Jansen, 7,500 . . . . | 39.50 | NR |

This Little Pig Went to Market
Photo courtesy of *Collectors News*

KETSUZAN–KILN JAPAN

Poetic Visions of Japan

1988	PLUM BLOSSOMS	39.93	BR
1989	A BUTTERFLY	39.93	NR
1989	SNOWY HERON	42.93	NR
1989	ORPHAN SPARROW	42.93	BR
1990	CHERRY FLOWERS	42.93	NR
1990	LEAVES	42.93	NR
1990	HARVEST MOON	44.93	BR
1990	CRYSTAL SPRING	44.93	NR

KHOLUI ART STUDIOS RUSSIA

Legend of the Snowmaiden

| 1989 | SNOWMAIDEN, SNEGUROCHKA . . . . | 35.87 | BR |
| 1990 | SNOWMAIDEN AND HER PARENTS . . . . | 35.87 | BR |

		Issue Price	Current Value
1990	JUDGMENT OF TSAR BERENDEY	38.87	BR
1990	A SONG OF LOVE	38.87	BR
1990	A DANCE OF FRIENDSHIP	38.87	BR
1990	LET'S SERENADE	38.87	BR
1991	LOVE'S FINALE	40.87	BR
1991	THE SNOWMAIDEN WITH SPRING AND WINTER	40.87	BR

Snowmaiden and Her Parents
Photo courtesy of *Collectors News*

Light of Christ

1993	JESUS WALKS ON WATER..........................	29.87	RI
1993	THE ASCENSION	29.87	RI
1993	THE BAPTISM OF CHRIST	29.87	RI
1993	THE ACT OF BLESSING..............................	29.87	RI

KING'S ITALY

Christmas

1973	ADORATION, Merli, 1,500	100.00	220.00
1974	MADONNA, Merli, 1,500	150.00	200.00
1975	HEAVENLY CHOIR, Merli, 1,500	160.00	215.00
1976	SIBLINGS, Merli, 1,500	200.00	230.00

Flowers

1973	CARNATION, Aldo Falchi, 1,000	85.00	130.00
1974	RED ROSE, Aldo Falchi, 1,000	100.00	145.00
1975	YELLOW DAHLIA, Aldo Falchi, 1,000	110.00	160.00
1976	BLUEBELLS, Aldo Falchi, 1,000	130.00	165.00
1977	ANEMONES, Aldo Falchi, 1,000	130.00	175.00

Mother's Day		Issue Price	Current Value
1973	DANCING GIRL, Merli, 1,500	100.00	185.00
1974	DANCING BOY, Merli, 1,500	115.00	185.00
1975	MOTHERLY LOVE, Merli, 1,500	140.00	200.00
1976	MAIDEN, Merli, 1,500	180.00	200.00

KIRK UNITED STATES

Bicentennial

1972	WASHINGTON, 5,000................................	75.00	NR
1972	CONSTELLATION, 825	75.00	NR

Chistmas

1972	FLIGHT INTO EGYPT, 3,500	150.00	NR

Mother's Day

1972	MOTHER AND CHILD, 3,500	75.00	NR
1973	MOTHER AND CHILD, 2,500	80.00	NR

Thanksgiving

1972	THANKSGIVING WAYS AND MEANS, 3,500	150.00	NR

JODI KIRK UNITED STATES

DeGrazia Series

1972	HEAVENLY BLESSING, 200	75.00	85.00

EDWIN M. KNOWLES UNITED STATES

Aesop's Fables

1988	THE GOOSE THAT LAID THE GOLDEN EGG, M. Hampshire, 150 days	27.90	NR
1988	THE HARE AND THE TORTOISE, M. Hampshire, 150 days	27.90	NR
1988	THE FOX AND THE GRAPES, M. Hampshire, 150 days ...	30.90	BR
1989	THE LION AND THE MOUSE, M. Hampshire, 150 days ...	30.90	NR
1989	THE MILK MAID AND HER PAIL, M. Hampshire, 150 days	30.90	BR
1989	THE JAY AND THE PEACOCK, M. Hampshire, 150 days ..	30.90	BR

American Innocents

1986	ABIGAIL IN THE ROSE GARDEN, Barbara Marsten and Valentin Mandrajji, 150 days	19.50	NR
1986	ANN BY THE TERRACE, Marsten and Mandrajji, 150 days	19.50	NR

		Issue Price	Current Value
1986	ELLEN AND JOHN IN THE PARLOR, Marsten and Mandrajji, 150 days	19.50	NR
1987	WILLIAM ON THE ROCKING HORSE, Marsten and Mandrajji, 150 days	19.50	45.00

American Jouney

1987	WESTWARD HO, Mort Kunstler, 150 days	29.90	NR
1988	KITCHEN WITH A VIEW, Mort Kunstler, 150 days	29.90	NR
1988	CROSSING THE RIVER, Mort Kunstler, 150 days	29.90	NR
1988	CHRISTMAS AT THE NEW CABIN, Mort Kunstler, 150 days	29.90	NR

Americana Holidays

1978	THE FOURTH OF JULY, Don Spaulding, 1 year	26.00	BR
1979	THANKSGIVING, Don Spaulding, 1 year	26.00	BR
1980	EASTER, Don Spaulding, 1 year	26.00	BR
1981	VALENTINE'S DAY, Don Spaulding, 1 year	26.00	BR
1982	FATHER'S DAY, Don Spaulding, 1 year	26.00	BR
1983	CHRISTMAS, Don Spaulding, 1 year	26.00	BR
1984	MOTHER'S DAY, Don Spaulding, 1 year	26.00	BR

Annie

1983	ANNIE AND SANDY, William Chambers, 100 days	19.00	BR
1983	DADDY WARBUCKS, William Chambers, 100 days	19.00	BR
1983	ANNIE AND GRACE, William Chambers, 100 days	19.00	BR
1984	ANNIE AND THE ORPHANS, William Chambers, 100 days	21.00	BR
1985	TOMORROW, William Chambers, 100 days	21.00	BR
1985	ANNIE AND MISS HANNIGAN, William Chambers, 100 days	21.00	BR

The Goose that Laid the Golden Egg
Photo courtesy of *Collectors News*

Annie and Miss Hannigan
Photo courtesy of *Collectors News*

		Issue Price	Current Value
1986	ANNIE, LILY AND ROOSTER, William Chambers, 100 days	24.00	NR
1986	GRAND FINALE, William Chambers, 100 days	24.00	BR

Baby Owls of North America

1991	PEEK—A—WHOO: SCREECH OWLS, J. Thornbrugh, 150 days	27.90	35.00
1991	FORTY WINKS: SAW—WHET OWLS, J. Thornbrugh, 150 days	27.90	40.00
1991	THE TREE HOUSE: NORTHERN PYGMY OWLS, J. Thornbrugh, 150 days	30.90	40.00
1991	THREE OF A KIND: GREAT HORNED OWLS, J. Thornbrugh, 150 days	30.90	40.00
1991	OUT ON A LIMB: GREAT GRAY OWLS, J. Thornbrugh, 150 days	30.90	50.00
1991	BEGINNING TO EXPLORE: BOREAL OWLS, J. Thornbrugh, 150 days	32.90	50.00
1992	THREE'S COMPANY: LONG—EARED OWLS, J. Thornbrugh, 150 days	32.90	RI
1992	WHOO'S THERE?: BARRED OWL, J. Thornbrugh, 150 days	32.90	RI

Backyard Harmony

1991	THE SINGING LESSON, J. Thornbrugh, 150 days	27.90	35.00
1991	WELCOMING A NEW DAY, J. Thornbrugh, 150 days	27.90	40.00
1991	ANNOUNCING SPRING, J. Thornbrugh, 150 days	30.90	55.00
1992	THE MORNING HARVEST, J. Thornbrugh, 150 days	30.90	RI
1992	SPRINGTIME PRIDE, J. Thornbrugh, 150 days	30.90	RI
1992	TREETOP SERENADE, J. Thornbrugh, 150 days	32.90	RI
1992	AT THE PEEP OF DAY, J. Thornbrugh, 150 days	32.90	RI
1992	TODAY'S DISCOVERIES, J. Thornbrugh, 150 days	32.90	RI

Bambi

1991	BASHFUL BAMBI, Disney Studios, 150 days	34.90	NR
1992	BAMBI'S NEW FRIENDS, Disney Studios, 150 days	34.90	RI
1992	HELLO LITTLE PRINCE, Disney Studios, 150 days	37.90	RI
1992	BAMBI'S MORNING GREETINGS, Disney Studios, 150 days ..	37.90	RI
1992	BAMBI'S SKATING LESSON, Disney Studios, 150 days ..	37.90	RI
1993	WHAT'S UP POSSUMS?, Disney Studios, 150 days	37.90	RI

Band's Songbirds of Europe

1987	THE CHAFFINCH, Ursula Band, 100 days	24.50	NR

Beauty and the Beast

1993	LOVE'S FIRST DANCE, Disney Studios, 150 days	29.90	NR

Biblical Mothers

1983	BATHSHEBA AND SOLOMON, Eve Licea, 1 year	39.50	NR
1984	JUDGMENT OF SOLOMON, Eve Licea, 1 year	39.50	NR
1984	PHARAOH'S DAUGHTER AND MOSES, Eve Licea, 1 year	39.50	BR

		Issue Price	Current Value
1985	MARY AND JESUS, Eve Licea, 1 year	39.50	BR
1985	SARAH AND ISAAC, Eve Licea, 1 year................	44.50	NR
1985	REBEKAH, JACOB AND ESAU, Eve Licea, 1 year........	44.50	NR

Birds of the Seasons

1990	CARDINALS IN WINTER, S. Timm, 150 days	24.90	35.00
1990	BLUEBIRDS IN SPRING, S. Timm, 150 days.............	24.90	NR
1991	NUTHATCHES IN FALL, S. Timm, 150 days.............	27.90	BR
1991	BALTIMORE ORIOLES IN SUMMER, S. Timm, 150 days ..	27.90	NR
1991	BLUE JAYS IN EARLY FALL, S. Timm, 150 days	27.90	40.00
1991	ROBINS IN EARLY SPRING, S. Timm, 150 days	27.90	NR
1991	CEDAR WAXWINGS IN FALL, S. Timm, 150 days	29.90	60.00
1991	CHICKADEES IN WINTER, S. Timm, 150 days	29.90	55.00

Birds of Your Garden, Encyclopedia Britannica

1985	CARDINAL, Kevin Daniel, 100 days....................	19.50	NR
1985	BLUE JAY, Kevin Daniel, 100 days	19.50	NR
1985	ORIOLE, Kevin Daniel, 100 days	22.50	NR
1986	CHICKADEES, Kevin Daniel, 100 days	22.50	BR
1986	ROBIN, Kevin Daniel, 100 days	22.50	NR
1986	BLUEBIRD, Kevin Daniel, 100 days	22.50	NR
1986	HUMMINGBIRD, Kevin Daniel, 100 days	24.50	NR
1987	GOLDFINCH, Kevin Daniel, 100 days..................	24.50	NR
1987	DOWNY WOODPECKER, Kevin Daniel, 100 days	24.50	NR
1987	CEDAR WAXWING, Kevin Daniel, 100 days.............	24.90	NR

Call of the Wilderness

1991	FIRST OUTING, Keven Daniel, 150 days	29.90	45.00

Bathsheba and Solomon
Photo courtesy of *Collectors News*

First Outing
Photo courtesy of *Collectors News*

		Issue Price	Current Value
1991	HOWLING LESSON, Kevin Daniel, 150 days	29.90	90.00
1991	SILENT WATCH, Kevin Daniel, 150 days	32.90	50.00
1991	WINTER TRAVELERS, Kevin Daniel, 150 days	32.90	50.00
1992	AHEAD OF THE PACK, Kevin Daniel, 150 days	32.90	RI
1992	NORTHERN SPIRITS, Kevin Daniel, 150 days	34.90	RI
1992	TWILIGHT FRIENDS, Kevin Daniel, 150 days	34.90	RI
1992	A NEW FUTURE, Kevin Daniel, 150 days	34.90	RI
1992	MORNING MIST, Kevin Daniel, 150 days	36.90	RI
1992	THE SILENT ONE, Kevin Daniel, 150 days	36.90	RI

Carousel

1987	IF I LOVED YOU, D. Brown, 150 days	24.90	NR
1988	MR. SNOW, D. Brown, 150 days	24.90	NR
1988	THE CAROUSEL WALTZ, D. Brown, 150 days	24.90	NR
1988	YOU'LL NEVER WALK ALONE, D. Brown, 150 days	24.90	NR

Casablanca

1990	HERE'S LOOKING AT YOU, KID, J. Griffin, 150 days	34.90	NR
1990	WE'LL ALWAYS HAVE PARIS, J. Griffin, 150 days	34.90	NR
1991	WE LOVED EACH OTHER ONCE, J. Griffin, 150 days	37.90	BR
1991	RICK'S CAFE AMERICAIN, J. Griffin, 150 days	37.90	NR
1991	A FRANC FOR YOUR THOUGHTS, J. Griffin, 150 days	37.90	50.00
1991	PLAY IT SAM, J. Griffin, 150 days	37.90	55.00

Cat Tales

1987	A CHANCE MEETING: WHITE AMERICAN SHORTHAIRS, Amy Brackenbury, 150 days	21.50	30.00
1987	GONE FISHING: MAINE COONS, Amy Brackenbury, 150 days 35.00		21.50
1988	STRAWBERRIES AND CREAM: CREAM PERSIANS, Amy Brackenbury, 150 days	24.90	40.00
1988	FLOWER BED: BRITISH SHORTHAIRS, Amy Brackenbury, 150 days	24.90	NR
1988	KITTENS AND MITTENS: SILVER TABBIES, Amy Brackenbury, 150 days	24.90	NR
1988	ALL WRAPPED UP: HIMALAYANS, Amy Brackenbury, 150 days	24.90	45.00

China's Natural Treasures

1991	THE SIBERIAN TIGER, T. C. Chiu, 150 days	29.90	40.00
1991	THE SNOW LEOPARD, T. C. Chiu, 150 days	29.90	NR
1991	THE GIANT PANDA, T. C. Chiu, 150 days	32.90	NR
1992	THE TIBETAN BROWN BEAR, T. C. Chiu, 150 days	32.90	RI
1992	THE ASIAN ELEPHANT, T. C. Chiu, 150 days	32.90	RI
1992	THE GOLDEN MONKEY, T. C. Chiu, 150 days	34.90	RI

Christmas in the City

		Issue Price	Current Value
1992	A CHRISTMAS SNOWFALL, A. Leimanis, 150 days	34.90	RI
1992	YULETIDE CELEBRATION, A. Leimanis, 150 days	34.90	RI
1993	HOLIDAY CHEER, A. Leimanis, 150 days................	34.90	RI
1993	THE MAGIC OF CHRISTMAS, A. Leimanis, 150 days	34.90	RI

Cinderella

1988	BIBBIDI – BOBBIDI – BOO, Disney Studios, 150 days ...	29.90	55.00
1989	A DREAM IS A WISH YOUR HEART MAKES, Disney Studios, 150 days	29.90	55.00
1989	OH SING SWEET NIGHTINGALE, Disney Studios, 150 days	32.90	50.00
1989	A DRESS FOR CINDERELLA, Disney Studios, 150 days ...	32.90	90.00
1989	SO THIS IS LOVE, Disney Studios, 150 days	32.90	65.00
1990	AT THE STROKE OF MIDNIGHT, Disney Studios, 150 days	32.90	55.00
1990	IF THE SHOE FITS, Disney Studios, 150 days	34.90	65.00
1990	HAPPILY EVER AFTER, Disney Studios, 150 days	34.90	NR

Classic Fairy Tales

1991	GOLDILOCKS AND THE THREE BEARS, Scott Gustafson, 150 days	29.90	50.00
1991	LITTLE RED RIDING HOOD, Scott Gustafson, 150 days ...	29.90	60.00
1991	THE THREE LITTLE PIGS, Scott Gustafson, 150 days	32.90	60.00
1991	THE FROG PRINCE, Scott Gustafson, 150 days	32.90	60.00
1992	JACK AND THE BEANSTALK, Scott Gustafson, 150 days .	32.90	RI
1992	HANSEL AND GRETEL, Scott Gustafson, 150 days	34.90	RI
1992	PUSS IN BOOTS, Scott Gustafson, 150 days............	34.90	RI
1992	TOM THUMB, Scott Gustafson, 150 days	34.90	RI

Classic Mother Goose

1992	LITTLE MISS MUFFET, Scott Gustafson, 150 days	29.90	RI
1992	MARY HAD A LITTLE LAMB, Scott Gustafson, 150 days..	29.90	RI
1992	MARY, MARY, QUITE CONTRARY, Scott Gustafson, 150 days ..	29.90	RI
1992	LITTLE BO PEEP, Scott Gustafson, 150 days	29.90	RI

Comforts of Home

1992	SLEEPYHEADS, H. Hollister Ingmire, 150 days	24.90	RI
1992	CURIOUS PAIR, H. Hollister Ingmire, 150 days	24.90	RI
1993	MOTHER'S RETREAT, H. Hollister Ingmire, 150 days	29.90	RI

Cozy Country Corners

1990	LAZY MORNING, H. Hollister Ingmire, 150 days	24.90	50.00
1990	WARM RETREAT, H. Hollister Ingmire, 150 days.........	24.90	30.00
1991	A SUNNY SPOT, H. Hollister Ingmire, 150 days..........	27.90	40.00
1991	ATTIC AFTERNOON, H. Hollister Ingmire, 150 days	27.90	40.00
1991	MIRROR MISCHIEF, H. Hollister Ingmire, 150 days	27.90	60.00
1991	HIDE AND SEEK, H. Hollister Ingmire, 150 days	29.90	40.00

		Issue Price	Current Value
1991	APPLE ANTICS, H. Hollister Ingmire, 150 days	29.90	70.00
1991	TABLE TROUBLE, H. Hollister Ingmire, 150 days	29.90	65.00

Csatari Grandparents

1980	BEDTIME STORY, Joseph Csatari, 1 year	18.00	BR
1981	SKATING LESSON, Joseph Csatari, 1 year	20.00	NR
1982	COOKIE TASTING, Joseph Csatari, 1 year	20.00	BR
1983	THE SWINGER, Joseph Csatari, 1 year	20.00	NR
1984	THE SKATING QUEEN, Joseph Csatari, 1 year	22.00	BR
1985	PATRIOT'S PARADE, Joseph Csatari, 1 year	22.00	BR
1986	THE HOME RUN, Joseph Csatari, 1 year	22.00	BR
1987	THE SNEAK PREVIEW, Joseph Csatari, 1 year	22.00	BR

Bibbidy–Bobbidy–Boo
Photo courtesy of *Collectors News*

The Swinger
Photo courtesy of *Collectors News*

Disney Treasured Moments Collection

1992	CINDERELLA, Disney Studios, 150 days	29.90	RI
1992	SNOW WHITE AND THE SEVEN DWARFS, Disney Studios, 150 days	29.90	RI
1993	ALICE IN WONDERLAND, Disney Studios, 150 days	32.90	RI

Enchanted Cottages

1993	FALLBROOKE COTTAGE, Thomas Kinkade, 95 days	29.90	RI

Fantasia (The Sorcerer's Apprentice) Golden Anniversary

1990	THE APPRENTICE'S DREAM, Disney Studios, 150 days ..	29.90	55.00
1990	MISCHIEVOUS APPRENTICE, Disney Studios, 150 days..	29.90	65.00
1991	DREAMS OF POWER, Disney Studios, 150 days	32.90	55.00

		Issue Price	Current Value
1991	MICKEY'S MAGICAL WHIRLPOOL, Disney Studios, 150 days ..	32.90	45.00
1991	WIZARDRY GONE WILD, Disney Studios, 150 days	32.90	40.00
1991	MICKEY MAKES MAGIC, Disney Studios, 150 days	34.90	55.00
1991	THE PENITENT APPRENTICE, Disney Studios, 150 days .	34.90	45.00
1992	AN APPRENTICE AGAIN, Disney Studios, 150 days	34.90	RI

Father's Love

1984	OPEN WIDE, B. Bradley, 100 days....................	19.50	NR
1984	BATTER UP, B. Bradley, 100 days	19.50	NR
1985	LITTLE SHAVER, B. Bradley, 100 days	19.50	BR
1985	SWING TIME, B. Bradley, 100 days	22.50	BR

The Apprentice's Dream
Photo courtesy of *Collectors News*

Batter Up
Photo courtesy of *Collectors News*

Field Puppies

1987	DOG TIRED — THE SPRINGER SPANIEL, L. Kaatz, 150 days ..	24.90	45.00
1987	CAUGHT IN THE ACT — THE GOLDEN RETRIEVER, L. Kaatz, 150 days	24.90	40.00
1988	MISSING/POINT — IRISH SETTER, L. Kaatz, 150 days ...	27.90	NR
1988	A PERFECT SET — LABRADOR, L. Kaatz, 150 days	27.90	50.00
1988	FRITZ'S FOLLY — GERMAN SHORTHAIRED POINTER, L. Kaatz, 150 days	27.90	35.00
1988	SHIRT TALES — COCKER SPANIEL, L. Kaatz, 150 days...	27.90	40.00
1989	FINE FEATHERED FRIENDS — ENGLISH SETTER, L. Kaatz, 150 days	29.90	NR
1989	COMMAND PERFORMANCE — WEIMARANER, L. Kaatz, 150 days	29.90	NR

		Issue Price	Current Value

Field Trips

Year	Title	Issue Price	Current Value
1990	GONE FISHING, L. Kaatz, 150 days	24.90	NR
1991	DUCKING DUTY, L. Kaatz, 150 days	24.90	NR
1991	BOXED IN, L. Kaatz, 150 days	27.90	NR
1991	PUPS 'N BOOTS, L. Kaatz, 150 days	27.90	NR
1991	PUPPY TALES, L. Kaatz, 150 days	27.90	NR
1991	PAIL PALS, L. Kaatz, 150 days	29.90	NR
1992	CHESAPEAKE BAY RETRIEVERS, L. Kaatz, 150 days	29.90	NR
1992	HAT TRICK, L. Kaatz, 150 days	29.90	BR

First Impressions

Year	Title	Issue Price	Current Value
1991	TAKING A GANDER, J. Giordano, 150 days	29.90	40.00
1991	TWO'S COMPANY, J. Giordano, 150 days	29.90	35.00
1991	FINE FEATHERED FRIENDS, J. Giordano, 150 days	32.90	45.00
1991	WHAT'S UP?, J. Giordano, 150 days	32.90	40.00
1991	ALL EARS, J. Giordano, 150 days	32.90	65.00
1992	BETWEEN FRIENDS, J. Giordano, 150 days	32.90	RI

Four Ancient Elements

Year	Title	Issue Price	Current Value
1984	EARTH, Georgia Lambert, limited	27.50	BR
1984	WATER, Georgia Lambert, limited	27.50	BR
1985	AIR, Georgia Lambert, limited	29.50	BR
1985	FIRE, Georgia Lambert, limited	29.50	40.00

Dog Tired – The Springer Spaniel
Photo courtesy of *Collectors News*

Earth
Photo courtesy of *Collectors News*

Frances Hook Legacy

Year	Title	Issue Price	Current Value
1985	FASCINATION, Frances Hook, 100 days	19.50	NR
1985	DAYDREAMING, Frances Hook, 100 days	19.50	NR

		Issue Price	Current Value
1985	DISCOVERY, Frances Hook, 100 days	22.50	NR
1985	DISAPPOINTMENT, Frances Hook, 100 days	22.50	NR
1985	WONDERMENT, Frances Hook, 100 days	22.50	NR
1985	EXPECTATION, Frances Hook, 100 days	22.50	NR

Free as the Wind

1992	SKYWARD, M. Budden, 150 days	29.90	RI
1992	ALOFT, M. Budden, 150 days	29.90	RI
1992	AIRBORNE, M. Budden, 150 days	32.90	RI
1993	FLIGHT, M. Budden, 150 days	32.90	RI
1993	ASCENT, M. Budden, 150 days	32.90	RI
1993	HEAVENWARD	32.90	RI

Friends I Remember

1983	FISH STORY, Jeanne Down, limited	17.50	BR
1984	OFFICE HOURS, Jeanne Down, limited	17.50	BR
1985	A COAT OF PAINT, Jeanne Down, limited	17.50	BR
1985	HERE COMES THE BRIDE, Jeanne Down, limited	19.50	NR
1985	FRINGE BENEFITS, Jeanne Down, limited	19.50	NR
1986	HIGH SOCIETY, Jeanne Down, limited	19.50	NR
1986	FLOWER ARRANGEMENT, Jeanne Down, limited	21.50	NR
1986	TASTE TEST, Jeanne Down, limited	21.50	NR

Daydreaming
Photo courtesy of *Collectors News*

A Coat of Paint
Photo courtesy of *Collectors News*

Friends of the Forest

1987	THE RABBIT, Kevin Daniel, 150 days	24.50	NR
1987	THE RACCOON, Kevin Daniel, 150 days	24.50	NR
1987	THE SQUIRREL, Kevin Daniel, 150 days	27.90	BR

		Issue Price	Current Value
1988	THE CHIPMUNK, Kevin Daniel, 150 days	27.90	BR
1988	THE FOX, Kevin Daniel, 150 days	27.90	BR
1988	THE OTTER, Kevin Daniel, 150 days	27.90	BR

Garden Cottages of England

1991	CHANDLER'S COTTAGE, Thomas Kinkade, 150 days	27.90	55.00
1991	CEDAR NOOK COTTAGE, Thomas Kinkade, 150 days	27.90	45.00
1991	CANDLELIT COTTAGE, Thomas Kinkade, 150 days	30.90	45.00
1991	OPEN GATE COTTAGE, Thomas Kinkade, 150 days	30.90	40.00
1991	MCKENNA'S COTTAGE, Thomas Kinkade, 150 days	30.90	45.00
1991	WOODSMAN'S THATCH COTTAGE, Thomas Kinkade, 150 days	32.90	45.00
1992	MERRITT'S COTTAGE, Thomas Kinkade, 150 days	32.90	RI
1992	STONEGATE COTTAGE, Thomas Kinkade, 150 days	32.90	RI

Garden Secrets

1993	NINE LIVES, Higgins Bond, 150 days	24.90	RI
1993	FLORAL PURR—FUME, Higgins Bond, 150 days	24.90	RI

Gone with the Wind

1978	SCARLETT, Raymond Kursar, 1 year	21.50	180.00
1979	ASHLEY, Raymond Kursar, 1 year	21.50	85.00
1980	MELANIE, Raymond Kursar, 1 year	21.50	40.00
1981	RHETT, Raymond Kursar, 1 year	23.50	35.00
1982	MAMMY LACING SCARLETT, Raymond Kursar, 1 year	23.50	50.00
1983	MELANIE GIVES BIRTH, Raymond Kursar, 1 year	23.50	55.00
1984	SCARLETT'S GREEN DRESS, Raymond Kursar, 1 year	25.50	45.00
1985	BONNIE AND RHETT, Raymond Kursar, 1 year	25.50	65.00
1985	SCARLETT AND RHETT: THE FINALE, Raymond Kursar, 1 year	29.50	50.00

Scarlett

Bonnie and Rhett

Photo courtesy of *Collectors News*

		Issue Price	Current Value

Great Cats of the Americas

1989	THE JAGUAR, L. Cable, 150 days	29.90	NR
1989	THE COUGAR, L. Cable, 150 days	29.90	NR
1989	THE LYNX, L. Cable, 150 days	32.90	NR
1990	THE OCELOT, L. Cable, 150 days	32.90	NR
1990	THE BOBCAT, L. Cable, 150 days	32.90	BR
1990	THE JAGUARUNDI, L. Cable, 150 days	32.90	BR
1990	THE MARGAY, L. Cable, 150 days	34.90	NR
1991	THE PAMPAS CAT, L. Cable, 150 days	34.90	NR

Heirlooms and Lace

1989	ANNA, C. Layton, 150 days	34.90	40.00
1989	VICTORIA, C. Layton, 150 days	34.90	60.00
1990	TESS, C. Layton, 150 days	37.90	70.00
1990	OLIVIA, C. Layton, 150 days	37.90	110.00
1991	BRIDGET, C. Layton, 150 days	37.90	105.00
1991	REBECCA, C. Layton, 150 days	37.90	90.00

Hibel Christmas

1985	THE ANGEL'S MESSAGE, Edna Hibel	45.00	NR
1986	GIFTS OF THE MAGI, Edna Hibel	45.00	NR
1987	THE FLIGHT INTO EGYPT, Edna Hibel	49.00	NR
1988	ADORATION OF THE SHEPHERD, Edna Hibel	49.00	NR
1989	PEACEFUL KINGDOM, Edna Hibel	49.00	NR
1990	NATIVITY, Edna Hibel	49.00	NR

Hibel Mother's Day

1984	ABBY AND LISA, Edna Hibel, 1 year	29.50	NR
1985	ERICA AND JAMIE, Edna Hibel, 1 year	29.50	NR
1986	EMILY AND JENNIFER, Edna Hibel, 1 year	29.50	NR

Erica and Jamie
Photo courtesy of *Collectors News*

		Issue Price	Current Value
1987	CATHERINE AND HEATHER, Edna Hibel, 1 year	34.50	NR
1988	SARAH AND TESS, Edna Hibel, 1 year	34.90	NR
1989	JESSICA AND KATE, Edna Hibel, 1 year	34.90	NR
1990	ELIZABETH, JORDAN AND JANIE, Edna Hibel, 1 year ...	36.90	NR
1991	MICHELE AND ANNA, Edna Hibel, 1 year	36.90	NR

Home for the Holidays

1991	SLEIGH RIDE HOME, Thomas Kinkade, 150 days	29.90	40.00
1991	HOME TO GRANDMA'S, Thomas Kinkade, 150 days	29.90	45.00
1991	HOME BEFORE CHRISTMAS, Thomas Kinkade, 150 days	32.90	40.00
1992	THE WARMTH OF HOME, Thomas Kinkade, 150 days	32.90	RI
1992	HOMESPUN HOLIDAY, Thomas Kinkade, 150 days	32.90	RI
1992	HOMETIME YULETIDE, Thomas Kinkade, 150 days	34.90	RI
1992	HOME AWAY FROM HOME, Thomas Kinkade, 150 days ..	34.90	RI
1992	THE JOURNEY HOME, Thomas Kinkade, 150 days	34.90	RI

Home Is Where the Heart Is

1992	HOME SWEET HOME, Thomas Kinkade, 150 days	29.90	RI
1992	A WARM WELCOME HOME, Thomas Kinkade, 150 days .	29.90	RI
1992	A CARRIAGE RIDE HOME, Thomas Kinkade, 150 days ...	32.90	RI
1993	AMBER AFTERNOON, Thomas Kinkade, 150 days	32.90	RI
1993	COUNTRY MEMORIES, Thomas Kinkade, 150 days	32.90	RI

Home Sweet Home

1988	THE VICTORIAN, R. McGinnis, 150 days	39.90	NR
1989	THE GREEK REVIVAL, R. McGinnis, 150 days	39.90	BR
1989	THE GEORGIAN, R. McGinnis, 150 days	39.90	NR
1990	THE MISSION, R. McGinnis, 150 days	39.90	NR

It's a Dog's Life

1992	WE'VE BEEN SPOTTED, L. Kaatz, 150 days	29.90	RI
1992	LITERARY LABS, L. Kaatz, 150 days	29.90	RI
1993	RETRIEVING OUR DIGNITY, L. Kaatz, 150 days	32.90	RI
1993	LODGING A COMPLAINT, L. Kaatz, 150 days	32.90	RI
1993	BARRELING ALONG	32.90	RI
1993	PLAY BALL..	34.90	RI

Jerner's Less Travelled Road

1988	THE WEATHERED BARN, Bart Jerner, 150 days	29.90	BR
1988	THE MURMURING STREAM, Bart Jerner, 150 days	29.90	NR
1988	THE COVERED BRIDGE, Bart Jerner, 150 days	32.90	NR
1989	WINTER'S PEACE, Bart Jerner, 150 days	32.90	NR
1989	THE FLOWERING MEADOW, Bart Jerner, 150 days	32.90	NR
1989	THE HIDDEN WATERFALL, Bart Jerner, 150 days........	32.90	NR

Jessie Wilcox Smith Childhood Holidays	Issue Price	Current Value
1986 EASTER, Jessie Wilcox Smith	19.50	NR
1986 THANKSGIVING, Jessie Wilcox Smith.................	19.50	NR
1986 CHRISTMAS, Jessie Wilcox Smith	19.50	NR
1986 VALENTINE'S DAY, Jessie Wilcox Smith	22.50	NR
1987 MOTHER'S DAY, Jessie Wilcox Smith	22.50	NR
1987 FOURTH OF JULY, Jessie Wilcox Smith	22.50	NR

Jewels of the Flowers

	Issue Price	Current Value
1991 SAPPHIRE WINGS, T. C. Chiu, 150 days	29.90	NR
1991 TOPAZ BEAUTIES, T. C. Chiu, 150 days.................	29.90	40.00
1991 AMETHYST FLIGHT, T. C. Chiu, 150 days	32.90	BR
1991 RUBY ELEGANCE, T. C. Chiu, 150 days	32.90	40.00
1991 EMERALD PAIR, T. C. Chiu, 150 days..................	32.90	45.00
1991 OPAL SPLENDOR, T. C. Chiu, 150 days	34.90	NR
1992 PEARL LUSTER, T. C. Chiu, 150 days	34.90	RI
1992 AQUAMARINE GLIMMER, T. C. Chiu, 150 days	34.90	RI

Keepsake Rhymes

	Issue Price	Current Value
1992 HUMPTY DUMPTY, Scott Gustafson, 150 days	29.90	RI
1993 PETER PUMPKIN EATER, Scott Gustafson, 150 days	29.90	RI
1993 PAT—A—CAKE, Scott Gustafson, 150 days	29.90	RI
1993 OLD KING COLE	29.90	RI

The King and I

	Issue Price	Current Value
1984 A PUZZLEMENT, William Chambers, 1 year	19.50	NR
1984 SHALL WE DANCE?, William Chambers, 1 year	19.50	NR
1985 GETTING TO KNOW YOU, William Chambers, 1 year	19.50	NR
1985 WE KISS IN A SHADOW, William Chambers, 1 year	19.50	NR

Thanksgiving
Photo courtesy of *Collectors News*

A Puzzlement
Photo courtesy of *Collectors News*

		Issue Price	Current Value

Lady and the Tramp

1992	FIRST DATE, Disney Studios, 150 days	34.90	RI
1992	PUPPY LOVE, Disney Studios, 150 days	34.90	RI
1992	DOG POUND BLUES, Disney Studios, 150 days	37.90	RI
1992	MERRY CHRISTMAS TO ALL, Disney Studios, 150 days	37.90	RI
1993	DOUBLE SIAMESE TROUBLE, Disney Studios, 150 days	37.90	RI
1993	RUFF HOUSE	39.90	RI
1993	TELLIING TALES	39.90	RI
1993	MOONLIGHT ROMANCE	39.90	RI

Lincoln, Man of America

1986	THE GETTYSBURG ADDRESS, Mort Kunstler, 150 days	24.50	BR
1987	THE INAUGURATION, Mort Kunstler, 150 days	24.50	BR
1987	THE LINCOLN—DOUGLAS DEBATES, Mort Kunstler, 150 days	27.50	NR
1987	BEGINNINGS IN NEW SALEM, Mort Kunstler, 150 days	27.90	NR
1988	THE FAMILY MAN, Mort Kunstler, 150 days	27.90	NR
1988	EMANCIPATION PROCLAMATION, Mort Kunstler, 150 days	27.90	NR

Little Mermaid

1993	A SONG FROM THE SEA, Disney Studios, 95 days	29.90	RI

Living with Nature

1986	THE PINTAIL, Bart Jerner, 150 days	19.50	30.00
1986	THE MALLARD, Bart Jerner, 150 days	19.50	40.00
1987	THE WOOD DUCK, Bart Jerner, 150 days	22.50	35.00
1987	THE GREEN—WINGED TEAL, Bart Jerner, 150 days	22.50	35.00
1987	THE NORTHERN SHOVELER, Bart Jerner, 150 days	22.90	30.00
1987	THE AMERICAN WIDGEON, Bart Jerner, 150 days	22.90	35.00
1987	THE GADWALL, Bart Jerner, 150 days	24.90	35.00
1988	THE BLUE—WINGED TEAL, Bart Jerner, 150 days	24.90	30.00

The Wood Duck
Photo courtesy of *Collectors News*

Majestic Birds of North America

		Issue Price	Current Value
1988	THE BALD EAGLE, David Smith, 150 days	29.90	BR
1988	PEREGRINE FALCON, David Smith, 150 days	29.90	NR
1988	THE GREAT HORNED OWL, David Smith, 150 days	32.90	BR
1989	THE RED—TAILED HAWK, David Smith, 150 days	32.90	BR
1989	THE WHITE GYRFALCON, David Smith, 150 days	32.90	BR
1989	THE AMERICAN KESTRAL, David Smith, 150 days.......	32.90	BR
1990	THE OSPREY, David Smith, 150 days	34.90	BR
1990	THE GOLDEN EAGLE, David Smith, 150 days............	34.90	NR

Mary Poppins

1989	MARY POPPINS, M. Hampshire, 150 days	29.90	45.00
1989	A SPOONFUL OF SUGAR, M. Hampshire, 150 days	29.90	40.00
1990	A JOLLY HOLIDAY WITH MARY, M. Hampshire, 150 days.	32.90	NR
1990	WE LOVE TO LAUGH, M. Hampshire, 150 days	32.90	40.00
1991	CHIM CHIM CHER—EE, M. Hampshire, 150 days	32.90	BR
1991	TUPPENCE A BAG, M. Hampshire, 150 days............	32.90	50.00

Mickey's Christmas Carol

1992	BAH HUMBUG!, Disney Studios, 150 days	29.90	RI
1992	WHAT'S SO MERRY ABOUT CHRISTMAS?, Disney Studios, 150 days	29.90	RI
1993	GOD BLESS US EVERY ONE, Disney Studios, 150 days ...	32.90	RI

Bah Humbug!
Photo courtesy of Collectors News

Gepetto Creates Pinocchio
Photo courtesy of Collectors News

My Fair Lady

1989	OPENING DAY AT ASCOT, William Chambers, 150 days ..	24.90	NR
1989	I COULD HAVE DANCED ALL NIGHT, William Chambers, 150 days	24.90	NR

		Issue Price	Current Value
1989	THE RAIN IN SPAIN, William Chambers, 150 days	27.90	BR
1989	SHOW ME, William Chambers, 150 days	27.90	BR
1990	GET ME TO THE CHURCH ON TIME, William Chambers, 150 days	27.90	BR
1990	I'VE GROWN ACCUSTOMED/FACE, William Chambers, 150 days	27.90	35.00

Nature's Child

1990	SHARING, M. Jobe, 150 days	29.90	NR
1990	THE LOST LAMB, M. Jobe, 150 days	29.90	NR
1990	SEEMS LIKE YESTERDAY, M. Jobe, 150 days	32.90	NR
1990	FAITHFUL FRIENDS, M. Jobe, 150 days	32.90	NR
1990	TRUSTED COMPANION, M. Jobe, 150 days	32.90	45.00
1991	HAND IN HAND, M. Jobe, 150 days	32.90	45.00

Nature's Garden

1993	SPRINGTIME FRIENDS, C. Decker, 95 days	29.90	RI

Nature's Nursery

1992	TESTING THE WATERS, J. Thornbrugh, 150 days	29.90	RI
1993	TAKING THE PLUNGE, J. Thornbrugh, 150 days	29.90	RI

Not So Long Ago

1988	STORY TIME, Jessie Wilcox Smith, 150 days	24.90	NR
1988	WASH DAY FOR DOLLY, Jessie Wilcox Smith, 150 days ..	24.90	NR
1988	SUPPERTIME FOR KITTY, Jessie Wilcox Smith, 150 days.	24.90	NR
1988	MOTHER'S LITTLE HELPER, Jessie Wilcox Smith, 150 days ...	24.90	NR

Oklahoma!

1985	OH, WHAT A BEAUTIFUL MORNIN', Mort Kunstler	19.50	NR
1986	SURREY WITH THE FRINGE ON TOP, Mort Kunstler	19.50	NR
1986	I CAN'T SAY NO, Mort Kunstler	19.50	NR
1986	OKLAHOMA!, Mort Kunstler	19.50	NR

Old—Fashioned Favorites

1991	APPLE CRISP, M. Weber, 150 days	29.90	70.00
1991	BLUEBERRY MUFFINS, M. Weber, 150 days	29.90	60.00
1991	PEACH COBBLER, M. Weber, 150 days	29.90	100.00
1991	CHOCOLATE CHIP OATMEAL COOKIES, M. Weber, 150 days ..	29.90	180.00

Old Mill Stream

1990	NEW LONDON GRIST MILL, C. Tennant, 150 days	39.90	BR
1991	WAYSIDE INN GRIST MILL, C. Tennant, 150 days	39.90	NR
1991	OLD RED MILL, C. Tennant, 150 days	39.90	BR
1991	GLADE CREEK GRIST MILL, C. Tennant, 150 days	39.90	NR

		Issue Price	Current Value

Once Upon a Time

1988	LITTLE RED RIDING HOOD, K. Pritchett, 150 days	24.90	NR
1988	RAPUNZEL, K. Pritchett, 150 days	24.90	NR
1988	THREE LITTLE PIGS, K. Pritchett, 150 days	27.90	NR
1989	THE PRINCESS AND THE PEA, K. Pritchett, 150 days	27.90	NR
1989	GOLDILOCKS AND THE THREE BEARS, K. Pritchett, 150 days .	27.90	NR
1989	BEAUTY AND THE BEAST, K. Pritchett, 150 days	27.90	45.00

Pinocchio

1989	GEPETTO CREATES PINOCCHIO, Disney Studios, 150 days	29.90	75.00
1990	PINOCCHIO AND THE BLUE FAIRY, Disney Studios, 150 days .	29.90	80.00
1990	IT'S AN ACTOR'S LIFE FOR ME, Disney Studios, 150 days	32.90	55.00
1990	I'VE GOT NO STRINGS ON ME, Disney Studios, 150 days	32.90	45.00
1991	PLEASURE ISLAND, Disney Studios, 150 days	32.90	45.00
1991	A REAL BOY, Disney Studios, 150 days................	32.90	50.00

Portraits of Motherhood

| 1987 | MOTHER'S HERE, William Chambers, 150 days .... | 29.50 | NR |
| 1988 | FIRST TOUCH, William Chambers, 150 days .... | 29.50 | NR |

Precious Little Ones

1988	LITTLE RED ROBINS, M. T. Fangel, 150 days	29.90	NR
1988	LITTLE FLEDGLINGS, M. T. Fangel, 150 days	29.90	NR
1988	SATURDAY NIGHT BATH, M. T. Fangel, 150 days	29.90	NR
1988	PEEK—A—BOO, M. T. Fangel, 150 days	29.90	NR

Proud Sentinels of the American West

1993	YOUNGBLOOD, N. Glazier, 150 days	29.90	RI
1993	CAT NAP, N. Glazier, 150 days	29.90	RI
1993	DESERT BIGHORN—MORMON RIDGE	32.90	RI
1993	CROWN PRINCE......................................	32.90	RI

Purrfect Point of View

1991	UNEXPECTED VISITORS, J. Giordano, 150 days.........	29.90	NR
1992	WISTFUL MORNING, J. Giordano, 150 days	29.90	RI
1992	AFTERNOON CATNAP, J. Giordano, 150 days	29.90	RI
1992	COZY COMPANY, J. Giordano, 150 days...............	29.90	RI

Pussyfooting Around

1991	FISH TALES, C. Wilson, 150 days	24.90	NR
1991	TEATIME TABBIES, C. Wilson, 150 days	24.90	NR
1991	YARN SPINNERS, C. Wilson, 150 days.................	24.90	NR
1991	TWO MAESTROS, C. Wilson, 150 days.................	24.90	NR

		Issue Price	Current Value

Romantic Age of Steam

1992	THE EMPIRE BUILDER, R. B. Pierce, 150 days	29.90	RI
1992	THE BROADWAY LIMITED, R. B. Pierce, 150 days	29.90	RI
1992	TWENTIETH CENTURY LIMITED, R. B. Pierce, 150 days..	32.90	RI
1992	THE CHIEF, R. B. Pierce, 150 days	32.90	RI
1992	THE CRESCENT LIMITED, R. B. Pierce, 150 days	32.90	RI
1993	THE OVERLAND LIMITED, R. B. Pierce, 150 days........	34.90	RI
1993	THE JUPITER	34.90	RI
1993	THE DAYLIGHT	34.90	RI

Santa's Christmas

1991	SANTA'S LOVE, T. Browning, 150 days	29.90	40.00
1991	SANTA'S CHEER, T. Browning, 150 days	29.90	40.00
1991	SANTA'S PROMISE, T. Browning, 150 days	32.90	65.00
1991	SANTA'S GIFT, T. Browning, 150 days	32.90	70.00
1992	SANTA'S SURPRISE, T. Browning, 150 days	32.90	RI
1992	SANTA'S MAGIC, T. Browning, 150 days	32.90	RI

Season for Song

1991	WINTER CONCERT, M. Jobe, 150 days	34.90	40.00
1991	SNOWY SYMPHONY, M. Jobe, 150 days	34.90	60.00
1991	FROSTY CHORUS, M. Jobe, 150 days	34.90	55.00
1991	SILVER SERENADE, M. Jobe, 150 days	34.90	50.00

Seasons of Splendor

1992	AUTUMN'S GRANDEUR, K. Randle, 150 days	29.90	RI
1992	SCHOOL DAYS, K. Randle, 150 days	29.90	RI
1992	WOODLAND MILL STREAM, K. Randle, 150 days	32.90	RI
1992	HARVEST MEMORIES, K. Randle, 150 days	32.90	RI
1992	A COUNTRY WEEKEND, K. Randle, 150 days	32.90	RI
1993	INDIAN SUMMER, K. Randle, 150 days	32.90	RI

Shadows and Light: Winter's Wildlife

1993	WINTER'S CHILDREN, N. Glazier, 150 days	29.90	RI
1993	CUB SCOUTS, N. Glazier, 150 days	29.90	RI
1993	LITTLE SNOWMAN, N. Glazier, 150 days	29.90	RI
1993	THE SNOW CAVE	29.90	RI

Singin' in the Rain

1990	SINGIN' IN THE RAIN, M. Skolsky, 150 days	32.90	NR
1990	GOOD MORNING, M. Skolsky, 150 days	32.90	NR
1991	BROADWAY MELODY, M. Skolsky, 150 days	32.90	40.00
1991	WE'RE HAPPY AGAIN, M. Skolsky, 150 days	32.90	50.00

		Issue Price	Current Value

Sleeping Beauty

1991	ONCE UPON A DREAM, Disney Studios, 150 days	39.90	50.00
1991	AWAKENED BY A KISS, Disney Studios, 150 days	39.90	100.00
1991	HAPPY BIRTHDAY BRIAR ROSE, Disney Studios, 150 days	42.90	50.00
1992	TOGETHER AT LAST, Disney Studios, 150 days	42.90	RI

Small Blessings

1992	NOW I LAY ME DOWN TO SLEEP, C. Layton, 150 days	29.90	RI
1992	BLESS US O LORD FOR THESE, THY GIFTS, C. Layton, 150 days	29.90	RI
1992	JESUS LOVES ME, THIS I KNOW, C. Layton, 150 days	32.90	RI
1992	THIS LITTLE LIGHT OF MINE, C. Layton, 150 days	32.90	RI
1992	BLESSED ARE THE PURE IN HEART, C. Layton, 150 days	32.90	RI
1993	BLESS OUR HOME, C. Layton, 150 days	32.90	RI

Snow White and the Seven Dwarfs

1991	THE DANCE OF SNOW WHITE AND THE SEVEN DWARFS, Disney Studios, 150 days	29.90	55.00
1991	WITH A SMILE AND A SONG, Disney Studios, 150 days	29.90	40.00
1991	A SPECIAL TREAT, Disney Studios, 150 days	32.90	50.00
1992	A KISS FOR DOPEY, Disney Studios, 150 days	32.90	RI
1992	THE POISON APPLE, Disney Studios, 150 days	32.90	RI
1992	FIRESIDE LOVE STORY, Disney Studios, 150 days	34.90	RI
1992	STUBBORN GRUMPY, Disney Studios, 150 days	34.90	RI
1992	A WISH COME TRUE, Disney Studios, 150 days	34.90	RI
1992	TIME TO TIDY UP, Disney Studios, 150 days	34.50	RI
1993	MAY I HAVE THIS DANCE?, Disney Studios, 150 days	36.90	RI

Songs of the American Spirit

1991	THE STAR SPANGLED BANNER, Higgins Bond, 150 days	29.90	NR
1991	BATTLE HYMN OF THE REPUBLIC, Higgins Bond, 150 days	29.90	50.00
1991	AMERICA THE BEAUTIFUL, Higgins Bond, 150 days	29.90	45.00
1991	MY COUNTRY 'TIS OF THEE, Higgins Bond, 150 days	29.90	45.00

Sound of Music

1986	SOUND OF MUSIC, Tony Crnkovich, 150 days	19.50	NR
1986	DO—RE—MI, Tony Crnkovich, 150 days	19.50	NR
1986	MY FAVORITE THINGS, Tony Crnkovich, 150 days	22.50	NR
1987	LAENDLER WALTZ, Tony Crnkovich, 150 days	22.50	NR
1987	EDELWEISS, Tony Crnkovich, 150 days	22.50	NR
1987	I HAVE CONFIDENCE, Tony Crnkovich, 150 days	22.50	BR
1987	MARIA, Tony Crnkovich, 150 days	24.90	BR
1987	CLIMB EV'RY MOUNTAIN, Tony Crnkovich, 150 days	24.90	BR

South Pacific

| 1987 | SOME ENCHANTED EVENING, E. Gignilliat, 150 days | 24.50 | NR |
| 1987 | HAPPY TALK, E. Gignilliat, 150 days | 24.50 | NR |

		Issue Price	Current Value
1987	DITES MOI, E. Gignilliat, 150 days	24.90	NR
1988	HONEY BUN, E. Gignilliat, 150 days	24.90	NR

Stately Owls

1989	THE SNOWY OWL, J. Beaudoin, 150 days	29.90	50.00
1989	THE GREAT HORNED OWL, J. Beaudoin, 150 days	29.90	50.00
1990	THE BARN OWL, J. Beaudoin, 150 days	32.90	BR
1990	THE SCREECH OWL, J. Beaudoin, 150 days	32.90	BR
1990	THE SHORT—EARED OWL, J. Beaudoin, 150 days	32.90	BR
1990	THE BARRED OWL, J. Beaudoin, 150 days	32.90	NR
1990	THE GREAT GREY OWL, J. Beaudoin, 150 days	32.90	NR
1991	THE SAW—WHET OWL, J. Beaudoin, 150 days.........	34.90	NR

Story of Christmas by Eve Licea

1987	THE ANNUNCIATION, Eve Licea, 1 year	44.90	NR
1988	THE NATIVITY, Eve Licea, 1 year	44.90	NR
1989	ADORATION OF THE SHEPHERDS, Eve Licea, 1 year	49.90	55.00
1990	JOURNEY OF THE MAGI, Eve Licea, 1 year	49.90	60.00
1991	GIFTS OF THE MAGI, Eve Licea, 1 year	49.90	65.00
1992	REST ON THE FLIGHT INTO EGYPT, Eve Licea, 1 year....	49.90	RI

Sundblom Santas

1989	SANTA BY THE FIRE, Haddon Sundblom, closed	27.90	40.00
1990	CHRISTMAS VIGIL, Haddon Sundblom, closed	27.90	50.00
1991	TO ALL A GOOD NIGHT, Haddon Sundblom, closed	32.90	50.00
1992	SANTA'S ON HIS WAY, Haddon Sundblom, closed	32.90	RI

The Annunciation
Photo courtesy of *Collectors News*

Christmas Vigil
Photo courtesy of *Collectors News*

A Swan Is Born

		Issue Price	Current Value
1987	HOPES AND DREAMS, L. Roberts, 150 days	24.50	NR
1987	AT THE BARRE, L. Roberts, 150 days	24.50	40.00
1987	IN POSITION, L. Roberts, 150 days	24.50	70.00
1988	JUST FOR SIZE, L. Roberts, 150 days	24.50	70.00

Sweetness and Grace

1992	GOD BLESS TEDDY, J. Welty, 130 days	34.90	RI
1992	SUNSHINE AND SMILES, J. Welty, 130 days	34.90	RI
1992	FAVORITE BUDDY, J. Welty, 130 days..................	34.90	RI
1992	SWEET DREAMS, J. Welty, 130 days	34.90	RI

Thomas Kinkade's Thomashire

1992	OLDE PORTERFIELD TEA ROOM, Thomas Kinkade, 150 days ..	29.90	RI
1992	OLDE THOMASHIRE MILL, Thomas Kinkade, 150 days ...	29.90	RI
1992	SWANBROOK COTTAGE, Thomas Kinkade, 150 days	32.90	RI
1992	PYE CORNER COTTAGE, Thomas Kinkade, 150 days	32.90	RI
1993	BLOSSOM HILL CHURCH, Thomas Kinkade, 150 days ...	32.90	RI
1993	OLDE GARDEN COTTAGE, Thomas Kinkade, 150 days ...	32.90	RI

Thomas Kinkade's Yuletide Memories

1992	THE MAGIC OF CHRISTMAS, Thomas Kinkade, 150 days	29.90	RI
1992	A BEACON OF FAITH, Thomas Kinkade, 150 days	29.90	RI
1993	MOONLIT SLEIGH RIDE, Thomas Kinkade, 150 days	29.90	RI
1993	SILENT NIGHT, Thomas Kinkade, 150 days	29.90	RI
1993	OLDE PORTERFIELD GIFT SHOPPE, Thomas Kinkade, 150 days	29.90	RI
1993	THE WONDER OF THE SEASON, Thomas Kinkade, 150 days ..	29.90	RI
1993	A WINTER'S WALK, Thomas Kinkade, 150 days.........	29.90	RI

The Magic of Christmas
Photo courtesy of *Collectors News*

		Issue Price	Current Value

Tom Sawyer

1987	WHITEWACIIINO TIIE FENCE, William Chambers, 150 days ..	27.90	NR
1987	TOM AND BECKY, William Chambers, 150 days	27.90	NR
1987	TOM SAWYER THE PIRATE, William Chambers, 150 days	27.90	NR
1988	FIRST PIPES, William Chambers, 150 days	27.90	BR

Under Mother's Wing

1992	ARCTIC SPRING: SNOWY OWLS, J. Beaudoin, 150 days .	29.90	RI
1992	FOREST'S EDGE: GREAT GRAY OWLS, J. Beaudoin, 150 days .	29.90	RI
1992	TREETOP TRIO: LONG—EARED OWLS, J. Beaudoin, 150 days	32.90	RI
1992	WOODLAND WATCH: SPOTTED OWLS, J. Beaudoin, 150 days	32.90	RI
1992	VAST VIEW: SAW–WHET OWLS, J. Beaudoin, 150 days .	32.90	RI
1992	LOFTY LIMB: GREAT HORNED OWL, J. Beaudoin, 150 days ...	34.90	RI
1993	PERFECT PERCH: BARRED OWLS, J. Beaudoin, 150 days	34.90	RI
1993	HAPPY HOME: SHORT—EARED OWL, J. Beaudoin, 150 days .	34.90	RI

Upland Birds of North America

1986	THE PHEASANT, W. Anderson, 150 days	24.50	NR
1986	THE GROUSE, W. Anderson, 150 days	24.50	NR
1987	THE QUAIL, W. Anderson, 150 days	27.50	NR
1987	THE WILD TURKEY, W. Anderson, 150 days	27.50	NR
1987	THE GRAY PARTRIDGE, W. Anderson, 150 days	27.50	NR
1987	THE WOODCOCK, W. Anderson, 150 days	27.50	BR

Windows of Glory

| 1993 | KING OF KINGS, J. Welty, 95 days .... | 29.90 | RI |

Wings Upon the Wind

| 1987 | THE FAMILY, Donald Pentz, 150 days .... | 24.80 | NR |

Wizard of Oz

1977	OVER THE RAINBOW, J. Auckland, 100 days	19.00	40.00
1978	IF I ONLY HAD A BRAIN, J. Auckland, 100 days	19.00	40.00
1978	IF I ONLY HAD A HEART, J. Auckland, 100 days	19.00	40.00
1978	IF I WERE KING OF THE FOREST, J. Auckland, 100 days ..	19.00	40.00
1979	WICKED WITCH OF THE WEST, J. Auckland, 100 days ...	19.00	50.00
1979	FOLLOW THE YELLOW BRICK ROAD, J. Auckland, 100 days ..	19.00	50.00
1979	WONDERFUL WIZARD OF OZ, J. Auckland, 100 days	19.00	55.00
1980	THE GRAND FINALE, J. Auckland, 100 days	24.00	50.00

Wizard of Oz: A National Treasure

1991	YELLOW BRICK ROAD, R. Laslo, 150 days	29.90	50.00
1991	I HAVEN'T GOT A BRAIN, R. Laslo, 150 days............	29.90	50.00
1991	I'M A LITTLE RUSTY YET, R. Laslo, 150 days	32.90	50.00
1992	I EVEN SCARE MYSELF, R. Laslo, 150 days	32.90	RI
1992	WE'RE OFF TO SEE THE WIZARD, R. Laslo, 150 days	32.90	RI

		Issue Price	Current Value
1992	I'LL NEVER GET HOME, R. Laslo, 150 days	34.90	RI
1992	I'M MELTING, R. Laslo, 150 days	34.90	RI
1992	THERE'S NO PLACE LIKE HOME, R. Laslo, 150 days	34.90	RI

Yesterday's Innocents

1992	MY FIRST BOOK, Jessie Wilcox Smith, 150 days	29.90	RI
1992	TIME TO SMELL THE ROSES, Jessie Wilcox Smith, 150 days ..	29.90	RI
1993	HUSH, BABY'S SLEEPING, Jessie Wilcox Smith, 150 days	32.90	RI
1993	READY AND WAITING, Jessie Wilcox Smith, 150 days ..	32.90	RI

KONIGSZELT BAYERN GERMANY

Deutches Fachwerk

1984	BAUERNHAUS, Karl Bedal	24.00	BR
1984	NIEDERSACHSENHAUS, Karl Bedal	24.00	NR
1985	MOSELHAUS, Karl Bedal	27.00	NR
1985	WESTFALENHAUS, Karl Bedal	27.00	BR
1986	MITTELFRANKENHAUS, Karl Bedal	27.00	BR
1986	BODENSEEHAUS, Karl Bedal	27.00	NR

Grimm's Fairy Tales

1981	RUMPELSTILZCHEN, Charles Gehm, 1 year	23.00	BR
1982	RAPUNZEL, Charles Gehm, 1 year	25.00	BR
1982	HANSEL AND GRETEL, Charles Gehm, 1 year	25.00	BR
1984	SHOEMAKER AND ELVES, Charles Gehm, 1 year	25.00	BR
1984	GOLDEN GOOSE, Charles Gehm, 1 year	29.00	BR
1985	SHOES THAT WERE DANCED, Charles Gehm, 1 year	29.00	BR
1986	SLEEPING BEAUTY, Charles Gehm, 1 year	29.00	BR
1987	SNOW WHITE, Charles Gehm, 1 year	29.00	BR

Hedi Keller Christmas

1979	THE ADORATION, Hedi Keller, 90 days	29.50	NR
1980	FLIGHT INTO EGYPT, Hedi Keller, 90 days	29.50	BR
1981	RETURN INTO GALILEE, Hedi Keller, 90 days	29.50	BR
1982	FOLLOWING THE STAR, Hedi Keller, 90 days	29.50	BR
1983	REST ON THE FLIGHT, Hedi Keller, 90 days	29.50	BR
1984	THE NATIVITY, Hedi Keller, 90 days	29.50	BR
1985	GIFT OF THE MAGI, Hedi Keller, 90 days	34.50	BR
1986	ANNUNCIATION, Hedi Keller, 90 days	34.50	BR

Love and Life

1986	SINCE I FIRST SAW HIM, Sulamith Wulfing, limited	29.85	NR
1986	HE, NOBLEST OF ALL, Sulamith Wulfing, limited	29.85	NR
1987	I CAN'T UNDERSTAND IT, Sulamith Wulfing, limited	29.85	NR

Sulamith's Christmas

		Issue Price	Current Value
1985	THE ANGEL'S VIGIL, Sulamith Wulfing	35.00	BR
1986	CHRISTMAS CHILD, Sulamith Wulfing	35.00	NR
1987	THE CHRISTMAS ANGELS	39.00	BR
1988	THE ANGEL'S ADORATION	39.00	BR
1989	HEAVEN'S GIFT	44.00	NR
1990	THE LIGHT OF THE HOLY NIGHT	44.00	NR
1991	MARIA AND JOSEPH	49.00	140.00
1992	SENT FROM HEAVEN	49.00	RI

Sulamith's Love Song

1982	MUSIC, Sulamith Wulfing, limited	29.00	BR
1983	PLEDGE, Sulamith Wulfing, limited	29.00	BR
1983	VISION, Sulamith Wulfing, limited	29.00	BR
1983	GIFT, Sulamith Wulfing, limited	29.00	NR
1984	THE CIRCLE, Sulamith Wulfing, limited	29.00	BR
1984	THE CENTRE	29.00	BR
1984	THE JOURNEY	29.00	BR
1984	THE COMPLETION	29.00	BR

Rest on the Flight
Photo courtesy of *Collectors News*

The Nativity
Photo courtesy of *Collectors News*

KOSCHERAK BROTHERS CZECHOSLOVAKIA

Christmas

1973	CHRISTMAS, Mary Gregory, 1,000	55.00	NR
1974	CHRISTMAS, Mary Gregory, 1,000	60.00	NR

		Issue Price	Current Value
1975	CHRISTMAS, Mary Gregory, 1,000	60.00	NR
1976	CHRISTMAS, Mary Gregory, 1,000	60.00	NR

Mother's Day

		Issue Price	Current Value
1973	MOTHER'S DAY, Mary Gregory, 500	55.00	NR
1974	MOTHER'S DAY, Mary Gregory, 300	60.00	NR
1975	MOTHER'S DAY, Mary Gregory, 300	60.00	NR
1976	MOTHER'S DAY, Mary Gregory, 500	65.00	NR

KPM—ROYAL BERLIN GERMANY

Christmas

		Issue Price	Current Value
1969	CHRISTMAS STAR, 5,000	28.00	380.00
1970	THREE KINGS, 5,000	28.00	300.00
1971	CHRISTMAS TREE, 5,000	28.00	290.00
1972	CHRISTMAS ANGEL, 5,000............	31.00	300.00
1973	CHRIST CHILD ON SLED, 5,000	33.00	280.00
1974	ANGEL AND HORN, 5,000	35.00	180.00
1975	SHEPHERDS, 5,000.................	40.00	165.00
1976	STAR OF BETHLEHEM, 5,000	43.00	140.00
1977	MARY AT CRIB, 5,000................	46.00	100.00
1978	THREE WISEMEN, 5,000	49.00	NR
1979	THE MANGER, 5,000	55.00	NR
1980	SHEPHERDS IN FIELDS, 5,000	55.00	NR

LAKE SHORE PRINTS UNITED STATES

Rockwell Series

		Issue Price	Current Value
1973	BUTTER GIRLS, Norman Rockwell, 9,433.........	14.95	140.00
1974	TRUTH ABOUT SANTA, Norman Rockwell, 15,141......	19.50	75.00
1975	HOME FROM FIELDS, Norman Rockwell, 8,500	24.50	60.00
1976	A PRESIDENT'S WIFE, Norman Rockwell, 2,500	70.00	80.00

LALIQUE FRANCE

Annual

		Issue Price	Current Value
1965	DEUX OISEAUX (TWO BIRDS), Marie—Claude Lalique, 2,000 .	25.00	1,250.00
1966	ROSE DE SONGFRIE (DREAMROSE), Marie—Claude Lalique, 5,000	25.00	110.00
1967	BALLET DE POISSON (FISH BALLET), Marie—Claude Lalique, 5,000.......	25.00	100.00

		Issue Price	Current Value
1968	GAZELLER FANTASIE (GAZELLE FANTASY), Marie—Claude Lalique, 6,000	25.00	75.00
1969	PAPILLON (BUTTERFLY), Marie—Claude Lalique, 6,000	20.00	50.00
1970	PAON (PEACOCK), Marie—Claude Lalique, 6,000	30.00	60.00
1971	HIBOU (OWL), Marie—Claude Lalique, 6,000	35.00	70.00
1972	COQUILLAGE (SHELL), Marie—Claude Lalique, 7,00	40.00	75.00
1973	PETIT GEAI (JAYLING), Marie—Claude Lalique, 7,500	42.50	100.00
1974	SOUS D'ARGENT (SILVER PENNIES), Marie—Claude Lalique, 7,500	47.50	95.00
1975	DUO DE POISSON (FISH DUET), Marie—Claude Lalique, 8,000	50.00	140.00
1976	AIGLE (EAGLE), Marie—Claude Lalique, 7,500	60.00	90.00

Papillon (Butterfly)

LANCE INTERNATIONAL UNITED STATES

American Expansion

1975	SPIRIT OF '76, Prescott W. Baston, closed, 6"	—	100.00
1975	AMERICAN INDEPENDENCE, Prescoot W. Baston, closed, 6"	—	100.00
1975	AMERICAN EXPANSION, Prescott W. Baston, closed, 6"	—	50.00
1975	THE AMERICAN WAR BETWEEN THE STATES, Prescott W. Baston, closed, 6"	—	150.00

Child's Christmas

1978	BEDTIME STORY, Albert Petitto, suspd	35.00	NR
1979	LITTLEST ANGELS, Albert Petitto, suspd	35.00	NR
1980	HEAVEN'S CHRISTMAS TREE, Albert Petitto, suspd	42.50	NR
1981	FILLING THE SKY, Albert Petitto, suspd	47.50	NR

		Issue Price	Current Value
Sebastian Plates			
1978	MOTIF NO. 1, Prescott W. Baston, closed	75.00	BR
1979	GRAND CANYON, Prescott W. Baston, closed	75.00	BR
1980	LONE CYPRESS, Prescott W. Baston, closed	75.00	160.00
1980	IN THE CANDY STORE, Prescott W. Baston, closed	39.50	NR
1981	THE DOCTOR, Prescott W. Baston, closed	39.50	NR
1983	LITTLE MOTHER, Prescott W. Baston, closed	39.50	NR
1984	SWITCHING THE FREIGHT, Prescott W. Baston, closed ..	42.50	90.00
Songs of Christmas			
1988	SILENT NIGHT, A. McGrory, suspd	55.00	NR
1989	HARK! THE HERALD ANGELS SING, A. McGrory, suspd .	60.00	NR
1990	THE FIRST NOEL, A. McGrory, suspd	60.00	NR
1991	WE THREE KINGS, A. McGrory, suspd	60.00	NR
'Twas the Night Before Christmas			
1982	NOT A CREATURE WAS STIRRING, Andrea Hollis, 10,000	47.50	NR
1983	VISIONS OF SUGAR PLUMS, Andrea Hollis, 10,000	47.50	NR
1984	HIS EYES HOW THEY TWINKLED, Andrea Hollis, 10,000 .	47.50	NR
1985	HAPPY CHRISTMAS TO ALL, Andrea Hollis, 10,000	47.50	NR
1986	BRINGING HOME THE TREE, J. Wanat, 10,000	47.50	NR
Walt Disney			
1986	GOD BLESS US, EVERY ONE, D. Everhart, suspd	47.50	NR
1987	THE CAROLING ANGELS, Albert Petitto, suspd	47.50	NR
1987	JOLLY OLD SAINT NICK, D. Everhart, suspd	55.00	NR
1988	HE'S CHECKING IT TWICE, D. Everhart, suspd	50.00	NR

LANGENTHAL CHINA WORKS SWITZERLAND

		Issue Price	Current Value
Anker's Heritage			
1986	THE FIRST SMILE, Albert Anker	34.86	NR
1986	GRANDFATHER TELLS A STORY, Albert Anker	34.86	NR
1987	GIRL FEEDING THE CHICKENS, Albert Anker	34.86	NR
1987	SCHOOL PROMENADE	34.86	NR
1987	THE CHEMIST	37.86	NR
1987	THE DAY NURSERY	37.86	NR
1987	THE SNOW BEAR	37.86	NR
1988	AT THE GRANDPARENTS	37.86	NR

LAPSYS UNITED STATES

		Issue Price	Current Value
Crystal Series			
1977	SNOWFLAKE, crystal, 5,000	47.50	75.00

	Issue Price	Current Value
1978 PEACE ON EARTH, crystal, 5,000	47.50	NR

LEGACY LIMITED UNITED STATES

Christmas

1986 CHRISTMAS 1986, Les Kouba, 5,000	39.50	NR

LENINGRAD PORCELAIN FACTORY RUSSIA

Firebird

1990 THE TSAREVICH AND THE FIREBIRD	29.87	NR
1990 PRINCESS ELENA AND IVAN	29.87	40.00
1990 THE WEDDING FEAST	32.87	45.00
1990 ELENA THE FAIR	32.87	NR
1990 THE GOLDEN BRIDLE	32.87	NR
1990 THE GOLDEN CAGE	32.87	40.00
1991 AWAITING THE FIREBIRD	34.87	NR
1991 IVAN'S CONQUEST	34.87	NR
1991 THE MAGNIFICENT FIREBIRD	34.87	60.00
1991 JOURNEY OF TSAREVICH EVAN/ELENA	36.87	50.00
1991 IN SEARCH OF THE FIREBIRD	36.87	65.00
1991 TSAREVICH IVAN AND THE GRAY WOLF	36.87	85.00

The Tsarevich and the Firebird
Photo courtesy of *Collectors News*

Princess Elena and Ivan
Photo courtesy of *Collectors News*

LENOX UNITED STATES

American Wildlife

		Issue Price	Current Value
1983	RED FOXES, N. Adams, 9,500	65.00	NR
1983	OCELOTS, N. Adams, 9,500	65.00	NR
1983	SEA LIONS, N. Adams, 9,500	65.00	NR
1983	RACCOONS, N. Adams, 9,500	65.00	NR
1983	DALL SHEEP, N. Adams, 9,500	65.00	NR
1982	BLACK BEARS, N. Adams, 9,500	65.00	NR
1982	MOUNTAIN LIONS, N. Adams, 9,500	65.00	NR
1982	POLAR BEARS, N. Adams, 9,500	65.00	NR
1982	OTTERS, N. Adams, 9,500	65.00	NR
1982	WHITE–TAILED DEER, N. Adams, 9,500	65.00	NR
1982	BUFFALO, N. Adams, 9,500	65.00	NR
1982	JACK RABBITS, N. Adams, 9,500	65.00	NR

Annual Holiday

1991	SLEIGH, 1 year	75.00	NR

Boehm Birds

1970	WOOD THRUSH, Edward Marshall Boehm, 1 year	35.00	100.00
1971	GOLDFINCH, Edward Marshall Boehm, 1 year	35.00	50.00
1972	MOUNTAIN BLUEBIRD, Edward Marshall Boehm, 1 year	37.50	45.00
1973	MEADOWLARK, Edward Marshall Boehm, 1 year	50.00	BR
1974	RUFOUS HUMMINGBIRD, Edward Marshall Boehm, 1 year	45.00	NR
1975	AMERICAN REDSTART, Edward Marshall Boehm, 1 year	50.00	BR
1976	CARDINALS, Edward Marshall Boehm, 1 year	53.00	NR
1977	ROBINS, Edward Marshall Boehm, 1 year	55.00	BR
1978	MOCKINGBIRDS, Edward Marshall Boehm, 1 year	58.00	NR
1979	GOLDEN—CROWNED KINGLETS, Edward Marshall Boehm, 1 year	65.00	90.00
1980	BLACK—THROATED BLUE WARBLER, Edward Marshall Boehm, 1 year	80.00	95.00
1981	EASTERN PHOEBES, Edward Marshall Boehm, 1 year	92.50	100.00

Boehm Birds/Young America

1972	EAGLET, Edward Marshall Boehm, 5,000	175.00	NR
1973	EAGLET, Edward Marshall Boehm, 6,000	175.00	NR
1975	EAGLET, Edward Marshall Boehm, 6,000	175.00	NR

Boehm Woodland Wildlife

1973	RACCOONS, 1 year	50.00	NR
1974	RED FOXES, 1 year	52.50	NR
1975	COTTONTAIL RABBITS, 1 year	58.50	NR
1976	EASTERN CHIPMUNKS, 1 year	62.50	NR
1977	BEAVERS, 1 year	67.50	NR
1978	WHITETAIL DEER, 1 year	70.00	NR

		Issue Price	Current Value
1979	SQUIRRELS, 1 year	76.00	NR
1980	BOBCATS, 1 year	82.50	NR
1981	MARTENS, 1 year	100.00	NR
1982	RIVER OTTERS, 1 year	100.00	NR

Butterflies and Flowers

1982	QUESTION MARK BUTTERFLY AND NEW ENGLAND ASTER, Val Roy Gerischer, 25,000	60.00	NR
1983	SONORAN BLUE BUTTERFLY AND MARIPOSA LILY, Val Roy Gerischer, 25,000	65.00	NR
1983	MALACHITE BUTTERFLY AND ORCHID, Val Roy Gerischer, 25,000	65.00	NR
1984	AMERICAN PAINTED LADY AND VIRGINIA ROSE, Val Roy Gerischer, 25,000	70.00	NR
1984	RUDDY DAGGERWING AND LANTANA, Val Roy Gerischer, 25,000	70.00	NR
1985	BUCKEYE BUTTERFLY AND BLUEBELLS, Val Roy Gerischer, 25,000	75.00	NR

Christmas Trees Around the World

1991	GERMANY, 1 year	75.00	NR
1992	FRANCE, 1 year	75.00	RI

Colonial Christmas Wreath

1981	COLONIAL VIRGINIA, 1 year	65.00	90.00
1982	MASSACHUSETTS, 1 year	70.00	90.00
1983	MARYLAND, 1 year	70.00	80.00
1984	RHODE ISLAND, 1 year	70.00	NR
1985	CONNECTICUT, 1 year	60.00	NR
1986	NEW HAMPSHIRE, 1 year	70.00	NR
1987	PENNSYLVANIA, 1 year	70.00	NR
1988	DELAWARE, 1 year	70.00	NR
1989	NEW YORK, 1 year	75.00	NR
1990	NEW JERSEY, 1 year	75.00	NR
1991	SOUTH CAROLINA, 1 year	75.00	NR
1992	NORTH CAROLINA, 1 year	75.00	RI

Confederacy

1972	STATES OF THE CONFEDERACY	900.00	NR

Confederacy Collection

1971	THE WHITE HOUSE OF THE CONFEDERACY, W. Schiener, 1,201	—	—
1971	THE GREAT SEAL OF THE CONFEDERACY, W. Schiener, 1,201	—	—
1971	A CALL TO ARMS, W. Schiener, 1,201	—	—
1971	THE GENERAL, W. Schiener, 1,201	—	—

		Issue Price	Current Value
1971	LEE AND JACKSON, W. Schiener, 1,201	—	—
1971	THE MERRIMAC, W. Schiener, 1,201	—	—
1971	J.E.B. STUART, W. Schiener, 1,201	—	—
1971	CONFEDERATE CAMP, W. Schiener, 1,201	—	—
1971	BLOCKADE RUNNER, W. Schiener, 1,201	—	—
1971	FORT SUMTER, W. Schiener, 1,201, set of 10	900.00	NR

Garden Birds

1988	CHICADEE, limited	48.00	NR
1988	BLUEJAY, limited	48.00	NR
1989	HUMMINGBIRD, limited	48.00	NR
1991	DOVE, limited	48.00	NR
1991	CARDINAL, limited	48.00	NR
1992	GOLDFINCH, limited	48.00	RI

Lenox Christmas Trees

1976	DOUGLAS FIR, 1 year	50.00	NR
1977	SCOTCH PINE, 1 year	55.00	NR
1978	BLUE SPRUCE, 1 year	65.00	NR
1979	BALSAM FIR, 1 year	65.00	NR
1980	BREWER'S SPRUCE, 1 year	75.00	NR
1981	CHINA FIR, 1 year	75.00	NR
1982	ALEPPO PINE, 1 year...............................	80.00	NR

Nature's Collage

1992	CEDAR WAXWING, AMONG THE BERRIES, C. McClung, open	34.50	RI
1992	GOLDFINCHES, GOLDEN SPLENDOR, C. McClung, open .	34.50	RI

Nature's Nursery

1982	SNOW LEOPARDS, Lynn Chase, 15,000	65.00	NR
1983	KOALAS, Lynn Chase, 15,000	65.00	NR
1983	LLAMAS, Lynn Chase, 15,000	70.00	NR
1984	BENGAL TIGERS, Lynn Chase, 15,000..................	70.00	NR
1985	EMPEROR PENGUINS, Lynn Chase, 15,000	75.00	NR
1985	POLAR BEARS, Lynn Chase, 15,000	75.00	NR
1986	ZEBRAS, Lynn Chase, 15,000	80.00	NR

LIGHTPOST PUBLISHING

Thomas Kinkade Signature Collection

1991	CHANDLER'S COTTAGE, Thomas Kinkade, 2,500	49.95	NR
1991	CEDAR NOOK, Thomas Kinkade, 2,500	49.95	NR
1991	SLEIGH RIDE HOME, Thomas Kinkade, 2,500	49.95	NR
1991	HOME TO GRANDMA'S, Thomas Kinkade, 2,500	49.95	NR

LIHS LINDER GERMANY

America the Beautiful

Year		Issue Price	Current Value
1975	INDEPENDENCE HALL, 1,500	42.00	NR
1975	STATUE OF LIBERTY, 1,500	42.00	NR
1975	NIAGARA FALLS, 1,500	42.00	NR
1975	GRAND CANYON, 1,500	42.00	NR
1975	GOLDEN GATE, 1,500	42.00	NR
1975	CAPITOL, 1,500	42.00	NR

Child's Christmas

1978	HOLY NIGHT, Ferner, 5,000	40.00	NR
1979	SHEPHERDS IN THE FIELD, Ferner, 5,000	40.00	NR

Christmas

1972	LITTLE DRUMMER BOY, Josef Neubauer, 6,000	25.00	35.00
1973	CAROLERS, Josef Neubauer, 6,000	25.00	NR
1974	PEACE, Josef Neubauer, 6,000	25.00	NR
1975	CHRISTMAS CHEER, Josef Neubauer, 6,000	30.00	NR
1976	JOY OF CHRISTMAS, Josef Neubauer, 6,000	30.00	NR
1977	HOLLY JOLLY CHRISTMAS, Josef Neubauer, 6,000	30.00	NR
1978	HOLY NIGHT, Josef Neubauer, 5,000	40.00	NR

Easter

1973	HAPPY EASTER, 1,500	22.00	45.00
1974	SPRINGTIME, 1,500	25.00	NR
1975	WITH LOVE, 1,500	28.00	NR

Golden Spike Centennial

1977	CENTRAL PACIFIC JUPITER, 1,500	25.00	NR
1977	UNION PACIFIC 119, 1,500	25.00	NR

History

1973	TRIBUTE TO FLAG, 3,000	60.00	120.00
1974	GOLDEN SPIKE CENTENNIAL, 1,500	40.00	NR

Mother's Day

1972	MOTHER AND CHILD, 1,000	20.00	90.00
1973	MOTHER AND CHILD, 2,000	24.00	BR
1974	BOUQUET, 2,000	25.00	NR
1975	HAPPINESS, 2,000	28.00	NR

Playmates

1976	TIMMY AND FRIEND	45.00	55.00
1977	HEIDI AND FRIEND	45.00	NR

Single Issues

		Issue Price	Current Value
1972	UNION PACIFIC RAILROAD, 1,500	22.00	NR
1973	UNIION PACIFIC BIG BOY, 1,500	25.00	NR
1973	FLAG, 3,000	60.00	140.00
1976	DRUMMER BOY, 1,500	45.00	55.00
1976	FREEDOM TRAIN, 1,500	45.00	60.00
1978	UNION PACIFIC 8444, 1,500	27.50	NR
1979	UNION PACIFIC CHALLENGER, 1,500	30.00	NR

LILLIPUT LANE, LTD.

American Landmarks

1990	COUNTRY CHURCH, R. Day, 5,000	35.00	NR
1990	RIVERSIDE CHAPEL, R. Day, 5,000	35.00	NR

LIMOGES—TURGOT FRANCE

Durand's Children

1978	MARIE—ANGE, Paul Durand, 1 year	36.50	NR
1979	EMILIE ET PHILIPPE, Paul Durand, 1 year	36.50	NR
1980	CHRISTIANE ET FIFI, Paul Durand, 1 year	36.50	NR
1980	CECILE ET RAOUL, Paul Durand, 1 year	36.50	NR

Les Enfants de la Fin du Siecle

1984	PAINTINGS AU TROCADERO, Bernard Peltriauz, limited	24.82	NR
1985	PETITS VOILIERS AU BASSIN DES TUILERIES, Bernard Peltriauz, limited	29.82	40.00
1985	GUIGNOL AU LUXEMBOURG, Bernard Peltriauz, limited	29.82	40.00
1986	MANAGE AUX CHAMPS—ELYSEES, Bernard Peltriauz, limited	29.82	NR

Quellier's Morals of Perrault

1983	CINDERELLA, Andre Quellier, limited	28.67	NR
1984	LITTLE TOM THUMB, Andre Quellier, limited	28.67	NR
1984	LITTLE RED RIDING HOOD, Andre Quellier, limited	28.67	NR
1985	SLEEPING BEAUTY, Andre Quellier, limited	28.67	NR

LINCOLN MINT UNITED STATES

Artists

1971	DALI UNICORN, gold, 100	1,500.00	1,600.00
1971	DALI UNICORN, silver, 5,000	100.00	NR
1972	DALI ATHENA, gold, 300	2,000.00	NR
1972	DALI ATHENA, vermeil, 2,500	1,150.00	NR

		Issue Price	Current Value
1972	DALI ATHENA, silver, 7,500	125.00	NR

Christmas
| 1978 | SANTA BELONGS TO ALL CHILDREN, 7,500 | 29.50 | NR |

Easter
1972	DALI, gold, 10,000	200.00	215.00
1972	DALI, silver, 20,000	150.00	BR
1974	DALI, pewter	45.00	NR

Madonnas
| 1972 | MADONNA DELLA SEGGIOLA, 3.000 | 125.00 | BR |

Mother's Day
| 1972 | COLLIES, gold on silver | 90.00 | 100.00 |
| 1972 | COLLIES, silver | 125.00 | BR |

LIONSHEAD MINT

Iditarod Race Champs
| 1984 | RICK MACKEY, George Rodgers, 5,000 | 35.00 | NR |

LITT UNITED STATES

Annual
| 1979 | APACHE SUNSET, enamel, 1,250 | 275.00 | NR |

Christmas
| 1978 | MADONNA AND CHILD, enamel, 1,000 | 200.00 | NR |
| 1979 | O HOLY NIGHT, 1,000 | 200.00 | NR |

LLADRO SPAIN

Christmas
1971	CAROLING, 1 year	27.50	NR
1972	CAROLERS, 1 year	35.00	NR
1973	BOY AND GIRL, 1 year	45.00	NR
1974	CAROLERS, 1 year	55.00	75.00
1975	CHERUBS, 1 year	60.00	NR
1976	CHRIST CHILD, 1 year	60.00	BR

		Issue Price	Current Value
1977	NATIVITY, 1 year	80.00	BR
1978	CAROLING CHILD, 1 year	80.00	BR
1979	SNOW DANCE, 1 year	90.00	BR

Lladro Plate Collection

1993	THE GREAT VOYAGE L5964G, Lladro, limited	50.00	RI
1993	LOCKING OUT L5998G, Lladro, limited	38.00	RI
1993	SWINGING L5999G, Lladro, limited	38.00	RI
1993	DUCK PLATE L6000G, Lladro, limited	38.00	RI

Mother's Day

1971	KISS OF THE CHILD, 800	27.50	75.00
1972	BIRDS AND CHICKS, 3,500	27.50	NR
1973	MOTHER AND CHILDREN, 2,000	35.00	NR
1974	NURSING MOTHER, 1 year	45.00	135.00
1975	MOTHER AND CHILDREN, 1 year	60.00	NR
1976	VIGIL, 1 year	60.00	BR
1977	MOTHER AND DAUGHTER, 1 year	67.50	BR
1978	NEW ARRIVAL, 1 year	80.00	BR
1979	OFF TO SCHOOL, 1 year	90.00	NR

LONGTON CROWN POTTERY GREAT BRITAIN

Canterbury Tales

1980	MAN OF LAW'S TALE, G. A. Hoover	29.80	NR
1982	FRANKLIN'S TALE, G. A. Hoover	31.80	NR
1982	KNIGHT'S TALE, G. A. Hoover	31.80	NR
1982	WIFE OF BATH'S TALE, G. A. Hoover	31.80	NR

LOUISIANA HERITAGE ART GALLERIES
UNITED STATES

Southern Backroads

| 1985 | MORNING MYSTIQUE, Barrie Van Osdell | 39.50 | NR |

JEAN—PAUL LOUP

Christmas

1971	NOEL, 300	125.00	1,000.00
1972	NOEL, 300	150.00	700.00
1973	NOEL, 300	175.00	500.00

		Issue Price	Current Value
1974	NOEL, 400	200.00	500.00
1975	NOEL, 250	250.00	500.00
1976	NOEL, 150	300.00	600.00

Mother's Day

1974	MOTHER AND CHILD, champleve, 500	250.00	1,100.00
1975	MOTHER AND CHILD, enamel, 400	285.00	550.00
1976	MOTHER AND CHILD, enamel, 150	300.00	600.00

LUND AND CLAUSEN   DENMARK

Christmas

1971	DEER, 1 year	13.50	NR
1972	STAVE CHURCH, 1 year	13.50	NR
1973	CHRISTMAS SCENE, 1 year	13.50	NR

Moon Series

1969	MOON LANDING, 1 year	10.00	NR
1971	APOLLO 13, 1 year	15.00	NR

Mother's Day

1969	ROSE, 1 year	10.00	18.00
1971	FORGET—ME—NOTS, 1 year	10.00	NR
1972	BLUEBELL, 1 year	15.00	NR
1973	LILY OF THE VALLEY, 1 year	16.00	NR

LYNELL   UNITED STATES

American Adventures

1979	THE WHALER, Endre Szabo, 7,500	50.00	60.00
1980	THE TRAPPER, Endre Szabo, 7,500	50.00	NR
1980	THE FORTY—NINER, 7,500	50.00	NR
1981	THE PIONEER WOMAN, 7,500	50.00	NR
1981	THE WAGON MASTER, 7,500	50.00	NR
1982	WAGON HO!, 7,500	50.00	NR

Betsy Bates Annual

1979	OLDE COUNTRY INN, 7,500	38.50	45.00
1980	VILLAGE SCHOOLHOUSE, 7,500	38.50	NR
1981	VILLAGE BLACKSMITH, 7,500	38.50	NR
1982	CHRISTMAS VILLAGE, Betsy Bates, 15,000	24.50	NR

		Issue Price	Current Value

Children's Moments

1981	OFFICIAL BABYSITTER, Mike Hagel, 15,000	24.50	NR
1981	COWBOY CAPERS, Mike Hagel, 15,000	24.50	NR
1982	NURSE NANCY, Mike Hagel, 15,000	24.50	NR

Circus Dreams

1982	TWO FOR THE SHOW, Susan Neelon, 19,500	24.50	NR

Famous Clowns of the Circus

1982	EMMETT, Robert Weaver, 1 year......................	38.50	NR
1982	LOU JACOBS, Robert Weaver, 1 year..................	38.50	NR
1982	FELIX ADLER, Robert Weaver, 1 year	38.50	NR
1982	OTTO GRIEBLING, Robert Weaver, 1 year	38.50	NR

Great Chiefs of Canada

1980	CHIEF JOSEPH BRANT, Murray Killman, 7,500	65.00	NR
1981	CHIEF CROWFOOT, Murray Killman, 7,500	65.00	NR
1982	TECUMSEH, Murray Killman, 7,500	65.00	NR

Hagel Christmas

1981	SH-H-H!, Mike Hagel, 17,500	25.90	NR
1982	A KISS FOR SANTA, Mike Hagel, 17,500	25.90	NR

Hagel Mother's Day

1982	ONCE UPON A TIME, Mike Hagel, 60 days ....,.	29.50	NR

Hobo Joe

1982	HOLD THE ONIONS, Ron Lee, 10,000	50.00	NR
1982	TRAVELING IN STYLE, Ron Lee, 10,000	50.00	NR

How the West Was Won

1981	PONY EXPRESS, Gayle Gibson, 19,500	38.50	NR
1981	THE OREGON TRAIL, Gayle Gibson, 19,500	38.50	NR
1982	CALIFORNIA GOLD RUSH, Gayle Gibson, 19,500	38.50	NR
1982	DRIVING THE GOLDEN SPIKE, Gayle Gibson, 19,500	38.50	NR
1982	CATTLE DRIVE, Gayle Gibson, 19,500	38.50	NR
1982	PEACE PIPE, Gayle Gibson, 19,500	38.50	NR

Little House on the Prairie

1982	WELCOME TO WALNUT CREEK, Eugene Christopherson, 1 year	45.00	NR
1982	COUNTRY GIRLS, Eugene Christopherson, 1 year	45.00	NR

Little Traveler

1978	ON HIS WAY, George Malick, 4,000....................	45.00	BR

	Issue Price	Current Value

1979   ON HER WAY, George Malick, 4,000 .... 45.00   BR

Norman Rockwell Christmas

1979   SNOW QUEEN, Norman Rockwell, 60 days .... 29.50   NR
1980   SURPRISES FOR ALL, Norman Rockwell, 60 days .... 29.50   NR
1982   GRANDPOP AND ME, Norman Rockwell, 60 days .... 29.50   NR

Norman Rockwell Collection of Legendary Art

1980   ARTIST'S DAUGHTER, Norman Rockwell, 1 year .... 65.00   NR
1980   POOR RICHARD'S ALMANAC, Norman Rockwell, 17,500 . 45.00   NR
1981   A DAILY PRAYER, Norman Rockwell, <1 year .... 29.50   NR

Norman Rockwell Mother's Day

1980   CRADLE OF LOVE, Norman Rockwell, 60 days 29.50   40.00
1981   A MOTHER'S BLESSING, Norman Rockwell, 30 days .... 29.50   NR
1982   MEMORIES, Norman Rockwell, 60 days .... 29.50   NR

North American Wildlife

1982   SNUGGLING COUGARS, Murray Killman, 7,500 .... 65.00   NR

Popeye's 50th Anniversary

1980   HAPPY BIRTHDAY POPEYE, 1 year .... 22.50   NR

Rockwell's Scotty

1981   SCOTTY'S STOWAWAY, Norman Rockwell, 17,500 ...... 45.00   NR
1982   SCOTTY STRIKES A BARGAIN, Norman Rockwell, 17,500 35.00   NR

Soap Box Derby

1979   LAST MINUTE CHANGES, Norman Rockwell, 1 year .... 24.50   NR
1980   AT THE GATE, Norman Rockwell, 1 year .... 24.50   NR
1982   IN THE STRETCH, Norman Rockwell, 1 year .... 24.50   NR

Special Celebrities

1981   REAGAN/BUSH, Mike Hagel, 17,500 .... 45.00   NR
1982   HOPE/THANKS FOR THE MEMORIES, Mike Hagel, limited 45.00   NR
1982   BURNS/YOUNG AT HEART, Mike Hagel, limited .... 45.00   NR
1982   I LOVE LUCY, Mike Hagel, limited .... 45.00   NR

Single Issues

1979   JOHN WAYNE TRIBUTE, Endre Szabo, 7,500 .... 45.00   NR
1980   HIS MASTER'S VOICE, <1 year .... 24.50   NR
1981   EYES OF THE SEASONS, 19,500, set of 4 .... 154.00   NR
1982   NORMAN ROCKWELL TRIBUTE, George Malik, 5,000 .... 55.00   NR

		Issue Price	Current Value
1982	BETTY BOOP, 15,000	24.50	NR
1982	WHITE HOUSE PANDA, Bogdan Grom, 15,000	38.50	NR

MANJUNDO JAPAN

Chinese Lunar Calendar

		Issue Price	Current Value
1972	YEAR OF THE RAT, 5,000	15.00	NR
1973	YEAR OF THE OX, 5,000	15.00	NR
1974	YEAR OF THE MONKEY, 5,000	15.00	NR

MARCH OF DIMES

Our Children, Our Future

		Issue Price	Current Value
1989	A TIME FOR PEACE, Donald Zolan, 150 days	29.00	NR
1989	A TIME TO LOVE, Sandra Kuck, 150 days	29.00	NR
1989	A TIME TO PLANT, John McClelland, 150 days	29.00	NR
1989	A TIME TO BE BORN, Gregory Perillo, 150 days	29.00	NR
1990	A TIME TO EMBRACE, Edna Hibel, 150 days	29.00	NR
1990	A TIME TO LAUGH, Abbie Williams, 150 days	29.00	NR

MARIGOLD

Picasso

		Issue Price	Current Value
1984	TETE APPUYEE SUR LES MAINS, 7,777	50.00	NR

World Stars

		Issue Price	Current Value
1984	MICKEY MANTLE, Pablo Carreno, 10,000	60.00	NR
1984	MICKEY MANTLE, Pablo Carreno, sgd, 1,000	100.00	NR

MARMOT GERMANY

Christmas

		Issue Price	Current Value
1970	POLAR BEAR, 5,000	13.00	45.00
1971	AMERICAN BUFFALO, 6,000	14.50	25.00
1971	BUFFALO BILL, 6,000	16.00	35.00
1972	BOY AND GRANDFATHER, 5,000	20.00	40.00
1973	SNOWMAN, 3,000	22.00	40.00
1974	DANCING, 2,000	24.00	30.00
1975	QUAIL, 2,000	30.00	NR
1976	WINDMILL, 2,000	40.00	NR

Father's Day

		Issue Price	Current Value
1970	STAG, 3,500	12.00	100.00
1971	HORSE, 3,500	12.50	40.00

Mother's Day

1972	SEAL, 6,000	16.00	45.00
1973	POLAR BEAR, 3,000	20.00	140.00
1974	PENGUINS, 2,000	24.00	35.00
1975	RACCOONS, 2,000	30.00	NR
1976	DUCKS, 2,000	40.00	NR

Presidents

1971	WASHINGTON, 1,500	25.00	NR
1972	JEFFERSON, 1,500	25.00	NR
1973	JOHN ADAMS, 1,500	25.00	NR

MARURI USA UNITED STATES

Eagle Plate

1984	FREE FLIGHT, W. Gaither, 995	150.00	160.00

MARY ENGELBREIT SOCIETY UNITED STATES

Believe Series

1986	SANTA'S TREASURE, Mary Engelbreit, 10,000	29.95	NR

MASON GREAT BRITAIN

Christmas

1975	WINDSOR CASTLE, 1 year	75.00	NR
1976	HOLYROOD HOUSE, 1 year	75.00	NR
1977	BUCKINGHAM PALACE, 1 year	75.00	NR
1978	BALMORAL CASTLE, 1 year	75.00	NR
1979	HAMPTON COURT, 1 year	75.00	NR
1980	SANDRINGHAM HOUSE, 1 year	75.00	NR

MASTER ENGRAVERS OF AMERICA UNITED STATES

Indian Dancers

1979	EAGLE DANCER, Don Ruffin, 2,500	300.00	320.00
1980	HOOP DANCER, Don Ruffin, 2,500	300.00	320.00

MASTERS OF PALEKH

Gifts of the Seasons

		Issue Price	Current Value
1993	THE TWELVE MONTHS	35.87	RI
1993	WOODLAND MAJESTY	35.87	RI
1993	A BASKET OF SNOWDROPS	35.87	RI
1993	THE WARMTH OF FRIENDSHIP	35.87	RI

MEISSEN GERMANY

Annual

1973	WINTER COUNTRYSIDE BY SLEIGH, 5,000	71.00	NR
1974	SLEEPING BEAUTY, 5,000	75.00	NR
1975	ARCHWAY TO ALBRECHT'S CASTLE, 5,500	92.00	NR
1976	DOGE'S PALACE IN VENICE, 5,000	92.00	NR
1977	FRA HOLLE, 5,000	114.00	NR
1978	ICE CRYSTAL WITH CHILDREN, 7,000	123.00	NR
1979	WINTER FAIRY TALE, 7,000	151.00	NR
1980	BOOTED CAT	155.00	NR

METAL ARTS COMPANY UNITED STATES

Children of Norman Rockwell (The Hamilton Collection)

1979	DOCTOR AND DOLL, Norman Rockwell, 19,750	21.00	NR
1979	KNUCKLES DOWN, Norman Rockwell, 19,750	21.00	NR
1979	GRANDPA'S GIRL, Norman Rockwell, 19,750	21.00	NR
1979	LEAPFROG, Norman Rockwell, 19,750	21.00	NR
1980	DOG GONE IT, Norman Rockwell, 19,750	21.00	NR
1980	LOOK OUT BELOW, Norman Rockwell, 19,750	21.00	NR
1980	BATTER UP, Norman Rockwell, 19,750	21.00	NR
1980	NO PEEKING, Norman Rockwell, 19,750	21.00	NR

Norman Rockwell Christmas (The Hamilton Collection)

1978	THE CHRISTMAS GIFT, Norman Rockwell, 1 year	48.00	NR
1979	THE BIG MOMENT, Norman Rockwell, 1 year	48.00	NR
1980	SANTA'S HELPERS, Norman Rockwell, 1 year	48.00	NR
1981	SANTA, Norman Rockwell, 1 year	48.00	NR

Norman Rockwell Man's Best Friend
(The Hamilton Collection)

1979	THE HOBO, Norman Rockwell, 9,500	40.00	60.00
1979	THE DOCTOR, Norman Rockwell, 9,500	40.00	NR
1979	MAKING FRIENDS, Norman Rockwell, 9,500	40.00	NR
1979	GONE FISHING, Norman Rockwell, 9,500	40.00	NR

	Issue Price	Current Value
1980 THE THIEF, Norman Rockwell, 9,500	40.00	NR
1080 PUPPY LOVE, Norman Rockwell, 9,500	40.00	NR

Winslow Homer's The Sea

1977 BREEZING UP, 9,500	29.95	NR

Single Issues

1977 AMERICA'S FIRST FAMILY — CARTERS, 9,500	40.00	NR
1977 WASHINGTON AT VALLEY FORGE, pewter, 9,500	95.00	NR
1977 WASHINGTON AT VALLEY FORGE, sterling silver, 500	225.00	NR

METAWA NETHERLANDS

Christmas

1972 ICE SKATERS, 3,000	30.00	NR
1973 ONE—HORSE SLEIGH, 1,500	30.00	NR
1974 SAILBOAT, 1 year	35.00	NR

METROPOLITAN MUSEUM OF ART UNITED STATES

Metropolitan Cat

1986 TWO CATS, Felix Vallotton	12.00	NR

Treasures of Tutankhamen

1977 KING TUT, 2,500	150.00	170.00

METTLACH GERMANY

Christmas

1978 CHRISTMAS, 20,000	175.00	BR
1979 MOTHER WITH CHILD, 10,000	298.00	BR
1980 MADONNA IN GLORY, 10,000	210.00	NR

Collectors Society

1980 SNOW WHITE AND SEVEN DWARFS, 1 year	60.00	NR

Mother's Day Plaque

1978 MOTHER'S DAY, 15,000	100.00	NR

MICHELON ENTERPRISES

Quiet Places

		Issue Price	Current Value
1981	DAY DREAMING, Tom Heflin, 5,000	75.00	NR
1981	TRY TO REMEMBER, Tom Heflin, 5,000	75.00	NR
1981	EMMETT'S GATE, Tom Heflin, 5,000	75.00	NR

MICHIGAN NATURAL RESOURCES UNITED STATES

Nature's Heritage

1982	WHITE—TAILED FAWN, Richard Timm, 14,500	37.50	NR

MINGOLLA/HOME PLATES UNITED STATES

Christmas

1973	CHRISTMAS, enamel on copper, 1,000	95.00	165.00
1974	CHRISTMAS, enamel on copper, 1,000	100.00	145.00
1974	CHRISTMAS, porcelain, 5,000	35.00	65.00
1975	CHRISTMAS, enamel on copper, 1,000	125.00	145.00
1975	CHRISTMAS, porcelain, 5,000	35.00	45.00
1976	CHRISTMAS, enamel on copper, 1,000	125.00	NR
1976	CHRISTMAS, porcelain, 5,000	35.00	NR
1977	WINTER WONDERLAND, enamel on copper, 2,000	200.00	NR

Four Seasons

1978	DASHING THROUGH THE SNOW, 2,000	150.00	NR
1978	SPRING FLOWERS, 2,000	150.00	NR
1978	BEACH FUN, 2,000	150.00	NR
1978	BALLOON BREEZES, 2,000	150.00	NR

MISTWOOD DESIGNS UNITED STATES

American Wildlife

1981	DESPERADO AT THE WATERHOLE, Skipper Kendricks, 5,000 NR		45.00
1982	BAYOU BUNNIES, Skipper Kendricks, 5,000	45.00	NR

MODERN CONCEPTS LIMITED UNITED STATES

Magic of the Sea

1983	FUTURE MISS, Lucelle Raad, limited	25.00	NR
1984	ONE, TWO, THREE!, Lucelle Raad, limited	26.50	NR

		Issue Price	Current Value

Nursery Rhyme Favorites

1984	SUGAR AND SPICE, Lucelle Raad, 7,500	38.50	NR
1984	SNIPS AND SNAILS, Lucelle Raad, 7,500	38.50	NR

Signs of Love

1983	WHEN HEARTS TOUCH, Lucelle Raad, 19,500	39.50	NR
1984	MY VERY OWN, Lucelle Raad, 19,500	39.50	NR

Special Moments

1982	DAVID'S DILEMMA, Lucelle Raad, 12,500	35.00	50.00
1983	SECRETS, Lucelle Raad, 12,500	35.00	NR
1983	ENOUGH FOR TWO, Lucelle Raad, 12,500	38.50	NR
1984	CHATTERBOX, Lucelle Raad, 12,500	38.50	NR

One, Two, Three!
Photo courtesy of *Collectors News*

Chatterbox
Photo courtesy of *Collectors News*

MODERN MASTERS UNITED STATES

Babes in the Woods

1982	NEWBORN FAWN, Sally Miller, 9,500	45.00	NR
1983	FIRST OUTING, Sally Miller, 9,500	45.00	NR
1983	BANDY BANDIT, Sally Miller, 9,500	50.00	NR
1984	MOMENT'S REST, Sally Miller, 9,500	50.00	BR

Child's Best Friend

1982	CHRISTI'S KITTY, Richard Zolan, 15 days	29.50	NR
1982	PATRICK'S PUPPY, Richard Zolan, 15 days	29.50	NR

Family Treasures

		Issue Price	Current Value
1981	CORA'S RECITAL, Richard Zolan, 18,500	39.50	NR
1982	CORA'S TEA PARTY, Richard Zolan, 18,500	39.50	NR
1983	CORA'S GARDEN PARTY, Richard Zolan, 18,500	39.50	NR

Floral Felines

1983	THE BARON, Julie Shearer, 9,500	55.00	NR
1984	HER MAJESTY, Julie Shearer, 9,500	55.00	NR
1984	DUCHESS, Julie Shearer, 9,500	55.00	NR
1984	HIS LORDSHIP, Julie Shearer, 9,500	55.00	NR

Horses of Fred Stone

1982	PATIENCE, Fred Stone, 9,500	55.00	100.00
1982	ARABIAN MARE AND FOAL, Fred Stone, 9,500	55.00	90.00
1982	SAFE AND SOUND, Fred Stone, 9,500	55.00	70.00
1983	CONTENTMENT, Fred Stone, 9,500	55.00	70.00

Little Baskets

1983	LAST OF THE LITTER, Sally Miller, limited	35.00	NR
1984	DOUBLE DELIGHT, Sally Miller, limited	35.00	NR
1984	TENDER TRIO, Sally Miller, limited	35.00	NR
1985	LITTER BUG, Sally Miller, limited	35.00	NR
1985	HIDE AND SEEK, Sally Miller, limited	35.00	NR
1985	POODLE PICNIC, Sally Miller, limited	35.00	NR

Little Ladies

1983	WHEN MOMMY'S AWAY, Claire Freedman, limited	29.50	NR
1984	BEFORE THE SHOW BEGINS, Claire Freedman, limited	29.50	NR

They Came to Adore Him
Photo courtesy of *Collectors News*

Twelve Days of Christmas
Photo courtesy of *Collectors News*

		Issue Price	Current Value

Sally Miller Christmas

| 1985 | THEY CAME TO ADORE HIM, Sally Miller, 5,000 . . . . | 39.50 | NR |

Through the Eyes of Love

1981	ENCHANTED EYES, Karin Schaefers, 9,500	55.00	NR
1982	SUMMER SECRETS, Karin Schaefers, 9,500	55.00	NR
1983	GARDEN GATHERING, Karin Schaefers, 9,500	55.00	NR

Will Moses' America

| 1982 | SEPTEMBER FAIR, Will Moses, 7,500 . . . . | 45.00 | NR |
| 1983 | SPRING RECESS, Will Moses, 7,500 . . . . | 45.00 | NR |

Wings of Nobility

1984	AMERICAN BALD EAGLE, 7,500	49.50	NR
1984	PEREGRINE FALCON, 7,500	49.50	NR
1984	RED—SHOULDERED HAWK, 7,500	49.50	NR

Single Issue

| 1983 | TWELVE DAYS OF CHRISTMAS, Will Moses, 12 days . . . . | 45.00 | NR |

MONACO PORCELAIN FACTORY MONACO

Day and Night

1983	LE NUIT, Erich Rozewica, 600	—	—
1983	LE JOUR, Erich Rozewica, 600	—	—
	Set of 2	200.00	NR

MORGANTOWN CRYSTAL UNITED STATES

Country Ladies

1981	ANGELICA, Michael Yates, 30,000	75.00	NR
1982	VIOLET, Michael Yates, 30,000	75.00	NR
1983	HEATHER, Michael Yates, 30,000	75.00	NR
1984	LAUREL, Michael Yates, 30,000	75.00	90.00

MOSER CZECHOSLOVAKIA

Christmas

1970	HRADCANY CASTLE, 400	75.00	170.00
1971	KARLSTEIN CASTLE, 1,365	75.00	NR
1972	OLD TOWN HALL, 1,000	85.00	NR
1973	KARLOVY VARY CASTLE, 500	90.00	100.00

		Issue Price	Current Value

Mother's Day
1971	PEACOCKS, 350	75.00	135.00
1972	BUTTERFLIES, 750	85.00	NR
1973	SQUIRRELS, 500	90.00	NR

MOUSSALLI UNITED STATES

Birds of Four Seasons
1977	CEDAR WAXWING, 1,000	375.00	450.00
1978	CARDINAL, 1,000	375.00	425.00
1978	WREN, 1,000	375.00	NR
1979	HUMMINGBIRD, 1,000	375.00	NR
1979	INDIGO BUNTING, 1,000	375.00	NR

Mother's Day
| 1979 | CHICKADEE, 500 | 450.00 | NR |

MUSEUM COLLECTIONS, INC.

American Family I
1979	BABY'S FIRST STEP, Norman Rockwell, 9,900	28.50	90.00
1979	HAPPY BIRTHDAY, DEAR MOTHER, Norman Rockwell, 9,900	28.50	55.00
1979	SWEET SIXTEEN, Norman Rockwell, 9,900	28.50	40.00
1979	FIRST HAIRCUT, Norman Rockwell, 9,900	28.50	40.00
1979	FIRST PROM, Norman Rockwell, 9,900	28.50	35.00
1979	WRAPPING CHRISTMAS PRESENTS, Norman Rockwell, 9,900	28.50	35.00
1979	THE STUDENT, Norman Rockwell, 9,900	28.50	35.00
1979	THE BIRTHDAY PARTY, Norman Rockwell, 9,900	28.50	35.00
1979	LITTLE MOTHER, Norman Rockwell, 9,900	28.50	35.00
1979	WASHING OUR DOG, Norman Rockwell, 9,900	28.50	35.00
1979	MOTHER'S LITTLE HELPERS, Norman Rockwell, 9,900	28.50	35.00
1979	BRIDE AND GROOM, Norman Rockwell, 9,900	28.50	35.00

American Family II
1980	NEW ARRIVAL, Norman Rockwell, 22,500	35.00	55.00
1980	SWEET DREAMS, Norman Rockwell, 22,500	35.00	NR
1980	LITTLE SHAVER, Norman Rockwell, 22,500	35.00	NR
1980	WE MISSED YOU DADDY, Norman Rockwell, 22,500	35.00	NR
1980	HOME RUN SLUGGER, Norman Rockwell, 22,500	35.00	NR
1980	GIVING THANKS, Norman Rockwell, 22,500	35.00	NR
1980	SPACE PIONEERS, Norman Rockwell, 22,500	35.00	NR
1980	LITTLE SALESMAN, Norman Rockwell, 22,500	35.00	NR
1980	ALMOST GROWN UP, Norman Rockwell, 22,500	35.00	NR
1980	COURAGEOUS HERO, Norman Rockwell, 22,500	35.00	NR

		Issue Price	Current Value
1980	AT THE CIRCUS, Norman Rockwell, 22,500	35.00	NR
1980	GOOD FOOD, GOOD FRIENDS, Norman Rockwell, 22,500 .	35.00	NR

Christmas

1979	DAY AFTER CHRISTMAS, Norman Rockwell, 1 year	75.00	85.00
1980	CHECKING HIS LIST, Norman Rockwell, 1 year	75.00	85.00
1981	RINGING IN GOOD CHEER, Norman Rockwell, 1 year . . .	75.00	85.00
1982	WAITING FOR SANTA, Norman Rockwell, 1 year	75.00	NR
1983	HIGH HOPES, Norman Rockwell, 1 year	75.00	NR
1984	SPACE AGE SANTA, Norman Rockwell, 1 year	55.00	NR

NASSAU ART GALLERY BAHAMAS

Collector Plates of the Bahamas

1982	BAHAMAS 1982, Elyse Wasile, 5,000	35.00	NR
1982	GREGORY'S ARCH, Elyse Wasile, 5,000	35.00	NR

NEWELL POTTERY COMPANY UNITED STATES

Calendar Series

1984	JUNE, Sarah Stilwell Weber, limited	19.00	NR
1985	JULY, Sarah Stilwell Weber, limited	19.00	NR
1985	AUGUST, Sarah Stilwell Weber, limited	19.00	NR
1985	SEPTEMBER, Sarah Stilwell Weber, limited	19.00	NR
1985	OCTOBER, Sarah Stilwell Weber, limited	19.00	NR
1985	NOVEMBER, Sarah Stilwell Weber, limited	19.00	NR

June
Photo courtesy of *Collectors News*

		Issue Price	Current Value
1986	DECEMBER, Sarah Stilwell Weber, limited	19.00	NR
1986	JANUARY, Sarah Stilwell Weber, limited	19.00	NR
1986	FEBRUARY, Sarah Stilwell Weber, limited	19.00	NR
1986	MARCH, Sarah Stilwell Weber, limited	19.00	NR
1986	APRIL, Sarah Stilwell Weber, limited	19.00	25.00
1986	MAY	19.00	50.00

NORITAKE JAPAN

Annual

1977	PARADISE BIRDS, 3,000	380.00	NR
1978	CHRYSANTHEMUMS, 3,000	494.00	NR
1979	CRANES, 3,000	556.00	NR
1980	WATER LILIES AND BUTTERFLIES, 3,000	575.00	NR

Christmas

1975	MADONNA WITH CHILD, 3,000	42.00	NR
1975	GRATIA HOSO KAWA, 3,000	54.00	NR
1977	JULIA OTAA, 3,000	83.00	NR
1978	AMAKUSA SHIRO, 3,000	109.00	NR
1979	MUNZIO ITO, 3,000	124.00	NR
1980	FURST TAKAYANA, 3,000	125.00	NR

NOSTALGIA COLLECTIBLES UNITED STATES

Elvis Presley Collection

1985	HOUND DOG, limited	15.00	NR
1985	LONESOME TONIGHT, limited	15.00	NR
1985	TEDDY BEAR, limited	15.00	NR
1985	DON'T BE CRUEL, limited	15.00	NR
	Set of 4	60.00	NR

James Dean Collection (Rockwell Museum)

1985	EAST OF EDEN, limited	15.00	NR
1985	REBEL WITHOUT A CAUSE, limited	15.00	NR
1985	GIANT, limited	15.00	NR
1985	JIM AND SPYDER, limited	15.00	NR
	Set of 4	60.00	NR

Shirley Temple Collectibles

1982	BABY TAKE A BOW, 22,500	75.00	100.00
1983	BABY TAKE A BOW, sgd, 2,500	100.00	160.00
1982	CURLY TOP, 22,500	75.00	100.00

		Issue Price	Current Value
1983	CURLY TOP, sgd, 2,500	100.00	150.00
1982	STAND UP AND CHEER, 22,500	75.00	100.00
1983	STAND UP AND CHEER, sgd, 2,500	100.00	NR

Shirley Temple Collection (Rockwell Museum)

1983	CAPTAIN JANUARY, William Jacobson, 25,000	35.00	NR
1984	HEIDI, William Jacobson, 25,000	35.00	NR
1984	LITTLE MISS MARKER, William Jacobson, 25,000	35.00	NR
1984	BRIGHT EYES, William Jacobson, 25,000	35.00	NR
1985	THE LITTLE COLONEL, William Jacobson, 25,000	35.00	NR
1985	REBECCA OF SUNNYBROOK FARM, William Jacobson, 25,000	35.00	NR
1986	POOR LITTLE RICH GIRL, William Jacobson, 25,000	35.00	NR
1986	WEE WILLIE WINKIE, William Jacobson, 25,000	35.00	NR

Special Commemorative Issues (Rockwell Museum)

1985	JAMES DEAN — AMERICA'S REBEL, William Jacobson, 10,000	45.00	NR
1985	ELVIS PRESLEY — THE ONCE AND FOREVER KING, William Jacobson, 10,000	45.00	NR

OHIO ARTS UNITED STATES

Norman Rockwell

1979	LOOKING OUT TO SEA, Norman Rockwell, 20,000	19.50	NR

O.K. COLLECTIBLES

Fantasy Farm

1984	LOWENA, Louise Sigle, 3,000	39.95	NR

Single Issues

1984	CHESTER, Ralph Waterhouse, 5,000	55.00	NR
1984	MIDWESTERN SUMMER, Jeanne Horak, 4,500	50.00	NR
1984	MORNING IN THE MARSHLAND, Evel Knievel, 15,000 ...	50.00	NR

OPA'S HAUS GERMANY

Annual German Christmas (Weihnachten)

1978	ANNUAL CHRISTMAS PLATE, 2,500	58.00	NR
1979	ANNUAL CHRISTMAS PLATE, 2,500	58.00	NR
1980	ANNUAL CHRISTMAS PLATE, 2,500	58.00	NR
1981	ANNUAL CHRISTMAS PLATE, 2,500	58.00	NR

		Issue Price	Current Value
1982	ANNUAL CHRISTMAS PLATE, 2,500	58.00	NR
1983	ANNUAL CHRISTMAS PLATE, 2,500	58.00	NR
1984	ANNUAL CHRISTMAS PLATE, 2,500	58.00	NR

ORREFORS SWEDEN

Annual Cathedral

1970	NOTRE DAME, 5,000	50.00	65.00
1971	WESTMINSTER ABBEY, 5,000	45.00	NR
1972	BASILICA DE SAN MAREO, 5,000	50.00	60.00
1973	COLOGNE CATHEDRAL, 5,000	50.00	65.00
1974	RUE DE LA VICTOIRE, 5,000	60.00	70.00
1975	BASILICA DE SAN PIETRO, 5,000	85.00	110.00
1976	CHRIST CHURCH, 3,000	85.00	NR
1977	MASJID—I—SHAH, 3,000	90.00	100.00
1978	SANTIAGO DE COMPOSTELA, 3,000	95.00	NR

Mother's Day

1971	FLOWERS FOR MOTHER, 1 year	45.00	60.00
1972	MOTHER AND CHILDREN, 1 year	45.00	NR
1973	MOTHER AND CHILD, 1 year	50.00	NR
1974	MOTHER AND CHILD, 1 year	50.00	NR
1975	MOTHER AND CHILD, 1 year	60.00	NR
1976	CHILDREN AND PUPPY, 1 year	75.00	BR
1977	CHILD AND DOVE, 1,500	85.00	NR
1978	MOTHER AND CHILD, 1,500	90.00	NR

OSIRIS PORCELAIN EGYPT

Cleopatra: Queen of Ancient Egypt

1991	CLEOPATRA MEETS ANTONY	39.84	70.00
1992	CLEOPATRA AND THE ASP	39.84	RI
1992	ADORNING THE QUEEN	39.84	RI
1992	ENTERTAINING CLEOPATRA	39.84	RI

Legend of Tutankhamun

1991	TUTANKHAMUN AND HIS PRINCESS	39.84	NR
1991	THE MARRIAGE OF TUTANKHAMUN	39.84	NR
1991	BANQUET IN THE ROYAL GARDENS	42.84	60.00
1991	GAME OF SENET	42.84	50.00
1991	ADORNMENTS FOR THE KING	42.84	50.00
1992	FISHING ON THE NILE	44.84	RI
1992	GIFTS FROM FARAWAY PLACES	44.84	RI

		Issue Price	Current Value
1992	TRUE LOVES OF THE NEW KINGDOM	44.84	RI

Splendors of an Ancient World

1993	GOLDEN MASK OF TUTANKHAMUN	79.00	RI
1993	NEFERTITI: THE ETERNAL BEAUTY	79.00	RI
1993	CLEOPATRA: EMPRESS AND ENCHANTRESS	84.00	RI
1993	RAMSES II — THE WARRIOR OF PHARAOH	84.00	RI
1993	THE REFORMER KING, AKHENATEN	84.00	RI
1993	HATSHEPSUT — THE PHARAOH QUEEN	84.00	RI

Tutankhamun and His Princess
Photo courtesy of *Collectors News*

PACIFIC ART LIMITED UNITED STATES

Just Like Daddy's Hats

1983	JESSICA, Franklin Moody, 10,000	29.00	NR

Victoria and Jason

1983	VICTORIA, Lee Dubin, 7,500	—	—
1983	JASON, Lee Dubin, 7,500, set of 2	—	—
	Set of 2	65.00	NR

Single Issues

1983	MAE WEST, Bob Harman, 5,000.......................	42.50	NR
1983	GUARDIAN ANGEL, Lily Cavell, 7,500	29.50	NR

PALISANDER DENMARK

Christmas

		Issue Price	Current Value
1971	RED ROBIN, 1,200	50.00	65.00
1972	FLYING GEESE, 1,200	50.00	60.00
1973	CHRISTMAS, 1,200	50.00	NR

Presidential

1971	WASHINGTON, 1,000	50.00	NR
1972	JEFFERSON, 1,000	50.00	NR
1973	JOHN ADAMS, 1,000	50.00	NR

Single Issue

1973	BICENTENNIAL, 250	50.00	NR

PAPEL

Olympics

1984	SPORTS PLATE, 1 year	30.00	NR
1984	STAR IN MOTION, 25,000	17.00	NR
1984	SAM THE OLYMPIC EAGLE, 25,000	17.00	NR

PARKHURST ENTERPRISES UNITED STATES

International Wildlife Foundation

1984	PANDAS, Violet Parkhurst, 1,000	60.00	NR
1984	GRIZZLIES, Violet Parkhurst, 1,000	60.00	NR
1984	ELEPHANTS, Violet Parkhurst, 1,000	60.00	NR
1984	BENGAL TIGERS, Violet Parkhurst, 1,000	60.00	NR
1984	POLAR BEARS, Violet Parkhurst, 1,000	60.00	NR
1984	SNOW LEOPARDS, Violet Parkhurst, 1,000	60.00	NR
1984	HARP SEALS, Violet Parkhurst, 1,000	60.00	NR
1984	GIRAFFES, Violet Parkhurst, 1,000	60.00	NR
1984	BACTRIAN CAMEL, Violet Parkhurst, 1,000	60.00	NR
1984	HIPPOS, Violet Parkhurst, 1,000	60.00	NR
1984	LIONS, Violet Parkhurst, 1,000	60.00	NR
1984	CHEETAHS, Violet Parkhurst, 1,000	60.00	NR

PARKHURST & BOWER UNITED STATES

Single Issue

1984	I LOVE TEDDY BEARS, Violet Parkhurst	39.50	NR

PAVILION OF T'SANG YING–HAUAN TAIWAN

Chinese Children's Games

		Issue Price	Current Value
1986	CHINESE CHESS	29.00	NR
1986	KITE FLYING	29.00	NR
1986	SPINNING TOPS	32.00	NR
1987	ROLLING HOOPS	32.00	NR
1987	BLIND MAN BLUFF	32.00	NR
1988	KICKING GAMES	32.00	NR

PAWNEE CREEK PRESS

Christmas Classics

1984	CARDINALS AND MISTLETOE, James Landenberger, 2,000	50.00	NR

PEMBERTON AND OAKES UNITED STATES

Adventures of Childhood

1989	ALMOST HOME, Donald Zolan, 44 days	19.60	50.00
1989	CRYSTAL'S CREEK, Donald Zolan, 44 days	19.60	45.00
1989	SUMMER SUDS, Donald Zolan, 44 days	22.00	30.00
1990	SNOWY ADVENTURE, Donald Zolan, 44 days	22.00	30.00
1991	FORESTS AND FAIRY TALES, Donald Zolan, 44 days	24.40	30.00

The Best of Zolan in Miniature

1985	SABINA IN THE GRASS, Donald Zolan, 22 days	12.50	115.00
1986	ERIK AND THE DANDELION, Donald Zolan, 22 days	12.50	80.00
1986	TENDER MOMENT, Donald Zolan, 22 days	12.50	60.00
1986	TOUCHING THE SKY, Donald Zolan, 22 days	12.50	50.00
1987	A GIFT FOR LAURIE, Donald Zolan, 22 days	12.50	50.00
1987	SMALL WONDER, Donald Zolan, 22 days	12.50	45.00

Childhood Discoveries — Miniature

1990	COLORS OF SPRING, Donald Zolan, 19 days	14.40	40.00
1990	AUTUMN LEAVES, Donald Zolan, 19 days	14.40	35.00
1991	ENCHANTED FOREST, Donald Zolan, 19 days	16.60	30.00
1991	JUST DUCKY, Donald Zolan, 19 days	16.60	30.00
1991	RAINY DAY PALS, Donald Zolan, 19 days	16.60	25.00
1992	DOUBLE TROUBLE, Donald Zolan, 19 days	16.60	RI

Childhood Friendship

1987	BEACH BREAK, Donald Zolan, 17 days	19.00	40.00
1987	LITTLE ENGINEERS, Donald Zolan, 17 days	19.00	45.00
1988	TINY TREASURES, Donald Zolan, 17 days	19.00	35.00
1988	SHARING SECRETS, Donald Zolan, 17 days	19.00	45.00

		Issue Price	Current Value
1988	DOZENS OF DAISIES, Donald Zolan, 17 days	19.00	40.00
1990	COUNTRY WALK, Donald Zolan, 17 days	19.00	35.00

Children at Christmas

1981	A GIFT FOR LAURIE, Donald Zolan, 15,000	48.00	NR
1982	A CHRISTMAS PRAYER, Donald Zolan, 15,000	48.00	NR
1983	ERIK'S DELIGHT, Donald Zolan, 15,000	48.00	NR
1984	CHRISTMAS SECRET, Donald Zolan, 15,000	48.00	NR
1985	CHRISTMAS KITTEN, Donald Zolan, 15,000	48.00	55.00
1986	LAURIE AND THE CRÈCHE, Donald Zolan, 15,000	48.00	NR

Christmas

1991	CANDLELIGHT MAGIC, Donald Zolan, open	24.80	NR

Christmas — Miniature

1993	SNOWY ADVENTURE, Donald Zolan, 19 days	16.60	RI

Companion to Brotherly Love

1989	SISTERLY LOVE, Donald Zolan, 15,000	48.00	NR

Easter — Miniature

1991	EASTER MORNING, Donald Zolan, 19 days	16.60	30.00

Father's Day

1986	DADDY'S HOME, Donald Zolan, 19 days	19.00	80.00

Grandparent's Day

1990	IT'S GRANDMA AND GRANDPA, Donald Zolan, 19 days .	24.40	35.00
1993	GRANDPA'S FENCE, Donald Zolan, 13 days	24.40	RI

Colors of Spring
Photo courtesy of *Collectors News*

		Issue Price	Current Value

Heirloom Ovals

1992	MY KITTY, Donald Zolan, 1 year	18.80	RI

Little Girls

1985	CURIOUS KITTEN, Robert Anderson	29.00	85.00
1986	MAKING MAGIC, Robert Anderson	29.00	55.00
1986	SUNNY UMBRELLA, Robert Anderson	29.00	NR
1987	APPLE BLOSSOM TIME, Robert Anderson	29.00	NR

March of Dimes: Our Children, Our Future

1989	A TIME FOR PEACE, Donald Zolan, 150 days	29.00	NR

Curious Kitten
Photo courtesy of *Collectors News*

A Time for Peace
Photo courtesy of *Collectors News*

Membership — Miniature

1987	FOR YOU, Donald Zolan, 19 days	12.50	40.00
1988	MAKING FRIENDS, Donald Zolan, 19 days	12.50	60.00
1989	GRANDMA'S GARDEN, Donald Zolan, 19 days	12.50	65.00
1990	A CHRISTMAS PRAYER, Donald Zolan, 19 days	14.40	65.00
1991	GOLDEN MOMENT, Donald Zolan, 19 days	16.60	40.00
1992	BROTHERLY LOVE, Donald Zolan, 19 days	16.60	RI
1993	NEW SHOES, Donald Zolan, 19 days	16.60	RI

Moments Alone

1980	THE DREAMER, Robert Bentley, <1 year	28.80	45.00
1981	REVERIE, Robert Bentley, <1 year	28.80	NR
1982	GENTLE THOUGHTS, Robert Bentley, <1 year	28.80	35.00
1983	WHEAT FIELDS, Robert Bentley, <1 year	28.80	NR

Moments to Remember — Miniature

		Issue Price	Current Value
1992	JUST WE TWO, Donald Zolan, 19 days	16.60	RI
1992	ALMOST HOME, Donald Zolan, 19 days................	16.60	RI
1993	TINY TREASURES, Donald Zolan, 19 days	16.60	RI
1993	FOREST FRIENDS, Donald Zolan, 19 days	16.60	RI

Mother's Day

1988	MOTHER'S ANGELS, Donald Zolan, 19 days	19.00	40.00

Mother's Day — Miniature

1990	FLOWERS FOR MOTHER, Donald Zolan, 19 days	14.40	45.00
1992	TWILIGHT PRAYER, Donald Zolan, 19 days	16.60	RI
1993	JESSICA'S FIELD, Donald Zolan, 19 days...............	16.60	RI

Nutcracker II

1981	GRANDE FINALE, Shell Fisher, <1 year	24.40	35.00
1982	THE ARABIAN DANCERS, Shell Fisher, <1 year	24.40	65.00
1983	DEW DROP FAIRY, Shell Fisher, limited	24.40	55.00
1984	CLARA'S DELIGHT, Shell Fisher, limited	24.40	45.00
1985	BEDTIME FOR NUTCRACKER, Shell Fisher, limited	24.40	45.00
1986	CROWNING OF CLARA, Shell Fisher, limited	24.40	35.00
1987	DANCE OF THE SNOWFLAKES, Donald Zolan, limited ...	24.40	50.00
1988	THE ROYAL WELCOME, Robert Anderson	24.40	NR
1989	THE SPANISH DANCER, Mary Vickers	24.40	NR

Bedtime for Nutcracker
Photo courtesy of *Collectors News*

Dance of the Snowflakes
Photo courtesy of *Collectors News*

Plaques

1991	NEW SHOES, Donald Zolan, 1 year....................	18.80	30.00

		Issue Price	Current Value
1992	GRANDMA'S GARDEN, Donald Zolan, 1 year	18.80	RI
1992	SMALL WONDER, Donald Zolan, 1 year	18.80	RI
1992	EASTER MORNING, Donald Zolan, 1 year	18.80	RI

Special Moments of Childhood

		Issue Price	Current Value
1988	BROTHERLY LOVE, Donald Zolan, 19 days	19.00	40.00
1988	SUNNY SURPRISE, Donald Zolan, 19 days	19.00	NR
1989	SUMMER'S CHILD, Donald Zolan, 19 days	22.00	NR
1989	MEADOW MAGIC, Donald Zolan, 19 days	22.00	NR
1990	CONE FOR TWO, Donald Zolan, 19 days	24.60	NR
1990	RODEO GIRL, Donald Zolan, 19 days	24.60	NR

Brotherly Love
Photo courtesy of *Collectors News*

Swan Lake

		Issue Price	Current Value
1983	SWAN QUEEN, Shell Fisher, 15,000	35.00	65.00
1984	SWAN MAIDENS, Shell Fisher, 15,000	35.00	45.00
1984	SWAN LAKE ADAGIO, Shell Fisher, 15,000	35.00	45.00
1984	THE BLACK SWAN, Shell Fisher, 15,000	35.00	45.00
1985	THE DYING SWAN, Shell Fisher, 15,000	35.00	65.00

Tenth Anniversary

		Issue Price	Current Value
1988	RIBBONS AND ROSES, Donald Zolan, 19 days	24.40	50.00

Thanksgiving Day

		Issue Price	Current Value
1987	I'M THANKFUL, TOO, Donald Zolan, 19 days	19.00	NR

Thanksgiving — Miniature

		Issue Price	Current Value
1993	I'M THANKFUL, TOO, Donald Zolan, 19 days	16.60	RI

		Issue Price	Current Value

Times to Treasure, Bone China — Miniature

| 1993 | LITTLE TRAVELER, Donald Zolan, 19 days .... | 16.60 | RI |
| 1993 | GARDEN SWING, Donald Zolan, 19 days............... | 16.60 | RI |

Valentine's Day — Miniature

| 1990 | FIRST KISS, Donald Zolan, 19 days.................... | 14.40 | 60.00 |
| 1993 | PEPPERMINT KISS, Donald Zolan, 19 days............. | 16.60 | RI |

Wonder of Childhood

1982	TOUCHING THE SKY, Donald Zolan, 22 days	19.00	NR
1983	SPRING INNOCENCE, Donald Zolan, 22 days	19.00	NR
1984	WINTER ANGEL, Donald Zolan, 22 days	22.00	NR
1985	SMALL WONDER, Donald Zolan, 22 days	22.00	NR
1985	GRANDMA'S GARDEN, Donald Zolan, 22 days..........	22.00	NR
1986	DAY DREAMER, Donald Zolan, 22 days	22.00	NR

Winter Angel
Photo courtesy of *Collectors News*

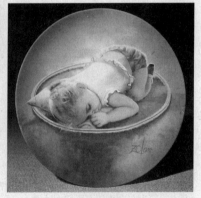

Day Dreamer
Photo courtesy of *Collectors News*

Zolan's Children

1978	ERIK AND THE DANDELION, Donald Zolan, 1 year	19.00	100.00
1979	SABINA IN THE GRASS, Donald Zolan, 1 year	22.00	90.00
1980	BY MYSELF, Donald Zolan, 1 year	24.00	NR
1981	FOR YOU, Donald Zolan, 1 year	24.00	NR

Zolan's Children and Pets

| 1984 | TENDER MOMENT, Donald Zolan, 28 days .... | 19.00 | NR |
| 1984 | GOLDEN MOMENT, Donald Zolan, 28 days .... | 19.00 | NR |

		Issue Price	Current Value
1985	MAKING FRIENDS, Donald Zolan, 28 days	19.00	NR
1985	TENDER BEGINNING, Donald Zolan, 28 days	19.00	NR
1986	BACKYARD DISCOVERY, Donald Zolan, 28 days	19.00	NR
1986	WAITING TO PLAY, Donald Zolan, 28 days	19.00	NR

Erik and the Dandelion
Photo courtesy of *Collectors News*

Tender Moment
Photo courtesy of *Collectors News*

Single Issue, Bone China — Miniature

1992	WINDOW OF DREAMS, Donald Zolan, 19 days	18.80	RI

Single Issue, Day to Day — Spode

1991	DAISY DAYS, Donald Zolan, 15,000	48.00	NR

Single Issues, Members Only — Miniature

1990	BY MYSELF, Donald Zolan, 19 days	14.40	60.00
1993	SUMMER'S CHILD, Donald Zolan, 10 days	16.60	RI

Single Issues — Miniature

1986	BACKYARD DISCOVERY, Donald Zolan, 22 days	12.50	65.00
1986	DADDY'S HOME, Donald Zolan, 19 days	12.50	85.00
1989	SUNNY SURPRISE, Donald Zolan, 19 days	12.50	60.00
1989	MY PUMPKIN, Donald Zolan, 19 days	14.40	60.00
1991	BACKYARD BUDDIES, Donald Zolan, 19 days	16.60	35.00
1991	THE THINKER, Donald Zolan, 19 days	16.60	30.00

Single Issue — Plaque

1991	FLOWERS FOR MOTHER, Donald Zolan, 1 year	16.80	25.00

PENDELFIN

Plate Series

		Issue Price	Current Value
XX	MOTHER WITH BABY, J. Heap, retrd	40.00	150.00
XX	FATHER, J. Heap, 7,500	40.00	NR
XX	WHOPPER, D. Roberts, 7,500	50.00	NR
XX	GINGERBREAD DAY, J. Heap, 7,500	55.00	NR
XX	CARAVAN, D. Roberts, 7,500	60.00	NR
XX	OLD SCHOOLHOUSE, J. Heap, 7,500	60.00	NR

PFAFF

Heritage

1977	GERMANY, 2,500	40.00	55.00
1978	HOLLAND, 2,500	40.00	NR
1979	SWITZERLAND, 2,500	40.00	NR
1980	NORWAY, 2,500	40.00	NR

PICKARD UNITED STATES

Christmas

1976	ALBA MADONNA, Raphael, 7,500	60.00	90.00
1977	THE NATIVITY, L. Lotto, 7,500	65.00	NR
1978	REST ON THE FLIGHT INTO EGYPT, G. David, 10,000	65.00	NR
1979	ADORATION OF THE MAGI, Botticelli, 10,000	70.00	NR
1980	MADONNA AND CHILD/INFANT ST. JOHN, Sodoma, 10,000 . .	80.00	NR
1981	MADONNA AND CHILD WITH ANGELS, Memling, 10,000	90.00	NR

The Nativity

Rest on the Flight into Egypt

Madonna and Child with the Infant Saint John

Madonna and Child with Angels

Children of Christmas Past

		Issue Price	Current Value
1983	SLEDDING ON CHRISTMAS DAY, 7,500	60.00	NR

Children of Mary Cassatt

		Issue Price	Current Value
1983	SIMONE IN WHITE BONNET, Mary Cassatt, 7,500	60.00	NR
1983	CHILDREN PLAYING ON BEACH, Mary Cassatt, 7,500	60.00	NR
1984	GIRL IN A STRAW HAT, Mary Cassatt, 7,500	60.00	NR
1984	YOUNG GIRLS, Mary Cassatt, 7,500	60.00	NR

Children of Mexico

		Issue Price	Current Value
1981	MARIA, J. Sanchez, 5,000	85.00	NR
1981	MIGUEL, J. Sanchez, 5,000	85.00	NR
1982	REGINA, J. Sanchez, 5,000	90.00	NR
1983	RAPHAEL, J. Sanchez, 5,000	90.00	NR

Children of Renoir

		Issue Price	Current Value
1978	GIRL WITH WATERING CAN, Auguste Renoir, 5,000	50.00	125.00
1978	CHILD IN WHITE, Auguste Renoir, 5,000	50.00	125.00
1979	GIRL WITH HOOP, Auguste Renoir, 5,000	55.00	75.00
1979	AT THE PIANO, Auguste Renoir, 5,000	55.00	75.00
1980	TWO LITTLE CIRCUS GIRLS, Auguste Renoir, 5,000	60.00	70.00
1980	ARTIST'S SON JEAN, Auguste Renoir, 5,000	60.00	65.00

Gardens of Monet

		Issue Price	Current Value
1986	SUMMER SPLENDOR, 3,500	85.00	NR
1987	A TIME GONE BY, 3,500	85.00	NR

Gems of Nature (Bradford Exchange)

		Issue Price	Current Value
1990	RUBY–THROATED WITH LILIES, 150 days	29.00	NR
1990	RUFOUS WITH APPLE BLOSSOMS, 150 days	29.00	NR
1990	BROAD–BILLED WITH PENSTEMON, 150 days	32.00	NR
1990	CALLIOPE WITH GLADIOLI, 150 days	32.00	45.00
1991	BLACK–CHINNED WITH FUCHSIA, 150 days	32.00	NR
1991	WHITE–EARED WITH PEONIES, 150 days	32.00	45.00
1991	ANNAS WITH PETUNIAS, 150 days	34.00	45.00
1991	COSTA'S WITH HOLLYHOCKS	34.00	60.00

Hawaiian Splendor (Bradford Exchange)

1992	TROPICAL ENCHANTMENT, 150 days	34.00	RI
1993	COASTAL HARMONY, 150 days	34.00	RI
1993	EVENING IN THE ISLANDS, 150 days	34.00	RI
1993	TWILIGHT PARADISE, 150 days	34.00	RI

Holiday Traditions

1992	CHRISTMAS HOMECOMING, 150 days	29.00	RI
1993	QUIET UNDER THE EAVES, 150 days	29.00	RI
1993	SNOWS OF YESTERYEAR, 150 days	29.00	RI
1993	HEART OF CHRISTMAS, 150 days	29.00	RI

Innocent Encounters (Bradford Exchange)

1988	MAKING FRIENDS, 150 days	34.00	NR
1988	JUST PASSING BY, 150 days	34.00	NR
1989	EYE TO EYE, 150 days	34.00	BR
1989	LET'S PLAY, 150 days	34.00	NR

Legends of Camelot

1982	MERLIN THE MAGICIAN, David Palladini, 12,500	62.50	NR
1982	THE SECRET ROMANCE, David Palladini, 12,500	62.50	NR
1982	I KNIGHT THEE SIR LANCELOT, David Palladini, 12,500	62.50	NR
1982	KING ARTHUR AND HIS QUEEN, David Palladini, 12,500	62.50	NR

Let's Pretend

1984	CLEOPATRA, Irene Spencer, 5,000	80.00	NR
1984	MARK ANTONY, Irene Spencer, 5,000	80.00	NR
1985	ROBIN HOOD, Irene Spencer, 5,000	80.00	NR
1985	MAID MARIAN, Irene Spencer, 5,000	80.00	NR

Lockhart Wildlife

1970	WOODCOCK and RUFFED GROUSE, James Lockhart, 2,000, pair 150.00		210.00
1971	GREEN–WINGED TEAL and MALLARD, James Lockhart, 2,000, pair	150.00	170.00
1972	CARDINAL and MOCKINGBIRD, James Lockhart, 2,000, pair	162.50	BR

Children Playing on Beach
Photo courtesy of *Collectors News*

Christmas Homecoming
Photo courtesy of *Collectors News*

A Time Gone By

Calliope with Gladioli

Green–Winged Teal

Mallard

Cardinal

Mockingbird

Great Horned Owl

American Panther

Red Fox

Courtship Flight

	Issue Price	Current Value
1973 PHEASANT and WILD TURKEY, James Lockhart, 2,000, pair ..	162.50	200.00
1974 AMERICAN BALD EAGLE, James Lockhart, 2,000, 13"....	150.00	675.00
1975 WHITE-TAILED DEER, James Lockhart, 2,500, 11".......	100.00	110.00
1976 AMERICAN BUFFALO, James Lockhart, 2,500, 13".......	165.00	BR
1977 GREAT HORNED OWL, James Lockhart, 2,500, 11".......	100.00	BR
1978 AMERICAN PANTHER, James Lockhart, 2,500, 13"	175.00	BR
1979 RED FOX, James Lockhart, 2,500, 11"	120.00	BR
1980 TRUMPETER SWAN, James Lockhart, 2,500, 13"	200.00	BR

Most Beautiful Women of All Time

1981 HELEN OF TROY, Oleg Cassini, 1 year..................	75.00	NR
1982 MARIE ANTOINETTE, Oleg Cassini, 1 year	75.00	NR
1983 LILLIE LANGTRY, Oleg Cassini, 1 year	75.00	NR
1984 SALOME, Oleg Cassini, 1 year	75.00	NR

Mother's Love

1980 MIRACLE, Irene Spencer, 7,500.......................	95.00	NR
1981 STORY TIME, Irene Spencer, 7,500....................	110.00	NR
1982 FIRST EDITION, Irene Spencer, 7,500.................	115.00	NR
1983 PRECIOUS MOMENT, Irene Spencer, 7,500.............	120.00	140.00

Nativity Triptych

1986 UNTO US A CHILD IS BORN, John Lawson, 3,500	95.00	NR

Pickard Commemorative

1982 GREAT SEAL OF THE UNITED STATES, 10,000...........	95.00	NR
1984 STATUE OF LIBERTY, 10,000	150.00	NR
1990 STAR SPANGLED BANNER, 10,000	150.00	NR

Great Seal of the United States

Truman

Presidential

		Issue Price	Current Value
1972	TRUMAN, 3,000	35.00	NR
1973	LINCOLN, 5,000	35.00	NR

Romantic Castles of Europe (The Hamilton Collection)

1990	LUDWIG'S CASTLE, 19,500	55.00	NR
1990	PALACE OF THE MOORS, 19,500	55.00	NR
1991	SWISS ISLE FORTRESS, 19,500	55.00	NR
1991	LEGENDARY CASTLE OF LEEDS, 19,500	55.00	NR
1991	LEONARDO DAVINCI'S CHAMBORD, 19,500	55.00	NR
1992	EILEAN DONAN, 19,500	55.00	RI
1992	ELTZ CASTLE, 19,500	55.00	RI
1992	KYLEMORE ABBY, 19,500	55.00	RI

Swiss Isle Fortress

Sanchez Miniatures

1985	CARMEN, J. Sanchez, 3,500	50.00	NR
1985	FELIPE, J. Sanchez, 3,500	50.00	NR

Symphony of Roses

1982	WILD IRISH ROSE, Irene Spencer, 10,000	85.00	95.00
1983	YELLOW ROSE OF TEXAS, Irene Spencer, 10,000	90.00	100.00
1984	HONEYSUCKLE ROSE, Irene Spencer, 10,000	95.00	115.00
1985	ROSE OF WASHINGTON SQUARE, Irene Spencer, 10,000	100.00	135.00

Wings of Freedom

1985	COURTSHIP FLIGHT, 2,500	250.00	NR
1986	WINGS OF FREEDOM, 2,500	250.00	NR

		Issue Price	Current Value
Single Issues (Paramount Classics)			
1977	CORONATION PLATE, 5,000	95.00	NR
1977	KING GEORGE III, 5,000	95.00	NR
1977	QUEEN ELIZABETH, 5,000	375.00	400.00
1977	QUEEN VICTORIA, 5,000	95.00	NR
1977	QUEEN OF ENGLAND, 5,000	95.00	NR

POILLERAT FRANCE

Calendar

1972	JANUARY, 1,000	100.00	115.00
1972	FEBRUARY, 1,000	100.00	115.00
1973	MARCH, 1,000	125.00	145.00
1973	APRIL, 1,000	125.00	145.00

Christmas

1972	THREE KINGS, 500	350.00	375.00
1973	ROSE, 500	350.00	375.00

POOLE POTTERY GREAT BRITAIN

Birds of North America

1979	GREAT HORNED OWL, 11,000	37.50	NR

Cathedrals

1973	CHRIST ON CROSS, 11,000	125.00	NR

Christmas

1973	ADORATION OF MAGI, 10,000	37.50	NR
1979	THREE WISEMEN, 10,000	37.50	NR

Medieval Calendar

1972	JANUARY — DRINKING WINE BY FIRE, 1,000	100.00	NR
1972	FEBRUARY — CHOPPING WOOD, 1,000	100.00	NR
1973	MARCH — DIGGING IN FIELDS AND SETTING SEEDS, 1,000 .	125.00	NR
1973	APRIL — CARRYING FLOWERING BRANCH, 1,000	125.00	NR
1974	MAY — HAWKING, 1,000	125.00	NR
1974	JUNE — MOWING HAY, 1,000	125.00	NR
1975	JULY — CUTTING CORN WITH SICKLE, 1,000	125.00	NR
1975	AUGUST — THRESHING WITH FLAIL, 1,000	125.00	NR
1976	SEPTEMBER — PICKING GRAPES, 1,000	125.00	NR
1976	OCTOBER — SOWING WINTER CORN, 1,000	125.00	NR
1977	NOVEMBER — GATHERING ACORNS TO FEED PIGS, 1,000 ..	125.00	NR
1977	DECEMBER — PIG KILLING, 1,000	125.00	NR

Mother's Day	Issue Price	Current Value
1979 TENDERNESS, 10,000	37.50	NR

PORCELAINE ARIEL UNITED STATES

Greatest Show on Earth (The Hamilton Collection)

1981 THE CLOWNS, Franklin Moody, 10 days	30.00	70.00
1981 THE ELEPHANTS, Franklin Moody, 10 days	30.00	NR
1981 THE AERIALISTS, Franklin Moody, 10 days	30.00	NR
1981 THE GREAT PARADE, Franklin Moody, 10 days	30.00	NR
1981 THE MIDWAY, Franklin Moody, 10 days	30.00	NR
1981 THE EQUESTRIANS, Franklin Moody, 10 days	30.00	NR
1981 THE LION TAMER, Franklin Moody, 10 days	30.00	NR
1982 THE GRAND FINALE, Franklin Moody, 10 days	30.00	NR

Tribute to Love — The Rubaiyat of Omar Khayyam

1980 A SHAFT OF LIGHT, Mossan Eskandar, 17,500	45.00	NR
1981 A JUG OF WINE, Mossan Eskandar, 17,500	45.00	NR
1981 SULTAN AFTER SULTAN, Mossan Eskandar, 17,500	45.00	NR
1982 THE BIRD IS ON THE WING, Mossan Eskandar, 17,500 ..	45.00	NR
1982 IF TODAY BE SWEET, Mossan Eskandar, 17,500	45.00	NR
1982 FLOWER THAT ONCE HAS BLOWN, Mossan Eskandar, 17,500	45.00	NR
1982 DOOR TO WHICH WE HAVE NO KEY, Mossan Eskandar, 17,500	45.00	NR
1982 AH, MY BELOVED FILL THE CUP, Mossan Eskandar, 17,500	45.00	NR
1982 THE MOVING FINGER WRITES, Mossan Eskandar, 17,500	45.00	NR

Waltzes of Johann Strauss (The Hamilton Collection)

1981 THE EMPEROR'S WALTZ, Marca America, 10 days	25.00	NR
1981 THE BLUE DANUBE, Marca America, 10 days	25.00	NR
1981 VOICES OF SPRING, Marca America, 10 days	25.00	NR
1981 VIENNA LIFE, Marca America, 10 days	25.00	NR
1981 ROSES OF THE SOUTH, Marca America, 10 days	25.00	NR
1982 WINE, WOMEN AND SONG, Marca America, 10 days...	25.00	NR
1982 ARTIST'S LIFE, Marca America, 10 days	25.00	NR
1982 TALES OF THE VIENNA WOODS, Marca America, 10 days	25.00	NR

PORCELANA GRANADA ARGENTINA

Christmas

1971 THE ANNUNCIATION, Tom Fennell Jr., 5,000	12.00	NR
1972 MARY AND ELIZABETH, Tom Fennell Jr., 5,000	12.00	NR
1973 ROAD TO BETHLEHEM, Tom Fennell Jr., 5,000	14.00	NR
1974 NO ROOM, Tom Fennell Jr., 5,000	16.00	NR

		Issue Price	Current Value
1975	SHEPHERDS IN THE FIELDS, Tom Fennell Jr., 5,000	16.50	NR
1976	NATIVITY, Tom Fennell Jr., 5,000	17.50	NR
1977	THREE KINGS, Tom Fennell Jr., 5,000	18.00	NR
1978	YOUNG CARPENTER, Tom Fennell Jr., 5,000	18.00	NR
1979	CALLING OF THE DISCIPLES, Tom Fennell Jr., 5,000	19.50	NR
1980	LOAVES AND FISHES, Tom Fennell Jr., 5,000	20.00	NR
1981	SUFFER THE LITTLE CHILDREN, Tom Fennell Jr., 5,000	20.00	NR
1982	TRIUMPHAL ENTRY, Tom Fennell Jr., 5,000	20.00	NR

PORSGRUND NORWAY

Castles
1970	HAMLET	13.00	NR
1971	ROSENBORG	13.00	NR

Christmas
1968	CHURCH SCENE, Gunnar Bratile, 1 year	12.00	120.00
1969	THREE KINGS, Gunnar Bratile, 1 year	12.00	NR
1970	ROAD TO BETHLEHEM, Gunnar Bratile, 1 year	12.00	NR
1971	A CHILD IS BORN, Gunnar Bratile, 1 year	12.00	NR
1972	HARK, THE HERALD ANGELS SING, Gunnar Bratile, 1 year	12.00	NR
1973	PROMISE OF THE SAVIOR, Gunnar Bratile, 1 year	12.00	NR
1974	THE SHEPHERDS, Gunnar Bratile, 1 year	15.00	35.00
1975	ROAD TO THE TEMPLE, Gunnar Bratile, 1 year	19.50	NR
1976	JESUS AND THE ELDERS, Gunnar Bratile, 1 year	22.00	NR
1977	DROUGHT OF THE FISH, Gunnar Bratile, 1 year	24.00	45.00
1983	CHRISTMAS NIGHT, Thorstein Rittun	42.00	BR

Christmas Deluxe
1970	ROAD TO BETHLEHEM, 3,000	50.00	NR
1971	A CHILD IS BORN, 3,000	50.00	NR
1972	HARK, THE HERALD ANGELS SING, 3,000	50.00	NR
1973	PROMISE OF THE SAVIOR, 3,000	50.00	NR

Easter
1972	DUCKS, 1 year	12.00	NR
1973	BIRDS, 1 year	12.00	NR
1974	BUNNIES, 1 year	15.00	NR
1975	CHICKS, 1 year	19.50	NR
1976	SHEEP, 1 year	22.00	NR
1977	BUTTERFLIES, 1 year	24.00	NR

Father's Day
1971	FISHING, 1 year	7.50	15.00

		Issue Price	Current Value
1972	COOKOUT, 1 year	8.00	15.00
1973	SLEDDING, 1 year	8.00	NR
1974	FATHER AND SON, 1 year............................	10.00	NR
1975	SKATING, 1 year..................................	12.50	NR
1976	SKIING, 1 year	15.00	NR
1977	SOCCER, 1 year	16.50	NR
1978	CANOEING, 1 year..................................	17.50	NR
1979	FATHER AND DAUGHTER, 1 year	19.50	NR
1980	SAILING, 1 year	21.50	NR

Jubilee

1970	FEMBORINGER, 1 year	25.00	NR

Mother's Day

1970	MARE AND FOAL, Gunnar Bratile, 1 year	7.50	15.00
1971	BOY AND GEESE, Gunnar Bratile, 1 year...............	7.50	NR
1972	DOE AND FAWN, Gunnar Bratile, 1 year	10.00	NR
1973	CAT AND KITTENS, Gunnar Bratile, 1 year	10.00	NR
1974	BOY AND GOATS, Gunnar Bratile, 1 year	10.00	NR
1975	DOG AND PUPPIES, Gunnar Bratile, 1 year	12.50	NR
1976	GIRL AND CALF, Gunnar Bratile, 1 year	15.00	NR
1977	BOY AND CHICKENS, Gunnar Bratile, 1 year	16.50	NR
1978	GIRLS AND PIGS, Gunnar Bratile, 1 year...............	17.50	NR
1979	BOY AND REINDEER, Gunnar Bratile, 1 year	19.50	NR
1980	GIRL AND SHEEP, Gunnar Bratile, 1 year..............	21.50	NR
1981	BOY AND BIRDS, Gunnar Bratile, 1 year	24.00	NR
1982	CHILD WITH RABBIT, Gunnar Bratile, 1 year	26.00	NR
1983	MOTHER AND KITTENS, Gunnar Bratile, 1 year	26.00	NR
1984	BY THE POND, Gunnar Bratile, 1 year	25.00	NR

Traditional Norwegian Christmas

1978	GUESTS ARE COMING, Gunnar Bratile, 1 year..........	27.00	NR
1979	HOME FOR CHRISTMAS, Gunnar Bratile, 1 year	30.00	NR
1980	PREPARING FOR CHRISTMAS, Gunnar Bratile, 1 year ...	34.00	NR
1981	CHRISTMAS SKATING, Gunnar Bratile, 1 year..........	38.00	NR
1982	WHITE CHRISTMAS, Gunnar Bratile, 1 year............	42.00	NR

Single Issue

1909	CHRISTMAS FLOWERS, rare	—	1,150.00

POVERTY BAY PORCELAIN

Henry's Loveable Model T

1984	PAPA'S NEW FORD, Randy Giovenale, 5,000............	29.95	NR

PRINCETON GALLERY

		Issue Price	Current Value

Arctic Wolves

		Issue Price	Current Value
1991	SONG OF THE WILDERNESS, J. Van Zyle, 90 days	29.50	NR
1992	IN THE EYE OF THE MOON, J. Van Zyle, 90 days	29.50	RI

Circus Friends

1989	DON'T BE SHY, R. Sanderson.........................	29.50	NR
1990	MAKE ME A CLOWN, R. Sanderson	29.50	NR
1990	LOOKS LIKE RAIN, R. Sanderson	29.50	NR
1990	CHEER UP MR. CLOWN, R. Sanderson	29.50	NR

Cubs of the Big Cats

1990	COUGAR CUB, Q. Lemond	29.50	NR
1991	LION CUB, Q. Lemond, 90 days	29.50	NR
1991	SNOW LEOPARD, Q. Lemond, 90 days	29.50	NR
1991	CHEETAH, Q. Lemond, 90 days.......................	29.50	NR
1991	TIGER, Q. Lemond, 90 days...........................	29.50	NR
1992	LYNX CUB, Q. Lemond, 90 days	29.50	RI
1992	WHITE TIGER CUB, Q. Lemond, 90 days	29.50	RI

Darling Dalmatians

1991	DALMATIAN, L. Picken, 90 days	29.50	NR
1992	FIREHOUSE FROLIC, L. Picken, 90 days	29.50	RI

Enchanted World of the Unicorn

1991	RAINBOW VALLEY, R. Sanderson, 90 days	29.50	NR
1992	GOLDEN SHORE, R. Sanderson, 90 days	29.50	RI

RAINBOW TREASURY

Tea Party

Games We Used to Play

		Issue Price	Current Value
1984	TEA PARTY, John Sloane	29.50	NR

RAM UNITED STATES

Boston 500

1973	EASTER, 500	30.00	NR
1973	MOTHER'S DAY, 500................................	30.00	NR
1973	FATHER'S DAY, 500.................................	30.00	NR
1973	CHRISTMAS, 500	30.00	NR

Great Bird Heroes

1973	CHER AMI, 1,000....................................	7.95	NR
1973	MOCKER, 1,000	7.95	NR

RARE BIRD CANADA

Canadian Dreams

1983	GOING TO THE RINK, Joan Healey, 7,500	45.00	NR
1984	LACING UP, Joan Healey, 7,500	45.00	NR

Going to the Rink
Photo courtesy of *Collectors News*

Christmas in Canada

1986	THE WINDMILL, Joan Healey, 5,000...................	45.00	NR

RAYNAUD–LIMOGES FRANCE

		Issue Price	Current Value
Castle			
1979	BODIAM CASTLE, 5,000	48.00	NR
1979	GLAMIS CASTLE, 5,000	48.00	NR
1979	TOWER OF LONDON, 5,000	48.00	NR
Children of the Season			
1985	THE HIKER, Michael Vincent, 7,500	40.00	NR
Wildlife			
1978	TIGER BOUQUET, Cowles, 1 year	50.00	NR

RECO INTERNATIONAL UNITED STATES

Americana			
1972	GASPEE INCIDENT, Stuart Devlin, 1,500	200.00	325.00
Arabelle and Friends			
1982	ICE DELIGHT, Carol Greunke, 15,000	35.00	NR
1983	FIRST LOVE, Carol Greunke, 15,000	35.00	NR
Arta Christmas			
1973	NATIVITY, 1,500	50.00	70.00
Arta Mother's Day			
1973	FAMILY WITH PUPPY, 1,500	50.00	70.00
Barefoot Children			
1987	NIGHT–TIME STORY, Sandra Kuck, 14 days	29.50	NR
1987	GOLDEN AFTERNOON, Sandra Kuck, 14 days	29.50	NR
1987	LITTLE SWEETHEARTS, Sandra Kuck, 14 days	29.50	NR
1988	CAROUSEL MAGIC, Sandra Kuck, 14 days	29.50	NR
1988	UNDER THE APPLE TREE, Sandra Kuck, 14 days	29.50	NR
1988	THE REHEARSAL, Sandra Kuck, 14 days	29.50	NR
1988	PRETTY AS A PICTURE, Sandra Kuck, 14 days	29.50	NR
1988	GRANDMA'S TRUNK, Sandra Kuck, 14 days	29.50	NR
Becky's Day			
1985	AWAKENING, John McClelland, 90 days	24.50	NR
1985	GETTING DRESSED, John McClelland, 90 days	24.50	NR
1985	BREAKFAST, John McClelland, 90 days	27.50	NR
1986	LEARNING IS FUN, John McClelland, 90 days	27.50	NR
1986	MUFFIN MAKING, John McClelland, 90 days	27.50	NR

		Issue Price	Current Value
1986	TUB TIME, John McClelland, 90 days	27.50	NR
1986	EVENING PRAYER, John McClelland, 90 days	27.50	NR

Getting Dressed
Photo courtesy of *Collectors News*

Breakfast
Photo courtesy of *Collectors News*

Bohemian Annual

1974	1974, 500	130.00	155.00
1975	1975, 500	140.00	160.00
1976	1976, 500	150.00	160.00

Castles and Dreams

1992	THE BIRTH OF A DREAM, J. Bergsma, 48 days	29.50	RI
1992	DREAMS COME TRUE, J. Bergsma, 48 days	29.50	RI
1993	BELIEVE IN YOUR DREAMS, J. Bergsma, 48 days	29.50	RI

Celebration of Love

1992	HAPPY ANNIVERSARY, J. Hall, 9¼"	35.00	RI
1992	10TH, J. Hall, 9¼"	35.00	RI
1992	25TH, J. Hall, 9¼"	35.00	RI
1992	50TH, J. Hall, 9¼"	35.00	RI
1992	HAPPY ANNIVERSARY, J. Hall, 6½"	25.00	RI
1992	10TH, J. Hall, 6½"	25.00	RI
1992	25TH, J. Hall, 6½"	25.00	RI
1992	50TH, J. Hall, 6½"	25.00	RI

Childhood Almanac

| 1985 | FIRESIDE DREAMS — JANUARY, Sandra Kuck, 14 days . | 29.50 | 40.00 |
| 1985 | BE MINE — FEBRUARY, Sandra Kuck, 14 days .... | 29.50 | NR |

		Issue Price	Current Value
1985	WINDS OF MARCH — MARCH, Sandra Kuck, 14 days...	29.50	NR
1985	EASTER MORNING, Sandra Kuck, 14 days............	29.50	45.00
1985	FOR MOM — MAY, Sandra Kuck, 14 days.............	29.50	45.00
1985	JUST DAYDREAMING, Sandra Kuck, 14 days..........	29.50	45.00
1985	STAR SPANGLED SKY — JULY, Sandra Kuck, 14 days ...	29.50	NR
1985	SUMMER SECRETS — AUGUST, Sandra Kuck, 14 days..	29.50	40.00
1985	SCHOOL DAYS — SEPTEMBER, Sandra Kuck, 14 days ..	29.50	45.00
1985	INDIAN SUMMER — OCTOBER, Sandra Kuck, 14 days ..	29.50	40.00
1985	GIVING THANKS — NOVEMBER, Sandra Kuck, 14 days .	29.50	40.00
1985	CHRISTMAS MAGIC — DECEMBER, Sandra Kuck, 14 days ..	29.50	40.00

Easter Morning
Photo courtesy of *Collectors News*

Christmas Magic
Photo courtesy of *Collectors News*

Children's Christmas Pageant

1986	SILENT NIGHT, Sandra Kuck, 1 year...................	32.50	NR
1987	HARK, THE HERALD ANGELS SING, Sandra Kuck, 1 year	32.50	BR
1988	WHILE SHEPHERDS WATCHED..., Sandra Kuck, 1 year ..	32.50	NR
1989	WE THREE KINGS, Sandra Kuck, 1 year	32.50	NR

Children's Garden

1993	GARDEN FRIENDS, John McClelland, 120 days	29.50	RI
1993	TEA FOR THREE, John McClelland, 120 days	29.50	RI
1993	TBA, John McClelland, 120 days.....................	29.50	RI

Days Gone By

1983	AMY'S MAGIC HORSE, Sandra Kuck, 14 days	29.50	BR
1983	SUNDAY BEST, Sandra Kuck, 14 days	29.50	40.00
1984	LITTLE TUDOR, Sandra Kuck, 14 days	29.50	BR

		Issue Price	Current Value
1984	LITTLE ANGLERS, Sandra Kuck, 14 days	29.50	BR
1985	AFTERNOON RECITAL, Sandra Kuck, 14 days	29.50	50.00
1985	EASTER AT GRANDMA'S, Sandra Kuck, 14 days	29.50	BR
1985	MORNING SONG, Sandra Kuck, 14 days	29.50	BR
1985	THE SURREY RIDE, Sandra Kuck, 14 days	29.50	BR

Dresden Christmas

1971	SHEPHERD SCENE, 3,500	15.00	50.00
1972	NIKLAS CHURCH, 6,000	15.00	25.00
1973	SCHWANSTEIN CHURCH, 6,000	18.00	35.00
1974	VILLAGE SCENE, 5,000	20.00	30.00
1975	ROTHENBURG SCENE, 5,000	24.00	30.00
1976	VILLAGE CHURCH, 5,000	26.00	35.00
1977	OLD MILL, 5,000	28.00	NR

Dresden Mother's Day

1972	DOE AND FAWN, Hans Waldheimer, 8,000	15.00	20.00
1973	MARE AND COLT, Hans Waldheimer, 6,000	16.00	25.00
1974	TIGER AND CUB, Hans Waldheimer, 5,000	20.00	25.00
1975	DACHSHUND FAMILY, Hans Waldheimer, 5,000	24.00	NR
1976	MOTHER OWL AND YOUNG, Hans Waldheimer, 5,000	26.00	NR
1977	CHAMOIS, Hans Waldheimer, 5,000	28.00	NR

Enchanted Norfin Trolls

1993	TROLL MAIDEN, C. Hipkins, 75 days	19.50	RI
1993	WIZARD TROLL, C. Hipkins, 75 days	19.50	RI

Flower Fairy

1979	THE LAVENDER FAIRY, Cicely Mary Barker, 21 days	35.00	50.00
1980	THE SWEET PEA FAIRY, Cicely Mary Barker, 21 days	35.00	NR
1980	THE CANDY TUFT FAIRY, Cicely Mary Barker, 21 days	35.00	NR
1981	THE HELIOTROPE FAIRY, Cicely Mary Barker, 21 days	35.00	NR
1981	THE BLACKTHORN FAIRY, Cicely Mary Barker, 21 days	35.00	NR
1981	THE APPLE BLOSSOM FAIRY, Cicely Mary Barker, 21 days	35.00	NR

Flower Fairy II

1985	COLUMBINE, Cicely Mary Barker, 21 days	35.00	NR
1985	CORNFLOWER, Cicely Mary Barker, 21 days	35.00	NR
1985	MALLOW, Cicely Mary Barker, 21 days	35.00	NR
1985	BLACK MEDICK, Cicely Mary Barker, 21 days	35.00	NR
1985	CANTERBURY BELL, Cicely Mary Barker, 21 days	35.00	NR
1985	FUCHSIA, Cicely Mary Barker, 21 days	35.00	NR

Four Seasons

1973	SPRING, J. Poluszynksi, 2,500	50.00	75.00

		Issue Price	Current Value
1973	SUMMER, J. Poluszynksi, 2,500	50.00	75.00
1973	FALL, J. Poluszynksi, 2,500	50.00	75.00
1973	WINTER, J. Poluszynksi, 2,500	50.00	75.00

Furstenberg Christmas

1971	RABBITS, 7,000	15.00	30.00
1972	SNOWY VILLAGE, 6,000	15.00	20.00
1973	CHRISTMAS EVE, 4,000	18.00	35.00
1974	SPARROWS, 4,000	20.00	30.00
1975	DEER FAMILY, 4,000	22.00	30.00
1976	WINTER BIRDS, 4,000	25.00	NR

Furstenberg Deluxe Christmas

1971	WISE MEN, E. Grossberg, 1,500	45.00	NR
1972	HOLY FAMILY, E. Grossberg, 2,000	45.00	NR
1973	CHRISTMAS EVE, E. Grossberg, 2,000	60.00	NR

Furstenberg Easter

1971	SHEEP, 3,500	15.00	100.00
1972	CHICKS, 6,500	15.00	40.00
1973	BUNNIES, 4,000	16.00	60.00
1974	PUSSYWILLOW, 4,000	20.00	30.00
1975	EASTER WINDOW, 4,000	22.00	NR
1976	FLOWER COLLECTING, 4,000	25.00	NR

Furstenberg Mother's Day

1972	HUMMINGBIRDS, 6,000	15.00	40.00
1973	HEDGEHOGS, 5,000	16.00	30.00
1974	DOE AND FAWN, 4,000	20.00	NR

Black Medick
Photo courtesy of *Collectors News*

		Issue Price	Current Value
1975	SWANS, 4,000	22.00	NR
1976	KOALA BEARS, 4,000	25.00	NR

Furstenberg Olympic

1972	MUNICH, J. Poluszynski, 5,000	20.00	65.00
1976	MONTREAL, J. Poluszynski, 5,000	37.50	NR

Games Children Play

1979	ME FIRST, Sandra Kuck, 10,000	45.00	NR
1980	FOREVER BUBBLES, Sandra Kuck, 10,000	45.00	NR
1981	SKATING PALS, Sandra Kuck, 10,000	45.00	NR
1982	JOIN ME, Sandra Kuck, 10,000	45.00	NR

Gardens of America

1992	COLONIAL SPLENDOR, Dot Barlowe, 48 days	29.50	RI

Colonial Splendor
Photo courtesy of *Collectors News*

English Country Garden
Photo courtesy of *Collectors News*

Gardens of Beauty

1988	ENGLISH COUNTRY GARDEN, Dot Barlowe, 14 days	29.50	NR
1988	DUTCH COUNTRY GARDEN, Dot Barlowe, 14 days	29.50	NR
1988	NEW ENGLAND GARDEN, Dot Barlowe, 14 days	29.50	NR
1988	JAPANESE GARDEN, Dot Barlowe, 14 days	29.50	NR
1989	ITALIAN GARDEN, Dot Barlowe, 14 days	29.50	NR
1989	HAWAIIAN GARDEN, Dot Barlowe, 14 days	29.50	NR
1989	GERMAN COUNTRY GARDEN, Dot Barlowe, 14 days	29.50	NR
1989	MEXICAN GARDEN, Dot Barlowe, 14 days	29.50	NR

		Issue Price	Current Value

Gift of Love Mother's Day Collection

| 1993 | MORNING GLORY, Sandra Kuck, 10,000 | 65.00 | RI |

Glory of Christ

1992	THE ASCENSION, C. Micarelli, 48 days	29.50	RI
1992	JESUS TEACHING, C. Micarelli, 48 days	29.50	RI
1993	THE LAST SUPPER, C. Micarelli, 48 days	29.50	RI
1993	THE NATIVITY, C. Micarelli, 48 days	29.50	RI
1993	THE BAPTISM OF CHRIST, C. Micarelli, 48 days	29.50	RI
1993	JESUS HEALS THE SICK, C. Micarelli, 48 days	29.50	RI
1993	JESUS WALKS ON WATER, C. Micarelli, 48 days	29.50	RI
1993	DESCENT FROM THE CROSS, C. Micarelli, 48 days	29.50	RI

God's Own Country

1990	DAYBREAK, I. Drechsler, 14 days	30.00	NR
1990	COMING HOME, I. Drechsler, 14 days	30.00	NR
1990	PEACEFUL GATHERING, I. Drechsler, 14 days	30.00	NR
1990	QUIET WATERS, I. Drechsler, 14 days	30.00	NR

Golf

| 1992 | PAR EXCELLENCE, John McClelland, 180 days | 35.00 | RI |

Grafburg Christmas

| 1975 | BLACK–CAPPED CHICKADEE, 5,000 | 20.00 | 60.00 |
| 1976 | SQUIRRELS, 5,000 | 22.00 | NR |

Grandparent Collector's Plate

| 1981 | GRANDMA'S COOKIE JAR, Sandra Kuck, 1 year | 37.50 | NR |
| 1981 | GRANDPA AND THE DOLLHOUSE, Sandra Kuck, 1 year | 37.50 | NR |

Great Stories from the Bible

1987	MOSES IN THE BULRUSHES, Garri Katz, 14 days	29.50	NR
1987	KING DAVID AND SAUL, Garri Katz, 14 days	29.50	NR
1987	JOSEPH'S COAT OF MANY COLORS, Garri Katz, 14 days	29.50	NR
1987	MOSES AND THE TEN COMMANDMENTS, Garri Katz, 14 days	29.50	NR
1987	REBEKAH AT THE WELL, Garri Katz, 14 days	29.50	NR
1987	DANIEL READS THE WRITING ON THE WALL, Garri Katz, 14 days	29.50	NR
1987	KING SOLOMON, Garri Katz, 14 days	29.50	NR
1987	THE STORY OF RUTH, Garri Katz, 14 days	29.50	NR

Guardians of the Kingdom

1990	RAINBOW TO RIDE ON, J. Bergsma, 17,500	35.00	NR
1990	SPECIAL FRIENDS ARE FEW, J. Bergsma, 17,500	35.00	NR
1990	GUARDIANS OF INNOCENT CHILDREN, J. Bergsma, 17,500	35.00	NR
1990	THE MIRACLE OF LOVE, J. Bergsma, 17,500	35.00	NR

		Issue Price	Current Value
1991	THE MAGIC OF LOVE, J. Bergsma, 17,500	35.00	NR
1991	ONLY WITH THE HEART, J. Bergsma, 17,500	35.00	NR
1991	TO FLY WITHOUT WINGS, J. Bergsma, 17,500	35.00	NR
1991	IN FAITH I AM FREE, J. Bergsma, 17,500	35.00	NR

Hearts and Flowers

1991	PATIENCE, Sandra Kuck, 120 days	29.50	45.00
1991	TEA PARTY, Sandra Kuck, 120 days	29.50	60.00
1991	CAT'S IN THE CRADLE, Sandra Kuck, 120 days	32.50	45.00
1992	CAROUSEL OF DREAMS, Sandra Kuck, 120 days........	32.50	RI

Moses in the Bulrushes
Photo courtesy of *Collectors News*

In Faith I Am Free
Photo courtesy of *Collectors News*

Carousel of Dreams
Photo courtesy of *Collectors News*

			Issue Price	Current Value
1992	STORYBOOK MEMORIES, Sandra Kuck, 120 days		32.50	RI
1993	DELIGHTFUL BUNDLE, Sandra Kuck, 120 days		34.50	RI
1993	EASTER MORNING VISITOR, Sandra Kuck, 120 days		34.50	RI
1993	ME AND MY PONY, Sandra Kuck, 120 days		34.50	RI

Heart of the Family

1992	SHARING SECRETS, J. York, 48 days	29.50	RI
1993	SPINNING DREAMS, J. York, 48 days	29.50	RI

In the Eye of the Storm

1991	FIRST STRIKE, W. Lowe, 120 days	29.50	NR
1992	NIGHT FORCE, W. Lowe, 120 days	29.50	RI
1992	TRACKS ACROSS THE SAND, W. Lowe, 120 days	29.50	RI
1992	THE STORM HAS LANDED, W. Lowe, 120 days	29.50	RI

J. Bergsma Mother's Day

1990	THE BEAUTY OF LIFE, J. Bergsma, 14 days	35.00	NR
1992	LIFE'S BLESSING, J. Bergsma, 14 days	35.00	RI
1993	MY GREATEST TREASURES, J. Bergsma, 14 days	35.00	RI

King's Christmas

1973	ADORATION, Merli, 1,500	100.00	220.00
1974	MADONNA, Merli, 1,500	150.00	200.00
1975	HEAVENLY CHOIR, Merli, 1,500	160.00	215.00
1976	SIBLINGS, Merli, 1,500	200.00	230.00

King's Flowers

1973	CARNATION, Aldo Falchi, 1,000	85.00	130.00
1974	RED ROSE, Aldp Falchi, 1,000	100.00	145.00
1975	YELLOW DAHLIA, Aldo Falchi, 1,000	110.00	160.00
1976	BLUEBELLS, Aldo Falchi, 1,000	130.00	165.00
1977	ANEMONES, Aldo Falchi, 1,000	130.00	175.00

King's Mother's Day

1973	DANCING GIRL, Merli, 1,500	100.00	185.00
1974	DANCING BOY, Merli, 1,500	115.00	185.00
1975	MOTHERLY LOVE, Merli, 1,500	140.00	200.00
1976	MAIDEN, Merli, 1,500	180.00	200.00

Little Professionals

1982	ALL IS WELL, Sandra Kuck, 10,000	39.50	50.00
1983	TENDER LOVING CARE, Sandra Kuck, 10,000	39.50	60.00
1984	LOST AND FOUND, Sandra Kuck, 10,000	39.50	NR
1985	READING, WRITING, AND..., Sandra Kuck, 10,000	39.50	NR

March of Dimes: Our Children, Our Future

		Issue Price	Current Value
1989	A TIME TO LOVE, Sandra Kuck, 150 days	29.00	NR
1989	A TIME TO PLANT, John McClelland, 150 days	29.00	NR

Marmot Christmas

1970	POLAR BEAR, 5,000	13.00	45.00
1971	AMERICAN BUFFALO, 6,000	14.50	25.00
1971	BUFFALO BILL, 6,000	16.00	35.00
1972	BOY AND GRANDFATHER, 5,000	20.00	40.00
1973	SNOWMAN, 3,000	22.00	40.00
1974	DANCING, 2,000	24.00	30.00
1975	QUAIL, 2,000	30.00	NR
1976	WINDMILL, 2,000	40.00	NR

Marmot Mother's Day

1972	SEAL, 600	16.00	45.00
1973	POLAR BEAR, 3,000	20.00	140.00
1974	PENGUINS, 2,000	24.00	35.00
1975	RACCOONS, 2,000	30.00	NR
1976	DUCKS, 2,000	40.00	NR

McClelland Children's Circus

1982	TOMMY, THE CLOWN, John McClelland, 100 days	29.50	40.00
1982	KATIE, THE TIGHTROPE WALKER, John McClelland, 100 days 45.00		29.50
1983	JOHNNY, THE STRONGMAN, John McClelland, 100 days	29.50	35.00
1984	MAGGIE, THE ANIMAL TRAINER, John McClelland, 100 days .	29.50	NR
1993	MY GREATEST TREASURES, J. Bergsma, 14 days	35.00	RI

Memories of Yesterday

1993	HUSH, Mabel Lucie Attwell	29.50	RI
1993	TIME FOR BED, Mabel Lucie Attwell	29.50	RI
1993	I'SE BEEN PAINTING, Mabel Lucie Attwell.............	29.50	RI
1993	JUST LOOKING PRETTY, Mabel Lucie Attwell	29.50	RI

Moser Christmas

1970	HRADCANY CASTLE, 400	75.00	170.00
1971	KARLSTEIN CASTLE, 1,365	75.00	NR
1972	OLD TOWN HALL, 1,000	85.00	NR
1973	DARLOVY VARY CASTLE, 500.........................	90.00	100.00

Moser Mother's Day

1971	PEACOCKS, 350	75.00	135.00
1972	BUTTERFLIES, 750	85.00	NR
1973	SQUIRRELS, 500	90.00	NR

Mother's Day

		Issue Price	Current Value
1985	ONCE UPON A TIME, Sandra Kuck, <1 year	29.50	55.00
1986	TIMES REMEMBERED, Sandra Kuck, <1 year	29.50	45.00
1987	A CHERISHED TIME, Sandra Kuck, <1 year	29.50	45.00
1988	A TIME TOGETHER, Sandra Kuck, <1 year	29.50	60.00

Mother Goose

1979	MARY, MARY, John McClelland, <1 year	22.50	70.00
1980	LITTLE BOY BLUE, John McClelland, <1 year	22.50	BR
1981	LITTLE MISS MUFFET, John McClelland, < year	24.50	BR
1982	LITTLE JACK HORNER, John McClelland, <1 year	24.50	BR
1983	LITTLE BO PEEP, John McClelland, <1 year	24.50	BR
1984	DIDDLE DIDDLE DUMPLING, John McClelland, <1 year .	24.50	BR
1985	MARY HAD A LITTLE LAMB, John McClelland, <1 year ..	27.50	BR
1986	JACK AND JILL, John McClelland, <1 year.............	27.50	BR

Little Boy Blue

Noble and Free

1993	GATHERING STORM, C. Kelly........................	29.50	RI

Nutcracker Ballet

1989	CHRISTMAS EVE PARTY, C. Micarelli, 14 days	35.00	NR
1990	CLARA AND HER PRINCE, C. Micarelli, 14 days	35.00	NR
1990	THE DREAM BEGINS, C. Micarelli, 14 days	35.00	NR
1991	DANCE OF THE SNOW FAIRIES, C. Micarelli, 14 days....	35.00	NR
1992	THE LAND OF SWEETS, C. Micarelli, 14 days	35.00	RI
1992	THE SUGAR PLUM FAIRY, C. Micarelli, 14 days	35.00	RI

Oscar and Bertie's Edwardian Holiday

1991	SNAPSHOT, Peter D. Jackson, 48 days	29.50	NR

			Issue Price	Current Value
1992	EARLY RISE, Peter D. Jackson, 48 days	....	29.50	RI
1992	ALL ABOARD, Peter D. Jackson, 48 days	....	29.50	RI
1992	LEARING TO SWIM, Peter D. Jackson, 48 days	....	29.50	RI

Our Cherished Seas

1992	WHALE SONG, Sy Barlowe, 48 days	....	37.50	RI
1992	LIONS OF THE SEA, Sy Barlowe, 48 days	....	37.50	RI
1992	FLIGHT OF THE DOLPHINS, Sy Barlowe, 48 days	....	37.50	RI
1992	PALACE OF THE SEALS, Sy Barlowe, 48 days	....	37.50	RI
1992	ORCA BALLET, Sy Barlowe, 48 days	....	37.50	RI
1993	EMPERORS OF THE ICE, Sy Barlowe, 48 days	....	37.50	RI
1993	TURTLE TREASURE, Sy Barlowe, 48 days	....	37.50	RI
1993	SPLENDOR OF THE SEA, Sy Barlowe, 48 days	....	37.50	RI

Plate of the Month Collection

1990	JANUARY, Sandra Kuck, 28 days	....	25.00	NR
1990	FEBRUARY, Sandra Kuck, 28 days	....	25.00	NR
1990	MARCH, Sandra Kuck, 28 days	....	25.00	NR
1990	APRIL, Sandra Kuck, 28 days	....	25.00	NR
1990	MAY, Sandra Kuck, 28 days	....	25.00	NR
1990	JUNE, Sandra Kuck, 28 days	....	25.00	NR
1990	JULY, Sandra Kuck, 28 days	....	25.00	NR
1990	AUGUST, Sandra Kuck, 28 days	....	25.00	NR
1990	SEPTEMBER, Sandra Kuck, 28 days	....	25.00	NR
1990	OCTOBER, Sandra Kuck, 28 days	....	25.00	NR
1990	NOVEMBER, Sandra Kuck, 28 days	....	25.00	NR
1990	DECEMBER, Sandra Kuck, 28 days	....	25.00	NR

Premier Collection I

1991	PUPPY, Sandra Kuck, 7,500	....	95.00	140.00
1991	KITTEN, Sandra Kuck, 7,500	....	95.00	175.00
1992	LA BELLE, Sandra Kuck, 7,500	....	95.00	RI
1992	LE BEAU, Sandra Kuck, 7,500	....	95.00	RI

Premier Collection II

1991	LOVE, John McClelland, 7,500	....	75.00	NR

Royale

1969	APOLLO MOON LANDING, 2,000	....	30.00	80.00

Royale Christmas

1969	CHRISTMAS FAIR, 6,000	....	12.00	60.00
1970	VIGIL MASS, 10,000	....	13.00	30.00
1971	CHRISTMAS NIGHT, 8,000	....	14.00	35.00

		Issue Price	Current Value
1972	ELKS, 8,000	16.00	40.00
1973	CHRISTMAS DOWN, 6,000	20.00	30.00
1974	VILLAGE CHRISTMAS, 5,000	22.00	30.00
1975	FEEDING TIME, 5,000	26.00	NR
1976	SEAPORT CHRISTMAS, 5,000	27.50	NR
1977	SLEDDING, 5,000	30.00	NR

Royale Father's Day

1970	U.S. FRIGATE CONSTITUTION, 5,000	13.00	60.00
1971	MAN FISHING, 5,000	13.00	35.00
1972	MOUNTAINEER, 5,000	16.00	50.00
1973	CAMPING, 4,000	18.00	25.00
1974	EAGLE, 2,500	22.00	35.00
1975	REGATTA, 2,500	26.00	NR
1976	HUNTING, 2,500	27.50	NR
1977	FISHING, 2,500	30.00	NR

Royale Game Plates

1972	SETTERS, J. Poluszynski, 500	180.00	200.00
1973	FOX, J. Poluszynski, 500	200.00	250.00
1974	OSPREY, W. Schiener, 250	250.00	NR
1975	CALIFORNIA QUAIL, W. Schiener, 250	265.00	NR

Royale Germania Christmas Annual

1970	ORCHID, 600	200.00	650.00
1971	CYCLAMEN, 1,000	200.00	325.00
1972	SILVER THISTLE, 1,000	250.00	290.00
1973	TULIPS, 600	275.00	310.00
1974	SUNFLOWERS, 500	300.00	320.00
1975	SNOWDROPS, 350	350.00	425.00
1976	FLAMING HEART, 350	450.00	NR

Royale Germania Mother's Day, Crystal

1971	ROSES, 250	135.00	650.00
1972	ELEPHANT AND YOUNGSTER, 750	180.00	250.00
1973	KOALA BEAR AND CUB, 600	200.00	225.00
1974	SQUIRRELS, 500	240.00	250.00
1975	SWAN AND YOUNG, 350	350.00	360.00

Royale Mother's Day

1970	SWAN AND YOUNG, 6,000	12.00	80.00
1971	DOE AND FAWN, 9,000	13.00	55.00
1972	RABBITS, 9,000	16.00	40.00
1973	OWL FAMILY, 6,000	18.00	40.00
1974	DUCK AND YOUNG, 5,000	22.00	30.00

		Issue Price	Current Value
1975	LYNX AND CUBS, 5,000	26.00	NR
1976	WOODCOCK AND YOUNG, 5,000	27.50	NR
1977	KOALA BEAR, 5,000	30.00	NR

Sophisticated Ladies

		Issue Price	Current Value
1985	FELICIA, Aldo Fazio, 21 days	29.50	NR
1985	SAMANTHA, Aldo Fazio, 21 days	29.50	NR
1985	PHOEBE, Aldo Fazio, 21 days	29.50	NR
1985	CLEO, Aldo Fazio, 21 days	29.50	NR
1986	CERISSA, Aldo Fazio, 21 days	29.50	NR
1986	NATASHA, Aldo Fazio, 21 days	29.50	NR
1986	BIANKA, Aldo Fazio, 21 days	29.50	NR
1986	CHELSEA, Aldo Fazio, 21 days	29.50	NR

Cerissa
Photo courtesy of *Collectors News*

Natasha
Photo courtesy of *Collectors News*

Special Occasions by Reco

		Issue Price	Current Value
1988	THE WEDDING, Sandra Kuck	35.00	NR
1989	WEDDING DAY, Sandra Kuck, 6¹/₂"	25.00	NR
1990	THE SPECIAL DAY, Sandra Kuck	25.00	NR

Special Occasions – Wedding

		Issue Price	Current Value
1991	FROM THIS DAY FORWARD, C. Micarelli, 9¹/₂"	35.00	NR
1991	FROM THIS DAY FORWARD, C. Micarelli, 6¹/₂"	25.00	NR
1991	TO HAVE AND TO HOLD, C. Micarelli, 9¹/₂"	35.00	NR
1991	TO HAVE AND TO HOLD, C. Micarelli, 6¹/₂"	25.00	NR

		Issue Price	Current Value

Springtime of Life

1985	TEDDY'S BATHTIME, Thornton Utz, 14 days	29.50	NR
1986	JUST LIKE MOMMY, Thornton Utz, 14 days	29.50	NR
1986	AMONG THE DAFFODILS, Thornton Utz, 14 days	29.50	NR
1986	MY FAVORITE DOLLS, Thornton Utz, 14 days	29.50	NR
1986	AUNT TILLIE'S HATS, Thornton Utz, 14 days	29.50	NR
1986	LITTLE EMILY, Thornton Utz, 14 days	29.50	NR
1986	GRANNY'S BOOTS, Thornton Utz, 14 days	29.50	NR
1986	MY MASTERPIECE, Thornton Utz, 14 days	29.50	NR

Sugar and Spice

| 1993 | BEST FRIENDS, Sandra Kuck, 95 days | 29.90 | RI |

Tidings of Joy

1992	PEACE ON EARTH	35.00	RI
1993	REJOICE	35.00	RI
1994	NOEL	38.00	RI

Town and Country Dogs

1990	FOX HUNT, Sy Barlowe, 36 days	35.00	NR
1991	THE RETRIEVAL, Sy Barlowe, 36 days	35.00	NR
1991	GOLDEN FIELDS (GOLDEN RETRIEVER), Sy Barlowe, 36 days	35.00	NR
1993	FAITHFUL COMPANIONS (COCKER SPANIEL), Sy Barlowe, 36 days	35.00	RI

Treasured Songs of Childhood

1988	TWINKLE, TWINKLE, LITTLE STAR, John McClelland, 150 days	29.50	BR
1988	A TISKET, A TASKET, John McClelland, 150 days	29.50	BR
1988	BAA, BAA, BLACK SHEEP, John McClelland, 150 days	32.90	BR
1989	ROUND THE MULBERRY BUSH, John McClelland, 150 days	32.90	BR
1989	RAIN, RAIN GO AWAY, John McClelland, 150 days	32.90	BR
1989	I'M A LITTLE TEAPOT, John McClelland, 150 days	32.90	BR
1989	PAT–A–CAKE, John McClelland, 150 days	34.90	BR
1990	HUSH LITTLE BABY, John McClelland, 150 days	34.90	BR

Vanishing Animal Kingdoms

1986	RAMA THE TIGER, Dot and Sy Barlowe, 21,500	35.00	NR
1986	OLEPI THE BUFFALO, Dot and Sy Barlowe, 21,500	35.00	NR
1987	COOLIBAH THE KOALA, Sy Barlowe, 21,500	35.00	NR
1987	ORTWIN THE DEER, Sy Barlowe, 21,500	35.00	NR
1987	YEN–POH THE PANDA, Sy Barlowe, 21,500	35.00	NR
1988	MAMAKUU THE ELEPHANT, Sy Barlowe, 21,500	35.00	60.00

Victorian Mother's Day

| 1989 | MOTHER'S SUNSHINE, Sandra Kuck, 1 year | 35.00 | 65.00 |
| 1990 | REFLECTION OF LOVE, Sandra Kuck, 1 year | 35.00 | 65.00 |

		Issue Price	Current Value
1991	A PRECIOUS TIME, Sandra Kuck, 1 year	35.00	60.00
1992	LOVING TOUCH, Sandra Kuck, 1 year	35.00	RI

Western Series

| 1974 | MOUNTAIN MAN, E. Berke, 1,000 .... | 165.00 | NR |

Wonder of Christmas

1991	SANTA'S SECRET, John McClelland, 28 days	29.50	NR
1992	MY FAVORTIE ORNAMENT, John McClelland, 28 days...	29.50	RI
1992	WAITING FOR SANTA, John McClelland, 28 days	29.50	RI
1993	CANDLELIGHT CHRISTMAS, John McClelland, 28 days .	29.50	RI

World of Children

1977	RAINY DAY FUN, John McClelland, 10,000	50.00	BR
1978	WHEN I GROW UP, John McClelland, 15,000	50.00	NR
1979	YOU'RE INVITED, John McClelland, 15,000	50.00	NR
1980	KITTENS FOR SALE, John McClelland, 15,000	50.00	NR

MAYNARD REECE

Waterfowl

1973	MALLARDS and WOOD DUCKS, 900, set of 2	250.00	375.00
1974	CANVASBACK and CANDIAN GEESE, 900, set of 2	250.00	375.00
1975	PINTAILS and TEAL, 900, set of 2	250.00	425.00

REED AND BARTON UNITED STATES

Annual

1972	FREE TRAPPER, 2,500	65.00	NR
1973	OUTPOST, 2,500	65.00	NR
1974	TOLL COLLECTOR, 2,500	65.00	NR
1975	INDIANS DISCOVERING LEWIS AND CLARK, 2,500	65.00	NR

Audubon

1970	PINE SISKIN, 5,000	60.00	175.00
1971	RED–SHOULDERED HAWK, 5,000	60.00	75.00
1972	STILT SANDPIPER, 5,000	60.00	70.00
1973	RED CARDINAL, 5,000	60.00	65.00
1974	BOREAL CHICADEE, 5,000	65.00	NR
1975	YELLOW–BREASTED CHAT, 5,000	65.00	NR
1976	BAY–BREASTED WARBLER, 5,000	65.00	NR
1977	PURPLE FINCH, 5,000	65.00	NR

	Issue Price	Current Value

Bicentennial

			Issue Price	Current Value
1972	MONTICELLO, damascene, silver, 1,000		75.00	80.00
1972	MONTICELLO, silver plate, 200		200.00	225.00
1973	MT. VERNON, 1 year		75.00	80.00

Christmas

		Issue Price	Current Value
1973	ADORATION OF THE KINGS, Roger van der Weyden, 7,500	60.00	65.00
1974	ADORATION OF THE MAGI, Fra Angelico and Fra Filippo Lippi, 7,500	65.00	NR
1975	ADORATION OF THE KINGS, Steven Lochner, 7,500	65.00	NR
1976	MORNING TRAIN, Maxwell Mays, 7,500	65.00	NR

Christmas Carols

		Issue Price	Current Value
1970	A PARTRIDGE IN A PEAR TREE, Robert Johnson, 2,500	55.00	210.00
1971	WE THREE KINGS OF ORIENT ARE, Robert Johnson, 7,500	60.00	75.00
1972	HARK! THE HERALD ANGELS SING, Robert Johnson, 7,500	60.00	65.00

Christmas — Old Fashioned

		Issue Price	Current Value
1976	MORNING TRAIN, Maxwell Mays, 7,500	65.00	NR
1977	DECORATING THE CHURCH, Maxwell Mays, 7,500	65.00	NR
1978	GENERAL STORE AT CHRISTMAS TIME, Maxwell Mays, 7,500	65.00	BR
1979	MERRY OLD SANTA CLAUS, Thomas Nast, 2,500	55.00	NR
1980	GATHERING CHRISTMAS GREENS, 2,500	65.00	NR
1981	THE SHOPKEEPER AT CHRISTMAS, W. L. Seppard, 2,500	75.00	BR

Currier & Ives

		Issue Price	Current Value
1972	VILLAGE BLACKSMITH, 1,500	85.00	NR
1972	WESTERN MIGRATION, 1,500	85.00	NR
1973	OAKEN BUCKET, 1,500	85.00	NR
1973	WINTER IN COUNTRY, 1,500	85.00	NR
1974	PREPARING FOR MARKET, 1,500	85.00	NR

Founding Fathers

		Issue Price	Current Value
1974	GEORGE WASHINGTON, 2,500	65.00	NR
1975	THOMAS JEFFERSON, 2,500	65.00	NR
1976	BEN FRANKLIN, 2,500	65.00	NR
1976	PATRICK HENRY, 2,500	65.00	NR
1976	JOHN HANCOCK, 2,500	65.00	NR
1976	JOHN ADAMS, 2,500	65.00	NR

Kentucky Derby

		Issue Price	Current Value
1972	NEARING FINISH, 1,000	75.00	85.00
1973	RIVA RIDGE, 1,500	75.00	85.00
1974	100TH RUNNING, 1,500	75.00	85.00

Missions of California

		Issue Price	Current Value
1971	SAN DIEGO, 1,500	75.00	NR
1972	CARMEL, 1,500	75.00	NR
1973	SANTA BARBARA, 1,500	60.00	NR
1974	SANTA CLARA, 1,500	60.00	NR
1976	SAN GABRIEL, 1,500	65.00	NR

Thomas Nast Christmas (Collector Creations)

1973	CHRISTMAS, 750	100.00	110.00

Single Issues

1970	ZODIAC, 1,500	75.00	NR
1972	ROAD RUNNER, 1,500	65.00	NR
1972	DELTA QUEEN, 2,500	75.00	NR
1973	ALICE IN WONDERLAND, 750	100.00	110.00
1973	CHICAGO FIRE, 1 year	60.00	NR
1975	MISSISSIPPI QUEEN, 2,500	75.00	NR

RHEA SILVA PORCELAIN COLLECTION
UNITED STATES

Child's Garden of Verse

1983	LAND OF COUNTERPANE, Tom Bharnson, 17,500	39.00	NR

Endangered Birds

1983	WHOOPING CRANES, Frank DeMatteis, 5,000	60.00	NR

Feline Favorites

1982	LONG–HAIRED LADIES, Patrick Oxenham, 10,000	47.00	NR
1983	SIAMESE AND APPLE BLOSSOMS, Patrick Oxenham, 10,000	47.00	NR

RHODES UNITED STATES

Bountiful Harvest

1992	BASKET FULL OF APPLES	39.00	RI
1992	BUSHEL OF PEACHES	39.00	RI
1993	PEARS FROM THE GROVE	39.00	RI
1993	FRESH OFF THE PLUM TREE	39.00	RI

Legendary Steam Trains

1989	AMERICAN STANDARD 4–4–0	64.00	75.00
1990	HUDSON J3 STREAMLINER 4–6–4	65.00	85.00

		Issue Price	Current Value
1990	BEST FRIEND CHARLESTON 0–4–0T	70.00	BR
1990	THE CHALLENGER CLASS 4-6-6-4	70.00	85.00
1991	THE K–28–8–2...	70.00	80.00
1991	THE K4 CLASS 4–6–2	70.00	NR

Miracles of Light

1992	NATIVITY OF LOVE..................................	85.00	RI
1992	NATIVITY OF PEACE	85.00	RI
1992	NATIVITY OF HOPE	90.00	RI
1992	NATIVITY OF JOY....................................	90.00	RI
1993	NATIVITY OF FAITH	90.00	RI
1993	NATIVITY OF PRAISE................................	90.00	RI

Sculptured Songbirds

1993	TENDING THE NEST	49.00	RI
1993	CHORUS OF HAPPINESS	49.00	RI
1993	MORNING FEEDING	54.00	RI
1984	BREAKFAST BLOSSOMS	54.00	RI
1994	SYMPHONY IN THE AZALEAS........................	54.00	RI

Treasures of the Dore Bible

1986	MOSES/TEN COMMANDMENTS	59.00	BR
1987	JACOB AND THE ANGEL	59.00	BR
1987	REBEKAH AT THE WELL	64.00	BR
1988	DANIEL IN THE LION'S DEN	64.00	BR
1988	JUDGMENT OF SOLOMON	64.00	BR
1988	ELIJAH AND CHARIOT OF FIRE......................	64.00	75.00

Village Lights

1993	HOLLY STREET BAKERY	49.00	RI
1993	MISTLETOE TOY SHOP	49.00	RI
1993	MRS. SUGARPLUM'S CHOCOLATES	54.00	RI
1993	CHURCH AT THE BEND	54.00	RI
1993	EVERGREEN BOOKS	54.00	RI
1994	KRINGLE'S GENERAL STORE........................	54.00	RI

Waterfowl Legacy

1991	MALLARD'S DESCENT	69.00	110.00
1992	IN FLIGHT	69.00	RI
1992	TAKING OFF......................................	74.00	RI
1992	WIND RIDERS...../...............................	74.00	RI
1993	FLYING IN	74.00	RI
1993	RISING UP.......................................	74.00	RI

RICKER–BARTLETT CASTING STUDIOS

UNITED STATES

		Issue Price	Current Value

America's Children

1981 DEL, Anthony Ricker, 5,000 .... 20.00 NR

Single Issue

1982 MOTHER'S DAY, Michael Ricker, 5,250 .... 65.00 NR

RIDGEWOOD UNITED STATES

Bicentennial

1974 FIRST IN WAR, 12,500 .... 40.00 NR

Christmas

1975 CHRISTMAS MORNING, J. C. Leyendecker, 10,000 ...... 24.50 40.00
1976 CHRISTMAS SURPRISE, 10,000 .... 26.50 40.00

Little Women

1976 SWEET LONG AGO, Lorraine Trester, 5,000 .... 45.00 65.00
1976 SONG OF SPRING, Lorraine Trester, 5,000 .... 45.00 75.00
1977 JOY IN THE MORNING, Lorraine Trester, 5,000 .... 45.00 50.00

Mother's Day

1976 GRANDMA'S APPLE PIE, J. C. Leyendecker, 5,000 ...... 24.50 NR
1977 TENDERNESS, J. C. Leyendecker, 10,000 .... 35.00 NR

Tom Sawyer

1974 TRYING A PIPE, Norman Rockwell, 3,000 .... 9.98 NR
1974 LOST IN CAVE, Norman Rockwell, 3,000 .... 9.98 NR
1974 PAINTING FENCE, Norman Rockwell, 3,000 .... 9.98 NR
1974 TAKING MEDICINE, Norman Rockwell, 3,000 .... 9.98 NR

Vasils Series

1976 ALL HALLOWS EVE, 5,000 .... 38.50 NR

Wild West

1975 DISCOVERY OF LAST CHANCE GULCH, 15,000 .... 16.25 NR
1975 DOUBTFUL VISITOR, 15,000 .... 16.25 NR
1975 BAD ONE, 15,000 .... 16.25 NR
1975 CATTLEMAN, 15,000 .... 16.25 NR

RIVER SHORE UNITED STATES

America at Work

		Issue Price	Current Value
1984	THE SCHOOL TEACHER, Norman Rockwell, 10 days	29.50	NR
1984	THE PIANO TUNER, Norman Rockwell, 10 days	29.50	NR
1984	THE ZOO KEEPER, Norman Rockwell, 10 days	29.50	NR
1984	THE CLEANING LADIES, Norman Rockwell, 10 days	29.50	NR
1984	THE HATCHECK GIRL, Norman Rockwell, 10 days	29.50	NR
1984	THE ARTIST, Norman Rockwell, 10 days	29.50	NR
1984	THE CENSUS TAKER, Norman Rockwell, 10 days	29.50	NR

Baby Animals Collection

1979	AKIKU, Roger Brown, 20,000	50.00	80.00
1980	ROOSEVELT, Roger Brown, 20,000	50.00	90.00
1981	CLOVER, Roger Brown, 20,000	50.00	65.00
1982	ZUELA, Roger Brown, 20,000	50.00	65.00

Della Robbia Annual

1979	ADORATION, Roger Brown, 5,000	550.00	NR
1980	VIRGIN AND CHILD, Roger Brown, 5,000	450.00	NR

Famous Americans

1976	BROWN'S LINCOLN, Rockwell–Brown, 9,500	40.00	NR
1977	ROCKWELL'S TRIPLE SELF–PORTRAIT, Rockwell–Brown, 9,500	45.00	NR
1978	PEACE CORPS, Rockwell–Brown, 9,500	45.00	NR
1979	SPIRIT OF LINDBERGH, Rockwell–Brown, 9,500	50.00	NR

Famous American Songbirds

1985	WESTERN TANGER, Linda Thompson, 14 days	19.50	NR
1985	PURPLE FINCHES, Linda Thompson, 14 days	19.50	NR
1985	MOUNTAIN BLUEBIRDS, Linda Thompson, 14 days	19.50	NR
1985	CARDINAL, Linda Thompson, 14 days	19.50	NR
1985	BARN SWALLOW, Linda Thompson, 14 days	19.50	NR
1985	CANYON WREN, Linda Thompson, 14 days	19.50	NR
1985	MOCKINGBIRD, Linda Thompson, 14 days	19.50	NR
1985	WOOD THRUSH, Linda Thompson, 14 days	19.50	NR

Grant Wood Single Issue

1982	AMERICAN GOTHIC, Grant Wood, 17,500	80.00	NR

Little House on the Prairie

1985	FOUNDER'S DAY PICNIC, Eugene Christopherson, 10 days	29.50	40.00
1985	WOMEN'S HARVEST, Eugene Christopherson, 10 days	29.50	NR
1985	MEDICINE SHOW, Eugene Christopherson, 10 days	29.50	NR
1985	CAROLINE'S EGGS, Eugene Christopherson, 10 days	29.50	NR
1985	MARY'S GIFT, Eugene Christopherson, 10 days	29.50	NR

		Issue Price	Current Value
1985	A BELL FOR WALNUT GROVE, Eugene Christopherson, 10 days	29.50	NR
1985	INGALL'S FAMILY, Eugene Christopherson, 10 days	29.50	NR
1985	THE SWEETHEART TREE, Eugene Christopherson, 10 days	29.50	NR

Lovable Teddies

1985	BEDTIME BLUES, M. Hague, 10 days	21.50	NR
1985	BEARLY FRIGHTFUL, M. Hague, 10 days	21.50	NR
1985	CAUGHT IN THE ACT, M. Hague, 10 days	21.50	NR
1985	FIRESIDE FRIENDS, M. Hague, 10 days	21.50	NR
1985	HARVEST TIME, M. Hague, 10 days	21.50	NR
1985	MISSED A BUTTON, M. Hague, 10 days	21.50	NR
1985	TENDER LOVING BEAR, M. Hague, 10 days	21.50	NR
1985	SUNDAY STROLL, M. Hague, 10 days	21.50	NR

Puppy Playtime

1987	DOUBLE TAKE, J. Lamb, 14 days	24.50	NR
1988	CATCH OF THE DAY, J. Lamb, 14 days	24.50	NR
1988	CABIN FEVER, J. Lamb, 14 days	24.50	NR
1988	WEEKEND GARDENER, J. Lamb, 14 days	24.50	NR
1988	GETTING ACQUAINTED, J. Lamb, 14 days	24.50	NR
1988	HANGING OUT, J. Lamb, 14 days	24.50	NR
1988	A NEW LEASH ON LIFE, J. Lamb, 14 days	24.50	NR
1988	FUN AND GAMES, J. Lamb, 14 days	24.50	NR

Remington Bronze

1977	BRONCO BUSTER, Roger Brown, 15,000	55.00	70.00
1978	COMING THROUGH THE RYE, Roger Brown, 15,000	60.00	NR
1980	CHEYENNE, Roger Brown, 15,000	60.00	NR
1981	THE MOUNTAIN MAN, Roger Brown, 15,000	60.00	NR

Rockwell Cats

| 1982 | JENNIE AND TINA, Norman Rockwell, 9,500 | 39.50 | NR |

Rockwell Four Freedoms

1981	FREEDOM OF SPEECH, Norman Rockwell, 17,000	65.00	75.00
1982	FREEDOM OF WORSHIP, Norman Rockwell, 17,000	65.00	70.00
1982	FREEDOM FROM FEAR, Norman Rockwell, 17,000	65.00	150.00
1982	FREEDOM FROM WANT, Norman Rockwell, 17,000	65.00	250.00

Rockwell Good Old Days

1982	OLD OAKEN BUCKET, Norman Rockwell	24.50	NR
1982	BOY FISHING, Norman Rockwell	24.50	NR
1982	BAREFOOT BOY, Norman Rockwell	24.50	NR

		Issue Price	Current Value
Rockwell Single Issues			
1979	SPRING FLOWERS, Norman Rockwell, 17,000	75.00	145.00
1000	LOOKING OUT TO SEA, Norman Rockwell, 17,000	75.00	150.00
1982	GRANDPA'S GUARDIAN, Norman Rockwell, 17,000	80.00	NR
1982	GRANDPA'S TREASURES, Norman Rockwell, 17,000	80.00	NR
Signs of Love			
1981	A KISS FOR MOTHER, Yin–Rei Hicks, <1 year	18.50	BR
1981	A WATCHFUL EYE, Yin–Rei Hicks, <1 year	21.50	BR
1982	A GENTLE PERSUASION, Yin–Rei Hicks, <1 year	21.50	BR
1983	A PROTECTIVE EMBRACE, Yin–Rei Hicks, <1 year	23.50	BR
1983	A TENDER COAXING, Yin–Rei Hicks, <1 year	23.50	BR
1984	A REASSURING TOUCH	23.50	BR
1985	A TRUSTING HUG	26.50	BR
1985	A LOVING GUIDANCE	26.50	BR
Timberlake's Christmas after Christmas			
1982	KAY'S DOLL, Bob Timberlake, 9,500	75.00	NR
Vignette			
1981	THE BROKEN WINDOW, Norman Rockwell, 22,500	19.50	NR
1982	SUNDAY BEST, Norman Rockwell, 22,500	19.50	NR
We the Children			
1987	THE FREEDOM OF SPEECH, Don Crook, 14 days	24.50	NR
1988	RIGHT TO VOTE, Don Crook, 14 days	24.50	NR
1988	UNREASONABLE SEARCH AND SEIZURE, Don Crook, 14 days	24.50	NR
1988	RIGTH TO BEAR ARMS, Don Crook, 14 days	24.50	NR
1988	TRIAL BY JURY, Don Crook, 14 days	24.50	NR
1988	SELF–INCRIMINATION, Don Crook, 14 days	24.50	NR
1988	CRUEL AND UNUSUAL PUNISHMENT, Don Crook, 14 days ...	24.50	NR
1988	QUARTERING OF SOLDIERS, Don Crook, 14 days	24.50	NR

ROCKFORD EDITIONS UNITED STATES

Little Mothers			
1985	LOVE IS BLIND, Bessie Pease Gutmann	29.95	NR
1985	FIRST STEP, Bessie Pease Gutmann	29.95	NR

ROCKWELL COLLECTORS CLUB UNITED STATES

Christmas			
1978	CHRISTMAS STORY, Norman Rockwell, 15,000	24.50	NR

ROCKWELL GALLERY

		Issue Price	Current Value
Rockwell's Centennial			
1993	THE TOY MAKER	39.90	RI
1993	THE COBBLER	39.90	RI
1994	THE LIGHTHOUSE KEEPER'S DAUGHTER	44.90	RI
1994	THE SHIP BUILDER	44.90	RI
1994	THE MUSIC MASTER	44.90	RI
1994	THE TYCOON	49.90	RI
1994	THE PAINTER	49.90	RI
1994	THE STORYTELLER	49.90	RI
Rockwell's Christmas Legacy			
1992	SANTA'S WORKSHOP, Norman Rockwell, 150 days	49.90	RI
1993	MAKING A LIST, Norman Rockwell, 150 days	49.90	RI
1993	WHILE SANTA SLUMBERS	54.90	RI
1993	VISIONS OF SANTA	54.90	RI
1993	FILLING EVERY STOCKING	54.90	RI
1993	SANTA'S MAGICAL VIEW	54.90	RI
Rockwell's Main Street			
1994	THE STUDIO	44.90	RI
1994	THE ANTIQUE SHOP	44.90	RI
1994	THE COUNTRY STORE	44.90	RI
1994	THE TOWN OFFICES	44.90	RI

ROCKWELL MUSEUM UNITED STATES

		Issue Price	Current Value
American Family I			
1979	BABY'S FIRST STEP, Norman Rockwell, 9,900	28.50	135.00
1979	HAPPY BIRTHDAY, DEAR MOTHER, Norman Rockwell, 9,900	28.50	60.00
1979	SWEET SIXTEEN, Norman Rockwell, 9,900	28.50	45.00
1979	FIRST HAIRCUT, Norman Rockwell, 9,900	28.50	45.00
1979	FIRST PROM, Norman Rockwell, 9,900	28.50	35.00
1979	WRAPPING CHRISTMAS PRESENTS, Norman Rockwell, 9,900	28.50	35.00
1979	THE STUDENT, Norman Rockwell, 9,900	28.50	35.00
1979	THE BIRTHDAY PARTY, Norman Rockwell, 9,900	28.50	35.00
1979	LITTLE MOTHER, Norman Rockwell, 9,900	28.50	35.00
1979	WASHING OUR DOG, Norman Rockwell, 9,900	28.50	35.00
1979	MOTHER'S LITTLE HELPERS, Norman Rockwell, 9,900	28.50	35.00
1979	BRIDE AND GROOM, Norman Rockwell, 9,900	28.50	35.00
American Family II			
1980	NEW ARRIVAL, Norman Rockwell, 22,500	35.00	55.00
1980	SWEET DREAMS, Norman Rockwell, 22,500	35.00	NR
1980	LITTLE SHAVER, Norman Rockwell, 22,500	35.00	NR

		Issue Price	Current Value
1980	WE MISSED YOU, DADDY, Norman Rockwell, 22,500	35.00	NR
1981	HOME RUN SLUGGER, Norman Rockwell, 22,500	35.00	NR
1981	GIVING THANKS, Norman Rockwell, 22,500	35.00	NR
1981	LITTLE SALESMAN, Norman Rockwell, 22,500	35.00	NR
1981	ALMOST GROWN UP, Norman Rockwell, 22,500	35.00	NR
1981	COURAGEOUS HERO, Norman Rockwell, 22,500	35.00	NR
1981	AT THE CIRCUS, Norman Rockwell, 22,500	35.00	NR
1981	GOOD FOOD, GOOD FRIENDS, Norman Rockwell, 22,500 .	35.00	NR

Christmas Collectibles

1979	THE DAY AFTER CHRISTMAS, Norman Rockwell, 1 year .	75.00	85.00
1980	CHECKING HIS LIST, Norman Rockwell, 1 year	75.00	85.00
1981	RINGING IN GOOD CHEER, Norman Rockwell, 1 year ...	75.00	85.00
1982	WAITING FOR SANTA, Norman Rockwell, 1 year	75.00	NR
1983	HIGH HOPES, Norman Rockwell, 1 year	75.00	NR
1984	SPACE AGE SANTA, Norman Rockwell, 1 year	55.00	NR

Classic Plate

1981	PUPPY LOVE, Norman Rockwell, 60 days	24.50	NR
1981	WHILE THE AUDIENCE WAITS, Norman Rockwell, 60 days	24.50	NR
1981	OFF TO SCHOOL, Norman Rockwell, 60 days	24.50	NR
1982	THE COUNTRY DOCTOR, Norman Rockwell, 60 days	24.50	NR
1982	SPRING FEVER, Norman Rockwell, 60 days	24.50	NR
1982	A DOLLHOUSE FOR SIS, Norman Rockwell, 60 days	24.50	NR

Elvis Presley Collection

1985	HOUND DOG, limited	15.00	NR
1985	LONESOME TONIGHT, limited	15.00	NR
1985	TEDDY BEAR, limited	15.00	NR
1985	DON'T BE CRUEL, limited	15.00	NR
	Set of 4	60.00	NR

Gene Autry Collection (Nostalgia Collectibles)

1984	AMERICA'S FAVORITE COWBOY, Norman Rockwell, 25,000	45.00	NR

James Dean Collection (Nostalgia Collectibles)

1985	EAST OF EDEN, limited	15.00	NR
1985	REBEL WITHOUT A CAUSE, limited	15.00	NR
1985	GIANT, limited	15.00	NR
1985	JIM AND SPYDER, limited	15.00	NR
	Set of 4	60.00	NR

Mother's Day

1982	A TENDER MOMENT, Norman Rockwell, 5,000	70.00	NR

High Hopes

Space Age Santa

Puppy Love

The Country Doctor

A Dollhouse for Sis

Captain January

Heidi

Poor Little Rich Girl

Wee Willie Winkie

Songs of Praise

Bedtime Prayers

Surprise Treat

Shirley Temple Collectibles

		Issue Price	Current Value
1982	BABY TAKE A BOW, 22,500	75.00	100.00
1983	BABY TAKE A BOW, sgd, 2,500	100.00	160.00
1983	CURLY TOP, 22,500	75.00	100.00
1983	CURLY TOP, sgd, 2,500	100.00	150.00
1982	STAND UP AND CHEER, 22,500	75.00	100.00
1983	STAND UP AND CHEER, sgd, 2,500	100.00	NR

Shirley Temple Collection

1983	CAPTAIN JANUARY, William Jacobson, 25,000	35.00	NR
1984	HEIDI, William Jacobson, 25,000	35.00	NR
1984	LITTLE MISS MARKER, William Jacobson, 25,000	35.00	NR
1984	BRIGHT EYES, William Jacobson, 25,000	35.00	NR
1985	THE LITTLE COLONEL, William Jacobson, 25,000	35.00	NR
1985	REBECCA OF SUNNYBROOK FARM, William Jacobson, 25,000	35.00	NR
1986	POOR LITTLE RICH GIRL, William Jacobson, 25,000	35.00	NR
1986	WEE WILLIE WINKIE, William Jacobson, 25,000	35.00	NR

Touch of Rockwell

1984	SONGS OF PRAISE, Norman Rockwell, 1 year	14.95	NR
1984	BEDTIME PRAYERS, Norman Rockwell, 1 year	14.95	NR
1984	FIRST DAY OF SCHOOL, Norman Rockwell, 1 year	14.95	NR
1984	SUPRISE TREAT, Norman Rockwell, 1 year	14.95	NR
1984	THE RUNAWAY, Norman Rockwell, 1 year	14.95	NR

World of Children Bas–Relief

1982	DOWNHILL RACER, Norman Rockwell, 15,000	45.00	NR
1982	VACATION OVER, Norman Rockwell, 15,000	45.00	NR
1982	LITTLE PATIENT, Norman Rockwell, 15,000	45.00	NR
1982	BICYCLE BOYS, Norman Rockwell, 15,000	45.00	NR

Celebration

With this Ring

		Issue Price	Current Value

Special Commemorative Issues

Year	Title	Issue Price	Current Value
1985	ELVIS PRESLEY — THE ONCE AND FOREVER KING, William Jacobson, 10,000	40.00	NR
1985	JAMES DEAN — AMERICA'S REBEL, William Jacobson, 10,000	45.00	NR

Single Issues

Year	Title	Issue Price	Current Value
1979	ROCKWELL REMEMBERED, Norman Rockwell, 30 days	45.00	NR
1982	CELEBRATION, Norman Rockwell, 9,900	55.00	NR
1983	A TRIBUTE TO JOHN F. KENNEDY, Norman Rockwell	39.50	NR
1983	WITH THIS RING, Norman Rockwell, 1 year	50.00	NR

ROCKWELL SOCIETY UNITED STATES

American Dream

Year	Title	Issue Price	Current Value
1985	A YOUNG GIRL'S DREAM, Norman Rockwell	19.90	BR
1985	A COUPLE'S COMMITMENT, Norman Rockwell	19.90	25.00
1985	A FAMILY'S FULL MEASURE, Norman Rockwell	22.90	30.00
1986	A MOTHER'S WELCOME, Norman Rockwell	22.90	BR
1986	A YOUNG MAN'S DREAM, Norman Rockwell	22.90	BR
1986	THE MUSICIAN'S MAGIC, Norman Rockwell	22.90	BR
1987	AN ORPHAN'S HOPE, Norman Rockwell	24.90	BR
1987	LOVE'S REWARD, Norman Rockwell	24.90	BR

Christmas

Year	Title	Issue Price	Current Value
1974	SCOTTY GETS HIS TREE, Norman Rockwell, 1 year	24.50	100.00
1975	ANGEL WITH A BLACK EYE, Norman Rockwell, 1 year	24.50	40.00
1976	GOLDEN CHRISTMAS, Norman Rockwell, 1 year	24.50	35.00
1977	TOY SHOP WINDOW, Norman Rockwell, 1 year	24.50	NR
1978	CHRISTMAS DREAM, Norman Rockwell, 1 year	24.50	BR
1979	SOMEBODY'S UP THERE, Norman Rockwell, 1 year	24.50	BR
1980	SCOTTY PLAYS SANTA, Norman Rockwell, 1 year	24.50	BR
1981	WRAPPED UP IN CHRISTMAS, Norman Rockwell, 1 year	25.50	BR
1982	CHRISTMAS COURTSHIP, Norman Rockwell, 1 year	25.50	BR
1983	SANTA IN THE SUBWAY, Norman Rockwell, 1 year	25.50	BR
1984	SANTA IN HIS WORKSHOP, Norman Rockwell, 1 year	27.50	BR
1985	GRANDPA PLAYS SANTA	27.50	BR
1986	DEAR SANTY CLAUS	27.90	BR
1987	SANTA'S GOLDEN GIFT	29.90	NR
1988	SANTA CLAUS	29.90	BR
1989	JOLLY OLD ST. NICK	29.90	BR
1990	A CHRISTMAS PRAYER	29.90	BR
1991	SANTA'S HELPERS	32.90	BR
1992	THE CHRISTMAS SURPRISE	32.90	RI
1993	THE TREE BRIGADE	32.90	RI
1994	CHRISTMAS MARVEL	32.90	RI
1995	FILLING THE STOCKINGS	32.90	RI

A Young Girl's Dream
Photo courtesy of *Collectors News*

A Christmas Prayer
Photo courtesy of *Collectors News*

Colonials—The Rarest Rockwell

		Issue Price	Current Value
1986	UNEXPECTED PROPOSAL, Norman Rockwell, 150 days..	27.90	BR
1986	WORDS OF COMFORT, Norman Rockwell, 150 days	27.90	BR
1987	LIGHT FOR THE WINTER, Norman Rockwell, 150 days ...	30.90	BR
1987	PORTRAIT FOR A BRIDEGROOM, Norman Rockwell,150 days .	30.90	BR
1987	THE JOURNEY HOME, Norman Rockwell, 150 days	30.90	BR
1987	CLINCHING THE DEAL, Norman Rockwell, 150 days	30.90	BR
1988	SIGN OF THE TIMES, Norman Rockwell, 150 days	32.90	BR
1988	YE GLUTTON, Norman Rockwell, 150 days	32.90	BR

Coming of Age

		Issue Price	Current Value
1990	BACK TO SCHOOL, Norman Rockwell, 150 days	29.90	45.00
1990	HOME FROM CAMP, Norman Rockwell, 150 days	29.90	50.00
1990	HER FIRST FORMAL, Norman Rockwell, 150 days	32.90	65.00
1990	THE MUSCLEMAN, Norman Rockwell, 150 days	32.90	BR
1990	A NEW LOOK, Norman Rockwell, 150 days	32.90	BR
1991	A BALCONY SEAT, Norman Rockwell, 150 days	32.90	BR
1991	MEN ABOUT TOWN, Norman Rockwell, 150 days	34.90	NR
1991	PATHS OF GLORY, Norman Rockwell, 150 days	34.90	BR
1991	DOORWAY TO THE PAST, Norman Rockwell, 150 days ...	34.90	NR
1991	SCHOOL'S OUT!, Norman Rockwell, 150 days	34.90	60.00

Heritage

		Issue Price	Current Value
1977	TOY MAKER, Norman Rockwell, 1 year	14.50	80.00
1978	THE COBBLER, Norman Rockwell, 1 year	19.50	40.00
1979	THE LIGHTHOUSE KEEPER'S DAUGHTER, Norman Rockwell, 1 year..	19.50	55.00
1980	THE SHIP BUILDER, Norman Rockwell, 1 year..........	19.50	BR

		Issue Price	Current Value
1981	THE MUSIC MASTER, Norman Rockwell, 1 year	19.50	BR
1982	THE TYCOON, Norman Rockwell, 1 year	19.50	BR
1983	THE PAINTER, Norman Rockwell, 1 year	19.50	BR
1984	THE STORYTELLER, Norman Rockwell, 1 year	19.50	BR
1985	THE GOURMET, Norman Rockwell, 1 year..............	19.50	BR
1986	THE PROFESSOR	22.90	BR
1987	THE SHADOW ARTIST	22.90	BR
1988	THE VETERAN.......................................	22.90	BR
1989	THE BANJO PLAYER	24.90	BR
1990	THE OLD SCOUT....................................	24.90	NR
1991	THE YOUNG SCHOLAR	24.90	NR
1992	THE FAMILY DOCTOR	27.90	RI
1993	THE JEWELER......................................	27.90	RI
1994	HALLOWEEN FROLIC...............................	27.90	RI
1994	THE APPRENTICE	29.90	RI
1994	THE MASTER VIOLINIST	29.90	RI

Back to School
Photo courtesy of *Collectors News*

The Young Scholar
Photo courtesy of *Collectors News*

Innocence and Experience

1991	THE SEA CAPTAIN, Norman Rockwell, 150 days	29.90	BR
1991	THE RADIO OPERATOR, Norman Rockwell, 150 days	29.90	NR
1991	THE MAGICIAN, Norman Rockwell, 150 days..........	32.90	NR
1992	THE AMERICAN HEROES, Norman Rockwell, 150 days ..	32.90	RI

A Mind of Her Own

1986	SITTING PRETTY, Norman Rockwell, 150 days	24.90	BR
1987	SERIOUS BUSINESS, Norman Rockwell, 150 days	24.90	BR
1987	BREAKING THE RULES, Norman Rockwell, 150 days	24.90	NR

			Issue Price	Current Value
1987	GOOD INTENTIONS, Norman Rockwell, 150 days	....	27.90	BR
1988	SECOND THOUGHTS, Norman Rockwell, 150 days	......	27.90	BR
1988	WORLDS AWAY, Norman Rockwell, 150 days	....	27.90	BR
1988	KISS AND TELL, Norman Rockwell, 150 days	....	29.90	BR
1988	ON MY HONOR, Norman Rockwell, 150 days	....	29.90	NR

Mother's Day

			Issue Price	Current Value
1976	A MOTHER'S LOVE, Norman Rockwell, 1 year	....	24.50	65.00
1977	FAITH, Norman Rockwell, 1 year	....	24.50	50.00
1978	BEDTIME, Norman Rockwell, 1 year	....	24.50	NR
1979	REFLECTIONS, Norman Rockwell, 1year	....	24.50	BR
1980	A MOTHER'S PRIDE, Norman Rockwell, 1 year	....	24.50	BR
1981	AFTER THE PARTY, Norman Rockwell, 1 year	....	24.50	BR
1982	THE COOKING LESSON, Norman Rockwell, 1 year	......	25.50	BR
1983	ADD TWO CUPS AND A MEASURE OF LOVE, Norman Rockwell, 1 year	....	25.50	NR
1984	GRANDMA'S COURTING DRESS, Norman Rockwell, 1 year	..	25.50	BR
1985	MENDING TIME, Norman Rockwell, 1 year	....	27.50	BR
1986	PANTRY RAID, Norman Rockwell, 1 year	....	27.50	BR
1987	GRANDMA'S SURPRISE, Norman Rockwell, 1 year	.....	29.90	BR

Rockwell's Christmas Legacy

			Issue Price	Current Value
1992	SANTA'S WORKSHOP, Norman Rockwell, 150 days	.....	49.90	RI
1993	MAKING A LIST, Norman Rockwell, 150 days	....	49.90	RI
1993	WHILE SANTA SLUMBERS	....	54.90	RI
1993	VISIONS OF SANTA	....	54.90	RI
1993	FILLING EVERY STOCKING	....	54.90	RI
1993	SANTA'S MAGICAL VIEW	....	54.90	RI

Reflections

Evening's Ease

Photo courtesy of *Collectors News*

Rockwell's Golden Moments

		Issue Price	Current Value
1987	GRANDPA'S GIFT, Norman Rockwell, 150 days	19.90	25.00
1988	GRANDMA'S LOVE, Norman Rockwell, 150 days	19.90	30.00
1988	END OF DAY, Norman Rockwell, 150 days	22.90	40.00
1988	BEST FRIENDS, Norman Rockwell, 150 days	22.90	BR
1989	LOVE LETTERS, Norman Rockwell, 150 days	22.90	BR
1989	NEWFOUND WORLDS, Norman Rockwell, 150 days	22.90	BR
1989	KEEPING COMPANY, Norman Rockwell, 150 days	22.90	BR
1989	EVENING'S REPOSE, Norman Rockwell, 150 days	22.90	BR

Rockwell's Light Campaign

1983	THE ROOM THAT LIGHT MADE, Norman Rockwell	19.50	BR
1984	GRANDPA'S TREASURE CHEST, Norman Rockwell	19.50	BR
1984	FATHER'S HELP, Norman Rockwell	19.50	BR
1984	EVENING'S EASE, Norman Rockwell	19.50	BR
1984	CLOSE HARMONY, Norman Rockwell	21.50	BR
1984	THE BIRTHDAY WISH, Norman Rockwell	21.50	BR

Rockwell on Tour

1983	WALKING THROUGH MERRIE ENGLANDE, Norman Rockwell	16.00	BR
1983	PROMENADE A PARIS, Norman Rockwell	16.00	BR
1983	WHEN IN ROME, Norman Rockwell	16.00	BR
1984	DIE WALK AM RHEIN, Norman Rockwell	16.00	BR

Rockwell's Rediscovered Women

1981	DREAMING IN THE ATTIC, Norman Rockwell	19.50	BR
1982	WAITING ON THE SHORE, Norman Rockwell...........	22.50	BR
1983	PONDERING ON THE PORCH, Norman Rockwell........	22.50	BR
1983	MAKING BELIEVE AT THE MIRROR, Norman Rockwell ..	22.50	BR
1983	WAITING AT THE DANCE, Norman Rockwell	22.50	BR
1983	GOSSIPING IN THE ALCOVE, Norman Rockwell	22.50	BR
1983	STANDING IN THE DOORWAY, Norman Rockwell	22.50	BR
1983	FLIRTING IN THE PARLOR, Norman Rockwell	22.50	BR
1983	WORKING IN THE KITCHEN, Norman Rockwell.........	22.50	BR
1984	MEETING ON THE PATH, Norman Rockwell	22.50	BR
1984	CONFIDING IN THE DEN, Norman Rockwell............	22.50	BR
1984	REMINISCING IN THE QUIET, Norman Rockwell	22.50	BR
1984	REMINISCING 'NEATH THE EAVES, Norman Rockwell ..	22.50	NR
	Set of 13	289.50	370.00

Rockwell's the Ones We Love

1988	TENDER LOVING CARE, Norman Rockwell, 150 days	19.90	25.00
1989	A TIME TO KEEP, Norman Rockwell, 150 days	19.90	25.00
1989	THE INVENTOR AND THE JUDGE, Norman Rockwell, 150 days	22.90	30.00
1989	READY FOR THE WORLD, Norman Rockwell, 150 days ...	22.90	30.00
1989	GROWING STRONG, Norman Rockwell, 150 days	22.90	30.00

		Issue Price	Current Value
1990	THE STORY HOUR, Norman Rockwell, 150 days.........	22.90	35.00
1990	THE COUNTRY DOCTOR, Norman Rockwell, 150 days ...	24.90	BR
1990	OUR LOVE OF COUNTRY, Norman Rockwell, 150 days ...	24.90	NR
1990	THE HOMECOMING, Norman Rockwell, 150 days	24.90	NR
1991	A HELPING HAND, Norman Rockwell, 150 days	24.90	BR

Rockwell's Treasured Memories

1991	QUIET REFLECTIONS, Norman Rockwell, 150 days	29.90	BR
1991	ROMANTIC REVERIE, Norman Rockwell, 150 days	29.90	NR
1991	TENDER ROMANCE, Norman Rockwell, 150 days	32.90	BR
1991	EVENING PASSAGE, Norman Rockwell, 150 days	32.90	BR
1991	HEAVENLY DREAMS, Norman Rockwell, 150 days	32.90	NR
1991	SENTIMENTAL SHORES, Norman Rockwell, 150 days ...	32.90	BR

The Inventor and the Judge
Photo courtesy of *Collectors News*

Quiet Reflections
Photo courtesy of *Collectors News*

ROMAN, INC.   UNITED STATES

Abbie Williams Collection

1991	LEGACY OF LOVE, Abbie Williams.....................	29.50	NR
1991	BLESS THIS CHILD, Abbie Williams, 14 days	29.50	NR

Catnippers

1986	CHRISTMAS MOURNING, Irene Spencer, 9,500	34.50	NR
1992	HAPPY HOLIDAZE, Irene Spencer, 9,500	34.50	RI

Legacy of Love
Photo courtesy of *Collectors News*

Cats

		Issue Price	Current Value
1984	GRIZABELLA, 30 days	29.50	NR
1984	MR. MISTOFFELEES, 30 days	29.50	NR
1984	RUM TUM TUGGER, 30 days	29.50	NR
1985	GROWLTIGER, 30 days	29.50	NR
1985	SKIMBLESHANKS, 30 days	29.50	NR
1985	MUNGOJERRIE AND RUMPELTEAZER, 30 days	29.50	NR

A Child's Play (Knowles China Co.)

1982	BREEZY DAY, Frances Hook, 30 days	29.95	35.00
1982	KITE FLYING, Frances Hook, 30 days	29.95	35.00
1984	BATHTUB SAILOR, Frances Hook, 30 days	29.95	35.00
1984	THE FIRST SNOW, Frances Hook, 30 days	29.95	35.00

A Child's World

1980	LITTLE CHILDREN, COME TO ME, Frances Hook, 15,000	45.00	NR

Fontanini Annual Christmas Plate

1986	A KING IS BORN, E. Simonetti, 1 year	60.00	NR
1987	O COME, LET US ADORE HIM, E. Simonetti, 1 year	60.00	NR
1988	ADORATION OF THE MAGI, E. Simonetti, 1 year	70.00	NR
1989	FLIGHT INTO EGYPT, E. Simonetti, 1 year	75.00	85.00

Frances Hook Collection — Set I

1982	I WISH, I WISH, Frances Hook, 15,000	24.95	40.00
1982	BABY BLOSSOMS, Frances Hook, 15,000	24.95	40.00

			Issue Price	Current Value
1982	DAISY DREAMER, Frances Hook, 15,000		24.95	40.00
1982	TREES SO TALL, Frances Hook, 15,000		24.95	40.00

Frances Hook Collection — Set II

1983	CAUGHT IT MYSELF, Frances Hook, 15,000		24.95	NR
1983	WINTER WRAPPINGS, Frances Hook, 15,000 ....,....		24.95	NR
1983	SO CUDDLY, Frances Hook, 15,000		24.95	NR
1983	CAN I KEEP HIM?, Frances Hook, 15,000		24.95	NR

Frances Hook Legacy (Knowles China Co.)

1985	FASCINATION, Frances Hook, 100 days		19.50	NR
1985	DAYDREAMING, Frances Hook, 100 days		19.50	NR
1985	DISCOVERY, Frances Hook, 100 days		22.50	NR
1985	DISAPPOINTMENT, Frances Hook, 100 days		22.50	NR
1985	WONDERMENT, Frances Hook, 100 days		22.50	NR
1985	EXPECTATION, Frances Hook, 100 days		22.50	NR

God Bless You Little One

1991	BABY'S FIRST BIRTHDAY (GIRL), Abbie Williams		29.50	NR
1991	BABY'S FIRST BIRTHDAY (BOY), Abbie Williams		29.50	NR
1991	BABY'S FIRST SMILE, Abbie Williams		19.50	NR
1991	BABY'S FIRST WORD, Abbie Williams		19.50	NR
1991	BABY'S FIRST STEP, Abbie Williams		19.50	NR
1991	BABY'S FIRST TOOTH, Abbie Williams		19.50	NR

Ice Capades Clown

1983	PRESENTING FREDDIE TRENKLER, George B. Petty, 30 days .		24.50	NR

Lord's Prayer

1986	OUR FATHER, Abbie Williams, 10 days		24.50	NR
1986	THY KINGDOM COME, Abbie Williams, 10 days		24.50	NR
1986	GIVE US THIS DAY, Abbie Williams, 10 days		24.50	NR
1986	FORGIVE OUR TRESPASSES, Abbie Williams, 10 days ...		24.50	NR
1986	AS WE FORGIVE, Abbie Williams, 10 days		24.50	NR
1986	LEAD US NOT, Abbie Williams, 10 days		24.50	NR
1986	DELIVER US FROM EVIL, Abbie Williams, 10 days		24.50	NR
1986	THINE IS THE KINGDOM, Abbie Williams, 10 days		24.50	NR

Love's Prayer

1988	LOVE IS PATIENT AND KIND, Abbie Williams, 14 days ...		29.50	NR
1988	LOVE IS NEVER JEALOUS OR BOASTFUL, Abbie Williams, 14 days		29.50	NR
1988	LOVE IS NEVER ARROGANT OR RUDE, Abbie Williams, 14 days		29.50	NR
1988	LOVES DOES NOT INSIST ON ITS OWN WAY, Abbie Williams, 14 days		29.50	NR

		Issue Price	Current Value
1988	LOVE IS NEVER IRRITABLE OR RESENTFUL, Abbie Williams, 14 days	29.50	NR
1988	LOVE REJOICES IN THE RIGHT, Abbie Williams, 14 days	29.50	NR
1988	LOVE BELIEVES ALL THINGS, Abbie Williams, 14 days	29.50	NR
1988	LOVE NEVER ENDS, Abbie Williams, 14 days	29.50	NR

Magic of Childhood

1984	SPECIAL FRIENDS, Abbie Williams, 10 days	24.50	NR
1985	FEEDING TIME, Abbie Williams, 10 days	24.50	NR
1985	BEST BUDDIES, Abbie Williams, 10 days	24.50	NR
1985	GETTING ACQUAINTED, Abbie Williams, 10 days	24.50	NR
1985	LOOK ALIKES, Abbie Williams, 10 days	24.50	NR
1985	LAST ONE IN, Abbie Williams, 10 days	24.50	NR
1985	A HANDFUL OF LOVE, Abbie Williams, 10 days	24.50	NR
1985	NO FAIR PEEKING, Abbie Williams, 10 days	24.50	NR

March of Dimes: Our Children, Our Future

1990	A TIME TO LAUGH, Abbie Williams, 150 days	29.00	NR

Masterpiece Collection

1979	ADORATION, Fra Filippo Lippi, 5,000	65.00	NR
1980	MADONNA WITH GRAPES, P. Mignard, 5,000	87.50	NR
1981	THE HOLY FAMILY, G. Delle Notti, 5,000	95.00	NR
1982	MADONNA OF THE STEETS, Robert Feruzzi, 5,000	85.00	NR

Precious Children

1993	BLESS BABY BROTHER, Abbie Williams	29.50	RI
1993	BLOWING BUBBLES, Abbie Williams	29.50	RI
1993	DON'T WORRY, MOTHER DUCK, Abbie Williams	29.50	RI
1993	TREETOP DISCOVERY, Abbie Williams	29.50	RI
1993	THE TEA PARTY, Abbie Williams	29.50	RI
1993	MOTHER'S LITTLE ANGEL, Abbie Williams	29.50	RI
1993	PICKING DAISIES, Abbie Williams	29.50	RI
1993	LET'S SAY GRACE, Abbie Williams	29.50	RI

Pretty Girls of the Ice Capades

1983	ICE PRINCESS, George B. Petty, 30 days	24.50	NR

Richard Judson Zolan Collection

1992	THE BUTTERFLY NET, R. J. Zolan, 100 days	29.50	RI
1994	THE RING, R. J. Zolan, 100 days	29.50	RI
1994	TERRACE DANCING, R. J. Zolan, 100 days	29.50	RI

Roman Memorial

1984	THE CARPENTER, Frances Hook, 1 year	100.00	135.00

Sweetest Songs

		Issue Price	Current Value
1986	A BABY'S PRAYER, Irene Spencer, 30 days	39.50	NR
1986	THIS LITTLE PIGGIE, Irene Spencer, 30 days	39.50	NR
1988	LONG, LONG AGO, Irene Spencer, 30 days	39.50	NR
1989	ROCKABYE, Irene Spencer, 30 days	39.50	NR

Tender Expressions

1992	THOUGHTS OF YOU ARE IN MY HEART, B. Sargent, 100 days .	29.50	RI

Single Issues

1983	THE KNEELING SANTA	29.50	NR
1985	FAIREST FLOWER OF PARADISE......................	45.00	NR

Fascination
Photo courtesy of *Collectors News*

The Holy Family
Photo courtesy of *Collectors News*

RORSTRAND   SWEDEN

Christmas

1968	BRINGING HOME THE TREE, Gunner Nylund, 1 year	12.00	475.00
1969	FISHERMEN SAILING HOME, Gunner Nylund, 1 year	13.50	25.00
1970	NILS WITH HIS GEESE, Gunner Nylund, 1 year	13.50	NR
1971	NILS IN LAPLAND, Gunner Nylund, 1 year	15.00	NR
1972	DALECARLIAN FIDDLER, Gunner Nylund, 1 year	15.00	NR
1973	FARM IN SMALAND, Gunner Nylund, 1 year	16.00	60.00
1974	VADSLENA, Gunner Nylund, 1 year	19.00	40.00
1975	NILS IN VASTMANLAND, Gunner Nylund, 1 year	20.00	30.00
1976	NILS IN UPPLAND, Gunner Nylund, 1 year	20.00	30.00
1977	NILS IN VARMLAND, Gunner Nylund, 1 year	29.50	NR

		Issue Price	Current Value
1978	NILS IN FJALLBACKA, Gunner Nylund, 1 year	32.50	40.00
1979	NILS IN VACOTERGOEILAND, Gunner Nylund, 1 year	38.50	NR
1980	NILS IN HALLAND, Gunner Nylund, 1 year	55.00	NR
1981	NILS IN GOTLAND, Gunner Nylund, 1 year	55.00	BR
1982	NILS AT SKANSEN, Gunner Nylund, 1 year	47.50	NR
1983	NILS IN OLAND, Gunner Nylund, 1 year	42.50	55.00
1984	NILS IN ANGERMANLAND, Gunner Nylund, 1 year	42.50	NR
1985	CHRISTMAS, Gunner Nylund, 1 year	42.50	BR
1985	NILS IN JAMTLAND, Gunner Nylund, 1 year	42.50	70.00
1986	NILS IN KARLSKRONA, Gunner Nylund, 1 year	42.50	NR
1987	DALSLAND, FORGET–ME–NOT, Gunner Nylund, 1 year	47.50	150.00
1988	NILS IN HALSINGLAND, Gunner Nylund, 1 year	55.00	NR
1989	NILS VISITS GOTHENBORG, Gunner Nylund, 1 year	60.00	NR
1990	NILS IN KVIKKJOKK, Gunner Nylund, 1 year	75.00	NR
1991	NILS IN MEDELPAD, Gunner Nylund, 1 year	85.00	NR
1992	GASTRIKLAND, LILY OF THE VALLEY, Gunner Nylund, 1 year	92.50	RI
1993	NARKE'S CASTLE, Gunner Nylund, 1 year	92.50	RI

Father's Day

1971	FATHER AND CHILD, 1 year	15.00	NR
1972	MEAL AT HOME, 1 year	15.00	25.00
1973	TILLING THE FIELDS, 1 year	16.00	25.00
1974	FISHING, 1 year	18.00	30.00
1975	PAINTING, 1 year	20.00	30.00
1976	PLOWING, 1 year	20.00	30.00
1977	SAWING, 1 year	27.50	NR
1978	IN THE STUDIO, 1 year	27.50	NR
1979	RIDING IN THE BUGGY, 1 year	27.50	NR
1980	MT ETCH–NOOK, 1 year	27.50	NR
1981	ESBJORN WITH PLAYMATE, 1 year	27.50	NR
1982	HOUSE SERVANTS, 1 year	36.00	NR
1984	FATHER WORKING, 1 year	42.50	NR

Jubilee

1980	1980, 1 year	47.50	NR

Julpoesi Series

1979	SILENT NIGHT, 1 year	38.50	NR
1980	ADORATION, 1 year	47.50	NR

Mother's Day

1971	MOTHER AND CHILD, 1 year	15.00	30.00
1972	SHELLING PEAS, 1 year	15.00	30.00
1973	OLD–FASHIONED PICNIC, 1 year	16.00	30.00
1974	CANDLE LIGHTING, 1 year	18.00	25.00

		Issue Price	Current Value
1975	PONTIUS ON THE FLOOR, 1 year	20.00	NR
1976	APPLE PICKING, 1 year	20.00	NR
1977	KITCHEN, 1 year	27.50	NR
1978	AZALEA, 1 year	27.50	NR
1979	STUDIO IDYLL, 1 year	27.50	NR
1980	LISBETH, 1 year	27.50	NR
1981	KARIN WITH BRITA, 1 year	27.50	NR
1982	BRITA, 1 year	36.00	NR
1983	LITTLE GIRL, 1 year	42.50	NR
1984	MOTHER SEWING, 1 year	42.50	NR

ROSENTHAL GERMANY

Christmas

1910	WINTER PEACE	—	550.00
1911	THREE WISE MEN	—	325.00
1912	STARDUST	—	255.00
1912	CHRISTMAS LIGHTS	—	235.00
1914	CHRISTMAS SONGS	—	350.00
1915	WALKING TO CHURCH	—	180.00
1916	CHRISTMAS DURING WAR	—	240.00
1917	ANGEL OF PEACE	—	200.00
1918	PEACE ON EARTH	—	200.00
1919	ST. CHRISTOPHER WITH THE CHRIST CHILD	—	225.00
1920	THE MANGER IN BETHLEHEM	—	325.00
1921	CHRISTMAS IN THE MOUNTAINS	—	200.00
1922	ADVENT BRANCH	—	200.00
1923	CHILDREN IN THE WINTER WOODS	—	200.00
1924	DEER IN THE WOODS	—	200.00
1925	THE THREE WISE MEN	—	200.00
1926	CHIRSTMAS IN THE MOUNTAINS	—	195.00
1927	STATION ON THE WAY	—	200.00
1928	CHALET CHRISTMAS	—	185.00
1929	CHRISTMAS IN THE ALPS	—	225.00
1930	GROUP OF DEER UNDER THE PINES	—	225.00
1931	PATH OF THE MAGI	—	225.00
1932	CHRIST CHILD	—	185.00
1933	THROUGH THE NIGHT TO LIGHT	—	190.00
1934	CHRISTMAS PEACE	—	190.00
1935	CHRISTMAS BY THE SEA	—	195.00
1936	NURNBERG ANGEL	—	195.00
1937	BERCHTESGADEN	—	195.00
1938	CHRISTMAS IN THE ALPS	—	195.00
1939	SCHNEEKOPPE MOUNTAIN	—	195.00

		Issue Price	Current Value
1940	MARIEN CHURCH IN DANZIG	–	250.00
1941	STRASSBURG CATHEDRAL	–	250.00
1942	MARIANBURG CASTLE	–	300.00
1943	WINTER IDYLL	–	300.00
1944	WOOD SCAPE	–	300.00
1945	CHRISTMAS PEACE	–	400.00
1946	CHRISTMAS IN AN ALPINE VALLEY	–	240.00
1947	THE DILLINGEN MADONNA	–	985.00
1948	MESSAGE TO THE SHEPHERDS	–	875.00
1949	THE HOLY FAMILY	–	185.00
1950	CHRISTMAS IN THE FOREST	–	185.00
1951	STAR OF BETHLEHEM	–	450.00
1952	CHRISTMAS IN THE ALPS	–	195.00
1953	THE HOLY LIGHT	–	195.00
1954	CHRISTMAS EVE	–	195.00
1955	CHRISTMAS IN A VILLAGE	–	195.00
1956	CHRISTMAS IN THE ALPS	–	195.00
1957	CHRISTMAS BY THE SEA	–	195.00
1958	CHRISTMAS EVE	–	195.00
1959	MIDNIGHT MASS	–	195.00
1960	CHRISTMAS IN A SMALL VILLAGE	–	195.00
1961	SOLITARY CHRISTMAS	–	225.00
1962	CHRISTMAS EVE	–	195.00
1963	SILENT NIGHT	–	195.00
1964	CHRISTMAS MARKET IN NURNBERG	–	225.00
1965	CHRISTMAS IN MUNICH	–	185.00
1966	CHRISTMAS IN ULM	–	275.00
1967	CHRISTMAS IN REGINBURG	–	185.00
1968	CHRISTMAS IN BREMEN	–	195.00
1969	CHRISTMAS IN ROTHENBURG	–	220.00
1970	CHRISTMAS IN COLOGNE	–	175.00
1971	CHRISTMAS IN GARMISCH	42.00	100.00
1972	CHRISTMAS IN FRANCONIA	50.00	95.00
1973	LUBECK–HOLSTEIN	77.00	105.00
1974	CHRISTMAS IN WURZBURG	85.00	100.00

Classic Rose Christmas

		Issue Price	Current Value
1974	MEMORIAL CHURCH IN BERLIN, Helmut Drexel	84.00	160.00
1975	FREIBURG CATHEDRAL, Helmut Drexel	75.00	NR
1976	CASTLE OF COCHEM, Helmut Drexel	95.00	BR
1977	HANOVER TOWN HALL, Helmut Drexel	125.00	NR
1978	CATHEDRAL AT AACHEN, Helmut Drexel	150.00	NR
1979	CATHEDRAL IN LUXEMBOURG, Helmut Drexel	165.00	NR
1980	CHRISTMAS IN BRUSSELS, Helmut Drexel	190.00	NR
1981	CHRISTMAS IN TRIER, Helmut Drexel	190.00	NR
1982	MILAN CATHEDRAL, Helmut Drexel	190.00	NR
1983	CHURCH AT CASTLE WITTENBERG, Helmut Drexel	195.00	NR

		Issue Price	Current Value
1984	CITY HALL OF STOCKHOLM, Helmut Drexel	195.00	NR
1985	CHRISTMAS IN AUGSBURG, Helmut Drexel	195.00	NR

Famous Women and Children

		Issue Price	Current Value
1980	PHARAOH'S DAUGHTER AND MOSES, Edna Hibel, gold, 2,500	350.00	390.00
1980	PHARAOH'S DAUGHTER AND MOSES, Edna Hibel, cobalt blue, 500	350.00	560.00
1981	CORNELIA AND JEWELS,Edna Hibel, gold, 2,500	350.00	NR
1981	CORNELIA AND JEWELS, Edna Hibel, cobalt blue, 500	350.00	NR
1982	ANNA AND CHILDREN OF KING OF SIAM, Edna Hibel, gold, 2,500	350.00	NR
1982	ANNA AND CHILDREN OF KING OF SIAM, Edna Hibel, cobalt blue 500	350.00	NR
1984	MOZART AND THE EMPRESS MARIA THERESA, Edna Hibel, gold, 2,500	350.00	395.00
1984	MOZART AND THE EMPRESS MARIA THERESA, Edna Hibel, cobalt blue, 500	350.00	975.00

Fantasies and Fables

1976	ORIENTAL NIGHT MUSIC, 10,000	50.00	NR
1977	MANDOLIN PLAYERS, 1 year	75.00	NR

Harvest Time

1976	PUMPKINS, John Falter, 5,000	70.00	NR
1977	HONEST DAY'S WORK, John Falter, 4,000	70.00	NR

Lorraine Trester Series

1975	SUMMERTIME, Lorraine Trester, 5,000	60.00	135.00
1977	ONE LOVELY YESTERDAY, Lorraine Trester, 5,000	70.00	90.00

Nobility of Children

1976	LA CONTESSA ISABELLA, Edna Hibel, 12,750	120.00	NR
1977	LE MARQUIS MAURICE–PIERRE, Edna Hibel, 12,750	120.00	NR
1978	BARONESSE JOHANNA, Edna Hibel, 12,750	130.00	140.00
1979	CHIEF RED FEATHER, Edna Hibel, 12,750	140.00	160.00

Oriental Gold

1973	YASUKO, Edna Hibel, 2,000	275.00	650.00
1976	MR. OBATA, Edna Hibel, 2,000	275.00	500.00
1978	SAKURA, Edna Hibel, 2,000	295.00	400.00
1979	MICHIO, Edna Hibel, 2,000	325.00	375.00

Runci Classic

1977	SUMMERTIME, Edward Runci, 5,000	95.00	NR
1978	SPRINGTIME, Edward Runci, 5,000	95.00	NR

	Issue Price	Current Value

Tribute to Classical Greek Beauty

1980	DIANA, Edna Hibel, 3,000	350.00	360.00

Wiinblad Christmas

1971	MARIA AND CHILD, Bjorn Wiinblad, 8,000	100.00	700.00
1972	CASPAR, Bjorn Wiinblad, 10,000	100.00	290.00
1973	MELCHIOR, Bjorn Wiinblad, 10,000	125.00	335.00
1974	BALTHAZAR, Bjorn Wiinblad, 10,000	125.00	300.00
1975	THE ANNUNCIATION, Bjorn Wiinblad, 1 year	195.00	NR
1976	ANGEL WITH TRUMPET, Bjorn Wiinblad, 1 year	195.00	NR
1977	ADORATION OF SHEPHERDS, Bjorn Wiinblad,1 year	225.00	NR
1978	ANGEL WITH HARP, Bjorn Wiinblad, 1 year	275.00	290.00
1979	EXODUS FROM EGYPT, Bjorn Wiinblad, 1 year	310.00	NR
1980	ANGEL WITH GLOCKENSPIEL, Bjorn Wiinblad,1 year	360.00	NR
1981	THE CHRIST CHILD VISITS THE TEMPLE, Bjorn Wiinblad, 1 year	375.00	NR
1982	CHRISTENING OF CHRIST, Bjorn Wiinblad, 1 year	375.00	NR

Wiinblad Crystal

1976	THE MADONNA, Bjorn Wiinblad, 2,000	150.00	400.00
1977	THE ANNUNCIATION, Bjorn Wiinblad, 2,000	195.00	285.00
1978	THREE KINGS, Bjorn Wiinblad, 2,000	225.00	270.00
1980	ANGEL WITH SHEPHERDS, Bjorn Wiinblad, 1 year	290.00	300.00
1981	ADORATION OF THE SHEPHERDS, Bjorn Wiinblad, 1 year	295.00	NR

ROYAL BAYREUTH GERMANY

Anniversary

1980	YOUNG AMERICANS, Leo Jansen, 5,000	125.00	NR

Antique American Art

1976	FARMYARD TRANQUILITY, 3,000	50.00	70.00
1977	HALF DOME, 3,000	55.00	65.00
1978	DOWN MEMORY LANE, 3,000	65.00	NR

Christmas

1972	CARRIAGE IN THE VILLAGE, 4,000	15.00	80.00
1973	SNOW SCENE, 4,000	16.50	NR
1974	THE OLD MILL, 4,000	24.00	NR
1975	FOREST CHALET "SERENITY," 4,000	27.50	NR
1976	CHRISTMAS IN THE COUNTRY, 5,000	40.00	NR
1977	PEACE ON EARTH, 5,000	40.00	NR
1978	PEACEFUL INTERLUDE, 5,000	45.00	NR
1979	HOMEWARD BOUND, 5,000	50.00	NR

		Issue Price	Current Value

L. Henry Series
| 1976 | JUST FRIENDS, 5,000 | 50.00 | 60.00 |
| 1977 | INTERRUPTION, 5,000 | 55.00 | NR |

Mother's Day
1973	CONSOLATION, Leo Jansen, 4,000	16.50	50.00
1974	YOUNG AMERICANS, Leo Jansen, 4,000	25.00	130.00
1975	YOUNG AMERICANS II, Leo Jansen, 5,000	25.00	105.00
1976	YOUNG AMERICANS III, Leo Jansen, 5,000	30.00	70.00
1977	YOUNG AMERICANS IV, Leo Jansen, 5,000	40.00	60.00
1978	YOUNG AMERICANS V, Leo Jansen, 5,000	45.00	50.00
1979	YOUNG AMERICANS VI, Leo Jansen, 5,000	60.00	65.00
1980	YOUNG AMERICANS VII, Leo Jansen, 5,000	65.00	75.00
1981	YOUNG AMERICANS VIII, Leo Jansen, 5,000	65.00	NR
1982	YOUNG AMERICANS IX, Leo Jansen, 5,000	65.00	NR

Sun Bonnet Babies
1974	MONDAY — WASHING DAY, 15,000	—	—
1974	TUESDAY — IRONING DAY, 15,000	—	—
1974	WEDNESDAY — MENDING DAY, 15,000	—	—
1974	THURSDAY — SCRUBBING DAY, 15,000	—	—
1974	FRIDAY — SWEEPING DAY, 15,000	—	—
1974	SATURDAY — BAKING DAY, 15,000	—	—
1974	SUNDAY — FISHING DAY, 15,000, set of 7	120.00	230.00

Sun Bonnet Babies Playtime
1981	SWINGING, 5,000	60.00	NR
1981	ROUND DANCE, 5,000	60.00	NR
1982	MARBLES, 5,000	60.00	NR
1982	PLAYING CATCH, 5,000	60.00	NR

ROYAL COPENHAGEN DENMARK

Christmas
1908	MADONNA AND CHILD, Christian Thomsen, 1 year	1.00	1,000.00
1909	DANISH LANDSCAPE, Stephn Ussing, 1 year	1.00	195.00
1910	THE MAGI, Christian Thomsen, 1 year	1.00	100.00
1911	DANISH LANDSCAPE, Oluf Jensen, 1 year	1.00	125.00
1912	ELDERLY COUPLE BY THE CHRISTMAS TREE, Christian Thomsen, 1 year	1.00	140.00
1913	SPIRE OF FREDERIK CHURCH, Arthur Boesen, 1 year	1.50	140.00
1914	HOLY SPIRIT CHURCH, Arthur Boesen, 1 year	1.50	250.00
1915	DANISH LANDSCAPE, Arnold Krog, 1 year	1.50	125.00
1916	THE SHEPHERDS IN THE FIELD, Richard Bocher, 1 year	1.50	140.00

Year	Title	Issue Price	Current Value
1917	THE TOWER OF OUR SAVIOUR'S CHURCH, Oluf Jensen, 1 year	2.00	170.00
1918	THE SHEPHERDS AND SHEEP, Oluf Jensen, 1 year	2.00	180.00
1919	IN THE PARK, Oluf Jensen, 1 year	2.00	135.00
1920	MARY WITH THE CHILD JESUS, Oluf Jensen, 1 year	2.00	170.00
1921	AABENRAA MARKETPLACE, Oluf Jenen, 1 year	2.00	180.00
1922	THREE SINGING ANGELS, Ellinor Selschau, 1 year	2.00	80.00
1923	DANISH LANDSCAPE, Oluf Jensen, 1 year	2.00	90.00
1924	CHRISTMAS STAR OVER THE SEA, Benjamin Olsen, 1 year	2.00	110.00
1925	STREET SCENE FROM CHRISTIANSHAVN, Oluf Jensen, 1 year	2.00	140.00
1926	CHRISTIANSHAVN CANAL, Richard Bocher, 1 year	2.00	180.00
1927	THE SHIP'S BOY AT THE TILLER CHRISTMAS NIGHT, Benjamin Olsen, 1 year	2.00	135.00
1928	THE VICAR — FAMILY ON THE WAY TO CHURCH, Gotfred Rode, 1 year	2.00	135.00
1929	THE GRUNDTVIG CHURCH, COPENHAGEN, Oluf Jensen, 1 year	2.00	140.00
1930	FISHING BOATS, Benjamin Olsen, 1 year	2.50	140.00
1931	MOTHER AND CHILD, Gotfred Rode, 1 year	2.50	175.00
1932	FREDERIKSBERG GARDENS WITH STATUE OF FREDERIK VI, Oluf Jensen, 1 year	2.50	120.00
1933	THE FERRY AND THE GREAT BELT, Benjamin Olsen, 1 year	2.50	225.00
1934	THE HERMITAGE CASTLE, Oluf Jensen, 1 year	2.50	325.00
1935	FISHING BOAT OFF KRONBORG CASTLE, Benjamin Olsen, 1 year	2.50	500.00
1936	ROSKILKDE CATHEDRAL, Richard Bocher, 1 year	2.50	300.00
1937	CHRISTMAS SCENE IN COPENHAGEN, Nils Thorsson, 1 year	2.50	235.00
1938	THE ROUND CHURCH IN OSTERLARS, Herne Nielsen, 1 year	3.00	460.00
1939	EXPEDITIONARY SHIP IN THE PACK ICE OF GREENLAND, Svend Nicolai Nielsen, 1 year	3.00	470.00
1940	THE GOOD SHEPHERD, Kai Lange, 1 year	3.00	185.00
1941	DANISH VILLAGE CHURCH, Theodor Kjolner, 1 year	3.00	500.00
1942	BELL TOWER OF OLD CHURCH IN JUTLAND, Nils Thorsson, 1 year	4.00	600.00
1943	THE FLIGHT OF THE HOLY FAMILY TO EGYPT, Nils Thorsson, 1 year	4.00	600.00
1944	TYPICAL DANISH WINTER SCENE, Viggo Olsen, 1 year	4.00	370.00
1945	A PEACEFUL MOTIF, Richard Bocher, 1 year	4.00	375.00
1946	ZEALAND VILLAGE CHURCH, Nils Thorsson, 1 year	4.00	280.00
1947	THE GOOD SHEPHERD, Kai Lange, 1 year	4.50	550.00
1948	NODEBO CHURCH, Theodor Kjolner, 1 year	4.50	260.00
1949	OUR LADY'S CATHEDRAL COPENHAGEN, Hans H. Hansen, 1 year	5.00	190.00
1950	BOESLUNDE CHURCH, Viggo Olsen, 1 year	5.00	210.00
1951	CHRISTMAS ANGEL, Richard Bocher, 1 year	5.00	250.00
1952	CHRISTMAS IN THE FOREST, Kai Lange, 1 year	5.00	175.00
1953	FREDERIKSBERG CASTLE, Theodor Kjolner, 1 year	6.00	265.00
1954	AMALIENBORG PALACE, COPENHAGEN, Kai Lange, 1 year	6.00	250.00
1955	FANO GIRL, Kai Lange, 1 year	7.00	350.00
1956	ROSENBORG CASTLE, Kai Lange, 1 year	7.00	270.00
1957	THE GOOD SHEPHERD, Hans H. Hansen, 1 year	8.00	125.00

Holy Spirit Church

Mary with the Child Jesus

Hojsager Mill

Christmas Rose and Cat

In the Desert

Choosing a Christmas Tree

Waiting for Christmas

Christmas Eve in Copenhagen
Photo courtesy of *Collectors News*

Sheperdhess and Chimney Sweep
Photo courtesy of *Collectors News*

A Loving Mother

An Outing with Mother

Reunion

		Issue Price	Current Value
1958	SUNSHINE OVER GREENLAND, Hans H. Hansen, 1 year .	9.00	130.00
1959	CHRISTMAS NIGHT, Hans H. Hansen, 1 year	9.00	180.00
1960	THE STAG, Hans H. Hansen, 1 year....................	10.00	185.00
1961	THE TRAINING SHIP DANMARK, Kai Lange, 1 year	10.00	240.00
1962	THE LITTLE MERMAID AT WINTERTIME, Kai Lange, 1 year...	11.00	195.00
1963	HOJSAGER MILL, Kai Lange, 1 year	11.00	50.00
1964	FETCHING THE CHRISTMAS TREE, Kai Lange, 1 year....	11.00	50.00
1965	LITTLE SKATERS, Kai Lange, 1 year	12.00	45.00
1966	BLACKBIRD AND CHURCH, Kai Lanage, 1 year	12.00	30.00
1967	THE ROYAL OAK, Kai Lange, 1 year	13.00	20.00
1968	THE LOST UMIAK, Kai Lange, 1 year	13.00	20.00
1969	THE OLD FARMYARD, Kai Lange, 1 year	14.00	20.00
1970	CHRISTMAS ROSE AND CAT, Kai Lange, 1 year.........	14.00	35.00
1971	HARE IN WINTER, Kai Lange, 1 year	15.00	NR
1972	IN THE DESERT, Kai Lange, 1 year	16.00	25.00
1973	TRAIN HOMEWARD BOUND, Kai Lange, 1 year.........	22.00	NR
1974	WINTER TWILIGHT, Kai Lange, 1 year	22.00	30.00
1975	QUEEN'S PALACE, Kai Lange, 1 year	27.50	BR
1976	DANISH WATERMILL, Kai Lange, 1 year	27.50	NR
1977	IMMERVAD BRIDGE, Kai Lange, 1 year	32.50	BR
1978	GREENLAND SCENERY, Kai Lange, 1 year.............	35.00	BR
1979	CHOOSING A CHRISTMAS TREE, Kai Lange, 1 year	42.50	BR
1980	BRINGING HOME THE CHRISTMAS TREE, Kai Lange, 1 year .	49.50	BR
1981	ADMIRING THE CHRISTMAS TREE, Kai Lange, 1 year ...	52.50	BR
1982	WAITING FOR CHRISTMAS, Kai Lange, 1 year.........	54.50	65.00
1983	MERRY CHRISTMAS, Kai Lange, 1 year...............	54.50	65.00
1984	JINGLE BELLS, Kai Lange, 1 year	54.50	NR
1985	SNOWMAN, Kai Lange, 1 year	54.50	80.00
1986	CHRISTMAS VACATION, Kai Lange, 1 year.............	54.50	85.00
1987	WINTER BIRDS, Sven Vestergaard, 1 year	59.50	NR
1988	CHRISTMAS EVE IN COPENHAGEN, Sven Vestergaard, 1 year	59.50	70.00
1989	THE OLD SKATING POND, Sven Vestergaard, 1 year	59.50	80.00
1990	CHRISTMAS AT TIVOLI, Sven Vestergaard, 1 year	64.50	170.00
1991	THE FESTIVAL OF SANTA LUCIA, Sven Vestergaard, 1 year...	69.50	BR
1992	THE QUEEN'S CARRIAGE, Sven Vestergaard, 1 year	69.50	RI
1993	CHRISTMAS GUESTS, Sven Vestergaard, 1 year........	69.50	RI
1994	CHRISTMAS SHOPPING, Sven Vestergaard, 1 year	72.50	RI

Christmas Jubilee

1983	CHRISTMAS MEMORIES, 1 year......................	95.00	NR

Hans Christian Andersen Fairy Tales

1983	SHEPHERDESS AND CHIMNEY SWEEP, Sven Vestergaard, 1 year	39.50	NR
1984	THUMBELINA, Sven Vestergaard, 1 year	39.50	NR
1985	MERMAID, Sven Vestergaard, 1 year	44.50	NR

	Issue Price	Current Value

Historical

		Issue Price	Current Value
1975	R. C. BICENTENNIAL, 1 year	30.00	NR
1976	U. S. BICENTENNIAL, 1 year	35.00	NR
1977	ELECTROMAGNETISM, 1 year	35.00	NR
1978	CAPTAIN COOK, 1 year	37.50	BR
1979	ADAM OEHLENSCHLEGER, 1 year	42.00	BR
1980	AMAGETORV, 1 year	57.50	BR
1983	ROYAL COPENHAGEN 75TH ANNIVERSARY, 1 year	95.00	NR

Motherhood

		Issue Price	Current Value
1982	MOTHER ROBIN WITH BABIES, Sven Vestergaard, 1 year	29.50	50.00
1983	MOTHER CAT AND KITTENS, Sven Vestergaard, 1 year	29.50	45.00
1984	MARE AND FOAL, Sven Vestergaard, 1 year	29.50	45.00
1985	MOTHER AND BABY RABBIT, Sven Vestergaard, 1 year	32.00	NR

Mother's Day

		Issue Price	Current Value
1971	AMERICAN MOTHER, Kamma Svensson, 1 year	12.50	130.00
1972	ORIENTAL MOTHER, Kamma Svensson, 1 year	14.00	65.00
1973	DANISH MOTHER, Arne Ungermann, 1 year	16.00	60.00
1974	GREENLAND MOTHER, Arne Ungermann, 1 year	16.00	60.00
1975	BIRD IN NEST, Arne Ungermann, 1 year	20.00	60.00
1976	MERMAIDS, Arne Ungermann, 1 year	20.00	55.00
1977	TWINS, Arne Ungermann, 1 year	24.00	55.00
1978	MOTHER AND CHILD, Ib Spang Olsen, 1 year	26.00	NR
1979	A LOVING MOTHER, Ib Spang Olsen, 1 year	29.50	NR
1980	AN OUTING WITH MOTHER, Ib Spang Olsen, 1 year	37.50	50.00
1981	REUNION, Ib Spang Olsen, 1 year	37.50	45.00
1982	CHILDREN'S HOUR, Ib Spang Olsen, 1 year	37.50	45.00

National Parks of America

		Issue Price	Current Value
1978	YELLOWSTONE, 5,000	75.00	NR
1979	SHENANDOAH, 5,000	75.00	NR
1981	MT. MCKINLEY, 5,000	75.00	NR
1981	THE EVERGLADES, 5,000	75.00	NR
1981	GRAND CANYON, 5,000	75.00	NR
1981	YOSEMITE, 5,000	75.00	NR

Nature's Children

		Issue Price	Current Value
1993	THE ROBINS, Jorgen Nielsen, 1 year	39.50	NR
1994	THE FAWN, Jorgen Nielsen, 1 year	39.50	NR

Special Issues

		Issue Price	Current Value
1967	VIRGIN ISLANDS, 1 year	12.00	25.00
1969	DANISH FLAG, 1 year	12.00	25.00
1969	APOLLO II, 1 year	15.00	NR
1970	REUNION, 1 year	12.00	25.00

		Issue Price	Current Value
1970	STATUE OF LIBERTY	15.00	25.00
1972	MUNICH OLYMPIAD	25.00	NR
1972	KING FREDERIK IX	25.00	NR

ROYAL CORNWALL UNITED STATES
(See also Haviland, Schumann, Wedgwood and Woodmere)

Alice in Wonderland

1979	ALICE AND THE WHITE RABBIT, Lawrence W. Whittaker, 27,500	45.00	NR
1979	ADVICE FROM A CATERPILLAR, Lawrence W. Whittaker, 27,500	45.00	NR
1980	THE CHESHIRE CAT'S GRIN, Lawrence W. Whittaker, 27,500 ..	45.00	NR
1980	MAD HATTER'S TEA PARTY, Lawrence W. Whittaker, 27,500 ..	45.00	NR
1980	QUEEN'S CROQUET MATCH, Lawrence W. Whittaker, 27,500 .	45.00	NR
1980	WHO STOLE THE TARTS?, Lawrence W. Whittaker, 27,500	45.00	NR

Beauty of Bouguereau

1979	LUCIE, William A. Bouguereau, 19,500	35.00	45.00
1980	MADELAINE, William A. Bouguereau, 19,500	35.00	NR
1980	FRERE ET SOEUR, William A. Bouguereau, 19,500	35.00	NR
1980	SOLANGE ET ENFANT, William A. Bouguereau, 19,500 ...	35.00	NR
1980	COLETTE, William A. Bouguereau, 19,500	35.00	65.00
1980	JEAN ET JEANETTE, William A. Bouguereau, 19,500	35.00	NR

Bethlehem Christmas

1977	FIRST CHRISTMAS EVE, Gerald R. Miller, 10,000	29.50	85.00
1978	GLAD TIDINGS, Robert Ahlcrona, 10,000	34.50	75.00
1979	THE GIFT BEARERS, Higgins Bond, 10,000	34.50	NR

Classic Christmas

1978	CHILD OF PEACE, 10,000	55.00	85.00
1978	SILENT NIGHT, 10,000	55.00	70.00
1978	MOST PRECIOUS GIFT, 10,000	55.00	65.00
1978	WE THREE KINGS, 10,000	55.00	65.00

Classic Collection

1980	ROMEO AND JULIET, J. C. Leyendecker, 17,500	55.00	65.00
1980	YOUNG GALAHAD, J. C. Leyendecker, 17,500	55.00	65.00
1980	AT LOCKSLEY HALL, J. C. Leyendecker, 17,500	55.00	NR
1980	ST. AGNES EVE, J. C. Leyendecker, 17,500	55.00	NR

Courageous Few

1982	THE FALL OF JERICHO, Yiannis Koutsis, 19,500	59.50	NR
1982	GIDEON'S FIVE HUNDRED, Yiannis Koutsis, 19,500	59.50	NR

		Issue Price	Current Value
1982	DESTRUCTION OF THE TEMPLE, Yiannis Koutsis, 10,500 .	59.50	NR
1982	RUTH AT THE HARVEST, Yiannis Koutsis, 19,500	59.50	NR
1982	DAVID AND GOLIATH, Yiannis Koutsis, 19,500	59.50	NR
1982	SOLOMON'S DECISION, Yiannis Koutsis, 19,500	59.50	NR
1982	BUILDING OF THE TEMPLE, Yiannis Koutsis, 19,500	59.50	NR
1982	ELIJAH AND HEAVENS' CHARIOT, Yiannis Koutsis, 19,500	59.50	NR
1982	JOB'S REWARD, Yiannis Koutsis, 19,500	59.50	NR
1983	PSALM OF DAVID, Yiannis Koutsis, 19,500	59.50	NR
1983	DANIEL AND THE LIONS, Yiannis Koutsis, 19,500	59.50	NR
1983	JONAH AND THE WHALE, Yiannis Koutsis, 19,500	59.50	NR

Creation

		Issue Price	Current Value
1977	IN THE BEGINNING, Yiannis Koutsis, 10,000	37.50	90.00
1977	IN HIS IMAGE, Yiannis Koutsis, 10,000	45.00	55.00
1978	ADAM'S RIB, Yiannis Koutsis, 10,000	45.00	55.00
1978	BANISHED FROM EDEN, Yiannis Koutsis, 10,000	45.00	NR
1978	NOAH AND THE ARK, Yiannis Koutsis, 10,000	45.00	NR
1980	TOWER OF BABEL, Yiannis Koutsis, 10,000	45.00	75.00
1980	SODOM AND GOMORRAH, Yiannis Koutsis, 10,000	45.00	NR
1980	JACOB'S WEDDING, Yiannis Koutsis, 10,000	45.00	NR
1980	REBEKAH AT THE WELL, Yiannis Koutsis, 10,000	45.00	75.00
1980	JACOB'S LADDER, Yiannis Koutsis, 10,000	45.00	75.00
1980	JOSEPH'S COAT OF MANY COLORS, Yiannis Koutsis, 10,000 . .	45.00	75.00
1980	JOSEPH INTERPRETS PHARAOH'S DREAM, Yiannis Koutsis, 10,000	45.00	75.00

Creation (Charter Release for Calhoun's Collector's Society)

		Issue Price	Current Value
1977	IN THE BEGINNING, Yiannis Koutsis, 19,500	29.50	155.00
1977	IN HIS IMAGE, Yiannis Koutsis, 19,500	29.50	120.00
1978	ADAM'S RIB, Yiannis Koutsis, 19,500	29.50	100.00
1978	BANISHED FROM EDEN, Yiannis Koutsis, 19,500	29.50	90.00
1978	NOAH AND THE ARK, Yiannis Koutsis, 19,500	29.50	90.00
1980	TOWER OF BABEL, Yiannis Koutsis, 19,500	29.50	80.00
1980	SODOM AND GOMORRAH, Yiannis Koutsis, 19,500	29.50	80.00
1980	JACOB'S WEDDING, Yiannis Koutsis, 19,500	29.50	80.00
1980	REBEKAH AT THE WELL, Yiannis Koutsis, 19,500	29.50	80.00
1980	JACOB'S LADDER, Yiannis Koutsis, 19,500	29.50	80.00
1980	JOSEPH'S COAT OF MANY COLORS, Yiannis Koutsis, 19,500 . .	29.50	80.00
1980	JOSEPH INTERPRETS PHARAOH'S DREAM, Yiannis Koutsis, 19,500	29.50	80.00

Crystal Maidens

		Issue Price	Current Value
1979	STRAWBERRY SEASON (SPRING), 2,500	57.50	80.00
1979	SUNSHINE SEASON (SUMMER), 2,500	57.50	80.00
1979	SCENIC SEASON (FALL), 2,500	57.50	80.00
1979	SNOWFLAKE SEASON (WINTER), 2,500	57.50	80.00

		Issue Price	Current Value

Dorothy's Day

1980	BRAND–NEW DAY, Bill Mack, 15,000	55.00	NR
1980	ALL BY MYSELF, Bill Mack, 15,000	55.00	NR
1981	OFF TO SCHOOL, Bill Mack, 15,000	55.00	NR
1981	BEST FRIENDS, Bill Mack, 15,000	55.00	NR
1981	HELPING MAMMY, Bill Mack, 15,000	55.00	NR
1981	BLESS ME TOO!, Bill Mack, 15,000	55.00	NR

Exotic Birds of Tropique

1981	SCARLET MACAWS, Konrad Hack, 19,500	49.50	NR
1981	TOCO TOUCAN, Konrad Hack, 19,500	49.50	NR
1981	GREATER SULFUR–CRESTED COCKATOO, Konrad Hack, 19,500	49.50	NR
1981	ROSY FLAMINGOS, Konrad Hack, 19,500	49.50	NR
1982	ULTRAMARINE KING, Konrad Hack, 19,500	49.50	NR
1982	RED–FAN PARROT, Konrad Hack, 19,500	49.50	NR
1982	GOLDIE'S BIRD OF PARADISE, Konrad Hack, 19,500	49.50	NR
1982	ANDEAN COCK–OF–THE–ROCK, Konrad Hack, 19,500	49.50	NR
1982	SEVEN–COLORED TANAGER, Konrad Hack, 19,500	49.50	NR
1982	SCARLET IBIS, Konrad Hack, 19,500	49.50	NR
1982	QUETZAL, Konrad Hack, 19,500	49.50	NR
1982	LONG–TAILED SYLPH, Konrad Hack, 19,500	49.50	NR

Five Perceptions of Weo Cho

1979	SENSE OF TOUCH, 19,500	55.00	125.00
1979	SENSE OF SIGHT, 19,500	55.00	85.00
1980	SENSE OF TASTE, 19,500	55.00	75.00
1980	SENSE OF HEARING, 19,500	55.00	75.00
1980	SENSE OF SMELL, 19,500	55.00	75.00

Four Seasons (Charter Release for Calhoun Collector's Society)

1978	WARMTH (WINTER), Gunther Granget, 17,500	60.00	NR
1978	VOICES OF SPRING (SPRING), Gunther Granget, 17,500	60.00	NR
1978	THE FLEDGLING (SUMMER), Gunther Granget, 17,500	60.00	NR
1978	WE SURVIVE (FALL), Gunther Granget, 17,500	60.00	NR

Golden Age of Cinema

1978	THE KING AND HIS LADIES, Lawrence W. Whittaker, 22,500	45.00	NR
1978	FRED AND GINGER, Lawrence W. Whittaker, 22,500	45.00	NR
1978	JUDY AND MICKEY, Lawrence W. Whittaker, 22,500	45.00	NR
1978	THE PHILADELPHIA STORY, Lawrence W. Whittaker, 22,500	45.00	NR
1979	THE THIN MAN, Lawrence W. Whittaker, 22,500	45.00	NR
1979	GIGI, Lawrence W. Whittaker, 22,500	45.00	NR

Golden Plates of the Noble Flower Maidens

| 1982 | IRIS MAIDEN, Kitagawa Utamaro, 19,500 | 65.00 | NR |
| 1982 | PLUM BLOSSOM, Kitagawa Utamaro, 19,500 | 65.00 | NR |

			Issue Price	Current Value
1982	QUINCE MAIDEN, Kitagawa Utamaro, 19,500		65.00	NR
1982	CHERRY BLOSSOM MAIDEN, Kitagawa Utamaro, 19,500		65.00	NR
1982	CRYSANTHEMUM MAIDEN, Kitagawa Utamaro, 19,500		65.00	NR
1982	AUGUST LILY MAIDEN, Kitagawa Utamaro, 19,500		65.00	NR

Impressions of Yesteryear

1982	MOON MIST, Dominic Mingolla, 19,500		59.50	NR
1982	FALL FLOWERS, Dominic Mingolla, 19,500		59.50	NR
1982	WISHING WELL, Dominic Mingolla, 19,500		59.50	NR
1982	THE LETTER, Dominic Mingolla, 19,500		59.50	NR
1982	SLEDDING, Dominic Mingolla, 19,500		59.50	NR
1982	RED TREE, Dominic Mingolla, 19,500		59.50	NR
1982	SWANS, Dominic Mingolla, 19,500		59.50	NR
1982	SAILBOAT, Dominic Mingolla, 19,500		59.50	NR
1982	WINTER PARK, Dominic Mingolla, 19,500		59.50	NR
1983	SEASHORE, Dominic Mingolla, 19,500		59.50	NR
1983	RED BALLOON, Dominic Mingolla, 19,500		59.50	NR
1983	SNOWMAN, Dominic Mingolla, 19,500		59.50	NR

Kitten's World

1979	JUST CURIOUS, Rudy Droguett, 27,500		45.00	80.00
1979	HELLO, WORLD, Rudy Droguett, 27,500		45.00	NR
1979	ARE YOU A FLOWER?, Rudy Droguett, 27,500		45.00	NR
1980	TALK TO ME, Rudy Droguett, 27,500		45.00	NR
1980	MY FAVORITE TOY, Rudy Droguett, 27,500		45.00	NR
1980	PURR–FECT PLEASURE, Rudy Droguett, 27,500		45.00	NR

Legend of the Peacock Maidens

1982	DANCE OF THE PEACOCK MAIDENS, 19,500		69.50	NR
1982	PROMISE OF LOVE, 19,500		69.50	NR
1982	THE BETRAYAL, 19,500		69.50	NR
1982	THE PRINCE AND THE PYTHON, 19,500		69.50	NR
1982	RETURN OF THE BRACELET, 19,500		69.50	NR
1982	THE MARRIAGE, 19,500		69.50	NR

Legendary Ships of the Sea

1980	THE FLYING DUTCHMAN, Alan D'Estrehan, 19,500		49.50	90.00
1981	THE REFANU, Alan D'Estrehan, 19,500		49.50	NR
1981	THE GASPEE BAY, Alan D'Estrehan, 19,500		49.50	NR
1981	THE RESCUE, Alan D'Estrehan, 19,500		49.50	NR
1981	THE COPENHAGEN, Alan D'Estrehan, 19,500		49.50	NR
1981	THE PALATINE, Alan D'Estrehan, 19,500		49.50	NR
1981	THE PRIDE, Alan D'Estrehan, 19,500		49.50	NR
1981	THE FOOCHOW SEA JUNK, Alan D'Estrehan, 19,500		49.50	NR
1981	THE ROTH RAMHACH, Alan D'Estrehan, 19,500		49.50	NR

		Issue Price	Current Value
1981	THE FRIGORIFIQUE, Alan D'Estrehan, 19,500	49.50	NR

Little People

1980	OFF TO THE PICNIC, Seima, 19,500	34.50	NR
1981	DECORATING THE TREE, Seima, 19,500	34.50	NR
1981	CRUISING DOWN THE RIVER, Seima, 19,500	34.50	NR
1981	THE SWEETEST HARVEST, Seima, 19,500	34.50	NR
1981	THE HAPPY CHORUS, Seima, 19,500	34.50	NR
1981	PAINTING THE LEAVES, Seima, 19,500	34.50	NR

Love's Precious Moments

1981	LOVE'S SWEET VOW, Robert Gunn, 17,500	55.00	NR
1981	LOVE'S SWEET VERSE, Robert Gunn, 17,500	55.00	NR
1981	LOVE'S SWEET OFFERING, Robert Gunn, 17,500	55.00	NR
1981	LOVE'S SWEET EMBRACE, Robert Gunn, 17,500	55.00	NR
1981	LOVE'S SWEET MELODY, Robert Gunn, 17,500	55.00	NR
1981	LOVE'S SWEET KISS, Robert Gunn, 17,500	55.00	NR

Memories of America by Grandma Moses

1980	BRINGING IN THE MAPLE SUGAR, Grandma Moses, 5,000 . . .	120.00	NR
1980	THE OLD AUTOMOBILE, Grandma Moses, 5,000	120.00	NR
1981	HALLOWEEN, Grandma Moses, 5,000	120.00	NR
1981	THE RAINBOW, Grandma Moses, 5,000	120.00	NR

Memories of the Western Prairies

1983	PICKING DAISIES, Rosemary Calder, 1 year	49.50	NR
1984	FEEDING THE COLT, Rosemary Calder, 1 year	49.50	NR

Mingolla Christmas

1977	WINTER WONDERLAND, Dominic Mingolla, 5,000	65.00	NR

Most Precious Gifts of Shen Lung

1981	FIRE, Sharleen Pederson, 19,500	49.00	NR
1981	WATER, Sharleen Pederson, 19,500	49.00	NR
1981	SUN, Sharleen Pederson, 19,500	49.00	NR
1981	MOON, Sharleen Pederson, 19,500	49.00	NR
1981	EARTH, Sharleen Pederson, 19,500	49.00	NR
1981	SKY, Sharleen Pederson, 19,500	49.00	NR

Promised Land

1979	PHARAOH'S DAUGHTER FINDS MOSES, Yiannis Koutsis, 24,500	45.00	NR
1979	THE BURNING BUSH, Yiannis Koutsis, 24,500	45.00	NR
1979	LET MY PEOPLE GO, Yiannis Koutsis, 24,500	45.00	NR

		Issue Price	Current Value
1979	THE PARTING OF THE RED SEA, Yiannis Koutsis, 24,500 .	45.00	NR
1980	MIRIAM'S SONG OF THANKSGIVING, Yiannis Koutsis, 24,500.	45.00	NR
1980	MANNA FROM HEAVEN, Yiannis Koutsis, 24,500	45.00	NR
1980	WATER FROM THE ROCK, Yiannis Koutsis, 24,500	45.00	NR
1980	THE BATTLE OF AMALEK, Yiannis Koutsis, 24,500	45.00	NR
1980	THE TEN COMMANDMENTS, Yiannis Koutsis, 24,500 . . .	45.00	NR
1980	THE GOLDEN CALF, Yiannis Koutsis, 24,500	45.00	NR
1980	MOSES SMASHES THE TABLET, Yiannis Koutsis, 24,500 .	45.00	NR
1980	THE GLORIOUS TABERNACLE, Yiannis Koutsis, 24,500 . . .	45.00	NR

Puppy's World

1982	FIRST BIRTHDAY, Rudy Droguett, 19,500	49.50	NR
1982	BEWARE OF DOG, Rudy Droguett, 19,500	49.50	NR
1982	TOP DOG, Rudy Droguett, 19,500	49.50	NR
1982	NEED A FRIEND?, Rudy Droguett, 19,500	49.50	NR
1982	DOUBLE TROUBLE, Rudy Droguett, 19,500	49.50	NR
1982	JUST CLOWNING, Rudy Droguett, 19,500	49.50	NR
1982	GUEST FOR DINNER, Rudy Droguett, 19,500	49.50	NR
1982	GIFT WRAPPED, Rudy Droguett, 19,500	49.50	NR

Remarkable World of Charles Dickens

1980	OLIVER TWIST AND FAGIN, Konrad Hack, 19,500	60.00	NR
1980	SCROOGE AND MARLEY'S GHOST, Konrad Hack, 19,500 .	60.00	NR
1980	BOB CRATCHIT AND TINY TIM, Konrad Hack, 19,500	60.00	NR
1980	DAVID COPPERFIELD AND GREAT–AUNT BETSY TROTWOOD, Konrad Hack, 19,500	60.00	NR
1980	MICAWBER DENOUNCING URIAH HEEP, Konrad Hack, 19,500	60.00	NR
1980	LITTLE NELL, Konrad Hack, 19,500	60.00	NR
1981	MADAME DEFARGE, Konrad Hack, 19,500	60.00	NR
1981	MR. PICKWICK AND FRIENDS, Konrad Hack, 19,500	60.00	NR
1981	NICHOLAS NICKLEBY, Konrad Hack, 19,500	60.00	NR
1982	LITTLE DORRIT, Konrad Hack, 19,500	60.00	NR
1982	BARKIS AND PEGGOTTY, Konrad Hack, 19,500	60.00	NR
1982	PIP AND MISS HAVISHAM, Konrad Hack, 19,500	60.00	NR

Treasures of Childhood

1979	MY CUDDLIES COLLECTION, Charlotte Jackson, 19,500. .	45.00	NR
1980	MY COIN COLLECTION, Charlotte Jackson, 19,500	45.00	NR
1980	MY SHELL COLLECTION, Charlotte Jackson, 19,500	45.00	NR
1980	MY STAMP COLLECTION, Charlotte Jackson, 19,500	45.00	NR
1980	MY DOLL COLLECTION, Charlotte Jackson, 19,500	45.00	NR
1980	MY ROCK COLLECTION, Charlotte Jackson, 19,500	45.00	NR

Two Thousand Years of Ships

1982	U.S.S. CONSTITUTION, Alan D'Estrehan	39.50	NR
1982	SANTA MARIA, Alan D'Estrehan.	39.50	NR

	Issue Price	Current Value
1983 MAYFLOWER, Alan D'Estrehan	39.50	NR
1983 DRAKAR, Alan D'Estrehan	39.50	NR
1983 CUTTY SARK THERMOPYLAE, Alan D'Estrehan	39.50	NR
1983 HMS ROYAL SOVEREIGN, Alan D'Estrehan	39.50	NR
1983 VASA, Alan D'Estrehan	39.50	NR
1983 HMS VICTORY, Alan D'Estrehan	39.50	NR
1983 ROYAL BARGE, Alan D'Estrehan	39.50	NR
1984 AMERICA, Alan D'Estrehan	39.50	NR
1984 GOLDEN HIND, Alan D'Estrehan	39.50	NR

Windows on the World

1980 THE GOLDEN GATE OF SAN FRANCISCO, Higgins Bond, 19,500	45.00	NR
1981 THE SNOW VILLAGE OF MADULAIN, Higgins Bond, 19,500 ...	45.00	NR
1981 RAINY DAY IN LONDON, Higgins Bond, 19,500	45.00	NR
1981 WATER FESTIVAL IN VENICE, Higgins Bond, 19,500	45.00	NR
1981 SPRINGTIME IN PARIS, Higgins Bond, 19,500	45.00	NR
1981 HARVESTIME IN THE UKRAINE, Higgins Bond, 19,500 ...	45.00	NR
1981 LUNCHTIME IN MICHELSTADT, Higgins Bond, 19,500 ...	45.00	NR
1981 FLAMENCO OF MADRID, Higgins Bond, 19,500	45.00	NR
1981 GREAT TUSKS OF THE SERENGETI, Higgins Bond, 19,500	45.00	NR
1981 CARNIVAL TIME IN RIO, Higgins Bond, 19,500	45.00	NR
1981 TOKYO AT CHERRY BLOSSOM TIME, Higgins Bond, 19,500	45.00	NR
1981 PALACE OF THE WINDS, JAIPUR, Higgins Bond, 19,500 .	45.00	\NR
1982 CARNIVAL TIME IN RIO, Higgins Bond, 19,500	45.00	\NR

ROYAL DELFT NETHERLANDS

Christmas (Large)

1915 CHRISTMAS BELLS, 1 year	2.25	6,250.00
1916 STAR–FLORAL DESIGN, 1 year	4.25	720.00
1916 CRADLE WITH CHILD, 1 year	4.25	370.00
1917 SHEPHERD, 1 year	6.00	450.00
1917 CHRISTMAS STAR, 1 year	4.25	290.00
1918 SHEPHERD, 1 year	7.50	375.00
1918 CHRISTMAS STAR, 1 year	5.50	275.00
1919 CHURCH, 1 year	12.50	400.00
1920 CHURCH TOWER, 1 year	12.50	390.00
1920 HOLLY WREATH, 1 year	7.50	290.00
1921 CANAL BOATMAN, 1 year	12.50	425.00
1921 CHRISTMAS STAR, 1 year	6.25	315.00
1922 LANDSCAPE, 1 year	10.00	425.00
1922 CHRISTMAS WREATH, 1 year	6.25	290.00
1923 SHEPHERD, 1 year	10.00	440.00
1924 CHRISTMAS STAR, 1 year	6.25	290.00

		Issue Price	Current Value
1924	SHEPHERD, 1 year	10.00	415.00
1925	TOWNGATE IN DELFT, 1 year	10.00	465.00
1925	CHRISTMAS STAR, 1 year	6.25	265.00
1926	WINDMILL LANDSCAPE, 1 year	12.50	465.00
1926	CHRISTMAS STAR, 1 year	6.25	290.00
1927	CHRISTMAS STAR, 1 year	6.25	300.00
1927	SAILBOAT, 1 year	10.00	475.00
1928	LIGHTHOUSE, 1 year	10.00	375.00
1928	CHRISTMAS POINSETTIA, 1 year	6.25	315.00
1929	CHRISTMAS BELL, 1 year	6.25	390.00
1929	SMALL DUTCH TOWN, 1 year	10.00	390.00
1930	CHURCH ENTRANCE, 1 year	10.00	350.00
1930	CHRISTMAS ROSE, 1 year	6.25	325.00
1931	CHRISTMAS STAR, 1 year	5.00	300.00
1931	SNOW LANDSCAPE, 1 year	8.00	375.00
1932	FIREPLACE, 1 year	8.00	440.00
1932	CHRISTMAS STAR, 1 year	5.00	390.00
1933	INTERIOR SCENE, 1 year	7.88	450.00
1934	INTERIOR SCENE, 1 year	7.75	475.00
1935	INTERIOR SCENE, 1 year	8.25	475.00
1936	INTERIOR SCENE, 1 year	8.25	490.00
1937	INTERIOR SCENE, 1 year	8.25	490.00
1938	INTERIOR SCENE, 1 year	8.25	485.00
1939	INTERIOR SCENE, 1 year	8.25	490.00
1940	CHRISTMAS TREE, 1 year	8.75	490.00
1941	INTERIOR SCENE, 1 year	8.75	440.00
1955	CHURCH TOWER, 200	24.00	440.00
1956	LANDSCAPE, 200	23.50	325.00
1957	LANDSCAPE, 225	23.50	325.00
1958	LANDSCAPE, 225	25.00	325.00
1959	LANDSCAPE, 250	26.25	325.00
1960	STREET IN DELFT, 250	25.00	350.00
1961	VILLAGE SCENE, 260	30.00	370.00
1962	TOWER IN LEEUWARDEN, 275	30.00	370.00
1963	TOWER IN ENKHUISEN, 275	35.00	370.00
1964	TOWER IN HOORN, 300	35.00	370.00
1965	CORN MILL IN RHOON, 300	35.00	370.00
1966	SNUFF MILL IN ROTTERDAM, 325	40.00	370.00
1967	TOWER IN AMSTERDAM 350	45.00	370.00
1968	TOWER IN AMSTERDAM, 350	60.00	365.00
1969	CHURCH IN UTRECHT, 400	60.00	340.00
1970	CATHEDRAL IN VEERE, 500	60.00	340.00
1971	"DOM" TOWER IN UTRECHT, 550	60.00	340.00
1972	CHURCH IN EDAM, 1,500	70.00	340.00
1973	"DE WAAG" IN ALKAMAR, 1,500	75.00	415.00
1974	KITCHEN IN HINDELOOPEN, 1,500	160.00	400.00
1975	FARMER IN LAREN, 1,500	250.00	390.00

		Issue Price	Current Value
1976	FARM IN STAPHORST, 1,500	220.00	375.00
1977	FARM IN SPAKENBURG, 1,500	277.00	370.00
1978	WINTER SKATING SCENE, 1,000	277.00	300.00
1979	CHRISTMAS RHENEN, 500	260.00	270.00
1980	WINTER SCENE, 500	245.00	260.00
1981	WINTER SCENE, 500	245.00	260.00
1982	WINTER SCENE, 500	245.00	NR
1983	EVENING TWILIGHT, 500	230.00	NR
1984	THE HOMECOMING, Jan Dessens, 500	230.00	NR
1985	CHURCH AT T'WOUDT, Mar de Bruijn, 500	270.00	NR
1986	ST. DIONYSIUS, Mar de Bruijn, 500	324.00	NR

Christmas (9")

		Issue Price	Current Value
1955	CHRISTMAS STAR, 1 year	11.75	175.00
1956	CHRISTMAS BELLS, 1 year	11.75	340.00
1957	FLOWER DESIGN, 1 year	11.75	140.00
1957	CHRISTMAS STAR, 1 year	12.25	140.00
1958	CHRISTMAS STAR, 1 year	12.25	140.00

Christmas (small)

		Issue Price	Current Value
1915	CHRISTMAS STAR, 1 year	1.50	3,630.00
1926	BELL TOWER, 1 year	3.00	225.00
1927	CHURCH TOWER, 1 year, 7"	3.00	300.00
1928	MILL, 1 year	3.00	325.00
1929	CHURCH SPIRE, 1 year	3.00	325.00
1930	SAILING BOAT, 1 year	3.00	225.00
1931	CHURCH TOWER, 1 year	3.00	300.00
1932	BELL TOWER, 1 year	3.00	300.00
1959	LANDSCAPE WITH MILL, 400	9.50	140.00
1960	LANDSCAPE, 400	11.25	170.00
1961	SNOW LANDSCAPE, 500	12.00	165.00
1962	TOWN VIEW, 500	12.00	165.00
1963	MILL IN ZEDDAM, 500	12.25	165.00
1964	TOWNGATE IN KAMPEN, 600	14.75	165.00
1966	TOWNGATE IN MEDEMBLIK, 600	14.75	165.00
1967	MILL IN HAZERSWOUDE, 700	16.75	165.00
1968	MILL IN SCHIEDAM, 700	18.00	165.00
1969	MILL NEAR GORKUM, 800	26.25	140.00
1970	MILL NEAR HAARLEM, 1,500	26.25	140.00
1971	TOWNGATE AT ZIERIKZEE, 3,500	30.00	140.00
1972	TOWNGATE AT ELBURG, 3,500	42.50	125.00
1973	TOWNGATE AT AMERSFOORT, 4,500	47.50	125.00
1974	WATERGATE AT SNEEK, 4,500	52.50	165.00
1975	TOWNGATE AT AMSTERDAM, 1,000	65.00	165.00
1976	TOWNGATE IN GORINCHEM, 4,500	72.50	165.00
1977	DROMEDARIS TOWER, 4,500	77.50	150.00

		Issue Price	Current Value
1978	CHRISTMAS FISHERMAN, 1,500	77.50	140.00
1979	GULF PLAYERS ON THE ICE, 1,000	97.50	130.00
1980	ICE SAILING, 1,000	117.50	130.00
1981	HORSE SLEDDING, 1,000	117.50	130.00
1982	ICE SKATING, 1,000	125.00	NR
1983	CAKE AND SOMETHING TO DRINK, 1,000	120.00	NR
1984	FIGURE SKATING, Jan Dessens, 1,000	120.00	NR
1985	THE FARMHOUSE, Mar de Bruijn, 1,000	140.00	NR
1986	FARMHOUSE, Mar de Bruijn, 1,000	168.00	NR

Easter

1973	DUTCH EASTER PALM, 3,500	75.00	150.00
1974	DUTCH EASTER PALM, 1,000	110.00	145.00
1975	DUTCH EASTER PALM, 1,000	125.00	180.00
1976	DUTCH EASTER PALM, 1,000	175.00	205.00

Father's Day

1972	FATHER AND SON, VOLENDAM, 1,500	40.00	75.00
1973	FATHER AND SON, HINDELOOPEN, 2,000	40.00	70.00
1974	FATHER AND SON, ZUID–BEVELAND, 1 year	80.00	105.00
1975	FATHER AND SON, SPAKENBURG, 1 year	140.00	BR

Mother's Day

1971	MOTHER AND DAUGHTER, VOLENDAM, 2,500	50.00	75.00
1972	MOTHER AND DAUGHTER, HINDELOOPEN, 2,500	40.00	80.00
1973	MOTHER AND DAUGHTER, MARKEN, 3,000	50.00	75.00
1974	MOTHER AND DAUGHTER, ZUID–BEVALAND, 1 year	80.00	100.00
1975	MOTHER AND DAUGHTER, SPAKENBURG, 1 year	100.00	120.00
1976	MOTHER AND DAUGHTER, SCHEVENINGEN, 1 year	115.00	125.00

Special Bicentenary

1976	GEORGE WASHINGTON, 2,500	350.00	NR
1976	EAGLE PLATE, 5,000	150.00	NR

Stars, Satellites and Space

1910	HALLEY'S COMET	22.50	750.00
1957	FIRST EARTH SATELLITE	22.50	90.00
1968	APOLLO 8	22.50	40.00
1969	APOLLO II	22.50	40.00
1974	SKYLAB AND COMET KOHOUTEK, 1,000	80.00	NR
1975	APOLLO SOYUZ	140.00	BR
1972	OLYMPIAD	70.00	BR

Valentine

1973	VALENTINE "ENDURING BEAUTY," 1,500	75.00	150.00

		Issue Price	Current Value
1974	VALENTINE, 1,000	125.00	135.00
1975	VALENTINE, 1,000	125.00	NR
1976	VALENTINE, 1,000	175.00	NR

Single Issue

1987	50TH WEDDING ANNIVERSARY OF PRINCESS JULIANA AND PRINCE BERNHARD, Mar de Bruijn, 500	337.50	350.00

ROYAL DEVON UNITED STATES

Norman Rockwell Christmas

1975	DOWNHILL DARING, Norman Rockwell, 1 year	24.50	30.00
1976	THE CHRISTMAS GIFT, Norman Rockwell, 1 year	24.50	35.00
1977	THE BIG MOMENT, Norman Rockwell, 1 year	27.50	50.00
1978	PUPPETS FOR CHRISTMAS, Norman Rockwell, 1 year ..	27.50	NR
1979	ONE PRESENT TOO MANY, Norman Rockwell, 1 year ...	31.50	NR
1980	GRAMPS MEETS GRAMPS, Norman Rockwell, 1 year ...	33.00	NR

Norman Rockwell Home of the Brave

1981	REMINISCING, Norman Rockwell, 18,000	35.00	75.00
1981	HERO'S WELCOME, Norman Rockwell, 18,000	35.00	50.00
1981	BACK TO HIS OLD JOB, Norman Rockwell, 18,000	35.00	NR
1981	WAR HERO, Norman Rockwell, 18,000	35.00	NR
1982	WILLIE GILLIS IN CHURCH, Norman Rockwell, 18,000 ...	35.00	NR
1982	WAR BOND, Norman Rockwell, 18,000	35.00	NR
1982	UNCLE SAM TAKES WINGS, Norman Rockwell, 18,000 ..	35.00	NR
1982	TAKING MOTHER OVER THE TOP, Norman Rockwell, 18,000 ..	35.00	NR

Norman Rockwell Mother's Day (The Hamilton Collection)

1975	DOCTOR AND DOLL, Norman Rockwell, 1 year	23.50	50.00
1976	PUPPY LOVE, Norman Rockwell, 1 year	24.50	75.00
1977	THE FAMILY, Norman Rockwell, 1 year	24.50	85.00
1978	MOTHER'S DAY OFF, Norman Rockwell, 1 year	27.00	35.00
1979	MOTHER'S EVENING OUT, Norman Rockwell, 1 year	30.00	NR
1980	MOTHER'S TREAT, Norman Rockwell, 1 year	32.50	NR

ROYAL DOULTON GREAT BRITAIN

All God's Children

1979	A BRIGHTER DAY, Lisette DeWinne, 10,000	60.00	75.00
1980	VILLAGE CHILDREN, Lisette DeWinne, 10,000	65.00	NR
1981	NOBLE HERITAGE, Lisette DeWinne, 10,000	85.00	NR
1982	BUDDIES, Lisette DeWinne, 10,000	85.00	NR
1983	MY LITTLE BROTHER, Lisette DeWinne, 10,000	95.00	NR

		Issue Price	Current Value
1984	SISTERLY LOVE, Lisette DeWinne, 10,000	95.00	NR

American Tapestries

1978	SLEIGH BELLS, C. A. Brown, 10,000	70.00	NR
1979	PUMPKIN PATCH, C. A. Brown, 10,000	70.00	NR
1980	GENERAL STORE, C. A. Brown, 10,000	95.00	NR
1981	FOURTH OF JULY, C. A. Brown, 10,000	95.00	NR

Annual Christmas

1983	SILENT NIGHT, Neil Faulkner	39.95	NR
1984	WHILE SHEPHERDS WATCHED THEIR FLOCKS BY NIGHT, Neil Faulkner	39.95	NR
1985	O, LITTLE TOWN OF BETHLEHEM, Neil Faulkner	39.95	NR
1986	WE SAW THREE SHIPS A–SAILING, Neil Faulkner	39.95	NR
1987	THE HOLLY AND THE IVY, Neil Faulkner	39.95	NR

Behind the Painted Masque

1982	PAINTED FEELINGS, Ben Black, 10,000	95.00	NR
1983	MAKE ME LAUGH, Ben Black, 10,000	95.00	NR

Beswick Christmas

1972	CHRISTMAS IN OLD ENGLAND, 15,000	35.00	NR
1973	CHRISTMAS IN MEXICO, 15,000	35.00	NR
1974	CHRISTMAS IN BULGARIA, 15,000	37.50	45.00
1975	CHRISTMAS IN NORWAY, 15,000	45.00	NR
1976	CHRISTMAS IN HOLLAND, 15,000	50.00	BR
1977	CHRISTMAS IN POLAND, 15,000	50.00	70.00
1978	CHRISTMAS IN AMERICA, 15,000	55.00	NR

Celebration of Faith

1982	ROSH HASHANAH, James Woods, 7,500	250.00	NR

Children of the Pueblo

1983	APPLE FLOWER, Mimi Jungbluth (She Cloud), 10,000	60.00	NR
1984	MORNING STAR, Mimi Jungbluth (She Cloud), 10,000	60.00	NR

Christmas Plates

1993	ROYAL DOULTON — TOGETHER FOR CHRISTMAS	45.00	RI
1993	ROYAL ALBERT — SLEIGH RIDE	45.00	RI

Commedia Dell' Arte

1974	HARLEQUIN, LeRoy Neiman, 15,000	50.00	80.00
1975	PIERROT, LeRoy Neiman, 15,000	60.00	75.00

Morning Star
Photo courtesy of *Collectors News*

Reunion
Photo courtesy of *Collectors News*

Gabriella

Michiko

Monika

Storytime

		Issue Price	Current Value
1977	COLUMBINE, LeRoy Neiman, 15,000	70.00	NR
1978	PUNCHINELLO, LeRoy Neiman, 15,000	70.00	NR

Encore
1985	GABRIELLA, Francisco Masseria, 10,000	95.00	NR

Family Christmas Plates
1991	DAD PLAYS SANTA, 1 year	60.00	NR

Festival Children of the World
1983	MARIANI, Brenda Bruke, 15,000	65.00	NR
1983	MICHICO, Brenda Bruke, 15,000	65.00	NR
1983	MAGDALENA, Brenda Bruke, 15,000	65.00	NR
1983	MONIKA, Brenda Bruke, 15,000	65.00	NR

Flower Garden
1975	SPRING HARMONY, Hahn Vidal, 15,000	60.00	80.00
1976	DREAMING LOTUS, Hahn Vidal, 15,000	65.00	90.00
1977	FROM THE POET'S GARDEN, Hahn Vidal, 15,000	70.00	NR
1978	COUNTRY BOUQUET, Hahn Vidal, 15,000	70.00	NR
1979	FROM MY MOTHER'S GARDEN, Hahn Vidal, 15,000	85.00	NR

Grandest Gift
1984	REUNION, MaGo, 10,000	75.00	NR

I Remember America
1977	PENNSYLVANIA PASTORALE, Eric Sloane, 15,000	70.00	90.00
1978	LOVE JOY BRIDGE, Eric Sloane, 15,000	70.00	80.00
1979	FOUR CORNERS, Eric Sloane, 15,000	75.00	NR
1980	MARSHLANDS, Eric Sloane, 15,000	95.00	BR

Jungle Fantasy
1980	THE ARK, Gustavo Novoa, 10,000	75.00	NR
1981	COMPASSION, Gustavo Novoa, 10,000	95.00	BR
1982	PATIENCE, Gustavo Novoa, 10,000	95.00	NR
1983	REFUGE, Gustavo Novoa, 10,000	95.00	NR

Leroy Neiman Special
1980	WINNING COLORS, Le Roy Neiman, 10,000	85.00	NR

Log of the Dashing Wave
1976	SAILING WITH THE TIDE, John Stobart, 15,000	65.00	120.00

		Issue Price	Current Value
1977	RUNNING FREE, John Stobart, 15,000	70.00	120.00
1978	ROUNDING THE HORN, John Stobart, 15,000	70.00	90.00
1979	HONG KONG, John Stobart, 15,000	75.00	90.00
1980	BORA BORA, John Stobart, 15,000	95.00	NR
1984	JOURNEY'S END, John Stobart, 15,000	95.00	NR

Mother and Child

		Issue Price	Current Value
1973	COLETTE AND CHILD, Edna Hibel, 15,000	40.00	460.00
1974	SAYURI AND CHILD, Edna Hibel, 15,000	40.00	165.00
1975	KRISTINA AND CHILD, Edna Hibel, 15,000	50.00	125.00
1976	MARILYN AND CHILD, Edna Hibel, 15,000	55.00	115.00
1977	LUCIA AND CHILD, Edna Hibel, 15,000	70.00	90.00
1982	KATHLEEN AND CHILD, Edna Hibel, 15,000	85.00	NR

Portraits of Innocence

		Issue Price	Current Value
1980	PANCHITO, Francisco Masseria, 15,000	75.00	200.00
1981	ADRIEN, Francisco Masseria, 15,000	85.00	125.00
1982	ANGELICA, Francisco Masseria, 15,000	95.00	110.00
1983	JULIANA, Francisco Masseria, 15,000	95.00	NR

Ports of Call

		Issue Price	Current Value
1975	SAN FRANCISCO, Doug Kingman, 15,000	60.00	90.00
1976	NEW ORLEANS, Doug Kingman, 15,000	65.00	80.00
1977	VENICE, Doug Kingman, 15,000	70.00	BR
1978	PARIS, Doug Kingman, 15,000	70.00	NR

Reflections on China

		Issue Price	Current Value
1976	GARDEN OF TRANQUILITY, Chen Chi, 15,000	70.00	90.00
1977	IMPERIAL PALACE, Chen Chi, 15,000	70.00	80.00
1978	TEMPLE OF HEAVEN, Chen Chi, 15,000	75.00	BR
1979	LAKE OF MISTS, Chen Chi, 15,000	85.00	NR

Victorian Childhood

		Issue Price	Current Value
1991	THE ORIGINAL "IN DISGRACE"	29.00	55.00
1991	BREAKFAST IN BED	29.00	70.00
1992	SAY, "PLEASE"	32.00	RI
1992	MY PRECIOUS BUNDLE	32.00	RI
1992	THE CONCERT	32.00	RI
1992	IN GOOD HANDS	34.00	RI
1992	TEMPTING FARE	34.00	RI
1992	A RIVAL ATTRACTION	34.00	RI

Victorian Christmas

		Issue Price	Current Value
1977	WINTER FUN, 1 year	25.00	55.00
1978	CHRISTMAS DAY, 1 year	25.00	NR

		Issue Price	Current Value
1979	SLEIGH RIDE, 1 year ..,,,.	29.95	NR
1980	SANTA'S VISIT, 1 year	42.00	NR
1981	CHRISTMAS CAROLERS, 1 year	37.50	NR
1982	CHRISTMAS, 1 year................................	39.95	NR

Single Issue

		Issue Price	Current Value
1981	COMMEMORATIVE WEDDING OF THE PRINCE OF WALES AND LADY DIANA SPENCER, 1,500	195.00	225.00

Juliana
Photo courtesy of *Collectors News*

The Original "In Disgrace"
Photo courtesy of *Collectors News*

ROYAL GRAFTON GEAT BRITAIN

Braithwaite Game Birds

		Issue Price	Current Value
1987	PHEASANTS IN FLIGHT	24.50	30.00
1987	RED–LEGGED PARTRIDGE	24.50	BR
1988	BLACK GROUSE	27.50	BR
1988	FLOCK OF PTARMIGAN.............................	27.50	NR
1988	QUAIL ON THE WING	27.50	NR
1988	CAPERCAILLIE	27.50	BR
1989	RED GROUSE	29.50	BR

Twelve Days of Christmas

		Issue Price	Current Value
1976	PARTRIDGE ON PEAR TREE, 3,000	17.50	NR
1977	TWO TURTLE DOVES, 3,000	17.50	NR
1978	THREE FRENCH HENS, 3,000	21.50	NR
1979	FOUR COLLY BIRDS, 3,000	26.50	NR

		Issue Price	Current Value
1980	FIVE GOLDEN RINGS, 3,000	35.00	NR

ROYAL LIMOGES FRANCE

Christmas

1972	NATIVITY, 5,000......................................	25.00	40.00
1973	THREE WISE MEN, 5,000	27.50	40.00

ROYAL OAKS LIMITED UNITED STATES

Love's Labor

1983	THE INTRUDER, James Landenberger, 15,000	50.00	NR

ROYAL ORLEANS UNITED STATES

Coca–Cola: The Classic Santa Claus

1983	GOOD BOYS AND GIRLS, Haddon Sundblom, 15,000.....	55.00	NR
1984	A GIFT FOR SANTA, Haddon Sundblom, 15,000	65.00	NR
1985	SANTA, PLEASE PAUSE HERE, Haddon Sundblom, 15,000	65.00	NR

Dynasty

1986	KRYSTLE, Shell Fisher	35.00	NR

Elvis in Concert

1984	ALOHA FROM HAWAII, Rick Grimes, 20,000	35.00	NR
1985	LAS VEGAS, Rick Grimes, 20,000......................	35.00	NR

Famous Movies

1985	CAT ON A HOT TIN ROOF, Rick Grimes, 20,000	35.00	NR

Marilyn — An American Classic

1983	THE SEVEN YEAR ITCH, Twentieth Century–Fox, 20,000 ..	35.00	NR
1984	GENTLEMEN PREFER BLONDES, Twentieth Century–Fox, 20,000	35.00	NR
1985	NIAGARA, Twentieth Century–Fox, 20,000..............	35.00	NR

Nostalgic Magazine Covers

1983	LADIES' HOME JOURNAL, Hayden Hayden, 12,500	35.00	NR

Pink Panther Christmas Collection

1982	SLEIGH RIDE, D. DePatie, 10,000	18.50	NR

		Issue Price	Current Value
1983	HAPPY LANDINGS, D. DePatie, 10,000	18.50	NR
1984	DOWN THE CHIMNEY, D. DePatie, 10,000	18.50	NR
1985	PASS THE BLAST, D. DePatie, 10,000	18.50	NR

In Trompe L'Oeil

1984	UP TO MISCHIEF, Carol Eytinge, 10,000	25.00	NR

TV

1983	THE M*A*S*H* PLATE, J. LaBonte, 1 year	25.00	NR
1983	DYNASTY, Shell Fisher,1 year	35.00	NR

Yorkshire Brontes

1984	WUTHERING HEIGHTS, 30 days	35.00	NR
1985	JANE EYRE, 30 days	35.00	NR

Ladies' Home Journal
Photo courtesy of *Collectors News*

ROYAL PORCELAIN — KINGDOM OF THAILAND THAILAND

Love Story of Siam

1991	THE BETROTHAL	29.92	NR
1991	THE MAGIC BOW..................................	29.92	50.00
1991	THE WEDDING DANCE	32.92	60.00
1992	THE CORONATION PREPARATIONS	32.92	RI
1992	THE EXILE	32.92	RI
1992	THE RETURN TO THE THRONE	32.92	RI

ROYAL PRINCESS

		Issue Price	Current Value
Christmas			
1973	THREE WISE MEN	10.00	NR

ROYAL TETTAU GERMANY

Christmas

1972	CARRIAGE IN THE VILLAGE	12.50	NR

Papal Series

1971	POPE PAUL VI, 5,000	100.00	175.00
1972	POPE JOHN XXIII, 5,000	100.00	150.00
1973	POPE PIUS XII, 5,000	100.00	125.00

ROYALWOOD UNITED STATES

Leyendecker

1978	CORNFLAKE BOY, J. C. Leyendecker, 10,000	25.00	NR
1978	CORNFLAKE GIRL, J. C. Leyendecker, 10,000	25.00	NR

Single Issue

1977	DOCTOR AND DOLL, Norman Rockwell, 1 year	21.50	NR

ROYAL WORCESTER GREAT BRITAIN

American History

1977	WASHINGTON'S INAUGURATION, 1,250	65.00	300.00

Audubon Birds

1977	WARBLER AND JAY, 5,000, set of 2	150.00	NR
1978	KINGBIRD AND SPARROW, 10,000, set of 2	150.00	NR

Doughty Birds

1972	REDSTART AND BEECH, D. Doughty, 2,750	150.00	NR
1973	MYRTLE WARBLER AND CHERRY, D. Doughty, 3,000	175.00	NR
1974	BLUE–GREY GNATCATCHERS, D. Doughty, 3,000	195.00	210.00
1975	BLACKBURNIAN WARBLER, D. Doughty, 3,000	195.00	NR
1976	BLUE–WINGED SIVAS AND BAMBOO, D. Doughty, 3,000	195.00	NR
1977	PARADISE WYDAH, D. Doughty, 3,000	195.00	NR
1978	BLUETITS AND WITCH HAZEL, D. Doughty, 3,000	195.00	NR
1979	MOUNTAIN BLUEBIRD AND PINE, D. Doughty, 3,000	195.00	NR

		Issue Price	Current Value

1980	CERULEAN WARBLERS AND BEECH, D. Doughty, 3,000..	315.00	NR
1981	WILLOW WARBLER, D. Doughty, 3,000	315.00	NR
1982	RUBY–CROWNED KINGLETS, D. Doughty, 3,000	330.00	NR
1983	WREN AND JASMINE, D. Doughty, 3,000	330.00	NR

English Christmas

1979	CHRISTMAS EVE, 1 year	60.00	NR
1980	CHRISTMAS MORNING, Ewnece, 1 year	65.00	NR
1980	CHRISTMAS DAY	70.00	NR

Fabulous Birds

| 1976 | PEACOCKS, 10,000 | 65.00 | NR |
| 1978 | PEACOCKS II, 10,000 | 65.00 | NR |

Kitten Classics

1985	CAT NAP, P. Cooper, 14 days	29.50	NR
1985	PURRFECT TREASURE, P. Cooper, 14 days	29.50	NR
1985	WILD FLOWER, P. Cooper, 14 days	29.50	NR
1985	BIRDWATCHER, P. Cooper, 14 days	29.50	NR
1985	TIGER'S FANCY, P. Cooper, 14 days	29.50	NR
1985	COUNTRY KITTY, P. Cooper, 14 days	29.50	NR
1985	LITTLE RASCAL, P. Cooper, 14 days	29.50	NR
1985	FIRST PRIZE, P. Cooper, 14 days	29.50	NR

Kitten Encounters

1987	FISHFUL THINKING, P. Cooper, 14 days	29.50	45.00
1987	PUPPY PAL, P. Cooper, 14 days	29.50	NR
1987	JUST DUCKY, P. Cooper, 14 days	29.50	NR
1987	BUNNY CHASE, P. Cooper, 14 days	29.50	NR
1987	FLUTTER BY, P. Cooper, 14 days	29.50	NR
1987	BEDTIME BUDDIES, P. Cooper, 14 days	29.50	NR
1988	CAT AND MOUSE, P. Cooper, 14 days	29.50	NR
1988	STABLEMATES, P. Cooper, 14 days	29.50	50.00

Water Birds of North America

1985	MALLARDS, J. Cooke, 15,000	55.00	NR
1985	CANVASBACKS, J. Cooke, 15,000	55.00	NR
1985	WOOD DUCKS, J. Cooke, 15,000	55.00	NR
1985	SNOW GEESE, J. Cooke, 15,000	55.00	NR
1985	AMERICAN PINTAILS, J. Cooke, 15,000	55.00	NR
1985	GREEN–WINGED TEALS, J. Cooke, 15,000	55.00	NR
1985	HOODED MERGANSERS, J. Cooke, 15,000	55.00	NR
1985	CANADA GEESE, J. Cooke, 15,000	55.00	NR

ROYAL WORCESTER UNITED STATES

Birth of a Nation

		Issue Price	Current Value
1972	BOSTON TEA PARTY, Prescott W. Baston, 10,000	45.00	275.00
1973	THE RIDE OF PAUL REVERE, Prescott W. Baston, 10,000 .	45.00	250.00
1974	INCIDENT AT CONCORD BRIDGE, Prescott W. Baston, 10,000 .	50.00	120.00
1975	SIGNING THE DECLARATION OF INDEPENDENCE, Prescott W. Baston, 10,000	65.00	125.00
1976	WASHINGTON CROSSING THE DELAWARE, Prescott W. Baston, 10,000...	65.00	125.00
1977	WASHINGTON'S INAUGURATION, 1,250..............	65.00	275.00

Currier & Ives

1974	ROAD IN WINTER, 10,000............................	59.50	NR
1975	OLD GRIST MILL, 10,000	59.50	NR
1976	WINTER PASTIME, 10,000	59.50	NR

Single Issue

1976	SPIRIT OF 1776, 10,000	65.00	NR

ROYALE GERMANY

Christmas

1969	CHRISTMAS FAIR, 6,000	12.00	60.00
1970	VIGIL MASS, 10,000	13.00	30.00
1971	CHRISTMAS NIGHT, 8,000	14.00	35.00
1972	ELKS, 8,000	16.00	40.00
1973	CHRISTMAS DAWN, 6,000	20.00	30.00
1974	VILLAGE CHRISTMAS, 5,000	22.00	30.00
1975	FEEDING TIME, 5,000................................	26.00	NR
1976	SEAPORT CHRISTMAS, 5,000	27.50	NR
1977	SLEDDING, 5,000	30.00	NR

Father's Day

1970	U.S. FRIGATE CONSTITUTION, 5,000	13.00	60.00
1971	MAN FISHING, 5,000	13.00	35.00
1972	MOUNTAINEER, 5,000	16.00	50.00
1973	CAMPING, 4,000....................................	18.00	25.00
1974	EAGLE, 2,500	22.00	35.00
1975	REGATTA, 2,500....................................	26.00	NR
1976	HUNTING, 2,500	27.50	NR
1977	FISHING, 2,500	30.00	NR

Game Plates

1972	SETTERS, J. Poluszynski, 500........................	180.00	200.00

		Issue Price	Current Value
1973	FOX, J. Poluszynski, 500 ...., ...	200.00	250.00
1974	OSPREY, J. Poluszynski, 250	250.00	NR
1975	CALIFORNIA QUAIL, J. Poluszynski, 250	265.00	NR

Mother's Day

1970	SWAN AND YOUNG, 6,000	12.00	80.00
1971	DOE AND FAWN, 9,000	13.00	55.00
1972	RABBITS, 9,000	16.00	40.00
1973	OWL FAMILY, 6,000	18.00	40.00
1974	DUCK AND YOUNG, 5,000	22.00	30.00
1975	LYNX AND CUBS, 5,000	26.00	NR
1976	WOODCOCK AND YOUNG, 5,000	27.50	NR
1977	KOALA BEAR, 5,000	30.00	NR

Single Issue

1969	APOLLO MOON LANDING, 2,000	30.00	80.00

ROYALE GERMANIA GERMANY

Christmas Annual

1970	ORCHID, 600	200.00	650.00
1971	CYCLAMEN, 1,000	200.00	325.00
1972	SILVER THISTLE, 1,000	250.00	290.00
1973	TULIPS, 600	275.00	310.00
1974	SUNFLOWERS, 500	300.00	320.00
1975	SNOWDROPS, 350	350.00	425.00
1976	FLAMING HEART, 350	450.00	NR

Mother's Day Crystal

1971	ROSES, 250	135.00	650.00
1972	ELEPHANT AND YOUNGSTER, 750	180.00	250.00
1973	KOALA BEAR AND CUB, 600	200.00	225.00
1974	SQUIRRELS, 500	240.00	250.00
1975	SWAN AND YOUNG, 350	350.00	360.00

JOHN A. RUTHVEN UNITED STATES

Moments of Nature

1980	SCREECH OWLS, John Ruthven, 5,000	39.50	NR
1980	CALIFORNIA QUAIL, John Ruthven, 5,000	39.50	NR
1981	CHICKADEES, John Ruthven, 5,000	39.50	NR

SABINO FRANCE

Annual Crystal		Issue Price	Current Value
1970	KING HENRY IV AND MARIA DE MEDICI, 1,500	65.00	75.00
1971	MILO AND THE BEASTS, 1,500	65.00	75.00

SANGO JAPAN

Christmas

1974	SPARK OF CHRISTMAS, Marvin Nye, 5,000	25.00	NR
1975	CHRISTMAS EVE IN COUNTRY, Marvin Nye, 5,000	27.50	NR
1976	MADONNA AND CHILD, Marvin Nye, 5,000	25.00	NR
1976	UNDESIRED SLUMBER, Marvin Nye, 7,500	25.00	55.00
1977	TOGETHERNESS, Marvin Nye, 7,500	25.00	40.00

Living American Artists

1976	SWEETHEARTS, Norman Rockwell, 10,000	30.00	60.00
1977	APACHE GIRL, Gregory Perillo, 5,000	35.00	290.00
1978	NATURAL HABITAT, 5,000	40.00	NR

Mother's Day

1976	SPRING DELIGHT, Leslie De Mille, 7,500	20.00	NR
1977	BROKEN WINGS, Leslie De Mille, 5,000	22.50	NR

SANTA CLARA SPAIN

Christmas

1970	CHRISTMAS MESSAGE, 10,000	18.00	40.00
1971	THREE WISE MEN, 10,000	18.00	35.00
1972	CHILDREN ON WOODS PATH, 10,000	20.00	40.00
1974	ARCHANGEL, 5,000	25.00	50.00
1974	SPIRIT OF CHRISTMAS, 5,000	25.00	NR
1975	CHRISTMAS EVE, 5,000	27.50	35.00
1976	MADONNA AND CHILD, 5,000	25.00	35.00
1977	MOTHER AND CHILD, 10,000	27.50	35.00
1978	ANGEL WITH FLOWERS, 10,000	32.00	NR
1979	MADONNA AND ANGELS, 10,000	34.50	NR

Mother's Day

1971	MOTHER AND CHILD, 10,000	12.00	30.00
1972	MOTHER AND CHILDREN, 12,000	12.00	40.00

SARAH'S ATTIC

Classroom Memories

		Issue Price	Current Value
1991	CLASSROOM MEMORIES, closed	80.00	NR

SARNA INDIA

Christmas

1975	HOLY FAMILY, 4,000	17.50	NR

SCHMID GERMANY

Beatrix Potter

1978	PETER RABBIT, Beatrix Potter, 5,000	50.00	NR
1979	JEMIMA PUDDLEDUCK, Beatrix Potter, 5,000	50.00	NR
1980	TALE OF BENJAMIN BUNNY, Beatrix Potter, 5,000	50.00	NR

Berta Hummel Christmas

1971	ANGEL, Berta Hummel, 1 year	15.00	NR
1972	ANGEL WITH FLUTE, Berta Hummel, 1 year	15.00	BR
1973	NATIVITY, Berta Hummel, 1 year	15.00	60.00
1974	GUARDIAN ANGEL, Berta Hummel, 1 year	18.50	BR
1975	CHRISTMAS CHILD, Berta Hummel, 1 year	25.00	BR
1976	SACRED JOURNEY, Berta Hummel, 1 year	27.50	BR
1977	HERALD ANGEL, Berta Hummel, 1 year	27.50	BR
1978	HEAVENLY TRIO, Berta Hummel, 1 year	32.50	BR
1979	STARLIGHT ANGEL, Berta Hummel, 1 year	38.00	BR
1980	PARADE INTO TOYLAND, Berta Hummel, 1 year	45.00	BR
1981	A TIME TO REMEMBER, Berta Hummel, 1 year	45.00	BR

A Message from Above
Photo courtesy of *Collectors News*

		Issue Price	Current Value
1982	ANGELIC PROCESSION, Berta Hummel, 1 year	45.00	BR
1983	ANGELIC MESSENGER, Berta Hummel, 1 year	45.00	BR
1984	A GIFT FROM HEAVEN, Berta Hummel, 1 year	45.00	BR
1985	HEAVENLY LIGHT, Berta Hummel, 1 year	45.00	BR
1986	TELL THE HEAVENS, Berta Hummel, 1 year	45.00	BR
1987	ANGELIC GIFTS, Berta Hummel, 1 year	47.50	NR
1988	CHEERFUL CHERUBS, Berta Hummel, 1 year	53.00	NR
1989	ANGELIC MUSICIAN, Berta Hummel, 1 year	53.00	BR
1990	ANGEL'S LIGHT, Berta Hummel, 1 year	53.00	BR
1991	A MESSAGE FROM ABOVE, Berta Hummel, 1 year	60.00	NR
1992	SWEET BLESSINGS, Berta Hummel, 1 year	65.00	RI

Berta Hummel Mother's Day

1972	PLAYING HOOKY, Berta Hummel, 1 year	15.00	NR
1973	LITTLE FISHERMEN, Berta Hummel, 1 year	15.00	35.00
1974	BUMBLEBEE, Berta Hummel, 1 year	18.50	NR
1975	MESSAGE OF LOVE, Berta Hummel, 1 year	25.00	NR
1976	DEVOTION TO MOTHER, Berta Hummel, 1 year	27.50	NR
1977	MOONLIGHT RETURN, Berta Hummel, 1 year	27.50	NR
1978	AFTERNOON STROLL, Berta Hummel, 1 year	32.50	NR
1979	CHERUB'S GIFT, Berta Hummel, 1 year	38.00	NR
1989	MOTHER'S LITTLE HELPERS, Berta Hummel, 1 year	45.00	55.00
1981	PLAYTIME, Berta Hummel, 1 year	45.00	55.00
1982	THE FLOWER BASKET, Berta Hummel, 1 year	45.00	NR
1983	SPRING BOUQUET, Berta Hummel, 1 year	45.00	55.00
1984	A JOY TO SHARE, Berta Hummel, 1 year	45.00	NR
1985	A MOTHER'S JOURNEY, Berta Hummel, 1 year	45.00	NR
1986	HOME FROM SCHOOL, Berta Hummel, 1 year	45.00	55.00

A Joy to Share
Photo courtesy of *Collectors News*

Young Reader
Photo courtesy of *Collectors News*

	Issue Price	Current Value
1987 MOTHER'S LITTLE LEARNER, Berta Hummel, 1 year.....	47.50	NR
1988 YOUNG READER, Berta Hummel, 1 year	52.50	80.00
1989 PRETTY AS A PICTURE, Berta Hummel, 1 year..........	53.00	75.00
1990 MOTHER'S LITTLE ATHLETE, Berta Hummel, 1 year	53.00	NR
1991 SOFT AND GENTLE, Berta Hummel, 1 year	55.00	NR

Carousel Fantasies

1983 A FAIRY TALE PRINCESS, Jessica Zemsky and Jack Hines, 7,500	50.00	NR

Davis Cat Tales

1982 RIGHT CHURCH WRONG PEW, Lowell Davis, 12,500.....	37.50	95.00
1982 COMPANY'S COMING, Lowell Davis,12,500	37.50	85.00
1983 ON THE MOVE, Lowell Davis, 12,500	37.50	75.00
1983 FLEW THE COOP, Lowell Davis, 12,500	37.50	75.00

Davis Country Christmas Annual

1983 HOOKER AT MAILBOX WITH PRESENT, Lowell Davis, 7,500 ..	45.00	90.00
1984 COUNTRY CHRISTMAS, Lowell Davis, 7,500	45.00	NR
1985 CHRISTMAS AT FOXFIRE FARM, Lowell Davis, 7,500	45.00	NR
1986 CHRISTMAS AT RED OAK, Lowell Davis, 7,500..........	45.00	NR
1987 BLOSSOM'S GIFT, Lowell Davis, 7,500	45.00	NR
1988 CUTTING THE FAMILY CHRISTMAS TREE, Lowell Davis, 7,500	47.50	75.00
1989 PETER AND THE WREN, Lowell Davis, 7,500	47.50	75.00
1990 WINTERING DEER, Lowell Davis, 7,500	47.50	NR
1991 CHRISTMAS AT RED OAK II, Lowell Davis, 7,500	55.00	NR
1992 BORN ON A STARRY NIGHT, Lowell Davis, 7,500	55.00	RI
1993 WAITING FOR MR. LOWELL, Lowell Davis, 7,500	55.00	RI

Christmas at Red Oak II
Photo courtesy of *Collectors News*

	Issue Price	Current Value

Davis Country Pride

1980	SURPRISE IN THE CELLAR, Lowell Davis, 7,500	35.00	150.00
1981	PLUM TUCKERED OUT, Lowell Davis, 7,500	35.00	100.00
1981	DUKE'S MIXTURE, Lowell Davis, 7,500	35.00	110.00
1981	BUSTIN' WITH PRIDE, Lowell Davis, 7,500	35.00	80.00

Davis Red Oak Sampler

1986	GENERAL STORE, Lowell Davis, 5,000	45.00	85.00
1987	COUNTRY WEDDING, Lowell Davis, 5,000	45.00	75.00
1989	COUNTRY SCHOOL, Lowell Davis, 5,000	45.00	NR
1990	BLACKSMITH SHOP, Lowell Davis, 5,000	52.50	NR

Davis Special Edition Plates

1983	THE CRITICS, Lowell Davis, 12,500	45.00	80.00
1984	GOOD OLE DAYS PRIVY SET II, Lowell Davis, 5,000	60.00	155.00
1986	HOME FROM MARKET, Lowell Davis, 7,500	55.00	120.00

Ferrandiz Beautiful Bounty

1982	SUMMER'S GOLDEN HARVEST, Juan Ferrandiz, 10,000 . .	40.00	NR
1982	AUTUMN BLESSING, Juan Ferrandiz, 10,000	40.00	NR
1982	A MIDWINTER'S DREAM, Juan Ferrandiz, 10,000	40.00	NR
1982	SPRING BLOSSOMS, Juan Ferrandiz, 10,000	40.00	NR

Ferrandiz Mother and Child

1977	ORCHARD MOTHER AND CHILD, Juan Ferrandiz, 10,000 .	65.00	NR
1978	PASTORAL MOTHER AND CHILD, Juan Ferrandiz, 10,000	75.00	NR
1979	FLORAL MOTHER, Juan Ferrandiz, 10,000	95.00	NR
1979	AVIAN MOTHER AND CHILD, Juan Ferrandiz, 10,000	100.00	NR

Ferrandiz Music Makers

1981	THE FLUTIST, Juan Ferrandiz, 10,000	25.00	NR
1981	THE ENTERTAINER, Juan Ferrandiz, 10,000	25.00	NR
1982	MAGICAL MEDLEY, Juan Ferrandiz, 10,000	25.00	NR
1982	SWEET SERENADE, Juan Ferrandiz, 10,000	25.00	NR

Ferrandiz Porcelain Christmas

1972	CHRIST IN THE MANGER, Juan Ferrandiz, 2,500	35.00	200.00
1973	CHRISTMAS, Juan Ferrandiz	40.00	225.00
1974	HOLY NIGHT, Juan Ferrandiz, 1 year	50.00	100.00
1975	FLIGHT INTO EGYPT, Juan Ferrandiz, 1 year	60.00	95.00
1976	TREE OF LIFE, Juan Ferrandiz, 1 year	60.00	NR
1976	MARY AND JOSEPH, Juan Ferrandiz, 1 year	60.00	199.00
1978	LEADING THE WAY, Juan Ferrandiz, 4,000	77.50	180.00
1979	THE DRUMMER, Juan Ferrandiz, 4,000	120.00	175.00
1980	REJOICE, Juan Ferrandiz, 4,000	150.00	160.00
1981	SPREADING THE WORD, Juan Ferrandiz, 4,000	150.00	NR

		Issue Price	Current Value
1982	THE SHEPHERD FAMILY, Juan Ferrandiz, 4,000	150.00	NR
1983	PEACE ATTEND THEE, Juan Ferrandiz, 4,000	150.00	NR

Ferrandiz Wooden Birthday

1972	BOY, Juan Ferrandiz, 1 year	15.00	70.00
1972	GIRL, Juan Ferrandiz, 1 year	15.00	70.00
1973	BOY, Juan Ferrandiz, 1 year	20.00	85.00
1973	GIRL, Juan Ferrandiz, 1 year	20.00	75.00
1974	BOY, Juan Ferrandiz, 1 year	22.00	75.00
1974	GIRL, Juan Ferrandiz, 1 year	22.00	75.00

Ferrandiz Wooden Jubilee

1979	SPRING DANCE, Juan Ferrandiz, 2,500	500.00	NR
1982	RIDING THRU THE RAIN, Juan Ferrandiz, 2,500	550.00	NR

Friends of Mine

1989	SUN WORSHIPPERS, Lowell Davis, 7,500	53.00	NR
1990	SUNDAY AFTERNOON TREAT, Lowell Davis, 7,500	53.00	NR
1991	WARM MILK, Lowell Davis, 7,500	55.00	NR
1992	CAT AND JENNY WREN, Lowell Davis, 7,500	55.00	RI

Gift of Happiness

1984	LILIES OF THE FIELD, Pati Bannister, 7,500	125.00	NR
1984	MORNING GLORIES, Juan Ferrandiz, 2,500	125.00	NR

Golden Moments

1978	TRANQUILITY, 15,000	250.00	NR
1981	SERENITY, 15,000	250.00	NR

Good Ol' Days

1984	WHEN MINUTES SEEM LIKE HOURS, Lowell Davis, 5,000	—	—
1984	WAITING FOR HIS MASTER, Lowell Davis, 5,000	—	—
	Set of 2	60.00	NR

Littlest Night

1993	THE LITTLEST NIGHT, Berta Hummel, 1 year	25.00	RI

My Name Is Star

1981	STAR'S SPRING, Jessica Zemsky, 10,000	30.00	NR
1981	STAR'S SUMMER, Jessica Zemsky, 10,000	30.00	NR
1982	STAR'S AUTUMN, Jessica Zemsky, 10,000	30.00	NR
1982	STAR'S WINTER, Jessica Zemsky, 10,000	30.00	NR

Pen Pals

		Issue Price	Current Value
1993	THE OLD HOME PLACE, Lowell Davis, 5,000	50.00	RI

Prairie Women

1982	THE MAIDEN, Jack Hines, 12,500	35.00	NR
1982	THE COURTSHIP BLANKET, Jack Hines, 12,500	35.00	NR
1982	MOTHER NOW, Jack Hines, 12,500....................	35.00	NR
1982	THE PASSING OF THE MOONS, Jack Hines, 12,500	35.00	NR

Reflections of Life

1980	QUIET REFLECTIONS, Juan Ferrandiz, 10,000	85.00	NR
1981	TREE OF LIFE, Juan Ferrandiz, 10,000	85.00	NR

Schmid Crystal Desevres

1978	THE SEA, 1,500	60.00	NR
1979	THE SKY, 1,500	80.00	NR
1980	THE EARTH, 1,500...................................	90.00	NR

Schmid Design

1971	FAMILY PORTRAIT, 5,000.............................	13.00	NR
1972	ON HORSEBACK, 5,000	15.00	NR
1973	BRINGING HOME TREE, 5,000	20.00	NR
1974	DECORATING TREE, 5,000............................	25.00	NR
1975	OPENING PRESENTS, 5,000	27.00	NR
1976	BY FIRESIDE, 5,000.................................	28.50	NR
1977	SKATING, 5,000....................................	28.50	NR
1978	FAMILY PICKING TREE, 5,000.........................	36.00	NR
1979	BREAKFAST BY TREE, 5,000	45.00	NR
1980	FEEDING ANIMALS, 5,000	55.00	NR

Schmid Father's Day

1975	BAVARIAN FATHER'S DAY	27.50	NR

Schmid Pewter Christmas Plates

1977	SANTA, 6,000	50.00	NR
1978	BEAUTIFUL SNOW, 6,000............................	50.00	NR
1979	I HEAR AMERICA SING, 6,000........................	50.00	NR
1980	A COUNTRY SLEIGH RIDE, 6,000	50.00	NR

Single Issues

1983	THE CRITICS, Lowell Davis, 12,500	45.00	65.00
1983	CHRISTMAS KINGDOM, Juan Ferrandiz, 10,000	45.00	NR
1986	HOME FROM MARKET, Lowell Davis, 7,000.............	55.00	NR

SCHMID JAPAN

Disney Annual

		Issue Price	Current Value
1983	SNEAK PREVIEW, Disney Studios, 20,000	22.50	NR
1984	COMMAND PERFORMANCE, Disney Studios, 20,000	22.50	NR
1985	SNOW BIZ, Disney Studios, 20,000	22.50	NR
1986	TREE FOR TWO, Disney Studios, 20,000	22.50	NR
1987	MERRY MOUSE MEDLEY, Disney Studios, 20,000........	25.00	NR
1988	WARM WINTER RIDE, Disney Studios, 20,000	25.00	NR
1989	MERRY MICKEY CLAUS, Disney Studios, 20,000	32.50	60.00
1990	HOLLY JOLLY CHRISTMAS, Disney Studios, 20,000	32.50	NR
1991	MICKEY AND MINNIE'S ROCKIN' CHRISTMAS, Disney Studios, 20,000	37.00	NR

Disney Bicentennial

1976	BICENTENNIAL PLATE, Disney Studios	13.00	NR

Disney Christmas

1973	SLEIGH RIDE, Disney Studios, 1 year	10.00	275.00
1974	DECORATING THE TREE, Disney Studios, 1 year	10.00	70.00
1975	CAROLING, Disney Studios, 1 year	12.50	NR
1976	BUILDING A SNOWMAN, Disney Studios, 1 year	13.00	NR
1977	DOWN THE CHIMNEY, Disney Studios, 1 year	13.00	20.00
1978	NIGHT BEFORE CHRISTMAS, Disney Studios, 1 year	15.00	25.00
1979	SANTA'S SURPRISE, Disney Studios, 15,000	17.50	30.00
1980	SLEIGH RIDE, Disney Studios, 15,000	17.50	35.00
1981	HAPPY HOLIDAYS, Disney Studios, 15,000	17.50	25.00
1982	WINTER GAMES, Disney Studios, 15,000	18.50	25.00

Disney Four Seasons of Love

1983	TICKETS ON THE FIFTY YARD LINE, Disney Studios, 10,000	17.50	NR
1983	LET IT SNOW, Disney Studios, 10,000.................	17.50	NR
1983	SPRING BOUQUET, 10,000	17.50	NR
1983	SHADES OF SUMMER, 10,000	17.50	NR

Disney Mother's Day

1974	FLOWERS FOR MOTHER, Disney Studios, 1 year	10.00	45.00
1975	SNOW WHITE AND DWARFS, Disney Studios, 1 year ...	12.50	50.00
1976	MINNIE MOUSE, Disney Studios, 1 year	13.00	25.00
1977	PLUTO'S PALS, Disney Studios, 1 year	13.00	20.00
1978	FLOWERS FOR BAMBI, Disney Studios, 1 year	15.00	40.00
1979	HAPPY FEET, Disney Studios, 10,000..................	17.50	NR
1980	MINNIE'S SURPRISE, Disney Studios, 10,000...........	17.50	30.00
1981	PLAYMATES, Disney Studios, 10,000	17.50	35.00
1982	A DREAM COME TRUE, Disney Studios, 10,000	18.50	40.00

Disney Special Edition

		Issue Price	Current Value
1978	MICKEY MOUSE AT FIFTY, Disney Studios, 15,000	25.00	80.00
1980	HAPPY BIRTHDAY PINOCCHIO, Disney Studios, 7,500	17.50	45.00
1981	ALICE IN WONDERLAND, Disney Studios, 7,500	17.50	NR
1982	HAPPY BIRTHDAY PLUTO, Disney Studios, 7,500	17.50	40.00
1982	GOOFY'S GOLDEN JUBILEE, Disney Studios, 7,500	18.50	30.00
1987	SNOW WHITE GOLDEN ANNIVERSARY, Disney Studios, 5,000	47.50	NR
1988	MICKEY MOUSE AND MINNIE MOUSE 60TH, Disney Studios, 10,000	50.00	110.00
1989	SLEEPING BEAUTY 30TH ANNIVERSARY, Disney Studios, 5,000	80.00	95.00
1990	FANTASIA — SORCERER'S APPRENTICE, Disney Studios, 5,000	59.00	80.00
1990	PINOCCHIO'S FRIEND, Disney Studios, 1 year	25.00	NR
1990	FANTASIA RELIEF PLATE, Disney Studios, 20,000	25.00	40.00

Disney Valentine's Day

1979	HANDS AND HEART, Disney Studio, 1 year	17.50	NR
1981	BE MINE, Disney Studios, 1 year	17.50	NR
1982	PICNIC FOR TWO, Disney Studios, 1 year	17.50	NR

Golden Anniversary

1987	SNOW WHITE AND THE SEVEN DWARFS, Disney Studios, 5,000	47.50	NR

Kitty Cucumber Annual

1989	RING AROUND THE ROSIE, M. Lillemoe, 20,000	25.00	45.00
1990	SWAN LAKE, M. Lillemoe, 20,000	25.00	45.00
1991	TEA PARTY, M. Lillemoe, 2,500	25.00	45.00
1992	DANCE 'ROUND THE MAYPOLE, M. Lillemoe, 2,500	25.00	RI

Nature's Treasures

1984	TULIP NEST — ROBIN, Mitsuko Gerhart, 5,000	45.00	NR
1984	ROSE HAVEN — CHIPPING SPARROW, Mitsuko Gerhart, 5,000	45.00	NR
1984	LEAFY BOWER — SPOTTED ORIOLE, Mitsuko Gerhart, 5,000	45.00	NR
1984	NESTING COMPANION — MOCKINGBIRD, Mitsuko Gerhart, 5,000	45.00	NR

Paddington Bear Annual

1979	PYRAMID OF PRESENTS, 25,000	12.50	30.00
1980	SPRINGTIME, 25,000	12.50	25.00
1981	SANDCASTLES, 25,000	12.50	25.00
1981	BACK TO SCHOOL, 25,000	12.50	NR

Paddington Bear Annual Christmas

1983	A BEAR'S NOEL, 10,000	22.50	NR
1984	HOW SWEET IT IS, 10,000	22.50	NR

Paddington Bear Musician's Dream

1982	THE BEAT GOES ON, 10,000	17.50	25.00

		Issue Price	Current Value
1982	KNOWING THE SCORE, 10,000	17.50	NR
1983	PERFECT HARMONY, 10,000	17.50	NR
1983	TICKLING THE IVORY, 10,000	17.50	NR

Peanuts Annual

1983	PEANUTS IN CONCERT, Charles Schulz, 20,000	22.50	NR
1984	SNOOPY AND THE BEAGLESCOUTS, Charles Schulz, 20,000 ..	22.50	NR
1985	CLOWN CAPERS, Charles Schulz, 20,000	22.50	NR
1986	LION TAMER SNOOPY, Charles Schulz, 20,000	22.50	NR
1987	BIG TOP BLAST OFF, Charles Schulz, 20,000	17.50	NR

Peanuts Christmas

1972	SNOOPY GUIDES THE SLEIGH, Charles Schulz, 20,000 ...	10.00	40.00
1973	CHRISTMAS EVE AT THE DOGHOUSE, Charles Schulz, 1 year .	10.00	85.00
1974	CHRISTMAS EVE AT THE FIREPLACE, Charles Schulz, 1 year .	10.00	40.00
1975	WOODSTOCK, SANTA CLAUS, Charles Schulz, 1 year ...	12.50	20.00
1976	WOODSTOCK'S CHRISTMAS, Charles Schulz, 1 year....	12.50	20.00
1977	DECK THE DOGHOUSE, Charles Schulz, 1 year	13.00	20.00
1978	FILLING THE STOCKING, Charles Schulz, 1 year	15.00	35.00
1979	CHRISTMAS AT HAND, Charles Schulz, 15,000	17.50	45.00
1980	WAITING FOR SANTA, Charles Schulz, 15,000	17.50	50.00
1981	A CHRISTMAS WISH, Charles Schulz, 15,000...........	17.50	30.00
1982	PERFECT PERFORMANCE, Charles Schulz, 15,000.......	18.50	40.00

Peanuts Mother's Day

1972	LINUS, Charles Schulz, 15,000	10.00	NR
1973	MOM?, Charles Schulz, 8,000	10.00	NR
1974	SNOOPY AND WOODSTOCK ON PARADE, Charles Schulz, 1 year	10.00	NR
1975	A KISS FOR LUCY, Charles Schulz, 1 year	12.50	NR
1976	LINUS AND SNOOPY, Charles Schulz, 1 year	13.00	35.00
1977	DEAR MOM, Charles Schulz, 1 year	13.00	30.00
1978	THOUGHTS THAT COUNT, Charles Schulz, 1 year	15.00	25.00
1979	A SPECIAL LETTER, Charles Schulz, 10,000.............	17.50	NR
1980	A TRIBUTE TO MOM, Charles Schulz, 10,000	17.50	NR
1981	MISSION FOR MOM, Charles Schulz, 10,000	17.50	NR
1982	WHICH WAY TO MOTHER?, Charles Schulz, 10,000......	18.50	NR

Peanuts Special Edition

1976	BICENTENNIAL, Charles Schulz, 1 year	13.00	30.00
1989	PEANUTS 30TH BIRTHDAY, Charles Schulz, 15,000	27.50	NR

Peanuts Valentine's Day

1977	HOME IS WHERE THE HEART IS, Charles Schulz, 1 year .	13.00	35.00
1978	HEAVENLY BLISS, Charles Schulz, 1 year	13.00	30.00
1979	LOVE MATCH, Charles Schulz, 1 year	17.50	30.00

Christmas Eve at the Doghouse

Christmas Eve at the Fireplace

Deck the Doghouse

Linus

		Issue Price	Current Value
1980	FROM SNOOPY, WITH LOVE, Charles Schulz, 1 year.....	17.50	25.00
1981	HEARTS–A–FLUTTER, Charles Schulz, 1 year	17.50	NR
1982	LOVE PATCH, Charles Schulz, 1 year	17.50	NR

Peanuts World's Greatest Athlete

1983	GO DEEP, Charles Schulz, 10,000	17.50	25.00
1983	THE PUCK STOPS HERE, Charles Schulz, 10,000	17.50	NR
1983	THE WAY YOU PLAY THE GAME, Charles Schulz, 10,000 .	17.50	NR
1983	THE CROWD WENT WILD, Charles Schulz, 10,000	17.50	NR

Prime Time

1984	LOVE BOAT, Shelly Mathers, limited	30.00	NR
1984	DALLAS, Shelly Mathers, limited	30.00	NR

		Issue Price	Current Value
Raggedy Ann Annual			
1980	SUNSHINE WAGON, 10,000	17.50	80.00
1981	THE RAGGEDY SHUFFLE, 10,000	17.50	45.00
1982	FLYING HIGH, 10,000	18.50	NR
1983	WINNING STREAK, 10,000	22.50	NR
1984	ROCKING RODEO, 10,000	22.50	NR

Raggedy Ann Bicentennial

1976	BICENTENNIAL PLATE, 1 year	13.00	45.00

Raggedy Ann Christmas

1975	GIFTS OF LOVE, 1 year	12.50	45.00
1976	MERRY BLADES, 1 year	13.00	40.00
1977	CHRISTMAS MORNING, 1 year	13.00	25.00
1978	CHECKING THE LIST, 1 year	15.00	20.00
1979	LITTLE HELPER, 15,000	17.50	NR

Raggedy Ann Mother's Day

1976	MOTHERHOOD, 1 year	13.00	NR
1977	BOUQUET OF LOVE, 1 year	13.00	NR
1978	HELLO MOM, 1 year	15.00	NR
1979	HIGH SPIRITS, 1 year	17.50	NR

Raggedy Ann Valentine's Day

1978	AS TIME GOES BY, 1 year	13.00	25.00
1979	DAISIES DO TELL, 1 year	17.50	NR

SCHOFIELD GALLERY UNITED STATES

Clowns, Klowns, Klonz

1986	PAINTING ON A SMILE, Mildred Schofield, 7,500	47.50	NR
1986	KEYSTONE KOP, Mildred Schofield, 7,500	47.50	NR

SCHUHAMANN GERMANY

Hidden Treasures of the Wood

1991	WILD STRAWBERRIES IN THE MOSS	29.72	NR
1991	BLUEBERRIES AMONGST THE UNDERGROWTH	29.72	40.00
1991	RASPBERRIES AMONGST THE GORSE	32.72	50.00
1992	BLACKBERRIES AMONGST THE HERBS	32.72	RI
1992	CRANBERRIES AMONGST THE GENTIAN	32.72	RI

SCHUMANN GERMANY

		Issue Price	Current Value

Christmas

1971	SNOW SCENE, 10,000	12.00	NR
1972	DEER IN SNOW, 15,000	12.00	NR
1973	WEIHNACHTEN, 5,000	12.00	NR
1974	CHURCH IN SNOW, 5,000	12.00	NR
1975	FOUNTAIN, 5,000	12.00	NR

Composers

1970	BEETHOVEN	12.00	NR
1972	MOZART	12.00	NR

Imperial Christmas (Royal Cornwall)

1979	LIEBLING, Marianne Stuwe, 10,000	65.00	100.00
1980	HALLELUJAH, Marianne Stuwe, 10,000	65.00	80.00
1981	STILLE NACHT, Marianne Stuwe, 10,000	75.00	80.00
1982	WINTER MELODIE, Marianne Stuwe, 10,000	75.00	80.00

SEBASTIAN UNITED STATES

America's Favorite

1978	MOTIF #1, 10,000	75.00	NR
1979	GRAND CANYON, 10,000	75.00	NR

SEELEY'S CERAMIC SERVICE UNITED STATES

Antique French Doll Collection

1979	THE BRU, Mildred Seeley, 5,000	39.00	200.00
1979	THE E. J., Mildred Seeley, 5,000	39.00	75.00
1979	THE A. T., Mildred Seeley, 5,000	39.00	55.00
1980	ALEXANDRE, Mildred Seeley, 5,000	39.00	45.00
1981	THE SCHMITT, Mildred Seeley, 5,000	39.00	45.00
1981	THE MARQUE, Mildred Seeley, 5,000	39.00	45.00
1983	BEBE HALO, Mildred Seeley, 5,000	39.00	NR
1984	BRU'S FAITH, Mildred Seeley, 5,000	39.00	NR
1984	STEINER'S EASTER, Mildred Seeley, 5,000	39.00	NR

Antique French Doll Collection II

1983	THE SNOW ANGEL, Mildred Seeley, 5,000	39.00	NR
1984	MARQUE'S ALYCE, Mildred Seeley, 5,000	39.00	NR
1984	JUMEAU'S GAYNELL, Mildred Seeley, 5,000	39.00	NR

Old Baby Doll Collection

		Issue Price	Current Value
1982	JDK HILDA, Mildred Seeley, 9,500	43.00	NR
1982	GOLDIE, Mildred Seeley, 9,500	43.00	NR
1983	LORI, Mildred Seeley, 9,500	43.00	NR
1983	BYE–LO, Mildred Seeley, 9,500	43.00	NR
1983	LAUGHING BABY, Mildred Seeley, 9,500	43.00	NR

Old German Doll Collection

1981	DEAR GOOGLY, Mildred Seeley, 7,500	39.00	NR
1981	LUCY, Mildred Seeley, 7,500	39.00	NR
1981	THE WHISTLER, Mildred Seeley, 7,500	39.00	NR
1982	APRIL, Mildred Seeley, 7,500	39.00	NR
1982	ELISE, Mildred Seeley, 7,500	39.00	NR

SELANDIA

Christmas

1972	WAY TO BETHLEHEM, sgd, 250	100.00	NR
1972	WAY TO BETHLEHEM, 4,750	30.00	50.00
1973	THREE WISE MEN, sgd, 200	100.00	NR
1973	THREE WISE MEN, 4,750	35.00	NR

SELTMANN VOHENSTRAUSS GERMANY

Romantic Village Views

1990	BY THE MILL STREAM	32.50	NR
1991	THE BAKEHOUSE	32.50	NR
1991	WASHDAY ON THE RIVER	34.50	NR
1991	BY THE OLD BRIDGE	35.50	NR
1991	DRINKING HORSES	35.50	NR
1992	THE VILLAGE POND	35.50	RI

SEVEN SEAS UNITED STATES

Christmas Carols

1970	I HEARD THE BELLS, 4,000	15.00	25.00
1971	OH TANNENBAUM, 4,000	15.00	20.00
1972	DECK THE HALLS, 1,500	18.00	25.00
1973	O HOLY NIGHT, 2,000	18.00	25.00
1974	JINGLE BELLS, 1,200	25.00	NR
1975	WINTER WONDERLAND, 1,500	25.00	NR
1976	TWELVE DAYS OF CHRISTMAS, 1,500	25.00	NR
1977	UP ON THE HOUSETOP, 1,500	25.00	NR

	Issue Price	Current Value
1978 LITTLE TOWN OF BETHLEHEM, 1,500	25.00	NR
1979 SANTA CLAUS IS COMING TO TOWN, 1,500	25.00	NR
1980 FROSTY THE SNOWMAN, 1,500	25.00	NR

Historical Events

1969 MOON LANDING — NO FLAG, 2,000	13.50	175.00
1969 MOON LANDING — WITH FLAG, 2,000	13.50	70.00
1970 YEAR OF CRISIS, 4,000	15.00	20.00
1971 FIRST VEHICULAR TRAVEL, 3,000	15.00	35.00
1972 LAST MOON JOURNEY, 2000	15.00	35.00
1973 PEACE, 3,000	15.00	35.00

Mother's Day

1970 GIRL OF ALL NATIONS, 5,000	15.00	20.00
1971 SHARING CONFIDENCES, 1,400	15.00	20.00
1972 SCANDINAVIAN GIRL, 1,600	15.00	20.00
1973 ALL–AMERICAN GIRL, 1,500	15.00	30.00

New World

1970 HOLY FAMILY, 3,5000	15.00	20.00
1971 THREE WISE MEN, 1,500	15.00	30.00
1972 SHEPHERDS WATCHED, 1,500	18.00	NR

Single Issue

1970 OBERAMMERGAU, 2,500	18.00	25.00

SIGNATURE COLLECTION

Angler's Dream

1983 BROOK TROUT, John Eggert, 9,800	55.00	NR
1983 CHINOOK SALMON, John Eggert, 9,800	55.00	NR
1983 LARGEMOUTH BASS, John Eggert, 9,800	55.00	NR
1983 STRIPED BASS, John Eggert, 9,800	55.00	NR

Baker Street

1983 SHERLOCK HOLMES, Mitchell Hooks, 9,800	55.00	NR
1983 DR. WATSON, 9,800	55.00	NR

Carnival

1983 KNOCK 'EM DOWN, Tom Newsom, 19,500	39.95	NR
1983 CAROUSEL, Tom Newsom, 19,500	39.95	NR
1983 FORTUNE TELLER, Tom Newsom, 19,500	39.95	NR
1983 RING THE BELL, Tom Newsom, 19,500	39.95	NR

Childhood Delights

		Issue Price	Current Value
1983	AMANDA, Rob Sauber, 7,500	45.00	NR

Grandma's Scrapbook

1983	COURTING, Robert Berran, 12,500	45.00	NR

How Do I Love Thee?

1983	ALAINA, Rob Sauber, 19,500	39.95	NR
1983	TAYLOR, Rob Sauber, 19,500	39.95	NR
1983	RENDEZVOUS, Rob Sauber, 19,500	39.95	NR
1983	EMBRACE, Rob Sauber, 19,500	39.95	NR

Legends

1983	PAUL BUNYAN, Carl Cassler, 10,000	45.00	NR
1983	RIP VAN WINKLE, Carl Cassler, 10,000	45.00	NR

Melodies of Childhood

1983	TWINKLE, TWINKLE, LITTLE STAR, Hector Girrado, 19,500	35.00	NR
1983	ROW, ROW, ROW YOUR BOAT, Hector Girrado, 19,500	35.00	NR
1983	MARY HAD A LITTLE LAMB, Hector Girrado, 19,500	35.00	NR

Songs of Stephen Foster

1984	OH! SUSANNAH, Rob Sauber, 3,500	60.00	NR
1984	I DREAM OF JEANIE WITH THE LIGHT BROWN HAIR, Rob Sauber, 3,500	60.00	NR
1984	BEAUTIFUL DREAMER, Rob Sauber, 3,500	60.00	NR

Unicorn Magic

1983	MORNING ENCOUNTER, Jeffrey Ferreson, 10,000	50.00	NR
1983	AFTERNOON OFFERING, Jeffrey Ferreson, 10,000	50.00	NR

Very Special Edition

1984	THE WEDDING, Rob Sauber	50.00	NR
1984	HAPPY BIRTHDAY, Rob Sauber	50.00	NR

SILVER CITY

Christmas

1969	WINTER SCENE	37.00	NR
1970	WATER MILL	25.00	NR
1971	SKATING SCENE	25.00	NR
1972	LOGGING IN WINTER	30.00	NR
1973	ST. CLAUDENS	20.00	NR

Single Issue

		Issue Price	Current Value
1972	INDEPENDENCE HALL	13.50	NR

SILVER CREATIONS UNITED STATES

Americana

1973	CLYDESDALES	150.00	NR

History

1972	CHURCHILLIAN HERITAGE, proof	550.00	575.00
1972	CHURCHILLIAN HERITAGE	150.00	200.00
1973	YALTA CONFERENCE, proof	550.00	575.00
1973	YALTA CONFERENCE	150.00	NR

SMITH GLASS UNITED STATES

Americana

1971	MORGAN SILVER DOLLAR, 5,000	10.00	NR

Christmas

1971	FAMILY AT CHRISTMAS	10.00	NR
1972	FLYING ANGEL	10.00	NR
1973	ST. MARY'S IN MOUNTAINS	10.00	NR

Famous Americans

1971	KENNEDY, 2,500	10.00	NR
1971	LINCOLN, 2,500	10.00	NR
1972	DAVIS, 5,000	11.00	NR
1972	LEE, 5,000	11.00	NR

SOUTHERN LIVING GALLERY UNITED STATES

Game Birds of the South

1983	BOBWHITE QUAIL, Antony Heritage, 19,500	39.95	NR
1983	MOURNING DOVE, Antony Heritage, 19,500	39.95	NR
1983	GREEN–WINGED TEAL, Antony Heritage, 19,500	39.95	NR
1983	RING–NECKED PHEASANT, Antony Heritage, 19,500	39.95	NR
1983	MALLARD DUCK, Antony Herltage, 19,500	39.95	NR
1983	AMERICAN COOT, Antony Heritage, 19,500	39.95	NR
1983	RUFFED GROUSE, Antony Heritage, 19,500	39.95	NR
1983	PINTAIL DUCK, Antony Heritage, 19,500	39.95	NR
1983	AMERICAN WOODCOCK, Antony Heritage, 19,500	39.95	NR
1983	CANADA GOOSE, Antony Heritage, 19,500	39.95	NR

		Issue Price	Current Value
1983	WILD TURKEY, Antony Heritage, 19,500	39.95	NR
1983	WOOD DUCK, Antony Heritage, 19,500	39.95	NR

Songbirds of the South

XX	AMERICAN GOLDFINCH, A. E. Ruffing, 19,500	39.95	NR
XX	TUFTED TITMOUSE, A. E. Ruffing, 19,500	39.95	NR
XX	RED–WINGED BLACKBIRD, A. E. Ruffing, 19,500	39.95	NR
XX	MOCKINGBIRD, A. E. Ruffing, 19,500	39.95	NR
XX	CARDINAL, A. E. Ruffing, 19,500	39.95	NR
XX	BLUEJAY, A. E. Ruffing, 19,500	39.95	NR
XX	ROBIN, A. E. Ruffing, 19,500	39.95	NR

Southern Forest Families

XX	EASTERN COTTONTAIL RABBIT, Sy and Dot Barlowe, 19,500 .	39.95	NR
XX	WHITE–TAILED DEER, Sy and Dot Barlowe, 19,500	39.95	NR
XX	RACCOON, Sy and Dot Barlowe, 19,500	39.95	NR
XX	STRIPED SKUNK, Sy and Dot Barlowe, 19,500	39.95	NR
XX	BOBCAT, Sy and Dot Barlowe, 19,500	39.95	NR
XX	FOX SQUIRREL, Sy and Dot Barlowe, 19,500	39.95	NR
XX	RED FOX, Sy and Dot Barlowe, 19,500	39.95	NR
XX	BLACK BEAR, Sy and Dot Barlowe, 19,500	39.95	NR
XX	OPOSSUM, Sy and Dot Barlowe, 19,500	39.95	NR
XX	CHIPMUNK, Sy and Dot Barlowe, 19,500	39.95	NR
XX	BEAVER, Sy and Dot Barlowe, 19,500	39.95	NR
XX	MINK, Sy and Dot Barlowe, 19,500	39.95	NR

Wildflowers of the South

XX	WILD HONEYSUCKLE, R. Mark, 19,500	39.95	NR
XX	FROST ASTER, R. Mark, 19,500	39.95	NR
XX	FLOWERING DOGWOOD, R. Mark, 19,500	39.95	NR
XX	BEE BALM, R. Mark, 19,500	39.95	NR
XX	QUEEN ANNE'S LACE, R. Mark, 19,500	39.95	NR
XX	BLUEBONNET, R. Mark, 19,500	39.95	NR
XX	SOUTHERN MAGNOLIA, R. Mark, 19,500	39.95	NR
XX	BIRDSFOOT VIOLET, R. Mark, 19,500	39.95	NR
XX	REGAL LILY, R. Mark, 19,500	39.95	NR
XX	LADY SLIPPER ORCHID, R. Mark, 19,500	39.95	NR
XX	BLACK–EYED SUSAN, R. Mark, 19,500	39.95	NR
XX	BUTTERCUP, R. Mark, 19,500	39.95	NR

SPODE GREAT BRITAIN

American Songbirds

1970	RUFUS–SIDED TOWHEE, Ray Harm, 5,000	–	–

		Issue Price	Current Value
1970	WINTER WREN, Ray Harm, 5,000	−	−
1971	EASTERN BLUEBIRD, Ray Harm, 5,000	−	−
1971	STELLAR'S JAY, Ray Harm, 5,000	−	−
1971	EASTERN MOCKINGBIRD, Ray Harm, 5,000	−	−
1971	BARN SWALLOW, Ray Harm, 5,000	−	−
1971	ROSE–BREASTED GROSBEAK, Ray Harm, 5,000	−	−
1971	CARDINAL, Ray Harm, 5,000	−	−
1972	WESTERN TANAGER, Ray Harm, 5,000	−	−
1972	WOODPECKER, Ray Harm, 5,000	−	−
1972	CHICKADEE, Ray Harm, 5,000	−	−
1972	AMERICAN GOLDFINCH, Ray Harm, 5,000	−	−
	Set of 12	350.00	765.00

Christmas

1970	PARTRIDGE, Gillian West, 1 year	35.00	NR
1971	ANGELS SINGING, Gillian West, 1 year	35.00	NR
1972	THREE SHIPS A–SAILING, Gillian West, 1 year	35.00	NR
1973	WE THREE KINGS OF ORIENT, Gillian West, 1 year	35.00	NR
1974	DECK THE HALLS, Gillian West, 1 year	35.00	NR
1975	CHRISTBAUM, Gillian West, 1 year	45.00	NR
1976	GOOD KING WENCESLAS, Gillian West, 1 year	45.00	NR
1977	HOLLY AND IVY, Gillian West, 1 year	45.00	NR
1978	WHILE SHEPHERDS WATCHED, Gillian West, 1 year	45.00	NR
1979	AWAY IN A MANGER, Gillian West, 1 year	50.00	BR
1980	BRINGING IN THE BOAR'S HEAD, P. Wood, 1 year	60.00	BR
1981	MAKE WE MERRY, P. Wood, 1 year	65.00	BR

Christmas Pastimes

1982	SLEIGH RIDE	75.00	NR

Maritime

1980	U.S.S. UNITED STATES AND HMS MACEDONIAN, 2,000	150.00	NR
1980	U.S.S. PRESIDENT AND HMS LITTLE BELT, 2,000	150.00	NR
1980	H.M.S. SHANNON AND USS CHESAPEAKE, 2,000	150.00	NR
1980	U.S.S. CONSTITUTION AND HMS GUERRIERE, 2,000	150.00	NR
1980	U.S.S. CONSTITUTION AND HMS JAVA, 2,000	150.00	NR
1980	H.M.S. PELICAN AND USS ARGUS, 2,000	150.00	NR

Noble Horse

1988	ENGLISH THOROUGHBRED	29.00	BR
1988	AUSTRIAN LIPIZZANER	29.00	NR
1988	THE AMERICAN QUARTERHORSE	32.00	BR
1988	THE ARABIAN	32.00	NR
1989	THE HANOVERIAN	32.00	NR
1989	THE CLEVELAND BAY	32.00	NR

		Issue Price	Current Value
1989	THE HACKNEY	34.00	BR
1990	THE APPALOOSA	34.00	NR

Single Issues

1969	PRINCE OF WALES, 1,500	65.00	NR
1970	DICKENS	70.00	80.00
1970	MAYFLOWER, 2,500	70.00	130.00
1970	LOEWSTOFT	70.00	BR
1971	IMPERIAL PERSIA, 10,000	125.00	NR
1971	CHURCHILL, 5,000	110.00	120.00
1972	PASSOVER, 5,000	59.00	BR
1972	CUTTY SARK	59.00	80.00
1973	DICKEN'S LONDON	70.00	BR

SPORTS IMPRESSIONS / ENESCO UNITED STATES

Baseball

1987	WADE BOGGS, Brian Johnson, 2,000	60.00	NR
1987	WADE BOGGS, Brian Johnson, sgd, 1,000	100.00	NR
1987	DARRYL STRAWBERRY, Robert Stephen Simon, 2,000	60.00	NR
1987	DARRYL STRAWBERRY, Robert Stephen Simon, sgd, 1,000	200.00	NR
1987	KEITH HERNANDEZ, Robert Stephen Simon, 2,000	60.00	NR
1987	KEITH HERNANDEZ, Robert Stephen Simon, sgd, 1,000	100.00	NR
1987	GARY CARTER "THE KID," Robert Stephen Simon, 2,000	60.00	NR
1987	GARY CARTER "THE KID," Robert Stephen Simon, 1,000	125.00	NR
1987	LENNY DYKSTRA, Robert Stephen Simon,1,000	60.00	NR
1987	LENNY DYKSTRA, Robert Stephen Simon, sgd, 1,000	100.00	NR
1987	CARL YASTREMSKI, Robert Stephen Simon, 3,000	60.00	NR
1987	MANTLE, "MICKEY AT NIGHT," Robert Stephen Simon, 3,500	60.00	NR
1987	MANTLE, "MICKEY AT NIGHT," Robert Stephen Simon, sgd, 1,500	100.00	NR

Basketball

1987	LARRY BIRD, Robert Stephen Simon, 5,000	60.00	NR

Don Mattingly

1987	PLAYER OF THE YEAR, Brian Johnson, 5,000	60.00	NR

Gold Edition Plates

1986	LARRY BIRD, Robert Stephen Simon, closed	125.00	150.00
1986	WADE BOGGS, Brian Johnson, closed	125.00	150.00
1986	MICKEY MANTLE AT NIGHT, Robert Stephen Simon, closed	125.00	275.00
1986	KEITH HERNANDEZ, Robert Stephen Simon, closed	125.00	175.00

		Issue Price	Current Value
1986	DON MATTINGLY, Brian Johnson, closed	125.00	175.00
1987	DARRYL STRAWBERRY #1, Robert Stephen Simon, closed	125.00	155.00
1987	TED WILLIAMS, Robert Stephen Simon, closed	125.00	495.00
1987	CARL YASTREMSKI, Robert Stephen Simon, closed	125.00	150.00
1987	MICKEY, WILLIE, AND DUKE, Robert Stephen Simon, closed ..	125.00	225.00
1988	BROOKS ROBINSON, Robert Stephen Simon, closed	125.00	225.00
1988	LARRY BIRD, Robert Stephen Simon, closed	125.00	275.00
1988	MAGIC JOHNSON, Robert Stephen Simon, closed	125.00	350.00
1988	YANKEE TRADITION, J. Catalano, closed	150.00	225.00
1989	MANTLE SWITCH HITTER, J. Catalano, closed	150.00	300.00
1989	WILL CLARK, J. Catalano, closed	125.00	195.00
1989	DARRYL STRAWBERRY #2, T. Fogarty, closed	125.00	195.00
1991	LARRY BIRD, J. Catalano, closed	150.00	195.00
1991	MAGIC JOHNSON, W. C. Mundy, closed	150.00	235.00
1991	MICHAEL JORDAN, J. Catalano, closed	150.00	250.00
1991	DREAM TEAM (1st TEN CHOSEN), L. Salk, closed	150.00	300.00
1992	DREAM TEAM, R. Tanenbaum, closed	150.00	RI
1992	MICHAEL JORDAN, R. Tanenbaum, closed	150.00	RI
1992	MAGIC JOHNSON, R. Tanenbaum, closed	150.00	RI
1993	MAGIC JOHNSON (4042–04), R. Tanenbaum, closed	150.00	RI

FRANZ STANEK

Single Issues

1969	MOON LANDING, 150	250.00	1,100.00
1972	MAYFLOWER, 60	250.00	650.00
1972	SANTA MARIA, 60	250.00	600.00
1973	EAGLE, 400	250.00	NR

STEIFF UNITED STATES

Bicentennial

1972	DECLARATION OF INDEPENDENCE, 10,000	50.00	NR
1974	BETSY ROSS, 10,000	50.00	NR
1975	CROSSING DELAWARE, 10,000	50.00	NR
1976	SERAPIA AND BON HOMME, 10,000	50.00	NR

STERLING AMERICA UNITED STATES

Christmas Customs

1970	YULE LOG, 2,500	18.00	30.00
1971	HOLLAND, 2,500	18.00	30.00

		Issue Price	Current Value
1972	NORWAY, 2,500	18.00	NR
1973	GERMANY, 2,500	20.00	NR
1974	MEXICO, 2,500	24.00	NR

Mother's Day

1971	MARE AND FOAL, 2,500	18.00	25.00
1972	HORNED OWL, 2,500	18.00	25.00
1973	RACCOONS, 2,500	20.00	NR
1974	DEER, 2,500	24.00	NR
1975	QUAIL, 2,500	24.00	NR

Twelve Days of Christmas

1970	PARTRIDGE, 2,500	18.00	25.00
1971	TURTLE DOVES, 2,500	18.00	25.00
1972	FRENCH HENS, 2,500	18.00	25.00
1973	COLLY BIRDS, 2,500	18.00	25.00
1974	FIVE RINGS, 2,500	24.00	NR
1975	SIX GEESE, 2,500	24.00	NR
1976	SEVEN SWANS, 2,500	24.00	NR
1977	EIGHT MAIDS, 2,500	28.00	BR

STRATFORD COLLECTION UNITED STATES

Famous Clowns

1982	EMMETT LOOKING OUT TO SEE, Robert Blottiaux, 10,000	35.00	NR
1982	JACK THUM AND CHILD, Robert Blottiaux, 10,000	35.00	NR

Four Seasons of the Unicorn

1983	UNICORN IN WINTER, Michele Livingstone, 10,000	45.00	NR

Real Children

1982	MICHAEL'S MIRACLE, Nancy Turner, 19,500	39.50	NR
1983	SUSAN'S WORLD, Nancy Turner, 19,500	45.00	NR

Young Wildlife

1982	SIBERIAN CUB AT PLAY, Robert Blottiaux, 15,000	35.00	NR
1982	CURIOUS RACCOON, Robert Blottiaux, 15,000	35.00	NR

STUART DEVLIN SILVER UNITED STATES

Americana

1972	GASPEE INCIDENT, 1,000	130.00	145.00

STUART INTERNATIONAL UNITED STATES

Childhood Secrets

		Issue Price	Current Value
1983	BILLY'S TREASURE, Nancy Turner, 19,500	39.50	NR

STUDIO DANTE DE VOLTERADICI ITALY

Benvenuti's Muses

1985	ERATO, Sergio Benvenuti	50.00	NR
1985	CLIO, Sergio Benvenuti	50.00	BR
1986	TERPSICHORE, Sergio Benvenuti	55.00	NR
1986	EUTERPE, Sergio Benvenuti.........................	55.00	NR

Christmas Crèche

1987	JOY TO THE WORLD	55.00	NR
1987	HARK, THE HERALD ANGELS SING	55.00	NR
1988	O COME ALL YE FAITHFUL	60.00	NR
1989	WE THREE KINGS	60.00	NR
1990	SILENT NIGHT, HOLY HIGHT	60.00	150.00
1991	ANGELS WE HAVE HEARD ON HIGH	60.00	105.00

Silent Night, Holy Night
Photo courtesy of *Collectors News*

Gates of Paradise

1989	GOD CREATES ADAM	75.00	85.00
1990	THE CREATION OF EVE	75.00	90.00
1990	THE ANGELS VISIT ABRAHAM	80.00	NR
1990	ISAAC BLESSING JACOB............................	80.00	95.00
1991	MOSES RECEIVES THE LAW	80.00	115.00
1991	SOLOMON AND THE QUEEN OF SHEBA	80.00	120.00

Ghilberti Doors

		Issue Price	Current Value
1983	ADORATION OF THE MAGI, Alberto Santangela	50.00	BR
1984	THE NATIVITY, Alberto Santangela....................	50.00	BR
1985	THE ANNUNCIATION, Alberto Santangela	50.00	BR
1985	CHRIST AMONG THE DOCTORS, Alberto Santangela....	55.00	BR
1986	CHRIST WALKS ON THE WATER, Alberto Santangela ...	55.00	BR
1986	THE EXPULSION OF THE MONEY CHANGERS, Alberto Santangela	55.00	NR
1987	CHRIST'S ENTRY INTO JERUSALEM	55.00	BR
1987	THE RAISING OF LAZARUS	55.00	BR

Grand Opera

		Issue Price	Current Value
1976	RIGOLETTO, Gino Ruggeri, 1 year	35.00	NR
1977	MADAME BUTTERFLY, Gino Ruggeri, 1 year	35.00	NR
1978	CARMEN, Gino Ruggeri, 1 year	40.00	NR
1979	AIDA, Gino Ruggeri, 1 year..........................	40.00	NR
1980	BARBER OF SEVILLE, Gino Ruggeri, 1 year	40.00	NR
1981	TOSCA, Gino Ruggeri, 1 year	40.00	NR
1982	I PAGLIACCI, Gino Ruggeri, 1 year	40.00	100.00

Madonne Viventi (Living Madonnas)

		Issue Price	Current Value
1978	MADONNA PENSOSA (PENSIVE MADONNA), Ado Santini ..	45.00	NR
1979	MADONNA SERENA (SERENE MADONNA), Ado Santini.	45.00	NR
1980	MADONNA BEATA (BEATIFIC MADONNA), Ado Santini .	45.00	NR
1981	MADONNA PROFETICA (PROPHETIC MADONNA), Ado Santini	45.00	NR
1982	MADONNA MODESTA (DEMURE MADONNA), Ado Santini ..	45.00	NR
1983	MADONNA SAGGIA (WISE MADONNA), Ado Santini ...	45.00	NR
1984	MADONNA TENERA (TENDER MADONNA), Ado Santini.	45.00	NR

Christ Among the Doctors
Photo courtesy of *Collectors News*

Madonna Saggia
Photo courtesy of *Collectors News*

Masterpiece Madonnas

		Issue Price	Current Value
1990	RAPHAEL'S MADONNA	60.00	75.00
1990	DELLA ROBBIA'S MADONNA	60.00	NR
1991	MICHELANGELO'S MADONNA	65.00	80.00
1991	BOTTICELLI'S MADONNA	65.00	80.00
1991	LEONARDO'S MADONNA	65.00	BR
1991	TITIAN'S MADONNA	65.00	110.00

Renaissance Madonnas: Gifts of Maternal Love

1986	THE GIFT OF WISDOM	65.00	BR
1987	THE GIFT OF FAITH	65.00	NR
1987	THE GIFT OF COMFORT	70.00	NR
1987	THE GIFT OF PATIENCE	70.00	NR
1988	THE GIFT OF DEVOTION	70.00	85.00
1988	THE GIFT OF TENDERNESS	70.00	80.00
1988	THE GIFT OF VIGILANCE	70.00	80.00
1988	THE GIFT OF SOLICITUDE	70.00	95.00

STUMAR GERMANY

Christmas

1970	ANGEL, 10,000	8.00	35.00
1971	THE OLD CANAL, 10,000	8.00	25.00
1972	COUNTRYSIDE, 10,000	10.00	25.00
1973	FRIENDSHIP, 10,000	10.00	20.00
1974	MAKING FANCY, 10,000	10.00	20.00
1975	CHRISTMAS, 10,000	10.00	20.00
1976	CHRISTMAS, 10,000	15.00	NR
1977	JOYFUL EXPECTATIONS, 10,000	15.00	NR
1978	CHRISTMAS, 10,000	19.50	NR

Egyptian

1977	ANCIENT EGYPTIAN TRILOGY, 5,000	45.00	NR
1978	CHARIOTEER, 5,000	54.00	NR

Mother's Day

1971	AMISH MOTHER AND DAUGHTER, 10,000	8.00	35.00
1972	CHILDREN, 10,000	8.00	25.00
1973	MOTHER SEWING, 10,000	10.00	20.00
1974	MOTHER, CRADLE, 10,000	10.00	20.00
1975	BAKING, 10,000	10.00	20.00
1976	READING TO CHILDREN, 10,000	15.00	NR
1977	COMFORTING CHILD, 10,000	15.00	NR
1978	TRANQUILITY, 10,000	19.50	NR

TIRSCHENREUTH GERMANY

Band's Songbirds of Europe

		Issue Price	Current Value
1985	BLUE TITMOUSE, Ursula Band, 100 days	19.50	NR
1986	FIRECREST, Ursula Band, 100 days	19.50	NR
1986	CORSICAN NUTHATCH, Ursula Band, 100 days	22.50	NR
1986	GOLDEN ORIOLE, Ursula Band, 100 days	22.50	BR
1986	GREAT TITMOUSE, Ursula Band, 100 days	22.50	BR
1986	RED ROBIN, Ursula Band, 100 days	22.50	NR
1986	CHAFFINCH, Ursula Band, 100 days	24.50	BR
1986	REDSTART, Ursulaa Band, 100 days	24.50	NR

Chaffinch
Photo courtesy of *Collectors News*

Christmas

1969	HOMESTEAD, 3,500	12.00	25.00
1970	CHURCH, 3,500	12.00	NR
1971	STAR OF BETHLEHEM, 3,500	12.00	NR
1972	ELK, 3,500	13.00	NR
1973	CHRISTMAS, 3,500	14.00	NR

TOPSY TURVY UNITED STATES

Storybook (From illustrations in antique storybooks)

1982	HARES AND HOUNDS, 10,000	19.50	NR
1982	OSTRICH AND ELEPHANT, 10,000	19.50	NR

TOWLE SILVERSMITHS UNITED STATES

Christmas

1972	WISE MEN, 2,500	250.00	NR

Valentines

		Issue Price	Current Value
1972	SINGLE HEART, 1 year	10.00	NR
1973	ENTWINED HEARTS, 1 year	10.00	NR

UNITED STATES GALLERY OF ART UNITED STATES

Single Issue

1984	INNOCENCE, Jack Woodson	24.50	NR

U.S. HISTORICAL SOCIETY UNITED STATES

Annual Historical

1977	GREAT EVENTS, 5,000	60.00	NR
1978	GREAT EVENTS, 10,000	75.00	NR

Annual Spring Flowers

1983	FLOWERS IN A BLUE VASE, J. Clark, 10,000	135.00	150.00
1984	SPRING FLOWERS, M. Wampler	135.00	NR

Annual Stained Glass and Pewter Christmas

1978	THE NATIVITY — CANTERBURY CATHEDRAL, 10,000	97.00	175.00
1979	FLIGHT INTO EGYPT — ST. JOHN'S, NEW YORK, 10,000	97.00	175.00
1980	MADONNA AND CHILD — WASHINGTON CATHEDRAL, 10,000	125.00	175.00
1981	THE MAGI — ST. PAUL'S, SAN FRANCISCO, 10,000	125.00	175.00
1982	FLIGHT INTO EGYPT — LOS ANGELES CATHEDRAL, 10,000	135.00	175.00
1983	SHEPHERDS AT BETHLEHEM — ST. JOHN'S, NEW ORLEANS, 10,000	135.00	150.00
1984	THE NATIVITY — ST. ANTHONY'S, ST. LOUIS, 10,000	135.00	NR
1985	GOOD TIDINGS OF GREAT JOY — BOSTON, 10,000	160.00	NR
1986	THE NATIVITY — OLD ST. MARY'S CHURCH, PHILADELPHIA, 10,000	160.00	NR
1987	O COME, LITTLE CHILDREN, 10,000	160.00	NR

Audubon's Birds

1986	AUDUBON AND THE BLUEJAY, Jack Woodson, 10,000	135.00	NR

Buffalo Bill's Wild West

1984	PONY EXPRESS, Jack Woodson, 5,000	55.00	NR
1984	ANNIE OAKLEY, Jack Woodson, 5,000	55.00	NR
1984	SITTING BULL, Jack Woodson, 5,000	55.00	NR
XX	BUFFALO HUNTER, Jack Woodson, 5,000	55.00	NR
XX	FAREWELL APPEARANCE, Jack Woodson, 5,000	55.00	NR
XX	DEADWOOD STAGE, Jack Woodson, 5,000	55.00	NR
XX	CONGRESS OF THE ROUGH RIDERS, Jack Woodson, 5,000	55.00	NR

		Issue Price	Current Value
XX	ROYAL VISIT, Jack Woodson, 5,000	55.00	NR

Christmas Carols

1982	DECK THE HALLS WITH BOUGHS OF HOLLY, J. Landis, 10,000 .	55.00	65.00
1983	O CHRISTMAS TREE, Jack Woodson, 10,000	55.00	65.00
1984	WINTER WONDERLAND, Jack Woodson, 10,000........	55.00	NR
1985	HERE WE COME A–CAROLING, Jack Woodson, 10,000 ..	55.00	NR
1986	THE CHRISTMAS SONG, Jack Woodson, 10,000	55.00	NR
1987	I HEARD THE BELLS ON CHRISTMAS DAY, Jack Woodson, 10,000..	55.00	NR

Good Tidings of Great Joy
Photo courtesy of *Collectors News*

The Christmas Song
Photo courtesy of *Collectors News*

Dacey Series

1984	MELODIES OF STEPHEN FOSTER, Robert Dacey........	19.50	NR

Easter

1987	THE GOOD SHEPHERD, Jack Woodson, 5,000	160.00	NR

Great American Sailing Ships

1983	OLD IRONSIDES, Jack Woodson, 10,000	135.00	150.00
1984	CHARLES W. MORGAN, Jack Woodson, 10,000	135.00	NR
1985	FLYING CLOUD, Jack Woodson, 10,000	135.00	NR

Stained Glass Cathedral Christmas

1978	CANTERBURY CATHEDRAL, 10,000....................	87.00	95.00
1979	FLIGHT INTO EGYPT, 10,000	97.00	NR
1980	MADONNA AND CHILD, 10,000	125.00	150.00
1981	THE MAGI, 10,000...................................	125.00	NR

		Issue Price	Current Value
1982	FLIGHT INTO EGYPT, 10,000	125.00	NR
1983	SHEPHERDS AT BETHLEHEM, 10,000	150.00	NR

Stained Glass Mother's Day

1987	A MOTHER'S LOVE, Nancy Noel, 5,000	160.00	NR

Stained Glass and Pewter Special Issues

1986	TEXAS SESQUICENTENNIAL COMMEMORATIVE, Jack Woodson, 10,000	135.00	NR
1986	STATUE OF LIBERTY, Jack Woodson, 10,000	135.00	NR

Two Hundred Years of Flight

1984	MAN'S FIRST FLIGHT, Jack Woodson, 5,000	48.75	NR
1984	MIRACLE AT KITTY HAWK, Jack Woodson, 5,000	48.75	NR
1984	CHINA CLIPPER, Jack Woodson, 5,000	48.75	NR
1984	MAN IN SPACE, Jack Woodson, 5,000	48.75	NR

Young America

1972	YOUNG AMERICA OF WINSLOW HOMER, Winslow Homer, 2,500, set of 6	425.00	1,100.00

V–PALEKH ART STUDIOS

Russian Legends

1988	RUSLAN AND LUDMILLA, G. Lubimov, 195 days	29.87	BR
1988	THE PRINCESS/SEVEN BOGATYRS, A. Kovalev, 195 days	29.87	BR
1989	THE GOLDEN COCKEREL, V. Vleshko, 195 days	32.87	BR
1989	LUKOMORYA, R. Belousov, 195 days	32.87	BR
1989	FISHERMAN AND THE MAGIC FISH, N. Lopatin, 195 days	32.87	NR
1989	TSAR SALTAN, G. Zhiryakova, 195 days	32.87	NR
1989	THE PRIEST AND HIS SERVANT, O. An, 195 days	34.87	NR
1990	STONE FLOWER, V. Bolshakova, 195 days	34.87	NR
1990	SADKO, E. Populor, 195 days	34.87	45.00
1990	THE TWELVE MONTHS, N. Lopatin, 195 days	36.87	45.00
1990	SILVER HOOF, S. Adeyanor, 195 days	36.87	60.00
1990	MOROZKO, N. Lopatin, 195 days	36.87	80.00

VAGUE SHADOWS UNITED STATES
(See also Artaffects)

Arabians

1986	SILVER STREAK, Gregory Perillo, 3,500	95.00	125.00

		Issue Price	Current Value

Arctic Friends

		Issue Price	Current Value
1982	SIBERIAN LOVE and SNOW PALS, Gregory Perillo, 7,500, set of 2	100.00	175.00

Chieftains I

1979	CHIEF SITTING BULL, Gregory Perillo, 7,500	65.00	325.00
1979	CHIEF JOSEPH, Gregory Perillo, 7,500	65.00	100.00
1980	CHIEF RED CLOUD, Gregory Perillo, 7,500	65.00	120.00
1980	GERONIMO, Gregory Perillo, 7,500	65.00	80.00
1981	CHIEF CRAZY HORSE, Gregory Perillo, 7,500	65.00	140.00

Chieftains II

1983	CHIEF PONTIAC, Gregory Perillo, 7,500	70.00	NR
1983	CHIEF VICTORIO, Gregory Perillo, 7,500	70.00	NR
1983	CHIEF TECUMSEH, Gregory Perillo, 7,500	70.00	NR
1983	CHIEF COCHISE, Gregory Perillo, 7,500	70.00	NR
1983	CHIEF BLACK KETTLE, Gregory Perillo, 7,500	70.00	NR

Child's Life

1983	SIESTA, Gregory Perillo, 10,000	45.00	NR
1984	SWEET DREAMS, Gregory Perillo, 10,000	45.00	NR

Indian Nations

1983	BLACKFOOT, Gregory Perillo, 7,500	35.00	65.00
1983	CHEYENNE, Gregory Perillo, 7,500	35.00	65.00
1983	APACHE, Gregory Perillo, 7,500	35.00	65.00
1983	SIOUX, Gregory Perillo, 7,500	35.00	65.00
	Set of 4	140.00	260.00

Legends of the West

1982	DANIEL BOONE, Gregory Perillo, 10,000	65.00	NR
1983	DAVY CROCKETT, Gregory Perillo, 10,000	65.00	NR
1983	KIT CARSON, Gregory Perillo, 10,000	65.00	NR
1983	BUFFALO BILL, Gregory Perillo, 10,000	65.00	NR

Masterpieces of Impressionism

1980	WOMAN WITH PARASOL, Claude Monet, 17,500	35.00	60.00
1981	YOUNG MOTHER SEWING, Mary Cassatt, 17,500	35.00	50.00
1982	SARA IN GREEN BONNET, Mary Cassatt,17,500	35.00	50.00
1983	MARGOT IN BLUE, Mary Cassatt, 17,500	35.00	45.00

Masterpieces of Rockwell

1980	AFTER THE PROM, Norman Rockwell, 17,500	42.50	90.00
1980	THE CHALLENGER, Norman Rockwell, 17,500	50.00	NR
1982	GIRL AT THE MIRROR, Norman Rockwell, 17,500	50.00	75.00

		Issue Price	Current Value
1982	MISSING TOOTH, Norman Rockwell, 17,500...........	50.00	NR

Masterpieces of the West

1980	TEXAS NIGHT HERDER, Frank T. Johnson, 17,500.......	35.00	55.00
1981	INDIAN TRAPPER, Frederic Remington, 17,500.........	35.00	45.00
1982	COWBOY STYLE, William R. Leigh, 17,500..............	35.00	NR
1982	INDIAN STYLE, Gregory Perillo, 17,500	35.00	75.00

Motherhood

1983	MADRE, Gregory Perillo, 10,000	50.00	75.00
1984	MADONNA OF THE PLAINS, Gregory Perillo, 10,000.....	50.00	75.00
1985	ABUELA, Gregory Perillo, 3,500	50.00	75.00
1986	NAP TIME, Gregory Perillo, 3,500	50.00	75.00

Nature's Harmony

1982	PEACEABLE KINGDOM, Gregory Perillo, 12,500.........	100.00	150.00
1982	ZEBRA, Gregory Perillo, 12,500	50.00	NR
1982	BENGAL TIGER, Gregory Perillo, 12,500...............	50.00	NR
1982	BLACK PANTHER, Gregory Perillo, 12,500	50.00	60.00
1982	ELEPHANT, Gregory Perillo, 12,500	50.00	70.00

Perillo Santas

1980	SANTA'S JOY, Gregory Perillo, 1 year	29.95	40.00
1981	SANTA'S BUNDLE, Gregory Perillo, 1 year	29.95	40.00

Plainsmen

1978	BUFFALO HUNT, Gregory Perillo, bronze, 2,500	350.00	375.00
1979	THE PROUD ONE, Gregory Perillo, bronze, 2,500	350.00	550.00

Pride of America's Indians

1986	BRAVE AND FREE, Gregory Perillo, 10 days	24.50	35.00
1986	DARK–EYED FRIENDS, Gregory Perillo, 10 days	24.50	BR
1986	NOBLE COMPANIONS, Gregory Perillo, 10 days	24.50	BR
1987	KINDRED SPIRITS, Gregory Perillo, 10 days	24.50	NR
1987	LOYAL ALLIANCE, Gregory Perillo, 10 days	24.50	45.00
1987	SMALL AND WISE, Gregory Perillo, 10 days	24.50	NR
1987	WINTER SCOUTS, Gregory Perillo, 10 days	24.50	NR
1987	PEACEFUL COMRADES, Gregory Perillo, 10 days	24.50	30.00

Princesses

1982	LILY OF THE MOHAWKS, Gregory Perillo, 7,500	50.00	85.00
1982	POCAHONTAS, Gregory Perillo, 7,500	50.00	65.00
1982	MINNEHAHA, Gregory Perillo, 7,500	50.00	65.00
1982	SACAJAWEA, Gregory Perillo, 7,500	50.00	85.00

		Issue Price	Current Value

Professionals

1979	THE BIG LEAGUER, Gregory Perillo, 15,000	29.95	45.00
1980	BALLERINA'S DILEMMA, Gregory Perillo, 15,000	32.50	45.00
1981	QUARTERBACK, Gregory Perillo, 15,000	32.50	50.00
1981	RODEO JOE, Gregory Perillo, 15,000	35.00	40.00
1982	MAJOR LEAGUER, Gregory Perillo, 15,000	35.00	50.00
1983	THE HOCKEY PLAYER, Gregory Perillo, 15,000	35.00	50.00

Storybook Collection

1980	LITTLE RED RIDING HOOD, Gregory Perillo, <1 year	29.95	45.00
1981	CINDERELLA, Gregory Perillo, <1 year	29.95	45.00
1981	HANSEL AND GRETEL, Gregory Perillo, <1 year	29.95	45.00
1982	GOLDILOCKS AND THE THREE BEARS, Gregory Perillo, 18 days 29.95		45.00

Thoroughbreds

1984	WHIRLAWAY, Gregory Perillo, 9,500	50.00	150.00
1984	SECRETARIAT, Gregory Perillo, 9,500	50.00	200.00
1984	MAN–OF–WAR, Gregory Perillo, 9,500	50.00	100.00
1984	SEABISCUIT, Gregory Perillo, 9,500	50.00	100.00

Tribal Ponies

1984	ARAPAHO, Gregory Perillo, 3,500	65.00	100.00
1984	COMANCHE, Gregory Perillo, 3,500	65.00	100.00
1984	CROW, Gregory Perillo, 3,500	65.00	150.00

War Ponies

1983	SIOUX, Gregory Perillo, 7,500	60.00	115.00
1983	NEZ PERCE, Gregory Perillo, 7,500	60.00	135.00
1983	APACHE, Gregory Perillo, 7,500	60.00	110.00

Single Issues

1981	APACHE BOY, Gregory Perillo, 5,000	95.00	175.00
1981	PERILLO LITHO BOOK, Gregory Perillo, 3,000	95.00	NR
1983	PAPOOSE, Gregory Perillo, 3,000	100.00	110.00
1984	NAVAJO GIRL, Gregory Perillo, 3,500	95.00	175.00
1986	NAVAJO BOY, Gregory Perillo, 3,500	95.00	125.00

VAL ST. LAMBERT BELGIUM

American Heritage

1969	PILGRIM FATHERS, 500	200.00	450.00
1970	PAUL REVERE'S RIDE, 500	200.00	225.00
1971	WASHINGTON ON DELAWARE, 500	200.00	225.00

Annual Old Masters	Issue Price	Current Value
1969 REUBENS and REMBRANDT, 5,000, set of 2	50.00	90.00
1969 VAN GOGH and VAN DYCK, 5,000, set of 2	50.00	85.00
1970 DA VINCI and MICHELANGELO, 5,000, set of 2..........	50.00	90.00
1971 EL GRECO and GOYA, 5,000, set of 2	50.00	85.00
1972 REYNOLDS and GAINSBOROUGH, 5,000, set of 2	50.00	70.00

Single Issue

1970 REMBRANDT	25.00	40.00

VENETO FLAIR ITALY

American Landscape

1979 HUDSON VALLEY, 7,500..............................	75.00	NR
1980 NORTHWEST CASCADE, 7,500	75.00	NR

Bellini Series

1971 MADONNA, Vincente Tiziano, 500	45.00	400.00

Birds

1972 OWL, 2,000..	37.50	100.00
1973 FALCON, 2,000.....................................	37.50	NR
1974 MALLARD, 2,000....................................	45.00	NR

Cats

1974 PERSIAN, 2,000....................................	40.00	55.00
1975 SIAMESE, 2,000	45.00	55.00
1976 TABBY, 2,000	45.00	55.00

Children's Christmas

1979 THE CAROLERS, Vincente Tiziano, 7,500	60.00	NR
1980 HEADING HOME, Vincente Tiziano, 7,500	75.00	NR
1981 THE NIGHT BEFORE, Vincente Tiziano, 7,500	95.00	NR
1982 A VISIT TO SANTA, Vincente Tiziano, 7,500.............	95.00	NR

Christmas

1971 THREE KINGS, Vincente Tiziano, 1,500	55.00	NR
1972 SHEPHERDS, Vincente Tiziano, 1,500	55.00	NR
1973 CHRIST CHILD, Vincente Tiziano, 1,500	55.00	NR
1974 ANGEL, Vincente Tiziano, 1,500	55.00	NR

Christmas Card

1975 CHRISTMAS EVE, Vincente Tiziano, 4,000	37.50	NR
1976 OLD NORTH CHURCH, Vincente Tiziano, 4,000	37.50	NR

		Issue Price	Current Value
1977	LOG CABIN CHRISTMAS, Vincente Tiziano, 4,000	37.50	NR
1978	DUTCH CHRISTMAS, Vincente Tiziano, 4,000	40.00	NR

Dogs

1972	GERMAN SHEPHERD, Vincente Tiziano, 2,000	37.50	75.00
1973	POODLE, Vincente Tiziano, 2,000	37.50	45.00
1974	DOBERMAN, Vincente Tiziano, 2,000	37.50	NR
1975	COLLIE, Vincente Tiziano, 2,000	40.00	NR
1976	DACHSHUND, Vincente Tiziano, 2,000	45.00	NR

Easter

1973	RABBITS, 2,000	50.00	90.00
1974	CHICKS, 2,000	50.00	NR
1975	LAMB, 2,000	50.00	NR
1976	COMPOSITE, 2,000	50.00	NR

Flower Children

1978	ROSE, 3,000	45.00	NR
1979	ORCHID, 3,000	60.00	NR
1980	CAMELIA, 3,000	65.00	NR

Four Seasons

1972	FALL, silver plate, 2,000	75.00	NR
1972	FALL, sterling silver, 2,000	125.00	NR
1973	SPRING, silver plate, 300	75.00	NR
1973	SPRING, sterling silver, 750	125.00	NR
1973	WINTER, silver plate, 2,000	75.00	NR
1973	WINTER, sterling silver, 250	125.00	NR
1974	SUMMER, silver plate, 300	75.00	NR
1974	SUMMER, sterling silver, 750	125.00	NR

Goddesses

1973	POMONA, 1,500	75.00	125.00
1974	DIANA, 1,500	75.00	NR

La Belle Femme

1978	LILY, 9,500	70.00	NR
1979	GIGI, 9,500	76.50	NR
1980	DOMINIQUE, 9,500	76.50	NR
1980	GABRIELLE, 9,500	76.50	NR

Lamincia Annual

1981	YOUNG LOVE, Franco Lamincia, 7,500	95.00	NR

Last Supper

		Issue Price	Current Value
1972	THREE APOSTLES, Vincente Tiziano, 2,000	100.00	NR
1973	THREE APOSTLES, Vincente Tiziano, 2,000	70.00	NR
1974	THREE APOSTLES, Vincente Tiziano, 2,000	70.00	NR
1975	THREE APOSTLES, Vincente Tiziano, 2,000	70.00	NR
1976	JESUS CHRIST, Vincente Tiziano, 2,000	70.00	85.00

Mosaic

1973	JUSTINIAN, Vincente Tiziano, 500	50.00	75.00
1974	PELICAN, Vincente Tiziano, 1,000	50.00	NR
1977	THEODORA, Vincente Tiziano, 500	50.00	NR

Mother and Child

1981	LOONS, Guilio Gialletti and Franco Lamincia, 5,000	95.00	NR
1981	POLAR BEAR, Guilio Gialletti and Franco Lamincia, 5,000	95.00	NR
1981	KOALAS, Guilio Gialletti and Franco Lamincia, 5,000	95.00	NR
1981	BUFFALOS, Guilio Gialletti and Franco Lamincia, 5,000	95.00	NR
1981	LIONS, Guilio Gialletti and Franco Lamincia, 5,000	95.00	NR
1981	ELEPHANTS, Guilio Gialletti and Franco Lamincia, 5,000	95.00	NR

Mother's Day

1972	MADONNA AND CHILD, Vincente Tiziano, 2,000	55.00	85.00
1973	MADONNA AND CHILD, Vincente Tiziano, 2,000	55.00	NR
1974	MOTHER AND SON, Vincente Tiziano, 2,000	55.00	NR
1975	DAUGHTER AND DOLL, Vincente Tiziano, 2,000	45.00	NR
1976	SON AND DAUGHTER, Vincente Tiziano, 2,000	55.00	NR
1977	MOTHER AND CHILD, Vincente Tiziano, 2,000	50.00	NR

Valentine's Day

1977	VALENTINE BOY, 3,000	45.00	60.00
1978	VALENTINE GIRL, 3,000	45.00	55.00
1979	HANSEL, 3,000	60.00	NR
1980	GRETEL, 5,000	67.50	NR

Wildlife

1971	DEER, Vincente Tiziano, 500	37.50	450.00
1972	ELEPHANT, Vincente Tiziano, 1,000	37.50	275.00
1973	PUMA, Vincente Tiziano, 2,000	37.50	65.00
1974	TIGER, Vincente Tiziano, 2,000	40.00	50.00

VERNONWARE UNITED STATES

Christmas

1971	PARTRIDGE, 1 year	15.00	60.00
1972	JINGLE BELLS, 1 year	17.50	30.00

	Issue Price	Current Value
1973 THE FIRST NOEL, 1 year	20.00	35.00
1974 UPON A MIDNIGHT CLEAR, 1 year	20.00	30.00
1975 O HOLY NIGHT, 1 year	20.00	30.00
1976 HARK! THE HERALD ANGELS, 1 year	20.00	30.00
1977 AWAY IN THE MANGER, 1 year	30.00	NR
1978 WHITE CHRISTMAS, 10,000	30.00	NR
1979 LITTLE DRUMMER BOY, 10,000	30.00	NR

Corvette Collector

1986 PACE CAR CONVERTIBLE, Bill Seitz, 2,000	29.95	NR
1987 '63 SPLIT WINDOW COUPE, Bill Seitz, 2,000	29.95	NR

VILETTA CHINA UNITED STATES
(See also Pemberton & Oakes)

Alice in Wonderland

1980 ALICE AND THE WHITE RABBIT, Robert Blitzer, 28 days .	25.00	NR
1980 ADVICE FROM A CATERPILLAR, Robert Blitzer, 28 days .	25.00	NR
1980 END OF A DREAM, Robert Blitzer, 28 days	25.00	NR
1981 MAD HATTER'S TEA PARTY, Robert Blitzer, 28 days	25.00	NR
1981 ALICE AND CHESHIRE CAT, Robert Blitzer, 28 days	25.00	NR
1981 ALICE AND CROQUET MATCH, Robert Blitzer, 28 days .	25.00	NR

Carefree Days

1982 AUTUMN WANDERER, Thornton Utz, 10 days	24.50	NR
1982 BEST FRIENDS, Thornton Utz, 10 days	24.50	NR
1982 FEEDING TIME, Thornton Utz, 10 days	24.50	NR
1982 BATHTIME VISITOR, Thornton Utz, 10 days	24.50	NR
1982 FIRST CATCH, Thornton Utz, 10 days	24.50	NR
1982 MONKEY BUSINESS, Thornton Utz, 10 days	24.50	NR
1982 TOUCHDOWN, Thornton Utz, 10 days	24.50	NR
1982 NATURE HUNT, Thornton Utz, 10 days	24.50	NR

Childhood Memories (Collector's Heirloom)

1978 JENNIFER BY CANDLELIGHT, William Bruckner, 5,000 ...	60.00	NR
1979 BRIAN'S BIRTHDAY, William Bruckner, 5,000	60.00	NR

Children's Series

1979 LAST OF THE NINTH, 5,000	45.00	NR

Christmas Annual

1978 EXPRESSION OF FAITH, 7,400	49.95	NR
1979 SKATING LESSON, 7,400	49.95	NR
1980 BRINGING HOME THE TREE, 7,400	49.95	NR

Coppelia Ballet (The Hamilton Collection)

Year	Title	Issue Price	Current Value
1980	FRANZ'S FANTASY LOVE, Renee Faure, 28 days	25.00	NR
1980	THE CREATION OF A DOLL, Renee Faure, 28 days	25.00	NR
1981	THE SECRET IS UNLOCKED, Renee Faure, 28 days	25.00	NR
1981	SWANILDA'S DECEPTION, Renee Faure, 28 days	25.00	NR
1981	AN UNEASY SLEEP, Renee Faure, 28 days	25.00	NR
1981	COPPELIA AWAKENS, Renee Faure, 28 days	25.00	NR
1982	A SHATTERED DREAM, Renee Faure, 28 days	25.00	NR
1982	THE WEDDING, Renee Faure, 28 days	25.00	NR

Days of the West

1978	COWBOY CHRISTMAS, 5,000	50.00	60.00

Disneyland

1976	SIGNING THE DECLARATION, 3,000	15.00	100.00
1976	CROSSING THE DELAWARE, 3,000	15.00	100.00
1976	BETSY ROSS, 3,000	15.00	100.00
1976	SPIRIT OF '76, 3,000	15.00	100.00
1979	MICKEY'S 50TH ANNIVERSARY, 5,000	37.00	50.00

Great Comedians (Warwick)

1978	THE LITTLE TRAMP, 7,500	35.00	NR
1978	OUTRAGEOUS GROUCHO, 7,500	35.00	NR

In Tribute to America's Great Artists

1978	DEGRAZIA, J. Marco, 5,000	65.00	NR

Israel's 30th Anniversary

1979	L'CHAYIM TO ISRAEL, 10,000	59.50	NR
1979	PROPHECY OF ISAIAH, 10,000	59.50	NR

Joys of Motherhood (Collector's Heirlooms)

1978	CRYSTAL'S JOY, William Bruckner, 7,500	60.00	BR

Making Friends

1978	FEEDING THE NEIGHBOR'S PONY, Irish McCalla, 5,000	45.00	NR
1979	COWBOYS 'N INDIANS, Irish McCalla, 5,000	47.50	NR
1980	SURPRISE FOR CHRISTY, Irish McCalla, 5,000	47.50	NR

Nutcracker Ballet

1978	CLARA AND THE NUTCRACKER, Shell Fisher, 28 days	29.50	40.00
1979	GIFT FROM GODFATHER, Shell Fisher, 28 days	29.50	NR
1979	SUGARPLUM FAIRY, Shell Fisher, 28 days	29.50	NR
1979	SNOW KING AND QUEEN, Shell Fisher, 28 days	29.50	NR
1980	WALTZ OF FLOWERS, Shell Fisher, 28 days	29.50	NR

		Issue Price	Current Value
1980	CLARA AND THE PRINCE, Shell Fisher, 28 days	29.50	NR

Olympics (Ghent Collection)

1980	WINTER OLYMPICS, 13 days	24.50	NR
1980	SUMMER OLYMPICS, <1 year	29.50	NR

The Performance (R. J. Ernst Enterprises)

1979	ACT I, Bonnie Porter, 5,000	65.00	NR

Portraits of Childhood (The Hamilton Collection)

1981	BUTTERFLY MAGIC, Thornton Utz, 28 days	24.95	NR
1982	SWEET DREAMS, Thornton Utz, 28 days	24.95	NR
1983	TURTLE TALK, Thornton Utz, 28 days	24.95	NR
1984	FRIENDS FOREVER, Thornton Utz, 28 days	24.95	NR

Precious Moments

1979	FRIEND IN THE SKY, Thornton Utz, 28 days	21.50	50.00
1980	SAND IN HER SHOE, Thornton Utz, 28 days	21.50	35.00
1980	SNOW BUNNY, Thornton Utz, 28 days	21.50	30.00
1980	SEASHELLS, Thornton Utz, 28 days	21.50	30.00
1981	DAWN, Thornton Utz, 28 days	21.50	30.00
1982	MY KITTY, Thornton Utz, 28 days	21.50	30.00

Rufus and Roxanne

1980	LOVE IS...., C. Kelly, 19,000	14.95	NR

Seasons of the Oak

1979	LAZY DAYS, Ralph Homan, 5,000	55.00	NR
1980	COME FLY WITH ME, Ralph Homan, 5,000	55.00	NR

Tender Moments

1978	OLD-FASHIONED PERSUASION, Eugene Christopherson, 7,500 NR		40.00
1980	DANDELIONS, Eugene Christopherson, 7,500	40.00	NR

Unicorn Fantasies

1979	FOLLOWERS OF DREAMS, K. Chin, 5,000	55.00	NR
1980	TWICE UPON A TIME, K. Chin, 5,000	55.00	NR
1981	FAMILIAR SPIRIT, K. Chin, 5,000	55.00	NR
1982	NOBLE GATHERING, K. Chin, 5,000	55.00	NR

Weddings Around the World

1979	HAWAIIAN WEDDING, Elke Sommer, 5,000	75.00	NR
1980	DUTCH WEDDING, Elke Sommer, 5,000	75.00	NR

Women of the West (R. J. Ernst Enterprises)

		Issue Price	Current Value
1979	EXPECTATIONS, Donald Putnam, 10,000	39.50	NR
1979	SILVER DOLLAR SAL, Donald Putnam, 10,000	39.50	NR
1980	FIRST DAY, Donald Putnam, 10,000	39.50	NR
1980	DOLLY, Donald Putnam, 10,000	39.50	NR
1982	SCHOOL MARM, Donald Putnam, 10,000	39.50	NR

Single Issues

1980	MAIL ORDER BRIDE, Irish McCalla, 5,000	60.00	NR
1980	THE DUKE (R. J. Ernst Enterprises), 27,500	29.75	NR
1983	PRINCESS GRACE, Thornton Utz, 21 days	75.00	NR

VILLEROY AND BOCH GERMANY

Christmas

1977	HOLY FAMILY, 10,000	175.00	200.00
1978	THREE HOLY KINGS, 20,000	175.00	200.00
1979	MARY WITH CHILD, 10,000	198.00	NR
1980	MADONNA IN GLORY, 10,000	200.00	NR

Flower Fairy

1979	THE LAVENDER FAIRY, Cicely Mary Barker, 21 days	35.00	50.00
1980	THE SWEET PEA FAIRY, Cicely Mary Barker, 21 days	35.00	NR
1980	THE CANDY TUFT FAIRY, Cicely Mary Barker, 21 days	35.00	NR
1981	THE HELIOTROPE FAIRY, Cicely Mary Barker, 21 days	35.00	NR
1981	THE BLACKTHORN FAIRY, Cicely Mary Barker, 21 days	35.00	NR
1981	THE APPLE BLOSSOM FAIRY, Cicely Mary Barker, 21 days	35.00	NR

Columbine
Photo courtesy of *Collectors News*

Flower Fairy II

1985	COLUMBINE, Cicely Mary Barker, 21 days	35.00	NR

			Issue Price	Current Value
1985	CORNFLOWER, Cicely Mary Barker, 21 days	....	35.00	NR
1985	MALLOW, Cicely Mary Barker, 21 days	....	35.00	NR
1985	BLACK MEDICK, Cicely Mary Barker, 21 days	....	35.00	NR
1985	CANTERBURY BELL, Cicely Mary Barker, 21 days	....	35.00	NR
1985	FUCHSIA, Cicely Mary Barker, 21 days	....	35.00	NR

Russian Fairy Tales — The Firebird

1981	IN SEARCH OF THE FIREBIRD, Boris Zvorykin, 27,500	....	70.00	NR
1981	IVAN AND TSAREVNA ON GREY WOLF, Boris Zvorykin, 27,500		70.00	NR
1981	THE WEDDING OF TSAREVNA ELENA THE FAIR, Boris Zvorykin, 27,500	....	70.00	100.00

Russian Fairy Tales — Maria Morevna

1982	MARIA MOREVNA AND TSAREVICH IVAN, Boris Zvorykin, 27,500	....	70.00	85.00
1983	KOSHCHEY CARRIES OFF MARIA MOREVNA, Boris Zvorykin, 27,500	....	70.00	NR
1983	TSAREVICH IVAN AND THE BEAUTIFUL CASTLE, Boris Zvorykin, 27,500	....	70.00	90.00

Russian Fairy Tales — The Red Knight

1981	THE RED KNIGHT, Boris Zvorykin, 27,500	....	70.00	BR
1981	VASSILISSA AND HER STEPSISTERS, Boris Zvorykin, 27,500	.	70.00	BR
1981	VASSILISSA IS PRESENTED TO THE TSAR, Boris Zvorykin, 27,500	....	70.00	BR

Russian Fairy Tales — Snow Maiden

1980	THE SNOW MAIDEN, Boris Zvorykin, 27,500	....	70.00	100.00
1981	SNEGUROCHKA AT THE COURT OF TSAR BERENDEI, Boris Zvorykin, 27,500	....	70.00	BR
1981	SNEGUROCHKA AND LEI THE SHEPHERD BOY, Boris Zvorykin, 27,500	....	70.00	BR

WALDENBURG PORCELAIN CANADA

Punkinhead, The Happy Little Bear

1983	PUNKINHEAD AND HIS FRIENDS, 4,000	....	34.50	NR
1983	PUNKINHEAD AND SANTA CLAUS, 4,000	....	34.50	NR

WATERFORD — WEDGWOOD

Avon Americana

1973	BETSY ROSS, 1 year	....	15.00	25.00
1974	FREEDOM, 1 year	....	15.00	25.00

Avon Christmas

		Issue Price	Current Value
1973	CHRISTMAS ON THE FARM, 1 year	15.00	40.00
1974	COUNTRY CHURCH, 1 year	16.00	30.00
1975	SKATERS ON POND, 1 year	18.00	25.00
1976	BRINGING HOME THE TREE, 1 year	18.00	NR
1977	CAROLERS IN THE SNOW, 1 year	19.50	NR
1978	TRIMMING THE TREE, 1 year	21.50	NR
1979	DASHING THROUGH THE SNOW, 1 year	24.00	NR

Avon Mother's Day

1974	TENDERNESS, 1 year	15.00	20.00
1975	GENTLE MOMENTS, 1 year	17.00	30.00

Avon North American Songbird

1974	CARDINALS, D. Eckelberry, 1 year	18.00	NR

Bicentennial

1972	BOSTON TEA PARTY, 1 year	40.00	NR
1973	PAUL REVERE'S RIDE 1 year	40.00	115.00
1974	BATTLE OF CONCORD 1 year	40.00	55.00
1975	ACROSS THE DELAWARE 1 year	40.00	105.00
1975	VICTORY AT YORKTOWN 1 year	45.00	55.00
1976	DECLARATION SIGNED, 1 year	45.00	NR

Blossoming of Suzanne

1977	INNOCENCE, Mary Vickers, 7,000	60.00	NR
1978	CHERISH, Mary Vickers, 7,000	60.00	NR
1979	DAYDREAM, Mary Vickers, 7,000	65.00	NR
1980	WISTFUL, Mary Vickers, 7,000	70.00	NR

Calendar

1971	VICTORIAN ALMANAC, 1 year	12.00	NR
1972	THE CAROUSEL, 1 year	12.95	NR
1973	BOUNTIFUL BUTTERFLY, 1 year	12.95	NR
1974	CAMELOT, 1 year	14.00	75.00
1975	CHILDREN'S GAMES, 1 year	15.00	NR
1976	ROBIN, 1 year	25.00	NR
1977	TONATIUH, 1 year	30.00	NR
1978	SAMURAI, 1 year	30.00	NR
1979	SACRED SCARAB, 1 year	35.00	NR
1980	SAFARI, 1 year	42.50	NR
1981	HORSES, 1 year	47.50	NR
1982	WILD WEST, 1 year	52.00	NR
1983	THE AGE OF THE REPTILES, 1 year	54.00	NR
1984	DOGS, 1 year	54.00	NR
1985	CATS, 1 year	54.00	NR

		Issue Price	Current Value
1986	BRITISH BIRDS, 1 year	54.00	NR
1987	WATER BIRDS, 1 year	54.00	NR
1988	SEA BIRDS, 1 year	54.00	NR

Cathedrals Christmas

1986	CANTERBURY CATHEDRAL, 1 year	40.00	NR

Child's Birthday

1981	PETER RABBIT, Beatrix Potter, 1 year	24.00	NR
1982	MRS. TIGG–WINKLE, Beatrix Potter, 1 year	27.00	NR
1983	PETER RABBIT AND BENJAMIN BUNNY, Beatrix Potter, 1 year	29.00	NR
1984	PETER RABBIT, Beatrix Potter, 1 year	29.00	NR
1985	PETER RABBIT, Beatrix Potter, 1 year	29.00	NR
1986	PETER RABBIT, Beatrix Potter, 1 year	29.00	NR
1987	OAKAPPLE WOOD, J. Partridge, 1 year	29.00	NR
1988	OAKAPPLE WOOD, J. Partridge, 1 year	29.00	NR

Child's Christmas

1979	CHILDREN AND SNOWMAN, 1 year	35.00	NR
1980	COLLECTING THE CHRISTMAS TREE, 1 year	37.50	NR
1981	CHILDREN SLEDDING, 1 year	40.00	NR
1982	SKATERS, 1 year	40.00	NR
1983	CAROL SINGING, 1 year	40.00	NR
1984	MIXING THE CHRISTMAS PUDDING, 1 year	40.00	NR

Children's Story

1971	THE SANDMAN, 1 year	7.95	25.00
1972	THE TINDER BOX, 1 year	7.95	NR
1973	THE EMPEROR'S NEW CLOTHES, 1 year	9.00	NR
1974	THE UGLY DUCKLING, 1 year	10.00	NR
1975	THE LITTLE MERMAID, 1 year	11.00	NR
1976	HANSEL AND GRETEL, 1 year	12.00	NR
1977	RUMPELSTILTSKIN, 1 year	15.00	NR
1978	THE FROG PRINCE, 1 year	15.00	25.00
1979	THE GOLDEN GOOSE, 1 year	15.00	NR
1980	RAPUNZEL, 1 year	16.00	NR
1981	TOM THUMB, 1 year	18.00	NR
1982	THE LADY AND THE LION, 1 year	20.00	NR
1983	THE ELVES AND THE SHOEMAKER, 1 year	20.00	NR
1984	KING ROUGHBEARD, 1 year	20.00	NR
1985	THE BRAVE LITTLE TAILOR, 1 year	20.00	NR

Christmas

1969	WINDSOR CASTLE, Tom Harper, 1 year	25.00	100.00
1970	TRAFALGAR SQUARE, Tom Harper, 1 year	30.00	NR

		Issue Price	Current Value
1971	PICCADILLY CIRCUS, Tom Harper, 1 year	30.00	NR
1972	ST. PAUL'S CATHEDRAL, Tom Harper, 1 year	35.00	NR
1973	TOWER OF LONDON, Tom Harper, 1 year	40.00	NR
1974	HOUSES OF PARLIAMENT, Tom Harper, 1 year	40.00	NR
1975	TOWER BRIDGE, Tom Harper, 1 year	45.00	NR
1976	HAMPTON COURT	50.00	NR
1977	WESTMINSTER ABBEY	55.00	NR
1978	HORSE GUARDS, Tom Harper, 1 year	60.00	NR
1979	BUCKINGHAM PALACE, 1 year	65.00	NR
1980	ST. JAMES'S PALACE, 1 year	70.00	NR
1981	MARBLE ARCH, 1 year	75.00	NR
1982	LAMBETH PALACE, 1 year	80.00	NR
1983	ALL SOULS, LANGHAM PALACE, 1 year	80.00	NR
1984	CONSTITUTION HILL, 1 year	80.00	NR
1985	THE TATE GALLERY, 1 year	80.00	NR
1986	THE ALBERT MEMORIAL, 1 year.......................	80.00	NR
1987	GUILDHALL, 1 year	80.00	NR
1988	THE OBSERVATORY/GREENWICH, 1 year	80.00	NR
1989	WINCHESTER CATHEDRAL, 1 year....................	80.00	NR

Colin Newman's Country Panorama

		Issue Price	Current Value
1987	MEADOWS AND WHEATFIELDS......................	29.00	NR
1987	THE MEANDERING STREAM.........................	29.00	NR
1987	VILLAGE IN THE VALLEY.............................	32.00	NR
1988	ROLLING HILLS AND GRASSLANDS	32.00	NR
1988	THE BEECHWOOD	32.00	NR
1988	THE FARM COTTAGE	32.00	NR
1988	THE HAYFIELD	34.00	NR
1988	THE LAKESIDE	34.00	NR

Eyes of the Child

		Issue Price	Current Value
XX	LITTLE LADY LOVE, Peter Fromme–Douglas, 15,000	65.00	NR
XX	MY BEST FRIEND, Peter Fromme–Douglas, 15,000	65.00	NR
XX	I WISH UPON A STAR, Peter Fromme–Douglas, 15,000 ..	65.00	NR
XX	IN A CHILD'S THOUGHT, Peter Fromme–Douglas, 15,000.	65.00	NR
XX	PUPPY LOVE, Peter Fromme–Douglas, 15,000	65.00	NR

Legends of King Arthur

		Issue Price	Current Value
1986	ARTHUR DRAWS THE SWORD, Richard Hook	39.00	NR
1986	ARTHUR CROWNED KING	39.00	NR
1987	EXCALIBUR..	42.00	NR
1987	WEDDING OF KING ARTHUR AND GUINEVERE.........	42.00	NR
1987	KNIGHTS OF THE ROUND TABLE	42.00	50.00
1987	LANCELOT AND GUINEVERE.........................	42.00	60.00
1988	MORGAN LE FAY AND MORDRED	44.00	75.00
1988	ARTHUR IS TAKEN TO AVALON	44.00	80.00

		Issue Price	Current Value

Mother's Day

1971	SPORTIVE LOVE, 1 year	20.00	NR
1972	THE SEWING LESSON, 1 year	20.00	NR
1973	THE BAPTISM OF ACHILLES, 1 year	20.00	NR
1974	DOMESTIC EMPLOYMENT, 1 year	30.00	NR
1975	MOTHER AND CHILD, 1 year	35.00	NR
1976	THE SPINNER, 1 year	35.00	NR
1977	LEISURE TIME, 1 year	35.00	NR
1978	SWAN AND CYGNETS, 1 year	40.00	NR
1979	DEER AND FAWN, 1 year	45.00	NR
1980	BIRDS, 1 year	47.50	NR
1981	MARE AND FOAL, 1 year	50.00	NR
1982	CHERUBS WITH SWING, 1 year	55.00	NR
1983	CUPID AND BUTTERFLY, 1 year	55.00	NR
1984	MUSICAL CUPIDS, 1 year	55.00	NR
1985	CUPIDS AND DOVES, 1 year	55.00	NR
1986	CUPIDS FISHING, 1 year	55.00	NR
1987	ANEMONES, 1 year	55.00	NR
1988	TIGER LILY, 1 year	55.00	NR
1989	IRISES, 1 year	65.00	NR
1991	PEONIES, 1 year	65.00	NR

My Memories

1981	BE MY FRIEND, Mary Vickers	27.00	NR
1982	PLAYTIME, Mary Vickers	27.00	NR
1983	OUR GARDEN, Mary Vickers	27.00	50.00
1984	THE RECITAL, Mary Vickers	27.00	50.00
1985	MOTHER'S TREASURES, Mary Vickers	27.00	35.00
1986	RIDING HIGH, Mary Vickers	29.00	NR

Peter Rabbit Christmas

1981	PETER RABBIT, Beatrix Potter, 1 year	27.00	NR
1982	PETER RABBIT, Beatrix Potter, 1 year	27.00	NR
1983	PETER RABBIT, Beatrix Potter, 1 year	29.00	NR
1984	PETER RABBIT, Beatrix Potter, 1 year	29.00	NR
1985	PETER RABBIT, Beatrix Potter, 1 year	29.00	NR
1986	PETER RABBIT, Beatrix Potter, 1 year	29.00	NR
1987	PETER RABBIT, Beatrix Potter, 1 year	29.00	NR

Portraits of First Love

| 1986 | THE LOVE LETTER, Mary Vickers | 27.00 | NR |

Queen's Christmas

| 1980 | WINDSOR CASTLE, A. Price, 1 year | 24.95 | NR |
| 1981 | TRAFALGAR SQUARE, A. Price, 1 year | 24.95 | NR |

		Issue Price	Current Value
1982	PICCADILLY CIRCUS, A. Price, 1 year	32.50	NR
1983	ST. PAUL'S, A. Price, 1 year	32.50	NR
1984	TOWER OF LONDON, A. Price, 1 year	35.00	NR
1985	PALACE OF WESTMINSTER, A. Price, 1 year	35.00	NR
1986	TOWER BRIDGE, A. Price, 1 year	35.00	NR

Street Sellers of London

1986	THE BAKED POTATO MAN, John Finnie	25.00	NR

Little Lady Love
Photo courtesy of *Collectors News*

WENDELL AUGUSTE FORGE UNITED STATES

Christmas

1974	CAROLER, bronze, 2,500	25.00	NR
1974	CAROLER, pewter, 2,500	30.00	NR
1975	CHRISTMAS IN COUNTRY, bronze, 2,500	30.00	NR
1975	CHRISTMAS IN COUNTRY, pewter, 2,500	35.00	NR
1976	LAMPLIGHTER, bronze, 2,500	35.00	NR
1976	LAMPLIGHTER, pewter, 2,500	40.00	NR
1977	COVERED BRIDGE, bronze, 2,500	40.00	NR
1977	COVERED BRIDGE, pewter, 2,500	45.00	NR

Great Americans

1971	KENNEDY, pewter, 500	40.00	NR
1971	KENNEDY, silver, 500	200.00	NR
1972	LINCOLN, pewter, 500	40.00	NR
1972	LINCOLN, silver, 500	200.00	NR

Great Moments

1972	LANDING OF PILGRIMS, pewter, 5,000	40.00	NR
1972	LANDING OF PILGRIMS, silver, 500	200.00	NR

		Issue Price	Current Value
1973	FIRST THANKSGIVING, pewter, 5,000	40.00	NR
1972	FIRST THANKSGIVING, silver, 500	200.00	NR
1974	PATRICK HENRY, pewter, 5,000	40.00	NR
1974	PATRICK HENRY, silver, 500	200.00	NR
1975	PAUL REVERE, pewter, 5,000	45.00	NR
1975	PAUL REVERE, silver, 500	200.00	NR
1976	SIGNING OF DECLARATION, pewter, 5,000	45.00	NR
1976	SIGNING OF DECLARATION, silver, 500	200.00	NR

Peace

1973	PEACE DOVES, 2,500	250.00	275.00

Wildlife

1977	ON GUARD, aluminum, 1,900	35.00	NR
1977	ON GUARD, bronze, 1,500	45.00	NR
1977	ON GUARD, pewter, 1,500	55.00	NR
1977	ON GUARD, silver, 100	250.00	NR
1978	THUNDERBIRD, aluminum, 1,900	40.00	NR
1978	THUNDERBIRD, bronze, 1,500	50.00	NR
1978	THUNDERBIRD, pewter, 1,500	60.00	NR
1978	THUNDERBIRD, silver, 100	250.00	NR

Wings of Man

1971	COLUMBUS' SHIPS, pewter, 5,000	40.00	NR
1971	COLUMBUS' SHIPS, silver, 500	200.00	NR
1972	CONESTOGA WAGON, pewter, 5,000	40.00	NR
1972	CONESTOGA WAGON, silver, 500	200.00	NR

WESTERN AUTHENTICS CANADA

Guns at Sea

1986	H.M.C.S. HAIDA, Robert Banks, 5,000	39.95	NR
1986	H.M.C.S. BONAVENTURE, Robert Banks, 5,000	39.95	NR

Iron Pioneers

1986	CPR NO. 374, Robert Banks, 15,000	39.95	NR
1986	COUNTESS OF DUFFERIN, Robert Banks, 15,000	39.95	NR

Tunes of Glory

1986	THE PIPER, Robert Banks, 15,000	42.50	NR
1986	PIPER AND DRUMMER, Robert Banks, 15,000	42.50	NR

Single Issues

1986	DOUGLASS DC–3, Robert Banks, 7,500	39.95	NR

		Issue Price	Current Value
1986	SCARLET AND GOLD, Robert Banks, 19,500	49.95	NR

WESTMINSTER COLLECTIBLES UNITED STATES

Holiday

1976	ALL HALLOWS EVE, 5,000	38.50	NR
1977	CHRISTMAS, 5,000	38.50	NR

WEXFORD GROUP UNITED STATES

Grandmother's World

1982	LITTLE TOY FRIENDS, Cynthia Knapton, 12,500	45.00	NR
1983	THE PROMENADE, Cynthia Knapton, 12,500	45.00	NR
1983	AFTERNOON TEA, Cynthia Knapton, 12,500	45.00	NR

Storyland Dolls

1984	MARY HAD A LITTLE LAMB, Cynthia Knapton, 5,000	39.50	NR

WILDLIFE INTERNATIONALE UNITED STATES

Owl Family

1983	SAW–WHET OWL FAMILY, John Ruthven, 5,000	55.00	NR
1983	GREAT HORNED OWL FAMILY, John Ruthven, 5,000	55.00	NR
1983	SNOWY OWL FAMILY, John Ruthven, 5,000	55.00	NR
1983	BARRED OWL FAMILY, John Ruthven, 5,000	55.00	NR

Sporting Dogs

1985	DECOY (LABRADOR RETRIEVER), John Ruthven, 5,000...	55.00	100.00
1985	RUMMY (ENGLISH SETTER), John Ruthven, 5,000.......	55.00	NR
1985	DUSTY (GOLDEN RETRIEVER), John Ruthven, 5,000	55.00	80.00
1985	SCARLETT (IRISH SETTER), John Ruthven, 5,000	55.00	100.00

Waterfowl

1983	WOOD DUCKS, John Ruthven, 5,000	65.00	NR

WINDEMERE COLLECTION UNITED STATES

Single Issue

1984	PIANO MOODS, Robert Olson, 7,500	60.00	NR

WOODMERE CHINA UNITED STATES

Children of the American Frontier

		Issue Price	Current Value
1986	IN TROUBLE AGAIN, Don Crook, 10 days	24.50	NR
1986	TUBS AND SUDS, Don Crook, 10 days................	24.50	NR
1986	A LADY NEEDS A LITTLE PRIVACY, Don Crook, 10 days ..	24.50	NR
1986	THE DESPERADOES, Don Crook, 10 days	24.50	NR
1986	RIDERS WANTED, Don Crook, 10 days................	24.50	NR
1987	A COWBOY'S DOWNFALL, Don Crook, 10 days	24.50	NR
1987	RUNAWAY BLUES, Don Crook, 10 days	24.50	NR
1987	A SPECIAL PATIENT, Don Crook, 10 days	24.50	NR

ZANOBIA

African Violet Miniatures

1985	HALF PINT, Zanobia, 5,000	29.50	NR
1985	LUVKINS, Zanobia, 5,000	29.50	NR

Violet Portraits

1987	CANADIAN SUNSET, Zanobia, 5,000	34.50	NR
1987	KISS'T, Zanobia, 5,000	34.50	NR

Artist Index

– A –

Aarestrup, 136, 142
Achtziger, Hans, 336, 338
Adachi, Yasuhiko, 297
Adams, Allen, 87, 88
Adams, N., 390
Adeyanor, S. , 534
Agnew, A., 316
Ahlcrona, Robert, 484
Akers, Roger, 344
Alexander, Cassidy J., 274, 278, 279
Allison, Betty, 82
Almazetta, 125
America, Marca, 430
An, O., 534
Anderson, Ivan, 274, 275
Anderson, N., 238
Anderson, Robert, 417, 418
Anderson, Susan, 166
Anderson, W., 383
Angelico, Fra, 451
Anglund, Joan Walsh, 192
Anguiano, Raul, 150
Anker, Albert, 388
Antonaccio, E., 237
Appleby, Gayle Bright, 343, 344
Appleby, Gregg, 125
Appleton, Jack, 160
Ard, Kurt, 142
Artisans of Incolay Studios, 343
Attwell, Mabel Lucie, 444
Auckland, J., 383
Audubon, John James, 219
Avey, Linda, 358

– B –

Baaring, Maggi, 347
Bahnsen, Frode, 267
Baldwin, Richard, 223
Balke, Don, 208, 209
Band, Ursula, 363, 531
Banks, Robert, 272, 551, 552
Bannister, Pati, 511
Banse, Glen, 195
Barbard, 269
Barker, Cicely Mary, 234, 320, 438, 544, 545
Barlowe, Dot, 440, 449, 523
Barlowe, Sy, 305, 446, 449, 523
Barnhouse, Dave, 285
Barratt, Isa, 211
Barratt, Peter, 215, 223, 224
Barrer, Gertrude, 94
Barson, J., 186
Baston, Prescott W., 387, 388, 504
Bates, Betsy, 397
Bauer, Kurt, 349, 350, 353, 354, 355
Beaudoin, J., 381, 383
Beaujard, Yves, 214, 220
Becker, Charlotte, 107, 113, 175, 176
Becker, H. T., 241, 242
Bedal, Karl, 384
Beecham, G., 237, 241
Bell, Deborah, 220
Bell, M., 295

Bellini, 318
Belousov, R., 234
Belski, Abram, 216, 224
Benger, B., 186
Beninati, Carlo, 188
Bentley, Robert, 417
Benvenuti, Sergio, 528
Béran, Lenore, 161, 278
Berger, Kathia, 334, 337
Bergsma, J., 436, 441, 442, 443, 444
Berke, E., 450
Bernadotte, Count Lennart, 93
Berran, Robert, 521
Beylon, C., 208
Bharnson, Tom, 452
Bialosky, P. and A., 289
Biel, 194
Bierly, Edward J., 254, 255, 354
Bishop, Jerold, 207
Black, Ben, 495
Blackshear, Thomas, 286, 297, 306, 310, 311, 315
Blandford, Wilfred, 182
Blaylock, T., 281
Blish, Carolyn, 164
Blitzer, Robert, 541
Blottiaux, Robert, 527
Blum, Hannelore, 349, 350, 353
Bobnick, D., 316
Bocher, Richard, 478, 479
Boehm Studio Artists, 146, 147, 148, 149, 150, 286, 287
Boehm, Edward Marshall, 390

Boesen, Arthur, 478
Bogart, M. H., 301, 314
Bohua, Zhu, 316
Bolshakova, V., 534
Bond, Higgins, 292, 313, 371, 380, 484, 490
Bonfils, Kjeld, 139, 142
Bonner, H., 251
Botticelli, 318, 422
Bouche, Andre, 202
Bouguereau, William A., 484
Bourgeault, Robert, 105
Boyer, Gene, 99, 210
Brackenbury, Amy, 365
Bradley, B., 368
Bragg, C. L., 174
Brastoff, Sascha, 164
Bratile, Gunnar, 431, 432
Brenders, C., 246, 247, 248
Brennan, Walter Jr., 89
Bridgett, J., 248
Brooks, P., 299
Brown, C. A., 495
Brown, D., 365
Brown, Roger, 172, 173, 455, 456
Browning, T., 379
Bruckner, T. Holter, 192
Bruckner, William, 541, 542
Bruijn, Mar de, 492, 493, 494
Bruke, Brenda, 497
Brunettin, Alan, 344
Budden, M., 370
Buffet, Bernard, 212
Burgues, Carol, 92
Burgues, Dr. Irving, 92, 93
Burke, B., 235, 242, 243
Bush, D., 239
Bush, G., 237
Butcher, Samuel, 193, 194, 306, 307
Byi, Charlot, 256

– C –

Cable, I., 372
Calder, Rosemary, 104, 343, 488
Calle, Paul, 211
Calvert, Lissa, 258
Cambier, Guy, 178, 179

Camm, Martin, 334, 335
Canaris, Patti, 319, 356
Capser, Mike, 285
Carlsen, Marin, 159
Carreno, Pablo, 400
Carroll, Mike, 359
Casay, A., 251
Caspari, Claus, 219
Cassatt, Mary, 112, 176, 423, 535
Cassini, Oleg, 427
Cassler, Carl, 521
Casson, A. J., 165
Catalano, J., 526
Cavell, Lily, 413
Cenkovcan, Ivo, 351
Chambers, William, 362, 363, 374, 376, 377, 378, 383
Chang, L., 240, 247
Chapple, Dave, 278
Chase, Beverly, 345
Chase, Lynn, 392
Cheng, J., 289, 290
Chi, Chen, 498
Chin, K., 543
Chiu, T. C., 365, 374
Choma, Edith McLennan, 255
Christie, B., 292
Christopherson, Eugene, 301, 398, 455, 456, 543
Christy, Howard Chandler, 119, 177
Chumley, John, 212
Clark, J., 532
Clark, Terry, 160
Clarke, Robert, 350
Cleary, Fergus, 130
Clymer, John, 261, 264
Cobane, R., 240
Colbert, June, 166
Cole, J. Kramer, 238, 250
Conche, Gina, 277
Cooke, J., 503
Cooper, A. Heesen, 141
Cooper, P., 303, 503
Copeland, Eric, 169
Corbin, Raymond, 181
Correggio, A., 302
Cowles, 435
Cranston, Toller, 259
Crnkovich, Tony, 380

Crook, Don, 291, 457, 553
Cross, Penni Anne, 104, 105
Crouch, Linda, 83
Csatari, Joseph, 367
Currier & Ives, 215

– D –

D'Estrehan, Alan, 100, 103, 104, 487, 488, 489, 490
Dacey, Robert, 533
Dali, Louis, 179, 180
Daly, James, 104
Danby, Ken, 93
Daniel, Kevin, 364, 365, 370, 371
Danielle, L., 302
David, G., 422
Davies, Will, 164
Da Vinci, L., 254, 302
Davis, Lowell, 509, 510, 511, 512
Day, Ray, 146, 394
De Mille, Leslie, 358, 506
De Winne, Lisette, 100, 101, 494, 495
Deas, Michael, 156
Decker, C., 377
DeGrazia, Ted, 121, 122, 123, 124, 125, 200, 201
DeHaan, C., 313
DeMatteis, Frank, 452
Dember, Sol, 355
Deneen, Jim, 109, 110, 175
DePatie, D., 500, 501
Dertner, E., 293
Dessens, Jan, 492, 493
Devlin, Stuart, 435
Devoche, Simon, 195
Didier, L., 281, 285
Dieckhoner, Gene, 164
Disney Studios, 96, 269, 363, 366, 367, 368, 375, 376, 378, 380, 513, 514
Dohanos, Steven, 211, 223
Dolph, John Henry, 114, 176
Donnelly, R., 259
Doughty, D., 502, 503
Down, Jeanne, 370
Doyle, Nancy, 164

Drayton, Grace G., 330, 331
Drechsler, I., 441
Drexel, Helmut, 475, 476
Droguett, Rudy, 487, 489
Dubin, Lee, 329, 413
Dumas, M., 281, 283
Durand, Paul, 394
Dutheil, Jean, 180
Dzenis, E., 241

– E –

Ebborn, Caroline, 215, 216
Ebihara, 300
Eckelberry, D., 546
Ede, Basil, 218, 225
Edison, Susan, 322
Eggert, John, 107, 114, 176, 520
Ellison, Pauline, 218, 219, 224
Emmett, B., 185, 186
Engelbreit, Mary, 401
Engstrom, Michael, 151
Eriksen, Edvard, 347
Ersgaard, C., 136, 142
Erte, 344
Escalera, Rudy, 167, 199, 272, 277, 278
Eskandar, Mossan, 430
Essenburg, Ben, 329
Etem, Sue, 88, 101, 102, 202, 276
Everard, Barbara, 219
Everhart, D., 388
Everson, Linda, 207
Ewnece, 503
Eytinge, Carol, 501

– F –

Falchi, Aldo, 360, 443
Falter, John, 159, 211, 476
Fangel, M. T., 378
Farnham, Alexander, 211
Faulkner, J., 237
Faulkner, Neil, 495
Faure, Renee, 542
Fausett, Dean, 211
Fazio, Aldo, 448
Felder, Bettie, 266
Fennell, Tom Jr., 430, 431
Fernandez, Mario, 211

Ferner, 393
Ferrandiz, Juan, 96, 97, 510, 511, 512
Ferreson, Jeffrey, 521
Feruzzi, Robert, 318, 471
Fina, Gloria, 205
Finnie, John, 550
Fisher, C., 250
Fisher, M., 328
Fisher, Shell, 305, 418, 419, 500, 501, 542, 543
Fisher, Virginia, 273
Flagg, James Montgomery, 119, 177
Flugenring, Hans, 136, 142
Fogarty, T., 526
Fogg, Howard, 195
Forbes, 231
Frace, Charles, 234, 241, 244, 245, 249, 252, 253, 254, 309
Fraley, Tobin, 286
Franca, Ozz, 274, 275, 278, 281, 283
Francis, J., 349
Frank, Grace Lee, 226
Frank, John, 225, 226
Frank, Joniece, 225, 226
Freedman, Claire, 406
Freeman, K., 307
Freeman, T., 288
Freuner, Willy, 349
Friis, Achton, 136,142
Fromme–Douglas, Peter, 548
Frudakis, Evangelos, 216
Fu, S., 341, 342

– G –

Gadino, V., 186, 249
Gainsborough, 264
Gaither, W., 401
Galli, Stanley, 167
Ganeau, Francois, 179
Garavani, Valentino, 105
Garde, Fanny, 136, 142
Gardner, S., 153
Garrido, Hector, 112, 236
Garrison, L., 248
Gaudin, Marguerite, 216
Gawantka, Wolfgang, 351
Gehm, Charles, 384
Geivette, G., 174

Gerardi, G., 293, 301, 302
Gerhart, Mitsuko, 514
Gerischer, Val Roy, 391
Ghislain, Charles, 219
Gialletti, Guilio, 540
Gibson, Gayle, 398
Gignilliat, E., 380, 381
Gilbert, Albert Earl, 254, 255
Gillies, C., 239
Giordano, G., 315
Giordano, J., 369, 378
Giorgio, Nate, 157, 184, 185
Giovenale, Randy, 432
Girrado, Hector, 521
Glazier, N., 378, 379
Glenice, 199
Gomez, Ignacio, 88
Gorham, 260, 265
Gossner, Gabriele, 219
Granget, Gunther, 255, 330, 336, 486
Graves, Oscar, 81
Gray, Holmes, 254
Green, D., 307, 308
Greenaway, Kate, 268
Greensmith, 274
Greenwood, Leslie, 217
Gregory, Mary, 385, 386
Greunke, Carol, 435
Grierson, Mary, 219, 225
Griffin, J., 365
Grimes, Rick, 500
Grom, Bogdan, 400
Grossberg, E., 227, 439
Grossman, J., 309, 314
Guidou, Jean–Calude, 179
Gunn, Robert, 488
Gustafson, Scott, 85, 366, 374
Gutmann, Bessie Pease, 107, 112, 113, 175, 290, 291, 307, 457
Gutshall, Charlotte, 277

– H –

Hack, Konrad, 486, 489
Hagara, Jan, 126, 166, 294, 295
Hagel, Mike, 398, 399
Hague, M., 456
Hall, J., 436

Hallett, Charlotte, 335, 336, 337, 338, 339
Hallett, William, 335, 336, 337, 338, 339
Hallin, Franz August, 133, 136, 142
Hamilton, Jack, 197
Hampshire, M., 361, 376
Hampton, B., 316
Hanks, Steve, 281, 285
Hansen, Derk, 358, 359
Hansen, Einar, 136
Hansen, Hans H., 144, 479, 482
Hara, N., 297
Harm, Ray, 252, 253, 523, 524
Harman, Bob, 413
Harper, Tom, 547, 548
Harris, Julian, 221
Harrison, B., 294, 305, 306
Harrison, J., 313, 314
Harvey, M., 233, 236
Havins, R., 208
Hayden, Hayden, 332, 500
Healey, Joan, 434
Heap, J., 422
Heflin, Tom, 404
Helland, John, 87, 88
Henderson, D., 188
Henri, Raphael, 219
Henson, Jim, 202
Hepple, W., 252
Heritage, Antony, 522, 523
Hershenburgh, Ann, 203
Hetreau, Remy, 317
Hibel, Edna, 93, 322, 323, 325, 327, 328, 334, 338, 372, 373, 400, 476, 477, 498
Hicks, Yin–Rei, 457
Hien, Harris, 329, 330
Hildebrandt, Tim, 170
Hines, Jack, 509, 512
Hipkins, C., 438
Hirata, T., 252, 302
Hirschfield, Al, 93
Hoffman, Leesa, 357
Hoffman, M., 174
Holden, Edith, 254
Holgate, Jeanne, 217, 219
Hollands–Robinson, Phyllis, 84

Hollis, Andrea, 333, 388
Homan, Ralph, 543
Homer, Winslow, 534
Hook, Frances, 369, 370, 469, 470, 472
Hook, Richard, 548
Hooks, Mitchell, 107, 520
Hoover, G. A., 396
Horak, Jeanne, 411
Horton, Joan, 276
Horton, Roger, 353
Hotta, Shigekasu, 296, 312
HuiMin, Z., 341, 342
Hulce, Claude, 161
Hummel, Berta, 507, 508, 509, 511
Hummel, M. I., 256, 257
Humphrey, M., 332
Humphrey, T., 245, 246
Hunter, Frances Tipton, 117, 177
Hurrell, David, 218
Hyldahl, Margrethe, 136, 139, 142

– I –

Icart, Louis, 322
Ingmire, H. Hollister, 366, 367
Innocenti, R., 188

– J –

Jackson, Anthony C., 346
Jackson, Charlotte, 489
Jackson, Peter D., 214, 445, 446
Jacobson, William, 411, 462, 463
Jacques, F., 209
Jagodits, C., 235
Jansen, Leo, 264, 357, 358, 359, 477, 478
Jarratt, Deborah Bell, 214, 215
Jennis, P., 236, 237, 246, 247
Jensen, Edvard, 139, 141
Jensen, L., 143
Jensen, Maureen, 225
Jensen, Oluf, 478, 479
Jensen, Peter Dahl, 133, 136, 142

Jerner, Bart, 373, 375
Jervis, Sharon, 331
Jobe, M., 377, 379
Johnson, Brian, 525, 526
Johnson, C., 171
Johnson, Diane, 204
Johnson, Frank T., 112, 176, 536
Johnson, H., 171, 233
Johnson, Laura, 200
Johnson, Robert, 451
Jondar, 332
Jones, Kate Lloyd, 214
Jones, Loretta, 318
Jones, Paul, 219
Jorgensen, J. Bloch, 136
Jorgensen, Povl, 136
Jungbluth, Mimi, 495

– K –

Kaatz, L., 236, 368, 369, 373
Kage, Senkin, 295, 300
Kage, Shuho, 295, 300
Kalan, 278
Kane, Margaret, 92, 93
Karn, Murray, 173
Katz, Garri, 441
Kaufman, Mico, 221
Kay, Sarah, 97
Keane, Bil, 331, 332
Keane, Margaret, 270
Keller, Hedi, 384, 385
Kelly, C., 197, 208, 274, 445, 543
Kemper, B., 89
Kendricks, Skipper, 404
Kent, Melanie Taylor, 165
Kerr, T., 208
Kethley, P., 174, 175
Kierstead, James, 165, 335, 355
Killen, J., 174, 304
Killman, Murray, 398, 399
Kilmer, D., 305
King, Dorothea, 354
Kingman, Doug, 498
Kinkade, Thomas, 158, 367, 371, 373, 382, 392
Kjolner, Theodor, 479
Knapton, Cynthia, 166, 552
Knievel, Evel, 411
Knox, 116

Kociber, N., 90
Koseki, 300
Kouba, Les, 389
Koutsis, Yiannis, 484, 485, 488, 489
Kovalev, A., 534
Krieghoff, 165
Kritz, J., 299, 300
Krog, Arnold, 478
Krumeich, Thaddeus, 94, 95
Kuck, Sandra, 400, 435, 436, 437, 438, 440, 441, 442, 443, 444, 445, 446, 448, 449, 450
Kuhnly, Scott, 195
Kunstler, Mort, 362, 375, 377
Kurkin, A. M., 210
Kursar, Raymond, 371
Kurz, G., 236, 239, 249

– L –

LaBonte, J., 501
Laetitia, 311
Lalique, Marie Claude, 386, 387
Lamb, J., 295, 296, 298, 310, 456
Lamb, R., 168
Lambert, Georgia, 369
Lambson, H., 233
Lamincia, Franco, 539, 540
Landenberger, James, 300, 415, 500
Landis, J., 533
Lange, Kai, 479, 482
Langeneckert, D., 90
Langton, B., 243
Lansdowne, James Fenwick, 212, 225
Lantz, Walter, 101
Larsen, Ove, 136, 139, 142
Larsen, T., 136, 142
Lasher, Mary Ann, 152
Laslo, R., 383, 384
Lawrence, R., 304, 305
Lawrence, Sir Thomas, 103
Lawson, Carol, 214, 216, 217, 218, 223, 224, 298
Lawson, John, 427
Laye, Tammy, 183
Layton, C., 372, 380

Lee, Nan, 321
Lee, Ron, 201, 390
Leigh, Susan, 82
Leigh, William R., 112, 176, 536
Leighton–Jones, Barry, 107, 269
Leimanis, A., 366
Lemond, Q., 290, 433
Leone, M., 109
LePage Eddie, 258
Letostak, John, 195
Leyendecker, J. C., 265, 454, 484, 502
Licea, Eve, 363, 364, 381
Lillemoe, M., 514
Lippi, Fra Filippo, 318, 451, 471
Littlejohn, John, 352
Liu, Lena, 156, 242, 245, 246, 250
Livingstone, Michele, 527
Lladro, 396
Lloyd–Jones, Kate, 220
Loates, Glen, 352
Lochner, Steven, 451
Lockhart, James, 424, 427
Lohmann, Adolf, 351, 353
Long, F. F., 255
Lopatin, N., 534
Lotto, L., 422
Loudin, Frank, 199
Lowe, W., 443
Lubimov, G., 534
Lucas, 193
Lundgren, Charles, 209
Lupetti, Lynn, 269

– M –

Maass, David, 266, 333
Mack, Bill, 486
MaGo, 110, 111, 112, 115, 116, 118
Malfertheiner, J., 95, 96
Malik, George, 398, 399
Mandrajji, Valentin, 361, 362
Manning, Douglas, 169, 289
Mano, Sadako, 272, 277, 278
Mao, A. Song, 341, 343
Maratti, Carlo, 350

Marchetti, L., 111, 116
Marco, J., 199, 542
Mark, R., 523
Marry–Kenyon, Ann, 196
Marsten, Barbara, 361, 362
Martin, John, 229, 232
Martin, Lisi, 301
Masseria, Francisco, 497, 498
Massey, R., 305
Mathers, Shelly, 516
Mathews, Jeffrey, 210
Matterness, Jay H., 254, 255
Maxwell, Elizabeth, 165
Mays, Maxwell, 451
McCalla, Irish, 274, 542, 544
McCarthy, Frank, 297, 314
McCarty, 104
McClelland, John, 315, 400, 435, 436, 437, 441, 444, 445, 446, 449, 450
McClung, C., 392
McDonald, M., 234
McEwan, Christopher, 212
McGinnis, R., 373
McGrory, A., 388
McKenzie, T. T., 224
McKernan, K., 352
Meger, J., 281
Memling, 422
Merli, 360, 361, 443
Micarelli, C., 297, 298, 441, 445, 448
Mignard, P., 302, 471
Miller, David, 88
Miller, Gerald R., 484
Miller, Sally, 405, 406, 407
Miller, Vel, 124
Miller, Vincent, 224
Miller–Maxwell, S., 110
Milnazik, K., 292
Mingolla, Dominic, 487, 488
Mitchell, James, 144, 145
Mix, Jo Anne, 166, 274, 275, 277, 278
Moeller, Harry J., 254, 255
Moltke, Harald, 136
Monet, Claude, 112, 175, 535

Money, Rusty, 124, 197, 198
Moody, Franklin, 299, 311, 413, 430
Morley, V., 239
Morrisseau, Norval, 92
Morton, Susie, 192, 195, 196, 197, 198, 199, 295, 308
Moses, Grandma, 488
Moses, Will, 407
Moss, P. Buckley, 91, 92, 95
Mowery, Geoff, 215
Mueller, Hans, 126, 127, 128
Munch, Verner, 144
Mundy, W. C., 526
Murillo, B. E., 302, 318
Murphy, Margaret, 214
Murray, Alan, 196, 198
Murray, G., 303

– N –

Nast, Thomas, 192, 451
Neelon, Susan, 398
Neiman, LeRoy, 495, 497
Nelson, W., 240, 242, 250
Neubacher, Gerda, 350, 351, 352, 353, 354
Neubauer, Josef, 393
Newman, Colin, 222, 223
Newman, M., 286
Newsom, Tom, 106, 108, 520
Ng, Kee Fung, 121
Nickerson, Richard, 202
Nielsen, Herne, 479
Nielsen, Jorgen, 141, 483
Nielsen, Svend Nicolai, 479
Nightingale, Sandy, 339
Nitschke, Detlev, 131
Nobata, Naoka, 213
Noel, Nancy, 294, 534
Northcott, Joann, 350
Notarile, C., 186, 187
Notti, G. Delle, 471
Novoa, Gustavo, 497
Nussbaum, J., 168
Nyce, Helen, 330
Nye, Linda, 358
Nye, Marvin, 357, 358, 506
Nylund, Gunner, 472, 473

– O –

O'Driscoll, D., 296
Oberstein, Chuck, 272, 278
Ohta, Yoai, 219
Oigaard, Nulle, 347
Okamoto, T., 224
Oliveira, Manuel de, 344, 345
Olsen, Benjamin, 479
Olsen, Cathinka, 136
Olsen, Spang, 483
Olsen, Viggo, 479
Olson, Robert, 552
Orosz, Ray, 88
Orr, R., 354
Osdell, Barrie Van, 396
Otto, Svend, 347
Oxenham, Patrick, 452

– P –

Pailthorpe, R., 260
Palladini, David, 424
Palma, P., 185
Palmieri, Frank, 159, 160
Paluso, Christopher, 231, 273, 279
Pape, Carl, 275
Paredes, Miguel, 103
Parker, Donna, 158
Parker, R., 303, 314
Parkhurst, Violet, 274, 275, 276, 277, 414
Partridge, J., 547
Paton, F., 251
Pearce, L. J., 214
Pearcy, Robert, 100, 101, 102
Pederson, Sharleen, 488
Peel, Paul, 165
Peltriauz, Bernard, 394
Penalva, J., 236
Pentz, Donald, 383
Perham, Michael, 104
Perillo, Gregory, 106, 107, 108, 109, 110, 111, 112, 113, 114, 115, 117, 118, 119, 120, 176, 292, 293, 357, 400, 506, 534, 535, 536, 537
Peter, Nori, 91, 353
Petitto, Albert, 333, 345, 387, 388

Petty, George B., 470, 471
Peynet, Raymond, 225
Phillips, Gordon, 211, 223
Picken, L., 302, 303, 433
Pierce, D., 237
Pierce, R. B., 379
Pike, John, 212
Pitcher, J., 306, 309
Plockross, Ingeborg, 136, 142
Plummer, William, 214
Poluszynski, J., 227, 438, 439, 440, 447, 504, 505
Poortvliet, Rien, 201, 202
Pope, Carl, 275
Populor, E., 534
Port, Beverly, 266
Porter, Bonnie, 197, 543
Potter, Beatrix, 507, 547, 550
Powell, William, 195
Pramvig, Borge, 139
Prechtel, D., 288
Price, A., 550
Price, Don, 166
Prince, Martha, 219
Pritchett, K., 378
Putnam, Donald, 198, 199, 544
Pyrah, J. K., 283, 285

– Q –

Quagon, F., 266
Quellier, Andre, 394
Quidley, Peter, 195

– R –

Raad, Lucelle, 404, 405
Rampel, Helen, 165
Randle, K., 379
Rane, W., 235
Raphael, 153, 318, 422
Redlin, Terry, 279, 281, 283
Reed, Hal, 347
Reed, Rex T., 255
Rembrandt, 264
Remington, Frederic, 112, 176, 253, 266, 536
Ren, C., 300, 303
Renoir, Auguste, 423
Restieau, Andre, 179

Restoueux, Rene, 217
Reynolds, Martha, 207
Richardson, E., 286
Richert, R., 233
Richter, Ludwig, 128
Ricker, Anthony, 454
Ricker, Michael, 454
Rickert, Paul, 211
Riemer-Gerbardt,
   Elizabeth, 219
Ries, Edward, 87
Riley, C. Ford, 302
Ritter, Julian, 104, 264
Rittun, Thorstein, 431
Roberton, Jon, 102
Roberts, D., 422
Roberts, E., 270
Roberts, Gilroy, 221
Roberts, James, 343
Roberts, L., 382
Robertson, 116
Rockwell, Norman, 112,
   113, 116, 119, 176,
   177, 200, 201, 221,
   222, 224, 254, 259,
   260, 261, 262, 263,
   266, 267, 269, 270,
   271, 287, 288, 308,
   309, 332, 386, 399,
   402, 403, 408, 409,
   411, 454, 455, 456,
   457, 458, 459, 462,
   463, 464, 465, 466,
   467, 468, 494, 502,
   506, 535, 536
Rode, Gotfred, 479
Rodgers, George, 395
Rogers, H., 240, 241
Rohn, Edward J., 166
Roller, C., 133
Romanelli, Carl, 343
Rosena, Anthony, 205
Rozewica, Erich, 407
Ruffin, Don, 121, 122, 123,
   124, 125, 167, 401
Ruffing, A. E., 523
Ruggeri, Gino, 529
Runci, Edward, 358, 476
Russell, Bob, 274
Russell, Charles, 260
Russell, Frank, 94
Rust, D., 208, 252
Ruthven, John, 102, 103,
   202, 338, 505, 552

– S –

Sabra, S., 136, 142
Salamanca, J., 247
Salk, L., 526
Sampson, S., 90
Sanchez, J., 423, 428
Sanderson, R., 433
Santangela, Alberto, 529
Santini, Ado, 529
Sanzio, R., 302
Sargent, B., 472
Sauber, Rob, 106, 107, 108,
   111, 113, 114, 115, 116,
   118, 119, 120, 160,
   175, 176, 177, 521
Sausmark, Gerhard, 346
Sawyer, 253
Sayer, Angela, 133
Schaefers, Karin, 407
Schenken, Rod, 105
Schiener, W., 391, 392, 447
Schlesinger, A., 349
Schmidt, Jay, 357
Schoener, Toni, 349, 350,
   352, 353
Schofield, Mildred, 517
Schulz, Charles, 515, 516
Schwartz, D., 248
Seeley, Mildred, 518, 519
Seerey-Lester, J., 234, 239,
   248, 304
Seima, 488
Seitz, Bill, 541
Selden, William, 277, 279
Selschau, Ellinor, 479
Seppard, W. L., 451
Shaefer, Gus, 223
Sharpe, H. Alvin, 316
Shearer, Julie, 406
Sheehan, Marion Ruff, 219
Shields, Adam, 196
Sias, J., 244, 249
Sickbert, Jo, 219
Sidoni, Anthony, 120, 121,
   200, 203
Sigle, Louise, 276, 277, 411
Simon, Robert Stephen,
   525, 526
Simonetti, E., 469
Singer, Arthur, 222, 223
Sivavec, D., 184
Sizemore, Ted, 231

Skelton, Red, 101, 103,
   104, 201
Skolsky, M., 319
Sloane, Eric, 497
Sloane, John, 434
Smith, C., 248
Smith, David, 272, 273,
   376
Smith, Jessie Wilcox, 297,
   331, 374, 377, 384
Smiton, David, 172
Snyder, Peter Etril, 169
Sodoma, 422
Soileau, Charles, 231
Soldwedel, Kipp, 107, 116,
   177
Sommer, Elke, 93, 543
Spaulding, Don, 362
Spencer, Irene, 202, 220,
   259, 264, 424, 427,
   428, 468, 472
St. Clair, 203
Stage, Mads, 347
Steele, M., 308
Stine, R., 251
Stobart, John, 497, 498
Stokes, Zoe, 85
Stone, Don, 211
Stone, Elisa, 318
Stone, Fred, 82, 83, 84, 85,
   318, 406
Stortz, T., 175
Stutzman, M., 152, 184
Stuwe, Marianne, 518
Suetomi, Shunsute, 226,
   297
Sundberg, Carl, 345
Sundblom, Haddon, 381,
   500
Sundin, Adelaid, 220
Sunyer, Oriol, 216
Susinno, M., 289
Svensson, Kamma, 483
Swanson, R., 307
Sweany, P. J., 288, 290
Sweet, D., 308, 309
Szabo, Endre, 397, 399

– T –

Tanenbaum, R., 288, 289,
   526
Taylor, Gage, 198

Taylor, M., 228, 229, 230, 231, 232, 233
Tellier, Liliane, 318
Tennant, C., 377
Terp, George, 329
Terreson, J., 119
Thayer, K., 294
Thelander, Henry, 133, 139, 142, 143
Therkelsen, A., 143
Theroux, C., 254
Thompson, Linda, 293, 455
Thomsen, Christian, 478
Thornbrugh, J., 363, 377
Thorpe, Clarence, 200, 203
Thorsson, Nils, 479
Timberlake, Bob, 457
Timm, Richard, 404
Timm, S., 364
Tiziano, Vincente, 538, 539, 540
Tjerne, Immanuel, 136
Tobey, Alton S., 109, 201, 211, 255
Tootle, Douglas, 182
Toschik, Larry, 124, 125
Trechslin, Anne Marie, 219
Trester, Lorraine, 265, 352, 355, 454, 476
Trumball, J., 349
Tsang, M., 313
Tseng, Mou-Sien, 292
Tuck, James, 161
Tuck, Janet, 207
Tudor, Guy, 254, 255
Turner, Nancy, 527, 528

– U –

Ungermann, Arne, 483
Unruh, D., 286
Uosikkinen, Raija, 99
Upton, Roger, 199
Urdahl, M., 90
Ussing, Stephen, 478
Utamaro, Kitagawa, 486, 487
Utz, Thornton, 290, 306, 310, 311, 312, 313, 316, 449, 541, 543

– V –

Valente, C., 247
Valenza, Dolores, 335
Vallotton, Felix, 403
van der Weyden, Roger, 451
Van Howd, Douglas, 87, 99, 100
Van Zyle, J., 433
Vargas, Alberto, 322
Vass, J. M., 293, 294
Vestergaard, Sven, 133, 145, 482, 483
Vickers, Mary, 418, 546, 549, 550
Vickery, Charles, 235, 240
Vidal, Hahn, 497
Vig, Rik, 183
Vincent, Michael, 272, 435
Vleshko, V., 534
Vlugenring, H., 133
Von Ault, 196

– W –

Waddey, R., 298, 299
Walczak, Jerome, 165
Waldheimer, Hans, 192, 438
Walker, Jason, 151
Wallin, Fred, 159
Walt Disney Studios, 152
Wampler, M., 532
Wanat, J., 388
Wasile, Elyse, 409
Waterhouse, Ralph, 411
Waugh, Carol–Lynn Rossel, 161
Weaver, John, 223
Weaver, Robert, 398
Weber, M., 377
Weber, Sarah Stilwell, 409, 410
Wegner, Fritz, 209
Wehrli, Mary Ellen, 91
Weidhorst, Olaf, 105
Weirs, Persis Clayton, 157
Weistling, M., 302, 311
Welty, J., 252, 382, 383
West, Gillian, 524

Whittaker, Lawrence W., 484, 486
Wieghorst, Olaf, 203
Wiinblad, Bjorn, 477
Wildermuth, P., 243
Williams, Abbie, 400, 468, 470, 471, 472
Williams, Frances Taylor, 125
Wilson, C., 378
Winslow, R., 231
Winther, Ole, 334, 335, 336, 337, 338, 339, 340
Wood, Grant, 455
Wood, P., 524
Woods, James, 495
Woodson, Jack, 141, 532, 533, 534
Wright, D., 304, 307
Wulfing, Sulamith, 384, 385
Wyeth, James, 219, 222
Wyeth, N. C., 253
Wyland, 299
Wysocki, Charles, 151

– X, Y, Z –

Xaras, Theodore, 168, 169, 298, 314, 315
Xue-Bing, J., 342, 343
Yang, Wei Tseng, 213
Yates, Michael, 407
York, J., 443
Young, Harland, 356, 357
Younger, Richard Evans, 213
Yu, Ren, 209
Zanobia, 553
Zapp, Marilyn, 160
Zemsky, Jessica, 509, 511
Zhiryakova, G., 534
Zolan, Donald, 83, 84, 85, 315, 316, 400, 415, 416, 417, 418, 419, 420, 421
Zolan, R. J., 472
Zolan, Richard, 82, 405, 406
Zuoren, Wu, 209
Zvorykin, Boris, 321, 322, 545
Zwierz, D., 187, 188

Series Index

– A –

A Child's World, 469
A Christmas Carol, 125, 151, 188
A Mind of Her Own, 465
A Swan Is Born, 382
Abbie Williams Collection, 468
Adventures of Childhood, 415
Adventures of Peter Pan, 106
Adventures of the Old West, 356
Aesop's Fables, 172, 361
African Violet Miniatures, 553
Africa's Beauties, 87
Age of Steam, 168
Al Barlick, 228
Alaska: The Last Frontier, 233
Alice in Wonderland, 329, 484, 541
All God's Children, 495
All-American Roses, 89
Allegro, 322
Allegro Ensemble, 334
Alliance, 203
Along an English Lane, 233
America at Work, 287, 455
America Has Heart, 166
America the Beautiful, 233, 329, 340, 393
American Adventures, 397
American Artists, 259
American Bicentennial Wildlife, 254
American Blues Special Occasions, 106
American Civil War, 288
American Craftsman Carnival, 203
American Dream, 463
American Expansion, 387
American Family, 408, 458
American Folk Art, 159
American Folk Heroes, 99
American Heritage, 255, 330, 537
American History, 503
American Innocents, 361

American Journey, 362
American Landmarks, 268, 394
American Landscape, 538
American Maritime Heritage, 107
American Memories, 279
American Milestones, 210
American Revolution, 211
American Rose Garden, 288
American Sail, 87
American Series, 172
American Silhouettes
    The Children, 91
    The Family, 91
    Valley Life, 91
American Songbirds, 523
American Steam, 169
American Tapestries, 495
American Trees of Christmas, 86
American Wildlife, 390, 404
Americana, 435, 522, 527
Americana Holidays, 362
America's Children, 454
America's Cup, 259
America's Favorite, 518
America's Greatest Sailing Ships, 288
America's Heritage of Flight, 87
America's Indian Heritage, 106
America's Most Beloved, 200
America's Pride, 233
America's Sailing Ships, 333
Andersen Fairy Tales, 346
Andy Griffith, 288
Angler's Dream, 107, 520
Angler's Prize, 289
Anker's Heritage, 388
Annie, 362
Anniversary, 346, 349, 477
Annual Cathedral, 412
Annual Crystal, 255, 330, 506
Annual German Christmas, 411

Annual Historical, 532
Annual Holiday, 390
Annual Old Masters, 538
Annual Spring Flowers, 532
Annual Stained Glass and Pewter
    Christmas, 532
Anthony Sidoni Series, 120
Antique American Art, 477
Antique French Doll Collection, 518
April Fool Annual, 254, 259
Arabelle and Friends, 435
Arabian Nights, 212
Arabians, 107, 534
Architects of Democracy, 345
Archives Plates, 90
Arctic Friends, 107, 535
Arctic Spring, 91
Arctic Wolves, 433
Art Deco, 234
Art Nouveau, 180
Arta Christmas, 435
Arta Mother's Day, 435
Arte Ovale, 322
Artists, 394
Arzberg, 334
As Free as the Wind, 211
Attwell's Silver Linings, 181
Audubon, 450
Audubon American Wildlife Heritage, 259
Audubon Birds, 503
Audubon Society, 212
Audubon's Birds, 532
Autumn Flights, 207
Aviation, 167
Avon
    Americana, 545
    Christmas, 546
    Mother's Day, 546
    North American Songbird, 546
Award–Winning Roses, 146, 286

– B –

Babes in the Woods, 405
Baby Animals Collection, 455
Baby Cats of the Wild, 234
Baby Owls of North America, 363
Baby's Firsts, 107
Backstage, 107
Backyard Harmony, 363
Baker Street, 107, 520
Bambi, 363
Band's Songbirds of Europe, 363, 531
Banquet of Blossoms and Berries, 147

Bare Innocence, 195
Barefoot Children, 435
Barrymore, 259
Bas Relief, 260
Baseball, 525
Baseball Record Breakers, 151
Bashful Bunnies, 91
Basketball, 525
Battle Wagons, 87
Bavarian Forest, 255, 330
Bear Feats, 166
Bear Tracks, 234
Beatles '67–'70, 184
Beatles Collection, 184
Beatrix Potter, 507
Beauties of the Red Mansion, 341
Beautiful Cats of the World, 99
Beautiful World, 195
Beauty and the Beast, 363
Beauty of Bouguereau, 484
Beauty of Polar Wildlife, 171
Beauty of Winter, 289
Becker Babies, 107, 175
Becky's Day, 435
Behind the Painted Masque, 497
Believe Series, 401
Bellini Series, 538
Beloved Hymns of Childhood, 234
Benvenuti's Muses, 528
Bernard Buffet, 212
Berta Hummel Christmas, 507
Berta Hummel Mother's Day, 508
Bessie's Best, 107
Best of Baseball, 289
Best of Fred Stone – Mare and Foal, 82
Best of Sascha, 164
Best of Zolan in Miniature, 415
Beswick Christmas, 497
Bethlehem Christmas, 485
Betsy Bates Annual, 397
Bialosky® & Friends, 289
Bible Series, 97
Biblical Mothers, 363
Bicentennial, 129, 132, 167, 212, 225,
    260, 317, 344, 348, 349, 361, 451,
    454, 513, 526, 546
Bicentennial Silver, 177
Big Cats of the World, 289
Big Top, 166
Bird Dogs, 349
Birds, 213, 538
Birds and Flowers of Beautiful Cathay, 213
Birds and Flowers of the Meadow and
    Garden, 208

Birds and Flowers of the Orient, 213
Birds of Fancy, 92
Birds of Four Seasons, 408
Birds of North America, 86, 429
Birds of Paradise, 334
Birds of Prey, 281
Birds of the North, 188
Birds of the Seasons, 364
Birds of the Temple Gardens, 289
Birds of Your Garden, Encyclopedia
  Britannica, 364
Birth of a Nation, 504
Birth Plates, 334
Black Tie Affair: The Penguin, 235
Blessed are the Children, 235
Blessings from a Chinese Garden, 341
Blossoming of Suzanne, 546
Blossoms of China, 209
Blue–Button Trains Christmas, 330
Bob Cousy, 228
Boehm Birds, 390
Boehm Owl Collection, 147
Boehm Woodland Wildlife, 390
Bohemian Annual, 436
Bonds of Love, 235
Boston 500, 434
Bountiful Harvest, 452
Bouquets of the Seasons, 334
Boy Scout, 260, 269
Braithwaite Game Birds, 500
Brastoff Series, 256
Brett and Bobby Hull, 228
Buck Hill Bears, 100
Buffalo Bill's Wild West, 532
Bundles of Joy, 290
Busy Bears, 195
Butterflies, 356
Butterflies and Flowers, 391
Butterflies of the World, 147, 214
Butterfly, 147
Butterfly Garden, 290
Bygone Days, 331

– C –

C. M. Russell, 97
Calendar, 214, 409, 429, 546
Call of the Wilderness, 364
Cambier Four Seasons, 178
Cameo Kittens, 290
Cameos of Childhood, 125
Canadian Dreams, 434
Canterbury Tales, 396
Capricious Clowns, 92

Carefree Days, 290, 541
Carl Larsson, 132, 133
Carl Yastrzemski — The Impossible
  Dream, 229
Carlton Fisk, 229
Carnival, 108, 520
Carol Lawson Annual, 214
Carousel, 365
Carousel Fantasies, 509
Casablanca, 365
Castles, 431, 435
Castles and Dreams, 436
Cat Portraits, 133
Cat Tales, 365
Catalina Island, 199
Cathedrals, 167, 429
Cathedrals Christmas, 547
Catnippers, 468
Cats, 469, 538
Cats for Cat Lovers, 82
Caverswall Christmas Carol, 254
Celebration, 92, 121
Celebration of Faith, 497
Celebration of Love, 436
Celebrity Clowns, 87
Centennial Collection, 133
Chagall Series, 346
Charles Russell, 260
Charles Vickery's Romantic Harbors, 235
Charles Wysocki's Peppercricket Grove,
  151
Charlot Byi Series, 256
Cherished Moments, 281
Cherished Traditions, 152
Chieftains, 108, 535
Child of America, 200
Childhood Almanac, 436
Childhood Delights, 108, 521
Childhood Discoveries — Miniature, 415
Childhood Friendship, 415
Childhood Memories, 349, 541
Childhood Reflections, 291
Childhood Secrets, 528
Childhood Sonatas, 159
Childhood Treasure, 204
Children at Christmas, 416
Children at Play, 121
Children of Aberdeen, 121
Children of Christmas Past, 423
Children of Don Ruffin, 121
Children of Mary Cassatt, 423
Children of Mexico, 423
Children of Mother Earth, 92
Children of Norman Rockwell, 402

Children of Renoir, 423
Children of the American Frontier, 91, 553
Children of the Classics, 164
Children of the Past, 195
Children of the Prairie, 109
Children of the Pueblo, 497
Children of the Seasons, 329, 435
Children of the Southwest, 357
Children of the Sun, 122
Children of the Week, 269
Children of the World, 122, 200
Children to Love, 88
Children's Christmas, 538
Children's Christmas Pageant, 437
Children's Day, 133
Children's Garden, 437
Children's Hour, 81
Children's Moments, 398
Children's Prayer, 349
Children's Series, 541
Children's Story, 547
Children's Television Workshop Christmas, 260
Child's Best Friend, 290, 405
Child's Birthday, 547
Child's Christmas, 333, 387, 393, 547
Child's Garden of Verse, 452
Child's Life, 108, 535
Child's Play, 469
Child's World, 357
China's Imperial Palace: The Forbidden City, 341
China's Natural Treasures, 365
Chinese and American Historical, 316
Chinese Blossoms of the Four Seasons, 291
Chinese Children's Games, 415
Chinese Lunar Calendar, 400
Chinese Symbols of the Universe, 292
Chosen Messengers, 152
Christian Collection, 109
Christian Fantasy, 170
Christmas, 6, 91, 95, 96, 98, 106, 114, 125, 126, 128, 129, 130, 132, 133, 145, 159, 160, 161, 165, 167, 173, 174, 178, 179, 191, 192, 194, 208, 209, 210, 214, 222, 225, 227, 258, 260, 265, 267, 269, 275, 276, 277, 279, 317, 323, 330, 334, 340, 345, 346, 349, 355, 360, 361, 372, 384, 385, 386, 389, 393, 395, 396, 397, 398, 399, 400, 401, 402, 403, 404, 407, 409, 410, 414, 416, 422, 429, 430, 431, 435, 438, 439, 443, 444, 446, 451, 454, 457, 463, 469, 472, 474, 477, 478, 485, 491, 492, 494, 495, 497, 500, 502, 505, 506, 507, 510, 513, 515, 518, 519, 521, 522, 524, 530, 531, 538, 540, 541, 544, 546, 548, 550
Christmas — International, 214
Christmas — Old Fashioned, 113, 126, 451
Christmas Card, 538
Christmas Carols, 451, 519, 533
Christmas Celebrations of Yesterday, 109
Christmas Classics, 415
Christmas Collectibles, 459
Christmas Crèche, 528
Christmas Customs, 526
Christmas Deluxe, 431
Christmas in America, 141, 204
Christmas in Canada, 434
Christmas in Kinderland, 256
Christmas in the City, 366
Christmas Jubilee, 482
Christmas Love, 193
Christmas Madonnas, 318
Christmas Memories, 152
Christmas Morning in Dingle Dell, 330
Christmas of Yesterday, 357
Christmas Pastimes, 524
Christmas Story, 145, 236
Christmas Trees Around the World, 391
Christmas Wildlife, 254
Christmas/Andersen Fairy Tales, 346
Cinderella, 366
Cinema Classics, 322
Circus Dreams, 398
Circus Friends, 433
Civil War, 90
Classic American Cars, 109
Classic American Trains, 109
Classic Cars, 152, 174
Classic Christmas, 485
Classic Circus, 175
Classic Collection, 485
Classic Fairy Tales, 366
Classic Mother Goose, 366
Classic Plate, 459
Classic Rose Christmas, 475
Classic Sporting Dogs, 292
Classic TV Westerns, 292
Classic Waterfowl, 236
Classical American Beauties, 272
Classroom Memories, 507
Classy Cars, 195
Cleopatra: Queen of Ancient Egypt, 412
Clipper Ships, 214
Clowns, 261
Clowns, Klowns, Klonz, 517
Coaching Classics — John Wooden, 229

Cobblestone Kids, 215
Coca–Cola: The Classic Santa Claus, 301
Coin Plates, 341
Colin Newman's Country Panorama, 548
Collector Plates of the Bahamas, 409
Collectors Society, 403
Colonial Christmas Wreath, 391
Colonials—The Rarest Rockwell, 464
Colts, 110
Columbus Discovers America: The 500th
    Anniversary, 236
Comforts of Home, 366
Coming of Age, 464
Commedia Dell' Arte, 497
Commemorating the King, 152, 184
Companion to Brotherly Love, 416
Companions, 100, 357
Competitive Sports, 347
Composers, 518
Composers of Classical Music, 141
Confederacy, 391
Constitution, 100
Copeland Remembers, 169
Coppelia Ballet, 542
Coral Paradise, 292
Corita Kent Annual, 272
Corvette, 174
Corvette Collector, 541
Cottages of Olde England, 182
Council of Nations, 110, 292
Country Birds of the Year, 334
Country Bouquets, 236
Country Cousins, 195
Country Diary, 215
Country Diary of an Edwardian Lady, 254
Country Doctors, 281
Country Friends, 165, 357
Country Garden Calendar Collection, 293
Country Garden Cottage, 293
Country Kitties, 293
Country Ladies, 407
Country Nostalgia, 236
Country Season of Horses, 293
Country Summer, 294
Country Year, 215
Courageous Few, 485
Cowboys, 261
Cozy Country Corners, 366
Craftsman Heritage, 88
Crazy Cats, 272
Creation, 485, 486
Critic's Choice: Gone with the Wind, 236
Crystal Maidens, 486
Crystal Series, 388

Csatari Grandparents, 367
Cubs of the Big Cats, 433
Curious Kittens, 294
Currier & Ives, 98, 205, 215, 451, 505
Currier & Ives Silver, 178

– D –

Da Vinci Series, 171
Dacey Series, 533
Daddy's Little Girl, 195
Dance, Ballerina, Dance, 350
Danish Church, 127
Darling Dalmatians, 433
Darryl Strawberry, 229
Daughter's of the Sun, 294
David Series, 323
David Winter Plate Collection, 328
Davis
    Cat Tales, 509
    Country Christmas Annual, 509
    Country Pride, 510
    Red Oak Sampler, 510
    Special Edition Plates, 510
Day and Night, 407
Days Gone By, 437
Days of Innocence, 164
Days of the Week, 215
Days of the West, 542
Days Remembered, 272
Days to Remember — Norman Rockwell,
    286
Dear to My Heart, 294
DeGrazia Series, 361
Delicate Balance: Vanishing Wildlife, 237
Delights of Childhood, 295
Della Robbia Annual, 455
Deluxe Christmas, 227
Der Ring des Nibelungen, 335
Designer Series, 205
Deutches Fachwerk, 384
Dickens' Village, 188
Discover Canada, 165
Disney
    Annual, 513
    Bicentennial, 513
    Christmas, 513
    Four Seasons of Love, 513
    Four Star Collection, 96
    Mother's Day, 513
    Musical Memories, 152
    Special Edition, 514
    Treasured Moments Collection, 367
    Valentine's Day, 514

Disneyland, 542
Dog Days, 152
Dogs, 539
Dolly Dingle World Traveler, 331
Don Mattingly, 525
Don Ruffin Series, 123
Dorothy's Day, 486
Doughty Birds, 503
Dr. Zhivago, 237
Dream Machines, 185
Dresden Christmas, 438
Dresden Mother's Day, 438
DU Great American Sporting Dogs, 174
Ducks Unlimited, 236
Durand's Children, 394
Dynasty, 501

– E –

Eagle, 129, 401
Early Discoveries, 272
Early Memories, 335
Early Works, 201
Easter, 81, 98, 160, 216, 227, 393, 395,
    416, 431, 439, 493, 533, 539
Edna Hibel Holiday, 323
Egyptian, 350, 530
Egyptian Commemorative, 147
Egyptian Treasures of Tutankhamen, 146
Eight Immortals, 168
Elegant Birds, 237
Elvira, 195
Elvis in Concert, 501
Elvis on the Big Screen, 185
Elvis Presley Collection, 410, 459
Elvis Presley Hit Parade, 185
Elvis Presley: In Performance, 185
Elvis Presley: Looking at a Legend, 185
Elvis Remembered, 295
Emmett Kelly Christmas, 269
Emmett Kelly, Jr., 208
Enchanted Cottages, 367
Enchanted Garden, 92, 237, 286
Enchanted Moments, 343
Enchanted Norfin Trolls, 438
Enchanted Seasons of a Unicorn, 335
Enchanted World of the Unicorn, 433
Enchantment, 335
Encore, 497
Encounters, Survival and Celebration, 261
Endangered Birds, 123, 452
Endangered Species, 272
English Christmas, 503

English Country Cottages, 295
English Countryside, 105
English Countryside Cats Collection, 331
Environmental, 174
Equestrian Love, 88
Eroica, 325
Erte Collection, 344
Escalera's
    Christmas, 167
    Father's Day, 272
Esteban Murillo Series, 127
Eternal Wishes of Good Fortune, 295
European Birds, 147
Everyone's Friends, 272
Exotic Birds of Tropique, 486
Expressions, 161
Eyes of the Child, 548
Eyes of the Wild, 237

– F –

Fabulous Birds, 503
Fabulous Cars of the Fifties, 186
Faces of Nature, 238
Faces of the World, 100
Fairies of the Fields and Flowers, 321
Fairy Tales, 216, 350
Fairy Tales of Old Japan, 296
Family Christmas, 168, 497
Family Circles, 152
Family Circus Christmas, 331
Family Treasures, 82, 406
Famous American Songbirds, 455
Famous Americans, 455, 522
Famous Clowns, 201, 527
Famous Clowns of the Circus, 398
Famous Fillies, 83
Famous Horses, 351
Famous Lullabies, 351
Famous Movies, 501
Famous Musicians, 181
Famous Parades, 165
Famous Personalities, 81
Famous Planes of Yesterday, 272
Famous Women and Children, 325, 476
Fancy Fowl, 147
Fantasia Golden Anniversary, 367
Fantasies and Fables, 476
Fantasy Cookbook, 170
Fantasy Farm, 411
Fantasy in Motion, 161
Farmyard Friends, 296
Fashions by Irene, 273

Father's Day, 81, 96, 98, 127, 130, 145,
     174, 272, 401, 416, 431, 447, 473, 494,
     505, 512
Father's Love, 368
Fausett Mural Plates, 255
Favorite American Songbirds, 296
Favorite Dreams, 273
Favorite Florals, 148
Favorite Pets, 357
Feathered Friends, 83
Federal Duck Stamps, 238
Feline Fancy, 238
Feline Favorites, 452
Ferrandiz Annual, 96
Ferrandiz
     Beautiful Bounty, 510
     Christmas, 96
     Mother and Child, 510
     Mother's Day, 96
     Music Makers, 510
     Porcelain Christmas, 510
     Wooden Birthday, 97, 511
     Wooden Jubilee, 511
     Wooden Wedding, 97
Festival Children of the World, 497
Fiddler's People, 183
Field Birds of North America, 239
Field Puppies, 368
Field Trips, 369
Fierce and the Free, The, 297
Fiesta of the Children, 123
Fifty Years of Oz, 297
Firebird, 389
First Impressions, 369
First Performers, 165
Fishing Boats, 195
Fitz and Floyd Annual Christmas Plate, 208
Five Perceptions of Weo Cho, 487
Flash of Cats, 239
Fleurs et Rubans, 317
Flights of Fancy: Ornamental Art of Old
     Russia, 161
Floral Fancies, 239
Floral Fantasies, 92
Floral Felines, 406
Floral Fiesta, 123
Flower Children, 539
Flower Fairy, 321, 438, 544
Flower Fantasies, 83
Flower Festivals of Japan, 297
Flower Garden, 498
Flower Girl Annual, 325
Flower Goddesses of China, 341

Flowers, 129, 148, 360
Flowers from Grandma's Garden, 239
Flowers of Count Bernadotte, 93
Flowers of the American Wilderness, 217
Flowers of the Year, 217
Flowers of Your Garden, 239
Flowers that Never Fade, 335
Fogg and Steam, 195
Fondest Memories, 196
Fontanini Annual Christmas Plate, 469
Footsteps of the Brave, 153
Forever Glamorous Barbie, 153
Founding Fathers, 451
Four Ancient Elements, 369
Four Elements, Micro Plate, 343
Four Freedoms, 86
Four Seasons, 172, 173, 181, 351, 404,
     438, 487, 539
     A Boy and His Dog, 261
     A Helping Hand, 262
     Ages of Love, 261
     Champleve, 217
     Dad's Boy, 262
     Going on Sixteen, 262
     Grand Pals, 262
     Grandpa and Me, 262
     Landscape, 262
     Life with Father, 262
     Me and My Pals, 263
     Old Buddies, 263
     Old Timers, 263
     Tender Years, 263
     Traveling Salesman, 263
     Young Love, 263
Four Seasons of the Unicorn, 527
Frances Hook Collection, 469, 470
Frances Hook Legacy, 369, 470
Fred Stone Classic, 83
Freddie the Freeloader, 101
Freddie's Adventure, 101
Free as the Wind, 370
Freedom Collection of Red Skelton, 101
French Collection Mother's Day, 317
Friends I Remember, 370
Friends of Mine, 511
Friends of the Forest, 273, 370
Friendship Annual, 335
Furstenberg
     Christmas, 439
     Deluxe Christmas, 439
     Easter, 439
     Mother's Day, 439
     Olympic, 440

– G –

Gallery of Masters, 264
Game Birds of the South, 522
Game Birds of the World, 218
Game Plates, 505
Gamebirds of North America, 148, 286
Games Children Play, 440
Games We Used to Play, 434
Garden and Songbirds, 351
Garden Birds, 392
Garden Birds of the World, 218
Garden Cottages of England, 371
Garden of Satin Wings, 342
Garden of the Lord, 239
Garden of Verses, 297
Garden Secrets, 371
Garden Year, 218
Gardens of America, 440
Gardens of Beauty, 440
Gardens of Monet, 423
Gardens of Paradise, 240
Gardens of the Orient, 297
Gardens of Victoria, 182
Gates of Paradise, 528
Gems of Nature, 424
Gene Autry Collection, 459
Gentle Arts of the Geisha, 297
Gentle Beginnings, 240
Gentle Love, 141
George Brett Gold Crown Collection, 229
Ghilberti Doors, 529
Gift Edition, 175
Gift of Happiness, 511
Gift of Love Mother's Day Collection, 441
Gifts of the Seasons, 402
Girl in the Moon, 174
Glen Loates' Feathered Friends, 352
Glorious Songbirds, 240
Glory of Christ, 297, 441
Glory of Christmas, 335
Glow Series, 281
Gnome Four Seasons, 201
Gnome Holiday, 201
Gnome Patrol, 255
Go for the Gold, 196
God Bless You Little One, 470
Goddesses, 539
God's Own Country, 441
Gold Edition Plates, 525
Gold Signature, 83
Golden Age of American Railroads, 298
Golden Age of Cinema, 487

Golden Age of Sail, 209
Golden Age of the Clipper Ships, 240
Golden Anniversary, 514
Golden Classics, 298
Golden Moments, 511
Golden Plates of the Noble Flower
    Maidens, 487
Golden Spike Centennial, 393
Golf, 441
Golfing Great, 274
Gone with the Wind, 371
Gone with the Wind: Golden Anniversary,
    240
Good Ol' Days, 511
Good Sports, 110, 298
Gordy Howe, 229
Gothic Romance, 332
Graduate, 352
Grafburg Christmas, 441
Grand Opera, 529
Grand Safari: Images of Africa, 241
Grandest Gift, 498
Grandma's Scrapbook, 521
Grandmother's World, 552
Grandpa and Me, 264
Grandparent Collector's Plate, 441
Grandparents, 274
Grandparent's Day, 416
Grant Wood, 268
Grant Wood Single Issue, 455
Great Achievements in Art, 357
Great American Masterpieces Silver, 178
Great American Sailing Ships, 533
Great American Trains, 110
Great Americans, 550
Great Atlantic Liners, 169
Great Bird Heroes, 434
Great Cats of the Americas, 372
Great Chiefs of Canada, 398
Great Comedians, 542
Great Fighter Planes of World War II, 298
Great Jewish Women, 348
Great Love Stories of Greek Mythology,
    183
Great Mammals of the Sea, 299
Great Moments, 551
Great Moments in Baseball, 153
Great Romances of History, 343
Great Stories from the Bible, 441
Great Trains, 110, 175
Greatest Show on Earth, 299, 430
Grimm's Fairy Tales, 218, 384
Growing Up Together, 299
Guardians of the Kingdom, 441

Guns at Sea, 551
Gunther Granget, 336

– H –

Hagel Christmas, 398
Hagel Mother's Day, 398
Hand Painted Christmas Classic, 206
Hans Achtziger, 336
Hans Christian Andersen, 141, 218, 483
Happy Art, 101
Happy Days, 352
Happy Village, 93
Hard Fruits, 148
Harmony and Nature, 352
Harvest Time, 476
Hawaiian Splendor, 424
Heart of the Family, 443
Heart of the Wild, 241
Heart to Heart, 153
Heartfelt Traditions, 189
Hearts and Flowers, 442
Hearts in Song, 254
Heavenly Angels, 110
Hedi Keller Christmas, 384
Heirloom Memories, 153
Heirloom Ovals, 417
Heirlooms and Lace, 372
Henry's Loveable Model T, 432
Heritage, 142, 348, 422, 464
Hibel Christmas, 372
Hibel Mother's Day, 372
Hidden Treasures of the Wood, 517
Hideaway Lake, 153
Hilda, 332
Historical, 131, 317, 483
Historical Events, 520
History, 393, 522
History of Santa Claus, 192
Hobo Joe, 201, 398
Holiday, 90, 123, 552
Holiday Mini Plates, 124
Holiday Scenes in Ireland, 129
Holiday Traditions, 424
Holiday Week of the Family Kappelmann, 131
Holidays Around the World, 88
Hollywood Greats, 196
Hollywood Squares, 166
Hollywood's Glamour Girls, 241
Hollywood's View of Christmas, 322
Holy Night, 168
Home for the Holidays, 373
Home Is Where the Heart Is, 373

Home Sweet Home, 373
Hometown Memories, 219, 241
Honor America, 148
Horses in Action, 274
Horses of Fred Stone, 84, 406
Horses of Harland Young, 357
How Do I Love Thee?, 111, 521
How the West Was Won, 398
Howe Christmas, 159
Huggable Moments, 274
Huggable Puppies, 101
Hummingbird Collection, 148, 287
Hummingbirds, 336

– I –

I Love Lucy Plate Collection, 299
I Remember America, 498
Ice Capades Clown, 470
Iditarod Race Champs, 395
Immortals of Early American Literature, 172
Imperial Christmas, 518
Impressions, 274
Impressions of Yesteryear, 487
In Appreciation, 168
In the Eye of the Storm, 443
In the Footsteps of the King, 186
In Tribute to America's Great Artists, 542
In Trompe L'Oeil, 502
Indian Bridal, 111
Indian Dancers, 167, 401
Indian Nations, 111, 535
Indiana Jones, 186
Indians, 253
Infinite Love, 101
Innocence and Experience, 465
Innocent Encounters, 424
Innocent Wonders, 286
International Gallery of Flowers, 219
International Mother Love, 93, 325
International Wildlife Foundation, 414
Irene Spencer, 264
Irish Wildlife, 129
Iron Pioneers, 551
Israeli Commemorative, 201
Israel's 30th Anniversary, 348, 542
It's a Dog's Life, 373

– J –

J. Bergsma Mother's Day, 443
James Dean Collection, 410, 459
James Wyeth, 219

Japanese Blossoms of Autumn, 300
Japanese Floral Calendar, 300
Jean–Paul Loup Christmas, 132
Jerner's Less Travelled Road, 373
Jerusalem Wedding, 348
Jessie Wilcox Smith Childhood Holidays, 374
Jeweled Hummingbirds, 300
Jewels of the Flowers, 374
Jewels of the Golden Ring, 162
Jewish Holidays, 348
Joe Montana, 230
John Falter Christmas, 159
John James Audubon, 219
Johnny Bench, 230
Josephine and Napoleon, 179
Joy of Christmas, 165
Joys of Childhood, 189
Joys of Motherhood, 93, 542
Joys of the Victorian Year, 220
Jubilee, 432, 473
Jubilee Five–Year Christmas, 142
Judaic Commemorative, 148
Julian Ritter, 264
Julian Ritter – Fall in Love, 264
Julian Ritter – To Love a Clown, 264
Julpoesi Series, 473
Jungle Fantasy, 498
Just Like Daddy's Hats, 413

– K –

Kalevala Series, 99
Kareem Abdul–Jabbar Sky–Hook Collection, 230
Kathia's Cats, 337
Keepsake Rhymes, 374
Keepsakes of the Heart, 156
Kelly's Stable, 274
Ken Griffey Jr., 230
Kennedy, 268, 316
Kentucky Derby, 451
King and I, The, 374
Kingdom of the Unicorn, 156
King's Christmas, 443
King's Flowers, 443
King's Mother's Day, 443
Kitten Classics, 503
Kitten Encounters, 504
Kitten's World, 487
Kitty Cats, 357
Kitty Cucumber Annual, 514
Knapp Series, 192
Kristi Yamaguchi, 230

– L –

L. Henry Series, 478
La Belle Femme, 539
Lady and the Tramp, 375
Lady and the Unicorn, 318
Lafayette Legacy, 179
Lamincia Annual, 539
Landfalls, 274
Lands of Fable, 255
Last of Their Kind: The Endangered Species, 242
Last Spike Centennial, 169
Last Supper, 540
Last Warriors, 300
Late to Party, 82
Leaders of Tomorrow, 264, 358
Legacy Series, 281
Legend of St. George, 337
Legend of the Gnomes, 201
Legend of the Peacock Maidens, 488
Legend of the Scarlet Flower, 162
Legend of the Snowmaiden, 359
Legend of Tsar Saltan, 162
Legend of Tutankhamun, 412
Legendary Animals, 337
Legendary Ships of the Sea, 488
Legendary Steam Trains, 452
Legends, 521
Legends of Baseball, 186
Legends of Camelot, 424
Legends of King Arthur, 548
Legends of the West, 111, 535
Legends of West Lake, 342
Lena Liu's Basket Bouquets, 242
Lena Liu's Country Accents, 156
Lena Liu's Flower Fairies, 242
Lena Liu's Hummingbird Treasury, 242
Lenore Béran Special, 161
Lenox Christmas Trees, 392
Leroy Neiman Special, 498
Les Enfants de la Fin du Siècle, 394
Les Femmes du Siècle, 179
Les Noels de France, 179
Les Sites Parisiens de Louis Dali, 179
Les Tres Riches Heures, 180
Let's Pretend, 424
Letter Writer's, 345
Lewis and Clark Expedition, 264
Leyendecker, 503
Leyendecker Annual Christmas, 265
Liebchen, 196
Life of Jesus, 111
Life's Best Wishes, 149

Life's Interludes, 343
Light of Christ, 360
Lil' Critters, 88
Lil' Peddlers, 329
Lincoln, Man of America, 375
Linda's Little Loveables, 358
Lisi Martin Christmas, 301
Little Angels, 242
Little Bandits, 156
Little Baskets, 406
Little Bible Friends, 193
Little Clowns, 159, 352
Little Friends, 274
Little Girls, 417
Little House on the Prairie, 301, 398, 455
Little Ladies, 301, 406
Little Men, 265, 352
Little Mermaid, 375
Little Misses Young and·Fair, 196
Little Mothers, 457
Little Orphans, 274
Little People, 488
Little Professionals, 443
Little Rascals, 301
Little Shopkeepers, 301
Little Traveler, 398
Little Women, 454
Littlest, The, 166
Littlest Night, 511
Living American Artists, 506
Living Dolls, 172
Living in Harmony, 111
Living with Nature, 375
Lladro Plate Collection, 396
Lockhart Wildlife, 424
Log of the Dashing Wave, 498
Long Road West, 202
"Loon," Voice of the North, 190
Loons, 281
Lords of the Plains, 202
Lords of the Wilderness, 189
Lord's Prayer, 470
Lore of the West, 302
Lorraine Trester Series, 476
Lovable Kittens, 102
Lovable Teddies, 456
Love, 347
Love and Life, 384
Love for All Seasons, 337
Love Sonnets of Shakespeare, 343
Love Story, 196
Love Story of Siam, 502
Loveables, 355
Lovers Collection, 281

Love's Labor, 501
Love's Prayer, 470
Love's Precious Moments, 488
Loving Look: Duck Families, 243
Lucy Collage, 302
Luekel's Idyllic Village Life, 170
Luis Aparicio, 231

– M –

Madonna and Child, 302
Madonna Plates, 226, 395
Madonne Viventi, 529
Magic Afternoons, 166
Magic Johnson Gold Rim Collection, 231
Magic of Childhood, 471
Magic of Marilyn, 186
Magic of the Sea, 404
Magic People, 269
Magical Moments, 112, 175
MaGo's Motherhood, 112
Maidens, 112
Maidens of the Folding Sky, 342
Majestic Birds of North America, 376
Majestic Birds of Prey, 302
Majestic Horse, 243
Majestic Wilderness, 286
Majesty of Flight, 302
Making Friends, 542
Man's Best Friend, 90, 302
March of Dimes: Our Children, Our Future,
    112, 325, 417, 444, 471
Mare and Foal, 84
Margaret Keane, 270
Marien Carlsen Mother's Day, 159
Marilyn — An American Classic, 501
Marilyn Monroe Collection, 187
Marilyn: The Golden Collection, 156
Maritime, 524
Mark Twain, 220
Marmot Christmas, 444
Marmot Mother's Day, 444
Mary Poppins, 376
Masquerade Fantasies, 93
Masterpiece Collection, 471
Masterpiece Madonnas, 530
Masterpiece Series, 151
Masterpieces of Impressionism, 112, 175,
    535
Masterpieces of Rockwell, 112, 176, 535
Masterpieces of the West, 112, 176, 536
McClelland Children's Circus, 444
Me and Mom, 197
Me and My Shadow, 156

Medieval Calendar, 429
Melodies of Childhood, 112, 521
Memorable Impressions, 274
Memories of a Victorian Childhood, 243
Memories of America by Grandma Moses, 489
Memories of Christmas, 352
Memories of the Heart, 165
Memories of the Western Prairies, 489
Memories of Yesterday, 193, 444
Memory Annual, 202
Men of the Rails, 169
Metropolitan Cat, 403
MI Hummel
    Annual Plates, 256
    Celebration, 256
    Collectibles Anniversary Plates, 256
    Friends Forever, 257
    Little Music Maker, 257
    The Little Homemakers, 257
Michelangelo Crystal, 178
Michelangelo Silver, 178
Mickey's Christmas Carol, 376
Mike Schmidt "500th" Home Run Edition, 231
Milestone Automobiles, 275
Mingolla Christmas, 489
Miniature Bas–Relief, 270
Miniature Roses, 149
Miracles of Light, 453
Mischief Makers, 102
Missions of California, 452
Mississippi River, 268
Mix Annual Christmas, 275
Mixed Company, 303
Modigliani Series, 345
Moments Alone, 417
Moments in Time, 166
Moments of Nature, 102, 505
Moments of Truth, 142
Moments to Remember, 418
Mommy and Me, 197
Moods of the Orient, 161
Moon, 355, 397
Moppets
    Anniversary, 265
    Christmas, 265
    Mother's Day, 265
Mosaic, 540
Moser Christmas, 444
Moser Mother's Day, 444
Most Beautiful Women of All Time, 427
Most Precious Gifts of Shen Lung, 489

Mother and Child, 275, 325, 337, 498, 540
Mother and Child Cats, 84
Mother Goose, 81, 445
Motherhood, 112, 483, 536
Mothers, 258
Mother's Day, 81, 86, 96, 97, 98, 106, 125, 128, 131, 132, 142, 145, 150, 159, 165, 174, 192, 206, 207, 209, 210, 220, 227, 253, 255, 265, 268, 276, 318, 327, 332, 333, 346, 347, 352, 355, 358, 361, 372, 386, 393, 395, 396, 397, 398, 399, 401, 403, 408, 412, 418, 430, 432, 435, 438, 439, 443, 444, 445, 447, 454, 459, 466, 473, 478, 483, 494, 495, 505, 506, 508, 512, 513, 520, 527, 530, 540, 546, 549
Mother's Day Crystal, 505
Mother's Day Five–Year Jubilee, 143
Mother's Day, Hand Painted, 207
Mother's Love, 113, 176, 427
Motorcar, 268
Mountain Majesty, 281
Muninger's Romantic Winter Impressions, 227
Museum Commemorative, 327, 338
Museum Doll, 265
Musical Maidens of the Imperial Dynasty, 149
Musical Moments from the Wizard of Oz, 156
My Fair Ladies, 197
My Fair Lady, 376
My Memories, 549
My Name Is Star, 511
Mysterious Case of Fowl Play, 156
Mystic Warriors, 303
Myth of Santa Claus, 208
Myths of the Sea, 125

– N –

N. C. Wyeth, 253
Nancy Doyle's Candy Girls, 164
Narrow Gauge, 197
National Parks of America, 484
Native American, 174, 270
Native Companions, 258
Nativity Triptych, 427
Natural History, 167
Nature Collection, 283
Nature's Beauty, 82
Nature's Child, 377
Nature's Children, 166, 484
Nature's Collage, 392

Nature's Garden, 377
Nature's Harmony, 113, 536
Nature's Heritage, 404
Nature's Legacy, 244
Nature's Lovables, 244
Nature's Nightime Realm, 303
Nature's Nobility, 157
Nature's Nursery, 377, 392
Nature's Playmates, 244
Nature's Poetry, 245
Nature's Quiet Moments, 303
Nature's Treasures, 514
Navajo Visions Suite, 283
Navajo Woman, 283
New Horizons, 157
New World, 520
1992 Olympic Team, 90
Nobility of Children, 327, 476
Nobility of the Plains, 81
Noble American Indian Women, 304
Noble and Free, 445
Noble Horse, 524
Noble Owls of America, 304
Noble Tribes, 84
Nordic Families, 327
Norman Rockwell, 411
    Christmas, 399, 402, 494
    Clowns, 332
    Collection, 270
    Collection of Legendary Art, 399
    Home of the Brave, 494
    Huckleberry Finn, 271
    Man's Best Friend, 402
    Mother's Day, 399, 495
    Salesman, 332
    Tom Sawyer, 271
North American Birds, 102
North American Ducks, 304
North American Game Birds, 304, 358
North American Waterbirds, 304
North American Wildlife, 113, 258, 399
Northwest Mounted Police, 130
Nostalgia, 332
Nostalgia – Children, 332
Nostalgic Magazine Covers, 332, 502
Nostalgic Memories, 160
Nosy Neighbors, 157
Not So Long Ago, 377
Notorious Disney Villains, 157
Now Is the Moment, 164
Nursery Pair, 113, 176
Nursery Rhyme Favorites, 405
Nutcracker, 151, 305, 418, 445, 542
Nymphea, 181

– O –

Oberammergau Passion Play, 333
Ocean Moods, 275
Ocean Stars, 275
Official Honeymooners Plate Collection, 305
Oklahoma!, 377
Old Baby Doll Collection, 519
Old Fashioned Christmas, 113, 126, 451
Old German Doll Collection, 519
Old Mill Stream, 377
Old Testament, 258
Old–Fashioned Christmas, 113, 126, 451
Old–Fashioned Country, 126
Old–Fashioned Favorites, 377
Old–Fashioned Mother's Day, 166
Olympiad Triumphs Collection, 199
Olympic Games, 143
Olympics, 227, 414, 440, 543
Omnibus Muralis, 265
On Golden Wings, 245
On Gossamer Wings, 245
On the Farm, 353
On the Road, 113, 176
On the Wing, 245
On Wings of Snow, 246
Once Upon a Barn, 146
Once Upon a Time, 378
1001 Arabian Nights, 318
Oriental Birds, 149, 347
Oriental Gold, 328, 476
Oriental Tranquility, 93
Oscar and Bertie's Edwardian Holiday, 445
Our Cherished Seas, 305, 446
Our Children, Our Future, 400
Our Woodland Friends, 246
Owl and the Pussycat, 278
Owl Collection, 287
Owl Family, 552

– P –

Pace Setters, 129
Paddington Bear Annual, 514
Paddington Bear Annual Christmas, 514
Paddington Bear Musician's Dream, 515
Panda, 149
Pandas of Wu Zuoren, 209
Papal Series, 502
Parkhurst
    Annual Christmas, 276
    Annual Mother's Day, 276
    Diamond Collection, 276

Passage to China, 305
Passing of Plains Indians, 202
Passion Play, 353
Passions of Scarlett O'Hara, 246
Pastoral Symphony, 266
Peace, 551
Peaceful Retreat, 276
Peanuts
    Annual, 515
    Christmas, 515
    Mother's Day, 515
    Special Edition, 515
    Valentine's Day, 515
    World's Greatest Athlete, 516
Pen Pals, 512
People of the Midnight Sun, 353
Performance, The, 197, 543
Perillo Christmas, 114
Perillo Santas, 114, 536
Perillo's Four Seasons, 114
Petal Pals, 247
Petals and Purrs, 305
Pete Rose Diamond Collection, 231
Pete Rose Platinum Edition, 231
Peter Rabbit Christmas, 549
Pewter, 178
Phil Esposito, 231
Picasso, 253, 316, 400
Pickard Commemorative, 427
Pink Panther Christmas Collection, 502
Pinocchio, 378
Plainsmen, 114, 536
Plaques, 151, 418
Plate of the Month, 338, 446
Playful Memories, 202, 276
Playful Pets, 114, 176
Playmates, 393
Poetic Cottages, 247
Poetic Visions of Japan, 359
Poor Richard, 220
Popeye's 50th Anniversary, 399
Portrait of Innocence, 358
Portraits, 114, 176
Portraits by Perillo, Mini Plates, 114
Portraits from Oz, 306
Portraits of American Brides, 114, 176
Portraits of Childhood, 103, 306, 543
Portraits of Christ, 247
Portraits of Exquisite Birds, 247
Portraits of First Love, 549
Portraits of Innocence, 498
Portraits of Motherhood, 378
Portraits of the Bald Eagle, 306

Portraits of the King, 187
Portraits of the Wild, 189
Ports of Call, 499
Postal Artists, 167
Prairie Children, 276
Prairie Women, 512
Precious Children, 471
Precious Little Ones, 378
Precious Moments, 306, 543
    Bible Story, 306
    Christmas Blessings, 193
    Christmas Collection, 194
    Classics, 307
    Four Seasons, 194
    Inspired Thoughts, 194
    Joy of Christmas, 194
    Mother's Love, 194
    Open Editions, 194
Precious Portraits, 307
Premier Collection, 446
Preserving a Way of Life, 169
Presidential, 266, 414, 428
Presidential Inaugural, 221
Presidents, 401
Pretty Girls of the Ice Capades, 471
Pride of America's Indians, 115, 536
Prime Time, 516
Princesses, 115, 536
Princesses of the Plains, 307
Prize Collection, 172
Professionals, 115, 537
Promised Land, 489
Proud Indian Families, 307
Proud Nation, 307
Proud Passage, 189
Proud Sentinels of the American West, 378
Proud Young Spirits, 115
Prowlers of the Clouds, 124
Punkinhead, The Happy Little Bear, 545
Puppy Playtime, 456
Puppy's World, 489
Purebred Horses of the Americas, 248
Purrfect Point of View, 378
Pussyfooting Around, 378
Puzzling Moments, 277

– Q –

Queen's Christmas, 550
Quellier's Morals of Perrault, 394
Quiet Moments of Childhood, 307
Quiet Places, 404
Quilted Countryside: Mel Steele Signature
    Collection, 308

R –

Racing for Pride and Profit, 353
Racing Legends, 84
Raggedy Ann
    Annual, 517
    Bicentennial, 517
    Christmas, 517
    Mother's Day, 517
    Valentine's Day, 517
Raggedy Ann & Andy, 208
Rare Encounters, 248
Rare Rockwell, 332
Real Children, 527
Realms of Wonder, 170
Reflection of Youth, 93
Reflections of Canadian Childhood, 189
Reflections of Innocence, 103
Reflections of Life, 512
Reflections of the Sea, 277
Reflections of Youth, 115
Reflections on China, 499
Remarkable World of Charles Dickens, 489
Remember When, 332
Remembering Elvis, 157
Remington Bronze, 456
Remington Series, 253
Remington Western, 266
Renaissance Madonnas: Gifts of Maternal
    Love, 530
Renaissance Masters, 168
Republic Pictures Film Library Collection,
    308
Retreat Series, 283
Rhythm and Dance, 93
Richard Judson Zolan Collection, 471
Richard Wagner, 338
Robert's Zodiac, 221
Robson Christmas, 258
Rockwell, 173, 386, 457
    American Sweethearts, 221
    Americana, 116, 177
    Cats, 456
    Christmas, 222
    Four Freedoms, 456
    Good Old Days, 456
    Home of the Brave, 308
    Mother's Day, 159
    On Tour, 467
    Trilogy, 116, 177
Rockwell's
    Centennial, 458
    Christmas Legacy, 458, 466
    Golden Moments, 467

    Light Campaign, 467
    Main Street, 458
    Rediscovered Women, 467
    Saturday Evening Post Baseball Plates,
        308
    Scotty, 399
    The Ones We Love, 467
    Treasured Memories, 468
Rod Carew, 231
Roger Staubach Sterling Collection, 231
Roger Tory Peterson, 86
Roman Memorial, 472
Romantic Age of Steam, 379
Romantic Castles of Europe, 308, 428
Romantic Cities of Europe, 116
Romantic Gardens, 248
Romantic Love, 94
Romantic Poets, 343
Romantic Portraits, 353
Romantic Victorian Keepsake, 309
Romantic Village Views, 519
Rose Wreaths, 116
Roses of Excellence, 149
Round Tripper, 232
Royal Canadian Police, 130
Royal Gainsborough, 105
Royal Literary Series, 105
Royal Wedding, 210
Royale, 446
    Christmas, 446
    Father's Day, 447
    Game Plates, 447
    Mother's Day, 447
Royale Germania
    Christmas Annual, 447
    Mother's Day, Crystal, 447
Rufus and Roxanne, 197, 543
Runci Classic, 476
Russian Fairy Tale Princesses, 163
Russian Fairy Tales
    Maria Morevna, 321, 544
    Snow Maiden, 322, 545
    The Firebird, 321, 544
    The Red Knight, 322, 545
Russian Legends, 534
Russian Seasons, 163
Ruthven Birds Feathered Friends, 202
Ruthven Songbirds, 338

– S –

Sacred Circle, 157
Sadako Mano's Christmas, 277
Sadako's Helpers, 277

Sailing Through History, 116, 177
Sally Miller Christmas, 407
Salvador Dali, 181
Sam Snead, 232
Sanchez Miniatures, 428
Santa Claus Collection, 144
Santa's Christmas, 379
Santa's Night Out, 170
Sarah Kay Annual, 97
Saturday Evening Post, 271
    Covers, 85
    Plate Collection, 309
Save the Whales, 277
Sawdust Antics, 88
Scandinavian Mother and Child, 328
Scenes from the Summer Palace, 343
Scenes of Christmas Past, 248
Schmid
    Crystal Desevres, 512
    Design, 512
    Father's Day, 512
    Pewter Christmas Plates, 512
School Days, 358
Sculptured Songbirds, 453
Seashells, 149
Season for Song, 379
Seasons, 283
Seasons of Splendor, 379
Seasons of the Bald Eagle, 309
Seasons of the Oak, 543
Seasons Remembered, 144
Sebastian Plates, 388
Secret World of the Panda, 248
Seed of the People, 164
Seems Like Yesterday, 197
Sensitive Moments, 277
Seven Sacraments, 160
Seven Seas, 222
Shades of Time, 198
Shadows and Light: Winter's Wildlife, 379
Shirley Temple, 410, 411, 462
Side by Side, 277
Signature Collection, 103
Signs of Love, 405, 457
Simpler Times, 116, 177
Singin' in the Rain, 379
Sisters, 355
Sleeping Beauty, 380
Small Blessings, 380
Small Wonders of the Wild, 309
Snow Babies, 277
Snow White and the Seven Dwarfs,
    269, 380
So Young, So Sweet, 198

Soap Box Derby, 399
Soaring Majesty, 249
Soft Fruits, 149
Songbirds, 319
Songbirds of North America, 338
Songbirds of the Four Seasons, 333
Songbirds of the South, 523
Songbirds of the World, 222
Songbirds of the World Miniatures, 222
Songs of Christmas, 388
Songs of Stephen Foster, 116, 521
Songs of the American Spirit, 380
Sonnets in Flowers, 249
Sophisticated Ladies, 448
Sound of Music, 380
Sound of Music: Silver Anniversary, 249
South Pacific, 380
Southern Backroads, 396
Southern Forest Families, 523
Southern Landmarks, 85
Sovereigns of the Wild, 158
Special Bicentenary, 494
Special Celebrities, 399
Special Heart, 88
Special Moments, 277, 405
Special Moments of Childhood, 419
Special Occasions, 117, 177, 448
Spencer Annual, 202
Spencer Special, 202
Spirit of Christmas, 249
Spirits of Nature, 117
Spirits of the Sky, 250
Splendors of an Ancient World, 413
Spock® Commemorative Wall Plaque, 309
Sport of Kings, 85
Sporting Dogs, 103, 552
Sporting Generation, 310
Spring in the World of Birds, 338
Springtime of Life, 310, 449
St. Patrick's Day, 130
Stained Glass and Pewter Special Issues,
    534
Stained Glass Cathedral Christmas, 533
Stained Glass Gardens, 310
Stained Glass Mother's Day, 534
Stallion, The, 85
Stamp Art, 345
Star Trek, 198
    25th Anniversary Commemorative, 310
Star Trek: The Next Generation, 310
Star Wars, 311
    10th Anniversary Commemorative, 311
    Trilogy, 311
Stars of the Circus, 311

Stars, Satellites and Space, 494
State Plates, 210
Stately Owls, 381
Statue of Liberty, 104, 144, 210
Story of Christmas by Eve Licea, 381
Story of Heidi, 311
Story of Noah's Ark, 311
Storybook, 117, 531, 537
Storyland Dolls, 552
Street Sellers of London, 550
Studies in Black and White, 117
Studies of Early Childhood, 118
Sugar and Spice, 358, 449
Sulamith's Christmas, 385
Sulamith's Love Song, 385
Summer at Skagen, 144
Summer Days of Childhood, 311
Summer Fun, 277
Sun Bonnet Babies, 277, 478
Sun Bonnet Babies Playtime, 478
Sunday Best, 278
Sundblom Santas, 381
Superheroes, 345
Superstars of Country Music, 158
Swan Lake, 419
Sweetest Songs, 472
Sweetheart Series, 124
Sweetness and Grace, 382
Symphony of Roses, 428
Symphony of Shimmering Beauty, 250

– T –

Take Me Out to the Ballgame, 188
Tale of Father Frost, 163
Tale of Genji, 312
Tales of Enchantment, 223
Tapestry I, 320
Teddy Bear Dreams, 158
Teenagers of the Bible, 226
Tender Expressions, 472
Tender Moments, 118, 543
Tenth Anniversary, 419
Thanksgiving, 98, 99, 128, 361
Thanksgiving — Miniature, 419
Thanksgiving by Dohanos, 223
Thanksgiving Day, 419
That Special Time, 283
The Best of Zolan in Miniature, 415
The Carnival, 108
The Constitution, 100
The Ducks Unlimited, 236
The Fierce and the Free, 297
The King and I, 374

The Littlest, 166
The Loon" Voice of the North, 190
The Performance, 197, 543
The Stallion, 85
The Tribute, 119
Theatre des Saisons, 318
This Land Is Our Land, 198
This Little Pig Went to Market, 358
This Ole Bear, 207
Thomas Kinkade
    Signature Collection, 392
    Scenes of Serenity, 158
    Thomashire, 382
    Yuletide Memories, 382
Thomas Nast Christmas, 452
Thornton Utz 10th Anniversary, 312
Thoroughbreds, 118, 537
Those Precious Years, 161
Three Graces, 104
Three Little Pigs 50th Anniversary, 269
Through the Eyes of Love, 407
Thundering Waters, 158
Tidings of Joy, 449
Time Machine Teddies, 266
Timeless Expressions of the Orient, 313
Timeless Love, 118
Timeless Moments, 203
Times of Our Lives, 119
Times to Treasure, Bone China —
    Miniature, 420
'Tis the Season, 250
To Life Annual, 328
To Mom with Love, 166
Tobin Fraley Carousels, 286
Toby Plate Collection, 182
Tom Sawyer, 172, 383, 454
Tom Seaver, 232
Tomorrow's Promise, 250
Touch of Rockwell, 462
Touching the Spirit, 250
Town and Country Dogs, 449
Toys from the Attic, 161
Traditional Christmas Cards, 318
Traditional Fairy Tales, 354
Traditional Norwegian Christmas, 432
Trains of the Great West, 158
Traveling Salesman, 266
Treasured Days, 313
Treasured Songs of Childhood, 449
Treasures of Childhood, 490
Treasures of the Arctic, 190
Treasures of the Chinese Mandarins, 313

Treasures of the Dore Bible, 453
Treasures of Tutankhamen, 354, 403
Treasury of Classic Children's Verse, 183
Treasury of Songbirds, 251
Tribal Companions, 359
Tribal Ponies, 119, 537
Tribute, 119, 177
Tribute to All Children, 328
Tribute to Award–Winning Roses, 150
Tribute to Ballet, 150
Tribute to Classical Greek Beauty, 477
Tribute to Love — The Rubaiyat of Omar
    Khayyam, 430
Tributes to the Ageless Arts, 125
Triptych Series, 94
True Love, 278
Tsarevich's Bride, 210
Tunes of Glory, 551
Turn of the Century, 198
Turn, Turn, Turn, 207
TV, 502
'Twas the Night Before Christmas, 333,
    388
Twelve Days of Christmas, 168, 208, 500,
    527
Two Hundred Years of Flight, 534
Two Thousand Years of Ships, 490

– U –

Ugly Duckling, 267
Unbridled Spirit, 313
Uncle Tad's Cat, 94
Uncle Tad's Golden Oldies, 94
Uncle Tad's Holiday Cats, 95
Uncle Tad's Tick Tock, 95
Under Mother's Wing, 383
Unicorn Fantasies, 543
Unicorn Magic, 119, 521
Unicorns in Dreamer's Garden, 338
Untamed Spirits, 158
Upland Birds of North America, 383
Utz Mother's Day, 313

– V –

Valentine, 494, 532
Valentine's Day, 207, 420, 540, 514
Vanishing Africa, 169
Vanishing American Barn, 329
Vanishing Americana, 203
Vanishing Animal Kingdoms, 449
Vanishing Animals, 164
Vanishing Gentle Giants, 251

Vanishing Paradises, 159
Vanishing Rural America, 313
Vanishing West, 88
Vasils Series, 454
Vel Miller Series, 124
Velvet Paws, 171
Very Special Edition, 521
Victoria and Jason, 413
Victorian Cat, 251
Victorian Cat Caper, 251
Victorian Childhood, 499
Victorian Christmas, 190, 500
Victorian Christmas Memories, 314
Victorian Mother's Day, 449
Victorian Playtime, 314
Vignette, 457
Village Life of Russia, 163
Village Lights, 453
Violet Portraits, 553
Visit from Saint Nicholas, 318
Voyage of Ulysses, 344

– W –

Wags to Riches, 173
Walt Disney, 388
Walter Brennan, 89
Waltzes of Johann Strauss, 430
War Ponies, 119, 537
War Ponies of the Plains, 119
Warabe No Haiku, 226
Water Birds, 150, 287
Water Birds of North America, 504
Water Fowl, 354
Waterbabies, 339
Waterbird Families, 278
Waterfowl, 450, 552
Waterfowl Legacy, 453
Wayne Gretzky, 232
We the Children, 457
Wedding, 339
Weddings Around the World, 543
Wells Fargo, 104
West of Frank McCarthy, 314
Western Series, 124, 223, 333, 450
When I Grow Up, 203
Where is England?, 105
Where is Scotland?, 105
Whitey Ford, 232
Wiinblad Christmas, 477
Wiinblad Crystal, 477
Wild and Free: Canada's Big Game, 191
Wild Beauties, 227
Wild Innocents, 252

Wild North, 169
Wild Spirits, 252
Wild West, 454
Wilderness Wings, 266, 333
Wildflowers, 354
Wildflowers of the South, 523
Wildlife, 226, 258, 354, 435, 540, 551
Wildlife Memories, 283
Will Moses' America, 407
Windjammers, 144
Windows of Glory, 252, 383
Windows on the World, 490
Windows to the Wild, 283
Winged Fantasies, 259
Winged Jewels: Chinese Cloisonné Birds, 168
Winged Reflections, 314
Wings of Freedom, 211, 428
Wings of Man, 551
Wings of Nobility, 407
Wings of the Wild, 333
Wings of Winter, 252
Wings Upon the Wind, 191, 383
Winner's Circle, 283
Winslow Homer's The Sea, 403
Winter Grotto Collection, 285
Winter Mindscape, 120
Winter Rails, 314
Winter Wildlife, 315
Winterfest, 175
Winter's Majesty, 252
Wizard of Oz, 315, 383
    A National Treasure, 383
Women of the West, 198, 544
Wonder of Childhood, 420
Wonder of Christmas, 315, 450
Wonderful World of Clowns, 278
Wonderland, 208
Wonders of the Sea, 252
Wondrous Years, 278
Woodland Birds of America, 150

Woodland Birds of the World, 223
Woodland Creatures, 354
Woodland Encounters, 315
Woodland Friends, 124
Woodland Year, 223
World I Love, 328
World of Beatrix Potter, 183
World of Children, 450
World of Children Bas–Relief, 462
World of Dance, 125
World of Game Birds, 124
World of Ozz Franca, 278
World of the Eagle, 159
World of Zolan, 315
World Stars, 400
World's Great Porcelain Houses, 224
World's Most Magnificent Cats, 253

– X, Y, Z –

Yachts, 354
Year of the Wolf, 316
Yesterday, 199
Yesterday Dreams, 160
Yesterday's Children, 126
Yesterday's Impressions, 278
Yesterday's Innocents, 384
Yesterday's World, 355
Yetta's Holidays, 161
Yogi Berra, 233
Yorkshire Brontes, 502
Young Adventurer Plate, 145
Young America, 534
Young Chieftains, 120
Young Emotions, 120
Young Wildlife, 527
Zodiac, 339
Zoe's Cats, 85
Zolan's Children, 420
Zolan's Children and Pets, 420
Zoological Garden, 359

THE ULTIMATE RESOURCE ON COLLECTIBLES!

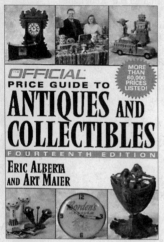

The Official Price Guide to Antiques and Collectibles contains the most comprehensive information on thousands of collector items.

- Over 60,000 current prices, from traditional antiques to the latest hot pop culture collectible

- Unique focus on baby-boomer collectibles

- Special tips on where and what to collect, regional preferences, and how to spot fakes and reproductions

- Fully illustrated

HOUSE OF COLLECTIBLES
SERVING COLLECTORS FOR MORE THAN THIRTY YEARS

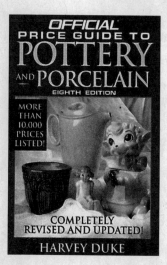